809.8973
St94

Phillips Library
Bethany College
Bethany, W. Va. 26032

STUDIES IN THE AMERICAN RENAISSANCE

1977

Author's Group

A photomontage by an unknown photographer, circa 1885. Represented are (from left to right) John Greenleaf Whittier, Oliver Wendell Holmes, Ralph Waldo Emerson, John Lothrop Motley, A. Bronson Alcott, Nathaniel Hawthorne, James Russell Lowell, Louis Agassiz and Henry Wadsworth Longfellow.

Collection of Joel Myerson.

STUDIES IN THE AMERICAN RENAISSANCE

1977

Edited by JOEL MYERSON

BOSTON:
TWAYNE PUBLISHERS

STUDIES IN THE AMERICAN RENAISSANCE

EDITOR

Joel Myerson

EDITORIAL ASSISTANTS

Robert Morace (1974–1975)
Robert E. Burkholder (1975–1977)

The editor would like to thank the College of Humanities and Social Sciences, Department of English, and the Office of Research of the University of South Carolina, and especially William H. Nolte, for their support.

STUDIES IN THE AMERICAN RENAISSANCE examines the lives and works of mid-nineteenth-century American authors and the circumstances in which they wrote, published, and were received. The Editor welcomes biographical, historical, and bibliographical articles on the literature, history, philosophy, art, religion, and general culture of America during the period 1830–1860. Editorial correspondence should be addressed to Joel Myerson, Department of English, University of South Carolina, Columbia, South Carolina 29208.

Copyright © 1978 by G. K. Hall & Co.
All rights reserved

ISSN 0149–015X

STUDIES IN THE AMERICAN RENAISSANCE is published annually by Twayne Publishers, a Division of G. K. Hall & Co., 70 Lincoln Street, Boston, Massachusetts 02111, and is available on a standing order basis. The price of this volume is $25.00. Orders from individuals must be accompanied by payment.

First Printing, May 1978

CONTENTS

ILLUSTRATIONS	vii
LIBRARY SYMBOLS	ix
The Ideology of Brook Farm *Richard Francis*	1
A Calendar of the Letters of Margaret Fuller *Robert N. Hudspeth*	49
Christopher Pearse Cranch, Robert Browning, and the Problem of Transcendental Friendship *David Robinson*	145
Origins of the American Renaissance: A Front-Page Story *C. E. Frazer Clark, Jr.*	155
Poe and Magazine Writing on Premature Burial *J Gerald Kennedy*	165
Poe's "The Spectacles": A New Text from Manuscript. Edited, with Textual Commentary and Notes. *Joseph J. Moldenhauer*	179
Poe's "Murders in the Rue Morgue": The Ingenious Web Unravelled *Burton R. Pollin*	235
A Guide to Primary Source Materials for the Study of Hawthorne's Old Manse Period *John J. McDonald*	261
Hawthorne: The Writer as Dreamer *Rita K. Gollin*	313

Daniel Ricketson's Sketch Book 327
    Thomas Blanding

Melville's Closet Skeleton: A New Letter about the
Illegitimacy Incident in *Pierre* 339
    Amy Puett Emmers

Harriet Beecher Stowe, John P. Jewett, and
Author-Publisher Relations in 1853 345
    Susan Geary

Louisa M. Alcott in Periodicals 369
    Madeleine B. Stern

Dr. Richard Maurice Bucke: A Religious Disciple of Whitman 387
    Artem Lozynsky

BOOKS RECEIVED 405
    Robert E. Burkholder

CONTRIBUTORS 410

ILLUSTRATIONS

Plate One: "The Buildings at Brook Farm as They Appear To-day"

Plate Two: "Sketch of the Edifice of a Phalanstery" (1840)

Plate Three: Hawthorne's earliest located appearance in print: "The Ocean" in the 26 August 1825 *Salem Gazette*

Plate Four: Hawthorne to Caleb Foote, 31 August 1840

Plate Five: Page one of Poe's "The Spectacles" manuscript

Plate Six: Last page of "The Spectacles" manuscript

Plate Seven: *Dollar Newspaper* first printing of "The Spectacles," 27 March 1844

Plate Eight: *Lloyd's Entertaining Journal* printing of "The Spectacles," 3 May 1845

Plate Nine: *Broadway Journal* printing of "The Spectacles," 22 November 1845

Plate Ten: First page of Griswold's 1850 text of "The Spectacles" in *The Works of the Late Edgar Allan Poe*

Plate Eleven: Title page of the spurious "Spectacles" pamphlet

Plate Twelve: Beginning of the spurious "Spectacles" pamphlet text dated "1842"

Plate Thirteen: "The Orang-Outang of Mr. Old Nick," from *The Spirit of the Times*, 16 January 1847

Plate Fourteen: Map of the Palais Royal environs

Plate Fifteen: Map of the "Rue Morgue" district

Plate Sixteen: Photogravure by A. D. McCormick illustrating "The Murders in the Rue Morgue"

Plate Seventeen: Self-portrait of Daniel Ricketson, September 1851

Plate Eighteen: Brooklawn, July 1858

Plate Nineteen: "H.D. Thoreau returning to his Shanty from Concord."

Plate Twenty: William Ellery Channing in 1856

Plate Twenty-One: Captain Thoreau, the Great Explorer of the Middleborough Lakes, 1856

Plate Twenty-Two: Back view of the Brady Farm, 1856

Plate Twenty-Three: Amos Bronson Alcott, 1857

Plate Twenty-Four: Amos Bronson Alcott, 1857

Plate Twenty-Five: William Ellery Channing in 1865

Plate Twenty-Six: Daniel Ricketson at age sixty

Plate Twenty-Seven: "A Shanty Man": Henry Thoreau, twenty-five years later

LIBRARY SYMBOLS

CSmH	Henry E. Huntington Library
CSt	Stanford University
CU-B	Bancroft Library, University of California, Berkeley
CaOLU	University of Western Ontario
Ct	Connecticut State Library
CtHNF	Nook Farm Research Library (Stowe-Day Foundation)
CtY	Yale University
DLC	Library of Congress
Ia-HA	Iowa State Department of History
IaU	University of Iowa
MB	Boston Public Library
MBAt	Boston Athenaeum
MC	Cambridge Public Library
MCR-S	Schlesinger Library, Radcliffe College
MCo	Concord Free Public Library
MH	Harvard University
MHarF	Fruitlands Museums
MHi	Massachusetts Historical Society
MNS	Smith College
MSaE	Essex Institute
MWelC	Wellesley College
MdHi	Maryland Historical Society
MeB	Bowdoin College

MeHi	Maine Historical Society
NBLiHi	Long Island Historical Society
NBu	Buffalo and Erie County Public Library
NCaS	Saint Lawrence University
NHi	New-York Historical Society
NN	New York Public Library
NNC	Columbia University
NNPM	Pierpont Morgan Library
NRU	University of Rochester
NcD	Duke University
NjP	Princeton University
OMC	Marietta College
PHC	Haverford College
PHi	Historical Society of Pennsylvania
PPL	Library Company of Philadelphia
PSt	Pennsylvania State University
RHi	Rhode Island Historical Society
RPA	Providence Athenæum
RPB	Brown University
ScU	University of South Carolina
TxU	University of Texas
ViU	University of Virginia
VtMiM	Middlebury College

THE IDEOLOGY OF BROOK FARM

Richard Francis

IT IS DIFFICULT TO DEFINE exactly what one means when referring to the phenomenon of New England Transcendentalism. Hawthorne well illustrates the movement's paradoxical combination of bulk and intangibility when he portrays Giant Transcendentalist in "The Celestial Rail-road" as "a heap of fog and duskiness."[1] A more recent student, William R. Hutchison, points out in his book *The Transcendentalist Ministers* that a description broad enough to accommodate the full complexity of the movement will also admit "all philosophical idealists from Plato through Bradley," while any attempt to be more specific will tend to disqualify various of the active participants: and he mentions that Orestes Brownson, Theodore Parker, Bronson Alcott, and even Ralph Waldo Emerson himself, have suffered this fate at different hands.[2] It is obviously much easier to make certain assumptions about the movement than to attempt a satisfactory definition of it. This can be an equally dangerous activity, however. Two of the most common assumptions about the Transcendentalists are that they were individualists, and that they tended to adopt a stance of genteel Bostonian aloofness toward society at large. Clearly there is a substantial amount of evidence to support these closely related points of view; and yet the picture they give us of the movement is not, finally, an accurate or even a helpful one. The Brook Farm experiment provides a perfect example of the difficulties such preconceptions can get us into.

One can easily establish that Brook Farm was born out of the authentic Transcendentalist impulse; the problem here is one of mapping the community's later route. The best way of validating the community's original claims is to sidestep the vexed question of ideology for a moment, and to follow Hutchison's example by pointing toward the participants involved. George Ripley, the founder and leader of the movement, had unchallengeable Transcendentalist qualifications. He had been one of the leading campaigners in the attack on Andrews Norton and orthodox Unitarianism since what Perry Miller calls the

PLATE ONE

"The Buildings at Brook Farm as They Appear To-day," from George Willis Cooke, "Brook Farm," *New England Magazine*, n.s. 17 (December 1897): 401.

"annus mirabilis" of 1836; indeed his review of Martineau's *Rationale of Religious Enquiry*, published in the *Christian Examiner* during that year, was one of the central documents of the miracles controversy.[3] He was one of the four graduates who originated the idea of the Transcendental Club during the bicentennial celebrations—also in 1836— of Harvard College.[4] It is true that when the Club heard his plan for a community in October 1840, the interest expressed by the members present was not supplemented by active support.[5] However, many other prominent Transcendentalists involved themselves in the community to a greater or lesser extent. John Sullivan Dwight, who had begun his career as a Unitarian minister and who was destined to become the most influential music critic in America; George P. Bradford, another disillusioned minister; and the young G. W. Curtis were among the members of the community, while William Henry Channing, nephew of the great Unitarian divine and precursor of Transcendentalism, William Ellery Channing, played an important part in its development, as we shall see later, even though he never took up full-time residence at the Farm. Margaret Fuller's younger brother and the children of George Bancroft and Orestes Brownson boarded at the Farm and attended the school. Theodore Parker had the neighboring parish of West Roxbury until 1845, and was frequently calling upon his friend

Ripley. Emerson, Bronson Alcott and his English colleague Charles Lane, Fuller, Brownson, and C. P. Cranch were among the many visitors.[6]

However, once scholars have accepted that Brook Farm was a manifestation of Transcendentalism, they have had some difficulty in coming to terms with the implications of its conversion to the doctrines of the French utopian thinker, Charles Fourier, in 1844. The problem revolves round the question of the Farmers' commitment to social reform. Put crudely, the difficulty seems to be this: if the community was a thoroughgoing Transcendentalist enterprise, then it had no business allying itself with a movement that aimed at complete (not to say half-baked) social reorganization. Alternatively, if the Farm is accepted as being sincerely committed to the establishment of a new order, then its links with Transcendentalism must be seen as rather tenuous, the result of a kind of historical and geographical coincidence.

Charles Crowe, in his excellent biography of George Ripley, inclines toward the latter view. He takes for granted that Ripley and the others were sincere in their desire to reestablish the whole of society on a different basis. He provides us with a well-balanced account of the history of the experiment, and devotes a chapter to showing how much time and energy the leading members of the community allocated to the administration and publicization of Fourierism on a national scale, and to allied radical movements like the National (Land) Reformers and the "Cooperators."[7] At the same time, he regards Transcendentalism and individualism as synonymous, and therefore detects a contradiction, or at least an inner tension, in the ideology of the Brook Farmers. "If they embraced Fourierism completely," he asks, "what became of the much-vaunted Transcendentalist individualism?"[8] His answer is, very little. He implies a development from Transcendentalism toward social

PLATE TWO

"Sketch of the Edifice of a Phalanx" by Victor Considerant, from Albert Brisbane, *Social Destiny of Man* (Philadelphia: C. F. Stollmeyer, 1840), p. 360.
Collection of Richard Francis

radicalism and indeed, in an earlier article, he claims that the "ideology of the Brook Farm leaders was from the beginning closer to Fourierism than to Transcendentalism."[9] While we are invited to consider the members as serious social reformers, therefore, we are for that very reason expected to conclude that they had in some way grown out of their earlier allegiances. We are left with a feeling that something fortuitous and unexpected has happened—that a group of Transcendentalists has revealed much more sense of responsibility than we, or they, thought they possessed.

Perry Miller in effect agrees with this verdict—although his allegiances are different from Crowe's. In one of the connecting passages of his anthology *The Transcendentalists* he claims that "Nobody knows what went on in Ripley's mind as he consented, by 18 January 1844, to change Brook Farm from a Transcendental picnic into a regimented Phalanx." He goes on to quote Lindsay Swift to the effect that Ripley must have come "to lay more stress on the method by which individual freedom was to become assured, than on the fact of personal liberty in itself."[10] In other words, the Farmers have given up their privileged and charming existence and for no good reason have imposed upon themselves a disciplined and even constricting way of life. Miller and Swift disapprove; Crowe applauds. But the three commentators agree that Transcendentalism and Fourierism do not really mix. This alleged incompatibility reflects no credit on either party. The assumption is either that the Transcendentalists were too frivolous, or that Fourierism was inhuman and bizarre—Miller describes the Brook Farm Phalanx as sitting "foreign and forlorn in West Roxbury."[11]

Neither charge is altogether baseless. It is clear that the Brook Farmers tended to have a good time, as Charles Lane's jaundiced account reveals when he describes going with Alcott "one evening to Roxbury where there are 80 or 90 persons playing away their youth and daytime in a miserably joyous and frivolous manner."[12] At the same time it is easy to find something at least un-American about the further reaches of Fourier's imagination—his notion that the seas will eventually change into lemonade, for example, or that a supple and elastic anti-lion will one day take people on long journeys at high speed.[13] We could, perhaps, total the main objections to the reconciliation of Fourierism with Transcendentalism by claiming that the escapism of the Brook Farmers, and the insane fanaticism of the protosocialist were opposites which would naturally repel each other.

They did not, however, and for a number of very good reasons. For one: throughout its history Brook Farm represented a sincere attempt to remove social injustice. It was, it is true, a middle-class enterprise in its conception and realization, a joint-stock company rather than a communist society. Like most attempts at reform via utopia, it was the inspiration of those with adequate means and education. But during both its phases it represented bourgeois ideals at their most generous: it was an attempt to extend the ranks, not to defend them. Moreover, the community's conversion into a phalanx was a perfectly logical development, and it can be understood not merely in the light of the social commitment of the Transcendentalists, but in that of their psychological, historical, and even religious preoccupations as well. A close examination of Fourier's basic ideas reveals that there are a number of inner connections between them and the beliefs of the Transcendentalists generally. Fourier's plan of labor organization locked much more neatly than might be expected into the pattern of behavior—of both work and play—that can be detected at the Farm during its earlier phase. Moreover—and this of course is a closely related point—his analysis of human identity, both individual and social, was closer than it might appear to certain lines of Transcendentalist inquiry, and it provided a relevant solution to some of the paradoxes encountered in the latter. Similarly, Fourier's account of the historical process chimed in harmoniously with a particular trend in the Transcendentalists' thinking of the subject.

Of course, Fourierism could not be swallowed by the Farmers in one monolithic mouthful—although Fourier himself, along with his American disciple, Albert Brisbane, took a firm take-it-or-leave-it attitude to prospective adherents. Despite their protestations, the Farmers were not quite able to accept Fourier's sternly utilitarian pursuit of happiness at all costs. Nevertheless, and this is probably as good a testimonial as any, Fourierism proved that it could accommodate a moral superstructure. The work of William Henry Channing—not a member, but an important influence on the intellectual and religious life of the community—shows perhaps better than any of the rather thin contemporary material pertaining to the experiment, how Fourierism looked to formerly Unitarian eyes.

In 1895 Charles Anderson Dana, then an old and famous journalist and reactionary, was invited by the University of Michigan to give an address on Brook Farm. He had joined the community as a young man in 1841, after his eyesight had been damaged by an overindulgence in Dickens while a Harvard student. He rapidly became Ripley's right-hand man and was one of the most important members of the Farm throughout almost the whole of its history. He was therefore well qualified to pass a verdict, and his later career as an aggressive polemicist for the political right indicates that he was under no temptation to exaggerate the community's reforming verve. And yet he is unequivocal in his judgment that the initial impulse and central doctrine of Brook Farm was an egalitarian one. The community was an essay in applied democracy:

> In this party of Transcendental philosophers the idea early arose—it was first stated by Mr. George Bancroft, the historian . . . that democracy, while it existed in the Constitution of the United States, while it had triumphed as a political party under Jefferson, and while it was then in possession of a majority of the governments of the States, and at times of the government of the United States, was not enough. . . . If democracy was the sublime truth which it was held up to be, it should be raised up from the sphere of politics, from the sphere of law and constitutions; it should be raised up into life and made social.[14]

Of course, there is no way of fully substantiating this claim that the Farm represented a deliberate and consistent attempt to interweave democratic ideals into the very texture of social life. To do so would require the kind of empirical approach that historians simply cannot achieve. It is impossible to know what the day-to-day experience of the Farmers was like—how, in the impromptu moment, the different elements of their society really treated each other. It certainly appears that from the beginning there were serious problems. Ora Gannet Sedgwick, who was present during the first years as a boarder at the school, unconsciously reveals the patronization and tension that must have been current during the pre-Fourierist period:

> Besides those whom I have mentioned others joined us, with well-trained hands, but not of such good New England blood. I recall among them two Irishwomen, one of whom, a fine cook, had lived with the Danas and others of the best families of Boston. This woman came to Brook Farm for the sake of her beautiful young daughter, an only child, who looked like a madonna and possessed much native delicacy. Her mother was desirous that she should be well educated. These women were perfectly welcome to sit at the table with us all, but they preferred not to sit down until the two courses had been put upon the table, if at all.[15]

The scope for the kind of unpleasant situation that Sedgwick describes was of course widened by the change to Fourierism. A certain amount of reshuffling inevitably occurred, and one assumes that among the departing were included the more troglodytic of the middle-class members.[16] However, the influx of a high proportion of "mechanics," as they were usually described, in turn served to increase the potential for social unrest. The adult male signatories of the Fourierist Constitution of 11 February 1844, which is now in the possession of the Massachusetts Historical Society, were required to record their previous work. Of the forty-nine occupations listed, there were two clergymen, three teachers, one student, one attorney-at-law, one clerk, and one broker. All the remaining previously employed members had been tradespeople, artisans, and laborers.[17] Some kind of class confrontation was at least in the cards, and if Arthur Sumner, who was about sixteen at the time, is to be trusted, the internecine social conflict rose for a time to a fairly serious level:

> Soon after this Fourierist agitation began, some very unpleasant people appeared upon the scene. They seemed to us boys to be discontented mechanics. They soon fell into a group by themselves. After dinner, they would collect together in the great barn, and grumble; and when the others passed through, the malcontents eyed them with suspicion, and muttered, "Aristocrats!" All because they knew themselves to be less cultivated and well-bred.

He adds innocently, "Yet there was the kindest feeling of brotherhood among the members; and it did not need that a man should be a scholar and a gentleman to be received and absorbed."[18]

A more mature and perhaps more representative attitude is provided by Marianne Dwight, sister of J. S. Dwight, in a letter to her friend Anna Q. T. Parsons. She is describing the wife of one of the community's carpenters, a Mrs. Cheswell, who was pregnant at the time:

> We have noble spirits here at Brook Farm. I have been much affected lately, by the noble devotedness of our good Mrs. Cheswell. This coarse woman, as I once thought her, and as she was, is really becoming very charming—a most zealous and untiring worker, full of nobleness and enthusiasm in a good cause, sweet and cheerful too, so that it does one good to look upon her. In her, we see what Association is going to do for the uneducated and rude.[19]

It is clear that working-class members were not to be accepted on their own terms. They were, however, to be accepted—and then manipulated and "improved" until they became more nearly the social equals of the middle-class members. Marianne Dwight is writing in 1845, a year into the Fourierist period, but her assumptions are those on which the community had rested from the beginning. They are stated in 1842 by the "distinguished literary lady" whose report on the Farm, together with an introduction by Orestes Brownson, appeared in the *Democratic Review* for November of that year. The Brook

Farmers, we find, are not hastening, lemming-like, toward a social lowest common denominator; instead, "true democratic equality may be obtained by *levelling up*, instead of *levelling down.*"[20]

It is easy to see this aspiration as an example of Brahminesque paternalism at its most naïve. From our present perspective we cannot automatically achieve imaginative sympathy with an egalitarian ideal that involves the extension, rather than the questioning, of bourgeois values. And yet an examination of the Brook Farm material reveals not merely that the members were dedicated to this cause, but also that their commitment involved a certain amount of courage, and the sense that they were taking up a revolutionary stance.

The school provides an excellent example of Brook Farm's good intentions, and its problems, since quite apart from being, throughout the history of the community, the most important of its "industries," it was also the one which involved the most give-and-take with the outside world. It provided education for children from four to college level; students could select the courses of study they wanted to take (the possibilities ranged from agriculture to "Intellectual and Natural Philosophy"); and it was a basic principle of the school that mental and manual labor should be combined.[21] Naturally, a progressive institution of this sort tended to attract parents who were themselves well educated, but this was certainly not exclusively the case. We have already seen in the Ora Gannet Sedgwick passage that the madonna-like daughter of the Irish cook had been brought to the Farm to get an education. A couple of months after the conversion to Fourierism, Charles Anderson Dana stated the principles of the school in his address to the General Convention of the Friends of Association in the United States (4 April 1844). It is clear that he is describing, not a new theory, but established policy. He affirms that every child, irrespective of his social and financial background, is entitled to a complete education at Brook Farm. Moreover, "It is not doled out to him as though he was a pupil of orphan assylums [sic] and almshouses—not as the cold benefice and bounty of the world—but as his right—a right conferred upon him by the very fact that he is born into this world a human being—and here we think we have made great advances."[22]

That these words are more than oratorical liberalism is implied in some interesting comments by James Kay of Philadelphia, one of the Farm's most important supporters and Ripley's business adviser. In a letter to J. S. Dwight dated 10 May 1844, he offers some proposals designed to aid the community in its fight for survival. He urges that the school should dismiss (among others) "those 3 or 4" pupils who are receiving board and education at half price. The numbers might seem rather insignificant, although it must be remembered that the older children could work in exchange for their education anyway (and their contribution perhaps represented a higher value in principle than in hard cash). Certainly Kay sees the assistance provided as a blind defiance of the rules of success ("No business in civilization could withstand such a drain").[23] However, his real worry becomes evident when he turns to a rather different question:

> I have one remark more to make, and that is, respecting the presence of impure children. My views, I know, are well understood; but I must claim the privilege of friendship to insist on them—if you will, "in season & out of season." Little importance as you attach to them, I am a true prophet when I say, that indifference or contumacy in this matter will break you down, if all other conditions were excellent. You cannot know how much harm has been done to you from this cause already; nor do you seem to be aware that the public are perhaps over-well informed of past events. I have heard much from time to time on the subject in Massachusetts; and strange as it may seem, more than a few here are better informed than they are willing to say. I know not where or from whom they procured their knowledge nor whether it is of truth; but the story is here. I say that this enormous evil ought to be abated.[24]

It is clear that Kay is alarmed because his son is a fellow pupil of these undesirables, and also annoyed that the Farmers have ignored his previous remonstrances on the subject. But even taking these two provocations into account, his expression still seems unduly violent, and testifies to the amount of popular hostility, in this and other respects, that the community must have had to face. His mention of impurity, of "enormous evil," his setting himself up as a "true prophet," implies that much more than economic efficiency, mere success, is at stake. His language is that of a man afraid in the presence of radical social change—of a man who views association from a certain aesthetic distance. In an earlier letter, he expressed his admiration of the new Fourierist constitution, "the beautiful structure which you have erected." He goes on to claim that "If it were simply a literary exercise, with no particular object, it would win universal applause for its author."[25] We get the picture of a dilettante at bay—a picnicking Brook Farmer. Kay, however, was a valetudinarian publisher from Philadelphia, and not a member of the community. Amelia Russell, who really had been one, confirms that he was not letting his imagination run away with him—talking of public suspicion of the school she says:

> People were shy of us; we were supposed to nourish some very fantastic views which encroached much on the decencies of society. I will not enumerate

all the absurd stories which were circulated with regard to us; and although our outside friends, who still continued to feel an interest in us, paid no heed to these ridiculous inventions, there were thousands who looked upon us as little less than heathens, who had returned to a state of semi-barbarism.[26]

It is clear that the Brook Farmers were willing, for the sake of their ideals, to take a certain number of risks, to occupy exposed ground.[27] Perhaps the reason why they have never really been given the benefit of the doubt—why, apart from the relevant chapters in Crowe's book, no serious and sustained treatment of the enterprise has been published since 1900[28]—is that there is so little primary material which sets out the aims and achievements of Brook Farm. Amelia Russell, writing on the *Home Life of the Brook Farm Association* more than thirty years after its collapse, poses a problem noticed by Hawthorne in his Preface to the *Blithedale Romance*[29] and by many of the other less important members when the time came for them to pen their memoirs:

> I cannot understand why no one of those who better comprehended all the machinery which kept the wheels going through many trying vicissitudes (though I suspect sometimes the operators themselves felt doubtful how it was done) has ever brought its interior life to view, since a real history of its aims and endeavours after a truer life has been asked for.[30]

Some years later, Arthur Sumner suggested that the cause of this lapse was "that it never had any result except upon the individual lives of those who dwelt there."[31] It is an answer that certainly plays into the hands of those who wish to see the community as symptomatic of a kind of death-wish, an attempt to "banish the world,"[32] particularly as he goes on to say: "It was a beautiful idyllic life which we led, with plenty of work and play and transcendentalism; and it gave place to the Roxbury poorhouse."[33]

The opposition established between "transcendentalism" and the "Roxbury poorhouse" is a suggestive one, but Sumner's explanation is not entirely satisfactory. For one thing, even in 1841 there were complaints that Ripley was not being audible enough on the subject of the experiment. In a letter to John Sullivan Dwight (who had not yet become a member) written in June of that year, a couple of months after the community was inaugurated, Elizabeth Palmer Peabody remarks of Ripley: "He enjoys the '*work*' so much that he does not clearly see that his plan is not in the way of being demonstrated any farther than that it is being made evident."[34] Moreover, although there were over six hundred articles by Brook Farmers in the *Harbinger*, a Fourierist journal which was published by the community every week between June 1845 and June 1847, only two give a direct account of Brook Farm, and they concern the calamitous destruction by fire of the nearly completed phalanstery in 1846.[35] This policy of omission is a deliberate one, and testifies not to any halfheartedness but, on the contrary, to the depth of the institution's commitment to Fourierism, and to the cause of Association generally. The journal is devoted to all the "socialisms" then prevalent, its articles and reviews covering the whole gamut of social wrongs and reforming possibilities.[36] In the first volume alone there are articles on, for example, capital punishment, the encroachment of capital upon labor, the abandonment of children in Boston, prisons and the reforming of criminals, the influence of machinery, the superiority of justice to charity, the conditions in Lowell, the advantages of a short working day, slavery, the Working Men's Association, the wrongs of women, and many other similar causes. Ripley explains the position in an editorial in the third issue:

> We trust that our brothers of the different Associations in the United States will not regard the Harbinger as the exclusive organ of the Brook Farm Phalanx. Although issued from its press, it is intended, that it should represent, as far as possible, the interests of the general movement which is now spreading with such encouraging progress throughout the land.[37]

The likeliest explanation of the subsequent silence on the part of the Farm's leaders is not that they did not want to break a butterfly upon a wheel, but that the almost simultaneous collapse of the community and of the national impetus toward Association must have had a traumatic effect on those who had invested their emotional and intellectual capital in the movement. By 1850 Ripley, Dwight, and Dana had embarked on careers which bore little or no relationship to their earlier ideals[38]—and to put a psychological distance between themselves and their unsuccessful experiment was a natural, and perhaps even necessary, undertaking.

By an irony that seems rather appropriate in view of Brook Farm's precarious stance between the world of fantasy and that of harsh social realities, one of the effects of this uneasy silence is that we have to rely heavily for information about the daily life of the community on writers who lay great stress on the fun they had during their time there. It is small wonder that Lindsay Swift should claim that "Enjoyment was almost from the first a serious pursuit of the community,"[39] when we see the emphasis laid on entertainment in most of the reminiscences. John Van Der Zee Sears devotes a whole chapter to the subject—it seems a long way from the *Harbinger*'s gritty sociology to his inauspicious opening: "Our slide down the knoll proved very popular"—and John Thomas Codman has one entitled "Fun Alive" which deals almost exclusively with the community's addiction to punning. The quantity, if not the quality, of this word-play inevitably bathes the Farm in an Illyrian glow. Ora Gannet Sedgwick, Amelia Russell, George P. Bradford, and Arthur Sumner all add their own lists of pleasures to the register.[40]

This apparent sybaritism can be explained away to some extent by pointing out that most of these writers were looking back to their youth from the standpoint of old age—indeed, all of them except for Amelia Russell and George P. Bradford, were teenagers during their time at the Farm. In any case, despite Charles Lane's grumbling, there is no real need to excuse the fact that there were pleasures available at the community—unless, like one commentator, you object to the fact that the members allowed only ten hours a day for work.[41] Perhaps the best defense of all is to point out that if one compares the kind of play the Farmers enjoyed with the way they organized their work, it becomes clear that the two activities were not merely compatible, but were each controlled by the same overriding concern. Whether they were at work or at play the Farmers were attempting to cement the bonds that joined them together and to create a new kind of communal consciousness.

It is worth looking at Brook Farm entertainment more closely. Probably the most vivid picture we have of it occurs in Hawthorne's *Blithedale Romance*. Of course, Hawthorne warns the reader in his Preface about taking his romance to be a record of the actual experiences of the Brook Farmers, and it would be an act of critical insensitivity to look too closely for parallels between the work of the imagination and historical reality. Particularly dangerous perhaps would be any attempt to manipulate the masks of Hawthorne's characters until they fit the known features of individual communitarians. At the same time it is fair to remark that Hawthorne's very obsession with masks, with play-acting, with the relationship between public and private identity, reflects one of the central features of Brook Farm life. For this reason it is worth looking at the scene presented in the chapter "The Masqueraders," particularly as there is substantial evidence that the masquerade described here actually took place.

Coverdale has been away from the community, and in this chapter we are given a rather odd description of his return. As he approaches Blithedale he begins to suspect that the farm has been abandoned. His anxiety is not a serious one, however, but a form of self-teasing which somehow serves to increase the shock when he finds that the buildings

The Ideology of Brook Farm

are actually deserted. His anticipation had resulted from his feeling that the community could hardly have existed in the first place:

> I indulged in a hundred odd and extravagant conjectures. Either there was no such place as Blithedale, nor ever had been, nor any brotherhood of thoughtful labourers, like what I seemed to recollect there, or else it was all changed during my absence. It had been nothing but dream work and enchantment. I should seek in vain for the old farmhouse, and for the greensward, the potato-fields, the root-crops, and the acres of Indian corn, and for all that configuration of the land which I had imagined. It would be another spot, and an utter strangeness.[42]

The community is still there, as it turns out, but Coverdale is right to anticipate "utter strangeness": he discovers "a concourse of strange figures beneath the overshadowing branches. They appeared, and vanished, and came again, confusedly, with the streaks of sunlight glimmering down upon them." This description, taken out of context, has a quality of Gothic menace about it. Rather uncharacteristically, however, Hawthorne has taken pains to drain the uneasy overtones from the situation—the wood "seemed as full of jollity as if Comus and his crew were holding their revels in one of its usually lonesome glades." When, therefore, we abruptly come across the masqueraders, the effect is one of benign surrealism (if the two terms do not cancel each other out):

> Among them was an Indian chief, with blanket, feathers, and war-paint, and uplifted tomahawk; and near him, looking fit to be his woodland bride, the goddess Diana, with the crescent on her head, and attended by our big lazy dog, in lack of any fleeter hound. . . . Another party consisted of a Bavarian broom-girl, a negro of the Jim Crow order, one or two foresters of the middle ages, a Kentucky woodsman in his trimmed hunting-shirt and deer-skin leggings, and a Shaker elder, quaint, demure, broad-brimmed, and square-skirted. Shepherds of Arcadia, and allegorical figures from the Faerie Queen, were oddly mixed up with these.[43]

Coverdale is more conscious than ever of being an outsider and while it is obviously simply chance that he should happen to return while the members of the community are merry-making in this fashion, the accident is of a deliberate and significant kind. These strange and apparently arbitrary juxtapositions, which he finds so alien and confusing, are characteristic of the community; in fact it was the intention of the Brook Farmers to create just such an atmosphere of cheerful, if slightly self-conscious, role-playing as that established in this scene.

Many of the reminiscences discuss the masquerade which provided the source of Hawthorne's description. Codman appends to his book a letter signed "Charles" which obviously describes the actual event: "One of the ladies personated Diana, and any one entering her wooded precincts was liable to be shot with one of her arrows." Ora Gannet Sedgwick attempts to correct the record in her version—apparently Hawthorne's "one variation from the facts was in making me, both there and in the American Note-book, the gypsy fortune-teller, whereas that part was really taken by Mrs. Ripley, and I was merely the messenger to bring persons to her," while Arthur Sumner, who actually joined the Farm after Hawthorne had left, remembers attending "a fancy dress picnic in the woods, which might have furnished Mr. Hawthorne his scene in the Blithedale Romance."[44]

There were many similar events, and they are recalled with a graphic detail which suggests the importance of the part they played in the life of the community. John Van Der Zee Sears claims that

> The finest pageant we ever had was arranged by the Festal Series, after the reorganization into a phalanx. It was historic in design, illustrating the Elizabethan period in England. Dr. Ripley personated Shakespeare; Miss Ripley, Queen Elizabeth, in a tissue paper ruff, which I helped to make; Mr. Dana, Sir Walter Raleigh; Mary Bullard, the most beautiful of our young women, Mary Queen of Scots, and Charles Hosmer, Sir Philip Sidney.[45]

Similarly, Amelia Russell describes another one, held at Christmas time, at which were impersonations of Hamlet, Greeks and Circasians, an Indian, Little Nell and her grandfather, and Spanish bolero dancers.[46] We also hear about other tableaus, charades, rural fetes, and a prodigious list of plays and operas performed in whole or in part by the Farmers: Byron's *Corsair*, Douglas Jerrold's *The Rent Day*, *The Midsummer Night's Dream*, the *Caliph of Baghdad*, *Zampa*, *Norma*, and so on. Of course, other activities—music, tobogganing, dancing—are mentioned, but those requiring acting of one sort or another seem to have been the most important, and the ones that had the deepest effect on the minds of the participants.[47]

We are already familiar with the equation Transcendentalism equals play. However, the significance of the kind of play described in the *Blithedale Romance* and in so many of the reminiscences is that it relates this formula to what could otherwise seem the opposing one of Fourierism equals work. There are interesting connections between the assumptions underlying masquerade and those that determine the Fourierist theory of labor; and the source of these connections can be traced to the inception of the community. From the very beginning, the Farmers were conscious that the individual's identity, or rather his sense of it, was unduly restricted by the rigidity of the social role that was forced on him in "civilization." They were aware of the problem of the dissociated sensibility and sought to solve it by creating a balance between physical and intellectual labor in the community. As a sympathetic contributor to the *Monthly Miscellany of Religion and Letters* demanded, in a very early account of the Farm, "How dare I sacrifice not only my own, but others' health, in sequestrating myself from my share of bodily labour, or neglecting a due mental cultivation?"[48] The descriptions we have of the pre-Fourierist period show us what this involved—we find Hawthorne uneasily shoveling manure or dealing with the transcendental heifer, and trying desperately to keep his writing going; George Ripley teaching in the school, administering the Farm, discussing intellectual topics with his neighbor Theodore Parker, and contemplatively milking cows; Charles Anderson Dana teaching, laboring, and organizing a corps of waiters; George P. Bradford leaving his hoeing to go and teach, only to find his pupil was still out hunting, and had forgotten the lesson.[49] Frothingham tells us that "When convenient, the men did the women's work,"[50] and indeed there are accounts of them doing the laundry, cooking, washing up, and hanging out the clothes. In any case, we are told, the women were able to cope with their duties because "By the wide distribution of these labors, no one has any great weight of any one thing."[51]

It is clear that the community was trying to make available to each member as wide a range of experience as possible. George Willis Cooke quotes Charles Anderson Dana as saying of the Brook Farmers that "in order to reform society, in order to regenerate the world and to realize democracy in the social relations, they determined that their society should first pursue agriculture, which would give every man plenty of out-door labor in the free air, and at the same time the opportunity of study, of becoming familiar with everything in literature and learning."[52] This desire to run the gamut of occupations and identities, to be everything from Diana to a schoolmarm, from a woodsman to an intellectual, is the Brook Farmers' most noticeable characteristic. It was one that could find complete fulfillment in Fourier's scheme. After the reorganization we find, by looking at the Brook Farm Account Book for June 1844 to April 1845, that, for example, C. A. Dana's typical working month (this one is May 1844) is divided up as follows: ten days (of ten hours each), three hours, agricultural; one day seven hours, domestic; six days nine hours educational; one day, six and a quarter hours miscellaneous; two days, eight and three-quarter hours, functional.[53] The women, needless to say, have a more restricted range of opportunities; indeed Marianne Dwight describes in a letter to her brother Frank, dated 14 April 1844, what would appear to be a desultory round of domestic occupations—if it were not for the manner in which she writes about them—:

> Now my business is as follows (but perhaps liable to frequent change): I wait on the breakfast table (½ hour), help M. A. Ripley clear away the breakfast things, etc. (1½ hours), go into the dormitory group until eleven o'clock,—dress for dinner—then over to the Eyrie and sew until dinner time,—half past twelve. Then from half past one or two o'clock until ½ past five I teach drawing in Pilgrim Hall and sew in the Eyrie. At ½ past five go down to the Hive, to help set the tea table, and afterwards I wash teacups, etc., till about ½ past seven. Thus I make a long day of it, but alternation of work and pleasant company and chats make it pleasant. I am about entering a flower garden group and assisting Miss Russell in doing up muslins.[54]

The precision of the times, the reference to "groups," above all the praise of "alternation of work" identify the Fourierist structure behind Marianne Dwight's working day. Fourier's scheme of industrial organization (like the rest of his universe) is based on the operation of series and groups, and these, with a gallant defiance of the laws of time and motion, dictate that all labor shall be broken up into small units, so that the individual can go from one occupation to another before he grows stale.

Oddly enough, this apparent dispersal of energies and indeed of identities in the Fourierist scheme is balanced by a doctrine which claims the underlying unity of all men and things. In fact, the latter is a necessary prelude to the former. The "Introductory Statement" to the second Brook Farm constitution states that "while on the one hand we yield an unqualified assent to that doctrine of Universal unity which Fourier teaches, so on the other, our whole observation has shown us the truth of the practical arrangements which he deduces therefrom." These practical arrangements boil down to "The law of groups and series," which "is, as we are convinced, the law of human nature, and when men are in true social relations their industrial organization will necessarily assume these forms."[55] At this point, it is worth looking closely at Fourier's doctrines in order to find out exactly what the Farmers mean when they talk about the "doctrine of Universal unity," the "law of groups and series," and so on. The best source of information, for us as well as for them, is undoubtedly the writings of Albert Brisbane, Fourier's most prominent American disciple. Because of the orthodoxy built into Fourier's scheme, almost all the material on him takes the form of translations or summaries. This means, of course, that there is a finite amount of work for his American protégés to produce. Brisbane cornered the market, as it were, and his *Social Destiny of Man*, his four *Democratic Review* articles on "Association and Attractive Industry," and his *Concise Exposition of the Doctrine of Association* provide a comprehensive account of the social implications of Fourierism.[56]

Brisbane was well qualified to be the leading American authority on the subject, since he was one of the few admirers to have seen the light while the master was still alive. He was born in upstate New York, of a well-to-do family, and spent a good part of his youth on a grand tour of Europe and Asia, during which he attended Cousin's lectures in Paris and Hegel's in Berlin. He became interested in St. Simonianism, and then Fourierism, and in 1832, shortly before the master's death, he actually met and studied with Fourier himself. On returning to America, he published *Social Destiny of Man* in 1840, and followed it with innumerable articles, including a weekly column in Greeley's *Tribune*.[57] His efforts brought a rich, if short-lived, harvest. John Humphrey Noyes, the founder of the Oneida Perfectionists, uses the data left by A. J. Macdonald, a contemporary student of Association, to show that there were approximately thirty-five phalanxes scattered about the country, with a total membership of over 3,000 people during the 1840s.[58] This takes no account, of course, of the many who were interested in, or even committed to, Fourierism, but who never put their beliefs to the test. Greeley, and indeed Brisbane himself, belong to this group. Nevertheless the latter was a frequent visitor to the Farm, staying there on one occasion for several months, and he was one of the editors of the *Harbinger*. Codman tells us that he did not regard Brook Farm as an ideal Fourieristic experiment (any more than did Ripley), but his influence on the later path of the community was enormous.[59] It may not have been exactly what he wanted, but he was responsible—to a large degree—for what it actually was.

Brisbane tells that a perfect society is possible as a result of Fourier's theory—or discovery, as the latter complacently put it[60]—that attractions are proportional to destinies. In other words, each individual has a certain number of drives or "passions"; each of these directs him toward a certain objective which has only to be achieved and he will be perfectly happy.[61] These passions can be analyzed and tabulated. They are as follows: five sensitive passions, one arising out of each of the senses, which have as their object "Elegance, Riches and Material Harmonies"; four affective passions—friendship, love, ambition, and paternity—which tend toward "Groups and passional Harmonies"; and, more obscurely, three "Distributive and Directing Passions," the "Emulative," "Alternating," and "Composite." These are, respectively, the desire for intrigue and rivalry; for variety of occupation; and for the double enjoyment of intellectual and emotional satisfaction; and they lead to

"Series and Concert of Masses." This whole nexus of desires can receive fulfillment only if work is arranged according to Fourier's blueprint.⁶²

The Harmonies—social and otherwise—are distributed according to groups and series. "Nature employs Series of Groups in the whole distribution of the Universe; the three kingdoms,—the animal, vegetable and mineral,—present us only Series of Groups."⁶³ In other words, despite the apparent variety of existing things, their composition and relationship to each other conforms to a consistent law. In his autobiography Brisbane describes the moment when he achieved an imaginative grasp of what this meant:

> I perceived that there was unity of law with great diversity of phenomena; that the laws manifested themselves differently according to the differences of the material spheres in which they acted. Hence unity of law and variety in manifestation. The same law, for instance, which governs the distribution, co-ordination, and arrangement of the notes of music governs the distribution, co-ordination, and arrangement of the planets and the solar system. As sounds are notes in musical harmony, so the planets are notes in a sidereal harmony. Continuing the analogy: the species in the animal or vegetable kingdom are the notes of a vast organic harmony; the bones in the human body are the notes of an osseous harmony, and these, with the muscles and other parts of the human organism, are the notes of a physical harmony. *Law is unchanging*, but there is infinite variety in its manifestations;—such manifestations being as rich and complex as are the varied spheres or departments of the Universe.⁶⁴

I have discussed elsewhere the Transcendentalists' fascination with the concept of "unity of law with diversity of phenomena."⁶⁵ Thoreau's assertion that the "Maker of this earth but patented a leaf," Emerson's gleeful account, in his essay on Swedenborg, of what appears to be the same osseous harmony that Brisbane describes—"spine on spine to the end of the world"—indicate the centrality of that "cordial truth" to be found in the "fable of Proteus." As Emerson's multi-tongued and athletic Sphinx (a creature as supple, surely, as Fourier's anti-lion) puts it:

> Through a thousand voices
> Spoke the universal dame;
> "Who telleth one of my meanings,
> Is master of all I am."⁶⁶

Naturally, since Fourier's law is unchanging, it must apply to industrial organization as well as everything else: labor is miserable and inefficient because it has not so far obeyed it. All working men are to be divided into groups, and series of groups. A group is the basic unit of labor and "should be composed of at least seven persons." These form three divisions or three sub-groups, the centre one of which should be stronger than the two wings or extremes. A group of seven persons will furnish the three following divisions: 2-3-2 (two persons at each wing and three in the centre). Each division would be engaged with some department of the work with which the Group was occupied.

A series is made up of groups in the same way that a group is composed of individuals. It "must contain at least three Groups—a Centre and two Wings: twenty-four persons is the least number with which a Series can be formed. The Central Group should be stronger than the Groups of the Wings."[67] This structure enables one's emulative passion to be fully engaged.

> The ascending wing will be occupied with the heaviest branch of a work, if the Series be engaged in manufactures, and with the largest variety, if engaged in the cultivation of grains, fruits, vegetables or flowers; the centre will be occupied with the most elegant and attractive branch or variety; and the descending wing with the lightest and smallest.[68]

The idea is that the two wings will unite to excel the center; they will have numbers on their side, while the center will have the satisfaction of producing the highest quality of article. This careful discrimination of function avoids the danger of easily resolved and therefore ineffective competition.

This organization of labor caters not merely for Emulation, but for all the other passions as well. One will never spend more than an hour or two on any particular activity: that deals with Alternation; the industrial system will be so highly specialized that each person will be able to do exactly the work he wants to do and will do it in the company of those who are also happy in their jobs: this provides the Composite Pleasure of interesting employment and good company. Friendship, Love, and Paternity are kept at full stretch because the mobility of the worker enables him to choose his company: he can work side by side with his wife if he wants to—and for as long as he wants to. Ambition is catered for by the possibilities of rivalry, and because the individual is making maximum use of his abilities. The five Sensitive Passions—Sight, Hearing, Smell, Taste, and Touch—can play on the beautiful environment that is the natural result of living in a community and thereby breaking down the distinction between home and work, and of the joint-stock system by which everyone receives his share in the whole and therefore possesses both the worker's needs and the proprietor's powers.[69]

Perhaps the oddest assumption behind this whole system is not that the deepest wishes of individuals can be identified and provided for, but that we are capable of achieving all the tasks we want to perform. Brisbane deals with this question in a passage in his *Concise Exposition*:

> It will be objected that if an individual takes part in so many branches of Industry, he will become perfect in none; this difficulty will be entirely obviated by the minute *division of labor*, which will take place, and by assigning to each individual of a Group the performance of a detail of the work with which it is engaged. In a Group of fruit-growers, for example, a person will attend to the grafting; now an intelligent person can learn to graft as well in a few days as in a lifetime, and his knowledge in this branch will enable him to belong to several Series of horticulturalists. Thus, while changes of scene and company would prevent monotony and apathy, the same detail of a work could be performed. A skilful turner could belong to Groups of chair-makers, without varying materially the nature of his work; a person skilled in working leather could belong to the Series of saddlers, glove-makers, and shoe-makers, and the part in which he excelled might be performed in each of the branches of Industry.[70]

The "division of labor" (technically speaking "parcelled exercise") is very minute indeed: one does not just want to work with, say, a flower, but with a specific part of a tulip, and one's taste will exactly complement that of one's colleagues: "for among twelve persons with a passion for the tulip, none of the twelve will have a love for the twelve functions connected with its cultivation; therefore unless they make a parcelled division of their work and distribute functions according to tastes, disagreements and discord will break out."[71]

After focusing on one's work with such microscopic intensity one would expect to feel something of a jolt when it came to switching occupations at the rate that is suggested:

> A man, for example, may be
> At five o'clock in the morning in a Group of Shepherds;
> At seven o'clock in a Group of gardeners;
> At nine o'clock in a Group of fishermen.[72]

However, Fourier is confident that the individual will fit exactly into each of the niches that have been made available for him. He asserts that "THERE IS NOTHING ARBITRARY IN THE SYSTEM WE PROPOSE, we resort to no laws or regulations of human invention; we make use of three of the twelve passions to direct the other nine with the freest and most economical of systems, that of Series of Groups, which system is a universal desire of the human heart, as well as the distribution followed in the whole order of known Nature."[73] The point is that the configuration of the individual's passions actually corresponds— on its own small scale—with the intricate topography of the natural

The Ideology of Brook Farm

order. He is like a piece of jigsaw puzzle, and when he interlocks with the other members of the phalanx, they provide together a miniature reproduction of the world itself. The phalanx is a self-sufficient community, able to cope with all life's needs. As Emerson sarcastically expressed it:

> It takes sixteen hundred and eighty men to make one Man, complete in all faculties; that is, to be sure that you have got a good joiner, a good cook, a barber, a poet, a judge, an umbrella-maker, a major and alderman, and so on. Your community should consist of two thousand persons, to prevent accidents of omission.[74]

Despite Emerson's sneer, however, the premise on which the phalanx is based has its points of resemblance with that underlying the individualistic variety of Transcendentalism. In this connection, it is worth looking at the following extract from a letter to John Sullivan Dwight written by George William Curtis, an ex-Brook Farmer who disapproved of Fourierism:

> Raphael could have sung as Shakespeare, and Milton have hewn as many forms as Angelo. Yet a divine economy rules these upper spiritual regions, as sure and steadfast as the order of the stars. Raphael must paint and Homer sing, yet the same soul gilds the picture and sweetens the song. So Venus and Mars shine yellow and red, but the same central fire is the light of each. In the capacity of doing all things well lies the willingness to serve one good. The Jack of all trades is sure to be good at none, for who is good at all is Jack of one only. It seemed a bitter thing to me, formerly, that painters must only paint and sculptors carve; but I see now the wisdom. In one thing well done lies the secret of doing all.[75]

The letter is dated 25 November 1843, shortly after Curtis left the community, and shortly before what he (as a Transcendentalist of the picnicking type) was to term the "earlier, golden age of the colony" gave way to the Fourierist period.[76]

Curtis has come to accept—at first unwillingly—that in order to achieve anything one must confine oneself strictly within a single discipline. Obviously, this is very different from Fourier's attitude, and yet there is a point in common. Curtis has an atomic view of the structure of the universe. Things are inextricably connected with each other in such a way that even though each of us deals with only a single point in the large pattern, the reverberations of our actions run right through the whole framework so that "In one thing well done lies the secret of doing all." Fourier believes that the basic unit of the social universe is an organized system which is composed of almost 2,000 people and which can be reproduced in the form of the phalanx; Curtis pins his faith on the individual. Both, however, assume that once you have mastered the part you have access to the whole. Both believe that the material and social universe has a consistent and repetitive order. Curtis sees the lowest common denominator of this system as an atom; Fourier finds that it is a molecule. The two men are simply disagreeing over the size and complexity of the basic component.

Curtis' description is the one we have come to associate with Transcendentalism: it is the Emersonian position. And yet Fourier's account, with its emphasis on communal identity, offered certain rewards that individualism could not provide. Emerson himself gives negative evidence of this, when he states in his "American Scholar" address that

> there is One Man,—present to all particular men only partially, or through one faculty; and . . . you must take the whole society to find the whole man. Man is not a farmer, or a professor, or an engineer, but he is all. Man is priest, and scholar, and statesman, and producer, and soldier. In the *divided* or social state these functions are parcelled out to individuals, each of whom aims to do his stint of the joint work, whilst each other performs his. The fable implies that the individual to possess himself, must sometimes return from his own labor to embrace all the other laborers. But, unfortunately, this original unit, this fountain of power, has been so distributed to multitudes, has been so minutely subdivided and peddled out, that it is spilled into drops, and cannot be gathered. The state of society is one in which the members have suffered amputation from the trunk and strut about so many walking monsters,—a good finger, a neck, a stomach, an elbow, but never a man.
>
> Man is thus metamorphosed into a thing, into many things.[77]

The phalanx admirably fulfills the implications of the fable. It provides a place where the individual can "return from his own labor to embrace all the other laborers." Actually, it does more even than that. The variety of occupations provides the individual with the opportunity of fulfilling so many different functions that he is no longer a mere member, but a man—or at least, more nearly one than he is in civilization. It is interesting to compare Emerson's metaphor of dismemberment with a much more matter-of-fact remark by Brisbane. He is pointing out that many kinds of work lead to physical illness—hernias, obesity, and so on—but that this danger will be avoided by the short occupations of phalansterian life. He goes on to say, almost in answer to Emerson's complaint, that the "health of man is promoted by this perpetual variety of functions, which exercising successively all parts of the body, all faculties of the mind, maintains activity and equilibrium."[78]

The attraction of role-playing for the Brook Farmers—whether it took the form of masquerade or of manual labor—becomes obvious. A simple accumulation of diverse activity frees the individual from a fixed and arbitrary social function, and enables him to become more nearly a whole person. Moreover, the phalanx integrates its members into a new unity—helps them to become what Emerson so much wanted everyone to be: one man. When one considers the latter's doctrine of a racial consciousness to which we all contribute, it seems odd that he should have been so unsympathetic to Fourierism. After all, the phalanx is a limited manifestation of that collective mind—a kind of finite over-soul.[79]

Fourier clearly had something to offer the Transcendentalists in his account of human identity and the relationship between the individual and the rest of society. He proved equally useful in another respect. The most difficult problem utopians are faced with, no matter where or when they perform their experiment, is that of the relationship between the good society and the historical process. Fourier, in his usual punctilious manner, showed the Brook Farmers exactly how such a relationship could be established.

Harold Clark Goddard, in his elderly but still useful *Studies in New England Transcendentalism*, puts his finger on the problem faced by the Transcendentalists. He exclaims at the fact that "at the very time when the historical way of regarding things was grounding itself in the minds of men, a movement should occur whose very essence was a denial of history," and remarks that while the world was learning that "society and civilization are the products of an evolution," the Transcendentalists were propounding the thesis "that both may be brought, outright, into perfect being."[80] Goddard's account is an oversimplification, of course, but an awareness of the full complexity of the Transcendentalists' position serves to deepen the paradox he has stated, rather than to solve it. The Newness, as its proponents were well aware, was not as new as all that. The Transcendentalists were much influenced by French and German thought and were perfectly *au fait* with doctrines of historical evolution. George Bancroft, who hovered on the periphery of the movement for a time, put the evolutionist's case succinctly:

> The world cannot retrograde; the dark ages cannot return. Dynasties perish; cities are buried; nations have been victims to error, or martyrs for right; Humanity has always been on the advance; its soul has always been gaining maturity and power.[81]

It is probably fair to say that Theodore Parker's great projected work on the history and development of religion is as much a product—or would have been, if he had completed it—of the movement's afflatus as Thoreau's wooden hut by Walden Pond.[82] Actually the famous last sentence of *Walden*—"The sun is but a morning star"—could stand as an assertion of progressivism if it were not qualified by the preceding passage:

> I do not say that John or Jonathan will realize all this; such is the character of that morrow which mere lapse of time can never make to dawn. The light which puts out our eyes is darkness to us. Only that day dawns to which we are awake.[83]

As it is, Thoreau seems to leave us with the doctrine of the "angle of vision": do not change things, just look at them aright. Nevertheless, in his notion that the light originally appears to be darkness, he is pointing toward a solution already adopted by many of the evolutionists, as we shall see shortly.

Emerson's essay on "History" plunges us into the very heart of the problem. By establishing an analogy between the growth of the individual and the development of civilization he implies an evolutionary view. The ancient Greek army, for example, is "a gang of great boys, with such a code of honour and such lax discipline as great boys have."[84] Different phases of civilization reflect different periods in an individual's life. Therefore the student of history "interprets the age of chivalry by his own age of chivalry, and the days of maritime adventure and circumnavigation by quite parallel miniature experiences of his own."[85] At the same time, however, there is a dimension of human experience which takes place outside the realm of history. Man "is the compend of time; he is also the correlative of nature."[86] Emerson appears to visualize a coming time that will be emancipated from the temporal order, a human destiny that will take place outside the historical process. Nature and history have been at odds; the latter does not participate in the harmonies which are embodied in the former. Emerson foresees a new historiography, one which will release man from the burden of his past by reestablishing him in the eternal natural world. This new perspective will bring about human redemption:

> Broader and deeper we must write our annals,—from an ethical reformation, from an influx of the ever new, ever sanative conscience,—if we would trulier express our central and wide related nature, instead of this old chronology of selfishness and pride to which we have too long lent our eyes. Already that day exists for us, shines in on us unawares, but the path of science and of letters is not the way into nature. The idiot, the Indian, the

child and the unschooled farmer's boy stand nearer to the light by which nature is to be read, than the dissector or the antiquary.[87]

Emerson has in fact extended his argument from history to human knowledge in general. Civilized man is out of step with the rest of creation, and therefore only those who by an accident of birth find themselves outside our cultural frame of reference can have access to nature. There is not much comfort to be derived from this diagnosis despite the hopeful rhythms of Emerson's prose. All may be well for the idiot and the Indian but for the rest of us, for John and Jonathan as Thoreau rather patronizingly put it, the future looks somewhat bleak.

At this point it is worth referring to one of the earlier products of the Transcendentalist movement: a review (published in the *Christian Examiner* in March 1834) by Frederic Henry Hedge of an address by Edward Everett on the subject of social progress.[88] Hedge's discussion of the problem involved in the progressive view of history deserves some respect, if for no other reason than because he was a central enough figure in the movement for the Transcendental Club to be frequently referred to as "Hedge's Club." There is another reason, as it happens: his account of historical development points toward the manner in which the utopian impulse could be accommodated in the evolutionary system.

Hedge admits that "Alternate civilization and barbarism make up the apparent history of man."[89] Nevertheless, he goes on to claim that society has never actually gone backward; at the worst it has stood still for a time. The point is that progress is not a consistent, accumulative phenomenon but is a matter of sporadic evolutionary developments. He calls these phases of growth "impulses" or "pulsations." They occur in a specific context and then, by a kind of chemical process, communicate themselves to society at large: "Each pulsation [of the human mind] has sent forth into the world some new sentiment or principle, some discovery or invention, which like small portions of leaven, have successively communicated their quickening energy to the whole mass of society."[90] Just as, in the natural world, the maker had to do no more than patent a leaf, so in society a single "invention" can gain universal currency. The utopian microcosm, if only it is correctly formulated (and the possibilities were to range from Thoreau alone in his hut to the plans for a full-scale phalanx), has the power of redeeming the macrocosm. Moreover, a sense of dissatisfaction with the modern world, a feeling that civilization is aimless and sterile, need not cast a shadow over the evolutionists' perspective—Hedge's theory of the alternation of civilization and barbarism sees to that. As Bronson Alcott expressed it in one of his "Orphic Sayings":

> The hunger of an age is alike a presentiment and pledge of its own supply. ... Now, men are lean and famishing; but, behold, the divine Husbandman has driven his share through the age, and sown us bread that we may not perish.[91]

It is not difficult to understand the appeal of Fourier's account of the historical process when one looks at the way in which certain of the Transcendentalists were grappling with the conflict between evolutionism and utopianism. Although Hedge was confident that there was nothing irregular or arbitrary about the occurrence of "pulsations," he did not pretend to have deciphered the historical pattern of which they formed part. Instead, he awaited the coming of a "philosophic historian" who would be able to "trace and exhibit these successive impulses. He who can do this, and he only will be able to furnish a systematic history of Man: something very different from, and infinitely more important than the histories we now have of dynasties and tribes."[92] Fourier provides just such a "systematic history of Man."

Fourier's series do not simply extend vertically as hierarchies of phenomena, and horizontally as equivalences between those different hierarchies: they have a third dimension, too—existence in time. Needless to say, the "Formula of the Movement of a Serie" (Brisbane sometimes found it convenient to distinguish between a singular and plural form of the word "series") is itself a "serie":

Ascending Transition	*or* **Birth**
First Phasis	*or* **Infancy**
Second Phasis	*or* **Youth**
Apogee	*or* **MATURITY**
Third Phasis	*or* **Decline**
Fourth Phasis	*or* **Decrepitude**
Descending Transition	*or* **Death**[93]

Human history has consisted of four of these temporal series so far: savage, patriarchal, barbarian, and civilized. The movement of the fourth, civilization, can be tabulated as in the table on page 27.

A clear indication of the way Fourierism manages to have the best of both worlds is that Brisbane can follow his account of this elaborately structured past by dismissing the confidence in "progress" that he detects in the contemporary historians of France and Germany because they "sanction the history of the past, the principles of which they wish to be the basis of all future improvement; they admire the dreary career of mankind as a magnificent achievement, and endeavour to read in their annals of blood a wisdom, which they claim to be Providence, but which is an illusive chimera of their own erroneous speculations."[94] The reason this attitude is possible is that the temporal

TABLE OF THE MOVEMENT OF CIVILIZATION, WITH
ITS FOUR AGES OR PHASES[95]

ASCENDING MOVEMENT.
>First age. *Infancy.*
>Exclusive marriage or Monogamy.
>Feudality of the Nobles.
>Pivot: Civil rights of the wife.
>Federation of the Great Barons.
>Illusions in chivalry.
>
>Second age. *Growth.*
>Privileges of free Towns and Cities.
>Cultivation of the Arts and Sciences.
>Pivot: Enfranchisement of the serfs or laboring classes.
>Representative System.
>Illusions in Liberty or Democratic Agitations.

Maturity: { Experimental Chemistry: Art of Navigation. National Loans: Clearing of Forests without excesses.

DESCENDING MOVEMENT.
>Third age. *Decline.*
>Commercial and Fiscal spirit.
>Stock companies.
>Pivot: Maratime Monopoly.
>Anarchical Commerce.
>Financial Illusions.
>
>Fourth age. *Decrepitude.*
>Agricultural Loaning Companies.
>Associated Farms; discipline system of cultivation.
>Pivot: Commercial and Industrial Feudality.
>Contractors of Feudal Monopoly: Oligarchy of Capital.
>Illusions in Association.

serie has what may be called organic form: in other words, it possesses a beginning, a middle, and an end, and serie follows serie, as generation follows generation. Thus history is not a simple success story, a matter of the cultural survival of the spiritually fittest. Instead, new stages of human development arise phoenix-like out of the ashes of the old. The structure of the serie is admirably suited to recording the successive "pulsations" of the human mind, while at the same time it provides a satisfactory explanation of the imperfections of the present social state. We are, in fact, in a period of decline; but for that very reason we are entitled to look forward to a more glorious future.

Another problem the evolutionary view of history brought with it was that of the status, and the freedom, of the individual. Fourier's position on this issue was not so easy for the Transcendentalists to accept. The Unitarianism on which they had been brought up may have been dry and inconsistent, but it represented a reaction against Calvinism and embodied Enlightenment values: it taught a respect for the powers of the human mind, man's ability to choose between good and evil, and his right to select his own destiny. The Transcendentalists emphasized these features, diminishing the power of authority in favor of a doctrine of personal responsibility. Although too much can be made of their individualism, it would be just as false to assume that they were blasé about free will. "Nothing can bring you peace but yourself," proclaims Emerson at the end of "Self-Reliance." "Nothing can bring you peace but the triumph of principles."[96] And yet it is very difficult to combine a belief in the possibility of moral choice with a doctrine of the approaching social millennium.

Since the human race is proceeding inevitably, if not necessarily on the most direct route, toward a heaven on earth, then surely, by taking our own contribution seriously, we are participating in the youthful error of Hawthorne's Holgrave "in fancying that it mattered anything to the great end in view, whether he himself should contend for it or against it."[97] It is a short step from saying, with Bancroft, that the "world cannot retrograde" to claiming that everything we do must be for the best; and an even shorter one from there to the belief that we are simply tools in the hands of Providence, without free will of our own. As usual, Emerson is a good representative of Transcendentalist confusion on the subject. His essay "The Over-Soul" provides an example of the ambiguous nature of the individual's status. Here we find that men possess enough independence of will to be able to "forsake their native nobleness" in "habitual and mean service to the world."[98] At the same time, however, we are told that the facts of experience, intractable though they may appear, will finally give way before our true destiny. We can be optimistic because "the argument which is always forthcoming to silence those who conceive extraordinary hopes of man, namely the appeal to experience, is forever invalid and vain. We give up the past to the objector, and yet we hope."[99] Despite everything—ourselves included—we have access to a higher life, the over-soul:

> By virtue of this inevitable nature, private will is overpowered, and maugre our efforts or our imperfections, your genius will speak from you, and mine from me. That which we are, we shall teach, not voluntarily but involuntarily. Thoughts come into our minds by avenues which we never left open, and

thoughts go out of our minds through avenues which we never voluntarily opened.[100]

Emerson has provided us with a kind of inverted fatalism: the individual is part of the "eternal ONE," whether he chooses to be so, or not.

Fourier shares this belief in insurmountable good. According to his table (see above), we are now in the third age of civilization, rapidly approaching the fourth. The new age will dawn because businessmen and speculators, unphilanthropic though they may be, will begin to find that Association is the most profitable social form. After a period of misguided experimentation (Owen's work at New Harmony, if not the more successful attempt at New Lanark, suggests an example), they will introduce the new order. It is not the over-soul, but the forces of history, as he interprets them, that will bring it about: "Thus the human race, to accomplish their Destiny, have to be urged on by force; the paths which lead to it are so rugged and the obstacles to be overcome are so great, that the attainment would be abandoned, if the double power—the political and monied, and the interest of those who wield it—did not force the mass to surmount these obstacles."[101] This being the case, there was not much point in doing anything except wait for things to happen. Fourier took little interest in the "partial" experiments done in his own time, just as, no doubt, he would have taken little interest in Brook Farm, the North American Phalanx, and the other American communities which attempted, imperfectly, to carry out his precepts. Instead, "Every day on the stroke of twelve he made a point of returning to his lodgings to wait for the appearance of the Maecenas who would somehow, of his own accord, arrive to consult with him on the practical details for the establishment of a model."[102]

The Transcendentalists were obviously impressed by the inexorable progress of Fourier's juggernaut. Its independence of individual volition appealed to that side of their thinking which viewed human history as the manifestation of God's will. But Fourier's answer could not satisfy them completely. The willingness to muddle through, with inadequate numbers and occupations, and only a vague approximation of Fourier's model, testifies to their continuing faith in the role of the individual in the broad historical effort, to their belief that one could exert leverage on the course of events by the power of one's will. The Transcendentalists' problem was basically that they suffered from an excess of optimism, which led simultaneously to confidence in a benevolent destiny, and at the same time to an increased respect for the individual's powers. The writings of Theodore Parker provide a particularly acute example of this paradox. The problem in his case was accentuated because he had to reconcile the Transcendental variety of optimistic evolutionism with his role as a deeply committed social agitator.

Parker shares Emerson's inability to take the possibility of evil completely seriously. When cornered, Emerson was quite prepared to pretend to be above the whole business: "if I am the Devil's child, I will live then from the Devil." Parker's equivalent gesture is to refer to sin, contemptuously, as "ngnsin-n-n-n."[103] As a result he is able to achieve an admirably ecological perspective on the natural world: "Earthquakes, volcanoes, hurricanes, tigers, lions, rattlesnakes, vipers—nobody has ever pretended that they did more harm than good; the leaning of science is quite the other way, to suspect that what we call evil is good in reality, only not comprehended yet."[104] The development of civilization takes place within the same comforting parameters that shield the natural world from the forces of evil, waste, and chaos. Parker asks: "How has the civilization of the world thus far been achieved?" and answers himself by claiming that it "has taken place in the providence of God, who, from perfect motives, of perfect material, for a perfect purpose, as a perfect means, created this human nature, put into it this reserve of power, put about it this reserve of material elements, wherewith to make a Jacob's ladder to clamber continually upwards towards God, our prayer being the hand which reaches up, while our practice is the foot which sustains the weight."[105] The occasional shuddering of this apparently perfect machinery is explained away by the fact that the Almighty has built a "margin for oscillation" into the system.[106] Human evolution is a conscious process and the mind can make mistakes. None of these can be crucial, however—they are part of the process of mankind's self-education:

> Look at the human race as one person: from the beginning till now man has been devising an instrument to produce welfare. Every experiment has been a partial success; each also a partial failure. So far as the attempt succeeded the result has been delightful; so far as it failed, painful. Suffering follows error; man abandons the error, abolishes the mischief, tries again, making out better next time. The pain has only been adequate to sharpen his wits, like hunger and thirst to make him work in other forms. Thus man gets political education and political enjoyment.[107]

When it comes to assessing an individual's behavior, therefore, the notion of sin has to be replaced by that of "wrong choice" because "No man loves the wrong for its own sake, but as a means for some actual good it is thought to lead to."[108]

The only trouble with this account of human behavior is that it does not seem to explain the stance that Parker himself took on issues

The Ideology of Brook Farm

that affected his society. Despite the rational framework which he provides for the historical process, Parker's temperament and his respect for human rights made it impossible for him to tolerate the social abuses of his own time and place. The upholders of the Fugitive Slave Law in Massachusetts are not allowed to get off as lightly as the volcanoes and rattlesnakes:

> Where shall I find a parallel with men who will do such a deed,—do it in Boston? I will open the tombs, and bring up the most hideous tyrants from the dead. Come, brood of monsters, let me bring you up from the deep damnation of the graves wherein your hated memories continue for all time their never-ending rot.[109]

A man who is prepared to speak in these terms is not merely one who is deeply concerned about the state of the society in which he finds himself, but also one who is willing to award the individual the privilege of being evil if he chooses to be so. A good example of this moral perspective is the memorial address on Daniel Webster in which Parker makes his subject a tragic figure, and clearly reprimands error— and thus acknowledges the possibility of waste and evil in a way that appears incompatible with his general account of human destiny.[110] This problem is a central one in Parker's philosophy, just as it is, in different ways, in the thinking of the other Transcendentalists, including the Brook Farmers. In this respect it is worth looking at William Henry Channing's contribution to the ideology of the community.[111]

Channing was a Fourierist and played an important part in the later history of Brook Farm—although, as Frothingham tells us, he was prevented by circumstances from becoming a fully fledged member:

> ... he resigned his ministry in New York in order to throw himself unburdened into this enterprise; he traced out a line of exposition; he meditated a permanent settlement in the pulpit of Theodore Parker, at West Roxbury. But his ill-health, domestic anxieties, a multitude of engagements, prevented him doing what he would.[112]

Nevertheless, for much of the Fourierist period, Channing was, in effect, Brook Farm's chaplain, living at the community for the last months of 1845, and then acting as minister at the West Roxbury church for a good part of the following year, and taking every opportunity to preach to and guide the Farmers. Frothingham tells us that during the stay at West Roxbury Channing was at the Farm "constantly, talking in private, preaching in public, in full sympathy with the highest aims of the community, stimulating those aims to the utmost extent of his power, and eulogizing Fourier as the discoverer of the method of organization."[113] Perhaps the best picture of Channing in action is provided by Codman:

> One Sabbath afternoon we were invited to meet with him in the nearby beautiful pine woods, for religious services; and like the Pilgrims and reformers of old, we there raised our voices in hymns of praise, and listened to a sermon of hopefulness from his eloquent lips. Would we had a picture of that marked company as they were seated around on the pine leaves that covered the ground, following their "attractions" by joining in groups with those they most admired or most sympathized with—young and old, bright and cheerful, as they mostly were . . . ; hearts and eyes illuminated with great thoughts; hands and faces browned with working for great, world-wide ideas. . . .
> . . . . After the music and an inspiring address under the trees, and the arches of Nature's temple, looking heavenwards, he said, "Let us all join hands and make a circle, the symbol of universal unity, and of the *at-one-ment* of all men and women, and here form the Church of Humanity that shall cover the men and women of every nation and every clime."[114]

Other members of the community seem to have been similarly impressed by him. Amelia Russell tells us that he "sanctified" the place, and even the reserved George Ripley admitted that his "presence with us . . . has been a source of unmingled satisfaction and benefit."[115] John Humphrey Noyes, in his shrewd account of the Farm, indicated Channing's importance in the history of the experiment:

> The connection of the Channings with Fourierism, then, stands thus: Dr. Channing, the first medium of the Unitarian afflatus, was the father (by suggestion) of the Brook Farm Association, which was originally called the West Roxbury Community. William H. Channing the second medium according to Miss Peabody, converted this community to Fourierism and changed it to a Phalanx.[116]

Channing's hold over the Farmers is not difficult to explain. For one thing, he was one of the leading Fourierists of the day. He was the Domestic Corresponding Secretary of the American Union of Associationists (he gives his address as Brook Farm in the notice of its constitution), and through his magazine the *Present*, his articles in the *Harbinger* (of which he was an editor), and his presence on the rostrum at all the major Fourierist conventions, he became an agitator second only in importance to Albert Brisbane.[117] But—and this is another source of his great appeal—he was not a blind fanatic: he was able to identify, on behalf of the Transcendentalists, Fourier's shortcomings. The latter, as we have seen, gave the individual no real control over his destiny and that of society; he recognized no moral distinctions but advocated instead the pursuit of pleasure; and he was thoroughly contemptuous of religion. Channing's contribution to his doctrine—and it was perhaps the only original one of the whole American movement—was to alter its stance in relation to all these issues. In short, he succeeded in endowing Fourierism with a moral dimension.

In 1842 Channing wrote a letter to Theodore Parker, thanking him for a copy of the *Discourse of Matters Pertaining to Religion* and offering some comments upon it. In the course of the letter, he complains that Parker has not done justice to "one conviction, which I presume you to hold, of course." The belief in question is, for Channing, "one of my deepest convictions, and is indeed the ground of my Christian faith—and my reconciliation with the Church":

> It is this: "That the Race is inspired as well as the Individual; that Humanity is a growth from a Divine Life as well as Man, and indeed that the true advancement of the individual is dependent upon the advancement of a generation, and that the law of this is providential, the direct act of the Being of beings."

He goes on to say, rather more tentatively:

> It is this: "That the Race is inspired as well as the Individual; that Humanity not demonstrate its truth—that not only all races, but all the myriads of men who have lived, and are living, or yet to live, are needed to express God's idea of man. Hence the shading which separates characters, and the formation which wide popular common sense, and yet more the direction which the impulsive enthusiasm of whole nations and ages, give to opinion and conduct, are sacred to me. The past justifies itself and explains itself in the present, and a perfected race alone will give adequate utterance to the "Word of God."[118]

Having established that progress is taking place on a racial level, that every individual has his foreordained part to play, Channing contradicts himself by suggesting that Parker join him in speeding up the process by means of "a little moral galvanism." At this point he obviously had not realized the problems a doctrine of comprehensive and inevitable evolutionary growth brings with it, although he does admit in a footnote that he may have been "too enthusiastic."[119]

By the following year, the confusion is even more apparent. In his *Statement of the Principles of the Christian Union* he is able to perpetrate the following non sequitur:

> The laws of Providence are living realities. They cannot be changed by our imaginations, nor made inert by our neglects. Man cannot fabricate a machine of society. Its germ of life, its organizing principles, its growth, is from God. Again, there is danger that the strong intellectual bias of our day towards tolerance and universality, sifting all systems, examining all science, as it does, may end in a vanity of varied knowledge, and a pride in powers of thought, more barren of results than untaught instinct, or even bigotry. The tree of knowledge, of good and evil, may again fill our minds with seeds of death.[120]

Channing contrasts mechanical and organic imagery to emphasize the impossibility of man's refuting the laws of Providence and determining his own future. Then without any grammatical acknowledgment of the transition, he proceeds to say exactly the opposite—the intellectual hubris that underlies the current eclecticism may lead to man's downfall. He appears to want man to eat the apple, and have it too.

This contradictoriness marks a transitional phase: by 1844 Channing has succeeded in making room in Fourierism to accommodate moral concepts and the free will that makes them meaningful. One can perhaps summarize his achievement by saying that he has removed the evil from the past and provided some for the future. On the one hand, he explains why the long and painful development of society with all its wasteful history of conflict, brutality, and war is actually necessary: why, in fact, God has allowed man to suffer evil in the first place. On the other hand, he shows that even when society has reached its final and perfect form, man will not have to live the life of a moral automaton, never having to make a choice between good and evil, never exercising his individual will. On the contrary, the price of his participation in the phalanx will be a conscious act of goodness.

Fourier had outlined the pattern of society's development from discord to association. He had also revealed that man will be perfectly happy in his new state because all his passions will have specific objects, and these will become available in the phalansterian system. He had, therefore, given one of the most detailed answers ever to the question, How? What he had omitted is a consideration of the equally pressing question, Why? He never quite gets around to explaining the purpose of the meticulously ordered development that he describes.

Like the Transcendentalists, Fourier is contemptuous of the doctrine of original sin, and resolutely opposes the "moralists" who offer it as an explanation of the unsatisfactoriness of life on earth. Brisbane puts the Fourierist case:

> It will be said, perhaps, that the passions were created good, but that when man fell, they became depraved. In answer, I will state, that the creator

does not give man control over his organic nature; he does not allow the finite being, by acts or will of his own, to vitiate the passions and attractions which he has given him. Man may perfect or degrade God's work, but he cannot change it organically. When he fell, his passions became deranged in their action, and took a false development; but he can regain his original condition, and restore the harmonies which were dissolved.[121]

This idea of sin as "false development," "a derangement," a dissolution of "harmonies" reminds one of Parker's "margin for oscillation." Without getting to the root of the matter, Brisbane elaborates his description by explaining the law of "Duality of Movement." This doctrine almost anticipates Freud's theory of repression. It states that the passions can move in one of two directions: either toward benign fulfillment, if society is correctly organized, or toward perversion and evil if circumstances frustrate them. Ambition, for example, leads the individual "to the fulfillment of numerous important social functions. But this passion is terrible in its false development; if perverted it leads to hatred, envy, revenge, and other outrages, and if misdirected in the minds of rulers, it leads to tyranny, injustice, war and devastation." Brisbane concludes that

> This great law will render an important service to the cause of the social elevation of the human race, as it will inspire the world with that faith which it requires most—FAITH IN MAN. It relieves human nature from the responsibility of those odious and fiendlike characteristics which result from perversion of the passions, and places it where it should rest—upon our false systems of society.[122]

This account achieves its verdict of not guilty by refusing to pursue the implications of the existence of "false systems of society." If we have, on the one hand, an essentially innocent human nature, and on the other a harmoniously ordered universe which should be able to impose order on human society with scrupulous efficiency, how on earth are we to explain how things went wrong in the first place—how the "accidental derangement," as Brisbane calls it, ever occurred? Why did not the dawn of Association, which is, after all, merely the social manifestation of an unchanging and universal law, coincide with the dawn of life on earth? Channing proposes an answer to that question. He attempts to "reconcile the necessary evil of the Finite with the necessary good of the Infinite,"[123] and to provide the process of historical evolution with a purpose, as well as a pattern.

First of all, he reminds us that harmony is not the same thing as unanimity—it is composed of different but interlocking parts. "What is an organization," he asks, "but an alliance,—a friendly grouping, a society of many forces conspiring to one common end?"[124] This is straightforward enough and agrees with Brisbane's emphasis on a fine discrimination of function in his discussion of the way in which work is to be organized. But Channing goes on to point out that this specialization, this useful differentiation between one unit and another, is the same as individualism, and we naturally expect individualism to lead to discord as a necessary consequence. The implication is obvious; he states it here in the form of rhetorical questions:

> Must every spirit be separated from good, before it can become united to it; must it feel its finiteness, before it seeks full exercise of power in co-operation with other limited existences, and perfect freedom, by obedience to him whose law of love is liberty; must it commence in disorder, ere it can learn how order binds all creatures, by mutual dependance [sic], into one living organization, and so through ignorance grow up to intelligent justice, and through destructive lawlessness, to power of creative beauty? ... He [God] would make us angels from the first, if he could do so. But the spirits, who come to blend their selfish discords in unison with him, must commence their journey far away in the chaos of extreme individualism. We must be men, before we can be angels.[125]

The uncertainties and disorder of the past have been useful, after all, because "Existing limitations are the means of growing unions. Accords are the blending of discords." Individualism has been necessary to create a sufficient variety within the race to enable people to complement each other's qualities, and render cooperation both meaningful and necessary.

Channing has certainly added some sort of dynamism to Fourier's account of the past, although his contribution basically resembles Parker's notion that the evils of history are part of an educational system. However, it is when he comes to turn his attention from the past to the future that Channing is able to confront the moral dilemma most effectively. The problem he has to face here is, once the perfect society has come about, have we anything left to live for? If it is a notorious fact that the anticipated joys of heaven, on reflection, become rather insipid, so that even Milton's imagination is engaged more fully by a vision of hell than by a view of paradise, the same is no less true of Fourier's plan for a heaven upon earth. It is this, perhaps, that Emerson is getting at when he states that "Fourier had skipped no fact but one, namely life."[126] Channing's major contribution to Fourierist ideology is to endow even phalansterian man with a sense of purpose.

In order to demonstrate how thoroughly apropos his argument is, it is worth preceding it with a look at Elizabeth Palmer Peabody's critique of Fourier's system. Her analysis is more sympathetic and more perceptive than Emerson's, and indeed is probably the most intelligent contemporary response to the movement by an outsider. In an article entitled "Fourierism" in the *Dial* of April 1844, she complains, in Emersonian fashion, that "Fourierism stops short, and, in so doing, proves itself to be, not a life, a soul, but only a body."[127] Though it is admirable to create a perfectly functioning organization, she argues that this is not enough. "The question is, whether the Phalanx acknowledges its own limitations of nature, in being an organization, or opens up any avenue into the source of life that shall keep it sweet, enabling it to assimilate to itself contrary elements, and consume its own waste; so that Phoenix-like it may renew itself forever in great and finer forms."[128] A little later, she reverts to one of her earlier contributions to the *Dial*, "A Glimpse of Christ's Idea of Society,"[129] in order to revise her conclusions about the place of the church in modern society, and in doing so she sheds further light on her objection to Fourierism:

> In a former article, we suggested the idea, that the Christian churches planted by the Apostles, were only initiatory institutions, to be lost, like the morning star, in the deeper glory of a kingdom of heaven on earth, which we then fancied Socialism would bring about.
> Since then, by the study of ancient nationalities, and also of Neander's History of the Churches of Christ up to the time of Constantine, together with observations on the attempt at West Roxbury, we have come to see that initiatory churches will have an office as long as men are born children; and that a tremendous tyranny is necessarily involved by constituting society itself the VISIBLE church of Christ. Those who have ideas, and who, individually, and free from human constraining, have pledged themselves to live by them alone, or die, must be a select body, in the midst of the instinctive life that is perpetually arriving on the shores of Being, and which it is not fair or wise to catch up and *christen* before it can understand its position, and give its consent. We must be men before we are Christians, else we shall never be either Christians or men.[130]

In the same month's edition of the *Present*, we find Channing making an almost identical point. Having shown that history makes sense when one realizes society had to go through the disruptive experience of warring factions as a necessary prelude to the harmony of Association, he narrows his perspective to a single life-span, and finds that the same process is a necessary part of the individual's development. Every man, even in Association, has to become aware of his own uniqueness. Only when he has done so can he offer it as a sacrifice to the community, for the good of his fellows: "His destiny is first to learn to know himself, as one of many in a Universe, and then to give himself away in ever enlarging communion with all creatures and with God, and so to become immortal."[131] Fourier would have been horrified at the proposal that a tension exists, or should exist, between the individual and the Association. Yet by insisting on it, Channing is superimposing a moral order onto the social structure, and enabling the individual, by an act of conscious self-sacrifice, to add a religious dimension to his experience.

Channing's views can be made a little clearer by reference to some of his writings in *The Spirit of the Age* a few years later, when his Fourierist theology had had time to crystallize in his mind.[132] In a series called "Criticism Criticized," which takes the form of a dialogue between Channing and Parke Godwin, on the subject of an earlier contribution by Channing which pointed out limitations in Fourier's philosophy, we find him expounding at some length on the latter's pantheism. He explains that in Fourier's scheme, "the Divine Being is complex" (which, if anything, seems to be putting it mildly). We are told that this complexity is comprised of the material world, which is "passive," of the spiritual world, which is "active," and of the "Order of Movement." This last category represents God's "Distributive" manifestation, "intermingling in endless variety and harmony all modes of existence," and its mood is neutral. Channing concludes that "one is constrained to say, that no writer in any land or age, has produced Pantheism in a more pure, perfect, uncompromising a [sic] form."[133]

Since the deity is no more than a principle of organization, it is quite impossible to distinguish Him from His world, and indeed it is impossible to make any sort of discrimination between subject and object. That this represents a criticism is made clear by an article of the previous week, entitled "The Church of God Within Us," in which Channing tells us, among other things, what pantheism is. He explains that in the current religious situation, we have to choose one out of three basic options, "CATHOLICISM, PANTHEISM, and DIVINE HUMANITY." He then proceeds to define his terms. The three ways all seem to aim at more or less the same destination, whether it is called "divine order," "harmonious joy," or "uniting in heavenly communion the perfected races of all globes." The principal difference between them lies in the routes they take.[134]

The account of Catholicism is conventional enough—it is a matter of "Super-human influence, hierarchically transmitted and diffused" and "sanctified obedience." Pantheism, meanwhile, "instinct with Natural impulse, amidst the ever-varying sphere of hourly circumstances, longs for unchecked freedom to realize the harmonious joy of earthly existence, in consummate art." The last phrase reads a little oddly—it implies some sort of substitute for the real thing. Our suspicions are confirmed by his third definition:

Divine Humanity, conscious of the everlasting series of descending and ascending mediations, whereby the One Absolute Good progressively fulfils his indefinitely benignant purpose of uniting in heavenly communion the perfected races of all globes, stands willing to do the exact work allotted to mankind, upon this globe, to day, assured of exhaustless growing good, and aspiring to the end of religious Unity and Art made one by perfect Love.[135]

The references to series, and to progression, make it clear that he is talking about the phalansterian system. It is also obvious that he finds this method superior to the others: it unites Catholic "Unity" and pantheistic "Art," "by perfect Love." Yet, a week later, he accuses Fourier of being a pantheist.

The criticism implied by this unexpected alignment is confirmed by some of Channing's remarks in a subsequent contribution to the series. He poses the question: "Is spontaneous, individual impulse or [i.e., "otherwise called"] Passional Attraction, the infallible indication of Divine Order?" He cannot accept Fourier's idea that the Association will be kept running efficiently by allowing the "passions" to operate freely. The main ground of his disagreement is that the consciousness is bound to impose its control eventually:

> . . . in action and reaction, each impulse encounters circumstances which it moulds, or is moulded by, and from all combined experience of pleasure and pain is formed a reflected image of the harmonious conditions of Integral existence. Finally, impulse, judgment, experience converge, intermingle, blend in a Character or Personality, which is inwardly conscious of being Manly, and felt by all men to be so, in proportion to its Unity. A man is loved by his fellows, as at once humane, natural, and divine, in degree as in deed, thought, feeling he progressively realizes unity in variety, and becomes a beautiful whole. And in the process of this development he ascends from a merely instinctive passionate existence, through consciously governed existence, to free co-operative existence.[136]

Obviously, in the course of this development, something is lost—the mind, triumphing over the emotions, is bound to place certain fulfillments out of reach. It is clear that when he uses the adjective "free," Channing is thinking not of the free gratification of the passions that Fourier sought but its antithesis, free will: when a person is faced with alternatives which are mutually exclusive, and is sufficiently liberated from merely instinctual existence to commit himself to one on moral and rational grounds. In Channing's sketch of human development, there is a hint of loss, of tragic possibilities, that Fourier's bland optimism could never envisage.

Channing goes on to stress the element of sacrifice:

> Not only is it true, then, that an individual man is approximately conformed to Divine Order in proportion as all his Passional Attractions are regulated by the Law of Right Reason, enacted and executed by a Unitary, Personal Will, fitly experienced, enlightened and sanctified; but yet more is it true, that a man fulfils the Divine Idea, just in degree as with loyal love he yields up his own personal inclination, judgment, interest, to the guidance of the Law of Right Reason in the Society of which he is a living member. The correlative of this is the complementary truth, that a Society can best attain to a knowledge of the Ideal Law of Justice, by duly respecting the highest conscience of each of its members. And both of these truths are involved in a third, that the various Societies of the Human Race, with all their constituent members, approach to an infallible science of Divine Wisdom, according to the entireness of their conformity to the Reason of Humanity, wherein the Word of God, hierarchically distributed through the whole Spiritual Universe, manifests Himself to Man.[137]

Without doing anything to alter the working of Fourier's system, Channing has managed to put the whole thing in an entirely new perspective. We have a kind of social contract—the individual must respect the "Right Reason" of his society; the society must respect the conscience of its members; and, summing it up, a man must listen to the voice of racial experience, in order to hear the word of God. Channing is basically repeating the old commandment of "love thy neighbor"—it retains its point in a world where, after all, one cannot do just as one wishes without hurting someone else.

During the autumn of 1845 Channing began his task of establishing a religious institution within the framework of the Brook Farm Phalanx. In a letter dated 5 October of that year, Marianne Dwight describes a meeting held at the Farm to discuss "our church." Channing wanted a place set aside for worship, although there was naturally a problem in finding a form that would satisfy everyone. The need, however, was clearly felt. The letter continues:

> Of course, the whole of life should be worship,—all labour, consecration, and not desecration,—and so all life should be poetry, should be music. But as we have a particular expression of poetry and of music, but adapted to these sentiments, why may we not have a form of worship peculiarly adapted to the religious sentiment?[138]

Marianne Dwight goes on to suggest that a perfect phalanx would have a worshiping series—in which one group would provide "the spirit of prayer," a second "song and thanksgiving," another "silent worship," and a fourth, preaching. This proposal almost certainly originated with Channing—it resembles his New York plan for a Christian Union, when the idea was to have three different kinds of meetings: the first

The Ideology of Brook Farm   41

under the guidance of a leader, the second of a wholly spontaneous character, and the third for "the frankest interchange of thought in conversation."[139]

At a meeting the following week, it was decided to consecrate one of the rooms in the phalanstery (then under construction) as a place of worship. The services were to begin and end with music, and to utilize books like "Mr. Clarke's and the Swedenborgian ritual or book of worship." A committee of seven was appointed to make the arrangements, and it was decided that "Mr. C. will not be considered as a priest—we do not want a priest." Instead, "The exercises will be left to the person who may conduct them for the day."[140] Appropriately enough, in view of Elizabeth Peabody's remarks on "a select body," and Channing's emphasis on a deliberate sacrifice of the self, the proposals caused a division at the Farm, and indeed only about twenty people attended the first meeting. These included some of the most important members of the community, however, since John Sullivan Dwight and Mrs. Ripley were among those appointed to the committee, and Ripley, John Allen, John Orvis, and others were added to it a fortnight later.[141] The machinery of the phalanx was now powered by volatile spiritual fuel, and an opportunity had been provided for the testing of Elizabeth Peabody's theory that "Christian churches in the midst of a Phalanx, might be the Dorian cities of another Greece."[142]

As it happened, however, the Christian church was never to be consecrated. For a while Fourierist Christianity was going strong: on 1 March 1846 Marianne Dwight tells of a "holy solemn afternoon," in which Channing made much of his theme of self-sacrifice:

> He compared our work with others that have demanded sacrifice; that of the crusaders, that of the religious brotherhoods and sisterhoods. As the crusaders sacrificed so much to restore the tomb of the buried Lord, how much more ought we to sacrifice, whose work it is to restore the whole earth that it may become the dwelling place of the living Lord.[143]

Two days later the Phalanstery, containing as it did the new church, burned to the ground. Another blow came when Channing lost his position at West Roxbury church—it was, according to Frothingham, "terminated suddenly by the active agency of a few."[144] Soon afterward Brook Farm itself broke up.

It is ironic that the community should fail as it was on the point of achieving the kind of "life" which Elizabeth Peabody had claimed it originally lacked. The reasons for the collapse have frequently been discussed: the fire, and its economic consequences; the increasing notoriety of Fourierism; the lagging enthusiasm of Brisbane and the movement's loss of impetus at the national level; the effect on the school of an outbreak of smallpox at the Farm; the disillusion of many of the members—a whole complex of factors led to the breakup.[145] A final evaluation will, however, have to take into account the fact that during its short existence it embodied, and indeed extended, some of the basic Transcendentalist ideas. As a phalanx it put into action a belief which individualistic members of the movement like Emerson and Thoreau manifested in a more passive mood when they set themselves up as representative men. The community assumed, with a literalness that is hard to take completely seriously now, that it constituted a perfectible microcosm of society, and that once Brook Farm was in proper running order it would inaugurate the reformation of the social macrocosm. This optimism may have been mistaken, but this does not mean that we are entitled to dismiss the experiment as a frivolous or escapist enterprise. Brook Farm was both a manifestation of the Transcendental impulse and an attempt to create a better world— there is no need to see a conflict between these two descriptions. Underlying the efforts of its members was a confidence in man: the Brook Farmers believed that the human race was adequate to its work, that people had only to behave as they were designed to and they would achieve a glorious destiny. For a short time near the end of the community's life, the Fourierist and Transcendental doctrine that man only had to express his innermost being—to be himself—in order to be perfect, was deepened under the influence of Channing. His contribution was the notion of self-sacrifice. The welfare of the many depended on the correct organization of the one: the complex harmony of the phalanx was provided by the appropriate relationships being maintained between its individual components. But for those relationships to be established, other possibilities, other rewards, had to be abandoned. Phalansterian man was called upon to sacrifice something for his fellows. Adherence to the law of the universe was, finally, not merely an evolutionary imperative but a moral one as well.

NOTES

1. "The Celestial Rail-road," *The Centenary Edition of the Works of Nathaniel Hawthorne*, ed. William Charvat et al., 11 vols. to date (Columbus: Ohio State University Press, 1962–), vol. 10, *Mosses from an Old Manse* (1974), p. 197.

2. William R. Hutchison, *The Transcendentalist Ministers* (New Haven: Yale University Press, 1959), pp. 22, 28.

3. Perry Miller, *The Transcendentalists: An Anthology* (Cambridge: Harvard University Press, 1950), pp. 129–32.

4. Charles Crowe, *George Ripley: Transcendentalist and Utopian Socialist* (Athens: University of Georgia Press, 1967), p. 81.

5. Crowe, *George Ripley*, p. 137.

6. See Lindsay Swift, *Brook Farm: Its Members, Scholars, and Visitors* (New York: Macmillan, 1900), for further details of these and others involved in the experiment.

7. Crowe, *George Ripley*, pp. 143–223.

8. Crowe, *George Ripley*, p. 173.

9. Charles R. Crowe, "Fourierism and the Founding of Brook Farm," *Boston Public Library Quarterly*, 12 (April 1960): 87. Morris Hillquit makes the same point in his *History of Socialism in the United States* (New York: Funk & Wagnalls, 1903), p. 103.

10. Miller, *The Transcendentalists*, p. 469. Swift's remark is from his *Brook Farm*, p. 135.

11. Miller, *The Transcendentalists*, p. 464.

12. Letter to the *New Age*, 30 July 1843, reprinted in F. B. Sanborn and William T. Harris, *A. Bronson Alcott: His Life and Philosophy* (Boston: Roberts, 1893), 2:382–83.

13. See the Introduction by Charles Gide to *Selections from the Works of Fourier*, trans. Julia Franklin (London: Swan-Sonnenschein, 1901), pp. 14–16.

14. "Brook Farm," an address delivered at the University of Michigan on 21 January 1895, printed as an Appendix to James Harrison Wilson, *The Life of Charles A. Dana* (New York: Harper's, 1907), p. 517. Besides Wilson's book there is a good account of Dana's later career in Candace Stone, *Dana and the Sun* (New York: Dodd, Mead, 1938), and a brief summary of his life in Swift, *Brook Farm*, pp. 145–52.

15. "A Girl of Sixteen at Brook Farm," *Atlantic Monthly*, 85 (March 1900): 396.

16. See, for example, John Thomas Codman, *Brook Farm: Historic and Personal Memoirs* (Boston: Arena, 1894), pp. 31, 57.

17. The manuscript does not provide information on the occupations of female members of the community.

18. "A Boy's Recollections of Brook Farm," *New England Magazine*, n.s. 16 (May 1894): 310.

19. Summer 1845, Marianne Dwight Orvis, *Letters from Brook Farm 1844–1847*, ed. Amy L. Reed (Poughkeepsie, N.Y.: Vassar College, 1928), p. 104.

20. "Brook Farm," *United States Magazine and Democratic Review*, n.s. 11 (November 1842): 491.

21. See Codman, *Brook Farm*, pp. 10–11.

22. *Phalanx*, 1 (20 April 1844): 114.

23. Letter to John Sullivan Dwight, 10 May 1846, Clarence Gohdes, "Three Letters by James Kay Dealing with Brook Farm," *Philological Quarterly*, 17 (October 1938): 383.

24. Gohdes, "Three Letters," 383.

25. Letter to Dwight, 14 March 1845, Gohdes, "Three Letters," 379.

26. Amelia E. Russell, *Home Life of the Brook Farm Association* (Boston: Little, Brown, 1900), p. 24. This book collects her articles originally published in the *Atlantic Monthly*, 42 (October, November 1878): 458–66, 556–63.

27. The Brook Farmers had to put up with a considerable amount of hostility as a result of their adoption of a Fourierist constitution. John Van Der Zee Sears, in his book *My Friends at Brook Farm* (New York: Desmond FitzGerald, 1912), claims that "there was bitter feeling against us among the old Puritans of Roxbury. They hated us and took occasion to annoy us and injure us in many mean ways" (p. 169). Codman mentions the press campaigns that were conducted against the community—usually on the grounds that Fourierism threatened the sanctity of marriage, which indeed it did, although not at Brook Farm (*Brook Farm*, p. 204).

28. That is since Lindsay Swift's book. Like other manifestations of Transcendentalism, Brook Farm has tended to invite superficial and gossipy treatment. See, if examples are required, Katherine Burton, *Paradise Planters: The Story of Brook Farm* (New York: Longmans, 1939) and Edith Roelker Curtis, *A Season in Utopia: The Story of Brook Farm* (New York: Thomas Nelson, 1961). A hostile but stimulating study of Brook Farm is contained in Jane Maloney Johnson, " 'Through Change and Through Storm': A Study of Federalist-Unitarian Thought, 1800–1860" (Ph.D. diss., Radcliffe College, 1958).

29. *The Centenary Edition of the Works of Nathaniel Hawthorne*, vol. 3, *The Blithedale Romance* (1964), p. 3.

30. Russell, *Home Life*, pp. 1–2.

31. Sumner, "A Boy's Recollections," 313.

32. Johnson, " 'Through Change and Through Storm,' " p. 277.

33. Sumner, "A Boy's Recollections," 313.

34. 24 June 1841, Zoltán Haraszti, *The Idyll of Brook Farm* (Boston: Boston Public Library, 1937), p. 18.

35. George Ripley, "Fire at Brook Farm," *Harbinger*, 2 (14 March 1846): 220–22; Ripley, "To Our Friends," *Harbinger*, 2 (21 March 1846): 237–38.

36. The plural of "socialism" is used in the title of John Humphrey Noyes, *History of American Socialisms* (Philadelphia: Lippincott, 1870). Virtually the only light relief for readers of the *Harbinger* was a translation of George Sand's *Consuelo*, running as an almost interminable serial.

37. "To Our Friends in Association," *Harbinger*, 1 (28 June 1845): 47.

38. Ripley became a journalist on Horace Greeley's *New York Tribune*, and, with Dana, edited the *New American Encyclopedia*, 16 vols. (New York: D. Appleton, 1858–63); see Crowe, *George Ripley*, pp. 224–63. Dwight edited *Dwight's Journal of Music* from 1853 to 1887; for information on his life see George Willis Cooke, *John Sullivan Dwight* (Boston: Small, Maynard, 1898).

39. Swift, *Brook Farm*, p. 53.

40. Sears, *My Friends*, Ch. 6, "Entertainments," pp. 80–106; Codman, *Brook Farm*, Ch. 5, pp. 172–85; Sedgwick, "A Girl of Sixteen," esp. 402; Russell, *Home Life*, esp. pp. 15–17, 43–44; George P. Bradford, "Reminiscences of Brook Farm, by a Member of the Community," *Century Magazine*, 45 (November 1892): 141; Sumner, "A Boy's Recollections," esp. 311–12.

41. Johnson, " 'Through Change and Through Storm,' " p. 198.

42. *Blithedale Romance*, p. 206.

43. *Blithedale Romance*, p. 209.

44. Codman, *Brook Farm*, p. 260; the letter is dated "Oct. 27th, B. F. Mass."; Sedgwick, "A Girl of Sixteen," 402; Sumner, "A Boy's Recollections," 311. Hawthorne's account of the original event can be found in his *American Notebooks*, ed. Randall Stewart (New Haven: Yale University Press, 1932), entry for 28 September 1841, pp. 78–79.

45. Sears, *My Friends,* p. 101.
46. Russell, *Home Life,* pp. 15–17.
47. See, for example, Bradford, "Reminiscences," 142; Sears, *My Friends,* pp. 80–106; Codman, *Brook Farm,* pp. 53–68.
48. "The Community at West Roxbury, Mass.," *Monthly Miscellany of Religion and Letters,* 5 (July 1841): 113–18, introduced by the editor as being "an extract from a letter written by a friend—not a member of the new Community—to a lady in England" (114).
49. The Brook Farm material is strong on anecdotes of this kind. See, for example, Hawthorne, *Passages from the American Notebooks,* ed. Sophia Hawthorne (Boston: Houghton, Mifflin, 1893), p. 229: this material is not included in more modern editions—see the prefatory note to Stewart's edition, pp. vii–viii; Swift, *Brook Farm,* passim; Bradford, "Reminiscences," 144; Sumner, "A Boy's Recollections," 311.
50. Octavius Brooks Frothingham, *George Ripley* (Boston: Houghton, Miffllin, 1883), p. 128.
51. "Brook Farm," *United States Magazine,* 494.
52. George Willis Cooke, "Brook Farm," *New England Magazine,* n.s. 17 (December 1897): 395.
53. MHi. Despite the title, the book begins with information for May 1844.
54. Orvis, *Letters,* pp. 7–8.
55. *Constitution of the Brook Farm Association for Industry and Education, West Roxbury, Mass., with an Introductory Statement. Second Edition with the By-Laws of the Association* (Boston: I. R. Butts, 1844).
56. *Social Destiny of Man; or, Association and Reorganization of Industry* (Philadelphia: C. F. Stollmeyer, 1840); "On Association and Attractive Industry," *United States Magazine and Democratic Review,* n.s. 10 (January, February, April, June 1842): 30–44, 167–82, 321–36, 560–80; *A Concise Exposition of the Doctrine of Association or Plan for the Reorganization of Society* (New York: J. S. Redfield, 1843).
57. For his life, see the account he dictated to his wife, *Albert Brisbane, A Mental Biography,* ed. Redelia Brisbane (Boston: Arena, 1893).
58. Noyes, *History of American Socialisms,* pp. 15–18. Noyes offers a perceptive, if not always accurate, account of Brook Farm.
59. He quotes a revealing letter from Brisbane, 9 December 1847 (Codman, *Brook Farm,* pp. 144–46).
60. See, for example, Brisbane, *Mental Biography,* p. 184: "It is interesting to remark in this connection how emphatically he [Fourier] condemns every semblance of speculation. In a hundred places in his works he asserts that he gives no theory of his own. 'It is not by speculation and theorizing,' he says, 'that men are to discover the normal organization of society: it is by going back to eternal laws in nature.'"
61. Brisbane, *Social Destiny,* pp. 245–52.
62. Brisbane, *Social Destiny,* Ch. 12, "The Passions," pp. 157–80, esp. the table on p. 160.
63. Brisbane, *Social Destiny,* p. 185.
64. Brisbane, *Mental Biography,* p. 258.
65. See Richard Francis, "Circumstances and Salvation: the Ideology of the Fruitlands Utopia," *American Quarterly,* 25 (May 1973): 213–15.
66. *The Writings of Henry D. Thoreau,* 3 vols. to date (Princeton: Princeton

University Press, 1971–), vol. 2, *Walden* (1971), ed. J. Lyndon Shanley, p. 308; "Swedenborg; or, the Mystic," *The Complete Works of Ralph Waldo Emerson,* 12 vols. (Boston: Houghton, Mifflin, 1903–1904), vol. 4, *Representative Men,* p. 107; "The Sphinx," *The Complete Works of Ralph Waldo Emerson,* vol. 9, *Poems,* p. 25.

67. Brisbane, *Concise Exposition,* p. 44.

68. Brisbane, *Concise Exposition,* p. 44. The work distribution within the groups is exactly the same.

69. Brisbane, *Social Destiny,* pp. 119–27.

70. Brisbane, *Social Destiny,* p. 47.

71. Brisbane, *Social Destiny,* p. 147.

72. Brisbane, *Social Destiny,* p. 184.

73. Brisbane, *Social Destiny,* p. 189.

74. "Historic Notes of Life and Letters in New England," *The Complete Works of Ralph Waldo Emerson,* vol. 10, *Lectures and Biographical Sketches,* p. 350.

75. *Early Letters of George Wm. Curtis to John S. Dwight,* ed. George Willis Cooke (New York: Harper's, 1898), pp. 127–28.

76. Curtis, *Early Letters,* quoted from an "Editor's Easy Chair" essay, p. 9.

77. *The Complete Works of Ralph Waldo Emerson,* vol. 1, *Nature, Addresses, and Lectures,* pp. 82–83.

78. Brisbane, *Social Destiny,* p. 154.

79. Crowe has some interesting comments on Brook Farm as an answer to Emerson's diagnosis of the divided personality of modern times. However, he is talking about Ripley's intentions at the time of the founding of the community, so that his discussion takes a rather general form (*George Ripley,* pp. 140–41).

80. Goddard, *Studies in New England Transcendentalism* (New York: Columbia University Press, 1908), p. 10.

81. George Bancroft, "On the Progress of Civilization," *Boston Quarterly Review,* 1 (October 1838): 389–407, excerpted in Miller, *The Transcendentalists,* p. 429.

82. John Weiss, *Life and Correspondence of Theodore Parker* (New York: D. Appleton, 1864), 2:50–52.

83. *Walden,* p. 333.

84. "History," *The Complete Works of Ralph Waldo Emerson,* vol. 2, *Essays, First Series,* p. 25.

85. "History," p. 27.

86. "History," pp. 35–36.

87. "History," pp. 40–41.

88. Hedge, "Review of Address . . . by E. Everett," *Christian Examiner,* 16 (March 1834): 1–21, excerpted in Miller, *The Transcendentalists,* pp. 72–74.

89. Miller, *The Transcendentalists,* p. 73.

90. Miller, *The Transcendentalists,* p. 73.

91. "Orphic Sayings," No. XXIV, *Dial,* 1 (July 1840): 91.

92. Miller, *The Transcendentalists,* p. 73.

93. Brisbane, *Social Destiny,* p. 228.

94. Brisbane, *Social Destiny,* p. 200.

95. Brisbane, *Social Destiny,* p. 284.

96. "Self-Reliance," *Essays, First Series,* p. 90.

97. *The Centenary Edition of the Works of Nathaniel Hawthorne,* vol. 2, *The House of the Seven Gables* (1965), p. 180.

98. "The Over-Soul," *Essays, First Series,* p. 278.
99. "The Over-Soul," p. 287.
100. "The Over-Soul," p. 286.
101. Brisbane, *Social Destiny,* p. 334.
102. Frank E. Manuel, *The Prophets of Paris* (Cambridge: Harvard University Press, 1962), p. 203.
103. "Self-Reliance," *Essays, First Series,* p. 50; Parker's comment quoted in John White Chadwick, *Theodore Parker: Preacher and Reformer* (Boston: Houghton, Mifflin, 1900), p. 196.
104. "God in the World of Matter," *The Works of Theodore Parker,* The Centenary Edition, 15 vols. (Boston: American Unitarian Association, 1907–16), vol. 6, *The World of Matter and the Spirit of Man,* ed. George Willis Cooke (1907), p. 263.
105. *Lessons from the World of Matter and the World of Man,* selected notes of unpublished sermons, ed. Rufus Leighton (Boston: C. W. Slack, 1865), pp. 29–32.
106. "Of Justice and the Conscience," *Ten Sermons of Religion* (Boston: Crosby, Nichols, 1853), pp. 52–53.
107. *The Works of Theodore Parker,* vol. 2, *Theism, Atheism, and the Popular Theology,* ed. Charles W. Wendte (1907), p. 301.
108. *Theism,* p. 379.
109. "The Chief Sins of the People," *The Works of Theodore Parker,* vol. 9, *Sins and Safeguards of Society,* ed. Samuel B. Stewart (n.d.), p. 37.
110. *A Discourse Occasioned by the Death of Daniel Webster* (Boston: B. B. Mussey, 1853).
111. I have discussed his role very briefly in "Circumstances and Salvation," 215–16.
112. Octavius Brooks Frothingham, *Memoir of William Henry Channing* (Boston: Houghton, Miffllin, 1886), p. 211.
113. Frothingham, *William Henry Channing,* p. 208.
114. Codman, *Brook Farm,* p. 72.
115. Russell, *Home Life,* p. 110; Orvis, *Letters,* p. 127; Ripley, "Fire at Brook Farm," 221.
116. Noyes, *History of American Socialisms,* p. 516.
117. See Frothingham, *William Henry Channing,* for a general account of his reforming activities, esp. pp. 171–252, and the *Present,* the *Harbinger,* passim.
118. 9 June 1842, Frothingham, *William Henry Channing,* pp. 174–75.
119. Frothingham, *William Henry Channing,* p. 176.
120. (New York: Hunt's Merchants' Magazine, 1843), pp. 8–9.
121. "On Association," *United States Magazine and Democratic Review,* n.s. 10 (February 1842): 179.
122. "On Association," 172–73.
123. "Heaven Upon Earth," *Present,* 1 (1 March 1844): 298.
124. "Heaven Upon Earth," 299.
125. "Heaven Upon Earth," 298.
126. "Historic Notes," p. 352.
127. *Dial,* 4 (April 1844): 481.
128. "Fourierism," 481–82.
129. *Dial,* 2 (October 1841): 214–28.
130. "Fourierism," 482–83.
131. "Heaven Upon Earth," *Present,* 1 (April 1844): 418.

132. Channing edited this magazine on a weekly basis between 7 July 1849 and 27 April 1850.
133. 1 (8 December 1849): 360.
134. 1 (1 December 1849): 344.
135. "The Church of God," 344.
136. "Criticism Criticized," *The Spirit of the Age*, 1 (15 December 1849): 377.
137. "Criticism Criticized," 377.
138. Orvis, *Letters*, p. 121.
139. *A Statement of the Principles of the Christian Union*, pp. 11–12.
140. Orvis, *Letters*, pp. 123–24.
141. Orvis, *Letters*, pp. 123, 125.
142. "Fourierism," 482.
143. Orvis, *Letters*, p. 144.
144. Frothingham, *William Henry Channing*, p. 193.
145. See, for example, Sears, *My Friends*, p. 166; Russell, *Home Life*, pp. 126–27; Swift, *Brook Farm*, pp. 280–81.

A CALENDAR OF THE LETTERS OF MARGARET FULLER

Robert N. Hudspeth

THIS CALENDAR of the letters of Sarah Margaret Fuller, Marchesa d'Ossoli, is both a research tool and a progress report for an edition of her collected letters. I have aimed at providing the reader with an accurate, comprehensive list complete with locations of all the extant letters written by Fuller. The Calendar is annotated to indicate the degree of completeness of each letter and the history of its publication, if any. To make the edition as complete as possible, I have canvassed over 1,100 domestic and foreign libraries and have received the help of many scholars, librarians, and collectors. Thus, while no edition is ever "complete," this one aims at being as comprehensive as possible. I hope this Calendar will be a useful guide to research until the edition is published.

The letters are arranged chronologically insofar as they can be dated. Letters dated only by year appear at the head of the year; those dated by month and year appear at the head of that month with the few exceptions of some letters whose contents put them later in the month. The undated letters are arranged at the end of the Calendar, first in a group that can be assigned a rough date (e.g., "after Brook Farm was founded"); then those presented alphabetically by recipient; finally the few having no indication of date or recipient.

Editorial insertions are marked with square brackets; there are no silent additions to the information. Thus, [?] indicates an addition made on less than full certainty; [ca.] indicates a less than exact date. I assume that all entries marked by [?] and [ca.] are open to more precise definition as the edition moves to completion.

A significant number of Fuller's letters which appeared in print in the last century have since disappeared. These letters, marked "Unrecovered," must be used with caution, for their accuracy is highly questionable. The chief group of such letters is found in the *Memoirs of Margaret Fuller Ossoli,* upon which, with much exasperation, every scholar of the period has had to rely. We all know this book to be a curse and a blessing, for not only is the printed version of a letter often incomplete, but separate letters are often silently joined; others are misdated or their recipients erroneously indicated; material from the *Tribune* essays is intermingled with letters; and Fuller's prose is often rewritten. Still, lacking some major discovery of Fuller holographs, and I believe the missing manuscripts were destroyed, the material in the *Memoirs* will continue to be used. Even though I cannot vouch for their accuracy, the letters therein appear in this Calendar and will appear in the complete edition. If we cannot go to a more reliable text, at least we can make some better use of what we have. The letters from the *Memoirs* can be put in the context of the other letters in a proper chronology; some recipients can be identified; many letters can be dated; some of them can be unscrambled. I know well that the law of averages dictates that some of the letters here identified as separate letters are, in fact, parts of the same letter; and that some letters indicated as written to one person at one time are probably fragments silently joined by the editors of the *Memoirs*. Using what remains of holographs and manuscript copies, I have tried to reduce the error as much as possible. Thus, in addition to dating and assigning names of recipients, I have on occasion conjectured the reconstruction of more complete versions of some of the printed fragments. (The reader will find, too, that I have sometimes been able to rejoin holograph fragments which over the years have become scattered.)

Following the date, place, and recipient comes a description of the length of the letter. I have arbitrarily distinguished between "Fragment" and "Incomplete" letters by assigning the former term to those partial letters having now two or less paragraphs and the latter term to an incomplete letter of more than two paragraphs. While this is a rather artificial distinction, it will alert the reader to a rough degree of length.

The location of the letter is given first by holograph, then by manuscript copy, and then by printed versions. When multiple copies exist, I give the most complete first, or, when equal, the Houghton Library of Harvard University, then the Boston Public Library, and then other locations. When the holograph no longer exists, but copies do, the most complete is given as the source. When both are equal, the Harvard copy is used as the reference, then the Boston Public Library copy. This is not meant to suggest any superiority of the copies in the Harvard collection, but merely that since it is larger, it is the more convenient to use.

The Harvard and Boston Public Library collections are identified by call numbers as they appear in the library. At Harvard, the most extensive collection is the Fuller Family Papers (fMS Am 1086) gathered in twenty-two manuscript volumes and four boxes. The Houghton reading room has a typed, bound index to the collection. The call number is followed in parentheses by the item number. Thus, fMS Am 1086 (9:150) is Fuller Family Papers, volume 9, page 150. The final five volumes in the collection are copybook volumes (called "Works") which contain a large number of Fuller's letters and journal fragments which were copied into the bound books. Thus, fMS Am 1086 (Works, 1:875) is Fuller Family Papers, copybook, volume 1, page 875. While a number of the original letters thus copied still survive, several have disappeared, leaving only the "Works" copy. I have given both the holograph and "Works" location for every Fuller letter in the collection. The "Box A" collection is a thick, uncatalogued sheaf of various papers including a few letters.

The next most extensive collection of Fuller's letters at Harvard is in the Emerson family papers. In addition to the surviving letters written to Emerson from Fuller, there exists the "Ossoli" journal which Emerson created for his part in the *Memoirs.* Into this small brown journal, he copied parts of her letters and journals which were in his possession or which were lent to him at the time. This journal (bMS Am 1280 [111]) is now in volume 11 of *The Journals and Miscellaneous Notebooks of Ralph Waldo Emerson.* Thus, bMS Am 1280 (111, p. 50) is "Ossoli" journal, manuscript page 50. Finally, there are six Fuller letters existing as copies in the Emerson collection which are uncatalogued and have the location number "Os 735."

The large collection of Fuller papers in the Boston Public Library is divided into two parts. The Ms. Am. 1450 collection was given the library by T. W. Higginson after he wrote his biography of Fuller. It contains holographs and copies, many of which had been earlier used during the preparation of the *Memoirs.* Anyone who has seen this collection vividly remembers the extensive, appalling liberties taken with the papers in the 1850s. We have now some fine holographs and a variety of inked and cut letters which were mutilated at the time the editors were writing the *Memoirs.* Formidable though the task appears, much of the inked over material has been recovered. The excised parts, however, are simply gone—a painful testament to a sensibility of another age.

The second part of the Boston Public Library collection contains the letters from Fuller to James Nathan. A few of these letters, too, were in part canceled at a later date, but virtually all of the lined matter has been recovered. The library has a very helpful typed catalogue of the Fuller collection.

A few final remarks: most of the printed versions of the letters, save those in Rusk and Wade and the few printed in scholarly journals, are unreliable to varying degrees. Dorothy Van Doren used the *Memoirs* versions for her book but let more errors creep into them. I have included the locations of printed letters from those authors who had access to the original letters and from the books where they have been most completely published. I have not noted excerpts printed in any biography since Higginson's.

Following her custom, I retain the second "t" in the given name of Fuller's mother because that was the way she wrote it. For consistency's sake, I have used the maiden names of Caroline Sturgis who married William Tappan and Ellen Fuller who married Ellery Channing.

The list of library symbols is derived from the National Union Catalog, with the addition of "NN (Berg)" for manuscripts in the Henry W. and Albert A. Berg Collection at the New York Public Library; the short title list is composed of the most frequent sources of printed Fuller letters. The Appendix is a list of letters Fuller is known to have written but which have never been recovered in any form. An Index of recipients and libraries follows the Calendar and is keyed to the chronological number of each letter. I would, of course, be deeply grateful for any further information about the whereabouts of Fuller manuscripts.

It is a distinct and deep pleasure to have an opportunity to identify and thank some of the people who have been so kind as to assist my research on the Fuller letters. First, I have received financial grants from the Graduate School and from the Summer Research fund of the University of Washington. I have also received grants from the Institute for the Arts and Humanistic Studies directed by Professor Stanley Weintraub of the Pennsylvania State University and from the Liberal Arts College Fund for Research administered by Dean Thomas Magner of the Pennsylvania State University. Obviously this project could not go forward without the frequent help given me by many librarians, most notably Miss Carolyn Jakeman and Mr. William Bond of the Houghton Library; Mr. John Alden and Mr. James Lawton of the Boston Public Library; and Mr. Stephen Riley of the Massachusetts Historical Society. Mr. Nelson White and Mr. Gene De Gruson have kindly given me photostats of Fuller letters in their collections. Mr. Howard N. Meyer has called to my attention a previously unknown letter. Mrs. Paula Blanchard made several helpful suggestions. Professor Eleanor Tilton and Miss Madeleine Stern have been unfailingly gracious in alerting me to the existence of Fuller materials. My especially deep gratitude is due Professor Joel Myerson, who not only has provided space for the publication of this Calendar, but who has been a constant source of information, aid, and encouragement.

SHORT TITLES

At Home and Abroad	*At Home and Abroad*, ed. Arthur B. Fuller. Boston: Crosby, Nichols, 1856.
Higginson	Thomas Wentworth Higginson. *Margaret Fuller Ossoli*. Boston: Houghton, Mifflin, 1884.
JMN, 11	*The Journals and Miscellaneous Notebooks of Ralph Waldo Emerson*, vol. 11, 1848–1851, ed. A. W. Plumstead, William H. Gilman, and Ruth H. Bennett. Cambridge: Harvard University Press, 1975.
Love-Letters	*Love-Letters of Margaret Fuller 1845–1846*. New York: D. Appleton, 1903.
Memoirs	*Memoirs of Margaret Fuller Ossoli*, ed. R. W. Emerson, W. H. Channing, and J. F. Clark. 2 vols. Boston: Phillips, Sampson, 1852; reprinted with additional material, 2 vols., Boston: Roberts, 1874; reprint ed., New York: Burt Franklin, 1973.
Miller	*Margaret Fuller: American Romantic*, ed. Perry Miller. New York: Doubleday, 1963; reprint ed., Ithaca, N.Y.: Cornell University Press, 1970.
Rusk	*The Letters of Ralph Waldo Emerson*, ed. Ralph L. Rusk. 6 vols. New York: Columbia University Press, 1939.
Wade	*The Writings of Margaret Fuller*, ed. Mason Wade. New York: Viking, 1941.
Woman in the Nineteenth Century	*Woman in the Nineteenth Century*, ed. Arthur B. Fuller. Boston: John P. Jewett, 1855.

A CALENDAR OF THE LETTERS OF MARGARET FULLER

1. 24 April [1817?]   [Cambridge]
   To Timothy Fuller. MH fMS Am 1086 (9:1); copy MH fMS Am 1086 (9:1).

2. 13 January 1818   Canton
   To Timothy Fuller. MH fMS Am 1086 (9:3).

3. 24 February 1818   [Cambridge?]
   To Timothy Fuller. MH fMS Am 1086 (9:3).

4. 5 March 1818   Canton
   To Timothy Fuller. MH fMS Am 1086 (10:86).

5. 16 December 1818   Cambridge
   To Timothy Fuller. MH fMS Am 1086 (9:4).

6. 6 January 1819   Cambridge
   To Timothy Fuller. MH fMS Am 1086 (9:5).

7. 8 January 1819   Cambridge
   To Timothy Fuller. MH fMS Am 1086 (9:6).
   Printed in Wade, p. 544.

8. 8 May [1819?]   Cambridge
   To Timothy Fuller. MH fMS Am 1086 (9:2).

9. 20 November 1819   Cambridge
   To Ellen Kilshaw. MH fMS Am 1086 (9:258).

10. 19 December 1819   Cambridge
    To Timothy Fuller. MH fMS Am 1086 (9:7).

11. 25 December 1819   Cambridge
    To Timothy Fuller. MH fMS Am 1086 (9:10).

12. [ca. 1820]   [Cambridge?]
    To Amelia Greenwood. PSt.

13. 16 January 1820   Cambridge
    To Timothy Fuller. MH fMS Am 1086 (9:11).

14. 3 February 1820   Cambridge
    To Timothy Fuller. MH fMS Am 1086 (9:13).

15. 21 March 1820   Cambridge
    To Timothy Fuller. MH fMS Am 1086 (10:87).

16. 17 April 1820   Cambridge
    To Margarett C. Fuller. MH fMS Am 1086 (9:14).

17. 7 August 1820   Cambridge
    To Mary Vose. MH fMS Am 1086 (9:15). Copy
    of unrecovered holograph.

18. 1 November 1820   Cambridge
    To Sarah B. Fuller. MH fMS Am 1086 (9:12).

19. 22 November 1820   Cambridge
    To Timothy Fuller. MH fMS Am 1086 (9:16).

A Calendar of the Letters of Margaret Fuller 55

20. 26 November 1820 — Cambridge
    To Timothy Fuller. MH fMS Am 1086 (6:92).

21. 4 December 1820 — Cambridge
    To Timothy Fuller. MH fMS Am 1086 (9:17).

22. 21 December 1820 — Cambridge
    To Timothy Fuller. MH fMS Am 1086 (6:104).

23. 5 January 1821 — Cambridge
    To Timothy Fuller. MH fMS Am 1086 (10:88).

24. 15 January 1821 — Cambridge
    To Timothy Fuller. MH fMS Am 1086 (9:18).

25. 25 January 1821 — Cambridge
    To Timothy Fuller. MH fMS Am 1086 (6:119).

26. 29 January 1821 — Cambridge
    To Timothy Fuller. MH fMS Am 1086 (6:121).

27. 14 February 1821 — Cambridge
    To Timothy Fuller. MH fMS Am 1086 (6:128).

28. 2 December 1821 — Boston
    To Margarett C. Fuller. MH fMS Am 1086 (9:19).

29. 9 December 1821 — Boston
    To Margarett C. Fuller. MH fMS Am 1086 (9:20).

30. 23 December 1821 — Boston
    To Margarett C. Fuller. MH fMS Am 1086 (9:21).

31. 13 March 1822 — Boston
    To Timothy Fuller. MH fMS Am 1086 (9:22).

32. 22 March 1822 — Canton
    To Timothy Fuller. MH fMS Am 1086 (7:26).

33. 29 March 1822 — Canton
    To Timothy Fuller. MH fMS Am 1086 (7:29).

34. 22 December 1822 — Cambridge
    To Timothy Fuller. MH fMS Am 1086 (10:89).

35. 30 December 1822 — Cambridge
    To Timothy Fuller. MH fMS Am 1086 (7:55).

36. 5 January 1823 — Cambridge
    To Timothy Fuller. MH fMS Am 1086 (7:58).

37. 12 January 1823 — Cambridge
    To Timothy Fuller. MH fMS Am 1086 (9:23).

38. 30 January 1823 — Cambridge
    To Timothy Fuller. MH fMS Am 1086 (7:67).

39. 2 February 1823   Cambridge
   To Timothy Fuller. MH fMS Am 1086 (10:90).

40. 18 December 1823   Cambridge
   To Timothy Fuller. MH fMS Am 1086 (10:91).

41. 23 December 1823   Cambridge
   To Timothy Fuller. MH fMS Am 1086 (7:86).

42. 25 January 1824   Cambridge
   To Timothy Fuller. MH fMS Am 1086 (9:24).

43. 17 February [1824?]   [Boston]
   To Amelia Greenwood. Unrecovered. Copy in collection of Robert N. Hudspeth.

44. 22 February 1824   Cambridge
   To Timothy Fuller. MH fMS Am 1086 (10:92).

45. 19 April 1824   Cambridge
   To Timothy Fuller. MH fMS Am 1086 (10:93).

46. 21 May 1824   Groton
   To Timothy Fuller. MH fMS Am 1086 (9:25).

47. 14 July 1824   Groton
   To Abraham W. Fuller. MH fMS Am 1086 (9:27).

48. 29 September 1824   Groton
   To Abraham W. Fuller. MH fMS Am 1086 (9:28).

49. 20 December 1824   Groton
   To Timothy Fuller. MH fMS Am 1086 (9:26).

50. 5 January 1825   Groton
   To Timothy Fuller. MH fMS Am 1086 (9:29).

51. 31 January 1825   Groton
   To Timothy Fuller. MH fMS Am 1086 (9:30).

52. 14 February 1825   Groton
   To Timothy Fuller. MH fMS Am 1086 (9:31).

53. 11 July 1825   Cambridge
   To [?]. Unrecovered. Incomplete. Printed in *Memoirs*, 1:52–54.

54. 5 March 1826   Cambridge
   To [?]. Unrecovered. Fragment. Printed in *Memoirs*, 1:54–55.

55. 14 May 1826   Cambridge
   To [?]. Unrecovered. Fragment. Printed in *Memoirs*, 1:55.

A Calendar of the Letters of Margaret Fuller 57

56. 10 January 1827   Cambridge
    To [?]. Unrecovered. Fragment. Printed in *Memoirs*,
    1:55–56.

57. 3 January 1828   Cambridge
    To [?]. Unrecovered. Incomplete. Printed in *Memoirs*,
    1:56–57.

58. 17 December 1829   [——?]
    To [?]. Incomplete. MH fMS Am 1086 (Box A).
    Copy of unrecovered holograph. Printed in *Memoirs*,
    1:222–24.

59. 19 December 1829   [——?]
    To [?]. Unrecovered. Fragment. Printed in *Memoirs*,
    1:80.

60. 1829–1830   [——?]
    To [?]. Unrecovered. Fragment. Printed in *Memoirs*,
    1:135–36.

61. 1829–1830   [——?]
    To [?]. Unrecovered. Fragment. Printed in *Memoirs*,
    1:115.

62. January 1830   Cambridge
    To [?]. Unrecovered. Fragment. Printed in *Memoirs*,
    1:57.

63. 16 March 1830   [——?]
    To [James F. Clarke]. Unrecovered. Printed in
    Memoirs, 1:62–63.

64. [ca. 26? March 1830]   [——?]
    To James F. Clarke. Unrecovered. Fragment. Printed
    in *Memoirs*, 1:66.

65. [28? March 1830]   [——?]
    To [James F. Clarke]. Unrecovered. Fragment.
    Printed in *Memoirs*, 1:66–68.

66. 1 May 1830   [——?]
    To [James F. Clarke]. Unrecovered. Fragment.
    Printed in *Memoirs*, 1:68–69.

67. 4 May 1830   [——?]
    To [James F. Clarke]. Unrecovered. Fragment.
    Printed in *Memoirs*, 1:69–70; Miller, pp. 28–29.

68. 21 August 1830   Cambridge
    To Timothy and Margarett C. Fuller. MH fMS Am
    1086 (10:94).

69. 19 November 1830   Cambridge
    To Almira P. Barlow. MH fMS Am 1086 (Works,

1:1–5). Copy of unrecovered holograph. Printed
in Higginson, pp. 39–40.

70. 1830–1831 [——?]
To [?]. Unrecovered. Fragment. Printed in *Memoirs*,
1:105–106.

71. 2 February 1831 [——?]
To [?]. Fragment. MB Ms. Am. 1450 (18). Copy in
Higginson's hand of unrecovered holograph.

72. 1832 [——?]
To [?]. Unrecovered. Fragment. Printed in *Memoirs*,
1:118. Probably written to James F. Clarke.

73. January 1832 [——?]
To [?]. Unrecovered. Fragment. Printed in *Memoirs*,
1:83–84.

74. 6 July 1832 [——?]
To [?]. Unrecovered. Fragment. Printed in *Memoirs*,
1:79.

75. [ca. 1 August 1832] [Groton]
To [James F. Clarke]. Unrecovered. Fragment. Printed
in *Memoirs*, 1:118–19.

76. 7 August 1832 [——?]
To [James F. Clarke]. Unrecovered. Incomplete.
Printed in *Memoirs*, 1:119–21.

77. September 1832 [——?]
To [?]. Unrecovered. Fragment. Printed in *Memoirs*,
1:123–24.

78. 14 December [1832] [Groton?]
To [?]. Fragment. NN. Bottom portion of the last sheet
of a letter written probably to a member of the Fuller
family.

79. 1833 Groton
To [?]. Unrecovered. Fragment. Printed in *Memoirs*,
1:145.

80. 25 April 1833 Groton
To Eliza R. Farrar. MH fMS Am 1086 (Box A); copy
MH fMS Am 1086 (Works, 3:351–53). Partially
printed in *Memoirs*, 1:146.

81. May 1833 Groton
To [James F. Clarke]. Unrecovered. Fragment. Printed
in *Memoirs*, 1:121.

82. June 1833 [Groton]
To [James F. Clarke?]. Unrecovered. Fragment. Printed
in *Memoirs*, 1:121.

83. 3 June 1833 [Groton]
To [James F. Clarke?]. Unrecovered. Fragment. Printed in *Memoirs*, 1:116–17.

84. [16? June 1833] [——?]
To [James F. Clarke]. MH bMS Am 1569.7 (462). Printed in *New England Quarterly*, 30 (September 1957): 378–79.

85. [18? June 1833] [——?]
To [James F. Clarke]. MH bMS Am 1569.7 (463).

86. [ca. July 1833] [Groton?]
To [?]. Unrecovered. Incomplete. Printed in *Memoirs*, 1:122–23. Probably written to James F. Clarke.

87. 4 July 1833 Groton
To Frederic H. Hedge. MH fMS Am 1086 (10:96); copies MH fMS Am 1086 (Works, 3:353–61); MB Ms. Am. 1450 (177). Partially printed in *Memoirs*, 1:146–47; Higginson, pp. 43–45, 141.

88. [August? 1833?] [Groton?]
To [James F. Clarke?]. Unrecovered. Fragment. Printed in *Memoirs*, 1:85–86. Dated by reference in Clarke to Fuller, 9 September 1833. In *The Letters of James Freeman Clarke to Margaret Fuller*, ed. John Wesley Thomas (Hamburg: Cram, de Gruyter and Co., 1957), p. 61.

89. 17 October 1833 Boston
To Richard F. Fuller. MH fMS Am 1086 (9:33); copy MH fMS Am 1086 (Works, 2:613–15).

90. 25 October 1833 Boston
To James F. Clarke. MH bMS Am 1569.7 (464). Partially printed in *New England Quarterly*, 30 (September 1957): 379.

91. [ca. 1834?] [——?]
To [?]. Unrecovered. Fragment. Printed in *Memoirs*, 1:167–68. May be two letters.

92. [1834] [Groton?]
To [?]. Unrecovered. Incomplete. Printed in *Memoirs*, 1:124–26. Probably written to James F. Clarke.

93. 9 March 1834 Groton
To Almira P. Barlow. MH fMS Am 1086 (Works, 1:7–11). Copy of unrecovered holograph. Printed in Wade, pp. 545–46.

94. 20 March 1834 Groton
To Amelia Greenwood. MH fMS Am 1086 (Box A); copy MH fMS Am 1086 (Works, 3:363–71). Partially printed in *Memoirs*, 1:149–51.

95. 4 June 1834   Boston
To Arthur B. Fuller. MH fMS Am 1086 (9:36);
copy MH fMS Am 1086 (Works, 1:611–13).

96. 28 September 1834   Boston
To James F. Clarke. MH bMS Am 1569.7 (467).
Partially printed in *New England Quarterly*, 30
(September 1957): 382.

97. 6 October 1834   Worcester
To Almira P. Barlow. MH fMS Am 1086 (Works,
1:13–17). Copy of unrecovered holograph. Partially
printed in Higginson, p. 62.

98. 9 November 1834   Groton
To Frederic H. Hedge. MH fMS Am 1086 (10:101).

99. 30 November 1834   Groton
To Frederic H. Hedge. MH fMS Am 1086 (10:98).
Partially printed in *Memoirs*, 1:151; Higginson, p. 63.

100. 26 December 1834   Groton
To Frederic H. Hedge. MH fMS Am 1086 (10:97).

101. 5 January 1835   Groton
To Almira P. Barlow. Incomplete. MH fMS Am 1086
(Works, 1:17–19). Copy of unrecovered holograph.

102. 1 February 1835   Groton
To James F. Clarke. MH bMS Am 1569.7 (466).

103. 1 February 1835   Groton
To Frederic H. Hedge. MH fMS Am 1086 (10:99).
Partially printed in *Memoirs*, 1:151.

104. 6 March 1835   Groton
To Frederic H. Hedge. MH fMS Am 1086 (10:100).
Partially printed in Higginson, pp. 48, 141–42.

105. 28 March 1835   [Groton?]
To Frederic H. Hedge. MH fMS Am 1086 (10:101).

106. [29 March 1835]   [Groton?]
To [James F. Clarke]. Unrecovered. Fragment. Printed
in *Memoirs*, 1:126–27.

107. 2 June 1835   Boston
To Timothy and Margarett C. Fuller. MH fMS Am 1086
(9:35); copy MH fMS Am 1086 (Works, 1:153–59).
Printed in Higginson, pp. 51–53.

108. 13 August 1835   Cambridge
To Timothy and Margarett C. Fuller. MH fMS Am
1086 (9:37).

A Calendar of the Letters of Margaret Fuller 61

109. 25 October 1835 [Groton]
 To [?]. Fragment. MH bMS Am 1280 (111, p. 200).
 Copy of unrecovered holograph. Printed in *JMN*, 11:491.

110. 3 November 1835 [———?]
 To [?]. Unrecovered. Fragment. Printed in *Memoirs*,
 1:157.

111. 6 November 1835 Groton
 To Abraham W. Fuller. MH fMS Am 1086 (9:39).

112. 17 November 1835 Groton
 To Abraham W. Fuller. MH fMS Am 1086 (9:36).

113. [13 December 1835] [Groton?]
 To [Eugene? Fuller]. Incomplete. MH fMS AM 1086
 (9:246).

114. [ca. 1836?] [———?]
 To [?]. Fragment. MH fMS Am 1086 (Box A).

115. [1836] [Groton?]
 To Eugene Fuller. Incomplete. MH fMS AM 1086
 (Box A).

116. 1836 [———?]
 To [?]. Unrecovered. Fragment. Printed in *Memoirs*,
 1:166–67.

117. 30 January 1836 [Groton?]
 To Eugene Fuller. Unrecovered. Fragment. Printed in
 Memoirs, 1:159.

118. [ca. 1 February 1836] [Groton]
 To [James F. Clarke]. Unrecovered. Fragment. Printed
 in *Memoirs*, 1:128–29, 127.

119. 1 February 1836 Groton
 To Almira P. Barlow. MH fMS Am 1086 (Works,
 1:19–20). Copy of unrecovered holograph. Partially
 printed in Higginson, p. 54.

120. 17 March 1836 [Groton]
 To [Eliza R. Farrar?]. Unrecovered. Fragment. Printed
 in *Memoirs*, 1:166.

121. 17 April 1836 [Groton?]
 To [Eliza R. Farrar]. Unrecovered. Fragment. Printed
 in *Memoirs*, 1:159–60.

122. [19 April 1836] [Groton?]
 To [James F. Clarke]. Unrecovered. Fragment. Printed
 in *Memoirs*, 1:129; Miller, p. 48.

123. 20 April 1836 — Groton
To Samuel G. Ward. Unrecovered. Incomplete? Printed in Higginson, pp. 56–58.

124. 21 April 1836 — Groton
To Ellen K. Fuller. MH fMS Am 1086 (9:40); copy MH fMS Am 1086 (Works, 1:159–63).

125. 23 May 1836 — [Groton?]
To [?]. Unrecovered. Incomplete. Printed in *Memoirs*, 1:160–61.

126. 14 July 1836 — Groton
To Elizabeth Hoar. Fragment. MH bMS Am 1280 (111, p. 120). Copy of unrecovered holograph. Printed in *JMN*, 11:479.

127. 25 August 1836 — Groton
To A. Bronson Alcott. MH 59m–312 (120).

128. 26 August [1836] — Groton
To Ellen K. Fuller. MH fMS Am 1086 (9:43).

129. 31 August 1836 — Groton
To Frederic H. Hedge. MH fMS Am 1086 (10:102).

130. 1 September 1836 — Groton
To R. W. Emerson. Fragment. MH bMS Am 1280 (111, p. 256). Copy of unrecovered holograph. Printed in *JMN*, 11:500.

131. 21 September 1836 — Boston
To R. W. Emerson. MH bMS Am 1280 (2335); copy MB Ms. Am. 1450 (62). Partially printed in Higginson, p. 68; printed entire in Rusk, 2:36–37.

132. [ca. late 1836] — [Boston]
To [?]. Unrecovered. Fragment. Printed in *Memoirs*, 1:175–76.

133. 1837 — [Boston?]
To Jane F. Tuckerman. Incomplete? MH fMS Am 1086 (Works, 1:73). Copy of unrecovered holograph. Printed in *Woman in the Nineteenth Century*, p. 352.

134. [ca. Spring 1837] — [——?]
To [?]. Unrecovered. Incomplete. Printed in *Memoirs*, 1:172–75.

135. [Spring 1837] — [Boston?]
To [?]. Unrecovered. Fragment. Printed in *Memoirs*, 1:176–77.

136. 6 April 1837 — Boston
To Frederic H. Hedge. Incomplete. Letter exists in four

A Calendar of the Letters of Margaret Fuller

parts which join as follows: MB Ms. Am. 1450 (79), (63), (162), Higginson, p. 78. Manuscript fragments are all copies of unrecovered holograph. Printed in Wade, pp. 547–48.

137. 11 April 1837   Boston
To R. W. Emerson. MH bMS Am 1280 (2336); copy MB Ms. Am. 1450 (64). Partially printed in Higginson, pp. 86–87; Rusk, 2:64–65.

138. [24? April 1837?]   [Boston]
To R. W. Emerson. TxU.

139. 2 May 1837   Concord
To Jane F. Tuckerman. MH fMS Am 1086 (Works, 1:83). Copy of unrecovered holograph. Printed in *Woman in the Nineteenth Century*, p. 351; partially printed in Higginson, p. 67.

140. 14 May 1837   Groton
To Caroline Sturgis. MH bMS Am 1221 (201).

141. 18 May 1837   Groton
To A. Bronson Alcott. MH 59m–312 (121); copy MB Ms. Am. 1450 (180).

142. 26 May 1837   Groton
To Elizabeth P. Peabody. PHi.

143. 30 May 1837   Groton
To R. W. Emerson. MH bMS Am 1280 (2337); copy MB Ms. Am. 1450 (65). Partially printed in Rusk, 2:78.

144. 31 May 1837   Groton
To John S. Dwight. MB Ms. E.4.1 (15).

145. [6 June 1837]   [Providence]
To R. W. Emerson. MH bMS Am 1280 (2338); copies MB Ms. Am. 1450 (19), (66).

146. 16 June 1837   Providence
To Jane F. Tuckerman. Incomplete? MH fMS Am 1086 (Works, 1:85–87). Copy of unrecovered holograph. Printed in *Woman in the Nineteenth Century*, pp. 357–58.

147. 18 June [1837?]   [Providence]
To Caroline Sturgis. Incomplete. MH bMS Am 1221 (202).

148. 27 June 1837   Providence
To A. Bronson Alcott. MH 59m–312 (122); copies MB Ms. Am. 1450 (16), (181). Partially printed in *The Critic*, 43 (October 1903): 340–41.

149. [Summer? 1837] [Providence?]
To Harriet Martineau. Unrecovered. Incomplete.
Printed in *Memoirs*, 1:192–94; Higginson, pp. 123–24.

150. 3 July 1837 Providence
To [R. W. Emerson?]. Fragment. MB Ms. Am. 1450
(160). Copy of unrecovered holograph. Partially printed
with the recipient identified as Emerson by Annie M.
Russell in *The Critic*, 43 (October 1903): 343.

151. 5 July 1837 Providence
To Arthur B. Fuller. MH fMS Am 1086 (9:44); copy
MH fMS Am 1086 (Works, 1:613–21). Printed, though
misdated as 25 July, in *The Critic*, 43 (October 1903):
342–43.

152. 8 July 1837 [Providence]
To Elizabeth P. Peabody. Unrecovered. Fragment.
Printed in Higginson, p. 81.

153. 12 July 1837 Providence
To Frederic H. Hedge. MH fMS Am 1086 (10:102).

154. 15 July 1837 Providence
To Caroline Sturgis. MH bMS Am 1221 (203).

155. 14 August 1837 Providence
To R. W. Emerson. MH bMS Am 1280 (2339); copy
MB Ms. Am. 1450 (161). Partially printed in Higginson,
p. 87; Rusk, 2:94–95.

156. 16 August 1837 Providence
To Caroline Sturgis. MH bMS Am 1221 (204).

157. 2 September 1837 Providence
To [?]. Fragment. MB Ms. Am. 1450 (160). Copy
of unrecovered holograph.

158. 5 September 1837 Concord
To Margarett C. Fuller. MH fMS Am 1086 (9:45); copy
MH fMS Am 1086 (Works, 1:163–69). Partially printed
in *Woman in the Nineteenth Century*, pp. 344–45.

159. 14 October 1837 Providence
To Caroline Sturgis. MH bMS Am 1221 (205).

160. 17 October 1837 Providence
To Caroline Sturgis. MH bMS Am 1221 (206).

161. 2 November 1837 Providence
To Caroline Sturgis. MH bMS Am 1221 (207).
Partially printed in *JMN*, 11:377.

162. 10 November 1837 Providence
To Caroline Sturgis. MH bMS Am 1221 (208).

A Calendar of the Letters of Margaret Fuller 65

163. 16 November 1837   Providence
 To Caroline Sturgis. MH bMS Am 1221 (209).

164. 18 November 1837   Providence
 To Margarett C. Fuller. MH fMS Am 1086 (9:56).

165. 22 December 1837   Providence
 To Anna Jameson. CtY.

166. 31 December 1837   Providence
 To Arthur B. Fuller. MH fMS Am 1086 (9:46); copy MH fMS Am 1086 (Works, 1:621–27). Partially printed in Higginson, p. 59; printed entire in Wade, pp. 549–50.

167. [ca. 1838]   [Providence]
 To [Albert G. Greene]. RPB.

168. 3 January 1838   Providence
 To Caroline Sturgis. MH bMS Am 1221 (210).

169. [February? 1838?]   Providence
 To Caroline Sturgis. Fragment. MH bMS Am 1221 (211).

170. 19 February 1838   Providence
 To Arthur B. Fuller. MH fMS Am 1086 (9:47); copy MH fMS Am 1086 (Works, 1:627–31). Partially printed in *Woman in the Nineteenth Century*, pp. 347–48.

171. 1 March 1838   Providence
 To R. W. Emerson. MH bMS Am 1280 (2341); copy MB Ms. Am. 1450 (76). Partially printed in Higginson, pp. 89–91.

172. 26 March 1838   Providence
 To Abraham W. Fuller. MH fMS Am 1086 (9:48).

173. 17 April 1838   Providence
 To Caroline Sturgis. ViU; copy MH fMS Am 1086 (Works, 3:253–61). Partially printed in *Memoirs*, 1:235.

174. 30 May 1838   Providence
 To Thesta [Dana]. CtY.

175. 28 June 1838   Providence
 To Arthur B., Richard F., and Lloyd Fuller. MH fMS Am 1086 (9:49); copy MH fMS Am 1086 (Works, 1:631–37).

176. [July? 1838?]   [Providence?]
 To R. W. Emerson. MH bMS Am 1280 (2340).

177. July 1838   Providence
 To Caroline Sturgis. MH bMS Am 1221 (212).

178. 19 August 1838 [——?]
To Lidian J. Emerson. MH bMS Am 1280.226 (3909).

179. 21 September 1838 Providence
To Jane F. Tuckerman. Incomplete? MH fMS Am 1086
(Works, 1:89–91). Copy of unrecovered holograph.

180. 27 September [1838?] [Providence?]
To Charles K. Newcomb. MH fMS Am 1086 (10:130).

181. October 1838 Providence
To Almira P. Barlow. Fragment. MH fMS Am 1086
(Works, 1:23). Copy of unrecovered holograph.

182. October 1838 [Providence]
To Caroline Sturgis. Fragment. MH bMS Am 1280
(111, p. 16). Copy of unrecovered holograph. Printed
in *Memoirs*, 1:286; *JMN*, 11:461.

183. 7 October 1838 Providence
To Mary. MH fMS Am 1086 (9:50); copy MH fMS
Am 1086 (Works, 1:171–77). Printed in *Woman in
the Nineteenth Century*, pp. 345–47.

184. 21 October 1838 Providence
To Jane F. Tuckerman. MH fMS Am 1086 (Works,
1:91–95). Copy of unrecovered holograph. Printed in
Woman in the Nineteenth Century, pp. 358–60.

185. 23 October 1838 [Providence]
To Charles K. Newcomb. MH fMS Am 1086 (10:126).

186. 30 October 1838 Providence
To Richard F. Fuller. MH fMS Am 1086 (9:51); copy
MH fMS Am 1086 (Works, 2:615–23).

187. 8 November 1838 Providence
To Almira P. Barlow. MH fMS Am 1086 (Works,
1:21–23). Copy of unrecovered holograph. Partially
printed in Higginson, p. 94.

188. 16 November 1838 Providence
To Mrs. [George H.] Calvert. MHi.

189 25 November [1838?] [Providence]
To Charles K. Newcomb. MH fMS Am 1086 (10:131).

190. 9 December 1838 Providence
To [William H. Channing?]. Incomplete. MB Ms. Am.
1450 (35). Partially printed in Higginson, pp. 91–92.

191. 7 January 1839 Groton
To R. W. Emerson. Fragment. Letter exists in two parts
which join as follows: MB Ms. Am. 1450 (67), Higgin-

son, p. 95. The manuscript portion is a copy of unrecovered holograph. Partially printed in Rusk, 2:178.

192. 8 January 1839   Groton
To James F. Clarke. Unrecovered. Incomplete. Printed in *Memoirs*, 1:73–74; partially printed in Miller, pp. 47–48.

193. 10 January 1839   Groton
To Caroline Sturgis. Incomplete? MH bMS Am 1221 (214).

194. 23 January 1839   [Groton?]
To Caroline Sturgis. MH bMS Am 1221 (215).

195. 24 January 1839   Groton
To Arthur B. Fuller. MH fMS Am 1086 (9:55); copy MH fMS Am 1086 (Works, 1:637–39).

196. 27 January 1839   Groton
To Caroline Sturgis. MH bMS Am 1221 (216).

197. 2 February 1839   Groton
To Caroline Sturgis. MH bMS Am 1221 (218). Partial copy, MH bMS Am 1280 (111, p. 220). Partially printed in *JMN*, 11:493.

198. 7 February [1839]   [Groton]
To Caroline Sturgis. MH bMS Am 1221 (219).

199. [21?] February 1839   [Groton?]
To Caroline Sturgis. MH bMS Am 1221 (217); copy MH bMS Am 1280 (111, p. 170). Printed in *Memoirs*, 1:295; *JMN*, 11:487–88.

200. 21 February [1839]   Groton
To George Ripley. VtMiM.

201. 4 March 1839   Groton
To R. W. Emerson. MH bMS Am 1280 (2343); copy MB Ms. Am. 1450 (68). Printed in Rusk, 2:190–91.

202. 4 March 1839   Groton
To Charles K. Newcomb. MH fMS Am 1086 (10:127).

203. 9 March 1839   Groton
To Caroline Sturgis. MH bMS Am 1221 (220). Printed in Wade, pp. 551–54.

204. 10 March 1839   Groton
To Arthur B. Fuller. MH fMS Am 1086 (9:57).

205. 31 March 1839   Concord
To Eugene Fuller. MH fMS Am 1086 (9:59).

206. 18 April 1839 — Jamaica Plain
To Charles K. Newcomb. MH fMS Am 1086 (10:128).

207. 23 April 1839 — [Jamaica Plain?]
To [?]. Fragment. MB Ms. Am. 1450 (17). Copy in Higginson's hand of unrecovered holograph.

208. 13 May 1839 — Jamaica Plain
To [?]. Fragment. MB Ms. Am. 1450 (159). Copy of unrecovered holograph.

209. 15 May 1839 — Jamaica Plain
To Elizabeth Hoar. Fragment. MH bMS Am 1280 (111, pp. 57–59). Copy of unrecovered holograph. Partially printed in *Memoirs*, 1:294; *JMN*, 11:469.

210. 29 May 1839 — Jamaica Plain
To Hiram Fuller. ViU.

211. 29 May 1839 — Jamaica Plain
To Charles K. Newcomb. MH fMS Am 1086 (10:129).

212. 3 June 1839 — Jamaica Plain
To R. W. Emerson. MH bMS Am 1280 (2344). Printed in Rusk, 2:202–203.

213. 8 June 1839 — [Jamaica Plain?]
To Eugene Fuller. MH fMS Am 1086 (9:172).

214. 10 June 1839 — Jamaica Plain
To Sarah H. Whitman. ViU.

215. [ca. 21?] June 1839 — Jamaica Plain
To Jane F. Tuckerman. Incomplete? MH fMS Am 1086 (Works, 1:99–103). Copy of unrecovered holograph. Printed in *Woman in the Nineteenth Century*, pp. 361–63.

216. 25 June 1839 — [Jamaica Plain]
To Caroline Sturgis. MH bMS Am 1221 (222).

217. [28? June 1839] — [Jamaica Plain]
To Caroline Sturgis. MH bMS Am 1221 (213).

218. July 1839 — [Jamaica Plain]
To [Caroline Sturgis?]. Fragment. MH bMS Am 1280 (111, p. 82). Copy of unrecovered holograph. Printed in *Memoirs*, 1:282; *JMN*, 11:473.

219. July 1839 — [Jamaica Plain]
To [Samuel G. Ward?]. Incomplete. MH fMS Am 1086 (Works, 1:179–81). Copy of unrecovered holograph.

A Calendar of the Letters of Margaret Fuller 69

220. 12 July 1839 [Jamaica Plain]
To Caroline Sturgis. Fragment. MH bMS Am 1221
(223).

221. August 1839 Jamaica Plain
To Jane F. Tuckerman. Incomplete? MH fMS Am 1086
(Works, 1:95–97). Copy of unrecovered holograph.
Printed in *Woman in the Nineteenth Century*, pp. 363–64.

222. 17 August 1839 Jamaica Plain
To Elizabeth Hoar. ViU.

223. 27 August 1839 Jamaica Plain
To [Sarah Ripley?]. Incomplete. MH fMS Am 1086
(9:61–62); copies MH fMS Am 1086 (Works, 1:197–
201); RPB. Printed in *Memoirs*, 1:324–28; partially
printed in Higginson, pp. 112–13.

224. [ca. 1] September 1839 [Jamaica Plain]
To [Samuel G. Ward?]. Incomplete. MH fMS Am 1086
(9:60); copy MH fMS Am 1086 (Works, 1:183–87).
Partially printed in Miller, pp. 50–52.

225. 7 October 1839 Jamaica Plain
To Caroline Sturgis. MH bMS Am 1221 (224).

226. 10 October 1839 [Jamaica Plain?]
To A. Bronson Alcott. MH 59m–312 (123);
copy MB Ms. Am. 1450 (1b).

227. 15 October 1839 [Jamaica Plain?]
To Samuel G. Ward. MH fMS Am 1086 (9:63);
copies MH fMS Am 1086 (Works, 1:187–93); MH
bMS Am 1280 (111, p. 160). Partially printed in
JMN, 11:487.

228. [ca. Autumn? 1839?] [Jamaica Plain?]
To [?]. Unrecovered. Fragment. Printed in
Memoirs, 1:332.

229. November 1839 [Jamaica Plain?]
To R. W. Emerson. Fragment. MH bMS Am 1280
(111, p. 104). Copy of unrecovered holograph. May
be part of no. 228. Printed in *JMN*, 11:477.

230. 12 November 1839 [Jamaica Plain?]
To R. W. Emerson. Fragment. MH bMS Am 1280
(111, p. 100). Copy of unrecovered holograph. Printed
in *JMN*, 11:476.

231. 24 November 1839 Jamaica Plain
To R. W. Emerson. MH bMS Am 1280 (2345); copy
MB Ms. Am. 1450 (69). Partially printed in Higginson,
pp. 69, 94; printed entire in Rusk, 2:238–40.

232. 25 November 1839   [Jamaica Plain?]
To[?]. Incomplete. MH bMS Am 1280 (111, pp. 101–
[103]). Copy of unrecovered holograph. Partially
printed in *Memoirs*, 1:266; 331–32. Printed in *JMN*,
11:476–77. Probably written to Emerson.

233. 26 December 1839   [Jamaica Plain?]
To R. W. Emerson. Unrecovered. Fragment. Printed in
Memoirs, 1:230–31. One sentence in MH bMS Am
1280 (111, p. 101). This printed in *JMN*, 11:476.

234. [1840?]   [——?]
To Caroline Sturgis. MH bMS Am 1221 (233).

235. [1840?]   [——?]
To Caroline Sturgis. MH bMS Am 1221 (234);
copy MH bMS Am 1280 (111, p. 82). Printed in
JMN, 11:473.

236. [1840?]   [——?]
To Caroline Sturgis. MH bMS Am 1221 (235).

237. 1840   [——?]
To [William H. Channing?]. Unrecovered. Incomplete.
Printed in *Memoirs*, 2:26–31; Miller, pp. 62–66.

238. 1840   [——?]
To R. W. Emerson. Unrecovered. Fragment.
Printed in *Memoirs*, 1:301.

239. 1 January 1840   Jamaica Plain
To William H. Channing. Incomplete. MB Ms. Am.
1450 (36). Partially printed in Higginson, p. 149;
printed entire in Wade, p. 555.

240. 1 January 1840   Jamaica Plain
To Frederic H. Hedge. MH fMS Am 1086 (10:103).
Partially printed in Higginson, pp. 149–50.

241. 14 January 1840   Boston
To Richard F. Fuller. MH fMS Am 1086 (9:52);
copy MH fMS Am 1086 (Works, 2:641–43).

242. 20 January 1840   [——?]
To R. W. Emerson. MH Os 735Laa 1840.1.20. Copy
in Emerson's hand of unrecovered holograph.
Printed in Rusk, 2:248–49.

243. 21 January 1840   Jamaica Plain
To [Sarah H.] Whitman. RHi. Printed in *American
Literature*, 1 (January 1930): 419–21.

244. 10 February [1840]   [Jamaica Plain?]
To Caroline Sturgis. MH bMS Am 1221 (236).

A Calendar of the Letters of Margaret Fuller 71

245. 23 February 1840 [Jamaica Plain]
To R. W. Emerson. Unrecovered. Incomplete.
Printed in *Memoirs*, 1:289-91.

246. 24 February 1840 Jamaica Plain
To Charles K. Newcomb. MH fMS Am 1086 (10:132).

247. 10 March 1840 Jamaica Plain
To Frederic H. Hedge. Unrecovered. Fragment. Printed
in Higginson, p. 150.

248. 22 March 1840 Jamaica Plain
To William H. Channing. Unrecovered. MB Ms. Am.
1450 (37). Partially printed in *Memoirs*, 2:24-25;
Higginson, p. 309.

249. April 1840 [Jamaica Plain]
To R. W. Emerson. Fragment. MH bMS Am 1280
(111, p. 88). Copy of unrecovered holograph. Printed
in *Memoirs*, 1:295; *JMN*, 11:474.

250. 12 April 1840 Jamaica Plain
To R. W. Emerson. MH bMS Am 1280 (2346); copy
MB Ms. Am. 1450 (71). Partially printed in Higginson,
p. 310; printed entire in Rusk, 2:280-81.

251. 19 April 1840 Jamaica Plain
To William H. Channing. Incomplete. MB Ms. Am.
1450 (38). Partially printed in *Memoirs*, 2:25-26;
Higginson, p. 151.

252. [25 April] 1840 Jamaica Plain
To R. W. Emerson. MH bMS Am 1280 (2347).
Printed in Rusk, 2:290-91.

253. 31 May 1840 Jamaica Plain
To R. W. Emerson. MH bMS Am 1280 (2338), (2383);
copy MB Ms. Am. 1450 (72). The second portion of
this letter is a postscript to the main body. Partially
printed in Higginson, p. 151; Rusk, 2:297-98.

254. June 1840 [Jamaica Plain?]
To A. Bronson Alcott. MH 59m-306 (10); another
copy MB Ms. Am. 1450 (1a). Copy of unrecovered
holograph.

255. 3 June 1840 Jamaica Plain
To Richard F. Fuller. MH fMS Am 1086 (9:67);
copy MH fMS Am 1086 (Works, 2:623-27).

256. [ca. July 1840] [Jamaica Plain?]
To [James F. Clarke]. Unrecovered. Fragment. Printed
in *Memoirs*, 1:165-66.

257. July 1840   Jamaica Plain
     To [Almira P. Barlow?]. MH fMS Am 1086 (Works,
     1:23). Copy of unrecovered holograph.

258. 5 July 1840   Jamaica Plain
     To R. W. Emerson. MH bMS Am 1280 (2349); copies
     MH bMS Am 1280 (111, p. 139); MB Ms. Am. 1450
     (73). Partially printed in Higginson, pp. 154–56; Rusk
     2:309–10; *JMN,* 11:483.

259. 12 July 1840   Jamaica Plain
     To Caroline Sturgis. MH bMS Am 1221 (237).

260. 19 July 1840   [Jamaica Plain?]
     To R. W. Emerson. MH bMS Am 1280 (2350);
     copy MB Ms. Am. 1450 (74). Partially printed in
     Higginson, pp. 157–58; Rusk, 2:315.

261. 25 July 1840   Jamaica Plain
     To John Neal. ViU.

262. 29 July 1840   Jamaica Plain
     To Caroline Sturgis. MH bMS Am 1221 (238).
     Partially printed in *Memoirs,* 1:76–77.

263. 16 August 1840   [Jamaica Plain?]
     To Caroline Sturgis. MH bMS Am 1221 (239).

264. 8 September [1840?]   Jamaica Plain
     To Caroline Sturgis. Incomplete? MH bMS Am 1221
     (240).

265. 26 September 1840   Jamaica Plain
     To Caroline Sturgis. MH bMS Am 1221 (241).

266. 29 September 1840   [Jamaica Plain?]
     To R. W. Emerson. MH Os 735Laa 1840.9.29.
     Copy in Emerson's hand of unrecovered holograph.
     Printed in Rusk, 2:340–41; Miller, pp. 53–55.

267. 2 October 1840   Jamaica Plain
     To [Albert G.] Greene. RPB. Partially printed in
     Higginson, p. 163.

268. 10 October 1840   [Jamaica Plain?]
     To [William H. Channing?]. Unrecovered. Fragment.
     Printed in *Memoirs,* 2:44.

269. 18 October 1840   [Jamaica Plain]
     To [William H. Channing?]. Incomplete. Letter exists
     in three parts which join as follows: *Memoirs,* 2:44;
     MB Ms. Am. 1450 (163); *Memoirs,* 2:47. Partially
     printed in *Memoirs,* 2:44–47.

A Calendar of the Letters of Margaret Fuller 73

270. 18 October [1840]   Jamaica Plain
 To Caroline Sturgis. MH bMS Am 1221 (226).

271. 19 October 1840   [Jamaica Plain?]
 To [William H. Channing?]. Unrecovered. Incomplete.
 Printed in *Memoirs*, 2:47–49.

272. 22 October 1840   [Jamaica Plain?]
 To Caroline Sturgis. MH bMS Am 1221 (242).

273. [ca. 25 October 1840]   [Jamaica Plain?]
 To [Caroline Sturgis]. MH bMS Am 1221 (225).
 Conjectural date, could be early 1840.

274. 25 October 1840   [Jamaica Plain?]
 To William H. Channing. Incomplete. Letter exists
 in three parts which join as follows: *Memoirs*, 2:50–52;
 Memoirs, 2:84–85; MB Ms. Am. 1450 (40). Partially
 printed in Higginson, pp. 183–84.

275. [ca. November 1840]   [Jamaica Plain?]
 To R. W. Emerson. MH bMS Am 1280 (2342); copy
 MB Ms. Am. 1450 (70). Printed in Rusk, 2:366;
 Miller, p. 56.

276. November 1840   Jamaica Plain
 To R. W. Emerson. Unrecovered. Fragment. Printed
 in *Memoirs*, 1:301.

277. 7 November 1840   Jamaica Plain
 To R. W. Emerson. MH bMS Am 1280 (2351). Printed
 in Rusk, 2:354.

278. 8 November [1840]   [Jamaica Plain]
 To [William H. Channing]. MB Ms. Am. 1450 (41);
 copy MH bMS Am 1280 (111, pp. 104–106). Partially
 printed in *Memoirs*, 1:339–40; *JMN*, 11:477.

279. 24 [November? 1840?]   [Jamaica Plain?]
 To Caroline Sturgis. MH bMS Am 1221 (232).

280. 1 December [1840]   [Jamaica Plain?]
 To Henry D. Thoreau. NNPM. Printed in F. B. Sanborn,
 Henry D. Thoreau (Boston: Houghton, Mifflin and Co.,
 1882), pp. 172–73, where it is misdated 1841. Printed
 also in *The Correspondence of Henry David Thoreau*, ed.
 Walter Harding and Carl Bode (New York: New York
 University Press, 1958), pp. 41–42.

281. 3 December 1840   [Jamaica Plain]
 To [William H. Channing?]. Unrecovered. Fragment.
 Printed in *Memoirs*, 2:53–54.

282. 6 December 1840 Jamaica Plain
To R. W. Emerson. MH bMS Am 1280 (2352).
Printed in Rusk, 2:362–63.

283. [8 December 1840?] [Jamaica Plain?]
To [William H. Channing?]. Incomplete. Letter exists
in two parts which join as follows: MB Ms. Am. 1450
(42); *Memoirs*, 2:54. This may be a journal entry rather
than a letter.

284. 10 December 1840 [Jamaica Plain?]
To William H. Channing. Unrecovered. Incomplete?
Printed in Higginson, pp. 120–21.

285. 13 December [1840] [Jamaica Plain?]
To [William H. Channing?]. Incomplete. MB Ms. Am.
1450 (43). Partially printed (with part misdated as 22
December) in *Memoirs*, 2:54–57; Higginson, p. 180.

286. 20 December 1840 Jamaica Plain
To Arthur B. Fuller. MH fMS Am 1086 (9:69);
copy MH fMS Am 1086 (Works, 1:641–45). Partially
printed in Higginson, pp. 83–84.

287. 26 December 1840 Jamaica Plain
To Maria W. Chapman. MB Ms.A.9.2, Vol. 14, no. 82.
Printed in Wade, pp. 556–57.

288. [ca. 1841?] [——?]
To [William H. Channing?]. Unrecovered. Fragment.
Printed in *Memoirs*, 2:41–42.

289. [1841?] [——?]
To R. W. Emerson. MH bMS Am 1280 (2381).

290. 24 January 1841 [Jamaica Plain?]
To Caroline Sturgis. MH bMS Am 1221 (243).

291. 30 January 1841 [Jamaica Plain?]
To [William H. Channing?]. Unrecovered. Fragment.
Printed in Higginson, pp. 97–98.

292. [ca. 1 February 1841] [Jamaica Plain?]
To [William H. Channing?]. Fragment. MB Ms. Am.
1450 (45). Partially printed in Higginson, p. 162.

293. [19 February 1841] [Jamaica Plain?]
To [William H. Channing]. Incomplete. Letter exists
in two parts which join as follows: *Memoirs*, 2:57–58;
MB Ms. Am. 1450 (27). Partially printed in Higginson,
pp. 191–92.

294. 20 February 1841 [Jamaica Plain?]
To Elizabeth Hoar. Fragment. MH bMS Am 1280

A Calendar of the Letters of Margaret Fuller 75

(111, p. 107). Copy of unrecovered holograph. Printed in *JMN*, 11:478.

295. 21 February 1841   [Jamaica Plain?]
To [William H. Channing?]. Unrecovered. Fragment. Printed in Higginson, pp. 101–102.

296. 29 March 1841   [Jamaica Plain?]
To [William H. Channing?]. Unrecovered. Fragment. Printed in *Memoirs*, 2:58–59.

297. [5?] April 1841   [Cambridge?]
To [William H. Channing]. Fragment. MB Ms. Am. 1450 (46).

298. 6 April 1841   Cambridge
To Richard F. Fuller. MH fMS Am 1086 (9:68); copy MH fMS Am 1086 (Works, 2:627–37).

299. [ca. 25] April 1841   [Cambridge?]
To R. W. Emerson. Fragment. MH bMS Am 1280 (111, p. 190). Copy of unrecovered holograph. Printed in *JMN*, 11:490.

300. 10 May 1841   [Cambridge]
To R. W. Emerson. MH bMS Am 1280 (2353); copy MB Ms. Am. 1450 (164). Partially printed in Higginson, pp. 181–82; Rusk, 2:398 prints the postscript.

301. 25 May 1841   Concord
To Richard F. Fuller. MH fMS Am 1086 (9:71); copy MH fMS Am 1086 (Works, 2:635–41). Partially printed in Miller, pp. 74–75.

302. [June? 1841?]   [Cambridge]
To Caroline Sturgis. MH bMS Am 1221 (228).

303. [June 1841?]   [Cambridge]
To Charles K. Newcomb. MH fMS Am 1086 (10:138).

304. 21 June 1841   Brookline
To R. W. Emerson. MH bMS Am 1280 (2554). Printed in Rusk, 2:408–409.

305. [July? 1841?]   [Cambridge?]
To [William H. Channing?]. MB Ms. Am. 1450 (165). Partially printed in *Memoirs*, 2:42–44; Higginson, pp. 72–74.

306. 18 July [1841]   [Roxbury?]
To Charles K. Newcomb. MH fMS Am 1086 (10:145).

307. 20 July 1841   Cambridge
To Margarett C. Fuller. MH fMS Am 1086 (9:58); copy MH fMS Am 1086 (Works, 2:525–31).

308. 22 July 1841 Cambridge
To Caroline Sturgis. MH bMS Am 1221 (244).

309. 29 July [1841] Cambridge
To Margarett C. Fuller. MH fMS Am 1086 (9:104);
copy MH fMS Am 1086 (Works, 2:255–57).

310. [31 July 1841] [Newport]
To [William H. Channing]. Fragment. MB Ms. Am.
1450 (47).

311. 5 August 1841 Newport
To Margarett C. Fuller. MH fMS Am 1086 (9:73);
copy MH fMS Am 1086 (Works, 2:531–39).

312. 6 August 1841 Newport
To William H. Channing. MB Ms. Am. 1450 (48).
Partially printed in *Memoirs*, 2:60–62.

313. 22 August 1841 Newport
To Margarett C. Fuller. MH fMS Am 1086 (9:74);
copy MH fMS Am 1086 (Works, 2:539–45).

314. [29? August 1841] [Cambridge]
To William H. Channing. Incomplete. MB Ms. Am.
1450 (49).

315. 31 August 1841 Cambridge
To Margarett C. Fuller. MH fMS Am 1086 (9:75);
copy MH fMS Am 1086 (Works, 2:545–51).

316. 8 September 1841 Cambridge
To R. W. Emerson. MH bMS Am 1280 (2355). Printed
in Rusk, 2:446.

317. 16 September 1841 Cambridge
To R. W. Emerson. MH bMS Am 1280 (2356). Printed
in Rusk, 2:449–50.

318. [October? 1841] [Concord]
To R. W. Emerson. MH bMS Am 1280 (2357); copy
MB Ms. Am. 1450 (75). Printed in *Publications of the
Modern Language Association*, 50 (June 1935): 590;
Rusk, 2:455.

319. [October? 1841] [Concord]
To R. W. Emerson. MH bMS Am 1280 (2358).
Printed in Rusk, 2:455–56; Miller, pp. 109–11.

320. 2 October 1841 Concord
To Charles K. Newcomb. MH fMS Am 1086 (10:137).

321. [3 October 1841] [Concord]
To Ellery Channing. MH fMS Am 1086 (9:82). Printed
in Wade, pp. 562–63, where it is incorrectly dated.

A Calendar of the Letters of Margaret Fuller 77

322. 5 October 1841   Concord
To Margarett C. Fuller. MH fMS Am 1086 (9:76);
copy MH fMS Am 1086 (Works, 2:551–55).

323. 10 October 1841   [——?]
To Caroline Sturgis. Fragment. MH bMS Am 1280
(111, pp. 59–60). Copy of unrecovered holograph.
Printed in *JMN*, 11:469.

324. 18 October 1841   [Newbury?]
To Henry D. Thoreau. TxU. Printed in Sanborn,
Henry D. Thoreau, pp. 169–72; *Correspondence of
Henry David Thoreau*, pp. 56–57.

325. [ca. 20? October 1841]   Newbury
To Elizabeth Hoar. Fragment. MH bMS Am 1280
(111, pp. 222–23). Copy of unrecovered holograph.
Printed in *Memoirs*, 1:315; *JMN*, 11:493–94.

326. 25 October 1841   Newbury
To Richard F. Fuller. MH fMS Am 1086 (9:72);
copy MH fMS Am 1086 (Works, 2:643–49). Partially
printed in Higginson, p. 111.

327. November 1841   [Boston?]
To R. W. Emerson. Fragment. MH bMS Am 1280
(111, pp. 139–40). Copy of unrecovered holograph.
Printed in *JMN*, 11:483–84.

328. 5 November 1841   Boston
To Richard F. Fuller. MH fMS Am 1086 (9:77).

329. [9?] November 1841   [Boston]
To R. W. Emerson. Fragment. MH bMS Am 1280
(111, p. 280). Copy of unrecovered holograph. Partially
printed in *Memoirs*, 1:207; printed in *JMN*, 11:503.

330. 9 November 1841   Boston
To R. W. Emerson. MH bMS Am 1280 (2359). Not
in Fuller's hand but dictated by her to Sarah Clarke.
Printed in Rusk, 2:461–62.

331. 17 November 1841   Boston
To Richard F. Fuller. MH fMS Am 1086 (9:78);
copy in MH fMS Am 1086 (Works, 2:655–61).

332. 25 November 1841   [Boston]
To Samuel G. Ward. MH bMS Am 1465 (919).

333. 1 December 1841   Boston
To Richard F. Fuller. MH fMS Am 1086 (9:85);
copy MH fMS Am 1086 (Works, 2:663–69).

334. [2 December 1841] [Boston?]
To Richard F. Fuller. MH fMS Am 1086 (9:85);
copy MH fMS Am 1086 (Works, 2:669-71).

335. [6 December 1841?] [Boston?]
To Samuel G. Ward. MH bMS Am 1465 (921).

336. 13 December [1841] Boston
To Margarett C. Fuller. MH fMS Am 1086 (9:106);
copy MH fMS Am 1086 (Works, 2:257-63).

337. [17? December 1841] Boston
To Margarett C. Fuller. MH fMS Am 1086 (9:105);
copy MH fMS Am 1086 (Works, 2:271-75).

338. 24 December [1841] [Boston]
To Margarett C. Fuller. Letter exists in two parts which
join as follows: MH fMS Am 1086 (9:79); MH bMS
Am 1610 (51). Copy MH fMS Am 1086 (Works,
2:285-93). Partially printed in Higginson, p. 165.

339. [30? December 1841] [Boston?]
To Richard F. Fuller. MH fMS Am 1086 (9:86);
copy MH fMS Am 1086 (Works, 2:649-55). Partially
printed in *Woman in the Nineteenth Century*, pp. 349-
50; Miller, pp. 76-77.

340. 1842 Canton
To Mary Rotch. Fragment. MH bMS Am 1280 (111,
pp. 26-27). Copy of unrecovered holograph. Printed
in *JMN*, 11:463-64.

341. 1 January 1842 [Boston]
To Margarett C. Fuller. MH fMS Am 1086 (9:80);
copy MH fMS Am 1086 (Works, 2:555-61).

342. 6 January [1842] [Boston]
To Richard F. Fuller. MH fMS Am 1086 (9:87);
copy MH fMS Am 1086 (Works, 2:671-75).

343. 8 January 1842 Boston
To Margarett C. Fuller. MH fMS Am 1086 (9:98);
copy MH fMS Am 1086 (Works, 2:561-69).

344. 15 January [1842] Boston
To Margarett C. Fuller. Incomplete. MH fMS Am 1086
(9:99); copy MH fMS Am 1086 (Works, 2:263-69).

345. [15? January? 1842?] [Boston?]
To Richard F. Fuller. MH fMS Am 1086 (9:77);
copy MH fMS Am 1086 (Works, 2:701-703). Partially
printed in Higginson, p. 106.

346. 22 January 1842 [Boston]
To Margarett C. Fuller. MH fMS Am 1086 (Works, 2:569–73). Copy of unrecovered holograph.

347. [ca. February? 1842] [Boston?]
To John S. Dwight. Collection of Gene De Gruson.

348. February 1842 [Boston?]
To [William H. Channing?]. Unrecovered. Incomplete. Printed in *Memoirs,* 2:62–63.

349. 5 February [1842] [Boston]
To Margarett C. Fuller. Incomplete. MH fMS Am 1086 (9:81); copy MH fMS Am 1086 (Works, 2:275–85).

350. [8?] March 1842 [Boston?]
To Elizabeth Hoar. Incomplete. MH bMS Am 1280 (111, pp. 165–66, 180–84). Copy of unrecovered holograph. Partially printed in *Memoirs,* 1:285–86, 309–10. Printed in *JMN,* 11:487, 488–89.

351. 8 March 1842 Boston
To R. W. Emerson. MH bMS Am 1280 (2362). Partially printed in Higginson, pp. 168–69; Rusk, 2:263; printed entire in Rusk, 3:28–29.

352. 15 March 1842 [Boston?]
To R. W. Emerson. MH Os 735Laa 1842.3.15. Copy in Emerson's hand of unrecovered holograph. Printed in *Memoirs,* 1:285.

353. [17? March 1842] [Boston?]
To R. W. Emerson. MH bMS Am 1280 (2361).

354. 20 March 1842 [Boston]
To Elizabeth Hoar. MHarF; copy MH bMS Am 1280 (111, pp. 146–48). Partially printed in *JMN,* 11:484.

355. April 1842 [Boston?]
To Caroline Sturgis. Fragment. MH bMS Am 1280 (111, pp. 15–16). Copy of unrecovered holograph. Printed in *JMN,* 11:461.

356. 7 April 1842 Boston
To Mary Rotch. Complete, but signature cut away. MH fMS Am 1086 (9:70); copies MH fMS Am 1086 (Works, 1:25–27); MH bMS Am 1280 (111, p. 128). Partially printed in *JMN,* 11:480.

357. 9 April 1842 Boston
To R. W. Emerson. MH bMS Am 1280 (2363). Printed in Rusk, 3:45–46; Wade, pp. 558–59.

358. 18 April 1842 Canton
To R. W. Emerson. MH bMS Am 1280 (2364); copy

MB Ms. Am. 1450 (77). Partially printed in Higginson, pp. 169–70.

359. 22 April 1842   Canton
To Richard F. Fuller. MH fMS Am 1086 (9:88); copy MH fMS Am 1086 (Works, 2:695–701).

360. 12 May 1842   Canton
To Richard F. Fuller. MH fMS Am 1086 (9:89); copy MH fMS Am 1086 (Works, 2:685–95). Partially printed in Higginson, p. 105.

361. 4 June [1842]   [Cambridge?]
To Sophia Peabody. NN (Berg).

362. 17 June 1842   Cambridge
To William H. Channing. Incomplete. MB Ms. Am. 1450 (50). Partially printed in *Memoirs*, 2:87; Higginson, pp. 309–10.

363. 19 June 1842   New Bedford
To Elizabeth Hoar. Unrecovered. Fragment. Printed in *The Journals and Miscellaneous Notebooks of Ralph Waldo Emerson*, ed. William H. Gilman et al. (Cambridge: Harvard University Press, 1960–), 8:184.

364. [ca. 23?] June 1842   [New Bedford]
To [William H. Channing?]. Unrecovered. Incomplete. Printed in *Memoirs*, 2:63–64.

365. 23 June 1842   New Bedford
To R. W. Emerson. MH bMS Am 1280 (2360). Printed in Rusk, 3:72–73.

366. 25 June [1842]   [New Bedford?]
To Richard F. Fuller. MH fMS Am 1086 (9:84); copy MH fMS Am 1086 (Works, 2:683–85).

367. July 1842   [——?]
To Caroline Sturgis. Fragment. MH bMS Am 1280 (111, p. 164). Copy of unrecovered holograph. Printed in *JMN*, 11:487.

368. 1 July 1842   Providence
To Charles K. Newcomb. MH fMS Am 1086 (10:136).

369. July 1842   Cambridge
To [William H. Channing?]. Unrecovered. Fragment. Printed in *Memoirs*, 2:64–65.

370. July 1842   Boston
To [William H. Channing?]. Unrecovered. Fragment. Printed in *Memoirs*, 2:65.

A Calendar of the Letters of Margaret Fuller 81

371. 25 July 1842   The White Mountains
To R. W. Emerson. Fragment. MH bMS Am 1280
(111, pp. 130–31). Copy of unrecovered holograph.
Printed in *Memoirs*, 1:264–65; *JMN*, 11:481.

372. 30 July 1842   Cambridge
To Charles K. Newcomb. MH fMS Am 1086 (10:139).

373. 31 July 1842   Cambridge
To James F. Clarke. Unrecovered. Fragment. Printed
in *Memoirs*, 1:74.

374. August 1842   Cambridge
To [William H. Channing?]. Unrecovered. Fragment.
Printed in *Memoirs*, 2:66.

375. [August?] 1842   Cambridge
To Elizabeth Hoar. Fragment. MH bMS Am 1280
(111, p. 95). Copy of unrecovered holograph. Partially
printed in *Memoirs*, 1:210; *JMN*, 11:475.

376. 5 August 1842   Cambridge
To Richard F. Fuller. MH fMS Am 1086 (9:90);
copy MH fMS Am 1086 (Works, 2:711–19). Partially
printed in *Woman in the Nineteenth Century*, pp. 365–
66; Miller, pp. 4–5.

377. 10 August 1842   Cambridge
To R. W. Emerson. MH bMS Am 1280 (2366). Partially
printed in Higginson, p. 182; Rusk, 3:79–80.

378. 11 August 1842   Cambridge
To Richard F. Fuller. MH fMS Am 1086 (9:83);
copy MH fMS Am 1086 (Works, 2:719–27). Partially
printed in Higginson, pp. 59–61; printed entire in Wade,
pp. 560–61; partially printed in Miller, pp. 34–35.

379. 16 August 1842   [Cambridge?]
To Caroline Sturgis. MH bMS Am 1221 (245).

380. 21 August 1842   Concord
To [Samuel G. Ward?]. MH fMS Am 1086 (9:91).

381. 25 August 1842   Concord
To [William H. Channing?]. Unrecovered. Incomplete.
Printed in *Memoirs*, 2:67–69.

382. September 1842   [——?]
To R. W. Emerson. MH Os 735Laa 1842.9. Copy of
unrecovered holograph.

383. September 1842   Brook Farm
To Charles K. Newcomb. MH fMS Am 1086 (10:140).

384. 9 September 1842   Concord
     To Caroline Sturgis. MHi.

385. October 1842   [Cambridge?]
     To [William H. Channing?]. Unrecovered. Incomplete.
     Printed in *Memoirs*, 2:69–71. May not be a letter.

386. 10 October [1842]   [Cambridge]
     To Charles K. Newcomb. MH fMS Am 1086 (10:141).

387. 16 October 1842   [Cambridge]
     To R. W. Emerson. MH bMS Am 1280 (2367).
     Printed in Rusk, 3:89–90; Wade, pp. 564–66.

388. November 1842   [Cambridge?]
     To [William H. Channing?]. Unrecovered. Fragment.
     Printed in *Memoirs*, 2:71.

389. November 1842   [Cambridge?]
     To Elizabeth Hoar. Fragment. MH bMS Am 1280
     (111, p. 108). Copy of unrecovered holograph.
     Partially printed in *Memoirs*, 1:350. Printed in
     JMN, 11:478.

390. November 1842   [Cambridge?]
     To Anna H. Clarke. MH bMS Am 1569.7 (472).

391. 8 November 1842   [Cambridge?]
     To R. W. Emerson. MH bMS Am 1280 (2368); copy
     MB Ms. Am. 1450 (78). Partially printed in Higgin-
     son, p. 171; printed entire in Rusk, 3:95–96.

392. [10?] December 1842   [Cambridge]
     To R. W. Emerson. Unrecovered. Fragment. Printed
     in *Memoirs*, 1:240–41.

393. 17 December 1842   Cambridge
     To George [T. Davis?]. MH fMS Am 1086 (9:91a).
     Copy of unrecovered holograph.

394. 17 December 1842   Cambridge
     To Frederic H. Hedge. MH fMS Am 1086 (10:104).

395. 26 [December?] 1842   Cambridge
     To [R. W. Emerson?]. Incomplete. Three fragments
     which join, I believe, as follows: *Memoirs*, 1:294–95;
     MH bMS Am 1280 (111, pp. 155–56); MH bMS Am
     1280 (2382). The first fragment is unrecovered; the sec-
     ond fragment is a copy of unrecovered holograph.
     Partially printed in *JMN*, 11:486.

396. [ca. 1843?]   [———?]
     To Charles K. Newcomb. MH fMS Am 1086 (10:134).

A Calendar of the Letters of Margaret Fuller 83

397. 1843 [——?]
To [James F. Clarke?]. Unrecovered. Incomplete.
Printed in *Memoirs*, 1:81–82.

398. 1843 [——?]
To [?]. Unrecovered. Fragment. Printed in *Memoirs*,
1:313–14.

399. 16 January [1843] [Cambridge]
To Elizabeth Hoar. Collection of Nelson C. White.
Complete but unsigned. Partial copy MH bMS Am 1280
(111, p. 150). Partially printed in *JMN*, 11:485.

400. 16 January 1843 Cambridge
To Nathaniel Hawthorne. NN (Berg).

401. 30 January 1843 Cambridge
To Elizabeth Hoar. MHarF.

402. 5 February 1843 Cambridge
To Mary Rotch. MH fMS Am 1086 (9:92); copy
MH fMS Am 1086 (Works, 1:27–29).

403. 7 February 1843 [——?]
To R. W. Emerson. Unrecovered. Fragment.
Printed in *Memoirs*, 1:284.

404. 16 February 1843 Cambridge
To Mary Rotch. MH fMS Am 1086 (9:93); copy
MH fMS Am 1086 (Works, 1:29–31).

405. 27 February 1843 Cambridge
To William H. Channing. Unrecovered. Incomplete.
Printed in Higginson, p. 110.

406. 16 April [1843?] [——?]
To Richard F. Fuller. MH fMS Am 1086 (Works,
2:623). Copy of unrecovered holograph. May be 1844.

407. 3 May 1843 Cambridge
To Henry W. Longfellow. MH bMS Am 1340.2 (4208).

408. 8 May 1843 Cambridge
To Sarah F. Clarke. MHi.

409. 9 May [1843] [Cambridge?]
To R. W. Emerson. MH bMS Am 1280 (2365).
Printed in Rusk, 3:170.

410. 22 May 1843 [Cambridge?]
To Charles K. Newcomb. MH fMS Am 1086 (10:142).

411. 30 May 1843 Niagara Falls
To [Elizabeth Hoar]. NRU.

412. 30 May 1843   Niagara Falls
     To Sarah Shaw. MH bMS Am 1417 (185).

413. 1 June 1843   Niagara Falls
     To R. W. Emerson. Unrecovered. Incomplete. Printed
     in *Memoirs,* 1:261–63.

414. 16 June 1843   Chicago
     To R. W. Emerson. MH bMS Am 1280 (2369); copy
     MB Ms. Am. 1450 (167). Partially printed in Higginson,
     pp. 196–97; Rusk, 3:177–78.

415. 29 July 1843   Milwaukee
     To Richard F. Fuller. MH fMS Am 1086 (9:96);
     copy MH fMS Am 1086 (Works, 2:675–83). Partially
     printed in *Woman in the Nineteenth Century,*
     pp. 366–67.

416. 3 August 1843   Milwaukee
     To Samuel G. Ward. MH bMS Am 1465 (922).

417. 4 August 1843   Chicago
     To R. W. Emerson. MH bMS Am 1280 (2370). Partially
     printed in Higginson, pp. 166, 193–94; Rusk, 3:194–95.

418. 7 August 1843   Chicago
     To Albert H. Tracy. MHarF.

419. 9 August 1843   Chicago
     To Mary Rotch. MH fMS Am 1086 (9:94); copies
     MH fMS Am 1086 (Works, 1:31–35); MH bMS Am
     1280 (111, pp. 133–35). Partially printed in *Woman in
     the Nineteenth Century,* pp. 367–69; *JMN,* 11:481–82.

420. 17 August 1843   Chicago
     To R. W. Emerson. MH bMS Am 1280 (2371).
     Printed in Rusk, 3:200–201; partially printed in Miller,
     pp. 112–13.

421. [18?] August 1843   [Chicago?]
     To William H. Channing. MB Ms. Am. 1450 (51).
     Partially printed in Higginson, p. 311.

422. 8 September [1843]   [Concord]
     To Richard F. Fuller. MH fMS Am 1086 (9:101);
     copy MH fMS Am 1086 (Works, 2:705–11).

423. 20 September 1843   Cambridge
     To Maria Rotch. MH fMS Am 1086 (9:97).

424. 25 September 1843   [Cambridge?]
     To Henry D. Thoreau. Unrecovered. Printed in *New
     England Quarterly,* 33 (September 1960): 372–73.
     Incomplete copy in Sanborn's hand MB Ms. Am. 1450

A Calendar of the Letters of Margaret Fuller 85

(181). Also printed in *Companion to Thoreau's Correspondence*, ed. Kenneth W. Cameron (Hartford, Conn.: Transcendental Books, 1964), pp. 182–83.

425. 26 September 1843   Cambridge
To Albert H. Tracy. MHarF.

426. 13 October 1843   West Roxbury
To Henry James, Sr. NN (Berg).

427. [ca. 16] October 1843   [Cambridge?]
To [Ralph Waldo Emerson]. Fragment. MH bMS Am 1280 (111, p. 108). Copy of unrecovered holograph. Printed in *JMN*, 11:478.

428. 23 October 1843   [Cambridge?]
To Marianne Clarke. MHarF.

429. 27 October 1843   Cambridge
To [William H. Channing?]. Incomplete. MB Ms. Am. 1450 (166). Partially printed in Higginson, pp. 285–86.

430. 6 November 1843   Cambridge
To Albert H. Tracy. Barnard College Library.

431. 12 November 1843   Cambridge
To R. W. Emerson. MH bMS Am 1280 (2372). Partially printed in Higginson, pp. 166–67; Rusk, 3:220–21; Miller, pp. 114–16.

432. 5 December 1843   Cambridge
To Mrs. Francis. MB Ch.B.4.57.

433. 12 December 1843   [Cambridge?]
To R. W. Emerson. Unrecovered. Fragment. Printed in *Memoirs*, 1:224.

434. 26 December 1843   Cambridge
To Anna B. Ward. MH bMS Am 1465 (926).

435. [1844]   [——?]
To Georgiana Bruce. Unrecovered. Fragment. Printed in Georgiana Bruce Kirby, *Years of Experience* (New York: Putnam's, 1887), pp. 207–208. This is a badly corrupted text. The first two paragraphs are from 15 August 1844; the remainder is unrecovered, though the accuracy of the text is highly doubtful.

436. Winter 1844   [——?]
To [?]. Unrecovered. Fragment. Printed in *Memoirs*, 2:119.

437. 10 January 1844   Cambridge
To Sarah Shaw. MH bMS Am 1417 (175).

438. 21 January 1844   Cambridge
     To Mary Rotch. MH fMS Am 1086 (9:115); copies
     MH fMS Am 1086 (Works, 1:37–41); MH bMS Am
     1280 (111, pp. 132–33). Partially printed in *Woman in
     the Nineteenth Century*, pp. 370–71; *JMN*, 11:481.

439. 22 January 1844   Cambridge
     To Maria Rotch. MH fMS Am 1086 (9:100).

440. 28 January 1844   Cambridge
     To R. W. Emerson. MH bMS Am 1280 (2373). Printed
     in Rusk, 3:235–38.

441. February 1844   [——?]
     To [William H. Channing]. Incomplete. MH bMS Am
     1280.226 (3908).

442. 2 February 1844   Boston
     To R. W. Emerson. MH bMS Am 1280 (2374).
     Printed in Rusk, 3:240.

443. 2 February 1844   Boston
     To Richard F. Fuller. MH fMS Am 1086 (9:102);
     copy MH fMS Am 1086 (Works, 2:729–31).

444. 13 March 1844   Boston
     To Lydia M. Child. MHarF.

445. 16 March 1844   Cambridge
     To Mrs. Stimson. RPA.

446. 21 March [1844]   [Cambridge?]
     To James [F. Clarke]. ViU.

447. [ca. April? 1844?]   [Cambridge?]
     To Elizabeth Hoar. Fragment. MH bMS Am 1280
     (111, p. 109). Copy of unrecovered holograph. Part
     of this letter is erroneously printed in *Memoirs*, 1:351,
     where it is given as the second sentence of a letter
     to William H. Channing. Printed in *JMN*, 11:478.

448. 2 April 1844   Cambridge
     To Frances Fuller. MH fMS Am 1086 (9:118); copy
     MH fMS Am 1086 (Works, 1:193–97).

449. 14 April [1844]   [Cambridge]
     To Anna B. Ward. MH bMS Am 1465 (924).

450. 22 April 1844   Cambridge
     To Arthur B. Fuller. MH fMS Am 1086 (9:64); copy
     MH fMS Am 1086 (Works, 1:645–55).

451. 28 April 1844   Cambridge
     To William H. Channing. Fragment. MH bMS Am

1280 (111, pp. 106–107). Copy of unrecovered holograph. Printed in *Memoirs*, 1:351; *JMN*, 11:478.

452. 3 May [1844?]   [Cambridge?]
To Caroline Sturgis. MH bMS Am 1569 (1350).

453. 7 May [1844]   [Cambridge?]
To Anna Loring. MCR-S.

454. [9 May 1844]   Cambridge
To R. W. Emerson. NNC.

455. 25 May [1844?]   [——?]
To Caroline Sturgis. MH bMS Am 1221 (246).

456. 30 May 1844   [Boston?]
To Mr. Little. NBLiHi.

457. 3 June [1844?]   [Boston?]
To Caroline Sturgis. MH bMS Am 1221 (200).

458. 3 June [1844]   [Boston?]
To Little and Brown, Co. ViU.

459. 9 June [1844?]   [——?]
To Charles K. Newcomb. MH fMS Am 1086 (10:143).

460. 15 June 184[4]   Cambridge
To Barbara [Channing?]. MBAt.

461. Midsummer 1844   [——?]
To [?]. Unrecovered. Fragment. Printed in *Memoirs*, 2:120.

462. 3 July 1844   Cambridge
To Arthur B. Fuller. MH fMS Am 1086 (9:122); copy MH fMS Am 1086 (Works, 1:655–63).

463. 8 July [1844?]   Cambridge
To Charles K. Newcomb. MH fMS Am 1086 (10:144).

464. [9? July 1844]   [Concord]
To Charles Lane. MHi. Copy by Fuller written in her journal of 1844.

465. 11 July [1844]   [Concord]
To Richard F. Fuller. MH fMS Am 1086 (9:95); copy MH fMS Am 1086 (Works, 2:703–705).

466. 13 July [1844]   Concord
To R. W. Emerson. MH fMS Am 1086 (9:109).

467. [16 July 1844]   [Concord]
To Georgiana Bruce. Unrecovered. Printed in *Years of Experience*, p. 210.

468. [ca. 20? July 1844?] [Concord]
To R. W. Emerson. MH bMS Am 1280 (2375). Partially printed and misdated in Higginson, pp. 70–71; partially printed in Rusk, 3:252–54; Miller, pp. 133–34.

469. 22 July 1844 Concord
To [Jane F. Tuckerman]. MH fMS Am 1086 (Works, 1:103–107). Copy of unrecovered holograph.

470. [26 July 1844] [Concord]
To Charles Lane. MHi. Copy by Fuller written in her journal of 1844.

471. 4 August [1844?] [Cambridge?]
To Caroline Sturgis. MH bMS Am 1221 (227).

472. [15? August 1844] [Cambridge?]
To Sarah Shaw. VtMiM.

473. 15 August 1844 Cambridge
To Georgiana Bruce. ViU. Partially printed in *Years of Experience*, p. 207.

474. [September 1844?] [Cambridge?]
To William H. Channing. MB Ms. Am. 1450 (53). Partially printed in Higginson, pp. 97–98, 101.

475. 1 September 1844 [Cambridge?]
To Sarah Shaw. MH bMS Am 1417 (176).

476. 20 September 1844 Cambridge
To Richard F. Fuller. MH fMS Am 1086 (9:107); copy MH fMS Am 1086 (Works, 2:731–35).

477. 25 September 1844 Cambridge
To Maria Rotch. MH fMS Am 1086 (9:103).

478. 27 September 1844 Cambridge
To Sarah H. Swan. MC.

479. Autumn 1844 Fishkill Landing
To [?]. Unrecovered. Fragment. Printed in *Memoirs*, 2:132–33.

480. Autumn 1844 Fishkill Landing
To [?]. Unrecovered. Fragment. Printed in *Memoirs*, 2:133.

481. [Autumn 1844] Fishkill Landing
To Christopher P. Cranch. MB Ms. Am. 1450 (59). Copy of unrecovered holograph.

482. 14 October 1844 [Fishkill Landing]
To R. W. Emerson. MH Os 735Laa 1844.10.14. Copy in Emerson's hand of unrecovered holograph. Printed in Rusk, 3:240–41.

A Calendar of the Letters of Margaret Fuller 89

483. 15 October 1844   Fishkill Landing
To Richard F. Fuller. Incomplete. Letter exists in two parts which join as follows: MH fMS Am 1086 (9:124); (9:107a); copy MH fMS Am 1086 (Works, 2:737–39); (Works, 2:779–83). Partially printed in *Memoirs*, 2:132.

484. 20 October 1844   Fishkill Landing
To Elizabeth Hoar. Incomplete. MH bMS Am 1280 (111, pp. 116–18). Copy of unrecovered holograph. Partially printed in *Memoirs*, 2:144–45, where it is mixed with 23 November 1844 to Richard F. Fuller. Printed in *JMN*, 11:479.

485. 20 October 1844   Fishkill Landing
To Georgiana [Bruce]. CSt. Partially printed in *Years of Experience*, p. 211.

486. [Late October? 1844]   Fishkill Landing
To the women inmates at Sing Sing. Unrecovered. Printed in *Years of Experience*, pp. 212–13.

487. 3 November 1844   [Fishkill Landing]
To William H. Channing. Incomplete. MB Ms. Am. 1450 (54).

488. 17 November 1844   [Fishkill Landing]
To [William H. Channing]. Incomplete. MB Ms. Am. 1450 (55). Partially printed in Higginson, pp. 201–202; printed entire in Wade, pp. 567–68.

489. 17 November 1844   Fishkill Landing
To R. W. Emerson. MH bMS Am 1280 (2376). Partially printed in Higginson, p. 201; printed entire in Rusk, 3:269–70.

490. 20 November 1844   Fishkill Landing
To Sarah Shaw. MH bMS Am 1417 (177). Printed in Wade, pp. 559–60.

491. 23 November 1844   Fishkill Landing
To Richard F. Fuller. MH fMS Am 1086 (9:108); copy MH fMS Am 1086 (Works, 2:739–49). Partially printed in *Woman in the Nineteenth Century*, p. 373; *Memoirs*, 2:144–45. The *Memoirs* version badly mixes the letter with 10 December 1845 to Richard F. Fuller.

492. 25 November 1844   Fishkill Landing
To Charles K. Newcomb. MH fMS Am 1086 (10:143). Partially printed in *Memoirs*, 1:264.

493. December 1844   New York
To [?]. Unrecovered. Fragment. Printed in *Memoirs*, 2:150–51.

494. [December? 1844]　　　　　　　　　　　　　　　　[New York]
To Georgiana Bruce. Unrecovered. Incomplete.
Printed in *Years of Experience,* pp. 205–206.

495. 3 December 1844　　　　　　　　　　　　　　　　New York
To R. W. Emerson. MH bMS Am 1610 (50).

496. 12 December 1844　　　　　　　　　　　　　　　　New York
To James F. Clarke. MH bMs Am 1569.7 (465).

497. 26 December 1844　　　　　　　　　　　　　　　　New York
To Elizabeth [Peabody]. MH fMS Am 1086 (Works,
3:261–69). Copy of unrecovered holograph. Another
copy MB Ms. Am. 1450 (81). Printed in Wade,
pp. 571–72.

498. 26 December 1844　　　　　　　　　　　　　　　　[New York]
To Anna Loring. MWelC.

499. 29 December 1844　　　　　　　　　　　　　　　　New York
To Samuel G. Ward. MH bMS Am 1465 (923).

500. 31 December [1844]　　　　　　　　　　　　　　　[New York]
To William [H. Channing]. MB Ms. Am. 1450 (57).
Partially printed in Higginson, p. 207.

501. [1845?]　　　　　　　　　　　　　　　　　　　　　[New York]
To [?]. Unrecovered. Fragment. Printed in *Memoirs,*
2:164.

502. [1845?]　　　　　　　　　　　　　　　　　　　　　[New York]
To [?]. Fragment. MH bMS Am 1280 (111, pp. 154–55).
Copy of unrecovered holograph. Printed in *Memoirs,*
1:309; *JMN,* 11:485. Conjectural date based on a reference
to Ellery Channing's homesickness. The letter thus could
fall between December 1844 and March 1845.

503. [1845?]　　　　　　　　　　　　　　　　　　　　　[New York?]
To Richard F. Fuller. MH fMS Am 1086 (9:248);
copy MH fMS Am 1086 (Works, 2:727–29).

504. [ca. January? 1845]　　　　　　　　　　　　　　　[New York]
To Anna Loring. MWelC.

505. 9 January 1845　　　　　　　　　　　　　　　　　New York
To Richard F. Fuller. MH fMS Am 1086 (9:110);
copy MH fMS Am 1086 (Works, 2:749–57). Partially
printed in Higginson, p. 209.

506. 12 January 1845　　　　　　　　　　　　　　　　　New York
To Margarett C. Fuller. MH fMS Am 1086 (9:112).

507. 15 January 1845　　　　　　　　　　　　　　　　　New York
To Mary Rotch. MH fMS Am 1086 (9:114); copy
MH fMS Am 1086 (Works, 1:41–47). Partially printed

in *Woman in the Nineteenth Century*, pp. 371–72; *Memoirs*, 2:151–52, 163–64; Higginson, pp. 212–13.

508. [ca. 1 February 1845] [New York]
To William [H. Channing]. Incomplete. MB Ms. Am. 1450 (52). Partially printed in Higginson, pp. 198–99.

509. [ca. 7? February 1845] [New York]
To James Nathan. MB Ms. Am. 1451 (1). Printed in *Love-Letters*, pp. 9–10.

510. [ca. 14? February 1845] New York
To James Nathan. MB Ms. Am. 1451 (2). Printed in *Love-Letters*, pp. 10–11.

511. 22 February [1845] [New York]
To James Nathan. MB Ms. Am. 1451 (3). Printed in *Love-Letters*, pp. 12–13.

512. 25 February 1845 New York
To Sarah Shaw. MH bMS Am 1417 (178). Printed in Wade, p. 573.

513. 27 February 1845[?] [New York]
To Georgiana Bruce. Fragment. ViU.

514. [ca. 28? February? 1845] [New York]
To James Nathan. MB Ms. Am. 1451 (4). Printed in *Love-Letters*, pp. 13–15.

515. [ca. 1? March? 1845] [New York]
To James Nathan. MB Ms. Am. 1451 (6). Printed in *Love-Letters*, pp. 15, 17.

516. 2 March 1845 Brooklyn
To Richard F. Fuller. MH fMS Am 1086 (9:111); copy MH fMS Am 1086 (Works, 2:757–63).

517. [6 March 1845] [New York]
To Richard F. Fuller. Fragment. MH fMS Am 1086 (9:111).

518. 9 March 1845 New York
To Eugene Fuller. MH fMS Am 1086 (9:116); copy MH fMS Am 1086 (Works, 2:763–71). Partially printed in Higginson, pp. 202–203, 208–209; printed entire in Wade, pp. 574–75.

519. 12 March 1845 New York
To David Thom. ViU.

520. 13 March 1845 New York
To Caroline Sturgis. MH bMS Am 1221 (247).

521. 14 March [1845] [New York]
To James Nathan. MB Ms. Am. 1451 (5). Printed
in *Love-Letters,* pp. 15–17.

522. [ca. mid-March? 1845?] [New York]
To Richard F. Fuller. MH fMS Am 1086 (9:124);
copy MH fMS Am 1086 (Works, 2:777–79).

523. 19 March [1845] [New York]
To James Nathan. MB Ms. Am. 1451 (8). Printed
in *Love-Letters,* pp. 17–18.

524. [ca. 23? March? 1845] [New York]
To James Nathan. MB Ms. Am. 1451 (9). Printed
in *Love-Letters,* pp. 18–21; partially printed in Miller,
pp. 203–204.

525. 31 March [1845] [New York]
To James Nathan. MB Ms. Am. 1451 (17). Printed
in *Love-Letters,* pp. 31–33.

526. [2? April? 1845] [New York]
To Richard F. Fuller. MH fMS Am 1086 (9:247).

527. 2 April 1845 New York
To Anna Loring. MWelC.

528. 2 April [1845] [New York]
To James Nathan. MB Ms. Am. 1451 (18). Printed
in *Love-Letters,* pp. 33–35.

529. 6 April 1845 [New York]
To James Nathan. MB Ms. Am. 1451 (19–22). Printed
in *Love-Letters,* pp. 35–39.

530. 8 April 1845 [New York]
To James Nathan. MB Ms. Am. 1451 (23–24). Printed
in *Love-Letters,* pp. 39–41.

531. 9 April [1845] [New York]
To James Nathan. MB Ms. Am. 1451 (25). Printed
in *Love-Letters,* pp. 41–43.

532. 14 April [1845] [New York]
To James Nathan. MB Ms. Am. 1451 (27–29). Printed
in *Love-Letters,* pp. 43–50.

533. [15? April? 1845] [New York]
To James Nathan. MB Ms. Am. 1451 (10–11). Printed
in *Love-Letters,* pp. 22–25.

534. 17 April 1845 [New York]
To Caroline Sturgis. MH bMS Am 1221 (248).

A Calendar of the Letters of Margaret Fuller   93

535. 19 April 1845 [New York]
      To James Nathan. MB Ms. Am. 1451 (30–32). Printed
      in *Love-Letters,* pp. 50–55.

536. 22 April [1845] [New York]
      To James Nathan. MB Ms. Am. 1451 (33–34). Printed
      in *Love-Letters,* pp. 55–59.

537. [ca. 24? April? 1845] [New York]
      To James Nathan. MB Ms. Am. 1451 (14). Printed
      in *Love-Letters,* pp. 25–31.

538. 27 April [1845] [New York]
      To James Nathan. MB Ms. Am. 1451 (35–37). Printed
      in *Love-Letters,* pp. 59–64.

539. 1 May [1845] [New York]
      To James Nathan. MB Ms. Am. 1451 (37). Printed
      in *Love-Letters,* pp. 64–65.

540. [2? May 1845] [New York]
      To James Nathan. MB Ms. Am. 1451 (38). Printed
      in *Love-Letters,* pp. 65-67.

541. [May? 1845] [New York]
      To James Nathan. MB Ms. Am. 1451 (39). Printed
      in *Love-Letters,* pp. 67–69. The contents will not date
      this letter precisely. It may fall later in May.

542. 7 [May 1845] [New York]
      To James Nathan. MB Ms. Am. 1451 (40). Printed
      in *Love-Letters,* pp. 69–73.

543. 9 May [1845] [New York]
      To James Nathan. MB Ms. Am. 1451 (43–44). Printed
      in *Love-Letters,* pp. 76–80.

544. [15? May 1845] [New York]
      To James Nathan. MB Ms. Am. 1451 (42). Printed
      in *Love-Letters,* pp. 73–75.

545. [16? May 1845] [New York]
      To James Nathan. MB Ms. Am. 1451 (45). Printed
      in *Love-Letters,* pp. 80–81.

546. 19 May [1845] [New York]
      To James Nathan. MB Ms. Am. 1451 (46). Printed
      in *Love-Letters,* pp. 81–83.

547. 22 May 1845 New York
      To R. W. Emerson. MH bMS Am 1280 (2377).
      Partially printed in Higginson, p. 199.

548. 22 May [1845] New York
      To Sophia and Nathaniel Hawthorne. NN (Berg).

549. 23 May [1845]   [New York]
     To James Nathan. MB Ms. Am. 1451 (48). Printed
     in *Love-Letters*, pp. 85–90.

550. 26 May [1845]   [New York]
     To James Nathan. MB Ms. Am. 1451 (50). Printed
     in *Love-Letters*, pp. 91–93.

551. [27? May 1845]   New York
     To James Nathan. MB Ms. Am. 1451 (47). Printed
     in *Love-Letters*, pp. 83–85.

552. [28? May? 1845]   [New York]
     To James Nathan. MB Ms. Am. 1451 (26). Printed
     in *Love-Letters*, p. 43.

553. 30 May 1845   [New York]
     To James Nathan. MB Ms. Am. 1451 (51–52). Printed
     in *Love-Letters*, pp. 93–97.

554. [31? May 1845]   [New York]
     To James Nathan. MB Ms. Am. 1451 (53). Printed
     in *Love-Letters*, pp. 97–98.

555. 5 June 1845   [New York]
     To James Nathan. MB Ms. Am. 1451 (54). Printed
     in *Love-Letters*, pp. 98–104.

556. 12 June [1845]   [New York]
     To Elizabeth Hoar. MHarF.

557. 12 June 1845   New York
     To James Nathan. MB Ms. Am. 1451 (55). Printed
     in *Love-Letters*, pp. 104–10.

558. 24 June 1845   New York
     To James Nathan. MB Ms. Am. 1451 (56–57). Printed
     in *Love-Letters*, pp. 110–21. This letter exists in two
     parts, the second of which is labeled "no. 2."

559. 29 June 1845   New York
     To Richard F. Fuller. MH fMS Am 1086 (9:117);
     copy MH fMS Am 1086 (Works, 2:771–77).

560. 1 July 1845   New York
     To Sarah Shaw. MH bMS Am 1417 (179).

561. 2 July 1845   [New York]
     To [?]. Fragment. MB Ms. Am. 1450 (18). Copy
     in Higginson's hand of unrecovered holograph.

562. 6 July 1845   New York
     To Elizabeth Hoar. MHarF.

563. 8 July 1845   New York
     To Richard F. Fuller. MH fMS Am 1086 (9:120).

564. 10 July 1845   New York
     To Caroline Sturgis. MH bMS Am 1221 (249).

565. 22 July 1845   New York
     To James Nathan. MB Ms. Am. 1451 (58–59). Printed
     in *Love-Letters,* pp. 121–35.

566. 26 July [1845]   [New York]
     To James Nathan. MB Ms. Am. 1451 (60). Printed
     in *Love-Letters,* pp. 135–40.

567. [27? July 1845]   [New York]
     To Georgiana Bruce. Unrecovered. Incomplete. Printed
     in *Years of Experience,* pp. 228–30.

568. 6 August 1845   New York
     To Richard F. Fuller. MH fMS Am 1086 (9:121);
     copy MH fMS Am 1086 (Works, 2:783–89).

569. 12 August 1845   New York
     To James Nathan. MB Ms. Am. 1451 (61–62). Printed
     in *Love-Letters,* pp. 140–49.

570. 22 August 1845   New York
     To Ellis G. and Louisa Loring. MWelC.

571. 31 August 1845   New York
     To James Nathan. MB Ms. Am. 1451 (63–64). Printed
     in *Love-Letters,* pp. 149–51; partially printed in Miller,
     p. 219.

572. [31 August 1845]   [New York]
     To Richard F. Fuller. Fragment. MH fMS Am 1086
     (9:253).

573. 13 September 1845   [New York]
     To James Nathan. MB Ms. Am. 1451 (65). Printed
     in *Love-Letters,* pp. 158–63.

574. 24 [September 1845]   [New York]
     To [Pliny] Earle. MCR-S.

575. 29 September 1845   New York
     To James Nathan. MB Ms. Am. 1451 (66). Printed
     in *Love-Letters,* pp. 164–68.

576. 8 October 1845   Cambridge
     To Sarah Shaw. MH Ac 85. St 317. 885p.

577. 17 October [1845]   Boston
     To Sarah [Shaw?]. MHi.

578. 26 October 1845   [Boston]
     To Sarah Shaw. MH bMS Am 1417 (180).

579. 16 November 1845   New York
     To Anna B. Ward. MH bMS Am 1465 (925).

580. 3 December 1845   New York
     To Richard F. Fuller. MH fMS Am 1086 (9:125);
     copy MH fMS Am 1086 (Works, 2:789–91).

581. 3 December 1845   New York
     To Anna [Loring]. MCR-S.

582. 10 December 1845   New York
     To Richard F. Fuller. MH fMS Am 1086 (9:126);
     copy MH fMS Am 1086 (Works, 2:793–97).

583. [15 December 1845]   [New York]
     To William H. Channing. Incomplete. MB Ms. Am.
     1450 (56). Partially printed in *Memoirs*, 2:121;
     Higginson, pp. 17–18.

584. [25 December? 1845]   [New York]
     To Mary Rotch. MH fMS Am 1086 (9:53).

585. 27 December 1845   [New York]
     To Richard F. Fuller. MH fMS Am 1086 (9:128).

586. 31 December 1845   New York
     To James Nathan. MB Ms. Am. 1451 (67–68). Printed
     in *Love-Letters*, pp. 168–75.

587. [1846?]   [New York?]
     To Georgiana Bruce. Unrecovered. Fragment. Printed
     in *Years of Experience*, p. 230.

588. [January? 1846]   [New York]
     To Richard F. Fuller. Incomplete. MH fMS Am 1086
     (9:127); copy MH fMS Am 1086 (Works, 1:119–23).

589. 9 January 1846   New York
     To Mary Rotch. MH fMS Am 1086 (9:123); copy
     MH fMS Am 1086 (Works, 1:47–51).

590. [ca. January? 1846]   [New York]
     To [Richard F. Fuller]. Incomplete. MH fMS Am 1086
     (9:249); copy MH fMS Am 1086 (Works, 1:113–19).

591. [ca. February? 1846]   [New York]
     To Evert A. Duyckinck. NN.

592. 9 [February? 1846]   [New York]
     To Caroline Sturgis. MH bMS Am 1221 (251).

593. 27 February [1846]   New York
     To Evert A. Duyckinck. NN.

A Calendar of the Letters of Margaret Fuller 97

594. [ca. 28 February 1846]   [New York]
To [Richard F. Fuller]. Incomplete. MH fMS Am 1086 (9:135).

595. [28? February 1846]   New York
To James Nathan. MB Ms. Am. 1451 (69–70). Printed in *Love-Letters,* pp. 175–79.

596. 3 March 1846   New York
To Samuel G. and Anna B. Ward. MH bMS Am 1465 (927).

597. 9 March 1846   New York
To Mary Rotch. MH fMS Am 1086 (9:130); copy MH fMS Am 1086 (Works, 1:51–55).

598. 18 March [1846]   [New York]
To Evert A. Duyckinck. NN.

599. 20 [March 1846]   [New York]
To Horace Greeley. NN (Berg).

600. 17 April 1846   [New York]
To Sarah Shaw. MH bMS Am 1417 (181).

601. 25 April 1846   [New York]
To James Nathan. Unrecovered. Printed in *Love-Letters,* pp. 180–84.

602. [25? April? 1846]   [New York]
To Mrs. Richard H. Manning. PHi.

603. 17 May 1846   New York
To Richard F. Fuller. MH fMS Am 1086 (9:127); copy MH fMS Am 1086 (Works, 1:129–31).

604. [ca. July 1846]   [New York]
To Evert A. Duyckinck. NN.

605. 4 July 1846   [New York]
To Richard F. Fuller. MH fMS Am 1086 (9:132); copy MH fMS Am 1086 (Works, 1:131–35).

606. 7 July 1846   [New York]
To Wiley and Putnam, Co. OMC.

607. 14 July 1846   New York
To Richard F. Fuller. MH fMS Am 1086 (9:133); copy MH fMS Am 1086 (Works, 1:135–39).

608. 14 July 1846   New York
To James Nathan. MB Ms. Am. 1451 (71–73). Printed in *Love-Letters,* pp. 184–86.

609. 14 July [1846]   [New York]
To Evert A. Duyckinck. NN.

610. 15 July 1846   New York
      To R. W. Emerson. MH bMS Am 1280 (2378). Partially
      printed in Higginson, p. 220; Rusk, 3:339.

611. [16? July? 1846]   New York
      To Evert A. Duyckinck. NN.

612. 20 July [1846]   New York
      To Evert A. Duyckinck. NN.

613. 20 July 1846   New York
      To Caroline Sturgis. MH bMS Am 1221 (250).

614. [21? July 1846]   [New York]
      To Evert A. Duyckinck. NN.

615. 25 July 1846   New York
      To Samuel G. Ward. MH bMS Am 1465 (928).

616. [28 July 1846]   [New York]
      To Evert A. Duyckinck. NN.

617. 28 July [1846]   [New York]
      To Richard F. Fuller. MH fMS Am 1086 (9:134);
      copy MH fMS Am 1086 (Works, 1:139).

618. 16 August 1846   Liverpool
      To Margarett C. Fuller. Unrecovered. Incomplete. Printed
      in *Memoirs*, 2:171–72; Dorothy Van Doren, ed., *The
      Lost Art: Letters of Seven Famous Women* (New York:
      Coward-McCann, 1929), pp. 285–86.

619. 17 August 1846   Adelphi
      To Alexander Ireland. CU-B.

620. 1 September 1846   Edinburgh
      To Thomas Delf. MSaE.

621. 27 September 1846   Birmingham
      To Richard F. Fuller. MH bMS Am 1086 (9:136);
      copy MH fMS Am 1086 (Works, 1:141–45).

622. Autumn 1846   London
      To Caroline Sturgis. Unrecovered. Incomplete. Printed
      in *Memoirs*, 2:172–73; partially printed in *The Lost Art*,
      pp. 286–89.

623. 2 October [1846]   London
      To Richard F. Fuller. MH fMS Am 1086 (9:250);
      copy MH fMS Am 1086 (Works, 1:145–47).

624. [2? October 1846]   [London]
      To Thomas Delf. MSaE.

625. 5 October 1846 London
To Alexander Ireland. NjP; copy NNC where it is
misdated as 6 October.

626. 8 October [1846] London
To Mary Howitt. PSt.

627. 29 October [1846] London
To Mr. Putnam. Ia-HA.

628. 30 October 1846 London
To Evert A. Duyckinck. NN. Printed in *Bulletin of the
New York Public Library*, 5 (January-December 1901):
455–56.

629. 30 October 1846 London
To R. W. Emerson. MH bMS Am 1280 (2379). Printed
in Rusk, 3:381.

630. 3 November 1846 London
To Richard F. Fuller. MH fMS Am 1086 (9:137);
copy MH fMS Am 1086 (Works, 1:147–49).

631. 10 November 1846 [Paris]
To John S. Dwight. MHi.

632. [ca. 10 November 1846] [Paris]
To Richard F. Fuller. MH fMS Am 1086 (9:251);
copy MH fMS Am 1086 (Works, 1:149–53).

633. 16 November 1846 Paris
To R. W. Emerson. Incomplete. MH fMS Am 1086
(9:216–17). Copy of unrecovered holograph. Another
copy MH fMS Am 1086 (Works, 1:209). Partially
printed in *Memoirs*, 2:184–87; Higginson, p. 172.

634. 24 December 1846 [Paris]
To [William H. Channing?]. Fragment. MB Ms. Am.
1450 (101). Copy of unrecovered holograph.

635. 26 December 1846 Paris
To Margarett C. Fuller. Unrecovered. Incomplete.
Printed in *Memoirs*, 2:191–93. Partial, slightly different
copy MH bMS Am 1280 (111, pp. 90–91), which is
printed in *JMN*, 11:474–75.

636. [1847?] [Paris]
To R. W. Emerson. Fragment. MH bMS Am 1280
(111, pp. 91–[92]). Copy of unrecovered holograph.
Printed in *JMN*, 11:475.

637. 1847 Paris
To Félicité Robert de Lamennais. Unrecovered.
Printed in *Memoirs*, 2:202–203.

638. 18 January 1847   Paris
To Elizabeth Hoar. Unrecovered. Incomplete. Printed in *Memoirs*, 2:193–99; partially printed in Miller, pp. 261–65.

639. 18 January 1847   Paris
To R. W. Emerson. Unrecovered. Incomplete. Printed in *Memoirs*, 2:201–202.

640. 31 January 1847   Paris
To Richard F. Fuller. MH fMS Am 1086 (9:252); copy MH fMS Am 1086 (Works, 2:803–809).

641. February 1847   [Paris]
To [James F. Clarke]. MH bMS Am 1569.7 (473). Written in French.

642. 3 February 1847   Paris
To Benjamin P. Poore. PHC.

643. 15 March 1847   Naples
To R. W. Emerson. Unrecovered. Fragment. Printed in *Memoirs*, 2:207–208.

644. 18 March 1847   Rome
To Sarah Shaw. MH bMS Am 1417 (182).

645. 15 April 1847   Rome
To Richard F. Fuller. MH fMS Am 1086 (9:251); copy MH fMS Am 1086 (Works, 2:799–803).

646. 16 April 1847   [Rome?]
To [?]. Fragment. MB Ms. Am. 1450 (18). Copy in Higginson's hand of unrecovered holograph.

647. 18 April 1847   Rome
To Mary Howitt. MeHi.

648. 23 April 1847   Rome
To [G. A. Ossoli?]. MH fMs Am 1086 (9:130); copy MH fMS Am 1086 (Works, 1:211–13). This letter is something of a puzzle. While it apparently is written to Ossoli ("Dear Youth"), it is in English which Ossoli could not read. Most probably it was a copy in English of another holograph in Italian.

649. 7 May 1847   Rome
To William H. Channing. Unrecovered. Fragment. Printed in *Memoirs*, 2:209.

650. 23 May 1847   Rome
To Evert A. Duyckinck. NN.

A Calendar of the Letters of Margaret Fuller 101

651. 23 May 1847 Rome
To Mary Rotch. MH fMS Am 1086 (9:131); copies MH fMS Am 1086 (Works, 1:57–59); bMS Am 1280 (111, p. 90). Partially printed in *JMN*, 11:474.

652. 23 May 1847 Rome
To Maria Rotch. MH fMS Am 1086 (9:112); copy MH bMS Am 1280 (111, p. 90). Printed in *JMN*, 11:474.

653. 20 June 1847 Florence
To R. W. Emerson. Incomplete. Letter exists in two parts which join as follows: *Memoirs*, 2:210; MH bMS Am 1280 (111, p. 124). The first part is unrecovered; the second is a copy of unrecovered holograph. The parts may be from two different letters, but, given Fuller's habits in Italy, the possibility is slight. Partially printed in *The Lost Art*, pp. 289–90; *JMN*, 11:480.

654. 1 July 1847 Florence
To Richard F. Fuller. MH fMS Am 1086 (9:138); copy MH fMS Am 1086 (Works, 2:809–17). Partially printed in *Memoirs*, 2:210–11.

655. 2 July 1847 [Florence?]
To George [Curtis?]. University Library of Amsterdam, Holland.

656. 10 July 1847 Venice
To Marcus and Rebecca Spring. MH fMS Am 1086 (9:218). Copy of unrecovered holograph. Another copy MH fMS Am 1086 (Works, 1:213–15).

657. [Late July 1847] Riva di Trento
To Richard F. Fuller. MH fMS Am 1086 (9:129).

658. 1 August 1847 Lago di Garda
To Margarett C. Fuller. Unrecovered. Incomplete. Printed in *Memoirs*, 2:212. Two sentences in MH bMS Am 1280 (111, p. 33) and printed in *JMN*, 11:465.

659. 9 August 1847 Milan
To Marcus Spring. Incomplete. MH fMS Am 1086 (9:218). Copy of unrecovered holograph. Another copy MH fMS Am 1086 (Works, 1:217–21). Partially printed in *Memoirs*, 2:212–13.

660. 10 August 1847 Milan
To R. W. Emerson. Unrecovered. Fragment. Printed in *Memoirs*, 2:213–14.

661. [ca. 22] August 1847 Bellagio
To [?]. Unrecovered. Incomplete. Printed in *At Home and Abroad*, pp. 425–26.

662. [ca. 22] August 1847   Bellagio
To Jane F. Tuckerman. Fragment. MH fMS Am 1086 (Works, 1:109). Copy of unrecovered holograph which includes, with no indication, the first paragraph of no. 695.

663. 22 August 1847   Bellagio
To Caroline Sturgis. MH bMS Am 1221 (252). Partially printed in *Memoirs*, 2:216–18.

664. 6 September 1847   Milan
To J. Westland Marston. NHi.

665. Mid-September 1847   Florence
To Elizabeth Hoar. MH fMS Am 1086 (Works, 2:823–29). Copy of unrecovered holograph. Another copy MH bMS Am 1280 (111, pp. 43–45). Partially printed in *Memoirs*, 2:219–20; *JMN*, 11:466–67.

666. 25 September 1847   Florence
To [Richard F. Fuller]. MH fMS Am 1086 (9:139); copy MH fMS Am 1086 (Works, 2:829–39). Partially printed in *Memoirs*, 2:218–19.

667. October 1847   Rome
To Marcus Spring. Unrecovered. Incomplete. Printed in *Memoirs*, 2:221–22. One sentence copied in MH bMS Am 1280 (111, p. 33) and printed in *JMN*, 11:465.

668. [16? October? 1847]   [Rome]
To Richard F. Fuller. MH fMS Am 1086 (Works, 2:797). Copy of unrecovered holograph. The copy book wrongly dates this letters as 1 December 1846. The contents clearly show Fuller in Rome for the second time and refer to the letter of 16 October to Margarett C. Fuller.

669. 16 October 1847   Rome
To Margarett C. Fuller. MH fMS Am 1086 (9:140); copy MH fMS Am 1086 (Works, 1:223–31).

670. 22 October 1847   Rome
To Mary Rotch. MH fMS Am 1086 (9:141); copy MH fMS Am 1086 (Works, 1:61–63).

671. [ca. 25 October 1847]   Rome
To Emelyn Story. TxU.

672. 25 October 1847   Rome
To Sarah Shaw. MH bMS Am 1417 (184). Printed in Wade, p. 578.

673. 25 October 1847   Rome
To Francis G. Shaw. MH bMS Am 1417 (183). Printed in Wade, pp. 576–77.

A Calendar of the Letters of Margaret Fuller 103

674. 28 October 1847   Rome
To R. W. Emerson. Unrecovered. Incomplete.
Printed in *Memoirs*, 2:220–21.

675. 29 October 1847   Rome
To Elizabeth Hoar. MHarF; partial, slightly altered
copy MH bMS Am 1280 (111, p. 47). Partially printed
in *JMN*, 11:467.

676. 29 October 1847   Rome
To Richard F. Fuller. MH fMS Am 1086 (9:142);
copy MH fMS Am 1086 (Works, 2:841–43). Partially
printed in *Memoirs*, 2:221; *The Lost Art*, pp. 290–91.

677. 17 November 1847   Rome
To [?]. Unrecovered. Fragment. Printed in *Memoirs*,
2:222–23.

678. 16 December 1847   Rome
To Margarett C. Fuller. Incomplete. Letter exists in two
parts which join as follows: MH bMS Am 1280 (111,
pp. 129–30); *Memoirs*, 2:223–24. The first part is a copy
of the unrecovered holograph; the second is unrecovered.
Partially printed in *The Lost Art*, pp. 291–92; *JMN*,
11:480–81, 491.

679. 16 December 1847   Rome
To Mr. and Mrs. Richard H. Manning. ViU.

680. 20 December 1847   Rome
To R. W. Emerson. Unrecovered. Incomplete. Printed
in *Memoirs*, 2:224–25. Printed as two letters, but
probably there was but one original. Partially printed
in *The Lost Art*, pp. 292–93; Miller, pp. 277–78.

681. [ca. 1848?]   [Rome?]
To [?]. Fragment. MB Ms. Am. 1450 (106). Copy of
unrecovered holograph. May be a journal fragment.

682. 1 January 1848   Rome
To Richard F. Fuller. MH fMS Am 1086 (9:143); copy
MH fMS Am 1086 (Works, 2:843–47).

683. 10 January [1848]   [Rome]
To Frederic H. Hedge. MH fMS Am 1086 (10:106).

684. 11 January 1848   Rome
To Caroline Sturgis. Unrecovered. Incomplete. Printed
in *Memoirs*, 2:231–33. Partial copy of unrecovered holograph MH bMS Am 1280 (111, pp. 51, 213–14). Partially
printed in *Memoirs*, 1:226; *JMN*, 11:468, 493.

685. 12 January 1848   Rome
To Ellen K. Fuller. MH fMS Am 1086 (9:113).

686. 12 January [1848] [Rome]
To [Richard F. Fuller?]. MH fMS Am 1086 (9:254);
copy MH fMS Am 1086 (Works, 2:877–79).

687. 14 January 1848 Rome
To Costanza Arconati Visconti. Unrecovered. Fragment.
Printed in *Memoirs,* 2:233.

688. 8 February 1848 Rome
To Richard F. Fuller. MH fMS Am 1086 (9:146);
copy MH fMS Am 1086 (Works, 2:849–55).

689. 9 February 1848 Rome
To Margaret Fuller Channing. MH fMS Am 1086
(9:144).

690. 8 March 1848 Rome
To Miss Stirling. NBu.

691. 8 March 1848 [Rome]
To Frederic H. Hedge. MH fMS Am 1086 (10:105).

692. 14 March 1848 Rome
To R. W. Emerson. Unrecovered. Fragment. Printed
in *Memoirs,* 2:233–34.

693. 17 March 1848 Rome
To Richard F. Fuller. MH fMS Am 1086 (9:147);
copy MH fMS Am 1086 (Works, 2:855–65).

694. 29 March 1848 Rome
To William H. Channing. Unrecovered. Fragment.
Printed in *Memoirs,* 2:235; *The Lost Art,* pp. 293–94,
where it is incorrectly dated as 29 March 1849 and
incorrectly ascribed as being to Emerson.

695. April 1848 Rome
To [Jane F. Tuckerman]. MB Ms. Am. 1450 (168).
Copy of unrecovered holograph. Another copy MH fMS
Am 1086 (Works, 1:111). Partially printed in *At
Home and Abroad,* pp. 426–27.

696. 7 April 1848 Rome
To Henry Coleman. ViU.

697. 22 April 1848 Rome
To Mrs. Rotch. VtMiM.

698. 30 April 1848 Rome
To [?]. Unrecovered. Incomplete. Printed in *Memoirs,*
2:236–38.

699. [ca. May? 1848] Rome
To [Mr. Page?]. MCR-S.

A Calendar of the Letters of Margaret Fuller 105

700. [ca. May? 1848] [Rome]
To R. W. Emerson. Fragment. MH bMS Am 1280 (2380).

701. 14 May 1848 Rome
To Elizabeth D. Cranch. MB Ms. Am. 1450 (60). Copy of unrecovered holograph. Printed in Leonora Cranch Scott, *The Life and Letters of Christopher Pearse Cranch* (Boston: Houghton, Mifflin, 1917), p. 142.

702. 17 May 1848 Rome
To Thomas Hicks. Incomplete. MB Ms. Am. 1450 (82). Copy of unrecovered holograph.

703. 19 May 1848 Rome
To R. W. Emerson. Unrecovered. Fragment. Printed in *Memoirs*, 2:239.

704. 20 May 1848 Rome
To Richard F. Fuller. MH fMS Am 1086 (9:148); copy MH fMS Am 1086 (Works, 2:865–71). Partially printed in *Memoirs*, 2:239–40.

705. 27 May 1848 Rome
To Costanza Arconati Visconti. Unrecovered. Incomplete. Printed in *Memoirs*, 2:240–41.

706. 29 May 1848 Tivoli
To Mary Rotch. MH fMS Am 1086 (9:145); copies MH fMS Am 1086 (Works, 1:63–71); bMS Am 1280 (111, p. 200). Partially printed in *JMN*, 11:490.

707. 22 June 1848 [Rieti]
To Costanza Arconati Visconti. Incomplete. Letter exists in two parts. The main body of the letter is unrecovered and printed in *Memoirs*, 2:242–43. At the end of the second paragraph, omitted matter MH bMS Am 1280 (111, p. 13) should be added. The latter fragment printed in *JMN*, 11:460.

708. 22 June 1848 [Rieti]
To Emelyn Story. MB Ms. Am. 1450 (147). Copy of unrecovered holograph.

709. 22 June 1848 [Rieti]
To Charles K. Newcomb. MB Ms. Am. 1450 (124). Partially printed with extensive changes in *Memoirs*, 2:294–95.

710. 27 [June?] 1848 [Aquila?]
To G. A. Ossoli. MH fMS Am 1086 (9:181); copy MH fMS Am 1086 (Works, 2:97–99). Holograph in Italian; copy in English.

711. 29 June [1848] Aquila
      To G. A. Ossoli. MH fMS Am 1086 (9:208); copy
      MH fMS Am 1086 (Works, 2:99–103). Holograph in
      Italian; copy in English. Partially printed in *Memoirs*,
      2:295.

712. 1 July 1848 [Aquila]
      To Richard F. Fuller. Unrecovered. Fragment. Printed
      in *Memoirs*, 2:241–42.

713. 3 July 1848 [Aquila]
      To Richard F. Fuller. MH fMS Am 1086 (9:149);
      copy MH fMS Am 1086 (Works, 2:817–23).

714. 8 July [1848] [Aquila]
      To G. A. Ossoli. MH fMS Am 1086 (9:198); copy
      MH fMS Am 1086 (Works, 1:107–11). Holograph in
      Italian; copy in English.

715. 11 July 1848 [Aquila]
      To R. W. Emerson. Incomplete. Letter exists in two
      parts which join as follows: *Memoirs*, 2:243–44; MH
      bMS Am 1280 (111, pp. 37–39). The first part is un-
      recovered; the second is a copy of unrecovered holo-
      graph and is printed in *Memoirs*, 2:244; *JMN*,
      11:465–66.

716. 13 July 1848 Aquila
      To G. A. Ossoli. MH fMS Am 1086 (9:178); copy
      MH fMS Am 1086 (Works, 2:103–105). Holograph
      in Italian; copy in English. Partially printed in *Memoirs*,
      2:295.

717. 15 July [1848] [Aquila]
      To G. A. Ossoli. MH fMS Am 1086 (9:198); copy
      MH fMS Am 1086 (Works, 2:111–13). Holograph in
      Italian; copy in English.

718. 18 [July 1848] [Aquila]
      To G. A. Ossoli. MH fMS Am 1086 (9:212); copy
      MH fMS Am 1086 (Works, 2:113–15). Holograph in
      Italian; copy in English.

719. 18 July 1848 [Aquila]
      To J. C. Hooker. Letter exists in two parts which join
      as follows: MH fMS Am 1086 (9:151); MH fMS Am
      1086 (Box A).

720. 22 July [1848] Aquila
      To G. A. Ossoli. MH fMS Am 1086 (9:199); copy
      MH fMS Am 1086 (Works, 2:105–107). Holograph
      in Italian; copy in English.

A Calendar of the Letters of Margaret Fuller 107

721. 27 July 1848 [Aquila]
To G. A. Ossoli. MH fMS Am 1086 (9:179); copy
MH fMS Am 1086 (Works, 2:115–17). Holograph in
Italian; copy in English.

722. 30 July 1848 Rieti
To G. A. Ossoli. MH fMS Am 1086 (9:180); copy
MH fMS Am 1086 (Works, 2:117–19). Holograph in
Italian; copy in English.

723. 30 July 1848 [Rieti]
To J. C. Hooker. MH fMS Am 1086 (9:150).

724. 2 August 1848 Rieti
To G. A. Ossoli. MH fMS Am 1086 (9:182); copy
MH fMS Am 1086 (Works, 2:119–21). Holograph in
Italian; copy in English.

725. 13 August 1848 Rieti
To G. A. Ossoli. MH fMS Am 1086 (9:183); copy
MH fMS Am 1086 (Works, 2:121–23). Holograph in
Italian; copy in English. Partially printed in *Memoirs*,
2:296–97.

726. [ca. 15? August? 1848] [Rieti?]
To [?]. Incomplete. MH fMS Am 1086 (9:237). Copy
of unrecovered holograph. Another copy MH fMS Am
1086 (Works, 1:337–39). Partially printed in *At
Home and Abroad*, p. 426.

727. 15 August 1848 Rieti
To G. A. Ossoli. MH fMS Am 1086 (9:184); copy
MH fMS Am 1086 (Works, 2:123–27). Holograph in
Italian; copy in English. Partially printed in *Memoirs*,
2:297.

728. 16 August 1848 [Rieti]
To Richard F. Fuller. MH fMS Am 1086 (9:152).

729. 17 August [1848] Rieti
To G. A. Ossoli. MH fMS Am 1086 (9:203); copy
MH fMS Am 1086 (Works, 2:127). Holograph in
Italian; copy in English.

730. 18 August [1848] Rieti
To G. A. Ossoli. MH fMS Am 1086 (9:200); copy
MH fMS Am 1086 (Works, 2:127–31). Holograph in
Italian; copy in English. Partially printed in *Memoirs*,
2:297–98; printed entire in Higginson, pp. 250–51.

731. 20 August [1848] [Rieti]
To G. A. Ossoli. MH fMS Am 1086 (9:204); copy
MH fMS Am 1086 (Works, 2:131–33). Holograph in

Italian; copy in English. Partially printed in Higginson, pp. 251–52.

732. 22 August 1848   Rieti
To G. A. Ossoli. MH fMS Am 1086 (9:184); copy MH fMS Am 1086 (Works, 2:133–35). Holograph in Italian; copy in English. Partially printed in *Memoirs*, 2:297; printed entire in Higginson, pp. 252–53; Wade, p. 579.

733. 25 August 1848   Rieti
To G. A. Ossoli. MH fMS Am 1086 (9:201); copy MH fMS Am 1086 (Works, 2:135–37). Holograph in Italian; copy in English. Partially printed in *Memoirs*, 2:296; printed entire in Higginson, p. 253.

734. 7 September 1848   Rieti
To G. A. Ossoli. MH fMS Am 1086 (9:185); copy MH fMS Am 1086 (Works, 2:137). Holograph in Italian; copy in English. Not in Fuller's hand, but dictated by her. Printed in Higginson, p. 254.

735. [9? September 1848]   Rieti
To G. A. Ossoli. MH fMS Am 1086 (9:210); copy MH fMS Am 1086 (Works, 2:137–39). Holograph in Italian; copy in English. Printed in Higginson, p. 254.

736. 10 September 1848   Rieti
To G. A. Ossoli. MH fMS Am 1086 (9:186); copy MH fMS Am 1086 (Works, 2:139–41). Holograph in Italian; copy in English.

737. [13? September? 1848]   Rieti
To G. A. Ossoli. MH fMS Am 1086 (9:201); copy MH fMS Am 1086 (Works, 2:141–43). Holograph in Italian; copy in English.

738. 15 September [1848]   [Rieti]
To G. A. Ossoli. MH fMS Am 1086 (9:202); copy MH fMS Am 1086 (Works, 2:143–45). Holograph in Italian; copy in English. Partially printed in Higginson, pp. 255–56.

739. 17 September [1848]   [Rieti]
To G. A. Ossoli. MH fMS Am 1086 (9:204); copy MH fMS Am 1086 (Works, 2:145–47). Holograph in Italian; copy in English. Partially printed in *Memoirs*, 2:298; printed entire in Higginson, pp. 256–57; Wade, p. 580.

740. 19 [September 1848]   Rieti
To G. A. Ossoli. MH fMS Am 1086 (9:195); copy MH fMS Am 1086 (Works, 2:147–49). Holograph in Italian; copy in English.

A Calendar of the Letters of Margaret Fuller 109

741. 21 [September 1848]   Rieti
To G. A. Ossoli. MH fMS Am 1086 (9:205); copy MH fMS Am 1086 (Works, 2:151–53). Holograph in Italian; copy in English.

742. 23 September [1848]   Rieti
To G. A. Ossoli. MH fMS Am 1086 (9:205); copy MH fMS Am 1086 (Works, 2:149–51). Holograph in Italian; copy in English. Partially printed in *Memoirs,* 2:298; printed entire in Higginson, p. 257.

743. 26 September [1848]   Rieti
To G. A. Ossoli. MH fMS Am 1086 (9:206); copy MH fMS Am 1086 (Works, 2:153–55). Holograph in Italian; copy in English. Partially printed in Higginson, p. 258.

744. 28 [September? 1848]   Rieti
To G. A. Ossoli. MH fMS Am 1086 (9:209); copy MH fMS Am 1086 (Works, 2:161). Holograph in Italian; copy in English. Partially printed in Higginson, p. 259.

745. 7 October 1848   Rieti
To G. A. Ossoli. MH fMS Am 1086 (9:188); copy MH fMS Am 1086 (Works, 2:155–59). Holograph in Italian; copy in English. Partially printed in Higginson, pp. 258–59.

746. 8 October 1848   Rieti
To G. A. Ossoli. MH fMS Am 1086 (9:187); copy MH fMS Am 1086 (Works, 2:161–63). Holograph in Italian; copy in English.

747. 11 October 1848   Rieti
To G. A. Ossoli. MH fMS Am 1086 (9:189); copy MH fMS Am 1086 (Works, 2:163–65). Holograph in Italian; copy in English.

748. 13 [October 1848]   Rieti
To G. A. Ossoli. MH fMS Am 1086 (9:195); copy MH fMS Am 1086 (Works, 2:167–69). Holograph in Italian; copy in English.

749. 15 October 1848   Rieti
To G. A. Ossoli. MH fMS Am 1086 (9:189); copy MH fMS Am 1086 (Works, 2:169–71). Holograph in Italian; copy in English. Partially printed in Higginson, p. 260.

750. 18 October 1848   Rieti
To G. A. Ossoli. MH fMS Am 1086 (9:190); copy MH fMS Am 1086 (Works, 2:171–77). Holograph in Italian; copy in English.

751. 20 October [1848] Rieti
     To G. A. Ossoli. MH fMS Am 1086 (9:191); copy
     MH fMS Am 1086 (Works, 2:177–79). Holograph in
     Italian; copy in English. Partially printed in a garbled
     version in *Memoirs*, 2:298.

752. 25 [October 1848] [Rieti]
     To G. A. Ossoli. MH fMS Am 1086 (9:199); copy
     MH fMS Am 1086 (Works, 2:179–83). Holograph in
     Italian; copy in English.

753. 27 [October 1848] Rieti
     To G. A. Ossoli. MH fMS Am 1086 (9:210); copy
     MH fMS Am 1086 (Works, 2:183–87). Holograph in
     Italian; copy in English.

754. [28 October 1848] [Rieti]
     To G. A. Ossoli. MH fMS Am 1086 (9:211); copy
     MH fMS Am 1086 (Works, 2:191–97). Holograph in
     Italian; copy in English. Partially printed in Higginson,
     p. 261.

755. 29 October 1848 [Rieti]
     To G. A. Ossoli. MH fMS Am 1086 (9:207); copy
     MH fMS Am 1086 (Works, 2:187–89). Holograph in
     Italian; copy in English.

756. 1 November [1848] Rieti
     To G. A. Ossoli. MH fMS Am 1086 (9:191); copy
     MH fMS Am 1086 (Works, 2:189–91). Holograph in
     Italian; copy in English.

757. 16 November 1848 Rome
     To Margarett C. Fuller. Unrecovered. Incomplete.
     Printed in *Memoirs*, 2:245–52; partially printed in *At
     Home and Abroad*, pp. 427–30.

758. 17 November 1848 Rome
     To Richard F. Fuller. MH fMS Am 1086 (9:154);
     copy MH fMS Am 1086 (Works, 2:871–77).

759. 23 November 1848 Rome
     To Marcus Spring. Unrecovered. Incomplete. Printed
     in *Memoirs*, 2:252–54.

760. 23 November 1848 Rome
     To [William H. Channing?]. Fragment. MB Ms. Am.
     1450 (102). Copy of unrecovered holograph.

761. 24 November 1848 Rome
     To Charles K. Newcomb. MB Ms. Am. 1450 (125);
     misdated copy MH bMS Am 1280 (111, pp. 33–34, 87).
     Partially printed in *JMN*, 11:465, 474.

A Calendar of the Letters of Margaret Fuller   111

762. 28 November 1848 — Rome
To Emelyn Story. Incomplete. NNC.

763. 7 December 1848 — Rome
To Richard F. Fuller. MH fMS Am 1086 (9:155).

764. 9 December 1848 — [Rome]
To William W. Story. Unrecovered. Incomplete. Printed in *Memoirs*, 2:254, 256–57. May be misdated in *Memoirs* and may thus be two separate letters.

765. [22? December? 1848] — Rieti
To G. A. Ossoli. MH fMS Am 1086 (9:207); copy MH fMS Am 1086 (Works, 2:197–201). Holograph in Italian; copy in English. Printed in Higginson, pp. 261–62.

766. 24 December [1848] — [Rieti]
To G. A. Ossoli. MH fMS Am 1086 (9:192); copy MH fMS Am 1086 (Works, 2:201–203). Holograph in Italian; copy in English.

767. 27 December 1848 — [Rieti]
To G. A. Ossoli. MH fMS Am 1086 (9:192); copy MH fMS Am 1086 (Works, 2:203–205). Holograph in Italian; copy in English.

768. January 1849 — Rome
To [Jane F. Tuckerman]. Fragment. MH fMS Am 1086 (Works, 1:111–13). Copy of unrecovered holograph. Another copy MB Ms. Am. 1450 (169).

769. 7 January 1849 — Rome
To Emelyn Story. MH fMS Am 1086 (9:224). Copy of unrecovered holograph. Another copy MH fMS Am 1086 (Works, 1:237–43).

770. 18 January 1849 — Rome
To Sarah Clarke. MH bMS Am 1569 (1349).

771. 19 January 1849 — Rome
To Margarett C. Fuller. MH fMS Am 1086 (9:151).

772. 19 January 1849 — Rome
To Richard F. Fuller. MH fMS Am 1086 (9:156); copy MH fMS Am 1086 (Works, 2:587–601). Printed in *At Home and Abroad*, pp. 430–32.

773. 20 January 1849 — Rome
To Arthur B. Fuller. MH fMS Am 1086 (9:153); copy MH fMS Am 1086 (Works, 1:663–67). Partially printed in *Woman in the Nineteenth Century*, p. 374.

774. 21 January 1849 — [Rome]
To R. W. Emerson. Collection of Nelson C. White.

775. 21 January 1849   Rome
     To Emelyn Story. TxU.

776. 3 February 1849   Rome
     To Maria Rotch. MH fMS Am 1086 (9:173).

777. 5 February 1849   Rome
     To Costanza Arconati Visconti. Unrecovered. In-
     complete. Printed in *Memoirs*, 2:257–59.

778. 23 February 1849   Rome
     To Richard F. Fuller. MH fMS Am 1086 (9:157); copy
     MH fMS Am 1086 (Works, 2:883–89). Partially printed,
     Memoirs, 2:259–60; Miller, pp. 281–82.

779. [ca. March? 1849]   [Rome]
     To Emelyn Story. MH fMS Am 1086 (9:174).

780. [3?] March 1849   Rome
     To Giuseppi Mazzini. MH fMS Am 1086 (9:105);
     copy MH fMS Am 1086 (Works, 1:233–37). Printed
     in *Woman in the Nineteenth Century*, pp. 374–76;
     Wade, pp. 581–82.

781. 8 March 1849   Rome
     To Caroline Sturgis. Incomplete. Letter exists in two
     parts which join as follows: *Memoirs*, 2:302; MB
     Ms. Am. 1450 (151). The first part is unrecovered; the
     second is a copy of unrecovered holograph. A severely
     altered version is printed in *Memoirs*, 2:299–300, 301,
     302 where it is silently joined to another letter.

782. 9 March 1849   Rome
     To Marcus Spring. Unrecovered. Incomplete. Printed
     in *Memoirs*, 2:262–63; *The Lost Art*, pp. 294–96.

783. 9 March 1849   Rome
     To Margarett C. Fuller. MH fMS Am 1086 (9:158).

784. 9 March 1849   Rome
     To Elizabeth D. Cranch. MB Ms. Am. 1450 (61). Copy
     of unrecovered holograph. Printed in *Life and Letters
     of Christopher Pearse Cranch*, pp. 168–70.

785. 10 March 1849   [Rome]
     To [William H. Channing]. Incomplete. MB Ms. Am.
     1450 (103). Copy of unrecovered holograph. Another
     copy MH bMS Am 1280 (111, pp. 273–74). Partially
     printed in *Memoirs*, 2:302; *JMN*, 11:503.

786. 13 March 1849   Rome
     To Ellen K. Fuller. MH fMS Am 1086 (9:174).

A Calendar of the Letters of Margaret Fuller 113

787. 16 March 1849 [Rome]
To Caroline Sturgis. Incomplete. MH fMS Am 1086
(9:170); copy MH bMS Am 1280 (111, p. 213).
Partially printed in *Memoirs*, 1:226; 2:266–67, 279–81,
300; Higginson, pp. 268–70, where it is wrongly ascribed
to Emelyn Story; Miller, pp. 282–86; *JMN*, 11:492.

788. 17 March 1849 Rome
To Richard F. Fuller. MH fMS Am 1086 (9:255);
copy MH fMS Am 1086 (Works, 2:889–97). Partially
printed in *At Home and Abroad*, pp. 432–33.

789. 18 March 1849 Rome
To Anna B. Ward. MH bMS Am 1465 (930).

790. 27 March [1849] Rieti
To G. A. Ossoli. MH fMS Am 1086 (9:194); copy
MH fMS Am 1086 (Works, 2:205–207). Holograph
in Italian; copy in English. Partially printed in
Higginson, p. 262.

791. 30 March 1849 Rieti
To G. A. Ossoli. MH fMS Am 1086 (9:194); copy
MH fMS Am 1086 (Works, 2:207–11). Holograph in
Italian; copy in English. Partially printed in Higginson, p. 263.

792. [1 April 1849] Rieti
To G. A. Ossoli. MH fMS Am 1086 (9:213); copy
MH fMS Am 1086 (Works, 2:215–17). Holograph in
Italian; copy in English.

793. 4 April 1849 Rieti
To G. A. Ossoli. MH fMS Am 1086 (9:196); copy
MH fMS Am 1086 (Works, 2:211–15). Holograph in
Italian; copy in English.

794. 6 April 1849 Rieti
To G. A. Ossoli. MH fMS Am 1086 (9:197); copy
MH fMS Am 1086 (Works, 2:217). Holograph in
Italian; copy in English.

795. 13 April [1849] Rieti
To G. A. Ossoli. MH fMS Am 1086 (9:197); copy
MH fMS Am 1086 (Works, 2:217–19). Holograph in
Italian; copy in English.

796. 15 April [1849] Rieti
To G. A. Ossoli. MH fMS Am 1086 (9:209); copy
MH fMS Am 1086 (Works, 2:219). Holograph in
Italian; copy in English.

797. 4 May [1849] [Rome]
To G. A. Ossoli. MH fMS Am 1086 (9:214); copy

MH fMS Am 1086 (Works, 2:219–21). Holograph in
Italian; copy in English. Printed in Higginson, p. 263.

798. [ca. late May 1849] [Rome]
To G. A. Ossoli. MH fMS Am 1086 (9:213); copy
MH fMS Am 1086 (Works, 2:223). Holograph in
Italian; copy in English. Printed in Wade, p. 583.

799. 20 May 1849 Rome
To Lewis Cass, Jr. MH fMS Am 1086 (Works,
1:341). Copy of unrecovered holograph.

800. [22? May? 1849] Rome
To Lewis Cass, Jr. MH fMS Am 1086 (9:193); copy
MH fMS Am 1086 (Works, 1:339).

801. 22 May 1849 Rome
To Richard F. Fuller. MH fMS Am 1086 (Works,
1:243–47). Copy of unrecovered holograph. Partially
printed in *At Home and Abroad*, pp. 433–34.

802. [24? May? 1849] Rome
To Lewis Cass, Jr. MH fMS Am 1086 (Works,
1:341). Copy of unrecovered holograph.

803. 28 May 1849 Rome
To Richard F. Fuller. MH fMS Am 1086 (9:160);
copy MH fMS Am 1086 (Works, 2:601–605).

804. 29 May 1849 Rome
To Emelyn Story. MH fMS Am 1086 (9:225). Copy
of unrecovered holograph. Another copy MH fMS
Am 1086 (Works, 1:247–53).

805. [ca. June? 1849] [Rome]
To Lewis Cass, Jr. MH fMS Am 1086 (Works, 1:339).
Copy of unrecovered holograph.

806. [ca. June? 1849] [Rome]
To Emelyn Story. Incomplete. MH fMS Am 1086
(9:234). Copy of unrecovered holograph.

807. [ca. June 1849] [Rome]
To G. A. Ossoli. MH fMS Am 1086 (9:215½); copy
MH fMS Am 1086 (Works, 2:223–25). Holograph in
Italian; copy in English. Printed in Higginson, pp. 264–
65; Wade, p. 583.

808. [June? 1849] Rome
To Arthur Hugh Clough. Bodleian Library. Printed
in *The Correspondence of Arthur Hugh Clough*, ed.
Frederick L. Mulhauser (Cambridge: Oxford University
Press, 1957), p. 262.

A Calendar of the Letters of Margaret Fuller 115

809. 4 June [1849] [Rome]
To G. A. Ossoli. MH fMS Am 1086 (9:215); copy MH fMS Am 1086 (Works, 2:221). Holograph in Italian; copy in English. Printed in Higginson, p. 264.

810. 6 June 1849 Rome
To Emelyn Story. Unrecovered. Fragment. Printed in *Memoirs*, 2:261–62.

811. 10 June 1849 Rome
To R. W. Emerson. Unrecovered. Incomplete. Printed in *Memoirs*, 2:264–66; *At Home and Abroad*, pp. 434–36; *The Lost Art*, pp. 296–99; Miller, pp. 295–98. In each printed version the final paragraph belongs not to this letter but to the one of 16 March 1849 to Caroline Sturgis.

812. 19 June 1849 Rome
To Ellen K. Fuller. Unrecovered. Printed in *At Home and Abroad*, p. 437; Miller, pp. 298–99.

813. [8? July 1849] [Rome]
To Lewis Cass, Jr. Unrecovered. Fragment. Printed in *Memoirs*, 2:271.

814. 8 July 1849 Rome
To Richard F. Fuller. MH fMS Am 1086 (9:160); copy MH fMS Am 1086 (Works, 2:879–83). Partially printed in *Memoirs*, 2:267, where it is incorrectly ascribed as being to William H. Channing and joined to another letter probably to him. Printed with the same error in *The Lost Art*, pp. 299–301.

815. 10 July [1849] [Rome]
To Lewis Cass, Jr. MH fMS Am 1086 (9:159); copy MH fMS Am 1086 (Works, 1:343–45).

816. 19 July 1849 Rieti
To Lewis Cass, Jr. MB Ms. Am. 1450 (29). Printed in Higginson, pp. 266–68.

817. [ca. late July? 1849] [Rieti?]
To [William H. Channing?]. Incomplete. Letter exists in several parts which join as follows: *Memoirs*, 2:269, 268–69; MB Ms. Am. 1450 (104). This arrangement is conjectural but suggested by the contents. The first three paragraphs of *Memoirs*, 2:267, are from 8 July to Richard F. Fuller. The first two parts above are unrecovered; the third is a copy of unrecovered holograph.

818. 30 July 1849 Rieti
To Lewis Cass, Jr. Incomplete. MB Ms. Am. 1450 (30). Copy of unrecovered holograph.

819. [Summer 1849] [Rieti]
To Margarett C. Fuller. Unrecovered. Incomplete.
Printed in *Memoirs*, 2:271–76; *The Lost Art*,
pp. 301–309.

820. [Summer? 1849] [Rieti?]
To Costanza Arconati Visconti. Incomplete. Letter
exists in two parts which join as follows: *Memoirs*,
2:314–15; MH fMS Am 1086 (9:232). The first part is
unrecovered; the second is a copy of unrecovered
holograph.

821. [ca. August? 1849?] [Rieti?]
To [Ellen K. Fuller?]. Unrecovered. Incomplete. Printed
in *Memoirs*, 2:254–56. Printed as "December 1848"
but two letters are joined. The other appears to be to
William W. Story written from Rome.

822. 8 August 1849 Rieti
To Lewis Cass, Jr. MH fMS Am 1086 (9:164); copy
MH fMS Am 1086 (Works, 1:345–47).

823. 9 August 1849 Rieti
To G. A. Ossoli. MH fMS Am 1086 (9:202); copy
MH fMS Am 1086 (Works, 2:225–27). Holograph in
Italian; copy in English.

824. 13 August 1849 Rieti
To Lewis Cass, Jr. Incomplete. MB Ms. Am. 1450 (31).
Copy of unrecovered holograph.

825. 25 August 1849 [Rieti]
To Horace Greeley. Unrecovered. Printed in Cecilia
Cleveland, *The Story of a Summer* (New York:
G. W. Carleton and Co., 1874), pp. 243–46.

826. 28 August 1849 Rieti
To William H. Channing. Unrecovered. Fragment.
Printed in *Memoirs*, 2:269–70. Partially printed in Miller,
pp. 299–300.

827. 28 August 1849 Rieti
To Caroline Sturgis. Fragment. MB Ms. Am. 1450
(152). Copy of unrecovered holograph. Printed in a
slightly different version in *Memoirs*, 2:301.

828. 31 August 1849 [Rieti]
To [Emelyn Story?]. Fragment. MB Ms. Am. 1450
(148). Copy of unrecovered holograph. Final portion
of the manuscript is a copy of 16 March 1849 to
Caroline Sturgis, but it is copied as though it were a
part of this letter.

829.	31 August 1849 To E. Welby. MH fMS Am 1086 (9:173).	Rieti
830.	[September? 1849] To [Lewis Cass, Jr.]. Fragment. MB Ms. Am. 1450 (171). Copy of unrecovered holograph. Another, partial, copy MH bMS Am 1280 (111, p. 210). Printed in *JMN,* 11:492.	[Perugia?]
831.	21 September 1849 To [E. Welby]. MH fMS Am 1086 (9:175).	Perugia
832.	30 September 1849 To Lewis Cass, Jr. Incomplete. MH fMS Am 1086 (9:236). Copy of unrecovered holograph. Partially printed in *Memoirs,* 2:303–304.	Florence
833.	[Autumn? 1849?] To [?]. Fragment. MB Ms. Am. 1450 (170a). Copy of unrecovered holograph. Printed in Higginson, p. 270.	[Florence?]
834.	[Autumn? 1849?] To [Elizabeth Hoar?]. Fragment. MB Ms. Am. 1450 (83). Copy of unrecovered holograph.	[Florence?]
835.	[Autumn? 1849?] To [William H. Channing?]. Fragment. Letter exists, I believe, in two parts which join as follows: MB Ms. Am. 1450 (109), (110). Both parts are copies of unrecovered holograph. A version of this is printed in *Memoirs,* 2:311, 334–35.	[Florence?]
836.	1 October 1849 To [?]. Fragment. MH bMS Am 1280 (111, p. 13). Copy of unrecovered holograph. Printed, erroneously, in no. 707 (*Memoirs,* 2:242); printed in *JMN,* 11:461.	Florence
837.	4 October 1849 To Lewis Cass, Jr. Fragment. MB Ms. Am. 1450 (32). Copy of unrecovered holograph.	Florence
838.	8 October 1849 To Lewis Cass, Jr. MH fMS Am 1086 (9:165); copy MH fMS Am 1086 (Works, 1:347–51).	Florence
839.	14 October 1849 To Margarett C. Fuller. Incomplete. Letter exists in two parts which join as follows: MH fMS Am 1086 (9:236); *Memoirs,* 2:306–307. The first part is a copy of unrecovered holograph; the second is unrecovered. The first is partially printed in *Memoirs,* 2:305–306, where it is incorrectly dated 7 November 1849. Partially printed in *The Lost Art,* pp. 310–12.	Florence

840. 16 October 1849   Florence
To Costanza Arconati Visconti. Incomplete. MH fMS Am 1086 (9:232). Copy of unrecovered holograph. Another, but longer, copy MH bMS Am 1280 (111, pp. 19–21). Emerson erroneously dates his copy "Apr. 6, 1850." The subject matter places the letter in 1849. Printed in *Memoirs*, 2:316–17; *JMN*, 11:462.

841. 21 October 1849   Florence
To Samuel G. Ward. MH bMS Am 1465 (931).

842. 25 October 1849   Florence
To George W. Curtis. MHarF.

843. 31 October [1849]   [Florence]
To Samuel G. Ward. MH bMS Am 1465 (932).

844. [November? 1849]   [Florence]
To [Emelyn Story]. MH fMS Am 1086 (9:230). Copy of unrecovered holograph. Another copy MH fMS Am 1086 (Works, 1:325–29). Partially printed in *Memoirs*, 2:304.

845. 8 November 1849   Florence
To [?]. ViU.

846. 18 November 1849   Florence
To Sarah F. Clarke. NjP.

847. 30 November 1849   Florence
To Emelyn Story. Incomplete. MH fMS Am 1086 (9:226). Copy of unrecovered holograph. Another copy MH fMS Am 1086 (Works, 1:253–57). Partially printed in *Memoirs*, 2:312–13; Miller, p. 301.

848. [December 1849]   [Florence]
To [Caroline Sturgis]. Incomplete. MH fMS Am 1086 (9:166); partial copy MH fMS Am 1086 (9:233). Partially printed in *Memoirs*, 2:307–10, 317–18, 319; Higginson, p. 271; *The Lost Art*, pp. 312–14, where it is incorrectly ascribed as being to Margarett C. Fuller; Miller, pp. 307–10.

849. 2 December 1849   Florence
To William W. Story. MH fMS Am 1086 (9:277). Copy of unrecovered holograph. Another copy MH fMS Am 1086 (Works, 1:259–65). Partially printed in *Memoirs*, 2:313–14; printed entire in Wade, pp. 584–86; partially printed in Miller, pp. 302–303.

850. 6 December [1849]   Florence
To Elizabeth B. Browning. VtMiM. Printed in *American Literature*, 9 (March 1937): 70–71.

851. 11 December 1849 — Florence
To Ellen K. Fuller. MH fMS Am 1086 (9:177); copies MH bMS Am 1280 (111, p. 204), MB Ms. Am. 1450 (105). Partially printed in *Memoirs*, 2:276–79, 301; Miller, pp. 303–306; *JMN*, 11:491.

852. 12 December 1849 — Florence
To Marcus and Rebecca Spring. MH fMS Am 1086 (9:219). Copy of unrecovered holograph. Other copies MH fMS Am 1086 (Works, 1:265–77); MH bMS Am 1280 (111, p. 41). Partially printed in *Woman in the Nineteenth Century*, pp. 376–78; *Memoirs*, 1:302–303; F. B. Sanborn, *Recollections of Seventy Years* (Boston: Richard G. Badger, 1909), pp. 410–11; printed entire in Wade, pp. 587–90; partially printed in *JMN*, 11:466.

853. 17 December 1849 — Florence
To [?]. Fragment. Letter exists, I believe, in two parts which join as follows: MB Ms. Am. 1450 (107), (58). Copy of unrecovered holograph. May be to William H. Channing.

854. [1850] — [Florence]
To [?]. Unrecovered. Fragment. Printed in *Memoirs*, 2:337.

855. 8 January 1850 — Florence
To Samuel G. and Anna B. Ward. MH bMS Am 1465 (933).

856. 8 January 1850 — Florence
To Richard F. Fuller. MH fMS Am 1086 (9:162); copy MH fMS Am 1086 (Works, 2:605–11). Partially printed in *Woman in the Nineteenth Century*, pp. 378–80; printed entire in Wade, pp. 591–92; partially printed in Miller, pp. 310–12.

857. 20 January 1850 — Florence
To Lewis Cass, Jr. MH fMS Am 1086 (9:167); copy MH fMS Am 1086 (Works, 1:351–53).

858. [ca. February? 1850?] — [Florence]
To [?]. Fragment. MB Ms. Am. 1450 (112). Copy of unrecovered holograph. Printed in Higginson, p. 273.

859. [ca. 1 February? 1850?] — [Florence]
To [?]. Fragment. MB Ms. Am. 1450 (173). Copy of unrecovered holograph. A highly altered version is printed in *Memoirs*, 2:310–11.

860. 5 February 1850 — Florence
To Marcus and Rebecca Spring. MH fMS Am 1086 (9:220). Copy of unrecovered holograph. Another copy

MH fMS Am 1086 (Works, 1:277-87). Partially printed in *Woman in the Nineteenth Century*, pp. 381-84; Sanborn, *Recollections*, pp. 411-12; Miller, pp. 312-14.

861. 5 February 1850   Florence
To Lewis Cass, Jr. Fragment. MB Ms. Am. 1450 (33). Copy of unrecovered holograph.

862. 6 February 1850   Florence
To Margarett C. Fuller. MH fMS Am 1086 (9:176); copy MH fMS Am 1086 (Works, 1:287-95). Partially printed in *At Home and Abroad*, pp. 438-39.

863. 6 February 1850   Florence
To [?]. Fragment. MB Ms. Am. 1450 (110). Copy of unrecovered holograph.

864. 15 February 1850   Florence
To Emelyn Story. Incomplete. Letter exists in two parts which join as follows: MB Ms. Am. 1450 (149); MH fMS Am 1086 (9:235). Both parts are copies of unrecovered holograph. Another copy of the second part MH fMS Am 1086 (Works, 1:329-35).

865. 16 February [1850]   [Florence]
To Arthur Hugh Clough. Bodleian Library. Printed in *The Correspondence of Arthur Hugh Clough*, pp. 280-81.

866. 24 February 1850   Florence
To Samuel G. Ward. MH bMS Am 1465 (934).

867. 24 February 1850   Florence
To Richard F. Fuller. MH fMS Am 1086 (9:135); copies MH fMS Am 1086 (Works, 1:123-27), MB Ms. Am. 1450 (81a). Partially printed in Higginson, p. 273.

868. 5 March 1850   [Florence]
To Lewis Cass, Jr. Fragment. MB Ms. Am. 1450 (81b). Copy of unrecovered holograph.

869. [Spring? 1850?]   [Florence]
To [William H. Channing?]. Incomplete. MB Ms. Am. 1450 (115). Copy of unrecovered holograph. Partially printed in *Memoirs*, 2:311-12, where it is joined to another letter.

870. [Spring? 1850?]   [Florence]
To [?]. Incomplete. I believe the letter eixsts in two parts which join as follows: *Memoirs*, 2:334; MB Ms. Am. 1450 (172). The first part is unrecovered; the second is copy of unrecovered holograph.

A Calendar of the Letters of Margaret Fuller 121

871. [March? 1850] [Florence]
To [Emelyn Story?]. Fragment. MB Ms. Am. 1450 (118). Copy of unrecovered holograph.

872. 15 March 1850 Florence
To Emelyn Story. MH fMS Am 1086 (9:228). Copy of unrecovered holograph. Another copy MH fMS Am 1086 (Works, 1:297–301).

873. 20 March [1850] Florence
To Lewis Cass, Jr. MH fMS Am 1086 (9:168); copy MH fMS Am 1086 (Works, 1:341–43).

874. 5 April [1850?] [Florence]
To Mrs. Greenough. ViU.

875. 6 April 1850 Florence
To Costanza Arconati Visconti. Incomplete. Letter exists in two parts which join, I believe, as follows: MB Ms. Am. 1450 (154); MH bMS Am 1280 (111, pp. 8–9). Both parts copies of unrecovered holograph. Partially printed in *Memoirs*, 2:337; Higginson, p. 274; *JMN*, 11:458–59. This conjectural combination is based on the common date assigned by the unknown copyist and by Emerson. Since, however, discrepancies exist between dates of other letters copied by both, this may be two separate letters.

876. 12 April 1850 Florence
To Costanza Arconati Visconti. Fragment. MB Ms. Am. 1450 (155). Copy of unrecovered holograph. Partially printed in *Memoirs*, 2:335–36.

877. 16 April 1850 Florence
To Emelyn Story. Letter exists in four parts which join as follows: MH fMS Am 1086 (9:233); MB Ms. Am. 1450 (150); MH fMS Am 1086 (9:223), (222 [where it is misdated as 17 May]). All parts are copies of unrecovered holograph. Other copy fragments are MH fMS Am 1086 (Works, 1:301–305, 321–25). Partially printed in *Woman in the Nineteenth Century*, pp. 385–86; *Memoirs*, 2:318–19; Miller, pp. 314–15.

878. [21 April 1850] [Florence]
To Costanza Arconati Visconti. Fragment. MB Ms. Am. 1450 (156). Copy of unrecovered holograph. Another, slightly different and misdated copy, MH bMS Am 1280 (111, pp. 6–8). Partially printed in *Memoirs*, 2:336; printed entire in Higginson, pp. 274–75; *JMN*, 11:458.

879. 25 April 1850 Florence
To Costanza Arconati Visconti. Fragment. MB Ms. Am. 1450 (157). Copy of unrecovered holograph.

880. 2 May 1850   Florence
To Lewis Cass, Jr. MH fMS Am 1086 (9:169); copy
MH fMS Am 1086 (Works, 1:355-57). Partially printed
in *Woman in the Nineteenth Century*, p. 384.

881. 10 May 1850   Florence
To William W. Story. MH fMS Am 1086 (9:229). Copy
of unrecovered holograph. Other copies MH fMS Am
1086 (Works, 1:305-11); NNPM.

882. 10 May 1850   [Florence]
To [J. C.?] Calvert. MH fMS Am 1086 (9:231). Copy
of unrecovered holograph. Another copy MH fMS Am
1086 (Works, 1:311-13).

883. [14] May 1850   Florence
To Marcus and Rebecca Spring. MH fMS Am 1086
(9:221). Copy of unrecovered holograph. Another
copy MH fMS Am 1086 (Works, 1:313-17).

884. 14 May 1850   Florence
To Margarett C. Fuller. MB Ms. Am. 1450 (80). Copy
of unrecovered holograph. Printed in *At Home and
Abroad*, p. 440; *Memoirs*, 2:337-38; *The Lost Art*,
pp. 314-15.

885. 3 June 1850   Gibraltar
To Marcus Spring. MH fMS Am 1086 (9:221). Copy
of unrecovered holograph. Another copy MH fMS Am
1086 (Works, 1:317-21). Printed in *Woman in the
Nineteenth Century*, pp. 387-88; Sanborn, *Recollections*,
pp. 413-14.

886. [18] June 1850   Gibraltar
To Mr. and Mrs. Samuel Thompson. MeHi. Printed
in *American Literature*, 5 (March 1933): 66-69. The
first portion of the letter is one from Catherine Hasty
dictated to Fuller who then added her own letter at
the end.

887. n.d.   [Cambridge?]
To Amelia Greenwood. MH fMS Am 2001 (41).
Written when a young girl.

888. n.d.   [Cambridge?]
To Amelia Greenwood. CtY. Written when a young girl.

889. n.d.   [Cambridge?]
To Amelia Greenwood. CtY. Written when a young girl.

890. n.d.   [Cambridge?]
To Anne W. Weston. MB Ms. A. 92, Vol. 14, no. 2.
Written, I think, while her residence was Groton.

891. n.d. [Boston?]
To Mary Rotch. ViU. This formal note was written early in their relationship.

892. n.d. [———?]
To [?]. Unrecovered. Fragment. Printed in *Memoirs*, 1:117. Probably written in 1830s to either Clarke, Hedge, or Emerson.

893. n.d. [———?]
To [?]. Unrecovered. Fragment. Printed in *Memoirs*, 1:121–22. Probably written in the 1830s to Clarke.

894. n.d. [———?]
To [?]. Unrecovered. Fragment. Printed in *Memoirs*, 1:122. Probably written in the 1830s to Clarke.

895. n.d. [Groton]
To [?]. Unrecovered. Fragment. Printed in *Memoirs*, 1:124. Probably written early in the 1830s to Clarke.

896. n.d. [———?]
To [?]. Unrecovered. Fragment. Printed in *Memoirs*, 1:127–28. Probably written between 1832 and 1836 to Clarke.

897. n.d. [———?]
To [?]. Unrecovered. Fragment. Printed in *Memoirs*, 1:148–49. Probably written between 1832 and 1836 to Clarke.

898. n.d. [———?]
To [?]. Unrecovered. Fragment. Printed in *Memoirs*, 1:164–65. Probably written between 1832 and 1837 to Clarke.

899. n.d. [———?]
To [James F. Clarke?]. Unrecovered. Incomplete. Printed in *Memoirs*, 1:168–69. Probably written in the 1830s in answer to the letter, n.d., printed in *The Letters of James Freeman Clarke to Margaret Fuller*, p. 35.

900. n.d. [———?]
To Charles K. Newcomb. MH fMS Am 1086 (10:125). Written after the founding of Brook Farm in 1841.

901. n.d. [———?]
To [William H. Channing]. MB Ms. Am. 1450 (44). Written before the death of William Ellery Channing in October 1842.

902. n.d. [———?]
To Sarah Shaw. MH bMS Am 1417 (174). Written while Fuller was still editor of the *Dial* (1840–1842).

903. n.d. [——?]
To [Caroline Sturgis]. MH bMS Am 1221 (230).
Written while editor of the *Dial*.

904. n.d. [——?]
To Georgiana Bruce. Fragment. TxU. Written after
founding of Brook Farm in 1841.

905. n.d. [New York]
To Horace Greeley. IaU. Written between December
1844 and July 1846.

906. n.d. Rome
To [?]. MH fMS Am 1086 (9:214). Written between
1847 and 1849.

907. n.d. [Rome?]
To [Mrs. Nicholas Brown]. RPB. Written between 1847
and 1849.

908. n.d. [——?]
To [?]. Unrecovered. Incomplete. Printed in Higginson,
pp. 111–12. May not be a letter.

909. n.d. [——?]
To [William H. Channing?]. Unrecovered. Fragment.
Printed in *Memoirs*, 2:65–66. May be a continuation
of July 1842 to [William H. Channing?] but probably not. May not be a letter.

910. n.d. [——?]
To [William H. Channing?]. Unrecovered. Incomplete.
Printed in *Memoirs*, 2:81–84.

911. n.d. [——?]
To [William H. Channing?]. Unrecovered. Fragment.
Printed in *Memoirs*, 2:110–11.

912. n.d. [——?]
To [William H. Channing?]. Unrecovered. Fragment.
Printed in *Memoirs*, 2:111–12.

913. n.d. [——?]
To James F. Clarke. MH bMS Am 1569.7 (469).

914. n.d. [——?]
To George T. Davis. Unrecovered. Fragment. Printed
in *American Transcendental Quarterly*, No. 17 (Winter
1973): 36.

915. n.d. [——?]
To G[eorge T.] D[avis]. Unrecovered. Fragment. MB
Ms. Am. 1450 (18). Copy in Higginson's hand of
unrecovered holograph.

916. n.d. [——?]
To R. W. Emerson. MH bMS Am 1280 (2384).

917. n.d. [——?]
To [R. W. Emerson?]. Unrecovered. Fragment. Printed in *Memoirs,* 1:265. May not be a letter.

918. n.d. [——?]
To [R. W. Emerson?]. Unrecovered. Fragment. Printed in *Memoirs,* 1:289.

919. n.d. [——?]
To Margarett C. Fuller. MH fMS Am 1086 (9:53); copy MH fMS Am 1086 (Works, 1:55, 177–79). The copyist assigns 1846 as the date.

920. n.d. [——?]
To Richard F. Fuller. MH fMS Am 1086 (9:125); copy MH fMS Am 1086 (Works, 2:789).

921. n.d. [——?]
To [Richard F. Fuller]. Fragment. ViU.

922. n.d. [——?]
To [?]. Unrecovered. Fragment. Printed in *Memoirs,* 1:77. Identified as written to "a brother."

923. n.d. [——?]
To [?]. Unrecovered. Fragment. Printed in *Memoirs,* 2:120–21. Identified as written to "a brother."

924. n.d. [——?]
To [?]. Unrecovered. Incomplete. Printed in *Memoirs,* 2:121–24. Identified as written to "a brother."

925. n.d. [——?]
To [?]. Unrecovered. Fragment. Printed in *Memoirs,* 2:125–27. Probably written to Richard F. Fuller.

926. n.d. [——?]
To [?]. Unrecovered. Fragment. Printed in *Memoirs,* 2:127. Probably written to Richard F. Fuller.

927. n.d. [——?]
To [?]. Unrecovered. Fragment. Printed in *Memoirs,* 2:129. Identified as written to "a brother."

928. n.d. [——?]
To [?]. Unrecovered. Fragment. Printed in *Memoirs,* 2:129–30. Identified as written to "a brother."

929. n.d. [——?]
To [?]. Unrecovered. Fragment. Printed in *Memoirs,* 2:131. Probably written to Richard F. Fuller.

930. n.d. [——?]
To Elizabeth Hoar. MHarF.

931. n.d. [——?]
To Theodore Parker. PHi.

932. n.d. [——?]
To [?]. CtY. The library assigns the letter to Elizabeth Peabody.

933. n.d. [——?]
To Charles K. Newcomb. MH fMS Am 1086 (10:125).

934. n.d. [——?]
To Charles K. Newcomb. MH fMS Am 1086 (10:133).

935. n.d. [——?]
To Charles K. Newcomb. MH fMS Am 1086 (10:135).

936. n.d. [——?]
To Charles K. Newcomb. MH fMS Am 1086 (10:138).

937. n.d. [——?]
To Charles K. Newcomb. MH fMS Am 1086 (10:144).

938. n.d. [——?]
To William W. Story. Collection of Gene De Gruson.

939. n.d. [——?]
To [Caroline Sturgis]. Fragment. MH bMS Am 1221 (199).

940. n.d. [——?]
To Caroline Sturgis. MH bMS Am 1221 (229).

941. n.d. [——?]
To [Caroline Sturgis]. MH bMS Am 1221 (231).

942. n.d. [——?]
To Jane F. Tuckerman. Incomplete. MH fMS Am 1086 (Works, 1:97–99). Copy of unrecovered holograph. Printed in *Woman in the Nineteenth Century*, pp. 364–65.

943. n.d. [——?]
To Anna B. [Ward]. Incomplete. MH fMS Am 1086 (Box A).

944. n.d. [Boston]
To Mary G. Ward. Copy of unrecovered holograph. Collection of Robert N. Hudspeth.

945. n.d. [——?]
To [?]. Incomplete. MB Ms. Am. 1450 (140).

946.	n.d. To [?]. Fragment. MB Ms. Am. 1450 (174). Copy of unrecovered holograph.	[——?]
947.	n.d. To [?]. Unrecovered. Fragment. Printed in *Memoirs*, 1:79.	[——?]
948.	n.d. To [?]. Unrecovered. Fragment. Printed in *Memoirs*, 1:79.	[——?]
949.	n.d. To [?]. Unrecovered. Fragment. Printed in *Memoirs*, 1:84.	[——?]
950.	n.d. To [?]. Unrecovered. Fragment. Printed in *Memoirs*, 1:84.	[——?]
951.	n.d. To [?]. Unrecovered. Fragment. Printed in *Memoirs*, 1:84–85.	[——?]
952.	n.d. To [?]. Unrecovered. Fragment. Printed in *Memoirs*, 1:98.	[——?]
953.	n.d. To [?]. Unrecovered. Incomplete. Printed in *Memoirs*, 1:98–101; partially printed in Miller, pp. 29–31.	[——?]
954.	n.d. To [?]. Unrecovered. Fragment. Printed in *Memoirs*, 1:149.	[——?]
955.	n.d. To [?]. Unrecovered. Fragment. Printed in *Memoirs*, 1:161–64. May not be a letter.	[——?]
956.	n.d. To [?]. Unrecovered. Fragment. Printed in *Memoirs*, 1:169–70.	[——?]
957.	n.d. To [?]. Unrecovered. Fragment. Printed in *Memoirs*, 1:194–95.	[——?]
958.	n.d. To [?]. Unrecovered. Fragment. Printed in *Memoirs*, 1:195–96.	[——?]
959.	n.d. To [?]. Unrecovered. Incomplete. Printed in *Memoirs*, 1:196–97.	[——?]

960. n.d. [——?]
To [?]. Unrecovered. Fragment. Printed in *Memoirs*, 1:206–207. May not be a letter.

961. n.d. [——?]
To [?]. Unrecovered. Incomplete. Printed in *Memoirs*, 1:225–26.

962. n.d. [——?]
To [?]. Unrecovered. Fragment. Printed in *Memoirs*, 1:242.

963. n.d. [——?]
To [?]. Unrecovered. Incomplete. Printed in *Memoirs*, 1:296–97. May not be a letter.

964. n.d. [——?]
To [?]. Unrecovered. Fragment. Printed in *Memoirs*, 1:311.

965. n.d. [——?]
To [?]. Unrecovered. Fragment. Printed in *Memoirs*, 1:314.

966. n.d. [——?]
To [?]. Unrecovered. Fragment. Printed in *Memoirs*, 1:314–15.

967. n.d. [——?]
To [?]. Unrecovered. Incomplete. Printed in *Memoirs*, 2:99–100. Identified as being to a "confidential female friend."

968. n.d. [——?]
To [?]. Unrecovered. Incomplete. Printed in *Memoirs*, 2:109–10.

969. n.d. [——?]
To [?]. Unrecovered. Fragment. Printed in *Memoirs*, 2:127–28.

970. n.d. [——?]
To [?]. Unrecovered. Fragment. Printed in *Memoirs*, 2:128–29.

APPENDIX: UNLOCATED LETTERS

971. 28 December 1819 [Cambridge]
To Timothy Fuller. Mentioned in 16 January 1820 to Timothy Fuller.

972. 13 November 1823 [1829?] [Cambridge]
To [George T. Davis?]. Mentioned by Higginson in a list of mss. MB Ms. Am. 1450 (18).

A Calendar of the Letters of Margaret Fuller 129

973. 7 February 1834 [Groton?]
To James F. Clarke. Mentioned in his letter of 7 April 1834 to Fuller. *The Letters of James Freeman Clarke to Margaret Fuller*, p. 74.

974. [ca. 1 May] 1835 [Groton?]
To James F. Clarke. Mentioned in his letter of 12 May 1835 to Fuller. *The Letters of James Freeman Clarke to Margaret Fuller*, p. 94.

975. [ca. August] 1835 [Trenton Falls, N.J.]
To Timothy and Margarett C. Fuller. Mentioned in 13 August 1835 to Timothy and Margarett C. Fuller.

976. [ca. August] 1835 [Trenton Falls, N.J.]
To Ellen K. Fuller. Mentioned in 13 August 1835 to Timothy and Margarett C. Fuller.

977. [27? September 1835] [Groton]
To James F. Clarke. Mentioned in his letter of 29 September [1835]. *The Letters of James Freeman Clarke to Margaret Fuller*, p. 104.

978. 11 October 1835 [Groton]
To James F. Clarke. Mentioned in his letter of 14 October 1835. *The Letters of James Freeman Clarke to Margaret Fuller*, p. 196.

979. 7 December 1835 [Groton?]
To James F. Clarke. Mentioned in his letter of 7 January 1836. *The Letters of James Freeman Clarke to Margaret Fuller*, p. 111.

980. 14 March 1836 [Groton?]
To James F. Clarke. Mentioned in his letter of 28 March 1836. *The Letters of James Freeman Clarke to Margaret Fuller*, p. 116.

981. [ca. April?] 1836 [Groton?]
To Margarett C. Fuller. Mentioned in 21 April 1836 to Ellen K. Fuller.

982. 25 May 1836 [Groton]
To James F. Clarke. Recorded as received in Clarke's ms. journal "March 1836–Feb. 10 1839." MHi.

983. [ca. 1 July] 1836 [Groton?]
To James F. Clarke. Mentioned in his letter of 26 July 1837. *The Letters of James Freeman Clarke to Margaret Fuller*, p. 125.

984. [ca. 18 September] 1836 [Boston?]
To R. W. Emerson. Mentioned in his letter of 20 September 1836. Rusk, 2:36.

985. [ca. 15 October] 1837   [Providence]
To R. W. Emerson. Mentioned in his letter of 24 October 1837. Rusk, 2:98.

986. [ca. November?] 1837   [Providence]
To Thesta Dana. Mentioned in 18 November 1837 to Margarett C. Fuller.

987. 2 November 1837   [Providence]
To James F. Clarke. Recorded as received in Clarke's ms. Journal "March 1836—Feb. 10 1839." MHi.

988. [ca. 30 November] 1837   [Providence]
To R. W. Emerson. Mentioned in his letter of 2 December 1837. Rusk, 2:104.

989. [ca. February] 1838   [Providence]
To James F. Clarke. Implied in his letter of 1 March 1838. *The Letters of James Freeman Clarke to Margaret Fuller*, p. 128.

990. [ca. 1 March] 1838   [Providence?]
To James F. Clarke. Mentioned in his letter of 29 March 1838. *The Letters of James Freeman Clarke to Margaret Fuller*, p. 130.

991. 13 May 1838   [Providence]
To James F. Clarke. Mentioned in his letter of 21 May 1838. *The Letters of James Freeman Clarke to Margaret Fuller*, p. 131.

992. [ca. 15 July?] 1838   [Providence]
To James F. Clarke. Mentioned in his letter of 6 August 1838. *The Letters of James Freeman Clarke to Margaret Fuller*, p. 133.

993. 17 September 1838   [Providence]
To R. W. Emerson. Mentioned in his letter of 28 September 1838. Rusk, 2:163.

994. [ca. 1 October] 1838   [Providence]
To R. W. Emerson. Mentioned in his letter of 12 October 1838. Rusk, 2:167.

995. 8 March 1839 [1840?]   [——?]
To Christopher P. Cranch. Mentioned in a list of mss. made by Leonora Cranch Scott. MHi. Christopher Pearse Cranch Papers.

996. [ca. 15 April] 1839   [Jamaica Plain]
To R. W. Emerson. Mentioned in his letter of 1 May 1839. Rusk, 2:197.

A Calendar of the Letters of Margaret Fuller 131

997. [ca. 20? July?] 1839 [Jamaica Plain]
To R. W. Emerson. Mentioned in his letter of 31?
July 1839. Rusk, 2:211.

998. [ca. September] 1839 [Jamaica Plain]
To James F. Clarke. Mentioned in his letter of 8
October 1839. *The Letters of James Freeman Clarke to
Margaret Fuller,* p. 136.

999. [ca. 1 September] 1839 [Jamaica Plain]
To R. W. Emerson. Mentioned in his letter of 6
September 1839. Rusk, 2:221.

1000. [ca. 29 September] 1839 [Jamaica Plain]
To R. W. Emerson. Mentioned in his letter of 1
October 1839. Rusk, 2:226.

1001. [ca. 14 October] 1839 [Jamaica Plain]
To R. W. Emerson. Mentioned in his letter of 16
October 1839. Rusk, 2:228. May be no. 228.

1002. [ca. 21 December] 1839 [Jamaica Plain]
To R. W. Emerson. Mentioned in his letter of 23
December 1839. Rusk, 2:245.

1003. [1840] [———?]
To James F. Clarke. Mentioned in his letter of [1840].
*The Letters of James Freeman Clarke to Margaret
Fuller,* p. 141.

1004. 1 January 1840 [Jamaica Plain]
To James F. Clarke. Mentioned in his letter to T. W.
Higginson, 8 October 1883. MB Ms. Am. 1450 (199).

1005. [ca. 13 March] 1840 [Jamaica Plain]
To R. W. Emerson. Mentioned in his letter of 17
March 1840. Rusk, 2:261.

1006. [ca. 27 March] 1840 [Jamaica Plain]
To R. W. Emerson. Mentioned in his letter of 30
March 1840. Rusk, 2:270.

1007. [ca. 6 April] 1840 [Jamaica Plain]
To R. W. Emerson. Mentioned in his letter of 8
April 1840. Rusk, 2:275.

1008. [ca. 20 April] 1840 [Jamaica Plain]
To R. W. Emerson. Mentioned in his letter of 24
April 1840. Rusk, 2:291.

1009. [ca. 25 July] 1840 [Jamaica Plain]
To R. W. Emerson. Mentioned in his letter of 27
July 1840. Rusk, 2:318.

1010. [ca. 14 August] 1840 [——?]
To R. W. Emerson. Mentioned in his letter of 16
August 1840. Rusk, 2:324.

1011. 26 August 1840 [——?]
To R. W. Emerson. Mentioned in his letter of 29
August 1840. Rusk, 2:327.

1012. [ca. 4 September] 1840 [Jamaica Plain]
To R. W. Emerson. Mentioned in his letter of 6
September 1840. Rusk, 2:329.

1013. [ca. 23 September] 1840 [Jamaica Plain]
To R. W. Emerson. Implied in his letter of 25 September
1840. Rusk, 2:337.

1014. [ca. 19? October] 1840 [Boston]
To Samuel G. and Anna B. Ward. Mentioned in
25 October to William H. Channing.

1015. [ca. 20? October 1840?] [——?]
To R. W. Emerson. Mentioned in his letter of 22?
October?1840?. Rusk, 2:351.

1016. [22? October] 1840 [Jamaica Plain?]
To R. W. Emerson. Mentioned in his letter of 24
October 1840. Rusk, 2:352. Mentioned also in 22
October 1840 to Caroline Sturgis.

1017. [ca. November] 1840 [Jamaica Plain]
To Bettine von Arnim. Mentioned in 7 November
1840 to R. W. Emerson.

1018. [ca. 9 November] 1840 [Jamaica Plain]
To R. W. Emerson. Mentioned in his letter of 10
November 1840. Rusk, 2:359. May be no. 276.

1019. [ca. 17 January] 1841 [Jamaica Plain]
To R. W. Emerson. Mentioned in his letter of 19
January 1841. Rusk, 2:377.

1020. 24 February 1841 [Jamaica Plain?]
To R. W. Emerson. Mentioned in his letter of 2
March 1841. Rusk, 2:383.

1021. [ca. 20 April] 1841 [Cambridge]
To R. W. Emerson. Mentioned in his letter of 22
April 1841. Rusk, 2:394.

1022. [ca. 11 July] 1841 [Cambridge]
To R. W. Emerson. Mentioned in his letter of 13
July 1841. Rusk, 2:422.

1023. [ca. 29 July] 1841 [Cambridge]
To R. W. Emerson. Mentioned in his letter of 31
July 1841. Rusk, 2:437.

A Calendar of the Letters of Margaret Fuller   133

1024. [ca. 14 August] 1841   [Newport]
To R. W. Emerson. Mentioned in his letter of 16 August 1841. Rusk, 2:441.

1025. [Late August? 1841]   [Cambridge?]
To Ellen K. Fuller. Mentioned in Ellery Channing's letter to Margaret Fuller, 17 September [1841]. MH fMS Am 1086.

1026. 13 September 1841   [Cambridge]
To [?]. Mentioned by Higginson in a list of mss. MB Ms. Am. 1450 (18).

1027. [ca. 1? November?] 1841   [Boston?]
To R. W. Emerson. Mentioned in 9 November 1841 to R. W. Emerson.

1028. [January?] 1842   [Boston?]
To Ellery Channing. Mentioned in his letter of 26 February 1842. MH fMS Am 1086.

1029. [ca. 28 January] 1842   [Boston?]
To R. W. Emerson. Mentioned in his letter of 2 February 1842. Rusk, 3:9.

1030. [ca. late February?] 1842   [Boston?]
To Ellery Channing. Mentioned in his letter of 20 March 1842. MH fMS Am 1086.

1031. [April?] 1842   [——?]
To Ellery Channing. Mentioned in his letter of 7 May 1842. MH fMS Am 1086 (9:128).

1032. [ca. 1 May] 1842   [Cambridge?]
To Margarett C. Fuller. Mentioned in her letter of 15 May 1842. MH fMS Am 1086.

1033. [ca. 1? June] 1842   [Cambridge?]
To R. W. Emerson. Mentioned in his letter of 9 June 1842. Rusk, 3:62.

1034. [ca. 7? June] 1842   [Cambridge]
To R. W. Emerson. Mentioned in his letter of 9 June 1842. Rusk, 3:62.

1035. [ca. 29 December] 1842   [Cambridge]
To R. W. Emerson. Mentioned in his letter of 31 December 1842. Rusk, 3:107.

1036. [ca. January? 1843?]   [Cambridge]
To R. W. Emerson. Mentioned in his letter of 31 January 1843. Rusk, 3:137. May be same letter as the following.

1037. [ca. 17 January] 1843 [Cambridge]
To R. W. Emerson. Mentioned in his letter of 20 January 1843 to Lidian Emerson. Rusk, 3:128.

1038. [ca. 1 February] 1843 [Cambridge]
To James F. Clarke. Mentioned in his letter of 24 February 1843. *The Letters of James Freeman Clarke to Margaret Fuller,* p. 142.

1039. [ca. 19 February] 1843 [Cambridge]
To R. W. Emerson. Mentioned in his letter of 23 February 1843. Rusk, 3:148.

1040. 13 April 1843 [Cambridge]
To [?]. C. F. Libbie and Co. catalogue, 10 January 1912, item 594, lists the letter. "A fine, friendly letter, signed 'Margaret F.,' an unusual signature."

1041. [July] 1843 [——?]
To R. W. Emerson. Mentioned in his letter of 7 August 1843. Rusk, 3:193.

1042. [July] 1843 [——?]
To Ellery Channing. Mentioned in his letter to Richard F. Fuller, 2 August 1843. MH fMS Am 1086 (9:130).

1043. [ca. 1 November?] 1843 [Cambridge]
To R. W. Emerson. Mentioned in his letter of 5 November 1843. Rusk, 3:220.

1044. 8 November 1843 [Cambridge]
To R. W. Emerson. Mentioned by Higginson in a list of mss. MB Ms. Am. 1450 (18).

1045. [ca. December?] 1843 [Cambridge]
To Mr. Crane [Fuller's uncle]. Mentioned in 26 December 1843 to Anna B. Ward.

1046. [ca. 14 February] 1844 [Boston]
To R. W. Emerson. Mentioned in his letter of 16 February 1844. Rusk, 3:240.

1047. 15 May 1844 [Cambridge?]
To Eugene Fuller. Mentioned in copy of diary 15 May 1844. MB Ms. Am. 1450 (99).

1048. 4 July 1844 [Concord]
To Caroline Sturgis. Mentioned in Fuller journal, 1844. MHi.

1049. 16 July 1844 [Concord]
To Samuel G. Ward. Mentioned in Fuller Journal, 1844. MHi.

1050. 31 July 1844 [Cambridge?]
To Sophia [Peabody?]. Mentioned in Fuller journal, 1844. MHi.

1051. 9 August 1844 [Cambridge?]
To Horace Greeley. Mentioned in Fuller journal, 1844. MHi.

1052. 22 July 1845 [New York]
To George Bancroft. Mentioned in 22 July 1845 to James Nathan.

1053. 15 August 1845 [New York]
To James Nathan. Mentioned in 31 August 1845 to Nathan.

1054. [ca. November?] 1845 [Boston?]
To Dr. Howe. Mentioned in 16 November 1845 to Anna B. Ward.

1055. [14? July] 1846 [New York]
To Edward Everett. Mentioned in 14 July 1846 to Richard F. Fuller.

1056. [ca. Autumn? 1846?] [London]
To Margaret and Mary Gillies. Implied in letter of Carlyle to Emerson, 14 May 1852. *The Correspondence of Emerson and Carlyle,* ed. Joseph Slater (New York: Columbia University Press, 1964), p. 479.

1057. [October 1846] [London]
To Jane Carlyle. Mentioned in her letter of [October 1846]. Emma Detti, *Margaret Fuller Ossoli e i suoi Corrispondenti* (Florence: Felice Le Monnier, 1942), p. 347.

1058. [November 1847] [London]
To Giuseppi Mazzini. Mentioned in his letter of [November 1846]. Detti, p. 264.

1059. [ca. 3 November] 1846 [London]
To [Eliza Farrar?]. Mentioned in 3 November 1846 to Richard F. Fuller.

1060. [ca. 3? November] 1846 [London]
To Arthur B. Fuller. Mentioned in 3 November 1846 to Richard F. Fuller.

1061. [ca. 3? November] 1846 [London]
To Margarett C. Fuller. Mentioned in 3 November 1846 to Richard F. Fuller.

1062. [ca. 1847?] [———?]
To Margarett C. Fuller. Mentioned in Emerson's letter

to Carlyle, 14 April 1852. *The Correspondence of Emerson and Carlyle,* p. 475.

1063. [ca. 15 March] 1847   [Naples]
To Elizabeth Hoar. Mentioned in September 1847 to Elizabeth Hoar.

1064. [ca. March?] 1847   [Rome?]
To Adam Mickiewicz. Mentioned in his letter, n.d. Leopold Wellisz, *The Friendship of Margaret Fuller d'Ossoli and Adam Mickiewicz* (New York: Polish Book Importing Co., 1947), p. 16; Detti, p. 312.

1065. [ca. March] 1847   [Rome]
To Carolne Sturgis. Mentioned in 22 August 1847 to Caroline Sturgis.

1066. [ca. April 1847]   [Rome]
To Adam Mickiewicz. Implied in his letter of 26 April [1847]. Wellisz, p. 19; Detti, p. 309.

1067. [ca. June] 1847   [Florence]
To Arthur B. Fuller. Mentioned in 1 July 1847 to Richard F. Fuller.

1068. [ca. 20? June?] 1847   [Florence?]
To Elizabeth Hoar. Mentioned in Emerson's letter of 29 August 1847. Rusk, 3:412.

1069. 22 June 1847   [Florence]
To Benedetta Mazzini. Mentioned in her letter of 5 July 1847. Detti, p. 348.

1070. [ca. late June?] 1847   [Florence]
To Benedetta Mazzini. Mentioned in her letter of 5 July 1847. Detti, p. 348.

1071. [July?] 1847   [——?]
To Adam Mickiewicz. Mentioned in his letter of 3 August 1847. Wellisz, p. 22; Detti, p. 310.

1072. [August? 1847]   [——?]
To Adam Mickiewicz. Mentioned in his letter of 16 September [1847]. Wellisz, p. 24; Detti, p. 313.

1073. [ca. 6? September] 1847   [Milan]
To Richard F. Fuller. Mentioned in 25 September 1847 to Richard F. Fuller.

1074. [ca. 13? September] 1847   [Milan]
To Richard F. Fuller. Mentioned in 25 September 1847 to Richard F. Fuller.

A Calendar of the Letters of Margaret Fuller   137

1075. [Late? September? 1847?]   [Florence]
       To Costanza Arconati Visconti. Mentioned in her letter
       of 25 September [1847]. Detti, p. 286.

1076. [October?] 1847   [Rome]
       To Adam Mickiewicz. Implied in his letter of 17
       November 1847. Wellisz, p. 27; Detti, p. 314.

1077. 21 October 1847   [Rome]
       To [?]. Mentioned by Higginson in a list of mss. MB
       Ms. Am. 1450 (18).

1078. [ca. November?] 1847   [Rome]
       To R. W. Emerson. Mentioned in Carlyle to Emerson,
       30 November 1847. *The Correspondence of Emerson
       and Carlyle,* p. 434.

1079. [ca. November?] 1847   [Rome]
       To Giuseppi Mazzini. Mentioned in Carlyle to Emerson,
       30 November 1847. *The Correspondence of Emerson
       and Carlyle,* p. 434.

1080. [ca. November?] 1847   [Rome]
       To Thomas Carlyle. Mentioned in his letter to Emerson,
       30 November 1847. *The Correspondence of Emerson
       and Carlyle,* p. 434.

1081. [November?] 1847   [Rome]
       To Richard H. Manning. Mentioned in 16 December
       1847 to Mr. and Mrs. Manning.

1082. [November? 1847]   [Rome]
       To Costanza Arconati Visconti. Mentioned in her letter
       of 30 December [1847]. Detti, p. 291.

1083. [ca. December? 1847?]   [Rome]
       To [Wendell] Phillips. Mentioned in Fuller's *Tribune*
       essay of 30 December 1847. *At Home and Abroad,*
       p. 270.

1084. [ca. January?] 1848   [Rome]
       To the American consul at Civita Vecchia. Mentioned in
       29 May 1848 to Mary Rotch.

1085. 8 January [1848]   [Rome]
       To Costanza Arconati Visconti. Mentioned in her letter
       of 12 January [1848]. Detti, p. 292.

1086. [ca. 25 February] 1848   [Rome]
       To Elizabeth B. Browning. Mentioned in her letter of
       3 March 1848. Detti, p. 349.

1087. [ca. March] 1848   [Rome]
       To M. Mentioned in Emerson's letter of 25 April
       1848. Rusk, 4:61.

1088. [8? March] 1848 [Rome]
       To Cristina di Belgioioso. Mentioned in 8 March 1848
       to Frederic H. Hedge.

1089. [April?] 1848 [Rome]
       To Adam Mickiewicz. Mentioned in his letter of 4
       May 1848. Wellisz, p. 33; Detti, p. 315.

1090. [ca. late April?] 1848 [Rome]
       To Adam Mickiewicz. Mentioned in his letter of 4
       May 1848. Wellisz, p. 33; Detti, p. 315.

1091. [ca. 25? May] 1848 [Rome]
       To Baring and Brothers, Co. Mentioned in 3 July
       1848 to Richard F. Fuller.

1092. 13 July [1848] [Aquila]
       To [?]. Mentioned in 15 July [1848] to G. A. Ossoli.

1093. 7? December 1848 [Rome]
       To Caroline Sturgis. Mentioned in 7 December 1848
       to Richard F. Fuller.

1094. [21? January 1849] [Rome]
       To Costanza Arconati Visconti. Mentioned in 21 January to Emelyn Story and in the letter from Costanza
       Arconati Visconti to Margaret Fuller, 31 January [1849].
       Detti, p. 300.

1095. [25? January] 1849 [Rome]
       To Mrs. Ames. Mentioned in 19 January 1849 to
       Richard F. Fuller.

1096. 27 February 1849 [Rome]
       To James F. Clarke. Recorded received in Clarke
       journal, "1848." MHi.

1097. [May?] 1849 [Rome]
       To Costanza Arconati Visconti. Mentioned in her letter
       of 2 June 1849. Detti, p. 301.

1098. [26? May] 1849 [Rome]
       To Eliza Farrar. Mentioned in 28 May 1849 to
       Richard F. Fuller.

1099. [June? 1849] [Rome]
       To Giuseppi Mazzini. Implied in his letter of 20 June
       [1849]. Detti, pp. 277-78.

1100. [ca. 13? July] 1849 [Rieti]
       To Thomas Carlyle. Mentioned in Carlyle's letter to
       Emerson, 13 August 1849. *The Correspondence of
       Emerson and Carlyle*, p. 456.

1101. [August] 1849 [Rieti]
To Adam Mickiewicz. Mentioned in his letter of 9 September 1849. Wellisz, p. 37; Detti, p. 316.

1102. [ca. 1 October] 1849 [Florence]
To Costanza Arconati Visconti. Mentioned in her letter of 5 October 1849. Detti, p. 302.

1103. [ca. 3? October] 1849 [Florence]
To Anna B. Ward. Mentioned in 21 October 1849 to Samuel G. Ward.

1104. [ca. November? 1849] [Florence]
To Margarett C. Fuller. Mentioned in 6 February 1850 to Margarett C. Fuller.

1105. [ca. March] 1850 [Florence]
To R. W. Emerson. Implied in Emerson's letter of 1 April 1850. Rusk, 4:198.

1106. [16? April] 1850 [Florence]
To Madame Mohl. Mentioned in 16 April 1850 to Emelyn Story.

1107. [18 January, n.y.] [——?]
To James F. Clarke. Recorded received in Clarke journal, n.d. MHi.

INDEX

This Index is divided into two parts: Recipients and Libraries. Included in the former are the unlocated letters listed in the Appendix (numbers 971–1107).

A. RECIPIENTS

Alcott, Amos Bronson, 127, 141, 148, 226, 254
Ames, Mrs., 1095
Arconati Visconti, Constanza, 687, 705, 707, 777, 820, 840, 875, 876, 878, 879, 1075, 1082, 1085, 1094, 1097, 1102
Arnim, Bettine von, 1017

Bancroft, George, 1052
Baring and Brothers, Company, 1091
Barlow, Almira Peniman, 69, 93, 97, 101, 119, 181, 187, 257
Belgioioso, Christina di, 1088

Brown, Mrs. Nicholas, 907
Browning, Elizabeth Barrett, 850, 1086
Bruce, Georgiana, 435, 467, 473, 485, 494, 513, 567, 587, 904

Calvert, J. C., 882
Calvert, Mrs. George H., 188
Carlyle, Jane, 1057
Carlyle, Thomas, 1080, 1100
Cass, Lewis, Jr., 799, 800, 802, 805, 813, 815, 816, 818, 822, 824, 830, 832, 837, 838, 857, 861, 868, 873, 880
Channing, Barbara, 460

Channing, Ellen. *See* Ellen Kilshaw Fuller.
Channing, Ellery (William Ellery Channing the Younger), 321, 1028, 1030, 1031, 1042
Channing, Margaret Fuller (Greta), 689
Channing, William Henry, 190, 237, 239, 248, 251, 268, 269, 271, 274, 278, 281, 283–85, 288, 291–93, 295–97, 305, 310, 312, 314, 348, 362, 364, 369, 370, 374, 381, 385, 388, 405, 421, 429, 441, 451, 474, 487, 488, 500, 508, 583, 634, 649, 694, 760, 785, 817, 826, 835, 869, 901, 909–12
Chapman, Maria Weston, 287
Child, Lydia Maria Francis, 444
Clarke, Anna Huidekoper, 390
Clarke, James Freeman, 63–67, 75, 76, 81–85, 88, 90, 96, 102, 106, 118, 122, 192, 256, 373, 397, 446, 496, 641, 899, 913, 973, 974, 977–80, 982, 983, 987, 989–92, 998, 1003, 1004, 1038, 1096, 1107
Clarke, Marianne, 428
Clarke, Sarah Freeman, 408, 770, 846
Clough, Arthur Hugh, 808, 865
Coleman, Henry, 696
Cranch, Christopher Pearse, 481, 995
Cranch, Elizabeth De Windt, 701, 784
Crane, Mr., 1045
Curtis, George William, 655, 842

Dana, Thesta, 174, 986
Davis, George Thomas, 393, 914, 915, 972
Delf, Thomas, 620, 624
Duyckinck, Evert Augustus, 591, 593, 598, 604, 609, 611, 612, 614, 616, 628, 650
Dwight, John Sullivan, 144, 347, 631

Earle, Pliny, 574
Emerson, Lydia Jackson, 178
Emerson, Ralph Waldo, 130, 131, 137, 138, 143, 145, 150, 155, 171, 176, 191, 201, 212, 229–31, 233, 238, 242, 245, 249, 250, 252, 253, 258, 260, 266, 275–77, 282, 289, 299, 300, 304, 316–19, 327, 329, 330, 351–53, 357, 358, 365, 371, 377, 382, 387, 391, 392, 395, 403, 409, 413, 414, 417, 420, 427, 431, 433, 440, 442, 454, 466, 468, 482, 489, 495, 547, 610, 629, 633, 636, 639, 643, 653, 660, 674, 680, 692, 700, 703, 715, 774, 811, 916–18, 984, 985, 988, 993, 994, 996, 997, 999–1002, 1005–1013, 1015, 1016, 1018–24, 1027, 1029, 1033–37, 1039, 1041, 1043, 1044, 1046, 1078, 1105
Everett, Edward, 1055

Farrar, Eliza Rotch, 80, 120, 121, 1059, 1098
Francis, Mrs., 432
Fuller, Abraham Williams, 47, 48, 111, 112, 172
Fuller, Arthur Buckminster, 95, 151, 166, 170, 175, 195, 204, 286, 450, 462, 773, 1060, 1067
Fuller, Ellen Kilshaw, 124, 128, 685, 786, 812, 821, 851, 976, 1025
Fuller, Eugene, 113, 115, 117, 205, 213, 518, 1047
Fuller, Frances (Mrs. William Henry), 448
Fuller, Hiram, 210
Fuller, James Lloyd, 175
Fuller, Margarett Crane, 16, 28–30, 68, 107, 108, 158, 164, 307, 309, 311, 313, 315, 322, 336–38, 341, 343, 344, 346, 349, 506, 618, 635, 658, 669, 678, 757, 771, 783, 819, 839, 862, 884, 919, 975, 981, 1032, 1061, 1062, 1104
Fuller, Richard Frederick, 89, 175, 186, 241, 255, 298, 301, 326, 328, 331, 333, 334, 339, 342, 345, 359, 360, 366, 376, 378, 406, 415, 422, 443, 465, 476, 483, 491, 503, 505, 516, 517, 522, 526, 559, 563, 568, 572, 580, 582, 585, 588, 590, 594, 603, 605, 607, 617, 621, 623, 630, 632, 640, 645, 654, 657, 666, 668, 676, 682, 686, 688, 693, 704, 712, 713, 728, 758, 763, 772, 778, 788, 801, 803, 814, 856, 867, 920, 921, 1073, 1074
Fuller, Sarah B., 18
Fuller, Timothy, 1–8, 10, 11, 13–15, 19–27, 31–42, 44–46, 49–52, 68, 107, 108, 971, 975

Gillies, Margaret, 1056
Gillies, Mary, 1056
Greeley, Horace, 599, 825, 905, 1051
Greene, Albert Gorton, 167, 267
Greenough, Mrs., 874
Greenwood, Amelia, 12, 43, 94, 887–89

Hawthorne, Nathaniel, 400, 548

Hawthorne, Sophia. See Sophia Peabody.
Hedge, Frederic Henry, 87, 98–100, 103–105, 129, 136, 153, 240, 247, 394, 683, 691
Hicks, Thomas, 702
Hoar, Elizabeth, 126, 209, 222, 294, 325, 350, 354, 363, 375, 389, 399, 401, 411, 447, 484, 556, 562, 638, 665, 675, 834, 930, 1063, 1068
Hooker, J. C., 719, 723
Howe, Dr., 1054
Howitt, Mary, 626, 647

Ireland, Alexander, 619, 625

James, Henry, Sr., 426
Jameson, Anna, 165

Kilshaw, Ellen, 9

Lamennais, Félicité Robert de, 637
Lane, Charles, 464, 470
Little, Mr., 456
Little and Brown, Company, 458
Longfellow, Henry Wadsworth, 407
Loring, Anna, 453, 498, 504, 527, 581
Loring, Ellis Gray, 570
Loring, Louisa, 570

Manning, Richard H., 679, 1081
Manning, Mrs. Richard H., 602, 679
Marston, J. Westland, 664
Martineau, Harriet, 149
Mazzini, Benedetta, 1069, 1070
Mazzini, Giuseppi, 780, 1058, 1079, 1099
Mickiewicz, Adam, 1064, 1066, 1071, 1072, 1076, 1089, 1090, 1101
Mohl, Madame, 1106

Nathan, James, 509–11, 514, 515, 521, 523–25, 528–33, 535–46, 549–55, 557, 558, 565, 566, 569, 571, 573, 575, 586, 595, 601, 608, 1053
Neal, John, 261
Newcomb, Charles King, 180, 185, 189, 202, 206, 211, 246, 303, 306, 320, 368, 372, 383, 386, 396, 410, 459, 463, 492, 709, 761, 900, 933–37

Ossoli, Giovanni Angelo, 648, 710, 711, 714, 716–18, 720–22, 724, 725, 727, 729–56, 765–67, 790–98, 807, 809, 823

Page, Mr., 699

Parker, Theodore, 931
Peabody, Elizabeth Palmer, 142, 152, 497
Peabody, Sophia, 361, 548, 1050
Phillips, Wendell, 1083
Poore, Benjamin Perley, 642
Putnam, Mr., 627

Ripley, George, 200
Ripley, Sarah, 223
Rotch, Maria, 423, 439, 477, 652, 776
Rotch, Mary, 340, 356, 402, 404, 419, 438, 507, 584, 589, 597, 651, 670, 706, 891
Rotch, Mrs., 697

Shaw, Francis G., 673
Shaw, Sarah, 412, 437, 472, 475, 490, 512, 560, 576–78, 600, 644, 672, 902
Spring, Marcus, 656, 659, 667, 759, 782, 852, 860, 883, 885
Spring, Rebecca, 656, 852, 860, 883
Stimson, Mrs., 445
Stirling, Miss, 690
Story, Emelyn Eldredge, 671, 708, 762, 769, 775, 779, 804, 806, 810, 828, 844, 847, 864, 871, 872, 877
Story, William Wetmore, 764, 849, 881, 938
Sturgis, Caroline, 140, 147, 154, 156, 159–63, 168, 169, 173, 177, 182, 193, 194, 196–99, 203, 216–18, 220, 225, 234–36, 244, 259, 262–65, 270, 272, 273, 279, 290, 302, 308, 323, 355, 367, 379, 384, 452, 455, 457, 471, 520, 534, 564, 592, 613, 622, 663, 684, 781, 787, 827, 848, 903, 939–41, 1048, 1065, 1093
Swan, Sarah Hodges, 478

Tappan, Caroline. See Caroline Sturgis.
Thom, David, 519
Thompson, Samuel, 886
Thompson, Mrs. Samuel, 886
Thoreau, Henry David, 280, 324, 424
Tracy, Albert H., 418, 425, 430
Tuckerman, Jane F., 133, 139, 146, 179, 184, 215, 221, 469, 662, 695, 768, 942

Vose, Mary, 17

Ward, Anna Barker, 434, 449, 579, 596, 789, 855, 943, 1014, 1103
Ward, Mary G., 944
Ward, Samuel Gray, 123, 219, 224, 227, 332, 335, 380, 416, 499, 596, 615, 841, 843, 855, 866, 1014, 1049

Welby, E., 829, 831
Weston, Anne Warren, 890
Whitman, Sarah Helen, 214, 243
Wiley and Putnam, Publishers, 606
Women Inmates of Sing Sing, 486

Unidentified, 53–62, 70–74, 77–79, 86, 91, 92, 109, 110, 114, 116, 125, 132, 134, 135, 157, 183, 207, 208, 228, 232, 398, 436, 461, 479, 480, 493, 501, 502, 561, 646, 661, 677, 681, 698, 726, 833, 836, 845, 853, 854, 858, 859, 863, 870, 892–98, 906, 908, 922–29, 932, 945–70, 1026, 1040, 1077, 1084, 1087, 1092

B. LIBRARIES

Amsterdam (Holland), University Library of, 655

Barnard College, 430
Bodleian (Oxford), 808, 865
Boston Athenæum, 460
Boston Public Library, 71, 87, 131, 136, 137, 141, 143–45, 148, 150, 155, 157, 171, 190, 191, 201, 207, 208, 226, 231, 239, 248, 250, 251, 253, 254, 258, 260, 269, 274, 275, 278, 283, 285, 287, 292, 293, 297, 300, 305, 310, 312, 314, 318, 358, 362, 391, 414, 421, 424, 429, 432, 474, 481, 487, 488, 497, 500, 508–11, 514, 515, 521, 523–25, 528–33, 535–46, 549–55, 557, 558, 561, 565, 566, 569, 571, 573, 575, 583, 586, 595, 608, 634, 646, 681, 695, 701, 702, 708, 709, 760, 761, 768, 781, 784, 785, 816–18, 824, 827, 828, 830, 833–35, 837, 851, 853, 858, 859, 861, 863, 864, 867–71, 875–79, 884, 890, 901, 915, 945, 946
Brown University, 167, 223, 267, 907
Buffalo and Erie County Public Library, 690

California, University of, at Berkeley, 619
Cambridge Public Library, 478
Columbia University, 454, 625, 762

Essex Institute, 620, 624

Fruitlands Museums, 354, 401, 418, 425, 428, 444, 556, 562, 675, 842, 930

Harvard University, 1–11, 13–42, 44–52, 58, 68, 69, 80, 84, 85, 87, 89, 90, 93–105, 107–109, 111–15, 119, 124, 126–31, 133, 137, 139–41, 143, 145–48, 151, 153–56, 158–64, 166, 168–73, 175–87, 189, 193–99, 201–206, 209, 211–13, 215–21, 223–27, 229–36, 240–42, 244, 246, 249, 250, 252–55, 257–60, 262–66, 270, 272, 273, 275, 277–79, 282, 286, 289, 290, 294, 298-304, 306–309, 311, 313, 315–23, 325–46, 349–60, 365–68, 371, 372, 375–80, 382, 383, 386, 387, 389–91, 393–96, 399, 402, 404, 406, 407, 409, 410, 412, 414–17, 419, 420, 422, 423, 427, 431, 434, 437–43, 447–52, 455, 457, 459, 462, 463, 465, 466, 468, 469, 471, 475–77, 482–84, 489–92, 495–97, 499, 502, 503, 505–507, 512, 516–18, 520, 522, 526, 534, 547, 559, 560, 563, 564, 568, 572, 576, 578–80, 582, 584, 585, 588–90, 592, 594, 596, 597, 600, 603, 605, 607, 610, 613, 615, 617, 621, 623, 629, 630, 632, 633, 635, 636, 640, 641, 644, 645, 648, 651–54, 656–59, 662, 663, 665–70, 672, 673, 675, 676, 678, 682–86, 688, 689, 691, 693, 695, 700, 704, 706, 707, 710, 711, 713–56, 758, 761, 763, 765–73, 776, 778–80, 783, 785–807, 809, 814, 815, 820, 822, 823, 829–32, 836, 838–41, 843, 844, 847–49, 851, 852, 855–57, 860, 862, 866, 867, 872, 873, 875, 877, 878, 880–83, 885, 887, 900, 902, 903, 906, 913, 916, 919, 920, 933–37, 939–43
Haverford College, 642

Iowa State Department of History, 627
Iowa, University of, 905

Long Island Historical Society, 456

Maine Historical Society, 647, 886
Marietta (Ohio) College, 606
Massachusetts Historical Society, 188, 384, 408, 464, 470, 577, 631
Middlebury College, 200, 472, 697, 850

New York Historical Society, 664

New York Public Library (Berg and Manuscripts Divisions), 78, 361, 400, 426, 548, 591, 593, 598, 599, 604, 609, 611, 612, 614, 616, 628, 650

Pennsylvania, Historical Society of, 142, 602, 931
Pennsylvania State University, 12, 626
Pierpont Morgan Library, 280, 881
Princeton University, 625, 846
Providence Athenæum, 445

Radcliffe College (Schlesinger Library), 453, 574, 581, 699

Rhode Island Historical Society, 243
Rochester, University of, 411

Stanford University, 485

Texas, University of, 138, 324, 671, 775, 904

Virginia, University of, 173, 210, 214, 222, 261, 446, 458, 473, 513, 519, 679, 696, 845, 874, 891, 921

Wellesley College, 498, 504, 527, 570

Yale University, 165, 174, 888, 889, 932

CHRISTOPHER PEARSE CRANCH, ROBERT BROWNING, AND THE PROBLEM OF "TRANSCENDENTAL" FRIENDSHIP

David Robinson

THE THIRTY YEAR INTERVAL between Christopher Pearse Cranch's first collection of verse, *Poems* (1844), and the successive publications of *Satan* (1874) and *The Bird and the Bell* (1875)[1] is marked by many apparent changes in a man characterized as one of the most restless of the Transcendentalists.[2] Much of this period was spent overseas, where Cranch, in the company of numerous other American intellectuals, was establishing himself as a successful, if not brilliant, landscape painter, and somewhat later in America, as an accomplished translator of the *Aeneid*.[3] But the themes to which he returned in his later poetry are remarkably similar to those of the early poems which won the praise of Emerson, and even Poe.[4] What is striking, however, in the second collection, *The Bird and the Bell*, is the personal flavor of many of the poems which are written to, or about, the literary figures Cranch had come to know in Europe. While the early poems have rightly been characterized as poetic paraphrases of Emersonian doctrine,[5] some of the later poems seem to test that doctrine in the vivid terms of a man whom Perry Miller characterizes as "a social being."[6]

Despite his social graces, and his continuing reputation as "the most delightful of the Transcendental group,"[7] Cranch was haunted by a conviction of loneliness, marred and imperfect friendship, and even rejection by others. One can note a hint of this feeling in "A Friend":

> We smile and clasp the hands
> With merry fellows o'er cigars and wine;
> We breakfast, walk, and dine
> With social men and women. Yes, we are friends;
> And there the music ends![8]

These may appear wistful, even maudlin sentiments until they are put in the context of one of the most striking, and puzzling, poems in the same volume, "Veils." The poem begins with the memory of a friendship that transcends ordinary social bounds:

> Once we called each other friends.
> 'T was no formal greeting
> When we clasped each other's hands;
> Soul with soul came meeting.
>
> (100)

Here the clasp of the hands, the sign of merely formal friendship in "A Friend," is the outward sign of a deeper communion of souls. But, turning away from the past, the poet depicts the current dissolution of this tie:

> Other friends now come between,
> Other love outstrips me.
> Can my light be then so dull
> That they all eclipse me?
> Often have I longed for you;
> Often have I wondered
> Why we two, whose thoughts were one,
> Ever should be sundered.
>
> (100)

The presence in the volume of so many other poems of personal reference raises the question of an actual biographical source for the poem, and perhaps intentionally, Cranch provides enough evidence to identify Robert Browning as the unnamed friend and subject of the poem.

Cranch, through an introduction by Margaret Fuller, had met Robert Browning in Florence, in December 1848, and was immediately impressed by his "true, social, healthy, open, frank nature," that of a man "entering into life and associating with men, while inwardly delicate and poetic."[9] When Browning returned Cranch's first visit with calls to his home and studio, Cranch called them "good, long, real and not formal visits."[10] After another visit of Browning to his studio in January 1849, he called him "a most genial man to whom I feel drawn exceedingly."[11] In these early meetings, at which Elizabeth Barrett Browning was sometimes present, Cranch saw Browning as someone beyond social formality, and was drawn to what he felt was the inner delicacy, or "soul," of the poet. As Cranch was to recall later in his "Personal Reminiscences" of Browning, "The natural feeling of remoteness in our first admission to the society of two such distinguished poets was soon dissipated by their frank and genial hospitality. We saw them often, and it is needless to say that the privilege of this acquaintance gave added charms to our residence that winter in Florence."[12]

The impact of these meetings was all the greater for Cranch when one considers his feeling that he "knew" Browning before meeting him through his writings. Thus in "Veils," the relationship is depicted as having begun before any actual meeting.

> Long ago I loved your books,
> (They first drew me to you);
> Loved you better than you thought;
> Ere I saw you knew you.
>
> (100)

Cranch himself dates the beginning of his knowledge of Browning in the mid-1840s in his "Reminiscences" of 1892: "My first acquaintance with Browning's works dates back to over forty-five years ago, when I was one of a comparatively small circle of the readers and admirers of the first of his books known in America. I well remember with what fresh delight and enthusiasm we read them."[13] Cranch is recounting in personal terms the impact of Browning on the Transcendentalists, one of the earliest phases of his growing American popularity. This regard for Browning's poetry was no transient enthusiasm for Cranch, who wrote in a letter of 1853 that "He is, in my opinion, the great poet of the day. I don't know anyone teeming with such rich life and thought as Browning."[14]

There is more, however, than the parallels of the relationship depicted in "Veils" and these 1848 and 1849 meetings to indicate Browning as its subject. Cranch closes the poem with the realization that the friendship can only continue in a realm totally apart from society, the imaginative realm where they first met as poet and reader:

> You and I will speak in dreams
> Loves not unrequited,
> As we met ten years ago,
> Happy and united.
>
> (105)

The specific mention of the meeting "ten years ago" is significant in light of the date Cranch affixes to the poem, "Rome, 1859." The growing possibility that the ten year period refers to the 1848–49 meetings of Cranch and Browning is confirmed by further evidence of their last meeting. Again in later years, Cranch briefly recalls the meeting: "I met Browning again in London in 1855—also in Paris—and in 1859 in Rome. But he was then moving much in aristocratic society, and we saw less both of him and his wife."[15] The reference is brief, but its lack of explanation is revealing. Cranch does not explain the apparent drifting apart because he himself fails to understand it. He only knows his own exclusion in favor of the "aristocrats" whom he feels do not really "know" the poet.

> There are those who cling to you
>   As their lamp and fuel,
> Or who wear you on their fronts
>   Like a glittering jewel;
> ....
> Happy if they can be seen
>   With you closely talking,
> Proud, if arm in arm with you
>   In the street they're walking.
>
> (101)

The time between the first and last meetings of Cranch and Browning were years of accelerating fame for both Brownings, which certainly accounts for the social success Cranch observed from without. *Men and Women* had been published in 1855, and the popularity of both the Brownings was growing. With poetic success came social success, and Browning's love for Rome's society was confirmed in the winter of 1858–59, when, as Louise Greer notes, "Browning was caught up in the social whirl which his wife considered much giddier than that of Paris, and hardly spent one night at home in a fortnight."[16] Cranch himself was in Rome at this time, painting and seeking buyers for his works, but also caught in the round of parties and balls that made the city such an attraction to foreigners. "Every evening this week past has been occupied with visits or parties, except one,"[17] he wrote his wife in January 1859. The immediate threat of war in Rome, and his eventual decision to return to America a few years later, prevented Cranch from returning, and, sadly, from meeting Browning again. Whatever prevented their satisfactory communication in Rome—the impenetrability of social forms, differing social circles, or in Cranch's words, "Time and space and circumstance" (102)—the split left Cranch to continue his relation with Browning only through Browning's works.

Whatever biographical interest the relation holds for us, it poses a much more important poetic problem, especially in light of Cranch's poetic career. It is significant that "The Bird and the Bell," the title poem of the volume containing "Veils," was read in manuscript and criticized by both Brownings, whose poetic opinion Cranch valued highly.[18] More important, however, is the obvious allusion of the title of "Veils" to Cranch's most widely popular poem, "Enosis." The second and third stanzas of "Enosis," probably its most memorable, pose in abstract terms the actual problem Cranch later faced in his relation with Browning:

> We are spirits clad in veils;
>   Man by man was never seen;
> All our deep communing fails
>   To remove the shadowy screen.
>
> Heart to heart was never known;
>   Mind with mind did never meet;
> We are columns left alone
>   Of a temple once complete.[19]

The "veils" of this poem are unmistakably the veils Cranch faces in his relation with Browning. But in "Veils," the metaphors of "Enosis" become less symbolic, and more literally descriptive. Thus the "shadowy screen" of "Enosis" becomes the shaded window barring Cranch from his friend:

> Time and space and circumstance
>   Barred me from your presence.
> Then behind your veils you seemed
>   Some dim phosphorescence.
> Half-transparent window shades
>   Told where you were sitting,
> And your astral lamp, half blurred,
>   Threw your shadow flitting
> Up against the curtain-folds.
>
> (102)

The similarity of both the theme and imagery of the two poems suggests a conscious echoing by Cranch, and as a result, a testing of transcendental doctrine. If "Enosis" suggested an Emersonian solution to the abstract question of isolation, "Veils" tests that solution emotionally in a concrete social situation.

The personal problem developing in the two decades between "Enosis" and "Veils" was what one critic has called Cranch's "extraordinary diffidence," an intense personal shyness that "made everyday life a trial."[20] One can, of course, account for Cranch's reputation as an engaging social personality in terms of a need to compensate for his deeper shyness, but, whatever its other causes and results, it has poetic and philosophical ramifications. The transcendental doctrine of the unity of man, which stressed an ultimate personal communion beyond ordinary social contact, offered Cranch a theoretical solution to his loneliness. Shyness or diffidence, viewed ideally, only meant the recognition of the infinity of the soul of each individual, ultimately unknowable in a social context because of its infinite nature. Interpreters of "Enosis" have tended to stress the opening despair and isolation of the poem rather than its closing affirmation, seeing it, in Levenson's terms, as an expression of "the atomistic side of Transcendental social theory."[21] Perhaps Cranch speaks more honestly of isolation than communion, or perhaps his images of isolation conform more readily to a modern view of human relations. His intention, however, was to depict the superficial isolation of individuals in order to emphasize their deeper, or higher, unity. Thus the poem turns when Cranch attacks the superficiality of society: "What is social company / But a babbling summer stream?" (*Poems*, p. 51). After this question, Cranch spends the last three stanzas establishing a communion transcending social intercourse, culminating the poem in a final image of unity rather than isolation:

> We like parted drops of rain
> Swelling till they meet and run,
> Shall be all absorbed again,
> Melting, flowing into one.
>
> (*Poems*, p. 52)

In abstract terms, then, Cranch affirms Emerson's "great discovery that there is one Mind common to all individual men; that what is individual is less than what is universal."[22]

But can one live out such a philosophy? The question plagued Emerson, who struggled against guilt for his "coldness," and almost every other Transcendentalist made at best a partial truce with the dilemma posed by the unsatisfactory nature of social relations and the unrequited need for human contact. Transcendental communion answered the problem philosophically, but how rare was the person who could, in Thoreau's unforgettable image, "talk across the pond to a visitor on the opposite side."[23]

Cranch's more concrete approach to the problem in the later poem, "Veils," suggests the emotional cost of trying to maintain a transcendental friendship. The three part structure of the poem suggested by Cranch's spatial divisions offers an opening meditation on the possible causes of the friendship's end (ll. 1–44), and a closing attempt to respond to the breakup (ll. 97–124), but centers on the actual social exclusion that signals the end of the friendship. Cranch pictures himself waiting for Browning who, "When the guests are gone" will "come / Where I'm waiting lonely" (102). The vision is one of restored communion, a reference to the four year interval (1855-59) since their last meeting.

> We will pace his garden-walks,
>   Of the past discoursing.
> All his heart will open, free
>   From convention's forcing
>
> (103)

But instead, Cranch feels a "chill between his [Browning's] words" as he asks him to return "to-morrow" (103). The pain he feels as a result is not, as he depicts it, the result of a social snub, but rather a realization that there is less in the relation than he expected or hoped. Again, fashionable society is the problem for Cranch, coming between real communion between the two men. Thus he begins the final section of the poem with a bitter admission of the "veils" between them:

> "Were we far from fashion's forms
>   In some desert gloomy,
> You might learn to know me then;
>   For you never knew me!"
>
> (104)

The poetry of "Veils" is far inferior to that of "Enosis," but the pain of loneliness seems more real, or at least more accessible. Perhaps for that reason, Cranch's final attempt to return to the purely ideal communion of poet and reader as a source of solace fails to convince even himself:

> "I will read your books again;
>   They at least will lead me
> Into walks where we may meet,
>   Though you do not need me."
>
> (105)

The final despairing line of this quatrain carries far more emotional weight than the earlier attempt at self-comfort. Similarly, the images of "cold estrangement" and "Loves not requited" in the last lines of the poem overshadow the "fancy" and "dreams" (105) which are left as alternatives to an actual relation between the men.

After reading "Veils" in the context of the friendship of Cranch and Browning, one cannot but be struck by the following brief passage from Cranch's late reminiscences after Browning's death:

At the time I first knew him he was thirty-seven years old. He wore no beard or moustache, and his hair was nearly black. This was his appearance the last time I saw him. The later photographs of him, with gray hair and full gray beard, do not help me in the least to a recollection of his face.[24]

This is Cranch in old age recalling as fact what, in earlier years, he only feared:

> "I will fancy you the same
> As in that bright weather
> Ere this cold estrangement came,—"
>
> (105)

NOTES

1. Christopher Pearse Cranch, *Poems* (Philadelphia: Carey and Hart, 1844); *Satan: A Libretto* (Boston: Roberts, 1874); *The Bird and the Bell, with Other Poems* (Boston: James R. Osgood, 1875). Cranch's volumes of poetry have recently been collected in a facsimile edition, *Collected Poems of Christopher Pearse Cranch*, ed. Joseph M. De Falco (Gainesville, Fla.: Scholars' Facsimiles and Reprints, 1971).

2. Elizabeth R. McKinsey, *The Western Experiment: New England Transcendentalists in the Ohio Valley* (Cambridge: Harvard University Press, 1973), pp. 36–39.

3. *The Aeneid of Virgil Translated into English Blank Verse*, trans. Cranch (Boston: James R. Osgood, 1872).

4. Emerson greeted Cranch's submission of two poems to the *Dial* in 1840 with a letter of acceptance calling them "true" and "brilliant" and "one more authentic sign—added to four or five I have reckoned already—of a decided poetic taste, and tendency to original observation in our Cambridge circle" (Leonora Cranch Scott, *The Life and Letters of Christopher Pearse Cranch* [Boston: Houghton Mifflin, 1917], p. 59; hereafter cited as *Life and Letters*). Poe offered grudging, but impressive, praise, considering his contempt for the Transcendentalists, calling Cranch, "one of the least intolerable of the school of Boston transcendentalists," possessing an "unusual vivacity of fancy and dexterity expression." Poe's liking for Cranch was so out of character that he concluded that Cranch "has at last 'come out from among them [the Transcendentalists],' abandoned their doctrines (whatever they are)." Poe's sketch of Cranch is included in "The Literati of New York City" (1846); see *The Complete Works of Edgar Allan Poe*, ed. James A. Harrison (New York: Thomas Y. Crowell, 1902; rpt. ed., New York: AMS Press, 1965), 15:69–72.

5. Perry Miller calls his contributions to the *Dial* "resolute attempts to turn Transcendental metaphysics into poetry" (*The Transcendentalists: An Anthology* [Cambridge: Harvard University Press, 1950], p. 385). J. C. Levenson, noting the Emersonian themes of Cranch's earlier poems, concludes that "Cranch's intellectual grasp of the richness and uses of symbolism was far less competent than Emerson's" ("Christopher Pearse Cranch: The Case History of a Minor Artist in America," *American Literature*, 21 [January 1950]: 421).

6. Miller, *The Transcendentalists*, p. 179.
7. Miller, *The Transcendentalists*, p. 179. The most well-known sketch of Cranch is that of Van Wyck Brooks who characterizes him as "the all-attractive entertainer" to the friends he visited in the commune at Brook Farm (*The Flowering of New England, 1815–1865* [New York: E. P. Dutton, 1936], p. 250).
8. *The Bird and the Bell*, p. 59; hereafter cited in the text by page.
9. *Life and Letters*, p. 156.
10. *Life and Letters*, p. 157.
11. *Life and Letters*, p. 157.
12. Cranch, "Personal Reminiscences," *In Memoriam; Memorial to Robert Browning* (Cambridge: Browning Society of Boston, 1892), p. 49; hereafter cited as "Personal Reminiscences."
13. "Personal Reminiscences," p. 48.
14. *Life and Letters*, p. 215.
15. "Personal Reminiscences," p. 49.
16. Louise Greer, *Browning and America* (Chapel Hill: University of North Carolina Press, 1952), p. 65.
17. *Life and Letters*, p. 237.
18. *Life and Letters*, pp. 157–61.
19. *Poems* (1844), p. 51. First published as "Stanzas" in the first issue of the *Dial*, 1 (July 1840): 98.
20. McKinsey, *The Western Experiment*, p. 38. McKinsey's characterization of Cranch is supported both by the evidence of his problematic friendship with Browning, and by Hazen C. Carpenter's discussion of his somewhat unsuccessful attempts to maintain a relation with Emerson. His letter of 1855 to Emerson, complaining of his "need of a voice and touch that come near to me in my solitude" is quoted at length by Carpenter in "Emerson and Christopher Pearse Cranch," *New England Quarterly*, 37 (March 1964): 34.
21. Levenson, "Cranch," 420. Paul O. Williams, "The Persistence of Cranch's 'Enosis,'" *Emerson Society Quarterly*, No. 57 (4th Quarter 1969): 44, concurs, arguing that "such laments for lost organic unity were common among transcendental poets." Carpenter, the exception here, stresses the affirmative ending of the poem (24).
22. *The Early Lectures of Ralph Waldo Emerson*, ed. Stephen E. Whicher, Robert E. Spiller, Wallace E. Williams (Cambridge: Harvard University Press, 1959–72), 2:11.
23. *The Writings of Henry D. Thoreau* (Princeton: Princeton University Press, 1971–), vol. 1, *Walden*, ed. J. Lyndon Shanley (1971), p. 141.
24. "Personal Reminiscenses," p. 49.

ORIGINS OF THE AMERICAN RENAISSANCE: A FRONT-PAGE STORY

C. E. Frazer Clark, Jr.

STUDIES IN THE AMERICAN RENAISSANCE should begin with long-overdue recognition of the indispensable and influential role of the American press in the promotion and spread of America's native literature.

The moving force behind the spirit of American literary independence and the first instrument of the American Renaissance was the American newspaper, where American authorship and literature were regularly front-page news. A knowledge of the existence and work of the writers who were creating American literature was important news at a time when the newspaper was the sole mass-media communication available. The earliest writings of a number of the chief authors of the American Renaissance first appeared in newspapers. Writings in books and periodicals, published in limited quantities, owned by the few, or available only to those with tickets to the local lyceum libraries, were first noticed, advertised, reviewed, and extracts printed and reprinted in the newspapers which, by the thousands, were delivered by the carrier boys to the homes of subscribers and avidly read by every member of the household. In addition to bringing American literature into the home of the broadest spectrum of American readers, the newspaper served as arbiter of taste in terms of the content and comment provided by the editor. The *Salem Gazette* was no less influential in the parlors of Hawthorne's neighbors than CBS news is in the family rooms of our neighbors.

By the time Longfellow was enthusiastically declaring at the 1825 Bowdoin College commencement that "Yes!—Palms are to be won by our native writers!"[1] his own work had already appeared in the Portland and Boston papers.[2] Longfellow's classmate, Nathaniel Hawthorne, listening with special interest to his friend's prophetic remarks about "Our Native Writers," had already had his first work published in the Salem papers.[3] Before Emerson's *Nature* (1836) and Hawthorne's *Twice-Told Tales* (1837) were published, writings by Cooper, Irving, Longfellow,

Bryant, Hawthorne, Poe, Whittier, and a number of lesser authors had widespread newspaper publication. And long before the appearance of such landmark American Renaissance titles as *Walden* (1854), *Moby-Dick* (1851), and *The Scarlet Letter* (1850) a host of American literary figures were familiar names to newspaper readers throughout New England.[4] In spite of Hawthorne's claim to the oft-quoted distinction of being "for a good many years, the obscurest man of letters of America,"[5] his dismissal from the Salem Custom House created a front-page furor of national proportions.[6] The political event was commonplace, except that the man thrown out of office was Nathaniel Hawthorne—and the newspapers had already established Hawthorne as front-page news.

An example of how newspapers served to promote American literature and contribute to an author's reputation is the way in which various editors looking for "filler" material appropriated and reprinted Hawthorne's popular tale, "A Rill from the Town Pump." The story first appeared as an anonymous contribution to the *New-England Magazine* (June 1835) and was collected two years later under Hawthorne's byline in *Twice-Told Tales*. The following is a selected list of newspaper reprintings:

> *Daily Evening Transcript*, Boston, 9 June 1835, p. 1. Unsigned.
> *Worcester Palladium*, 17 June 1835, p. 1. Unsigned.
> *Old Colony Memorial*, Plymouth, Mass., 4 July 1835, p. 1. Unsigned.
> *The Athenæum*, London, 413 (26 September 1835), p. 728. Unsigned.
> ———, Hawthorne identified as author with publication of *Twice-Told Tales* (6–7 March 1837).
> *Essex Register*, Salem, 16 March 1837, p. 1. "By Nathaniel Hawthorne."
> *Evening Mercury*, Salem, 18 September 1839, p. 1. As "The Town Pump," unsigned.
> *The Madisonian*, Washington City, 7 August 1841, p. 1. "By Nathaniel Hawthorne."
> *Supplement to the Courant*, Hartford, 2 October 1841, p. 362. Taken from the *New London Advocate*.
> *National Anti-Slavery Standard*, New York, 7 July 1842, p. 20. "From the Concord *Republican*."
> *Massachusetts Cataract*, 6 July 1848, p. 1. "By Nathaniel Hawthorne. From the *New England Magazine*."

In Boston, Worcester, Plymouth, Salem, and Washington, editors assigned "A Rill from the Town-Pump," with and without Hawthorne's byline, front-page space; literature was page-one copy. Hawthorne benefited both from the high-visibility positioning of his work and by the increased exposure gained through newspaper publication. The number of reprintings represented a readership many times greater

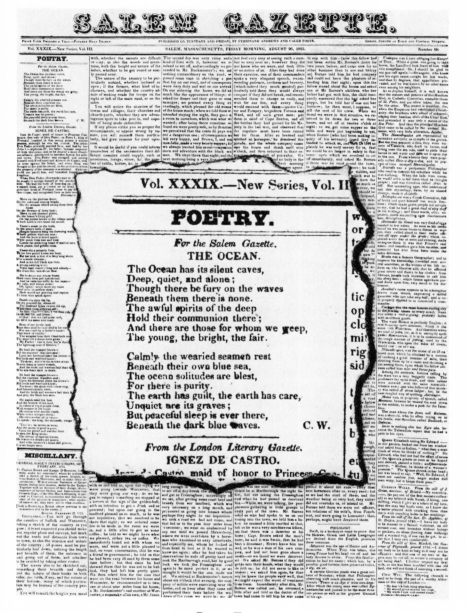

PLATE THREE

Hawthorne's earliest located appearance in print: "The Ocean," *Salem Gazette*, 26 August 1825, p. 1. Signed with the initials, "C. W."

Collection of C. E. Frazer Clark, Jr.

than that reached through the distribution and sale of the *New-England Magazine* and *Twice-Told Tales*. Also, the newspapers involved were serving markets many of which were not readily accessible through normal book and periodical distribution channels; newspapers were making Hawthorne's name and writings known to a significant number of readers who could be reached in no other way. The impact of Hawthorne's work was multiplied not only by the number of papers reprinting a given title, but by the frequency with which selections from Hawthorne appeared in the same paper. Editors found Hawthorne's work popular, and since the price was right (no royalties were paid for these "borrowings"), they freely appropriated the author's work to meet content, space, or deadline requirements. If newspaper editors were pirating Hawthorne's work to their own advantage, they were repaying him with another kind of literary currency by keeping his name and writings regularly before the mass-market reading public.

"A Rill from the Town-Pump," a popular title with buccaneering editors, was more widely reprinted in newspapers than were many of Hawthorne's other works. However, what happened to "Rill" was typical of the use the press made of the great majority of Hawthorne's tales and sketches which appeared prior to publication of *The Scarlet Letter* (1850). How typical "Rill" is as an example of how extensively the press published specific works of all of the other important figures in the American Renaissance is new study for scholars of these authors to pursue. I do know, from my Hawthorne research, that the same editors who pirated Hawthorne's writings were equally cavalier in their treatment of the work of other authors, major and minor, as evidenced by page-one bylines in the papers I have searched.

American newspapers performed another vital function in the service of a native literature by providing aspiring authors access to first publication. Longfellow's first poems were published in the *Portland Gazette* late in 1820 before he had entered Bowdoin College.[7] By 1825, Longfellow had become a regular contributor to *The United States Literary Gazette* where his poems often appeared beside the early poems of William Cullen Bryant.[8] While Hawthorne contributed verse to his home-town paper as early as 1825, he was also encouraged by the *Salem Gazette*'s acceptance and publication in rapid sequence of his first six tales and sketches, two of which were immediately picked up and reprinted by others:

> "The Battle Omen," *Salem Gazette*, 2 November 1830, p. 1. Unsigned. Reprinted in the *Daily Chronicle*, Philadelphia, 8 November 1830, p. 1. Unsigned. *Lowell Journal*, Lowell, Mass., 10 November 1830, p. 1. Unsigned.

"The Hollow of the Three Hills," *Salem Gazette*, 12 November 1830, p. 1. Unsigned. Reprinted in the *Lowell Journal*, Lowell, Mass., 8 December 1830, p. 1. Unsigned.
"Sir William Phips," *Salem Gazette*, 23 November 1830, pp. 1–2. Unsigned.
"Mrs. Hutchinson," *Salem Gazette*, 7 December 1830, p. 4.
"An Old Woman's Tale," *Salem Gazette*, 21 December 1830, pp. 1–2. Unsigned.
"Dr. Bullivant," *Salem Gazette*, 11 January 1831, pp. 1–2. Unsigned.

Bryant went on to a career in journalism; he assumed the editorship of the New York *Evening Post* in 1828 and remained associated with the paper until his death in 1878. Whittier and Lowell, besides their various associations with periodicals, fulfilled newspaper editorial stints, including successive assignments with the *Pennsylvania Freeman*. Whittier also edited and published the *Anti-Slavery Record*. Longfellow and Hawthorne considered journalistic careers as editors and publishers of a newspaper. Longfellow had been attracted to the idea of a literary newspaper as offering both an outlet for his work and as a source of income: "I must write for some paper where the remuneration will be certain, and not small; as my necessities point that way."[9] He discussed plans to found a literary newspaper with Jared Sparks, Samuel Ward, and Joseph Green Cogswell in the summer of 1838.[10] Sparks reported the idea to Hawthorne. Writing Longfellow on 12 January 1839 about a proposed collaboration on a book of fairy tales, Hawthorne endorsed the idea for a paper:

> I saw Mr. Sparks . . . some time since, and he said you were thinking of a literary paper. Why not? Your name would go a great way towards insuring its success; and it is intolerable that there should not be a single belles-lettres journal in New-England. And whatever aid a Custom-House officer could afford, should always be forthcoming. By the way, 'The Inspector' would be as good a title for a paper as 'The Spectator.'[11]

Several weeks after writing Longfellow, Hawthorne moved to Boston to assume the duties of measurer at the custom house. The move made it convenient for the two authors to renew their Bowdoin friendship and they were often together. Longfellow's dissatisfaction with Harvard, and Hawthorne's distaste for his custom-house duties made the idea of a paper an attractive escape possibility. Longfellow had made Hawthorne partner in the proposed adventure, and plans had progressed to a point where Hawthorne wrote his friend Caleb Foote, co-owner of the *Salem Gazette*, on 31 August 1840 to ask advice in the matter:

> Professor Longfellow and myself contemplate establishing a paper in Boston; and we are desirous of gaining some lights upon the subject, from your

> Boston, August 31st. 1840.
>
> Dear Sir,
>
> Professor Longfellow and myself contemplate establishing a paper in Boston, and we are desirous of gaining some lights upon the subject, from your experience. Our plans are yet in embryo; but we think of a daily evening paper, upon the cash principle, together with a weekly sheet. Will you be kind enough to give us an estimate of the cost of such a paper — say of the size of the Transcript? We should likewise be glad of your advice, whether to confide the printing, distributing, and other business of the paper, to a publisher, or to keep that department in our own hands. In short, no advice in the premises can come amiss.
>
> I will endeavor to see you at my next visit to Salem; but in the meantime should feel obliged by a few lines from you.
>
> Very truly Yours,
> Nath. Hawthorne
>
> Hon. Caleb Foote,
> Salem.

PLATE FOUR
Hawthorne to Caleb Foote, co-owner of the *Salem Gazette*, 31 August 1840.
Collection of C. E. Frazer Clark, Jr.

experience. Our plans are yet in embryo; but we think of a daily evening paper upon the cash principle, together with a weekly sheet. Will you be kind enough to give us an estimate of the cost of such a paper—say of the size of the [Boston] Transcript? We should likewise be glad of your advice, whether to confide the printing, distributing, and other business of the paper, to a publisher, or to keep that department in our own hands.[12]

Whatever Caleb Foote's counsel to the aspiring journalists, the Longfellow–Hawthorne paper never came into being. What we do have is the knowledge that in 1840, after discussing it with other members of the literary profession, Longfellow and Hawthorne sufficiently believed in the merits of a daily literary newspaper to consider undertaking it as a career.

As Mott has pointed out, the period roughly corresponding to Longfellow and Hawthorne's graduation from Bowdoin in 1825 and the publication of *The Scarlet Letter* in 1850 "... was emphatically a newspaper era—the era in which most of the greater American newspapers were founded and brought to influential positions."[13] According to 1828 figures published in the New York *Mirror*, there were ten daily papers in the city with an average circulation of 1,850; by 1850, the *Herald* and the *Tribune* were purported to have daily circulations between 20,000 and 30,000.[14] The primary business of the papers enjoying this remarkable growth was politics, but political papers did not neglect literature, some even solicited original contributions. The *National Era*, a Washington abolitionist paper, paid Hawthorne $25 for "The Great Stone Face" ("inadequate compensation," according to Whittier, an editor of the *Era*, who apologized to Hawthorne for the sum paid).[15] The *Era* was influential in bringing the story before a broad segment of the reading public:

National Era, 24 January 1850, p. 16. Signed "For the National Era. By Nathaniel Hawthorne."
The Essex County Mercury and Danvers Courier, Salem, 6 February 1850, pp. 1–2. "By Nathaniel Hawthorne. From the National Era."
National Aegis, Worcester, 13 February 1850, p. 1. "By Nathaniel Hawthorne. From the National Era."
The Age, Augusta, Maine, 14 February 1850, p. 1. "By Nathaniel Hawthorne. From the National Era."
Lowell Weekly Journal and Courier, Lowell, Mass., 1 March 1850, p. 4, and 8 March 1850, p. 4. "By Nathaniel Hawthorne."

As newspapers grew in circulation, they became increasingly successful commercial ventures. Advertising brought in substantial revenues. Newspaper earnings were newsworthy; the *Whig Review* pointed with awe at the *Tribune*'s 1850 dividend of $70,000.[16] Prospects of success created keen competition between rival newspapers, particularly where papers were competing for the same subscribers. Pressured by publishers looking for good return on their investments, harried editors working against recurring deadlines aggressively sought content that would build their paper's popularity. Politics, news, commerce, and religion were market segments largely defined by the editorial slant of the paper; literature had the kind of general market appeal that represented circulation-building opportunities. The result was that aggressive newspaper editors assumed a practice common to magazine editors, that of borrowing English writings of established popularity from sources unprotected by any copyright agreement. However, there were significant differences between the borrowing practices of magazines and newspapers. Predatory magazine editors concentrated on pirating unprotected English writings largely as a matter of economic necessity. The mortality rate among magazines was high; circulations were not large (except for such few exceptions as *Godey's*, up to 40,000 in 1849),[17] subscription fees seemed high, and delinquent subscribers created perpetual collection and cash-flow problems. Also, magazines were more expensive to distribute, did not enjoy the same low-cost mailing privileges as newspapers, did not have access to the advertising revenues, and were burdened with the expense of the "exchange list" (*Godey's*, for example, sent free copies to 1,500 newspapers in exchange for notices they expected to get in the papers).[18] Magazines, operating on narrow margins and hard pressed to pay contributors (late payments and no payments were common practice), had to borrow to survive; they could not afford to pay for American literature. As N. P. Willis put it in the announcement of his projected *Corsair*:

> As to original American production, we shall, as the publishers do, take what we can get for nothing (that is good), holding, as the publishers do, that while we can get Boz and Bulwer for a thank-ye or less, it is not pocket-wise to pay much for Halleck and Irving.[19]

In a terminating editorial statement in the last number of the *New-England Magazine* (December 1835), Park Benjamin, who had regularly published Hawthorne's work, told his readers that the chief reason why American periodical literature could not be compared with that of England was the inability of the American magazines to pay for contributions.[20] Where magazines were pirating English writings because they could not afford to pay for American writings, newspapers were borrowing English work because it was available and free for the taking. Also, newspapers did not restrict themselves to pirating English work, they borrowed with equal license from the pages of American magazines American writings that the magazines had paid for the privilege of publishing. This was a general practice fostered by the legal uncertainty surrounding ownership of a magazine's contents. This practice troubled publishers as well as authors: "It has often been a subject of complaint," reported the *Mirror*, "that editors in this country are in the constant habit of copying articles without giving credit to the journals from which they are extracted."[21] The publishers, for the most part, seemed to welcome the free advertising the newspaper borrowings represented, provided the source was credited. Authors like Hawthorne resented any unpaid use of their work. Things changed in 1845 when two of the best sources for newspaper borrowings, *Graham's* and *Godey's*, decided to protect their investment in contributions by copyrighting their contents. Newspapers, like magazines, depended heavily on their ability to borrow good material freely in an effort to secure a competitive edge in the market. In addition, newspapers, like their mass-market communications counterpart today—television—reached a point where they were consuming enormous amounts of copy and creating great demand for new copy. Borrowing from all available sources was essential to the continued growth of the American press, which meant not only a greater use of imported literary product, but increased consumption of America's native literary product.

The freebooting editors of the American press were effective agents in the cause of American literary independence. Through their efforts the newspaper served as a formative instrument of the American Renaissance by creating a general public awareness of literature, by making American literature important, and by working to make a market among readers for the future writings of American authors whose work was the day's front-page story.

NOTES

1. Longfellow's remarks were made as part of the formal program at the Bowdoin College commencement 7 September 1825. Longfellow's oration, scheduled as twelfth in the Order of Exercises of Candidates for the degree of Bachelor of Arts, listed in the printed program as "The Life and Writings of Chatterton," was changed to "Our Native Writers" some time between the printing of the program and the commencement; the new title is written in on some of the surviving copies of the program.

2. Longfellow's first published poem appeared in the *Portland Gazette*; see Richard Harwell, comp., *Hawthorne and Longfellow: A Guide to an Exhibit* (Brunswick, Maine: Bowdoin College, 1966), p. 9. Longfellow's pregraduation work also appeared in *Boston Prize Poems, And other Specimens of Dramatic Poetry* (Boston: J. T. Buckingham, 1824), and *The United States Literary*

Gazette; see Carroll A. Wilson, *Thirteen Author Collections of the Nineteenth Century*, ed. Jean C. S. Wilson and David A. Randall, 2 vols. (New York: Scribner's, 1950), 1:175–77.

3. Hawthorne's verses "The Ocean," "The Battle Ground," and "Moonlight" appeared in the *Salem Gazette* (26, 30 August, 2 September 1825), all p. 1. The work was signed with various initials; Hawthorne's name did not appear. In a letter to his sister Maria Louisa, dated Salem, 28 September 1819, Hawthorne alludes to newspaper publication of his work.

4. A sampling of authors whose work appears on the front page of the 1843 *Salem Gazette* includes Hawthorne, Lowell, Bryant, Harriet Beecher Stowe, N. P. Willis, Lydia H. Sigourney, Joseph C. Neal, T. S. Arthur, Catharine Sedgwick, William B. Tappan, Ann S. Stephens, Seba Smith, Charles Fenno Hoffman, Emma C. Embury, Frances S. Osgood, and J. R. Chandler.

5. *The Centenary Edition of the Works of Nathaniel Hawthorne*, ed. William Charvat, et al., 11 vols. to date (Columbus: Ohio State University Press, 1962–), vol. 9, *Twice-Told Tales* (1974), p. 3.

6. "The dismissal of Mr. Surveyor Hawthorne became a *cause célèbre* throughout New England. Arguments and counterarguments, charges and countercharges filled the metropolitan and country presses during the summer months of 1849. 'Mr. Hawthorne's name,' Sophia told her mother, 'is ringing through the land. All the latent feeling about him now comes out, and he finds himself very famous'" (Randall Stewart, *Nathaniel Hawthorne: A Biography* [New Haven: Yale University Press, 1948], p. 88).

7. See note 2, above.

8. See note 2, above.

9. *The Letters of Henry Wadsworth Longfellow*, ed. Andrew Hilen, 4 vols. to date (Cambridge: Harvard University Press, 1966–), 2:148.

10. Arlin Turner, "Hawthorne and Longfellow: Abortive Plans for Collaboration," *The Nathaniel Hawthorne Journal 1971*, ed. C. E. Frazer Clark, Jr. (Washington: NCR Microcard Editions, 1971), pp. 3–11.

11. Hawthorne to Longfellow, 12 January 1839, MH.

12. Hawthorne to Caleb Foote, 31 August 1840, Collection of C. E. Frazer Clark, Jr.

13. Frank Luther Mott, *A History of American Magazines 1741–1850* (Cambridge: Harvard University Press, 1957), p. 465.

14. Mott, *History*, p. 465.

15. Stewart, *Hawthorne*, p. 93.

16. Mott, *History*, p. 465.

17. Mott, *History*, p. 514.

18. Mott, *History*, p. 515.

19. Mott, *History*, pp. 504–505.

20. Mott, *History*, p. 505.

21. Mott, *History*, p. 502.

POE AND MAGAZINE WRITING ON PREMATURE BURIAL

J. Gerald Kennedy

FROM THE EARLY TRAVESTY "Loss of Breath" (1832) to the late classic "The Cask of Amontillado" (1846), living entombment remained a persistent and horrifying motif in Poe's fiction. To this fate he consigned Berenice, Monos, and the one-eyed black cat; he caused Arthur Gordon Pym and the narrator of "The Pit and the Pendulum" to undergo symbolic burial; he sent Morella, Ligeia, and Madeline Usher to early though apparently temporary graves. And at the height of his career, he produced his consummate sepulchral study, "The Premature Burial" (1844). The prevalence of the theme has inspired lengthy biographical speculation about Poe's necrophilia and his longing for the maternal womb;[1] it has also prompted such critical claims as D. H. Lawrence's that "all this underground vault business in Poe only symbolizes that which takes place *beneath* the consciousness."[2] But little has been written about Poe's conscious, journalistic motives—a surprising oversight since similar narratives abounded in contemporary periodicals.

Clearly, hasty interment evoked powerful and legitimate fears in Poe's day. One inventor, a "Mr. Eisenbrant of Baltimore," even constructed a "life-preserving coffin," to "guard against the occurrence of burial before life is extinct."[3] Frequent accounts of premature burial, factual and fictional, appeared in respected journals, feeding popular interest in a subject that alternately amused and terrified readers. Poe must have encountered numerous burial stories, for his various editorial positions required him to keep abreast of periodical writing. Evidence of this familiarity appears in his 1838 satire "How to Write a Blackwood Article," and A. H. Quinn has shown that two magazine pieces had a probable influence on "The Premature Burial."[4]

Oddly neglected by Poe scholars, this tale warrants reexamination as a complex response to the traditional magazine tale of living entombment. Deftly combining narrative techniques, Poe perhaps fashioned the story as an underground sequel to "The Balloon Hoax."[5] His

165

seemingly factual opening pages lead to a firsthand description of living burial; but the final paragraphs take an unexpected turn, as the "buried" narrator awakens to find himself the victim of a nightmare and vows to read no more "'Night Thoughts'—no fustian about church-yards— no bugaboo tales—*such as this.*"[6] G. R. Thompson points out that this "illusion-breaking reference" to the narrative itself typifies Poe's ironic attitude toward his Gothic materials.[7] But the comment also pokes fun at the graveyard school in general and "bugaboo tales" about living entombment in particular. In several respects, "The Premature Burial" draws upon the tradition that it finally satirizes; an examination of that tradition will clarify the nature of Poe's response to it.

If burial literature possessed a focal theme, it reflected diversity in style and substance. Accounts ranged from quasi-medical reports about suspended animation to the hysterical recollections of self-proclaimed survivors. Following Robert Scholes' useful theory of fictional modes, we can distinguish three basic forms: the historical, the satirical, and the romantic.[8] Accounts of the historical type concern "actual events and real people": concrete details about premature burials in the world of daily experience. In the satirical mode, however, the event is reduced to situation comedy; burial creates a temporary inconvenience for the "corpse," whose reanimation produces laughable encounters with the living. Conversely, the romantic mode elevates the action to melodrama or tragedy and in hyperbolic language portrays the almost superhuman suffering of the victim. In short, writers of burial narratives aimed primarily to inform, to amuse, or to excite their readers, though some tales, as we shall see, reveal a mixed purpose.

Particularly during outbreaks of yellow fever or cholera, newspapers in such cities as New York and Philadelphia often reported cases of living inhumation. Such catastrophes resulted from hasty postmortem examinations or, as a writer complained in 1817, from the sometimes scandalous burial practices of the time:

> Persons supposed to be dead are frequently buried with a haste that is highly reprehensible. This blameable precipitation has often been followed by the most shocking and disgusting consequences; it has frequently happened that persons supposed to be dead (but who in reality were only in a state of lethargy) have come to life without being able to obtain light, and perished in convulsions and despair, as the subsequent inspection of their bodies has proved. Repeated remonstrances have not had the effect of preventing the pernicious custom of burying the dead, the moment that the breath is supposed to be out of the body; it is customary to wrap up the corpse with a sheet which is sewed from head to foot in such a way

as to prevent the admission of air. The following is a recent and terrible example.

A man named *Tessier*, of the Parish of Saint Anne, in the district of Three Rivers, supposed to be dead, was carried to church about twenty-four hours after, where his funeral service was performed, [and] he was then placed in the charnel house, which is the ordinary custom in the country during the winter. About eight days after, it became again necessary to open the charnel house, and the coffin was found open, the feet out, the hands were torn, the left hand grasped *into* the right shoulder, and the body was turned upon the right side.[9]

This report from Montreal identifies two recurring causes of mishaps: hurried interments and burial shrouds, which effectively suffocated a still-living person. The Tessier account is paradigmatic of the historical mode in that little effort has been made to arrange or embellish the facts for narrative effect.

Narrative figures more prominently, however, in "The Lady Buried Alive," which compares two European stories about the apparent death of a woman forced to dismiss her suitor to marry a wealthy tax collector.[10] At several points, the account verges on melodrama; for example, the author attributes the woman's collapse to heartbreak: "The melancholy brought on by an engagement so fatal to her happiness, threw her into a disorder in which her senses were so locked up that she was taken up for dead and interred as such." He lapses into sentimentality again, depicting the woman's reunion with her first love: "Ginevra, tearing the shroud from her face, exclaimed with an agonizing voice, 'I am no spirit, Antonio! I am that Ginevra you once loved but was buried—buried alive!' She could say no more, but dropped senseless into his arms."

But despite the overblown language, "The Lady Buried Alive" purports to be historical scholarship. The author begins, "In the *Causes Célèbres*, we find the following romantic story related as having actually occurred in France, and been the cause of a judicial proceeding in the courts of that country." After summarizing the story, he registers several objections: "It is not said when it happened, or what court it came before; and to account for the want of any record of the judgment pronounced on the case, the parties are made to evade judgment by flying into a foreign country." In the interest of historical accuracy, the author shows that the French story is derivative: "It is in fact, altogether but an imperfect version of the accident which is said really to have occurred, not anywhere in France, but at Florence, during the great plague, in the year 1460. Dominico Mara Manni, who relates the story, says that the sepulchre in which the lady was entombed alive 'is pointed out even to this day.'" Though rife with romantic elements, "The Lady Buried Alive" essentially treats living entombment as a matter of fact.

The currency of European burial stories may also be observed in "Burying Alive," which enumerates ten instances of living burial "collected from medical history."[11] The piece opens with some reflections, by a Philadelphia editor, on the plague of 1793:

> During the prevalence of the yellow fever in this city, in the year 1793, we have every reason to believe, that many persons, suffering with disease, were removed from their houses and interred before the vital spark had fled. So general was this desolating scourge, that those who officiated as undertakers, acted without any check or responsibility, and if in entering a house, the door of which was marked with the fatal characters of the disease, the dying were taken with the dead, to avoid the trouble of a second visit; there was none to call them to account.

This grim reminiscence precedes the report of "an intelligent French gentleman" from New York, which lists the maladies associated with premature burial: "The diseases in which a partial and momentary suspension of life most often manifests itself, are Asphyxia, Hysterics, Lethargy, Hypochondria, Convulsions, Syncope, Catalepsis, excessive loss of blood, Tetanus, Apoplexy, Epilepsy, and Ecstasy." Ten "particularly striking" case histories follow.

Easily the most provocative concerns a "Mr. Rousseau of Rouen," who returned from a journey to find his fourteen-year-old bride about to be buried. Removing her body from the coffin, he ordered twenty-five incisions to be made: "At the twenty-sixth, probably deeper than the others, the deceased exclaimed, 'How severely you hurt me!' Medical assistance was immediately given. The lady had afterward twenty-six children." Despite his supposed acumen, the "intelligent French gentleman" fails to clarify the implied relationship between incisions and children, thus inviting skepticism, if not ribald speculation. But taken as a whole, his report provides a compendium of medical and historical evidence which suggests the range of contemporary knowledge about premature interment. Moreover, the mingling of medical information and apparently traditional lore reflects the proximity of fact and fiction in such periodical writing. Scientific theorists had not yet taught the reading public to distinguish between empirical and imaginative truth.

From the early 1820s, the cult of sentiment ruled the magazine world, popularizing a preciosity of language and sensibility alien to all humor except whimsy. But it is instructive to observe some writers struggling against the current, trying to convert a sentimental preoccupation—death and burial—into a subject of mirth. In "Dead Alive," a tale from Portugal, the apparent demise of a nun hides her clandestine affair with a group of monks.[12] The first sentence parenthetically injects a satirical tone: "A nun of St. Clara, whose conduct made everyone regard her as a saint, (for, instead of one confessor from the adjoining monastery, she had three or four,) died to all appearance, or rather it was given out she had died." But when her "corpse" shows no signs of decomposition, simple villagers worship her as a dead saint: "Hundreds of cripples and invalids came to touch her garments, and fancied themselves cured; while others, paid by the priests, pretended to be stone blind, and to recover their sight, on merely touching her habit." The writer playfully suggests that, but for the soldiers posted at the church door, "it is probable that the new saint, would soon have been stripped of her clothes—owing to the anxiety of everyone to get a scrap of something belonging to her." When a sentry overhears the woman complaining to her "confessors," the truth comes out:

> The fact of the matter was, the unhappy nun had been confessing too much to the purpose with these holy miscreants, who, in order to avoid the inconvenience and danger which were attendant on their rendezvous with her, when in different establishments, had agreed to make a dead saint of her, and bury her to all appearance, in their vaults. By this arrangement, one great object would be gained: the great honor, which would accrue to both monastery and convent, by the production of a saint.

The satire of "Dead Alive" thus cuts two ways, mocking the gullibility of believers and the blasphemous deeds of the clergy. By portraying the desecration of a church, the debasing of sainthood, and the violation of holy vows, the writer reveals an antisacerdotal impulse typical in Gothic fiction. Of equal interest to Poe scholars is the implicit connection between the burial vault and sexual intercourse, which anticipates the funereal eroticism of "Berenice," "Ligeia," and "The Fall of the House of Usher."

Hasty interment becomes the subject of a comical discussion between an inebriate and two grave diggers in the anecdote "Coffined Alive."[13] The narrative opens with a solemn reminder: "That persons, during the raging of a pestilence and the hurry of burials, have sometimes been earthed alive, there is very little doubt." But the tone abruptly changes when the writer tells us his account concerns "the coffining of a man, who, as will appear in the sequel, could not be persuaded that he was a proper subject for burial." Having been mistakenly consigned to the "dead room" of a hospital, a drunk awakens to find himself being nailed in a coffin by two Irishmen. When the tippler protests that he is not dead, one Irishman retorts, "Not dead! . . . ain't that a pretty extravagant assartion for a corpse to make? Not dead? And sure you can't be in your right mind to say so. Come, lie down, if ye plase, and we'll nail ye up and bury ye dacently." Finding himself unable to reason with the persistent Hibernians, the drunk leaps from the coffin and escapes. The satirical butt, of course, is the stereotyped Irish bogtrotter, then a common target for ethnic ridicule. But the appeal of "Coffined Alive" goes beyond the superficial matter of comic dialogue; however improbable and absurd, the action embodies a potent psychological theme: the avoidance of burial. As we shall see, the fear of death and desire for immortality seem to underlie the literature of living entombment.

The escape-from-the-tomb motif figures in another comic anecdote, "The Dead Alive."[14] Presented as "fact"—an actual event in "a country town south of the Potomack"—the piece tells of a meek country parson, hounded for years by a termagant wife. On the evening after the woman's burial, the parson's solitude is shattered by a knock at the door: "There, wrapped in her winding sheet, stood the formidable figure of his worst half—alive, and breathing vengeance upon her devoted lord for having prematurely consigned her to the tomb." The writer explains, "It had been a case merely of suspended animation, and the coffin having been imperfectly screwed, and the door of the vault left unlocked, its rebellious inmate had burst her cerements, and reappeared upon the scene of her former triumphs of temper!" The woman returned to bedevil her husband "until again her tongue and digital members were arrested in their career of mischief—when (as the story relates), profiting by the past, her much-abused and long-suffering lord directed the coffin to be *nailed*." Behind the witty portrayal of a parson's miseries, one discovers a pattern of action similar to such Poe tales as "Morella" and "The Fall of the House of Usher": the interment of a willful woman who returns to haunt the man who buried her.

According to Scholes' typology, the satirical mode presents base, "subhuman" characters in an absurd, chaotic world.[15] In the narratives examined above, we see that the humor depends partially upon the baseness of the victim; the debauched nun, the inebriate, and the shrew in some sense all deserve their misfortunes and evoke little sympathy. And in the preposterous world of burial satire, entombment is never permanent anyway, for comic necessity mandates the victim's survival. Escape from the tomb permits the improbable confrontation between the "deceased" and his survivors, which forms the crux of burial humor.

But through this absurd confrontation, we also experience the secret satisfaction of coffin comedy: the symbolic victory over death, dramatized by revivification.

Unlike the satirical mode, the romantic invites sympathetic identification with the victim; close description of his perceptions draws the reader into the subjective experience. Indeed, psychological anguish provides the focal interest, as the protagonist struggles to retain life and consciousness. Poe referred to such narratives as "tales of effect" (11:109), and through his fictional Mr. Blackwood, he once identified their essential ingredient: "Sensations are the great things after all. Should you ever be drowned or hung, be sure and make a note of your sensations—they will be worth to you ten guineas a sheet. If you wish to write forcibly,... pay minute attention to the sensations" (2:274).

Mr. Blackwood bases his advice upon the success of a popular burial tale, "'The Dead Alive,' a capital thing!—the record of a gentleman's sensations when entombed before the breath was out of his body." Poe evidently had in mind an import from *Blackwood's Magazine*, "The Buried Alive," which features the impressions of a man who has experienced "death," burial, and accidental rescue by grave robbers.[16] Indeed, after paralysis strikes the narrator in the second paragraph, the "action" consists mainly of sensory perceptions:

> One day toward the evening, the crisis took place.—I was seized with a strange and indescribable quivering—a rushing sound was in my ears—I saw around my couch, innumerable strange faces; they were bright and visionary, and without bodies. There was light and solemnity, and I tried to move, but could not.—For a short time a terrible confusion overwhelmed me, and when it passed off, all my recollection returned with the most perfect distinctness; but the power of motion had departed. I heard the sound of weeping at my pillow—and the voice of the nurse say, 'He is dead.'—I cannot describe what I felt at these words.—I exerted my utmost power of volition to stir, but could not move an eyelid. After a short pause my friend drew near; and sobbing, and convulsed with grief, drew his hand over my face, and closed my eyes.—The world was then darkened, but I still could hear, and feel, and suffer.

The account is not without grotesque humor; after the narrator's apparent demise, he suffers the indignities of two undertakers: "They laughed at one another as they turned me from side to side, and treated what they believed to be a corpse with the most appalling ribaldry." But as Poe correctly realized, the force of "The Buried Alive" comes from the writer's "minute attention to the sensations," particularly the auditory sensations of burial:

> I heard the cords of the coffin moved—I felt it swing as dependent by them—
> It was lowered, and rested on the bottom of the grave—the cords were
> dropped upon the lid—I heard them fall. Dreadful was the effort I then
> made to exert the power of action, but my whole frame was immovable. Soon
> after, a few handfuls of earth were thrown upon the coffin, then there was
> another pause; after which the shovels were employed, and the sound of the
> rattling mould, as it covered me, was far more tremendous than thunder.

The narrator mournfully concludes: "This is death, ... and I am doomed to remain in the earth until the resurrection." But his subsequent meditations on "the epicurean worm" are interrupted, not by Judgment Day, but by the arrival of "resurrection men," whose ghoulish activities ironically save the narrator's life. Lugged off to a medical school, the "corpse" recovers during a galvanic experiment. Evidently one of Poe's favorite magazine tales, "The Buried Alive" apparently furnished the details for the "Edward Stapleton" case in "The Premature Burial." More importantly, it illustrated for Poe the dynamics of underground emotion which he would explore in that tale and "The Colloquy of Monos and Una."

Another narrative of the *Blackwood's* type, "Living Inhumation," depicts the ordeal as a progression of psychological states.[17] Purportedly an extract "from the unpublished diary of C. Hodgson, Esq. lately deceased, formerly of Bristol, (Eng.)," the account traces, more closely than "The Buried Alive," the emotional changes and levels of awareness experienced by the victim. The opening sentence introduces the crucial theme of "consciousness": "I had been subject to epileptic fits from my youth upwards, which, though they did not deprive me of animation in the sight of those about me, completely annihilated my consciousness." Hodgson's entombment occurs after just such a fit, and the recovery of consciousness brings first terror, then despair:

> When the real truth flashed upon me in all its fearful energy, I never
> can forget the thrill of horror that struck through me! It was as if a bullet
> had perforated my heart, and all the blood in my body gushed through the
> wound! Never, never, can hell be more terrible than the sensations of that
> moment! I lay motionless for a time, petrified with terror. Then a clammy
> dampness burst forth from every pore of my body. My horrible doom seemed
> inevitable; and so strong at length became this impression—so bereft of hope
> appeared my situation—that I ultimately recovered from it only to plunge
> into the depths of a calm, resolute despair.

Thus the narrator depicts the flux of emotion. His charged rhetoric, wearisome in its total effect, reaches a grotesque climax: "I shrieked with horror: I plunged my nails into my thighs and wounded them; the coffin was soaked with my blood; and by tearing the wooden sides of my prison with the same maniacal feeling. I lacerated my fingers and wore the nails to the quick, soon becoming motionless from exhaustion." Like the narrator of "The Buried Alive," Hodgson receives his deliverance through the chance intervention of a grave robber—the standard *deus ex machina* of the burial tale. But "Living Inhumation" at least possesses a clear thematic focus: as would Poe's tales a few years later, it portrays the burial experience as a struggle for orientation and sanity. The torture derives less from physical confinement than from the imaginative horrors and incipient madness which entombment evokes.

One narrative which Poe almost certainly knew—and used—was James F. Otis' "Buried Alive: An Ower True Tale."[18] Published under the rubric "Young Mortality's Memories," the story draws heavily upon Gray and Goldsmith, as well as Scott, in evoking a mood of churchyard melancholy. The narrator's "penchant for burying grounds" one day leads him to witness a bizarre scene. With a funeral cortege looking on, a sexton opens a family burial vault: "As he did so, there fell outwards, at his feet,—nay, upon them, as he stood on the stones,—a fleshless skeleton!" The long hair covering the skull indicates the sex of the victim, whose shattered coffin lies on the floor of the vault. Upon learning the woman's identity, the narrator imagines her ordeal:

> Oh! what a waking must have been hers! Confined within the narrow limits of a coffin,—arrayed in the robes of the dead,—the companion of the mouldering dust of the departed,—doomed to a slow, lingering, miserable,—perhaps a maddened and desperate death! Methought, as I went on my musing way, methought I could see her, with almost superhuman energy, bursting open her horrible prison, and tearing off the revolting cerements in which she had been wrapped, and, applying herself to the iron door of her living tomb, attempting to break it from its hinges, screaming the while, in agony, for succour,—alas! alas! how vainly!

This sketch likely furnished Poe with one of the case histories cited in "The Premature Burial"—the account of a Baltimore woman whose skeleton falls into the arms of her husband as he opens the family vault.[19] Thoroughly conventional in language and sentiment, Otis' tale closes with a somewhat cryptic moral tag: "What a lesson, writ on the great page of life's constantly unfolding volume! And yet, stranger, I doubt you have read it less as a lesson than as a legend!"

A more explicitly sententious tale, "Premature Interment," recounts "the familiar story of the sexton and the lady's ring," an event said to have occurred in Cologne in 1547.[20] The action is simple enough: a debt-ridden sexton attempts to steal a ring from the body of a woman recently entombed in a cathedral, but when the "corpse" seizes his wrist, he flees in terror. As she regains consciousness, the lady perceives her situation and fears that "her dead ancestors were then to be her last companions; and her last occupation was to be that of tracing with her nails upon the black walls the melancholy progress of her real death." But the sexton has left the vault unlocked; the lady escapes, struggles to the altar of the cathedral, and revives herself—appropriately—with sacramental wine: "No true believer had ever set the cup to his lips with more sincere devotion and gratitude toward his Creator, than she did thus administer the cheering draught to herself." "Premature Interment" thus amounts to a didactic tale, illustrating the mysterious ways of Providence: the sexton's attempted crime frees the woman from her tomb and restores her faith. Like other romantic burial narratives though, it dwells intently on the subjective response of the victim and the pathos of her situation to realize the full melodramatic potential of the theme.

By the time Poe published "The Premature Burial" in 1844, the living entombment narrative had already become a cliché. Indeed, judging from the scarcity of later burial accounts, one can almost say that Poe had the last word on the subject. Hence, his conscious use of earlier material and his blending of realistic, romantic, and satirical elements smack of journalistic showmanship—a demonstration of Poe's ability to improvise on a popular, if shopworn motif.

A ruse from the outset, "The Premature Burial" begins: "There are certain themes of which the interest is all-absorbing, but which are too entirely horrible for the purposes of legitimate fiction. These the mere romanticist must eschew, if he do not wish to offend, or to disgust. They are with propriety handled, only when the severity and majesty of Truth sanctify and sustain them" (5:255). Poe's invocation of "Truth" and his feigned contempt for fiction dealing with "horrible" themes invite belief in the authenticity of his narrative. He assures the reader that "in these accounts, it is the fact—it is the reality—it is the history which excites. As inventions, we should regard them with simple abhorrence." Poe labors to remove suspicion that "The Premature Burial" may be just such an "invention" by parading four examples of living entombment, culled from published magazine accounts and replete with verisimilar detail. And he concludes this scholarly exercise by arguing that one's interest in premature burial "very properly and very peculiarly depends upon our conviction of the *truth* of the matter narrated" (5:264).

As in any hoax, the claim of "Truth" forms an integral part of the larger deception. The narrator moves from documentation to firsthand description with an ingenuous testimonial: "What I have now to tell, is of my own actual knowledge—of my own positive and personal experience" (5:264). In Scholes' terminology, Poe shifts from the historical to the romantic mode, turning gradually to the subjective experience, the inner drama. In the tradition of "The Buried Alive" and "Living Inhumation," the narrator explains his susceptibility to paralysis and then recollects the first sensations of consciousness:

> Slowly—with a tortoise gradation—approached the faint gray dawn of the psychal day. A torpid uneasiness. An apathetic endurance of dull pain. No care—no hope—no effort. Then, after a long interval, a ringing in the ears; then after a lapse still longer, a prickling or tingling sensation in the extremities; then a seemingly eternal period of pleasurable quiescence, during which the awakening feelings are struggling into thought; then a brief re-sinking into non-entity; then a sudden recovery. At length the slight quivering of an eyelid, and immediately thereupon, an electric shock of a terror, deadly and indefinite, which sends the blood in torrents from the temples to the heart. (5:269-70)

Here Poe himself follows the advice of Mr. Blackwood, paying "minute attention to the sensations." After struggling against his physical confines, the narrator concludes that he has been "nailed up in some common coffin—and thrust, deep, deep, and forever, into some ordinary and nameless *grave*" (5:271).

But the narrator's shriek, at the height of his romantic agony, prompts a series of ludicrous exclamations:

> "Hillo! hillo, there!" said a gruff voice in reply.
> "What the devil's the matter now?" said a second.
> "Get out o' that!" said a third.
> "What do you mean by yowling in that ere kind of style, like a cattymount?" said a fourth. (5:271-72)

Shifting into the satirical mode, Poe presents the stock confrontation scene: the narrator faces a band of angry sailors, awakened by his screams aboard a sloop. His "coffin" proves to be a narrow wooden berth and his premature burial, a bad dream. Employing virtually the same formula he used in *The Narrative of Arthur Gordon Pym* (1838), Poe destroys the illusion of factuality at the last moment—in this case, leaving the reader holding the shroud. The narrator's vow henceforth to read no more tales of living entombment, "no bugaboo tales—*such as this*," comprises an ironic and mocking comment on the tradition which he exploited so fully.[21]

By mid-century, the living entombment narrative had virtually disappeared from American periodicals. However, its lengthy vogue prompts several observations about popular culture in the early nineteenth century. It indicates the broad appeal of sentiment and melancholy and the persistence of the graveyard sensibility made fashionable by English poets like Young, Blair, and Gray. It mirrors a general romantic interest in the life-in-death motif and the folklore of ghosts, vampires, and other undead creatures. And in a sociological sense, the burial tale represents a literary protest against slipshod medical practices and funeral customs.

However, these narratives continue to engage the reader, not because they illustrate the aesthetic and social attitudes of the period, but because they give form to universal fears and fantasies. In *The Denial of Death*, Ernest Becker argues that man's primal instinct—more basic even than the sexual urge—is the denial of his own mortality. This death anxiety alienates him from his own flesh, since the body provides a constant reminder that one is, in Yeats' words, "fastened to a dying animal." Ultimately this avoidance of death deprives one of vitality; as Becker observes, "The irony of man's condition is that the deepest need is to be free from the anxiety of death and annihilation; but it is life itself which awakens it, and so we must shrink from being fully alive."[22] Man's search for immortality, actual or symbolic, thus becomes a crucial response to the problem of mortality.

In light of Becker's work, the modern reader discovers in the literature of living entombment a graphic expression of our deepest human impulses: the often-repressed fear of dying and the desperate longing for a means of transcendence. For all of its generic diversity, burial fiction finally presents only two significant patterns of action: the victim perishes or he survives. Pieces such as "Buried Alive: An Ower True Tale," which depicts the horrors of underground death, affect us despite the wearisome rhetoric, because the ordeal conceptualizes the primal struggle to escape the prison of the flesh. Literally, the victim has been betrayed by his body through catalepsy or paralysis; living entombment constitutes the terminal trap. Conversely, narratives of escape make use of "resurrection men" to liberate the victim and to underscore the element of redemption. Deliverance from the grave often implies spiritual renewal (in the story of the sexton and the lady's ring) or sexual revitalization (in the case of Mrs. Rousseau's twenty-six children). The return from the tomb imaginatively fulfills the human craving for a myth of rebirth. Becker notes that the pan-cultural hero has traditionally been "the man who could go into the spirit world, the world of the dead, and return alive."[23] While few victims in burial literature seem especially heroic, their victories over the grave nonetheless carry a profound symbolic meaning.

For Poe, the living entombment motif possessed a peculiar importance; Thompson has written that "Poe's image of man is that of a forlorn, perverse sentient being buried alive in the incomprehensible tomb of the universe."[24] In the predicament of living inhumation, Poe united the central ideas of alienation and mortality, which are, as Becker has demonstrated, finally the same problem. But Poe pulled the theme of premature burial not from the recesses of a neurotic imagination, as some have supposed, but from the periodicals of his time. This widespread literary vogue, which the modern mind has ironically regarded as an unhealthy preoccupation, expresses a cultural openness to death anxiety, a willingness to confront and experience feelings about dying. In some respects, the literature of living entombment seems a more sanguine response to man's fate than our contemporary denial of death.[25]

NOTES

1. See Marie Bonaparte, *The Life and Works of Edgar Allan Poe: A Psycho-Analytic Interpretation*, trans. John Rodker (London: Imago, 1949), pp. 586–87. A Bonaparte enthusiast, Daniel Hoffman says "The Premature Burial" reveals Poe's inability to escape "the feeling of fatal and foetal enclosure" (*Poe Poe Poe Poe Poe Poe Poe* [Garden City, N.Y.: Doubleday, 1972], p. 221).

2. *Studies in Classic American Literature* (New York: Viking, 1964), p. 79.

3. W. T. Bandy, "A Source for Poe's 'The Premature Burial,'" *American Literature*, 19 (April 1947): 167.

4. *Poe: A Critical Biography* (New York: D. Appleton-Century, 1941), p. 418n.

5. In a letter to the *Columbia Spy*, Poe confessed his enjoyment of the balloon hoax; see Quinn, *Poe*, p. 410. In "The Premature Burial," published about three months after the balloon piece, Poe shared his private joke with the few readers capable of recognizing his parody.

6. "The Premature Burial," *The Complete Works of Edgar Allan Poe*, ed. James A. Harrison (New York: Thomas Y. Crowell, 1902), 5:273. All subsequent references to Poe's writings are to the Harrison edition and are cited in the text. "The Premature Burial" first appeared in the Philadelphia *Dollar Newspaper*, 31 July 1844.

7. *Poe's Fiction: Romantic Irony in the Gothic Tales* (Madison: University of Wisconsin Press, 1973), p. 15.

8. "Toward a Poetics of Fiction," *Novel*, 2 (Winter 1969): 104–105.

9. *Niles Weekly Register*, 12 (17 May 1817): 185.

10. *The Casket*, 2 (September 1827): 340–42. This account, as noted by Quinn, is presumably the source for Poe's remarks about "Victorine Lafourcade" in "The Premature Burial."

11. *The Casket*, 9 (October 1834): 379.

12. *New-York Mirror, and Ladies' Literary Gazette*, 4 (19 August 1826): 26–27.
13. *The Casket*, 7 (November 1832): 492.
14. *New-York Mirror*, 14 (10 December 1836): 191.
15. "Toward a Poetics of Fiction," 105.
16. *The Casket*, 1 (September 1826): 257–58. The tale first appeared in *Blackwood's Magazine*, 20 (October 1821): 262–64.
17. *Saturday Evening Post*, 7 (24 May 1828): 1–2.
18. *Southern Literary Messenger*, 3 (June 1837): 338–40. The tale appeared just six months after Poe left his editorial position with the Richmond magazine.
19. Poe also describes the fragmented coffin and from this evidence reconstructs the woman's final struggle.
20. *New-York Mirror*, 17 (3 August 1839): 42.
21. Shortly after "The Premature Burial" appeared, a review article, "Burying Alive," was published in *The Rover*, 3 (17 August 1844): 380–81. The writer cites the recent case of "Mr. Muhlenberg," once a candidate for governor of Pennsylvania, whose funeral was delayed "because the corpse still retained a life-like appearance and people could not be satisfied that he was dead." Expressing complete faith in the veracity of Poe's narrative, the reviewer speaks of "The Premature Burial" as "a collection of very remarkable cases of premature burials, well-authenticated." He reprints a dozen paragraphs from the opening pages but omits any reference to the satirical conclusion.
22. *The Denial of Death* (New York: Macmillan, 1973), p. 66.
23. *The Denial of Death*, p. 12.
24. *Poe's Fiction*, p. 182.
25. I wish to thank the LSU Council on Research for the 1974 Summer Research Grant which supported early work on this essay. A shorter version of this paper was read at the 1976 SCMLA Convention in Dallas.

POE'S "THE SPECTACLES": A NEW TEXT FROM MANUSCRIPT

EDITED, WITH TEXTUAL COMMENTARY AND NOTES

Joseph J. Moldenhauer

I. HISTORY OF THE TEXT

UNDER THE CAPTION "Series of Prize Stories," Edgar A. Poe's "The Spectacles" was printed in the *Dollar Newspaper* on 27 March 1844. Poe thus appeared for the second time in the elephant-folio-sized Philadelphia weekly, which had published "The Gold-Bug" the previous June as the best story submitted in a $100-premium contest.[1] Both the author and the *Dollar Newspaper* benefited amply from "The Gold-Bug": Poe later declared that the tale had achieved a circulation of more than 300,000 copies.[2] After presenting it in two installments (21 June and 28 June 1843), the *Dollar Newspaper*'s editor, Joseph Sailer, reprinted it in a supplement to the 12 July issue. In an overlapping republication, it was serialized in the Philadelphia *Saturday Courier* on 24 June, 1 July, and 8 July; and within six weeks it was dramatized as *The Gold Bug; or, the Pirate's Treasure* at Philadelphia's Walnut Street Theatre.[3] Shortly after "The Raven" achieved notoriety, Poe told his friend F. W. Thomas, "'The Raven' has had a great 'run', Thomas—but I wrote it for the express purpose of running—just as I did the 'Gold-Bug', you know. The bird beat the bug, though, all hollow."[4]

Exploiting his former triumph, Sailer identified Poe in the byline of "The Spectacles" as "author of the prize story, 'The Gold-Bug,' etc." and inserted a puff in the same issue:

> We publish this week from the pen of Edgar A. Poe, Esq., a story under the title of "The Spectacles", to which we call the attention of the readers of the "Newspaper" under the assurance that they will join us in the opinion that it is one of the best from his chaste and able pen and second only to the popular prize production, "The Gold Bug." Who will go without "Spectacles" when an article so handsomely furnished may be obtained for 3 cents?[5]

Whether Poe actually received a prize for "The Spectacles" I have been unable to determine.[6] The 31 July issue contained the first printing of "The Premature Burial." One of the later reprintings of "The Raven" during Poe's lifetime occurred in the 1 November 1848 issue.

Almost simultaneously with the *Dollar Newspaper* printing of "The Spectacles," Poe took steps to place the tale in a British magazine. Robertson notes that "Poe was ambitious, and in his desire to be known to English readers, he made an attempt, through Dickens, to enter the ranks of the contributors to 'Blackwoods.'"[7] Charles Dickens' letter to Poe from London, 27 November 1842, alludes to a "mission" with which Poe had charged him, both by letter and orally during Dickens' American visit earlier that year: he had attempted, without success, to interest a London publisher in a volume of Poe's tales.[8] Now Poe approached another, if less celebrated, British writer, the poet and dramatist Richard Henry Horne. After an adventurous young manhood, Horne (1803–84) published literary essays in the early 1830s, edited the *Monthly Repository* in 1836–37, wrote two tragedies in the latter year, supplied an introduction to Black's translation of Schlegel's *Lectures on Dramatic Art and Literature*, and published *Gregory VII, a Tragedy* in 1840. The following year he provided an introduction and three texts to a modernized edition of Chaucer, a project to which Elizabeth Barrett also contributed; and in 1843 appeared his epic poem in three books, *Orion*.[9] An immediate success, *Orion* went into a fourth edition before the end of 1843; and it was this edition that Poe reviewed in *Graham's Magazine*, March 1844. In the first paragraph Poe acknowledged Horne's literary associations and declared his familiarity with and appreciation of Horne's more important earlier compositions: "We have been among the earliest readers of Mr. Horne—among the most earnest admirers of his high genius;—for a man of high, of the highest genius, he unquestionably is."[10] The "Review of *Orion*" is chiefly interesting for its anticipations of the concepts and even the phrases of Poe's late lecture-essay, "The Poetic Principle"; and by the criteria for "pure" poetic utterance that Poe announces in the review, *Orion* falls short of authenticity. Horne has been infected, according to Poe, by the cant of mystics, progressives, and transcendentalists, a "junto of dreamers" that "badgered" Horne "into the attempt at commingling the obstinate oils and waters of Poetry and of Truth."[11] *Orion*, in brief, is an allegory—a poem written for the sake of ideas:

> Mr. Horne conceived . . . that to compose a poem merely for that poem's sake—and to acknowledge such to be his purpose—would be to subject

PLATE FIVE
Page one of the
"Spectacles" manuscript.
Courtesy TxU

PLATE SIX
The last page of the
"Spectacles" manuscript.
Courtesy TxU

himself to the charge of imbecility—of triviality—of deficiency in the true dignity and force; but, had he listened to the dictates of his own soul, he could not have failed to perceive, at once, that under the sun there exists no work more intrinsically noble, than this very poem *written solely for the poem's sake*.[12]

By implication, then, *Orion* is a profoundly flawed work, defective in its very conception. But the weight of Poe's attack falls on Horne's philosophical acquaintances rather than upon the poet himself. In the second half of the review Poe indulges in fervid praise, qualifying his panegyrics only with a few remarks on minor defects in the poem. Notwithstanding the apparent contradiction with his earlier statements about Horne's improper purposes, Poe declares his

deliberate opinion that, in all that regards the loftiest and holiest attributes of the true Poetry, "Orion" has *never* been excelled. Indeed we feel strongly inclined to say that it has never been *equaled*. Its imagination—that quality which is all in all—is of the most refined—the most elevating—the most august character.[13]

Milton's picture of Hell in *Paradise Lost* is "*altogether inferior* in graphic effect, in originality, in expression, in the true imagination," Poe asserts, to a descriptive passage in *Orion*. And the poem as a whole, he concludes, "will be admitted, by every man of genius, to be one of the noblest, if not the very noblest poetical work of the age. Its defects are trivial and conventional—its beauties intrinsic and *supreme*."[14]

Poe's decision to solicit Horne's help with the British editors was thus not surprising. Lacking Horne's address, he wrote on 15 March to Cornelius Mathews, one of the New York literati and a friend of Horne's, requesting this information and mentioning that he had "a letter and small parcel" for Horne, then praising Mathews' pamphlet on "the International Copy-Right Question."[15] Aside from wishing to extend his reputation abroad, Poe was concerned to profit by English publication of his works: the absence of equitable copyright agreements left Poe, and his contemporaries on both sides of the Atlantic, vulnerable to piracy.

The "small parcel" Poe sent to Horne near the end of March contained a manuscript of "The Spectacles." Horne replied on 16 April:

I have received your letter this morning, and shall feel now, and at all times happy in forwarding your views here, so far as I am able, in these matters of literary engagement. Just at this time, however, and probably for some months to come, I shall not be *likely* to have the power. If you have seen the "New Spirit of the Age" you will readily understand that a

SERIES OF PRIZE STORIES

[Written for the Philadelphia Dollar Newspaper.]

THE SPECTACLES.

BY EDGAR A. POE, AUTHOR OF THE PRIZE STORY, "THE GOLD-BUG," ETC.

Many years ago, it was the fashion to ridicule the idea of "love at first sight;" but those who think not less than those who feel deeply, have always advocated its existence. Modern discoveries, indeed, in what may be termed ethical magnetism or magnetoæsthetics, render it probable that the most natural, and, consequently, the truest and most intense of the human affections, are those which arise in the heart as if by electric sympathy—in a word, that the brightest and most enduring of the psychal fetters are those which are riveted by a glance. The confession I am about to make will add another to the already almost innumerable instances of the truth of the position.

My story requires that I should be somewhat minute. I am still a very young man—not yet twenty-two years of age. My name, at present, is a very usual and rather plebeian one—Simpson. I say "at present;" for it is only lately that I have been so called—having legislatively adopted this surname within the last year, in order to receive a large inheritance left me by a distant male relative, Adolphus Simpson, Esq The bequest was conditioned upon my taking the name of the testator;—the family, not the Christian name; my Christian name is Napoleon Buonaparte—or, more properly, these are my first and middle appellations.

I assumed the name, Simpson, with some reluctance, as in my true patronym, Froissart, I felt a very pardonable pride; believing that I could trace a descent from the immortal author of the "Chronicles." While on the subject of names, by the by, I may mention a singular coincidence of sound attending the names of some of my immediate predecessors. My father was a Monsieur Froissart, of Paris. His wife, my mother, whom he married at fifteen, was a Mademoiselle Croissart, eldest daughter of Croissart, the banker; whose wife, again, being only sixteen when married, was the eldest daughter of one Victor Voissart. Monsieur Voissart, very singularly, had wedded a lady of similar name—a Mademoiselle Moissart. She, too, was quite a child when married; and her mother, also, Madame Moissart, was only fourteen when led to the altar. These early marriages are usual in France. Here, however, are Moissart, Voissart, Croissart, and Froissart, all in the direct line of descent. My own name, though, as I say, became Simpson, by act of Legislature, and with so much repugnance on my part that, at one period, I actually hesitated about accepting the legacy with the useless and annoying *proviso* attached.

As to personal endowments I am by no means deficient. On the contrary, I believe that I am well made, and possess what nine tenths of the world would call a handsome face. In height I saw—I felt—I knew that I was deeply, madly, irrecoverably in love—and this even before seeing the face of the person beloved. So intense, indeed, was the passion that consumed me, that I really believe it would have received little if any abatement had the features, yet unseen, proved of merely ordinary character; so anomalous is the nature of the only true love—of the love at first sight—and so little really dependent is it upon the external conditions which only seem to create and control it.

While I was wrapped in admiration of this lovely vision, a sudden disturbance among the audience caused her to turn her head partially towards me, so that I beheld the entire profile of the face. Its beauty even exceeded my anticipations—and yet there was something about it which disappointed me without my being able to tell exactly what it was. I said "disappointed," but this is not altogether the word. My sentiments were at once quieted and exalted. They partook less of transport and more of calm enthusiasm—of enthusiastic repose. This state of feeling arose, perhaps, from the Madonna-like and matronly air of the face; and yet I at once understood that it could not have arisen entirely from this. There was something else—some mystery which I could not develope—some expression about the countenance which slightly disturbed me while it greatly heightened my interest. In fact, I was just in that condition of mind which prepares a young and susceptible man for any act of extravagance. Had the lady been alone, I should undoubtedly have entered her box and accosted her at all hazards; but, fortunately, she was attended by two companions—a gentleman, and a strikingly beautiful woman, to all appearance a few years younger than herself.

I revolved in mind a thousand schemes by which I might obtain, hereafter, an introduction to the elder lady, or, for the present, at all events, a more distinct view of her beauty. I would have removed my position to one nearer her own; but the crowded state of the theatre rendered this impossible, and the stern decrees of Fashion, had, of late, imperatively prohibited the use of the opera-glass, in a case such as this, even had I been so fortunate as to have one with me—but I had not, and was thus in despair.

At length I bethought me of applying to my companion.

"Talbot," I said, "*you* have an opera-glass. Let me have it."

"An opera glass! no! what do you suppose I would be doing with an opera-glass?—low!—very." Here he turned impatiently towards the stage.

"But, Talbot," I continued, pulling him by the shoulder, "listen to me, will you? Do you see the stage-box?—there!—no, the next—did you ever behold as lovely a woman?"

"She is very beautiful, no doubt," he said.

"I wonder who she can be!"

"Why, in the name of all that is angelic, do n't you *know* who she is? 'Not to know her argues yourself unknown.' She is the celebrated Madame Lalande—the beauty of the day *par excellence*, and the talk of the whole town. seemed absorbed in the performances. At the expiration of this period, however, I was thrown into an extremity of agitation by seeing her unfold, for the second time, the eye-glass which hung at her side, fully confront me as before, and, disregarding the renewed buzz of the audience, survey me, from head to foot, with the the same miraculous composure which had previously so delighted and confounded my soul.

This extraordinary behaviour, by throwing me into a perfect fever of excitement—into an absolute delirium of love—served rather to embolden than to disconcert me. In the mad intensity of my devotion I forgot every thing but the presence and the majestic loveliness of the vision which confronted my gaze. Watching my opportunity, when I thought the audience were fully engaged with the opera, I at length caught the eyes of Madame Lalande, and, upon the instant, made a slight but unmistakeable bow.

She blushed very deeply—then averted her eyes—then slowly and cautiously looked around, apparently to see if my rash action had been noticed—then leaned over towards the gentleman who sat by her side.

I now felt a burning sense of the impropriety I had committed, and expected nothing less than instant exposure; while a vision of pistols upon the morrow floated rapidly and uncomfortably through my brain. I was greatly and immediately relieved, however, when I saw the lady merely hand the gentleman a playbill, without speaking; but the reader may form some feeble conception of my astonishment—of my profound amazement—my delirious bewilderment of heart and soul—when, instantly afterwards, having again glanced furtively around, she allowed her bright eyes to settle fully and steadily upon my own, and then, with a faint smile disclosing a bright line of her pearly teeth, made two distinct, pointed and unequivocal affirmative inclinations of the head.

It is useless, of course, to dwell upon my joy—upon my transport—upon my illimitable ecstasy of heart. If ever man was mad with excess of happiness, it was myself at that moment. I loved. This was my *first* love—so I felt it to be. It was love supreme—indescribable. It was "love at first sight;" and, at first sight too, it had been appreciated and—*returned*.

Yes, returned. How and why should I doubt it for an instant? What other construction could I possibly put upon such conduct, on the part of a lady so beautiful—so wealthy—evidently so accomplished—of so high breeding—of so lofty a position in society—in every regard so entirely respectable as I felt assured was Madame Lalande? Yes, she loved me—she returned the enthusiasm of my love, with an enthusiasm as blind—as uncompromising—as uncalculating—as abandoned—and as utterly unbounded as my own! These delicious fancies and reflections, however, were now interrupted by the falling of the drop-curtain. The audience arose; and the usual tumult immediately supervened. Quitting Talbot abruptly, I made every endeavor to force my way into closer proximity with Madame Lalande. Having failed in this, on ac- in a condition little short of madness. Madame Lalande, I had been told, was a Parisian—had lately arrived from Paris—might she not suddenly return?—return before Talbot came back—and might she not be thus lost to me forever? The thought was too terrible to bear. Since my future happiness was at issue, I resolved to act with a manly decision. In a word, upon the breaking up of the play, I traced the lady to her residence, noted the address, and the next morning sent her a full and elaborate letter, in which I poured out my whole heart.

I spoke boldly, freely—in a word, I spoke with passion. I concealed nothing—nothing even of my weakness. I alluded to the romantic circumstances of our first meeting—even to the glances which had passed between us. I went so far as to say that I felt assured of her love; while I offered this assurance, and my own intensity of devotion, as two excuses for my otherwise unpardonable conduct. As a third, I spoke of my fear that she might quit the city before I could have the opportunity of a formal introduction. I concluded the most wildly enthusiastic epistle ever penned, with a frank declaration of my worldly circumstances—of my affluence—and with an offer of my heart and of my hand.

In an agony of expectation I awaited the reply. After what seemed the lapse of a century it came.

Yes, actually *came*. Romantic as all this may appear, I really received a letter from Madame Lalande—the beautiful, the wealthy, the idolized Madame Lalande. Her eyes—her magnificent eyes—had not belied her noble heart. Like a true Frenchwoman, as she was, she had obeyed the frank dictates of her reason—the generous impulses of her nature—despising the conventional pruderies of the world. She had *not* scorned my proposals. She had *not* sheltered herself in silence. She had *not* returned my letter unopened. She had even sent me, in reply, one penned by her own exquisite fingers. It ran thus:

Monsieur Simpson will pardonne me for not compose de butefulle tong of his contrée so well as might. It is only de late dat I am arrive, and not yet have de opportunite for to—l'etudier.

Wid dis apologie for de maniere, I vill now say dat, hélas! Monsieur Simpson ave guess but de too true. Need I say de more? *Hélas!* am I not ready speak de too moshe?

EUGENIE LALANDE.

This noble-spirited note I kissed a million times, and committed no doubt, on its account, a thousand other extravagances that have now escaped my memory. Still Talbot *would* not return. Alas! could he have formed even the vaguest idea of the suffering his absence occasioned his friend, would not his sympathizing nature have flown immediately to my relief? Still, however, he came *not*. I wrote. He replied. He was detained by urgent business—but would now shortly return. He begged me not to be impatient—to moderate my transports—to read soothing books—to drink nothing stronger than Hock—and to bring the consolations of philosophy to my aid. The fool! if he could not come himself, why, in the name of every thing rational, could he not have enclosed

missible and indeed as even pr
had always entertained the belief
of the wife should *never* exceed ir
of the husband. A discrepancy o
ral kind gave rise too frequently,
of unhappiness. Now she was a
own age did not exceed two and t
on the contrary, perhaps, was *not*
years of my Eugénie extended
ably beyond that sum.

About all this there was a nobi
dignity of candor—which delight
chanted me—which eternally
chains. I could scarcely restrain
transport which possessed me.

"My sweetest Eugénie," I cr
all this about which you are disc
years surpass in some measure
what then? The customs of the
many conventional follies. To t
as ourselves, in what respect diff
an hour? I am twenty-two, you
indeed you may as well call me, a
three. Now you yourself, my de
can have numbered no more th
numbered no more than—no mor
than—than—"

Here I paused for a brief inst
pectation that Madame Lalande v
me by supplying her true age.
woman is seldom direct, and h
way of answer to an embarrassi
little practical reply of her own.
instance, Eugénie, who, for a
past, had seemed to be searching
in her bosom, at length let fall up
miniature, which I immediately
presented.

"Keep it," she said, with one
vishing smiles. "Keep it for my
sake of her whom it too flatterin
Besides, upon the back of the tri
discover, perhaps, the very in
seem to desire. It is now, to be
rather dark—but you can exan
leisure, in the morning. In the n
shall be my escort home to-nigh
here, are about holding a little m
can promise you, too, some good
French are not nearly so punc
Americans, and I shall have r
smuggling you in, in the characte
quaintance."

With this, she took my arm
her home. The mansion was qu
and, I believe, furnished in good
latter point, however, I am scarc
judge; for it was just dark as w
in American mansions of the be
seldom, during the heat of summ
appearance at this the most plea
the day. In about an hour after
be sure, a single shaded solar la
the principal drawing room; and
I could thus see, was arranged
good taste and even splendor;
rooms of the suite, and in which
chiefly assembled, remained, du
evening, in a very agreeable sh

PLATE SEVEN
A portion of the *Dollar Newspaper* first printing, 27 March 1844.
Courtesy MdHi

great many critics here, and some authors, are far from pleased with me. The attacks and jeers in Magazines and newspapers (though several have treated me very fairly) are nearly all written by friends of the angry parties, or influenced by them. Perhaps I may say a word on this point in the Second Edition now preparing. I mention this to show you *why* I can do little at present. I need not say to an American, that when the storm has blown over, those trees that are not blown down, nor injured, look all the fresher among the wrecks. I dare say I shall be able to do what you wish before long. I should prefer to do this so that you are fairly remunerated; but if the parties are *not* in a "paying condition" then I will put you in direct communication with them to arrange the matter yourself.

I could, most probably, obtain the insertion of the article you have sent, in "Jerrold's Illuminated Magazine." Jerrold has always spoken and written very handsomely and eloquently about me, and there would be no difficulty. But—I fear this magazine is not doing at all well. I tell you this *in confidence*. They have a large, but inadequate circulation. The remuneration would be scarcely worth having—10 guineas a sheet, is poor pay for such a page! And now, perhaps, they do not even give that. I will see. My impression, however, is that for the reasons stated previously, I shall not, *at present*, be able to assist you in the way I could best wish.

Your name is well known to me in the critical literature of America, although I have not seen any American magazine for some months. I have ordered the last two Nos of "Graham's Magazine" but have not yet received them from my booksellers.

I am very grateful for the noble and generous terms in which you speak of my works.

I have written you a business-like, and not a very 'spiritual' letter, you will think. Still, as you are kind enough to give me credit for some things of the latter kind, it seemed best at this distance to reply to some wishes, practically.[16]

It seems probable that Poe mentioned his review of *Orion* in the letter (now lost) accompanying "The Spectacles"; he may have sent a copy, in another communication, before receiving Horne's reply dated 16 April. Horne wrote again on the 27th, directing his remarks chiefly to the review:

When I replied to your letter . . . I had not seen the No of "Graham" for March, containing the review of "Orion." Mr C. Mathews, of New York, had been so good as to inform me there would be a review; and he, at the same time, mentioned that he had sent me a copy of the Magazine in question. My friend Miss E. B. Barrett also sent me a note to the same effect. But . . . the Magazine never reached me. . . .

Your M.S. of the "Spectacles" is safely lodged in my iron chest with my own M.S.S. till I find a favorable opportunity for its use.

I have carefully read and considered the review. . . . It would be uncandid in me to appear to agree to all the objections; and, amidst such high praise, so independantly and courageously awarded, it would be un-

THE SPECTACLES.

BY EDGAR A. POE.

MANY years ago, it was the fashion to ridicule the idea of "love at first sight;" but those who think not less than those who feel deeply, have always advocated its existence. Modern discoveries, indeed, in what may be termed ethical magnetism, or magnetœsthetics, render it probable that the most natural, and, consequently, the truest and most intense of the human affections, are those which arise in the heart as if by electric sympathy—in a word, that the brightest and most enduring of the psychal fetters are those which are rivetted by a glance. The confession I am about to make will add another to the already almost innumerable instances of the truth of the position.

My story requires that I should be somewhat minute. I am still a very young man—not yet twenty-two years of age. My name, at present, is a very usual and rather plebeian one, —Simpson. I say "at present;" for it is only lately that I have been so called—having legislatively adopted this surname within the last year, in order to receive a large inheritance left me by a distant male relative, Adolphus Simpson, Esq. The bequest was conditioned upon my taking the name of the testator—the family, not the Christian name; my Christian name is Napoleon Buonaparte—or, more properly, these are my first and middle appellations.

I assumed the name, Simpson, with some reluctance, as in my true patronym, Froissart, I felt a very pardonable pride; believing that I could trace a descent from the immortal author of the "Chronicles." While on the subject of names, by-the-bye, I may mention a singular coincidence of sound attending the names of some of my immediate predecessors. My father was a Monsieur Froissart, of Paris. His wife, my mother, whom he married at fifteen, was a Mademoiselle Croissart, eldest daughter of Croissart, the banker; whose wife, again, being only sixteen when married, was the eldest daughter of one Victor Voissart. Monsieur Voissart, very singularly, had wedded a lady of similar name—a Mademoiselle Moissart. She, too, was a child when married; and her mother, also, Madame Moissart, was only fourteen when led to the altar. These early marriages are usual in France. Here, however, are Moissart, Voissart, Croissart, and Froissart, all in the direct line of descent. My own name, though, as I say, became Simpson, by act of legislature, and with so much repugnance on my part, that, at one period, I actually hesitated about accepting the legacy with the useless and annoying *proviso* attached.

As to personal endowments, I am by no means deficient. On the contrary, I believe that I am well made, and possess what nine-tenths of the world would call a handsome face. In height, I am five feet eleven. My hair is black and curling. My nose is sufficiently good. My eyes are large and gray; and although, in fact, they are weak to a very inconvenient degree, still no defect in this regard would be suspected from their appearance. The weakness itself, however, has always much annoyed me, and I have resorted to every remedy—short of wearing glasses. Being youthful and good-looking, I naturally dislike these, and have resolutely refused to employ them. I know nothing, indeed, which so disfigures the countenance of a young person, or so impresses every feature with an air of demureness, if not altogether of sanctimoniousness and of age. An eye-glass, on the other hand, has a savour of downright foppery and affectation. I have hitherto managed as well as I could without either. But there is something too much of these merely personal details, which, after all, are of little importance. I will content myself with saying, in addition, that my temperament is sanguine, rash, ardent, enthusiastic—and that all my life I have been a devoted admirer of the women.

One night, last winter, I entered a box at the C—— theatre, in company with a friend, Mr. Talbot. It was an opera night, and the bills presented a very rare attraction, so that the house was excessively crowded. We were in time, however, to obtain the front seats which had been preserved for us, and into which, with some little difficulty, we elbowed our way.

For two hours, my companion, who was a musical *fanatico*, gave his undivided attention to the stage; and, in the meantime, I amused myself by observing the audience, which consisted, in chief part, of the very *elite* of the city. Having satisfied myself upon this point, I was about turning my eyes to the *prima donna*, when they were arrested and rivetted by a figure in one of the private boxes which had escaped my observation.

If I live a thousand years, I can never forget the intense emotion with which I regarded this figure. It was that of a female, the most exquisite I had ever beheld. The face was so far turned towards the stage that, for some minutes, I could not obtain a view of it; but the form was *divine*—no other word can sufficiently express its magnificent proportion, and even the term "divine" seems ridiculously feeble as I write it.

The magic of a lovely form in woman—the necromancy of female gracefulness—was always a power which I had found it impossible to resist; but here was grace personified, incarnate—the *beau ideal* of my wildest and most enthusiastic visions. The figure, nearly all which the construction of the box permitted to be seen, was somewhat above the medium height, and nearly approached, without positively reaching, the majestic. Its perfect fulness and *tournure* were delicious. The head, of which only the back was visible, rivalled in outline that of the Greek Psyche, and was rather displayed than concealed by an elegant cape of *gaze aerienne*, which put me in mind of the *ventum textilem* of Apuleius. The right arm hung over the balustrade of the box, and thrilled every nerve of my frame with its exquisite symmetry. Its upper portion was draperied by one of the loose open sleeves then in fashion. This extended but little below the elbow. Beneath it was worn an under one of some frail material, close fitting, and terminated by a cuff of rich lace, which fell gracefully over the top of the hand, revealing only the delicate fingers, upon one of which sparkled a diamond ring, which I at once saw was of extraordinary value. The admirable roundness of the wrist was well set off by a bracelet which encircled it, and which also was ornamented and clasped by a magnificent *aigrette* of jewels—telling, in words that could not be mistaken, at once of the wealth and fastidious taste of the wearer.

I gazed at this queenly apparition for at least half an hour, as if I had been suddenly converted to stone; and, during this period, I felt the full force and truth of all that has been said or sung concerning "love at first sight." My feelings were totally different from any which I had hitherto experienced, in the presence of even the most celebrated specimens of female loveliness. An unaccountable, and what I am compelled to consider a *magnetic* sympathy of soul for soul, seemed to rivet, not only my vision, but my whole powers of thought and feeling, upon the admirable object before me. I saw—I felt—I knew that I was deeply, madly, irrecoverably in love, —and this even before seeing the face of the person beloved. So intense, indeed, was the passion that consumed me, that I really believe it would have received little, if any, abatement, had the features, yet unseen, proved of merely ordinary character; so anomalous is the nature of the only true love—of the love at first sight—and so little really dependent is it upon the external conditions which only seem to create and control it.

While I was wrapped in admiration of this lovely vision, a sudden disturbance among the audience caused her to turn her head partially towards me, so that I beheld the entire

PLATE EIGHT

First page of the *Lloyd's Entertaining Journal* printing, 3 May 1845.

Courtesy CtY

grateful in me to offer any self-justificatory remark on any such objections. I shall, therefore, only observe that there are *some* objections from which I can *derive advantage* in the way of revision—which is more than I can say of any of the critiques written on this side of the waters.[17]

The manuscript that now rested in Horne's strongbox was not the printer's copy from which the *Dollar Newspaper* text had been set during the week preceding 27 March, and which had probably been discarded in the printshop or in Sailer's office. It was, rather, a clean holograph Poe prepared in mid-March or before, either from a working draft or from the manuscript that would serve as *Dollar Newspaper* setting copy. It remained among Horne's papers until Horne gave it to his friend and literary executor, the Keats and Shelley scholar Henry Buxton Forman (1842–1917).[18] In the 1920 sale of Forman's library by the Anderson Galleries, the manuscript entered the collection of Frank Brewer Bemis (1861–1935), whose bookplate, with Forman's, is attached to the binding.[19] The next owner was Frank J. Hogan (1877–1944), a Washington attorney and collector of American authors, whose library was auctioned by Parke-Bernet Galleries on 23 and 24 January 1945. As a result of the Hogan sale, William H. Koester, the noted Baltimore collector of Poe, obtained "The Spectacles" and a fair copy of "The Domain of Arnheim," plus three other literary manuscripts and an authorially annotated copy of *Eureka*. In 1966, two years after Koester's death, his collection was acquired by the University of Texas.[20] The "Spectacles" holograph, written in black ink, occupies thirty-eight pages of a forty-page booklet, 4½ by 7 inches, blind-stamped with a hand-and-flower design, and sewn into a marbled paper cover. Poe added his name below the title after writing page one, in a darker ink matching that of the final paragraphs. By courtesy of the Humanities Research Center, The University of Texas at Austin, the manuscript text of "The Spectacles" is here printed.

On 30 March, three days after "The Spectacles" was published in Philadelphia, Poe approached James Russell Lowell about the biographies of contemporary American authors that George R. Graham, his former employer, was commissioning for *Graham's Magazine*. (At the time, Poe expected to write Lowell's sketch; Lowell in fact wrote Poe's for the February 1845 issue.) After asking if Lowell had read *Orion*, Poe lamented the lack of international copyright agreements and of a literary monthly of the sort Poe was forever attempting to establish under the title the *Penn Magazine* or the *Stylus*. With his letter he enclosed "a 'Dollar Newspaper', containing a somewhat extravagant tale of my own. I fear it will prove little to your taste."[21] By the morning of 7 April Poe was in New York with his wife Virginia,

THE BROADWAY JOURNAL.

VOL. 2.   EDGAR A. POE, 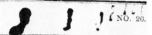 NO. 20.
EDITOR AND PROPRIETOR.

NEW-YORK, SATURDAY, NOVEMBER 22, 1845.

Sister Mine.

Sister mine—Sister mine!
  Why art so dear?
Why throbs this heart of mine,
Like the strong-tendrilled vine,
Clinging so close to thine
  When thou art near,
    Sister mine?

Sister mine—Sister mine!
  Why art so dear?
Chill is this heart of mine,
Till that sweet smile of thine
Wakes it to life divine,
  When thou art near,
    Sister mine.

Sister mine—Sister mine!
  Why art so dear?
Light is this heart of mine,
As is the sparkling wine
Bright in its crimson-shine,
  When thou art near,
    Sister mine.

Sister mine—Sister mine!
Thou art so dear
By that wierd spell of thine,
Wreathed round this heart of mine
Till our twin spirits twine
  When thou art near,
    Sister mine!
          R. H. DANA.

The Spectacles.

MANY years ago, it was the fashion to ridicule the idea of "love at first sight;" but those who think, not less than those who feel deeply, have always advocated its existence. Modern discoveries, indeed, in what may be termed ethical magnetism or magnetœsthetics, render it probable that the most natural, and, consequently the truest and most intense of the human affections, are those which arise in the heart as if by electric sympathy—in a word, that the brightest and most enduring of the psychal fetters are those which are riveted by a glance. The confession I am about to make will add another to the already almost innumerable instances of the truth of the position.

My story requires that I should be somewhat minute. I am still a very young man—not yet twenty-two years of age. My name, at present, is a very usual and rather plebeian one—Simpson. I say "at present;" for it is only lately that I have been so called—having legislatively adopted this surname within the last year, in order to receive a large inheritance left me by a distant male relative, Adolphus Simpson, Esq. The bequest was conditioned upon my taking the name of the testator:—the family, not the Christian name; my Christian name is Napoleon Buonaparte—or, more properly, these are my first and middle appellations.

I assumed the name, Simpson, with some reluctance, as in my true patronym, Froissart, I felt a very pardonable pride; beleiving that I could trace a descent from the immortal author of the "Chronicles." While on the subject of names, by the bye, I may mention a singular coincidence of sound attending the names of some of my immediate predecessors. My father was a Monsieur Froissart, of Paris. His wife, my mother, whom he married at fifteen, was a Mademoiselle Croissart, eldest daughter of Croissart the banker; whose wife, again, being only sixteen when married, was the eldest daughter of one Victor Voissart. Monsieur Voissart, very singularly, had married a lady of similar name—a Mademoiselle Moissart. She, too, was quite a child when married; and her mother, also, Madame Moissart, was only fourteen when led to the altar. These early marriages are usual in France. Here, however, are Moissart, Voissart, Croissart, and Froissart, all in the direct line of descent. My own name, though, as I say, became Simpson, by act of Legislature, and with so much repugnance on my part that, at one period, I actually hesitated about accepting the legacy with the useless and annoying *proviso* attached.

As to personal endowments I am by no means deficient. On the contrary, I believe that I am well made, and possess what nine tenths of the world would call a handsome face. In height I am five feet eleven. My hair is black and curling. My nose is sufficiently good. My eyes are large and gray; and although, in fact, they are weak to a very inconvenient degree, still no defect in this regard would be suspected from their appearance. The weakness, itself, however, has always much annoyed me, and I have resorted to every remedy—short of wearing glasses. Being youthful and good-looking, I naturally dislike these, and have resolutely refused to employ them. I know nothing, indeed, which so disfigures the countenance of a young person, or so impresses every feature with an air of demureness, if not altogether of sanctimoniousness and of age. An eye-glass, on the other hand, has a savor of downright foppery and affectation. I have hitherto managed as well as I could without either. But something too much of these merely personal details, which, after all, are of little importance. I will content myself with saying, in addition, that my temperament is sanguine, rash, ardent, enthusiastic—and that all my life I have been a devoted admirer of the women.

One night, last winter, I entered a box at the P—— theatre, in company with a friend, Mr. Talbot. It was an opera night, and the bills presented a very rare attraction, so that the house was excessively crowded. We were in time, however, to obtain the front seats having left Philadelphia even before Lowell could have responded to Poe's request for biographical data. When a letter from Lowell, including his offer to write the sketch of Poe's life and letters, was forwarded to Poe late in May, Poe declared his intention to live in New York "for the future" and provided Lowell with a list of his more recent published and unpublished tales. "The Spectacles" is the first item in the list, while "The Gold-Bug" and "Thou Art the Man" (which would not be printed until November) are the two final entries.[22]

Although Poe's hopes for the manuscript he sent to Horne failed to materialize, "The Spectacles" did, in fact, appear in a British magazine. *Lloyd's Entertaining Journal*, a London penny publication, reprinted "Raising the Wind; or, Diddling Considered as One of the Exact Sciences" from the *Saturday Courier* of 14 October 1843 in its 4 January 1845 issue, and reprinted "The Spectacles" from the *Dollar Newspaper* on 3 May 1845. Neither reprinting credits the American periodical source, and both, apparently, were piracies.[23] Meanwhile, Poe had joined John Bisco, a New York magazinist, in Bisco's *Broadway Journal* venture. This magazine of literature and the arts had commenced publication on 4 January 1845, under the editorship of Charles F. Briggs. Poe contributed reviews (some reprinted, but most original) to the early numbers, in which also appeared a reprint of "The Raven" (8 February) and a first publication of his "Some Secrets of the Magazine Prison-House" (15 February). His two-part review of Elizabeth Barrett's *The Drama of Exile, and Other Poems* occupied a prominent place in the maiden issues of 4 and 11 January. This piece, whose laudatory language sometimes echoes the review of *Orion* ("of all the friends of the fair author, we doubt whether one exists, with more profound—with more enthusiastic reverence and admiration of her genius, than the writer of these words"),[24] drew responses from both Horne and Elizabeth Barrett. It would seem that Poe sent a copy of the *Broadway Journal* columns to Horne with his letter (now lost) of 25 January 1845, for Horne responded from London, on 17 May, as follows:

> After so long a delay of my last letter to you, I am at all events glad to hear that it reached you. . . . your present letter of the date of Jany 25th/45 only reached my house at the latter end of April. . . .
> I have only just returned from a nine months' absence in Germany. . . .
> As I thought your letter to me contained more of the bright side of criticism than the 'Broadway Journal" I sent it to my friend Miss Barrett. She returned it with a note—half of which I tear off, and send you (*confidentially*) that you may see in what a good and noble spirit she receives the critique—in which as you say, the shadows do certainly predominate. . . .

THE SPECTACLES.

MANY years ago, it was the fashion to ridicule the idea of "love at first sight;" but those who think, not less than those who feel deeply, have always advocated its existence. Modern discoveries, indeed, in what may be termed ethical magnetism or magnetœsthetics, render it probable that the most natural, and, consequently, the truest and most intense of the human affections, are those which arise in the heart as if by electric sympathy—in a word, that the brightest and most enduring of the psychal fetters are those which are riveted by a glance. The confession I am about to make, will add another to the already almost innumerable instances of the truth of the position.

My story requires that I should be somewhat minute. I am still a very young man—not yet twenty-two years of age. My name, at present, is a very usual and rather plebeian one—Simpson. I say "at present;" for it is only lately that I have been so called—having legislatively adopted this surname within the last year, in order to receive a large inheritance left me by a distant male relative, Adolphus Simpson, Esq. The bequest was conditioned upon my taking the name of the testator;—the family, not the Christian name; my Christian name is Napoleon Buonaparte—or, more properly, these are my first and middle appellations.

I assumed the name, Simpson, with some reluctance, as in my true patronym, Froissart, I felt a very pardonable pride—believing

PLATE TEN
First page of Griswold's 1850 text in *The Works of the Late Edgar Allan Poe*, vol. 2.
Courtesy TxU

THE SPECTACLES
Short Story By
EDGAR ALLAN POE

PLATE ELEVEN
Title page of the spurious "Spectacles" pamphlet.
Courtesy TxU

CAREY & LEA
Philadelphia
1842

> Miss Barrett has read the "Raven" and says she thinks there is a fine lyrical melody in it. When I tell you that this lady "says" you will be so good as understand that I mean "writes"—for although I have corresponded with Miss Barrett these 5 or 6 years, I have never seen her to this day. Nor have I been *nearer* to doing so, than talking with her father and sisters.[25]

In response to questions and comments by Poe, Horne remarks on his acquaintance with and high opinion of Tennyson, sends a copy of *Orion* with a view to possible American publication, presents Poe with an endorsed copy of *Gregory VII* and two copies of his introduction to *A New Spirit of the Age* (critical essays on distinguished living authors, 1844), offers to transmit any of his other writings, and volunteers "a short poem or two for your Magazine"—the perennial *Stylus*, one imagines—"directly it is established, or for the 1st No, if there be time for you to let me know."[26] There is no mention of the "Spectacles" manuscript or of the reprinting in *Lloyd's*.

Eager to gain an interest in the *Broadway Journal* despite his chronic impecuniosity, Poe signed an agreement with Bisco on 21 February 1845 to assist Briggs in editing the weekly, to be listed as one of the editors, and to furnish at least one printed page of copy per week, in return for a third of the profits.[27] He is first listed as an editor, together with Briggs and Henry C. Watson, in the tenth issue of Volume I, 8 March 1845, for which number he provided the opening installment (of an eventual five) of his "Reply to Outis" concerning Longfellow and plagiarism. Heartman and Canny observe that Poe and Watson were joint editors from the issue of 1 March through that of 18 October;[28] Briggs' name, however, remained on the masthead through the last number of Volume I, 28 June 1845. In Volume II, number 1 (12 July), with the names of Poe and Watson as editors, there appeared a note to the public remarking on the one-week suspension of publication and observing that Watson remained in control of the "Musical Department," while Poe alone managed the "editorial conduct." Both before and after the removal of Briggs' name, Poe supplied large quantities of copy to the *Journal*—chiefly reviews at first, but reprinted stories and poems in increasing numbers during the spring and summer. As his influence in the *Journal* expanded, so did his hopes for making of it the kind of periodical he had envisaged in the *Penn* and *Stylus*. On 24 October, without adequate funds, Poe bought out Bisco for $50 and the assumption of current debts in a three-month note.[29] Bisco transferred Poe's note for $100, written on the same day as the agreement of sale, to W. H. Starr on 13 December, perhaps at a deep discount.[30]

The masthead of the 25 October issue of the *Broadway Journal*

PLATE TWELVE
Beginning of the spurious pamphlet text dated "1842."
Courtesy TxU

Mr. Editor.

Sir,—There is one epithet which seems made expressly to describe my aunt. She was a very romantic old lady. Had the word "romatic" never existed before, it must have been invented expressly on her account. At nineteen she refused a baronet with ten thousand a year, and married on love and nothing. I never understood how she and her husband lived, the twelvemonth before he was killed in Spain. An ensign's pay, now-a-days, will scarcely find him in epaulettes. But live they did, for at the end of this said year he was shot, leading a forlorn hope, and leaving a widow and child, as his monument stated 'inconsolable.' Mrs. Loraine never forced the marble to lie—under a mistake. She wore black, and white pocket handkerchiefs, to the last. The death of a distant relation made her quite independent; and she forthwith established herself in the prettiest cottage that Richmond, the modern Arcady of pretty cottages, ever invented. A willow on the lawn dropped the rain of its green leaves into the Thames, roses looked in at the windows, and geraniums out at the doors. Some people said it was damp; but, as my aunt justly observed "Some people have no soul.'" Here she devoted herself to the education of Lucy, her pretty little fairy of a daughter:—that is to say, she always curled Lucy's long fair hair herself; and instead of the usual recitation of "Pity the Sorrows of a Poor Old Man," and "Oh Hear a Pensive Prisoner's Prayer!" the little creature repeated, "If you would view fair Melrose aright" and Childe Harold's "Good Night." Certainly her system was not conducted on the most approved principles:—"there was no bread and water, no -ographies, and her botany only distinguished a rose from a lily, and developed itself in a taste for violets. Still is succeeded, for at seventeen Lucy was the nearest approach to an Angel that I, at least, ever saw. How well I remember the summer parlour, into which daylight never entered! My aunt had a lingering weakness in favour of a still fine complexion. Nature and art alike lent their aid; there were French blinds, and a Virginian creeper in great profusion; a harp stood in one window, where I generally stood too; while a stand of myrtles and roses occupied the other. My aunt's armchair was drawn a little aside towards a small work-table, on which usually lay an open volume of some favorite poet; near was a stool for her feet, and her daughter, for there Lucy delighted to sit, reading aloud page after page, and expecting every one read "Edgar A. Poe, Editor and Proprietor." Poe announced in the same number, under "Editorial Miscellany," that he had assumed sole proprietary and editorial control of the magazine. His own identifiable contributions of copy remained, naturally enough, at a high level. Besides "Critical Notices," reviews, and "Editorial Miscellany," he reprinted (to choose examples from a single month) "Some Words with a Mummy" on 1 November, "The Devil in the Belfry" on 8 November, and "A Tale of the Ragged Mountains" on 29 November.

"The Spectacles" was reprinted, with a few authorial changes and some corruptions, in the 22 November issue: Poe's printer's copy was the 1844 *Dollar Newspaper* text. Under the heading "Editorial Miscellany" Poe apologized for "the insufficient variety of the present number. We were not aware of the great length of 'The Spectacles' until too late to remedy the evil." The remainder of the editor's column was devoted to a skirmish in Poe's war with the Bostonians, dating from his "delivery" of poems before the Boston Lyceum on 16 October. Poe reacted to attacks by the Boston *Transcript* in several issues of the *Broadway Journal*. Just after announcing his proprietorship in the 25 October number, Poe observed that he had been "quizzing [i.e., hoaxing] the Bostonians." The next week he accused the editor of the *Transcript*, Cornelia M. Walter,[31] of having told "fibs" about him:

> The facts of the case seem to be these:—We *were* invited to "deliver" (stand and deliver) a poem before the Boston Lyceum. . . . We occupied some fifteen minutes with an apology for not "delivering" . . . a didactic poem. . . . After some farther words—still of apology—for the "indefinitiveness" and "general imbecility" of what we had to offer—all so unworthy a *Bostonian* audience—we commenced. . . .
>
> We like Boston. We were born there—and perhaps it is just as well not to mention that we are heartily ashamed of the fact. . . . Their hotels are bad. Their pumpkin pies are delicious. Their poetry is not so good.[32]

Poe went on to declare that the poem he had chosen to read, "Al Aaraaf," had been composed and published before his tenth birthday.

Resuming his counterattack in the 22 November "Editorial Miscellany," Poe cited a defense of his poetic and critical talents from the Charleston *Patriot* before ridiculing the taste and intelligence of his Yankee critics:

> Never was a "bobbery" more delightful than that which we have just succeeded in "kicking up" all around about Boston Common. We never saw the Frog-Pondians so lively in our lives. They seem absolutely to be upon the point of waking up. In about nine days the puppies may get open their eyes.

We had *tact* enough not to be "taken in and done for" by the Bostonians.... We knew very well that, among a certain *clique* of the Frogpondians, there existed a predetermination to abuse us under *any* circumstances.... We read before them a "juvenile"—a *very* "juvenile" poem—and thus the Frogpondians were *had*.... Never were a set of people more completely demolished.[33]

To Miss Walter's sneering accusation that he had been drunk during his delivery, Poe responded in kind, ironically declaring himself "willing to admit either that we *were* drunk, or that we set fire to the Frog-pond, or that once upon a time we cut the throat of our grandmother."[34] This was the context in which "The Spectacles" made its third—and second authorized—appearance in print.

Poe seems to have hoped, however, for another, and more profitable and prestigious, reprint of the tale in 1845. He had submitted to the publishers Wiley and Putnam a large selection of his tales for publication as a sequel to *Tales of the Grotesque and Arabesque* (1840). Evert A. Duyckinck, an energetic and scholarly editor and critic, served as Wiley and Putnam's chief literary reader. Poe complained retrospectively to Philip P. Cooke: "The last selection of my Tales was made from about 70, by . . . Duyckinck. He has what he thinks a taste for ratiocination, and has accordingly made up the book mostly of analytic stories. But this is not *representing* my mind in its various phases—it is not giving me fair play. In writing these Tales one by one, at long intervals, I have kept the book-unity always in mind—that is, each has been composed with reference to its effect as part of a *whole*. In this view, one of my chief aims has been the widest diversity of subject, thought, & especially *tone* & manner of handling."[35] It is reasonable to assume that the hitherto ungathered tales Duyckinck considered included "The Spectacles," especially since Poe, in his 8 January 1846 letter to Duyckinck (five days after the failure of the *Broadway Journal*) urging the publication of yet another volume of Tales that spring, sent a "collection" comprising " 'Sheherazade', 'The Spectacles', 'Tarr and Fether,' etc."[36]

Tales By Edgar A. Poe was published by Wiley and Putnam in June 1845 as the second item in the house's "Library of American Books." At least with respect to the humorous tales Poe had offered, his dissatisfaction with Duyckinck's choice of contents is justified: *Tales* contained "The Gold-Bug," "The Black Cat," "Mesmeric Revelation," "Lionizing," "The Fall of the House of Usher," "A Descent into the Maelström," "The Colloquy of Monos and Una," "The Conversation of Eiros and Charmion," "The Murders in the Rue Morgue," "The Mystery of Marie Rogêt," "The Purloined Letter," and "The Man of the Crowd." Either the modest success of *Tales* or considerations of literary allegiance and patronage induced Duyckinck to accept a selection of Poe's verse, *The Raven and Other Poems*, for Wiley and Putnam.[37] It was issued on 19 November 1845 as number 8 in the "Library of American Books," but no other volume of *Tales* would appear until after Poe's death.[38]

"The Spectacles" was finally collected in the second volume, "Poems and Miscellanies," of *The Works of the Late Edgar Allan Poe: with notices of his life and genius. By N. P. Willis, J. R. Lowell, and R. W. Griswold* (New York: J. S. Redfield, 1850). Rufus Griswold's edition (projected for two volumes, but including a third in 1850 and a fourth in 1856) was publicly known to be in progress by 29 October 1849—twenty-two days after Poe's death—when the Richmond (Virginia) *Weekly Examiner* mentioned it. On the 31st Griswold informed Lowell that six typesetters were at work on the copy and urged speed in Lowell's preparation of a biographical sketch.[39] The first two volumes appeared in January 1850.[40] Griswold's text of "The Spectacles" was that of the *Broadway Journal*, to which a few additional substantive corruptions were added. There is no evidence whatever that Poe supplied Griswold, his literary executor, with authorially corrected copy of the tale.

One last early printing of "The Spectacles" appeared in the 27 August 1850 issue of the Richmond *Semi-Weekly Examiner*, without assignment of a printed source or even an identification of authorship. The *Examiner*, weekly and semi-weekly, was edited by John M. Daniel, whom Poe told Mrs. Clemm he challenged to a duel in Richmond in 1848,[41] and with whom, in 1849, he reputedly made an agreement to furnish literary copy.[42] In Daniel's columns "The Raven" received reprinting on 25 September 1849—the last lifetime print and, according to Daniel's prefatory comments, "the only correct copy ever published," from a text supplied personally by Poe. A biographical and critical sketch appeared just after Poe's death in the issues for 12 and 19 October. "Dreamland," "To My Mother," and "MS. Found in a Bottle" were also reprinted in October issues. Despite the suggestion by Heartman and Canny that Poe was "engaged in revising some of his early works" for Daniel at the time he died, the *Semi-Weekly Examiner*'s "Spectacles" text demonstrably derives from Griswold's edition. The collation of substantives illustrates this genealogy; in addition, Daniel's text shares misprints ("uncompomising," "Madamoiselle") with Griswold's.

The text of "The Spectacles" in James A. Harrison's monumental, and still for most purposes "standard" edition, *Complete Works of Edgar Allan Poe* (New York: Thomas Y. Crowell, 1902), 5:177–209, derives from the *Broadway Journal* printing, as does the text in Arthur

Hobson Quinn and Edward H. O'Neill's *The Complete Poems and Stories of Edgar Allan Poe* (New York: Alfred A. Knopf, 1946), 1:495–514. I am informed that Griswold's edition will be copy-text for "The Spectacles" in the forthcoming Belknap Press of Harvard University Press edition of the fiction, edited by the late Thomas Ollive Mabbott, volume three in *Collected Works of Edgar Allan Poe*.

The publication here of Poe's manuscript of "The Spectacles" will bring the tale's textual history down to the present. One earlier and curious chapter—perhaps more properly termed a digression—remains to be told. The New York pulp magazine *Liberty* published, in its issue for 24 September 1938, the text of a tale entitled "The Spectacles" and attributed to Poe. The magazine's cover proclaims, "Edgar Allan Poe's Lost Short Story—Found at Last! Read it exclusively in this issue." Over the byline of Edward Doherty appear the captions "Hidden 100 years! Liberty presents a remarkable literary discovery. How the Story Was Found." The tale itself, printed on pages 12 and 13, bears no relation to the text in the established Poe canon. Doherty's accompanying account identifies it as one of the original eleven Tales of the Folio Club, and "one of the first [Poe] ever wrote. It has been hidden for more than a hundred years, unread, unnoticed, unhonored—and unsigned—within the yellowed pages of an antique Philadelphia magazine."[43] Supposedly it had disappeared at the offices of the Philadelphia publishers, Carey & Lea. The "discoverer" was Richard Gimbel, president of the International Poe Society and an important collector, "one of the wealthiest men in the country," who purchased "tons and tons" of old newspapers and periodicals and "pored over the musty pages," "day after day and night after night," in his quest for the eleventh Folio Club tale. Doherty ends his article with the observation that "The name of the magazine in which the story was found is being withheld for a short time to permit of additional research and of copyright protection."[44] Gimbel himself issued this tale in a pamphlet printing dated July 1938, and described by Heartman and Canny, who justifiably grumbled that the collector had never disclosed his source. They even conjectured that "a whole magazine or periodical" might have been "forged and passed on Mr. Gimbel."[45] One unequivocal forgery—which Heartman and Canny take pains to dissociate from Gimbel—is a four-page pamphlet, THE SPECTACLES | SHORT STORY BY | EDGAR ALLEN (*sic*) POE. | Carey & Lea | Philadelphia | 1830.[46] Another forgery, using the same text, was obtained by William Koester and is stored with the authentic "Spectacles" manuscript. The title page of this pamphlet reads THE SPECTACLES | Short Story By | EDGAR ALLAN POE | CAREY & LEA | Philadelphia | 1842. The text occupies seven pages; the pages measure approximately $3\frac{5}{16}$ by $4\frac{5}{8}$ inches.

II. THE MANUSCRIPT AS COPY-TEXT; EDITORIAL PROCEDURES

By the criteria of copy-text choice advanced by W. W. Greg and Fredson Bowers—criteria widely accepted in modern textual editing, and standard for the editions of American authors in progress under the supervision of the Modern Language Association—the "Spectacles" manuscript Poe sent to Horne is the most reliable basis for a text of the tale: all other versions over which Poe did exercise, or could have exercised, control are printed forms. In addition to demonstrable printer's errors (compounded as one printing was set from an earlier one, as with the *Dollar Newspaper*-*Broadway Journal*-Griswold-*Examiner* sequence), the printed texts doubtless contain unidentifiable instances of house styling, regularization, "indifferent" alterations of the substantives and accidentals by editors and typesetters, and other consequences of nonauthorial discretion and inattentiveness. For its accidentals, at least, the fair manuscript possesses the highest authority as copy-text. That is to say, of all documentary forms of the text it comes nearest to embodying the author's intention.

The case of "The Spectacles" is anomalous inasmuch as Poe produced *two* fair-copy manuscripts, of which one, the archetype for the *Dollar Newspaper* text, has disappeared. Most of the verbal differences between the manuscript and the first printing appear to be authorial variants. They are numerous, but they rarely involve distinct changes of meaning. Since the procedures of modern scholarly editing have been designed to capture the author's *final* intention, thus allowing for emendation of a copy-text with later substantives that can be proven authorial, the editor must take more than a passing interest in the relative ages of the surviving "Spectacles" manuscript and the lost fair copy reflected in the *Dollar Newspaper* printing.[47] Three basic genealogical hypotheses present themselves. First, that Poe drew both fair copies independently from his working draft (unfortunately, no draft material survives). Second, that he prepared the Horne manuscript from his draft, and then copied the *Dollar Newspaper* manuscript from the surviving holograph. Third, that he prepared the *Dollar Newspaper* manuscript from draft, and then copied the Horne manuscript from that fair copy. The physical evidence in the surviving holograph is slender and inconclusive, but leans slightly toward the first or third hypothesis. One of Poe's corrections, late in the manuscript, involves the last four letters of the word "posture," written over a thorough erasure of other characters. These characters may have been "ition," and the *Dollar Newspaper* reading at this point in the text is "position."

Judgments based on internal evidence—critical judgments of the relative superiority or inferiority of the manuscript text to the *Dollar Newspaper* where they differ—are necessarily subjective. I will not argue that each variant in the manuscript is a pronounced improvement over the printed text; the bulk of them are "indifferent," though almost surely authorial, variations. Taken as a whole, however, the manuscript readings seem to me to *tend* in the direction of improvement by removing unnecessary verbiage, reducing or avoiding repetition (as with the word "exquisite"), establishing more effective phrase-order (as "dreary, snail-paced"), eliminating awkward constructions (such as "The figure, nearly all which the construction of the box permitted to be seen"), or achieving greater precision in a given context (as "say something"). By and large, the manuscript introduces elaborations in the more important scenes and tends toward greater brevity than the *Dollar Newspaper* text in passages of lesser dramatic significance. In one instance, the manuscript reading ("a few days") is markedly superior to the print ("a few weeks"). If the elder Madame Lalande came to the American city from Paris to seek out her great-great-grandson and heir, the narrator, her having resided there "a few weeks" without discovering that well-known young man raises questions of verisimilitude which "a few days" avoids. In both versions, however, Poe overlooked a more glaring chronological inconsistency. The opening scene, at the opera, occurs in winter. After "the lapse of a fortnight" the narrator writes to Madame Lalande, receives a reply, fails in a necessarily brief and desperate effort to obtain an introduction from his friend Talbot, and resolves to accost the lady directly. This he does "in the grey uncertainty of a Midsummer gloaming" as she walks in the groves of a public park. The lighting of the house to which he escorts her from the park is customary in "American mansions of the better sort" on evenings "during the heat of the summer." The inconsistency, shared by the manuscript and the *Dollar Newspaper* text, stood unrecognized by Poe and unaltered in all lifetime printings of the tale, and is thus a feature of all subsequent editions.

Of the three dozen substantive variants between the *Broadway Journal* and *Dollar Newspaper* texts, a large majority are positive corruptions or indifferent changes attributable to the typesetters. Poe's hand is unmistakably evident only in the correction of "donned" (an error which also occurs in the manuscript) to "doffed"; this substantive change is adopted as an emendation in the present text.

The text is presented in clear rather than diplomatic form. No editorial symbols or footnotes occur in the text; emendations and authorial alterations are reported as end-matter in lists keyed to the text. The editor has followed a conservative policy of emendation, making no effort to modernize or regularize Poe's accidentals, and correcting only positive errors in the copy-text. Rationale for the more interesting or problematic emendations (or decisions not to emend) appears in textual notes.

The only editorial changes not individually recorded in the list of emendations are the omission of Poe's pagination numbers (all arabic, and underlined, in the manuscript); the lowering of superscribed elements in "Mr" and "Mrs" (the lower-case characters in these abbreviations are almost invariably superscribed, at least slightly, in the manuscript); and the imposition of a uniform four-em dash in such constructions as "S———" (town name) or "——— theatre" (in the manuscript these dashes are not consistently any longer than dashes used as marks of punctuation to set off phrases). Poe often placed close-quotation marks almost directly above periods or commas. The editor has transcribed quotation marks as inside or outside the terminal punctuation according to his best judgment of each case. The lineation and pagination of the manuscript are of course disregarded; this is not a type-facsimile presentation of the tale. Compound constructions hyphenated at the end of the line in the copy-text have been resolved (printed with the hyphen or as continuous words) on the grounds of other appearances of the same terms, or analogous ones, elsewhere in the manuscript. They are reported in the first part of a list of line-end hyphenations, appearing there in the form which the editor gave them in the text. The second part of the line-end hyphenation report, List B, presents those compounds hyphenated at the end of a line in the current printing which appeared, in the copy-text, as containing hyphens. Any term hyphenated at the end of a line in this printing and *not* recorded in List B should be construed as an unhyphenated continuous word, and so quoted or reprinted.

The list of alterations reports the few physical changes Poe made while writing the manuscript. The historical collation reports substantive variants between the six early forms of the text: manuscript, *Dollar Newspaper, Lloyd's, Broadway Journal,* Griswold, and *Semi-Weekly Examiner.* Where a variant reading is shared by two or more forms of the text, the associated accidentals are those of the earlier text; the later text (or texts) may differ in accidentals. The format of entries in the historical collation is as follows: page-and-line citation; reading in the present text; close bracket; source of reading (abbreviated); semicolon; variant reading; source of variant reading (abbreviated). In the list of emendations the page-and-line citation, reading in the present text, and close-bracket are followed by the source or authority for the emendation (abbreviated), a semicolon, and the copy-text reading.

The editor's collation copies, preceded by the abbreviations used in the apparatus, were the following:

D *The Dollar Newspaper*, 2, number 10 (27 March 1844): [1]–[2], negative photostat, MdHi
L *Lloyd's Entertaining Journal*, 3, number 63 (3 May 1845): [161]–67, electroprint, CtY A88/L66
B *The Broadway Journal*, 2, number 20 (22 November 1845): [299]–307, Koester Collection, TxU, 7–3 D Vol. 1; plus other Koester copies
G *The Works of the Late Edgar Allan Poe*, ed. Rufus W. Griswold (New York: J. S. Redfield, 1850), 2:322–46, TxU, Parsons *1114.
R Richmond (Va.) *Semi-Weekly Examiner*, 3, number 86 (27 August 1850), p. [4], Collections Deposit Library, TxU.

The editor expresses his gratitude to the Humanities Research Center of The University of Texas at Austin, to the Maryland Historical Society, to the Yale University Library, and to the Boston Public Library, for their cooperation in making available manuscripts and rare printed materials bearing on this study.

THE SPECTACLES.

By Edgar Allan Poe.

Some persons ridicule the idea of "love at first sight"; but those who think clearly, not less than those who feel deeply, have always advocated its existence. Modern discoveries, indeed, in what may be termed ethical magnetism, or magnetæsthetics, render it probable that the most natural, and, consequently, the most real and the most intense of the human affections, are those which arise in the heart as if by electric sympathy—in a word, that the brightest and most enduring of the psychal fetters are those which are riveted at a glance. The confession I am about to make, will add another to the already numerous instances of the truth of this position.

It is necessary that I be somewhat minute. I am still a young man—not yet twenty-two. My name, at present, is a very usual and rather plebeian one—Simpson. I say "at present"; for it is only lately that I have been so called—having legislatively adopted this surname, within the last year, in order to receive an inheritance left me by a distant male relative—Adolphus Simpson, Esquire. The bequest was conditioned upon my taking the name of the testator;—the family, not the Christian name. My Christian or baptismal names are Napoleon Buonaparte. I am now Napoleon Buonaparte Simpson. I assumed the "Simpson" with much reluctance; for in my true patronym, Froissart, I felt a very pardonable pride; believing that I could trace a descent from the immortal author of the "Chronicles." While on the subject of names, by the bye, I may as well mention a singular coincidence of sound, attending the names of some of my immediate predecessors. My father was a Monsieur George *Froissart*, of Paris. His wife, my mother, whom he married at fifteen, was a Mademoiselle *Croissart*, eldest daughter of Croissart, the banker. *His* wife, again, only sixteen when married, was the eldest daughter of one Monsieur *Voissart*; and this gentleman, very singularly, had wedded a lady of similar name—a Mademoiselle *Moissart*. She, too, was quite a child when married; and her mother, also, Madame Moissart, was only fourteen when led to the altar. These early marriages are usual in France. But what I speak of now is the coincidence. Observe! Here are *Moissart, Voissart,*

Croissart, and *Froissart*—all in the direct line of descent. My own name, though, as I say, became Simpson by Act of the Pennsylvania Legislature; but with so much repugnance on my part, that, at one period, I actually hesitated about accepting the legacy with the annoying and useless *proviso* attached.

As to personal endowments, I am so, so. I believe that I am well made, and that I possess what nine tenths of the world would call a handsome face. I am five feet eleven. My hair is black and curling. My nose is sufficiently good. My eyes are large and grey; and although, in fact, they are weak to a very inconvenient degree, still no defect in this regard would be suspected from their appearance. The weakness itself, however, has always much annoyed me; and I have resorted to every remedy—*short of wearing spectacles*. Being youthful and good-looking, I naturally dislike these, and have resolutely refused to employ them. I know nothing, indeed, which so disfigures the countenance of a young person, or which so impresses every feature with an air of demureness, if not exactly of sanctimoniousness. An eye-glass, on the other hand, has a savor of downright foppery and affectation. I have hitherto managed, as well as I could, without either. But something too much of these merely personal details, which, after all, are of little importance. I will content myself with saying, in addition, that my temperament is sanguine, rash, ardent, enthusiastic—and that all my life I have been a devout admirer of the gentle sex.

One night, last winter, I entered a box at the ——— theatre, in company with a friend, Mr Talbot. It was an opera night; the bills presented a very rare attraction; and thus the house was excessively crowded. We were in time, however, to obtain the front seats which had been preserved for us, and into which, with some little difficulty, we elbowed our way.

For two hours my companion, who was a musical *fanatico*, gave his undivided attention to the stage; and, in the meantime, I amused myself by observing the audience, which consisted, in chief part, of the very *élite* of the city. Having satisfied myself upon this point, I was about turning my eyes to the *prima donna*, when they were arrested and riveted by a figure in one of the private boxes which had escaped my observation.

If I live a thousand years I can never forget the intense emotion with which I gazed at this figure. It was that of a female, the most exquisite imaginable. The face was so far turned towards the stage that for some minutes I could not obtain a view of it—but the form was *divine*—no other word can sufficiently express its magnificent proportion; and even the term "divine" seems ridiculously feeble as I write it.

The magic of a lovely form in woman—the necromancy of female gracefulness—was always a power which I had found it impossible to resist; but here was Grace personified—incarnate—the *beau idéal* of my wildest and most enthusiastic visions. The construction of the box permitted nearly all the person to be seen. It was somewhat above the medium height, and nearly approached, without positively reaching, the majestic. Its perfect fulness and *tournure* were delicious. The head, of which only the back was visible, rivalled, in outline, that of the Greek Psyche, and was rather displayed than concealed by an elegant cap of *gaze aérienne*, which put me in mind of the *ventum textilem* of Apuleius. The right arm hung over the balustrade of the box, and thrilled every nerve of my frame with its delicious symmetry. Its upper portion was draperied by one of the loose open sleeves now in fashion. This extended but little below the elbow. Beneath it was worn an under one, of some gossamer material, close-fitting, and terminated by a cuff of rich lace, which fell gracefully over the top of the hand, revealing only the delicate fingers, upon one of which sparkled a diamond ring, which, I at once saw, was of extraordinary value. The admirable roundness of the wrist was well set off by a bracelet which encircled it, and which, also, was ornamented and clasped by a magnificent *aigrette* of jewels—telling, in words not to be misunderstood, at once of the wealth and of the fastidious taste of the wearer.

I gazed at this queenly apparition for at least half an hour, as if I had been suddenly converted to stone; and, during this period, I felt the full force of all that has been said or sung about "love at first sight". My feelings were totally different from any which I had hitherto experienced, in the presence of even the most celebrated specimens of female loveliness. An unaccountable, and what I am compelled to consider a *magnetic* sympathy of soul for soul, seemed to rivet, not only my vision, but my whole powers of thought and feeling, upon the admirable object before me. I saw—I felt—I knew that I was deeply, madly, irrecoverably in love—and this even before seeing the face of the one beloved. So intense, indeed, was the passion that consumed me, that I really believe it would have received little if any abatement, had the features yet unseen proved of merely ordinary character. So anomalous is the nature of the only true love—of the love at first sight—and so little really dependent is it upon the external conditions which only *seem* to create and control it.

While I was wrapped in admiration of this enchanting vision, a sudden disturbance among the audience caused her to turn her head partially towards me, so that I beheld the entire profile of the face.

Its beauty even exceeded my anticipations—and yet there was something about it which disappointed me, without my being able to tell exactly what it was.

I said "disappointed"—but this is not altogether the word. My sentiments were at once exalted and subdued. They partook less of transport, and more of a calm enthusiasm—of an enthusiastic repose. This state of feeling arose, perhaps, from the Madonna-like—from the matronly air of the face; and yet I at once understood that it could not have arisen *entirely* from this. There was something behind—some mystery I could not develope—some expression about the countenance which slightly disturbed me, while it heightened my interest. In fact, I was just in that condition of mind which prepares a young and susceptible man for any act of extravagance. Had the lady been alone, I should undoubtedly have entered her box and accosted her at all hazards; but, fortunately, she was attended by two companions—a gentleman, and a strikingly beautiful woman, to all appearance a few years younger than herself.

I revolved in mind a thousand schemes by which I might obtain, hereafter, an introduction to the elder lady, or, for the present at all events, a more distinct view of her beauty. I would have removed my position to one nearer her own; but the crowded state of the theatre rendered this impossible, and the stern decrees of Fashion had, of late, imperatively prohibited the use of the opera-glass, in a case such as this. But even if this had not been so, I had no glass with me, and was thus in despair.

At length I bethought me of applying to my companion, whose very existence I had for some time forgotten.

"Talbot," I said, "*you* have a *lorgnette*—let me have it."

"A *lorgnette*!—no!—what do you suppose I would be doing with a *lorgnette*?" Here he turned impatiently towards the stage.

"But, Talbot," I resumed, pulling him by the shoulder—"listen to me, will you? Do you see the stage-box?—there!—no, the next—did you ever behold so lovely a woman?"

"No doubt she is very beautiful," he said.

"I wonder who she can be."

"Why, in the name of all that is angelic, don't you *know* who she is? 'Not to know her argues yourself unknown'. She is the celebrated Madame Lalande—the beauty of the day *par excellence*, and the talk of the whole town. Immensely wealthy, too,—a widow, and a great match. Has just arrived from Paris."

"Do you know her?"

"I have the honor."

"Will you present me?"

"Assuredly. When shall it be?"

"To-morrow—at one—I will call upon you at B―――'s."

"Very good!—and now oblige me by just holding your tongue—*if you can.*"

In this latter respect I was forced to put Talbot under the obligation desired; for he remained obstinately deaf to every further question or suggestion, and occupied himself exclusively, for the rest of the evening, with what was transacting upon the stage.

In the meantime I kept my eyes riveted upon Madame Lalande, and, at length, had the good fortune to obtain a full front view of her face. It was supremely lovely—this, of course, my heart had told me before, even had not Talbot fully satisfied me upon the point—but still there was the unintelligible something which disturbed me. I finally concluded that my imagination was impressed by a certain air of gravity, of sadness, or, still more properly, of weariness, which took something from the youth and freshness of the countenance, only to endow it with a seraphic tenderness and majesty—and thus, to my enthusiastic and romantic temperament, with an interest ten-fold.

While I thus feasted my eyes, I perceived, at last, to my great trepidation, by an almost imperceptible start on the part of the lady, that she had become aware of the intensity of my gaze. Nevertheless, I was absolutely fascinated, and could not withdraw it, even for an instant. She averted her face; and, again, I saw only the chiselled contour of the back portion of the head. After some minutes, as if urged by curiosity to see if I was still looking, she gradually brought her face again round, and again encountered my burning gaze. Her large dark eyes fell instantly, and a deep blush mantled her cheek. But what was my astonishment at perceiving that she not only did not a second time turn aside her head, but that she actually took from her girdle a double eye-glass, elevated it, and regarded me through it, intently and deliberately, for the space of several minutes.

Had a thunderbolt fallen at my feet, I could not have been more thoroughly astounded—astounded *only*—not offended or disgusted in the slightest degree; although an action so bold, in any other woman, would have been sure to offend or to disgust. But the whole thing was done with so much quietude—so much *nonchalance*—so much repose—in short, with so evident an air of the highest breeding—that nothing of mere effrontery was perceptible, and my sole sentiments were those of admiration and surprise.

I observed that, upon her first elevation of the glass, she had seemed satisfied with a momentary inspection of my person, and was withdrawing the instrument, when, as if struck by a second thought, she resumed it, and so continued to regard me, with fixed attention, for several minutes—for five minutes at the very least, I am sure.

The action, so remarkable in an American theatre, attracted universal observation, and gave rise to an indefinite movement, or buzz, among the audience, which, for a moment, filled me with confusion, but produced no visible effect upon the countenance of Madame Lalande.

Having satisfied her curiosity—if such it was—she dropped the glass, and, quietly, gave her attention again to the stage;—her profile being now turned towards myself, as before. I continued to watch her unremittingly, although I was fully conscious of my rudeness in so doing. Presently I saw the head slowly and slightly change its position; and soon I became convinced that the lady, while pretending to look at the stage, was, in fact, attentively regarding myself. It is needless to say what effect this conduct, on the part of so fascinating a woman, had upon my excitable mind.

She scrutinized me thus for, perhaps, a quarter of an hour, and then suddenly addressed the gentleman who attended her. While she spoke, I saw distinctly, by the glances of both, that the conversation had reference to myself. Upon its conclusion, she again turned towards the stage, and, for a few minutes, seemed absorbed in the performances. At the expiration of this period, however, I was thrown into an extremity of agitation, by seeing her unfold, for the second time, the eye-glass which hung at her side—fully confront me, as before,—and, disregarding the renewed buzz of the audience, survey me, from head to foot, with the same miraculous composure which had previously so delighted and confounded my soul.

This extraordinary behaviour, by throwing me into a perfect fever of excitement—into an absolute delirium of love—served rather to embolden than to disconcert me. In the mad intensity of my devotion, I forgot everything but the presence and the majestic loveliness of the vision which confronted my gaze. Watching my opportunity, when I thought the audience were fully engaged with the opera, I at length caught the eyes of Madame Lalande, and, upon the instant, made a slight but unmistakeable *bow*.

She blushed very deeply—then averted her eyes—then slowly and cautiously looked around, apparently to see if my rash action had been noticed—then leaned over to the gentleman who sat by her side.

I now felt a burning sense of the impropriety I had committed, and expected nothing less than instant exposure; while a vision of pistols upon the morrow, flitted rapidly and uncomfortably through my brain. I was immediately relieved, however, when I saw the lady merely hand the gentleman a play-bill, without speaking;—but the reader may form some feeble conception of my astonishment—of my profound amazement—of my delirious bewilderment of heart and soul—when, instantly afterwards, having again glanced furtively around, she allowed her bright eyes to settle fully and steadily upon my own, and then, with a faint smile, disclosing a bright line of her pearly teeth, made two distinct, pointed, and unequivocal *nods*.

It is useless, of course, to dwell upon my joy—upon my transport—upon my illimitable ecstasy. If ever man was mad with excess of happiness, it was myself at that moment.

I loved. This was my first love—so I felt it to be. It was love supreme—indescribable. It was *"love at first sight"*. At first sight, too, it had been appreciated, and was *returned*.

Yes;—returned. How, and why should I doubt it for an instant? What other construction could I possibly put upon such conduct, on the part of a lady so beautiful—so wealthy—evidently so accomplished—of so high breeding—so refined—of so lofty a position in society—in every regard so entirely respectable as I felt assured was Madame Lalande? Yes!—she loved me—she returned the enthusiasm of my love, with an enthusiasm as blind, as uncalculating, as uncompromising, as abandoned, and as utterly unbounded as my own!

These delicious fancies and reflections, however, were now interrupted by the falling of the drop curtain. The audience arose; and the usual tumult supervened. Quitting Talbot abruptly, I made every endeavour to force my way into proximity with Madame Lalande. Having failed in this attempt, on account of the crowd, I at length gave up the chase, and bent my steps homewards; consoling myself for not having been able to touch even the hem of her robe, with the reflection that I should be introduced by Talbot, in due form, upon the morrow.

This morrow at last came;—that is to say, a day finally dawned upon a long and weary night of impatience; and then the hours until "one" were dreary, snail-paced, and innumerable. But "even Stamboul," it is said, "shall have an end", and there came an end to this long delay. The clock struck. As its last echo ceased, I stepped into B———'s and inquired for Talbot.

"Out"; said a footman—Talbot's own.

"Out!" I replied, staggering back half a dozen paces, "out!—let me tell you, my fine fellow, that this thing is thoroughly impossible and impracticable. Mr Talbot is *not* out. What do you mean?"

"Nothing, Sir; only Mr Talbot is not in—that's all. He rode over to

S——, immediately after breakfast, and left word that he should not be in town again for a week".

I stood petrified with horror and rage. I endeavoured to say something, but my tongue refused its office. At length I turned on my heel, livid with wrath, and inwardly consigning the whole tribe of the Talbots to the innermost regions of Erebus. It was evident that my considerate friend, *il fanatico*, had quite forgotten his appointment with myself; perhaps, indeed, he had forgotten it as soon as it was made. At no time had he been a very scrupulous man of his word. There was no help for it; so, smothering my vexation as well as I could, I strolled moodily up the street, propounding futile inquiries about Madame Lalande to every acquaintance I met. By report, I found, she was known to all—by sight to many—but she had been in town only a few days, and thus there were not more than one or two who professed a personal knowledge. These, being still comparatively strangers, could not, or would not take the liberty of introducing me with the formality of a morning call. While I stood, however, in despair, conversing with a trio of friends upon the all-absorbing subject of my heart, it so happened that the subject itself passed by.

"As I live, there she is!" cried one.

"How surpassingly beautiful!" exclaimed the second.

"An angel upon earth!" ejaculated the third.

I looked; and, in an open carriage, which approached us as it passed slowly down the street, sate the enchanting vision of the opera, accompanied by the younger lady who had occupied a portion of her box.

"Her companion, also, wears remarkably well", said the one of my trio who had spoken first.

"Astonishingly", said the second; "has still quite a brilliant air; but art will do wonders. Upon my word, she looks better than she did at Paris five years ago. A lovely woman still;—do n't you think so, Froissart?—Simpson, I mean."

"Still!" said I, "and why not? But, compared with her friend, she is a rush-light to the Evening Star—a glow-worm to Antares."

Here the whole trio laughed.

"Ha! ha! ha!" said the third, "why, Simpson, you have an astonishing tact at making discoveries—original ones, I mean;" and here, as we separated, he commenced humming a gay *vaudeville*, of which I caught only the lines:

Ninon, Ninon, Ninon à bas! —
A bas Ninon de L'Enclos!

During this little scene, however, one thing had served greatly to console me, although it fed the passion by which I was consumed. As the carriage of Madame Lalande rolled by our group, I had observed that she recognized me; and, more than this, she had blessed me, by the most seraphic of smiles, with no equivocal mark of the recognition.

As for an introduction, I was forced to abandon all hope of it until such time as Talbot should think proper to return from the country. In the meantime, I perseveringly frequented every reputable place of public amusement, and, at length, at the theatre where I first saw her, I had the supreme bliss of meeting her, and of exchanging glances with her, once again.

This did not occur, however, until after the lapse of a fortnight. Every day in the *interim*, I had inquired for Talbot at his Hotel; and every day had been thrown into a spasm of wrath, by the everlasting "Not come home yet" of his footman.

Upon the evening in question, therefore, I was in a condition little short of madness. Madame Lalande, I had been told, was a Parisian—had lately arrived from Paris—might she not suddenly return?—return before Talbot came back—and might she not thus be lost to me forever? The thought was too terrible to bear. Since my future happiness was at issue, I resolved to act with a manly decision. In a word, upon the breaking up of the play, I traced the lady to her residence, noted her address, and, next morning, sent her a full and elaborate letter, in which I poured out my whole heart.

I spoke boldly—freely—in a word, I spoke with passion. I concealed nothing—nothing even of my folly. I alluded to the romantic circumstances of our first meeting—even to the glances which had passed between us. I went so far as to say that I felt assured of her love; while I offered this assurance, and my own intensity of devotion, as two excuses for my otherwise unpardonable conduct. As a third, I spoke of my fear that she might leave the city before I could have the opportunity of a formal presentation. I concluded the most wildly enthusiastic epistle ever penned, with a frank declaration of my worldly circumstances—of my affluence—and with an offer of my hand, as of my heart.

In an agony of expectation I awaited the reply. After what seemed the lapse of a century, it came.

Yes;—came. Romantic as all this may appear, I really received a letter from Madame Lalande—from the beautiful, the wealthy, the idolized Madame Lalande. Her eyes—her magnificent eyes—had not belied her heart. Like a true Frenchwoman, as she was, she had obeyed the frank dictates of her reason—the generous impulses of her nature—despising the conventional pruderies of the world. She had *not* scorned my proposal. She had *not* sheltered herself in silence. She had *not* returned my letter unopened. She had even sent me, in reply, one penned by her own exquisite fingers. It ran thus:

"Monsieur Simpson vill pardonne me for not compose de butefulle tong of his contrée so vell as might. It is only of de late dat I am arrive, and not yet ave de opportunité for to learn.

"Vid dis apologie for de manière of dis leetle note, I vill now say dat, hélas! Monsieur Simpson ave guess but de too true. Vat is need I say de more? Hélas! am I not ready speake de too moshe?

Eugénie Lalande."

This noble-spirited letter I kissed a million times, and committed, no doubt, on its account, a thousand other extravagances which have now escaped my memory.

And still Talbot *would* not return. Alas! could he have formed even the vaguest idea of the suffering his absence occasioned his friend, would not his sympathising nature have flown instantly to my relief? Still, however, he came not. I wrote. He replied. He was detained by urgent business, but would now shortly return. He begged me not to be impatient—to moderate my transports—to read soothing books—to drink nothing stronger than Hock—and to bring the consolations of philosophy to my aid. The fool! I had acquainted him with the exigencies of the case, and, if he could not come himself, why, in the name of everything rational, could he not enclose me an introduction? I wrote again, entreating him to forward one forthwith. My letter was returned by *that* footman, with the following endorsement in pencil:

"Mr Talbot left S—— yesterday for parts unknown. Did n't say where, or when be back—so thought best to return letter, knowing your hand-writing, and as how you is always more or less in a hurry.

Yours sincerely,
Stubbs"

After this, it is needless to say that I devoted to the Infernal Deities both master and valet; but there was little use in anger, and no consolation at all in complaint.

I had yet a resource left me, however, in my constitutional audacity. Hitherto it had served me well, and I resolved to make it avail me to the end. Besides, after the correspondence which had passed between us, what act of mere informality *could* I commit, within bounds, that ought to be regarded as indecorous by Madame Lalande? Since the affair of the letter, I had been in the custom of watching her house, and thus discovered that, about twilight every fine evening, it was her practice to promenade, attended only by a negro in livery, in a certain one of our public squares overlooked by the windows of her residence. Here, amid the luxuriant and overshadowing grove, in the grey uncertainty of a Midsummer gloaming—here, at length, watching my opportunity, I accosted her.

The better to deceive the servant in attendance, I did this with the assured air of an old and familiar acquaintance. With a presence of mind truly Parisian, she took the cue at once, and, to welcome me, held out the most bewitchingly diminutive of hands. The valet at once fell into the rear;—and now, with hearts full to overflowing, we discoursed long and unreservedly of our love.

As Madame Lalande spoke English even much less fluently than she wrote it, our conversation was necessarily in French. In this sweet tongue, so adapted to passion, I gave loose to all the impetuous enthusiasm of my nature, and, with all the eloquence I could command, besought her consent to an immediate union.

At this impatience she smiled. She urged the old story of decorum— that bug-bear which deters so many from bliss, until the opportunity for bliss has forever departed. What would the world say? I had most imprudently made it known among my friends, she observed, that I desired her acquaintance—thus, of course, that I did not possess it:—thus, again, there was no possibility of concealing the *date* of our first knowledge of each other. And then she adverted, with a blush, to the extreme recency of this date. To wed immediately, would be improper—would be indecorous—would be *outré*. All this she said with an air of *naïveté* which enraptured, while it grieved and convinced me. She went even so far as to accuse me, laughingly, of rashness—of imprudence. She bade me remember that I really even knew not who she was—what were her prospects—her connexions—her standing in society. She begged me—but with a sigh—to re-consider my proposal, and termed my love an infatuation—a Will-o' the Wisp—a phantasy of the moment—a baseless and unstable creation, rather of the imagination than of the heart. These things she uttered as the shadows of the sweet twilight gathered darkly and more darkly around us—and then, with a gentle pressure of her fairy-like hand, overthrew, in a single sweet instant, all the fabric of argumentation she had reared.

I replied as I best could—as only a true lover can. I spoke at length, and perseveringly, of my passion—of my devotion—of her exceeding beauty and of my own enthusiastic adoration. In conclusion, I dwelt, with a convincing energy, upon the perils that encompass the course of true love—that "course of true love" that "never did run smooth", and thus deduced the danger of rendering that course unnecessarily long.

This latter argument seemed, finally, to soften the rigor of her resistance. She relented;—but there was yet an obstacle, she said, which she felt assured I had not sufficiently considered. This was a delicate point—for a woman to urge, especially delicate. In touching upon it, she saw that she must make a sacrifice of her feelings—of the finest sensibilities of her nature;—still, for *me*, every sacrifice should and would be willingly made. She alluded to the topic of *age*. Was I aware—was I fully aware of the discrepancy between us? That the age of the husband should surpass, by a few years—even by fifteen or twenty—the age of the wife, was regarded by the world as admissible, and indeed as very proper; but she had always entertained the belief that the years of the wife should, under *no* circumstances, exceed in number those of the husband. A discrepancy of this unnatural kind, gave rise, too frequently, alas! to a life of unhappiness. Now, she was aware that my own age did not exceed two-and-twenty; and I, on the contrary, perhaps, was *not* aware that the years of my Eugénie extended very considerably beyond that sum.

About all this there was a nobility of soul—a dignity and candor—which delighted—which enchanted me—which eternally riveted my chains. I could scarcely restrain the excessive transport which possessed me.

"Dearest", I cried, "what is all this about which you are discoursing? Your age surpasses, in some measure, my own. What then? The customs of the world—what are they, after all, but so many conventional impertinences? To those who love as we do, in what respect differs a year from an hour? I am twenty-two, you say; granted:—indeed you may as well call me, at once, twenty-three. Now you yourself, my sweetest Eugénie, can have numbered no more than—can have numbered no more than—no more than—than—than"—

Here I paused for an instant, in the expectation that Madame Lalande would interrupt me by supplying her true age. But a Frenchwoman is seldom direct, and has always, by way of answer to an embarrassing question, some little practical reply of her own. In the present instance Eugénie, who, for a few moments past, had seemed to be searching for something in her bosom, at length let fall upon the grass a miniature, which I immediately picked up and presented.

"Keep it", she said, with one of her most ravishing smiles;—"keep it for my sake—for the sake of her whom it too flatteringly represents.

Besides—upon the back of the trinket you may discover, perhaps, the information you seem just now to desire. It is growing rather dark, to be sure,—but you can examine it, at your leisure, in the morning. In the meantime, you shall be my escort home, to-night. My friends here are about holding a little musical *levée*. I can promise you some good singing. We French are not nearly so punctilious as you Americans, and I shall have no difficulty in smuggling you in, in the character of an old acquaintance."

With this, she took my arm, and I attended her home. The mansion, which belonged to one of her relatives, was quite a fine one, and, I believe, furnished in good taste. Of this latter point, however, I am scarcely qualified to judge; for it was just dark as we arrived; and, in American mansions of the better sort, lights seldom, during the heat of the summer, make their appearance at this the most pleasant period of the twenty-four hours. Not long after my arrival, to be sure, a single shaded solar lamp was lit in the principal drawing-room; and this apartment, I could thus see, was arranged with unusual good taste, and even splendor; but two other rooms of the *suite*, and in which the company chiefly assembled, remained, during the whole evening, in a very agreeable shadow. This is a well-conceived custom, giving the individual members of a party at least a choice of light or shade—a custom which our friends over the water could not do better than immediately adopt.

The evening thus spent was, unquestionably, the most delicious of my life. Madame Lalande had not over-rated the musical abilities of her friends; and the singing I here heard, I had never heard excelled in any private circle out of Vienna. The instrumental performers were many and of superior talents. The vocalists were chiefly ladies, and no individual sang less than well. At length, upon a peremptory call for Madame Lalande, she arose at once, without affectation of demur, from the *chaise longue* upon which she had been sitting by my side, and, accompanied by one or two gentlemen and her female companion at the opera, repaired to the piano in the main drawing-room. I would have escorted her thither myself, but felt that, under the peculiar circumstances of my introduction to the house, it might be more agreeable to Madame Lalande that I should remain unobserved where I was. I was thus deprived of the pleasure of seeing, although not of hearing her, sing.

The impression she produced upon the company was electrical—but the effect upon myself was even more. I know not how adequately to describe it. It arose in part, no doubt, from the sentiment of love with which I was imbued, but chiefly from my conviction of the extreme sensibility of the singer. It is beyond the reach of art to endow either air or recitative with more impassioned *expression* than was hers. Her utterance of the romance in "Otello"—the tone with which she gave the words "*Sul mio sasso*" in the "Capuleti"—are ringing in my memory yet. Her lower tones were absolutely miraculous. Her voice embraced three complete octaves, extending from the contralto D to the D upper soprano; and, though sufficiently powerful to have filled the San Carlos, it executed, with the minutest precision, every difficulty of vocal composition—ascending and descending scales, cadences, or *fioriture*. In the *finale* of the "Sonnambula" she wrought a most remarkable effect at the words,

> Ah! non giunge uman pensiero
> Al contento ond' io son piena.

Here, in imitation of Malibran, she modified the original phrase of Bellini, so as to let her voice descend to the tenor G, when by a rapid transition, she struck the G above the treble stave, springing over an interval of two octaves.

Upon rising from the piano after these miracles of vocal execution, she resumed her seat by my side—when I expressed to her, in terms of the deepest enthusiasm, my delight at her performance. Of my surprise I said nothing—and yet was I most unfeignedly surprised; for a certain feebleness, or, rather, a certain tremulous indecision of voice, in ordinary conversation, had prepared me to imagine that, in singing, she would not acquit herself with any remarkable ability.

Our conversation was now long, earnest, uninterrupted, and totally unreserved. She made me relate many of the earlier passages of my life, while she listened, with breathless attention, to every word of the narrative. I concealed nothing—I felt that I had a right to conceal nothing from her confiding affection. Encouraged by her candor upon the delicate point of her age, I entered, with perfect frankness, not only into a detail of my many minor vices, but made full confession of those moral, and even of those physical infirmities, the disclosure of which, in demanding so much higher a degree of courage, is so much more acceptable an evidence of love.

I touched upon my college indiscretions—upon my extravagances—upon my carousals—upon my flirtations—even upon my personal defects. I went so far as to speak of a slightly hectic cough with which at one time I had been troubled; of a chronic rheumatism—of a twinge of hereditary gout—and, in conclusion, of the disagreeable and inconvenient, but hitherto carefully concealed weakness of my eyes.

"Upon this latter point", said Madame Lalande, laughingly, "you have surely been injudicious in coming to confession; for I take it for granted that, without the confession, you would never have been suspected of the crime. By the bye", she continued, "have you any remembrance"—and here I fancied that a blush, even through the gloom of the apartment, became distinctly visible upon her cheek— "have you any recollection, *mon cher ami*, of this little ocular assistant— of this little aid to vision, which now depends from my neck?"

As she spoke, she twirled in her fingers the identical double eye-glass which had so overwhelmed me with confusion at the opera, while she had employed it with so magnificent a *nonchalance*.

"Full well—alas! too well do I remember it", I exclaimed, pressing passionately the delicate hand which offered the glass, or rather glasses, for my inspection. They formed a gorgeous and complex toy, richly chased and fillagreed, and gleaming with jewels, which, even in the deficient light, I could not help perceiving were of high value.

"*Eh bien, mon ami*", she resumed, with a certain *empressement* of manner that somewhat surprised me,—"*Eh bien, mon ami*, you have earnestly besought of me a favor which you have been pleased to denominate priceless. You have demanded of me my hand upon the morrow. Should I yield to your entreaties—and, I may add, to the pleadings of my own bosom—would I not be entitled to demand of you a little—a *very* little boon in return?"

"Name it!" I exclaimed, with an energy that had nearly drawn upon us the observation of the company, and restrained by their presence alone from throwing myself impetuously at her feet—"Name it, my beloved, my Eugénie, my own! —name it! —but, alas! it is already yielded ere named."

"You shall conquer, then," she said, "for the sake of the Eugénie whom you love, this little weakness which you have last confessed— this weakness rather moral than physical—this weakness so unbecoming the nobility of your real nature—so inconsistent with the candor of your usual character—and which, if permitted farther control, will assuredly involve you, sooner or later, in some very disagreeable scrape. You shall conquer, for my sake, this paltry affectation, which leads you, as you yourself acknowledge, to the tacit or implied denial of your infirmity of vision;—for, this infirmity you virtually deny, in refusing to employ the customary means for its relief. You will understand me to say, then, that I wish you *to wear spectacles*:—ah, hush!— you have already consented to wear them *for my sake*. You shall accept the little toy which I now hold in my hand, and which, although admirable as an aid to vision, is really of no very great value intrinsically.

You perceive that by a trifling modification—thus—the jewels with which it is set, disappear, and it assumes the form of ordinary *spectacles*; by sliding it thus, again, it re-appears in the more gaudy dress, and more tonnish shape, of an eye-glass. It is in the former arrangement, however, and habitually, that you have consented to wear it, *for my sake.*"

This request—must I confess it?—confused and annoyed me in no small degree; but the condition with which it was coupled, rendered hesitation, of course, a matter altogether out of the question.

"It is done"! I cried, with all the enthusiasm I could muster at the moment. "It is done—it is most cheerfully agreed. I sacrifice every feeling for your sake. To-night, I wear this dear eye-glass, *as* an eye-glass, in my waistcoat-pocket, and upon my heart; but, with the earliest dawn of that morning which gives me the privilege of calling you 'wife', I will place it upon my—upon my nose—and there wear it, ever afterwards, in the less romantic and less fashionable, but certainly in the more serviceable form, which you desire."

The conversation now turned upon the details of our arrangement for the morrow. Talbot, I learned from my betrothed, had just arrived in town. I was to see him at once, and procure a carriage. The *soirée* would scarcely break up before two; and by this hour the vehicle was to be at the door—when, in the confusion occasioned by the departure of the company, Madame L. could easily enter it unobserved. We were then to call at the house of a clergyman who would be in waiting; there be married, drop Talbot, and proceed on a short tour to the East—leaving the fashionable world at home to make whatever comments upon the matter it thought best.

Having planned all this, I immediately took leave and went in search of Talbot; but, on the way, I could not refrain from stepping into an Hotel, for the purpose of inspecting the miniature; and this I did by the powerful aid of the glasses.

The countenance was a surpassingly beautiful one. Those large luminous eyes!—those resplendent teeth!—that proud Grecian nose!—those dark luxuriant curls!—"ah!" said I exultingly to myself, "this is indeed the speaking image of my beloved!" I turned the reverse, and discovered the words—"*Eugénie Lalande—aged twenty-seven years and seven months."*

I found Talbot at home, and proceeded at once to acquaint him with my good fortune. He professed excessive astonishment, of course, but congratulated me most cordially, and proffered every assistance in his power. In a word, we carried out our arrangements to the letter; and, at two in the morning, just ten minutes after the ceremony, I found myself in a close carriage with Madame Lalande—with Mrs

Simpson, I should say—and driving at a great rate out of town, in a direction North East and by North half North.

It had been determined for us by Talbot that, as we were to be up all night, we should make our first stop at C———, a village about twenty miles from the city, there to get an early breakfast, and some repose, before proceeding upon our route. At four precisely, therefore, the carriage drew up at the door of the principal inn. I handed my adored wife out, and ordered breakfast forthwith. In the meantime we were shown into a small parlor, and sate down.

It was now nearly, if not altogether, daylight; and as I gazed, enraptured, at the angel by my side, the singular idea came, all at once, into my head, that this was really the very first moment, since my acquaintance with the celebrated loveliness of Madame Lalande, that I had enjoyed a near inspection of that loveliness by daylight.

"And now, *mon ami*", said she, taking my hand, and thus interrupting my reflections, "and now, *mon cher ami*, since we are, at length, indissolubly one—since I have yielded to your passionate entreaties—since I have performed my portion of our agreement—I presume you have not forgotten that *you*, also, have a little favor to bestow—a little promise which it is your intention to keep. Ah!—let me see!—let me remember! Yes; full easily do I call to mind the precise words of the dear promise you made to Eugénie last night. Listen! You spoke thus:

"'It is done', you said,—'it is most cheerfully agreed! I sacrifice every feeling for your sake. To-night, I wear this dear eye-glass in my waistcoat-pocket, and upon my heart; but, with the earliest dawn of that morning which gives me the privilege of calling you "wife", I will place it upon my—upon my nose—and there wear it, ever afterwards, in the less romantic and less fashionable, but certainly in the more serviceable form, which you desire'.—These were the exact words, my beloved husband; were they not?"

"They were", I replied—"by the bye, you have a capital memory—and assuredly, my beautiful Eugénie, there is no disposition on my part to evade the performance of the trivial promise these words imply. See! Behold! They are becoming—*rather*—are they not?"

Here, taking the glasses from my waistcoat-pocket, and arranging them in the ordinary form of spectacles, I applied them, gingerly, in their proper position; while Mrs Simpson, adjusting her cap, and folding her arms, sat bolt upright in her chair, in a somewhat stiff and prim, and indeed, I am sorry to say, in a rather undignified posture.

"Goodness gracious me!" I exclaimed, almost at the very instant that the rim of the spectacles settled upon my nose—"My!—goodness gracious me!—why, what *can* be the matter with these glasses?"—and, taking them hurriedly off, I wiped them carefully with a silk handkerchief, and adjusted them again. While I was doing all this, Mrs Simpson said not a word, and moved not a muscle, but looked very serious and very solemn, and continued to sit bolt upright, as before.

Well, I adjusted the glasses and put them on again; but if, in the first instance, there had occurred something which occasioned me surprise, in the second, this surprise became elevated into astonishment—and this astonishment was immense—was profound—was extreme—indeed I may as well say, at once, it was *horrific*! What, in the name of everything hideous, did this mean? Could I believe my eyes?—*could* I? that was the question. Was that—was that—was that *rouge*? and were those—were those—were those *wrinkles* upon the visage of Eugénie Lalande? And oh, Jupiter! and every one of the Gods and Goddesses, little and big!—what, what, what—*what* had become of her teeth? I dashed the spectacles to the ground, and, leaping to my feet, stood erect in the middle of the floor, confronting Mrs Simpson, and grinning and foaming, but at the same time utterly speechless and helpless, with terror and with rage.

Now I have already said that Madame Eugénie Lalande—that is to say, Simpson—spoke the English language but very little better, if not a great deal worse, than she wrote it; and, for this reason, very properly, she never attempted to speak it upon ordinary occasions. But rage will carry a lady to any extreme; and, in the present case, it carried Mrs Simpson to the very extraordinary extreme of attempting to hold a conversation in a tongue she knew nothing about.

"Vell, Monsieur", said she, after surveying me, with great disdain, for some moments—"Vell, Monsieur, and vat den?—vat de matter now?—is it de dance of de Saint Vitusse dat you ave?—if not like me, vat for vy buy de pig in de poke?"

"You wretch!" said I, catching my breath,—"you—you—you villanous old hag!"

"Ag!—ole!—me not so *ver* ole, after all—me not von day more dan de eighty-doo!"

"*Eighty-two*!" I ejaculated, staggering to the wall—"eighty-two hundred thousand of she baboons!—the miniature said twenty-seven years and seven months."

"To be sure!—dat is so!—ver true!—but den de portraite has been take for dis fifty-five year. Ven I go marry my segonde usbande, Monsieur Lalande, at dat time I had de portraite take for my daughter by my first usbande, Monsieur Moissart."

"Moissart!" said I.

"Yes, Moissart, Moissart," said she, mimicking my pronunciation, which, to speak the truth, was none of the best—"and vat den?—vat *you* know bout de Moissart?"

"Nothing, you old fright,—I know nothing about him at all—only I had an ancestor of that name, once upon a time."

"Dat name!—and vat you ave for say to dat name? 'Tis ver goot name—and so is Voissart—dat is ver goot name too. My daughter, Ma'mselle Moissart, she marry von Monsieur Voissart—and de name is bote *ver* respectaable name."

"Moissart!" I exclaimed, "and Voissart!—why, what is it you mean?"

"Vat I mean?" said she, putting her arms akimbo—"vy, I mean Moissart, and Voissart; and, for de matter of dat, I mean Croissart and Froissart, too, if I only tink proper for to mean it. My daughter's daughter, Ma'mselle Voissart, she marry von Monsieur Croissart; and, den agin, my daughter's grande-daughter, Ma'mselle Croissart, she marry von Monsieur Froissart—and I suppose you say dat *dat* is not von *ver* respectaable name!"

"Froissart!" said I, beginning to faint, "why surely you don't say Moissart, and Voissart, and Croissart, and Froissart!"

"Yes," she replied, shaking her head up and down, as some people do when very much in a passion,—"Yes! Yes!—Moissart, and Voissart, and Croissart, and Froissart! But Monsieur Froissart, who married my grande-daughter, he was von *ver* big vat you call de fool—he vas von *ver* great big donce like youself—for he lef *la belle France,* for com to dis stoopide *Amérique*—and, ven he get here, he vent and ave von *ver* stoopide—von *ver ver* stoopide sonn—so I hear—for I not yet ad de plaisir to meet vid him—neider me nor my companion, de Madame Stéphanie Lalande. He is name, dough, de Napoleon Buonaparte Froissart —and I sooppose you say dat *dat*, too, is not de von *ver* respectaable name."

Either the length or the nature of this speech, had the effect of working up Mrs Simpson into a very stupendous excitement, indeed; and as, with great labor, she made an end of it, she jumped up from her chair like somebody bewitched; dropping upon the floor an entire universe of bustle as she jumped. Once upon her feet, she gnashed her gums, brandished her arms, rolled up her sleeves, shook her fist in my face, and concluded the performance by tearing the cap from her head, and, with it, an immense wig of valuable black hair, the whole of which she dashed upon the floor with a yell—there trampling and dancing a fandango upon it, in an absolute ecstasy and agony of rage.

Meantime, I sank aghast into the chair which she had vacated.

"Moissart and Voissart!" I repeated, musingly, as she cut one of her pigeon-wings, and "Croissart and Froissart!" as she completed another—"Moissart, and Voissart, and Croissart, and Napoleon Buonaparte Froissart!—why, you ineffable old wretch, that's *me*. D'ye hear?—that's *me*—that's *mee*" [Here I shouted at the top of my voice]—"that's *me-e-e-e*! *I* am Napoleon Buonaparte Froissart, and if I hav n't married my great-great-grandmother, I wish I may be everlastingly confounded!!"

Madame Eugénie Lalande, *quasi* Simpson, formerly Moissart, was, in sober fact, my great, great, grandmother. In her youth she had been beautiful, and, even at eighty-two, retained the majestic height, the sculptural contour of head, the fine eyes, and the Grecian nose of her girlhood. By the aid of these—of rouge, of pearl-powder, of false hair, false teeth, and false *tournure*, as well as of the most skilful *modistes* of Paris, she easily contrived to hold a respectable footing among the beauties *un peu passées* of the French metropolis. In this respect, indeed, she might have been regarded as little less than the equal of the celebrated Ninon de L'Enclos.

She was immensely wealthy; and, being left for the second time a widow, with no surviving children, she bethought herself of my existence in America, and resolved, in a freak of fancy, to make me her heir. For this purpose she paid a visit to the United States, in company with a very lovely and accomplished friend—a distant relative of her second husband—a Madame *Stéphanie* Lalande.

At the opera, my great-great-grandmother's attention was arrested by my notice; and, upon surveying me through her eye-glass, she was struck with a certain family resemblance to herself. Thus interested, and knowing that the heir she sought was actually in the city, she made inquiries of her party respecting me. The gentleman who attended her knew my person, and told her who I was. The information thus obtained, induced her to renew her scrutiny; and it was this scrutiny which emboldened me to behave in the absurd manner already detailed. She returned my bow, however, under the impression that, by some odd accident, I had discovered her identity. When, deceived by my weakness of vision and the arts of the toilet, in respect to the age and charms of the strange lady, I demanded so enthusiastically of Talbot who she was, he concluded, as a matter of course, that it was the younger beauty whom I meant. He therefore told me, with perfect sincerity, that she was "the celebrated widow, Madame Lalande."

In the street, next morning, my great-great-grandmother encountered Talbot, an old Parisian acquaintance; when the conversation, very naturally, turned upon myself. My deficiencies of vision were then explained—for these were notorious, although I was entirely ignorant of their notoriety. My good old relative thus discovered, much to her chagrin, that she had been deceived in supposing me aware of her identity, and that I had been merely making a fool of myself, in making open love, in a theatre, to an old woman unknown.

By way of punishing me for this imprudence, she concocted, with Talbot, a plot. To avoid giving me an introduction, he purposely kept out of my way. My street inquiries, about "the lovely widow, Madame Lalande", were supposed to refer to the younger lady, of course; and thus will be understood my conversation with the three gentlemen whom I encountered upon leaving Talbot's Hotel. Thus, also, is explained the allusion of one of them to Ninon de L'Enclos.

I had no opportunity of seeing Madame Lalande closely during daylight; and, at the musical *soirée*, my silly weakness, in refusing the aid of glasses, effectually prevented me from making a discovery of her age. When "Madame Lalande" was called upon to sing, Madame *Stéphanie* Lalande was intended; and it was she who arose to obey the call;—my great-great-grandmother, to further the deception, arising at the same moment, and accompanying her to the piano in the main drawing-room. Had I decided upon escorting her thither, it had been her design to suggest the propriety of my remaining where I was; my own prudential views, however, rendered this unnecessary. The songs which I so much admired, and which so confirmed my impressions of the youth of my mistress, were executed, of course, by Madame *Stéphanie* Lalande.

The eye-glass was presented by way of adding a reproof to the hoax—a sting to the epigram of the deception. Its presentation afforded an opportunity for the lecture upon affectation with which I was so especially edified. It is almost superfluous to add that the *glasses* of the instrument, as worn by the old lady, had been exchanged by her for a pair better adapted to my years. They suited me, in fact, to a T.

The "clergyman", who merely pretended to tie the fatal knot, was a boon companion of Talbot's, and no priest. He was an excellent "whip", however; and, having doffed his cassock to put on a great coat, he drove the hack which conveyed the "happy couple" out of town. Talbot took a seat at his side. The two scoundrels were thus "in at the death", and, through a half open window of the back parlor of the inn, amused themselves in grinning at the *dénouement* of the drama. I believe I shall have to call them both out.

Nevertheless—I am *not* the husband of my great-great-grandmother; and this is a reflection which affords me infinite relief;—but I *am* the husband of Madame Lalande—of Madame *Stéphanie* Lalande—with whom my good old relative (besides making me her sole heir when she dies—if she ever does) has been at the trouble of concocting me a match.

In conclusion, I am done with *billets-doux*, and am never to be seen without SPECTACLES.

TEXTUAL NOTES

200.6   magnetæsthetics] The manuscript reading may have an o, rather than an a, as the first element in the ligature. In either event the term is a neologism, not listed in the OED. *Dollar Newspaper* and *Broadway Journal* have œ but the type fonts from which they were set might not have included a separate character for æ.

202.10   aérienne] Thus pointed in a number of French lexicons from the late eighteenth and nineteenth centuries consulted by the editor. The copy-text and all early printed forms of the tale read *äerienne*. This emendation, like that at 210.31, *naiveté*, is anticipated by Harrison, *Complete Works*, 5:180, 5:193.

213.4   Capuleti] So spelled in all printed references to Bellini's opera consulted by the editor, including an Italian-English libretto (New York: John Douglas, 1848) and an Italian-German score for voice and piano (Leipzig and Berlin: C. F. Peters, n.d. but nineteenth century). Romeo's phrase, "Sul mio sasso," occurs in the final scene.

213.10   fioriture] Harrison, *Complete Works*, 5:197, anticipates this emendation to the correct plural form of *fioritura*. The copy-text and all early printings have *fiorituri*.

213.12   giunge] Spelled *guinge* in the copy-text and all early printings. Harrison, 5:197, anticipates the emendation.

216.25–26   To-night . . . heart] Either by design or, more likely, through inadvertence, Poe does not have Madame Lalande echo precisely the narrator's earlier speech. She omits the phrase "*as* an eye-glass." In the *Dollar Newspaper* printing and the texts deriving from it, the phrase "in my waistcoat-pocket" is omitted from both speeches, and "as an eye-glass" occurs in both.

217.31   villanous] Thus in the copy-text, *Dollar Newspaper*, and *Lloyd's*. Although *Broadway Journal* prints villainous, the copy-text spelling is a tolerated variant or the favored form in standard American lexicons of the period.

EMENDATIONS

*202.10   aérienne] ed.; *äerienne*
203.21   her own] D; my own
203.40   Paris."] D; Paris"

207.37	vaudeville] D; vaude ville (divided at line-end without hyphen)
209.8	manière] B; maniére
210.9	Midsummer] D (midsummer); Midsum- (at line-end)
210.31	naïveté] ed.; näiveté
*213.4	Capuleti] ed.; Capuletti
*213.10	fioriture] ed.; fiorituri
*213.12	giunge] ed.; guinge
213.13	ond' io] ed.; ond 'io
216.27	"wife"] ed.; 'wife'
216.30	.—] ed.; (period and dash continuous)
218.25	Amérique] B (Amérique); Amerique
220.35	doffed] B; donned

ALTERATIONS IN THE MANUSCRIPT

201.8	black] preceded by erased bl at left margin, first line of page; remainder of line blank
213.40	eyes.] altered from eye-sig by erasure and overwriting
214.4	By the bye] altered from Bye the by by erasure and overwriting
216.24	'It . . . done' . . . 'it] single quotation marks written over erased double quotation marks
216.30	more] written over unrecoverable erased letters
216.40	posture.] last four letters and period written over erased matter, perhaps ition.
220.1	deficiencies] last four letters written over unrecoverable erased letters
220.28	Its] written over erased word, perhaps This

HISTORICAL COLLATION

200.1	lacking] MS, L, B, G, R; [Written for the Philadelphia Dollar Newspaper.] D
200.2	By Edgar Allan Poe.] MS; BY EDGAR A. POE, AUTHOR OF THE PRIZE STORY, "THE GOLD-BUG," ETC. D; BY EDGAR A. POE. L; lacking B, G, R
200.3	Some persons ridicule] MS; Many years ago, it was the fashion to ridicule D, L, B, G, R
200.4	think clearly, not] MS; think not D, L, B, G, R
200.5	indeed] MS, D, L, B, G; lacking R
200.7	most real and the most] MS; truest and most D, L, B, G, R
200.10	at a glance] MS; by a glance D, L, B, G, R
200.12	numerous] MS; almost innumerable D, L, B, G, R
200.12	this position] MS; the position D, L, B, G, R
200.13	It is necessary that I be] MS; My story requires that I should be D, L, B, G, R
200.13	a young] MS; a very young D, L, B, G, R
200.14	twenty-two.] MS; twenty-two years of age. D, L, B, G, R

200.17	an inheritance] MS; a large inheritance D, L, B, G, R
200.20	Christian or baptismal names are] MS; Christian name is D, L, B, G, R
200.20–21	Buonaparte.] MS; Buonaparte—or, more properly, these are my first and middle appellations. D, L, B, G, R
200.21	I am now Napoleon Buonaparte Simpson.] MS; *lacking*, D, L, B, G, R
200.21–22	the "Simpson" with] MS; the name, Simpson, with D, L, B, G, R
200.22	much] MS; some D, L, B, G, R
200.22	for in] MS; as in D, L, B, G, R
200.25	may as well mention] MS; may mention D, L, B, G, R
200.27	Monsieur George *Froissart*] MS; Monsieur Froissart D, L, B, G, R
200.29	*His* wife, again, only] MS; whose wife, again, being only D, L, B, G, R
200.30–31	one Monsieur *Voissart*; and this gentleman, very] MS; one Victor Voissart. Monsieur Voissart, very D, L, B, G, R
200.31	wedded] MS, D, L; married B, G, R
200.32	was quite a] MS, D, B, G, R; was a L
200.34–35	But what I speak of now is the coincidence. Observe!] MS; *lacking* D, L, B, G, R
200.35	Here are] MS; Here, however, are D, L, B, G, R
201.2–3	Act of the Pennsylvania Legislature] MS; act of Legislature D, L, B, G, R
201.3	but with] MS; and with D, L, B, G, R
201.4–5	the annoying and useless] MS; the useless and annoying D, L, B, G, R
201.6	am so, so] MS; am by no means deficient D, L, B, G, R
201.6	I believe] MS; On the contrary, I believe D, L, B, G, R
201.7	and that I possess] MS; and possess D, L, B, G, R
201.8	I am five] MS; In height I am five D, L, B, G, R
201.13	*spectacles*] MS; glasses D, L, B, G, R
201.14	dislike] MS, D, L, B, G; disliked R
201.16	or which so] MS; or so D, L, B, G, R
201.17	exactly] MS; altogether, D, L, B, G, R
201.17	sanctimoniousness.] MS; sanctimoniousness and of age. D, L, B, G, R
201.19	But something] MS, D, B, G, R; But there is something L
201.23	devout] MS; devoted D, L, B, G, R
201.23	the gentle sex] MS; the women D, L, B, G, R
201.24	——— theatre] MS; C——— theatre D, L; P——— theatre B, G, R
201.25	night; the] MS; night, and the D, L, B, G, R
201.26	and thus the] MS; so that the D, L, B, G, R
201.28	preserved] MS, D, L; reserved B, G, R
201.38	gazed at] MS; regarded D, L, B, G, R
201.39	imaginable] MS; I had ever beheld D, L, B, G; that I had ever beheld R
202.4–5	The construction of the box permitted nearly all the person to be seen. It was] MS; The figure, nearly all which the construction of the box permitted to be seen, was D, L; The figure, almost all of which the construction of the box permitted to be seen, was B, G, R
202.12–13	delicious symmetry] MS; exquisite symmetry D, L, B, G, R
202.14	now] MS, D, B, G, R; then L
202.15	gossamer] MS; frail D, L, B, G, R
202.19	was well set] MS, D, L, B, G; was set R
202.21–22	not to be misunderstood] MS; that could not be mistaken D, L, B, G, R

202.22	and of the fastidious] MS; and fastidious D, L, B, G, R
202.25	to stone] MS, D, L, B, G; to a stone R
202.26	force of] MS; force and truth of D, L, B, G, R
202.26	about] MS; concerning D, L, B, G, R
202.33	irrecoverably] MS, D, L; irrevocably B, G, R
202.34	one] MS; person D, L, B, G, R
202.40	wrapped] MS, D, L; thus wrapped B, G, R
202.40	enchanting] MS; lovely D, L, B, G, R
203.5	exalted and subdued] MS; quieted and exalted D, L, B, G, R
203.6	of a calm] MS; of calm D, L, B, G, R
203.6	of an enthusiastic] MS; of enthusiastic D, L, B, G, R
203.7–8	Madonna-like—from the matronly] MS; Madonna-like and matronly D, L, B, G, R
203.9	behind] MS; else D, L, B, G, R
203.10	mystery I] MS; mystery which I D, L, B, G, R
203.11	it heightened] MS; it greatly heightened D, L, B, G, R
203.18	in mind] MS, D, L; in my mind B, G, R
203.21	her own] D, L, B, G, R; my own MS
203.24–25	this. But even if this had not been so, I had no glass with me, and was thus] MS; this, even had I been so fortunate as to have one with me—but I had not, and was thus D, L, B, G, R
203.26–27	companion, whose very existence I had for some time forgotten.] MS; companion. D, L, B, G, R
203.28	a *lorgnette*] MS; an opera-glass D, L, B, G, R
203.29	A *lorgnette*] MS; An opera-glass D, L, B, G, R
203.29–30	a *lorgnette*?" Here] MS; an opera-glass?—low!—very." Here D, L; an opera-glass?" Here B, G, R
203.31	resumed] MS; continued D, L, B, G, R
203.33	so lovely] MS, L; as lovely D, B, G, R
203.34	No doubt she is very beautiful] MS; She is very beautiful, no doubt D, L, B, G, R
203.42	I have] MS; Yes; I have D, L, B, G, R
204.1	present] MS; introduce D, L, B, G, R
204.2	Assuredly. When] MS; Assuredly; with the greatest pleasure; when D, L, B, G, R
204.4	good!—and now oblige me by just holding your] MS; good; and now *do* hold your D, B, G, R; good," returned Talbot; and now *do* hold your L
204.6–7	put Talbot under the obligation desired] MS; take Talbot's advice D, L, B, G, R
204.10	upon] MS, D, L; on B, G, R
204.12	supremely] MS; exquisitely D, L, B, G, R
204.14	still there was the unintelligible something which disturbed] MS; still the unintelligible something disturbed D, L, B, G, R
204.15	imagination was] MS; senses were D, L, B, G, R
204.16	gravity, of sadness] MS; gravity, sadness D, L, B, G, R
204.18	thus, to] MS; thus, of course, to D, L, B, G, R
204.22	become aware] MS; become suddenly aware D, L, B, G, R
204.22	Nevertheless] MS; Still D, L, B, G, R
204.24	averted] MS; turned aside D, L, B, G, R

Poe's "The Spectacles" 225

204.27	round] MS, D, L; around B, G, R
204.30	turn aside] MS; avert D, L, B, G, R
204.31	elevated it, and regarded] MS; elevated it—adjusted it—and then regarded D, L, B, G, R
204.32	the space] MS, D, B, G, R; she space L
204.36	sure] MS; likely D, L, B, G, R
204.36	or to disgust] MS; or disgust D, L, B, G, R
204.38	in short] MS; *lacking* D, L, B, G, R
204.38	breeding—that] MS; breeding, in short—that D, L, B, G, R
204.39–40	sentiments were] MS, L, B, G, R; sentiments was D
205.2–3	for several] MS; for the space of several D, L, B, G, R
205.4	The] MS, D, L; This B, G, R
205.4	universal] MS; very general D, L, B, G, R
205.9–10	being now] MS; now being D, L, B, G, R
205.10	towards] MS, D, L; toward B, G, R
205.17	She scrutinized me thus] MS; Having thus scrutinized me D, L, B, G, R
205.17–18	and then suddenly addressed] MS; the fair object of my passion addressed D, L, B, G, R
205.18	her. While] MS; her, and while D, L, B, G, R
205.20	she] MS; Madame Lalande D, L, B, G, R
205.26	the same] MS, L, B, G, R; the the same D
205.30	than to disconcert] MS, D, L, G, R; than disconcert B
205.38	to] MS; towards D, L, B, G, R
205.41	flitted] MS; floated D, L, B, G, R
205.42	was immediately] MS; was greatly and immediately D, L, B, G, R
206.3	amazement—of my delirious] MS; amazement—my delirious D, L, B, G, R
206.7	nods] MS; affirmative inclinations of the head D, L, B, G, R
206.9	ecstasy.] MS; ecstasy of heart. D, L, B, G, R
206.12	*sight"*. At first] MS; sight;" and, at first D, L, B, G, R
206.13	and was *returned*] MS; and—*returned* D, L, B, G, R
206.17	so refined] MS; *lacking* D, L, B, G, R
206.20	as uncalculating, as uncompromising] MS; as uncompromising—as uncalculating D, L, B, G, R
206.24	tumult supervened] MS; tumult immediately supervened D, L, B, G, R
206.25	endeavour] MS, D, L; effort B, G, R
206.25	into proximity] MS; into closer proximity D, L, B, G, R
206.26	this attempt, on] MS; this, on D, L, B, G, R
206.27–28	myself for not] MS; myself for my disappointment in not D, L, B, G, R
206.28	robe, with] MS; robe, by D, L, B, G, R
206.33	dreary, snail-paced] MS; snail-paced, dreary D, L, B, G, R
206.35	its last] MS; the last D, L, B, G, R
206.37	a footman] MS; the footman D, L, B, G, R
206.38	paces, "out!—let] MS; paces—"let D, L, B, G, R
207.1	should] MS, D, L; would B, G, R
207.3–4	say something] MS; reply D, L, B, G, R
207.5	consigning] MS, D, L, B, G; consigned R
207.8	myself; perhaps, indeed, he had forgotten it] MS; myself—had forgotten it D, B, G, R; myself–forgotten it L
207.9	had he been] MS; was he D, L, B, G, R

207.12	every acquaintance] MS; every male acquaintance D, L, B, G, R
207.12–13	By report, I found, she was known to] MS; By report she was known, I found, to D, L, B, G, R
207.13	by sight to many] MS; to many by sight D, L, B, G, R
207.14	few days] MS; few weeks D, L, B, G, R
207.14	and thus there were not more than one or two who] MS; and there were very few, therefore, who D, L, B, G, R
207.15	professed a personal knowledge] MS; claimed her personal acquaintance D, L, B, G, R
207.15	These, being] MS; These few, being D, L, B, G, R
207.17	with] MS; through D, L, B, G, R
207.17	however] MS; thus D, L, B, G, R
207.21	How surpassingly] MS; Surpassingly D, L, B, G, R
207.21	the second] MS; a second D, L, B, G, R
207.22	the third] MS, D, L; a third B, G, R
207.23–24	as it passed] MS; passing D, L, B, G, R
207.28	second; "has still quite] MS; second; still quite D, L, B, G, R
207.30	lovely] MS; beautiful D, L, B, G, R
207.32	why not] MS; why should n't she be D, L, B, G, R
207.32–33	is a rush-light] MS, D, L; is as a rushlight B, G, R
207.34	Here the whole trio laughed.] MS; *lacking* D, L, B, G, R
207.35	ha!" said the third, "why] MS; ha! why D, L, B, G, R
207.36–37	and here, as we separated, he] MS; And here we separated, while one of the trio D, L, B, G, R
207.37	commenced] MS; began D, L, B, G, R
208.5	of smiles] MS; of all imaginable smiles D, L, B, G, R
208.5	of the recognition] MS, D, L, B, G; of recognition R
208.6	forced] MS; obliged D, L, B, G, R
208.12	until after the lapse] MS, D, L; until the lapse B, G, R
208.19	thus be] MS; be thus D, L, B, G, R
208.23	her address] MS; the address D, L, B, G, R
208.23	and, next] MS; and the next D, L, B, G, R
208.26	folly] MS; weakness D, L, B, G, R
208.31	leave] MS; quit D, L, B, G, R
208.32	presentation] MS; introduction D, L, B, G, R
208.34–35	my hand, as of my heart] MS; my heart and of my hand D, L, B, G, R
208.38	Yes;—came] MS; Yes, actually *came* D, L, B, G, R
208.39	Lalande—from the] MS; Lalande—the D, L, B, G, R
208.41	her heart] MS; her noble heart D, L, B, G, R
209.2	proposal] MS; proposals D, L, B, G, R
209.6	only of de] MS; only de D, L, B, G, R
209.7	learn] MS; l'etudier D, L, B, G, R
209.8	de manière of dis leetle note, I vill] ed., MS; de maniere, I vill, D, L, B, G, R
209.9–10	Vat is need I say de more] MS; Need I say de more D, L, B, G, R
209.12	letter] MS; note D, L, B, G, R
209.13	which] MS; that D, L, B, G, R
209.15	And still] MS; Still D, L, B, G, R
209.17	instantly] MS; immediately D, L, B, G, R

209.22–23	fool! I had acquainted him with the exigencies of the case, and, if] MS; fool! if D, L, B, G, R
209.24–25	not enclose me an introduction] MS; not have enclosed me a letter of presentation D, L, B, G, R
209.27–28	pencil: "Mr Talbot left S———] MS; pencil. The scoundrel had joined his master in the country: "Left S——— D, L, B, G, R
209.28	Did n't] MS; did not D, L, B, G, R
209.36	I had yet a resource left me, however, in] MS; But I had yet a resource left in D, L, B, G, R
209.37	and I resolved] MS; and I now resolved D, L, B, G, R
210.4	custom] MS; habit D, L, B, G, R
210.5	every fine evening] MS; *lacking* D, L, B, G, R
210.6	practice] MS; custom D, L, B, G, R
210.6–7	in a certain one of our public squares] MS; in a public square D, L, B, G, R
210.7–8	by the windows of her residence] MS; by her windows D, L, B, G, R
210.8	overshadowing grove] MS; shadowing groves D, L, B, G, R
210.9	grey uncertainty] MS; gray gloom D, L, B, G, R
210.9	Midsummer gloaming] ed.; Midsum-/gloaming MS; sweet midsummer evening D, L, B, G, R
210.9–10	here, at length, watching my opportunity, I accosted] MS; I observed my opportunity and accosted D, L, B, G, R
210.12	old and familiar acquaintance] MS, D, L, B, G; old acquaintance R
210.13	welcome] MS; greet D, L, B, G, R
210.14	diminutive of hands] MS; little of hands D, B, G, R; little pair of hands L
210.17	even much less] MS; even less D, L, B, G, R
210.19	to all the] MS, D, L; to the B, G, R
210.21	union] MS; marriage D, L, B, G, R
210.24	departed] MS; gone by D, L, B, G, R
210.24	What would the world say?] MS; *lacking* D, L, B, G, R
210.26	thus, of course, that] MS; thus that D, L, B, G, R
210.31	an air] MS; a charming air D, L, B, G, R
210.32	went even] MS, D, L, B, G; even went R
210.35	me—but with] MS, D, L, B, G; me, with R
210.36	a phantasy] MS; a fancy or fantasy D, L, B, G, R
210.38	These things she] MS, D, L, B, G; These she R
210.41	fabric of argumentation] MS; argumentative fabric D, L, B, G, R
210.42	I best] MS, D, L; best I B, G, R
211.1	my passion—of my devotion] MS; my devotion, of my passion D, L, B, G, R
211.2	adoration] MS; admiration D, L, B, G, R
211.3–4	of true love—] MS; of love— D, L, B, G, R
211.5	the danger] MS; the manifest danger D, L, B, G, R
211.6	This latter argument] MS, D, L, B, G; This argument R
211.7	resistance] MS; determination D, L, B, G, R
211.8	sufficiently] MS; properly D, L, B, G, R
211.9	delicate.] MS; so. D, L, B, G, R
211.9–10	touching upon] MS; mentioning D, L, B, G, R
211.10–11	of the finest sensibilities of her nature] MS; *lacking* D, L, B, G, R

211.11–12	should and would be willingly made] MS; should be made D, L, B, G, R
211.16	very] MS; even D, L, B, G, R
211.17	under *no* circumstances] MS; *never* D, L, B, G, R
211.23	dignity and candor] MS; dignity of candor D, L, B, G, R
211.23–24	candor—which delighted—which enchanted] MS, D, L, B, G; candor —which enchanted R
211.26	Dearest] MS; My sweetest Eugénie D, L, B, G, R
211.27	age surpasses] MS; years surpass D, L, B, G, R
211.27	What then] MS; But what then D, L, B, G, R
211.28	world—what are they, after all, but so] MS; world are so D, L, B, G, R
211.29	impertinences] MS; follies D, L, B, G, R
211.29	we do] MS; ourselves D, L, B, G, R
211.30	twenty-two] MS, D, L, B, G; twenty one R
211.32	sweetest] MS; dearest D, L, B, G, R
211.32–33	than—can have numbered no more than—no] MS, D, B, G, R; than—no L
211.33	than—than—than"—] MS; than—than—than—than—" D, L, B, G; than—than—than—than—than—' R
211.34	an instant] MS, B, G, R; a brief instant D, L
211.37	question] MS; query D, L, B, G, R
211.40	presented.] MS, D, L; presented to her. B, G, R
212.1–2	the information] MS; the very information D, L, B, G, R
212.2	seem just now to desire] MS; seem to desire D, L, B, G, R
212.2–3	is growing rather dark, to be sure] MS; is now, to be sure, growing rather dark D, L, B, G, R
212.4–5	friends here are] MS, D, L; friends are B, G, R
212.5	you some] MS; you, too, some D, L, B, G, R
212.10	which belonged to one of her relatives] MS; *lacking* D, L, B, G, R
212.14	of the summer] MS; of summer D, L, B, G, R
212.15	twenty-four hours] MS; day D, L, B, G, R
212.15	Not long] MS; In about an hour D, L, B, G, R
212.20–21	the individual members of a party] MS; the party D, L, B, G, R
212.21–22	a custom] MS; and one D, L, B, G, R
212.29	sang] MS, D, B, G, R; sung L
212.30	she arose] MS, D, L, B, G; she rose R
212.30	affectation of demur] MS, D, L; affectation or demur B, G, R
212.31	*chaise*] MS, D, B, G, R; *chasse* L
212.31	had been sitting] MS; had sate D, L, B, G, R
212.32–33	companion at] MS; friend of D, L, B, G, R
212.33	the main drawing-room] MS, D, L, B, G; the drawing-room R
212.34	her thither myself] MS; her myself D, L, B, G, R
212.34–35	the peculiar circumstances] MS, D, L; the circumstances B, G, R
212.35–36	it might be more agreeable to Madame Lalande that I should remain] MS; I had better remain D, L, B, G, R
212.37	the pleasure of] MS, D, L, B, G; *lacking* R
212.39	was] MS; seemed D, L, B, G, R
212.40	was even] MS; was something even D, L, B, G, R
213.4	are ringing] MS, D, L; is ringing B, G, R
213.8	Carlos, it executed] MS; Carlos, executed D, L, B, G, R
213.10	wrought] MS; brought about D, L, B, G, R

Poe's "The Spectacles" 229

213.12	*non*] MS, D, L, B, G; nou R
213.13	*ond' io*] ed., MS, D, L, B, G; onn 'io R
213.17	of two octaves] MS, D, L, B, G; of some two or more octaves R
213.23	imagine] MS; anticipate D, L, B, G, R
213.27	while she listened] MS; and listened D, L, B, G, R
213.33	higher a degree] MS, D, B, G, R; higher degree L
213.34	more acceptable] MS; surer D, L, B, G, R
213.36	carousals—upon my flirtations] MS; carousals—upon my debts—upon my flirtations D, L, B, G, R
213.36–37	flirtations—even upon my personal defects. I went] MS; flirtations. I even went D, L, B, G, R
214.2	surely been] MS; been surely D, L, B, G, R
214.2–4	for I take it for granted that, without the confession, you would never have been suspected of] MS; for, without the confession, I take it for granted that no one would have accused you of D, L, B, G, R
214.5	remembrance] MS; recollection D, L, B, G, R
214.8	of this little aid to vision] MS; *lacking* D, L, B, G, R
214.10–11	while she had employed it with so magnificent a *nonchalance*] MS; *lacking* D, L, B, G, R
214.12	alas! too well do I] MS, D, L; alas! do I B, G, R
214.13	the glass, or rather glasses] MS; the glasses D, L, B, G, R
214.14	gorgeous and complex] MS; complex and magnificent D, L, B, G, R
214.18	somewhat] MS; rather D, L, B, G, R
214.23	a little—a *very* little] MS; a very—a very little D, L, B, G; a very, very little R
214.29	then," she] MS; then, *mon ami*," she D, L, B, G, R
214.31	rather moral] MS; more moral D, L, B, G, R
214.31	this weakness so unbecoming] MS; and which, let me assure you, is so unbecoming D, L, B, G, R
214.35	this paltry affectation] MS; this affectation D, L, B, G, R
214.41	although] MS, D, L; though B, G, R
214.42	great] MS; immense D, L, B, G, R
214.42	intrinsically] MS; as a gem D, L, B, G, R
215.1–4	thus—the jewels with which it is set, disappear, and it assumes the form of ordinary *spectacles*; by sliding it thus, again, it re-appears in the more gaudy dress, and more tonnish shape, of an eye-glass] MS; thus—or thus—it can be adapted to the eyes in the form of spectacles, or worn in the waistcoat pocket as an eye-glass D, L, B, G, R
215.4	arrangement] MS; mode D, L, B, G, R
215.5	have consented] MS; have already consented D, L, B, G, R
215.6	confused and annoyed me] MS; confused me D, L, B, G, R
215.7	small] MS; little D, L, B, G, R
215.8	hesitation, of course, a] MS, D, B, G, R; hesitation a L
215.9	enthusiasm I] MS, D, L; enthusiasm that I B, G, R
215.12	in my waistcoat-pocket] MS; *lacking* D, L, B, G, R
215.13	privilege] MS, D, L; pleasure B, G, R
215.17	The] MS; Our D, L, B, G, R
215.17	arrangement] MS, D, L; arrangements B, G, R
215.25	whatever] MS, D, B, G, R; *lacking* L
215.29	an Hotel] MS; a hotel D, L, B, G, R

215.31	was a surpassingly beautiful one] MS, D, B, G, R; was surpassingly beautiful L
215.32	those resplendent teeth!] MS; *lacking* D, L, B, G, R
215.40	arrangements] MS; arrangement D, L, B, G, R
216.2	North East and by North] MS, D, L, B; North-east by North G, R
216.5	there to get] MS; and there get D, L, B, G, R
216.14	near] MS, D, L, B, G; neat R (*broken type, probably t*)
216.14	daylight.] MS; daylight at all. D, L, B, G, R
216.15	thus] MS; so D, L, B, G, R
216.16	my reflections] MS; this train of reflection D, L, B, G, R
216.16–17	at length] MS; *lacking* D, L, B, G, R
216.18	since I have performed] MS; and performed D, L, B, G, R
216.24	done', you said,—'it] MS; done!—it D, L, B, G, R
216.25–26	in my waistcoat-pocket] MS; as an eye-glass D, L, B, G, R
216.32	replied] MS; said D, L, B, G, R
216.32	"by the bye, you] MS; "you D, L, B, G, R
216.32	a capital] MS; an excellent D, L, B, G, R
216.34	these words] MS; they D, L, B, G, R
216.36–37	Here, taking the glasses from my waistcoat-pocket, and arranging them in the ordinary] MS; And here, having arranged the glasses in the ordinary D, L, B, G, R
216.38	Mrs] MS; Madame D, L, B, G, R
216.39	bolt] MS, D, L, B, G; bold R
216.40	I am sorry to say] MS; *lacking* D, L, B, G, R
216.40	rather] MS; somewhat, D, L, B, G, R
216.40	posture] MS; position D, L, B, G, R
216.42	spectacles settled] MS; spectacles had settled D, L, B, G, R
217.2	hurriedly] MS; quickly D, L, B, G, R
217.3–5	While I was doing all this, Mrs Simpson said not a word, and moved not a muscle, but looked very serious and very solemn, and continued to sit bolt upright, as before.] MS; *lacking* D, L, B, G, R
217.6	Well, I adjusted the glasses and put them on again;] MS; *lacking* D, L, B, G, R
217.9	was immense] MS; *lacking* D, L, B, G, R
217.10	I may as well say, at once, it] MS; I may say it D, L, B, G, R
217.13	—were those—] MS, D, L, B; —and were those— G, R
217.16	spectacles to] MS; spectacles violently to D, L, B, G, R
217.17–18	Simpson, and] MS; Simpson, with my arms set a-kimbo, and D, L, B, G, R
217.18–19	speechless and helpless, with] MS, D, B, G, R; speechless with L
217.20	Madame Eugénie Lalande] MS, D, L, B, G; Madame Lalande R
217.21–22	if not a great deal worse] MS; *lacking* D, L, B, G, R
217.22–23	very properly, she] MS; she very properly D, L, B, G, R
217.26	she knew nothing about] MS; that she did not altogether understand D, L, B, G, R
217.27	with great disdain] MS; in great apparent astonishment D, L, B, G, R
217.33	von day] MS; one single day D, L, B, G, R
217.36	thousand of she baboons] MS, D, L; thousand baboons B, G, R
217.39	dis] MS; dese D, L, B, G, R
217.41	Moissart."] MS, D, L, B; Moissart?" G; Moissart!' R

218.1	"Yes, Moissart, Moissart] MS, D, L, B; "Yes, Moissart G, R
218.7	name—and so is Voissart—dat is ver goot name too] MS, D, B, G, R; name too L
218.8	de name] MS, B, G, R; de names D, L
218.11	mean?" said she, putting her arms akimbo—"vy, I] MS; mean?—I D, L, B, G, R
218.13	proper for to] MS; proper to D, L, B, G, R
218.20–21	shaking her head up and down, as some people do when very much in a passion] MS; leaning fully back in her chair, and stretching out her lower limbs at great length D, L, B, G, R
218.21	"Yes! Yes!] MS; "yes, D, L, B, G, R
218.22–23	who married my grande-daughter] MS; *lacking* D, L, B, G, R
218.23	call de fool] MS; call fool D, L, B, G, R
218.24	youself] MS; yourself D, L, B, G, R
218.26	for I not yet ad] MS; dough I not yet ave ad D, L, B, G, R
218.28	name, dough, de] MS; name de D, L, B, G, R
218.29	not de von] MS; not von D, L, B, G, R
218.32	stupendous excitement] MS; extraordinary passion, D, L, B, G, R
218.33	as, with great labor, she made an end of it] MS; as she made an end of it, with great labor D, L, B, G, R
218.38	of valuable black] MS; of the most valuable and beautiful black D, L, B, G, R
218.39	floor] MS; ground D, L, B, G, R
218.39–40	there trampling and dancing] MS; and there trampled and danced D, L, B, G, R
218.42	she had vacated] MS, B, G, R; she vacated D, L
219.1	musingly] MS; thoughtfully D, L, B, G, R
219.4	wretch] MS; serpent D, L, B, G, R
219.4	that's *me*. D'ye] MS; that's *me*—that's *me*—d'ye D, L, B, G, R
219.4–5	hear?—that's *me*—that's *mee*"] MS; hear?—that's *me*" D, L, B, G, R
219.5	shouted] MS; screamed D, L, B, G, R
219.13	of rouge, of pearl-powder] MS; of pearl-powder, of rouge D, L, B, G, R
219.14	hair, false] MS, D, L, B, G; hair, of false R
219.15	she easily contrived] MS, D, L; she contrived B, G, R
219.20	with no surviving] MS; without D, L, B, G, R
219.21–22	and resolved, in a freak of fancy, to make me her heir. For this purpose she paid] MS; and, for the purpose of making me her heir, paid D, L, B, G, R
219.23–24	a very lovely and accomplished friend—a distant relative of] MS; a distant and exceedingly lovely relative of D, L, B, G, R
219.24	husband] MS; husband's D, L, B, G, R
219.31–32	it was this scrutiny] MS; this scrutiny it was D, L, B, G, R
219.32	which emboldened me to behave] MS; which so emboldened me that I behaved D, L, B, G, R
219.37–38	concluded, as a matter of course, that it was the younger beauty whom I meant. He therefore told me] MS; concluded that I meant the younger beauty, as a matter of course, and so informed me D, L, B, G, R
219.39	sincerity] MS; truth, D, L, B, G, R
219.41	when] MS; and D, L, B, G, R

220.2	for] MS, D, L, B, G; or R
220.3	My good old relative thus discovered] MS; and my good old relative discovered D, L, B, G, R
220.5	been merely making a fool] MS, D, L, B, G; been merely a fool R
220.8–9	To avoid giving me an introduction, he purposely kept out of my way] MS; He purposely kept out of my way, to avoid giving me the introduction D, L, B, G, R
220.11	thus will be understood my conversation] MS; thus the conversation D, L, B, G, R
220.12	upon] MS; shortly after D, L, B, G, R
220.12–13	Hotel. Thus, also, is explained the allusion of one of them to] MS; hotel, will be easily explained, as also their allusion to D, L, B, G, R
220.15	the musical] MS; her musical D, L, B, G, R
220.17–18	Madame *Stéphanie* Lalande] MS; the younger lady D, L, B, G, R
220.22–23	my own prudential views, however, rendered] MS; but my own prudential views rendered D, L, B, G, R
220.24	impressions] MS, D, L; impression B, G, R
220.25	of course] MS; *lacking* D, L, B, G, R
220.29	an] MS, D, B, G, R; another L
220.35	doffed] B, G, R; donned MS, D, L
220.40	have to] MS; be forced to D, L, B, G, R
221.5	done with] MS; done forever with D, L, B, G, R
221.6	seen] MS; met D, L, B, G, R
221.6	*lacking*] MS, D, L, G, R; Edgar A. Poe. B

LINE-END HYPHENATION

List A: Copy-Text			
204.14	something	218.23	grande-daughter
204.31	eye-glass	219.10	grandmother
205.18	gentleman	219.40	great-grandmother
207.1	breakfast	220.19	great-grandmother
210.8	overshadowing	220.41	great-great
210.24	forever		
210.36	Will-o'	*List B: Present Edition*	
217.2–3	handkerchief	201.13–14	good-looking
217.7	something	202.15–16	close-fitting
		219.6–7	great-great

NOTES

1. For accounts of Poe's having sold it to Graham and withdrawn it for use in the contest, see John W. Robertson, *Bibliography of the Writings of Edgar A. Poe* (San Francisco: Russian Hill Private Press, 1934), 2 vols., 2 (*Commentary on the Bibliography*): 208; Arthur Hobson Quinn, *Edgar Allan Poe: A Critical Biography* (New York: D. Appleton-Century, 1941), p. 392; Charles F. Heartman and James R. Canny, comps., *A Bibliography of First Printings of the Writings of Edgar Allan Poe*, rev. ed. (Hattiesburg, Miss.: The Book Farm, 1943), p. 181.

2. Poe to J. R. Lowell, 28 May 1844, in *The Letters of Edgar Allan Poe*, ed. John Ward Ostrom, rev. ed. (New York: Gordian Press, 1966), 1:253.

3. Quinn, *Poe*, p. 392.

4. 4 May 1845, *The Letters*, 1:287.

5. Quoted by Robertson, 2:210. The puff must appear on page 3 or 4 of the two-sheet issue; I have seen only the first two pages, on which the text of the tale is printed.

6. Robertson writes (2:209), "In September [1843], other prizes amounting to $300 were offered by this paper [*Dollar Newspaper*]. If Poe entered the competition he did not gain an award."

7. Robertson, 2:209.

8. Printed in *Complete Works of Edgar Allan Poe*, ed. James A. Harrison, 17 vols. (New York: Thomas Y. Crowell, 1902), 17:124–25.

9. *The Dictionary of National Biography*, rpt. ed. (London: Oxford University Press, 1937–38), vol. 9.

10. *Graham's Magazine*, 25 (March 1844): 136.

11. *Graham's Magazine*, 25: 137.

12. *Graham's Magazine*, 25: 138.

13. *Graham's Magazine*, 25: 139–40.

14. *Graham's Magazine*, 25: 141.

15. *The Letters*, 1:245.

16. MS, MB, Department of Rare Books and Manuscripts. Printed by courtesy of the Trustees of the Boston Public Library. Superscribed characters have been lowered to the line.

17. MS, MB. The entire letter is printed in *Complete Works*, 17:167–69.

18. See Anderson Galleries (New York) catalogue, No. 1480, of *The Library of the Late H. Buxton Forman [Part One]*, p. 5.

19. Anderson Galleries catalogue No. 1480, p. 130. Major sources of information on Bemis, the great collector of books and manuscripts, are Charles E. Goodspeed, *Yankee Bookseller* (Boston: Houghton Mifflin, 1937), pp. 146–50, and *Proceedings of the American Antiquarian Society*, n.s. 45 (1935): 8–10.

20. See Joseph J. Moldenhauer, comp., *A Descriptive Catalog of Edgar Allan Poe Manuscripts* (Austin: The University of Texas, 1973; also as a bound-in supplement to *The Texas Quarterly*, Vol. 16, No. 3 [Autumn 1973]), for descriptions of the ninety-seven manuscripts, plus others at TxU not from the Koester Collection, and for a general account of Koester and his Poe archives, pp. xiii–xvii.

21. *The Letters*, 1:247.

22. *The Letters*, 1:253.

23. Although this reprint of "Raising the Wind" is reported in several bibliographies of Poe, the *Lloyd's* printing of "The Spectacles" is not listed in Robertson, Heartman and Canny, John Cook Wyllie, "A List of the Texts of Poe's Tales," *Humanistic Studies in Honor of John Calvin Metcalf*, University of Virginia Studies, Vol. 1 (Charlottesville, 1941), pp. 322–38, or "Bibliographical and Textual Notes" to *The Complete Poems and Stories of Edgar Allan Poe*, ed. Arthur Hobson Quinn and Edward H. O'Neill (New York: Alfred A. Knopf, 1946), Vol. 2. It was brought to my attention by Mrs. Thomas Ollive Mabbott in personal correspondence, 7 July 1974.

24. *Broadway Journal*, 1 (4 January 1845): 5.

25. MS, MB. The entire letter is printed in *Complete Works*, 17:208–10.

26. The enclosure by Elizabeth Barrett survives (in MB) and is printed in Quinn, *Poe*, pp. 451–52. See also her letter to Poe, April 1846 (printed in *Complete Works*, 17: 229–30), acknowledging his gift to her of a bound double copy of *Tales* and *The Raven and Other Poems*. The printed dedication of the *Raven* volume reads "To the noblest of her sex— . . . to Miss Elizabeth Barrett Barrett, of England, . . . with the most enthusiastic admiration and with the most sincere esteem." Poe's presentation copy is in the New York Public Library (Quinn, *Poe*, p. 485n).

27. Koester Collection, TxU; see Moldenhauer, *Descriptive Catalog*, p. 79, item 96.

28. Heartman and Canny, *Bibliography*, p. 160.

29. Koester Collection, TxU; see Moldenhauer, *Descriptive Catalog*, p. 80, item 97.

30. Koester Collection, TxU; see Moldenhauer, *Descriptive Catalog*, pp. 80–81. item 98.

31. Quinn, *Poe*, p. 488. Poe calls her "Miss Walters."

32. *Broadway Journal*, 2 (1 November 1845): 262.

33. *Broadway Journal*, 2 (22 November 1845): 310.

34. *Broadway Journal*, 2:311.

35. 9 August 1846, in *The Letters*, 2:328–29. For an account of Duyckinck's key role in the New York magazine wars and the "Young America" movement of the 1840s, including his connections with Mathews, Poe, and Melville, see Perry Miller, *The Raven and the Whale* (New York: Harcourt, Brace, 1956).

36. *The Letters*, 2:309.

37. See Poe to Duyckinck, 10 September 1845, in *The Letters*, 1:297. Claude Richard, in "Poe and 'Young America,'" *Studies in Bibliography*, 21 (1968): 25–58, argues persuasively that Duyckinck's acceptance of *Tales* and the *Raven* volume represents the *quid* for the *quo* of Poe's services, in the columns of the *Broadway Journal* and elsewhere, in behalf of the "Young America" group. These services included his tortured encomiums for Mathews' British friends, Horne and Elizabeth Barrett.

38. "It may be some years," Poe wrote to George W. Eveleth on 15 December 1846, "before I publish the rest of my Tales, essays &c. The publishers cheat—and I must wait till I can be my own publisher. The collection of tales issued by W. & P. were selected by a gentleman whose taste does not coincide with my own . . ." (*The Letters*, 2:332).

39. Quinn, *Poe*, p. 659. Quinn also prints (p. 754) the legal document that Griswold secured from Mrs. Clemm on 15 October, in which she identifies him as Poe's posthumous editor and grants him power of attorney to contract with publishers.

40. Quinn, *Poe*, p. 660.

41. Poe to Maria Clemm, 28–29 (?) August 1849, in *The Letters*, 2:458.

42. Quinn, *Poe*, p. 625; Heartman and Canny, *Bibliography*, pp. 182–83.

43. *Liberty*, 15 (24 September 1938): 12.

44. *Liberty*, 15: 14.

45. Heartman and Canny, *Bibliography*, p. 31.

46. Heartman and Canny, *Bibliography*, p. 29.

47. It is possible, of course, to ignore the problem of priority, and to regard the manuscript and *Dollar Newspaper* texts as two *versions* of the same tale, both authorial and each with its own independent merits.

POE'S "MURDERS IN THE RUE MORGUE": THE INGENIOUS WEB UNRAVELLED

Burton R. Pollin

THE FIRST of Poe's tales featured in *Graham's Magazine* upon his assuming the editorship for the issue of April 1841 was "The Murders in the Rue Morgue." This "model" for the genre of detective fiction[1] immediately captured the interest of the reading public and of critics cherished by Poe, such as Frederic W. Thomas and Park Benjamin, whose statements Poe proudly quoted in the biographical sketch of 1843.[2] Whatever his own initial estimate of the tale, he came to speak of it as one of his best works; he planned to begin his newly projected volume of tales with it, and likewise the projected "Phantasy-Pieces" of 1842. It was the first of the two published *Prose Romances*, a pamphlet of 1843,[3] and finally, it was reissued in his *Tales* of 1845. As the two-fold translation of "Murders" in Paris became, in 1846, the subject of charges of plagiarism in the law courts, Poe believed that the story gave him a passport to international fame; in his "Marginalia" article in *Graham's Magazine* of November 1846 on Eugene Sue's *The Mysteries of Paris*, Poe suggests Sue's borrowing a major plot element from his tale and erroneously claims that the Paris *Charivari* had copied his entire work. The latter notion enters into Poe's letter to Evert A. Duyckinck on 30 December 1846 (Ostrom, 2:336). Poe must have swelled with pride to read in William T. Porter's widely circulated New York weekly, *The Spirit of the Times*, of 16 January 1847, a translation of a humorous account of the plagiarism case taken from *L'Entr'acte*, a Parisian theatrical journal, with an editorial note that obviously relies upon Poe's misinformation in *Graham's Magazine*. This amusing article (see Plate Thirteen) has apparently never been noted by students of Poe.[4]

Before these developments, however, Poe, who was not always modest in his claims, was generally reserved about his aims and even achievements in the tale, early declaring its theme to be "the exercise of ingenuity in the detection of a murderer" and not hinting at any allegorical undercurrent involving split personalities or subliminal death

THE ORANG-OUTANG OF MR. OLD NICK.
Translated from "L' Entr'Acte," a Parisian Theatrical Journal,
FOR THE "SPIRIT OF THE TIMES."

The other day a large paper accused Mr. Old Nick of having purloined an Orang-Outang. This interesting animal was being exhibited in the feuilleton of "*la Quotidienne*," when Mr. Old Nick saw him, found him suited to his taste, and took possession of him. No doubt our brother Nick was in want of a valêt. Every body knows that, for a long time past, the English have cultivated Orang-Outangs, and instructed them in the art of bringing in notes on porcelain waiters, as well as of varnishing boots. According to the large paper in question, it appears that, after having pilfered his Orang-Outang from "*la Quotidienne*," Mr. Old Nick was willing to yield it up to "*la Commerce*," as property belonging to *that* journal. Now, this accusation surprised us; for we know Mr. Old Nick to be a talented and honorable fellow, altogether too well off to think of appropriating the Orang-Outang of other people. "After all," we said to ourselves, "there have been stranger monomanias than this. The great Bacon could never see a stick of sealing-wax without stealing it; and, in a conference at the Tuilleries with M. Metternich, the Emperor caught the Austrian diplamatist slipping wafers in his pocket. Mr. Old Nick, for his part, has merely a passion for Orang-Outangs." We were in daily expectation of seeing "*la Quotidienne*" vomit fire and flames and demand his man of the woods with loud cries. We must observe, however, that we had read the history of this animal in "*la Commerce*," and were delighted with its genius, style, energy, and analysis. "La Quotidienne" had also published it, but in three *feuilletons*. The Orang-Outang of "*la Commerce*" had only nine columns. Was this latter, then, *another* literary quadruped? In faith, no! it was the very same; only it is the property neither of "*la Quotidienne*" nor of "*la Commerce*." Mr. Old Nick had purloined it from an American novelist, whom the "*Revue des Deux-Mondes*" is just discovering. This novelist's name is Poë—we do not pretend to deny it. But here is a writer who avails himself of his legitimate privilege to *arrange** the work of an American novelist upon whom he has hit; and straightway he is accused of plagiarism—of robbing the feuilletons—and the friends of these latter are frightened into the belief that the writer is possessed by a monomania for stealing Orang-Outangs! By Courchamps! that appears to us *cool*. Mr. Old Nick has written a reply to the journal in question, by way of re-establishing his character for morality, so scandalously attacked in relation to this matter of the Orang-Outang. This Orang-Outang, of late days, has thrown the whole literary world into commotion. No body, for one instant, has thought anything of the accusation which they have endeavored to bring against Mr. Old Nick—and still less, because he had taken pains to point out, of his own accord, the cage from which he had taken his Orang-Outang. This affair will impart new strength to the party who believe in American romance-writers. The prepossession in favor of COOPER will acquire fresh impulse. Meantime, while awaiting the whole truth, we are constrained to admit that this Poë is a fellow of great acuteness and spirituality—although he *has* been arranged by Mr. Old Nick.

Note.—"*L' Entr'Acte*," it will be seen, prints Mr. Poe's name with a diœresis (Poë)—the true spelling. Mr. P. is descended from the French naturalist of that name. The tale referred to, about the Orang-Outang, is "*The Murders in the Rue Morgue.*" It appeared originally in "Graham's Magazine" for April, 1841; was copied immediately, or at all events noticed, and a digest given of it, in the "Charivari," and Suë, in his "*Mysteries of Paris*," has been largely indebted to it for the epistle of "Gringalêt et Coupe en Deux." Subsequently, the story was included in the volume of Poe's Tales, published by Wiley & Putnam. There is an elaborate review of this book in the "*Revue des Deux Mondes*," and from this latter source, probably, the French journals have, each and all, taken the story. Who Mr. "Old Nick" is, we cannot tell—but no doubt he is an Englishman.

---

* Can this mean ' *dramatize?*'—Ed.

PLATE THIRTEEN
The Spirit of the Times,
16 (16 January 1847): 1.
Courtesy Burton R. Pollin and NN

urges or racial stereotypes (Ostrom, 1:99, 201). Indeed, in his 9 August 1846 reply to the comments of the esteemed Southern aristocrat and man of letters, Philip P. Cooke, concerning Dupin's hair-splitting,[5] Poe spoke plainly about the small credit due the hero of the tale or its author:

> Thank you . . . not because you praise me (for others have praised me more lavishly) but because I feel that you comprehend and discriminate. You are right about the hair-splitting of my French friend:—that is all done for effect. These tales of ratiocination owe most of their popularity to being something in a new key. I do not mean to say that they are not ingenious—but people think them more ingenious than they are—on account of their method and *air* of method. In the "Murders in the Rue Morgue", for instance, where is the ingenuity of unravelling a web which you yourself (the author) have woven for the express purpose of unravelling? The reader is made to confound the ingenuity of the supposititious Dupin with that of the writer of the story.[6] (Ostrom, 2:328)

Poe is surely being rather disingenuous here, for the detective stories are certainly worthy of admiration and praise. He is unquestionably highly ingenious in imagining settings, characters, situations, and episodes which will lead to the denouement that he himself first decided upon before evolving the plot to lead up to it. This, at least, was the procedure that he elaborated in his "Philosophy of Composition"[7] and that he specified in a review of his *Tales* of 1845 that has been largely neglected. While attributed to Thomas Dunn English, it bears many of the earmarks of Poe in style and facts. We find: "The incidents in the 'Murders in the Rue Morgue' are purely imaginary. Like all the rest, it is written backward."[8] Now just what is meant by "purely imaginary"? I believe that it corresponds to Poe's mention of his "method and *air* of method"; obviously he refers to Dupin's close observation, sifting of clues, and elimination of the least likely of many possibilities until arriving at the one best befitting the circumstances, whether it be how to escape from a sealed room or how to hide on the premises an object requiring preservation (in "The Purloined Letter"). But the ingenuity of the author is something else again, for here his apparent method is less obvious, although not extremely devious or subtle. It consists of joining the familiar, the possible, and the realistic to the impossible, the unknown, the incredible, and the incomprehensible. The first elements are given effective focus through rhetorical and dramatic devices, flourishes, and stresses so that the second are accepted without question. Before our disbelief or skepticism can be aroused, as readers we are hurried into a new series of amalgams of the possible and the impossible, and then into another. Thus we move along from stepping stone to stepping stone, none of which is allowed to form a stumbling block (the word is Poe's, p. 179) until we can mount even the highest of them, the escape of the orang, from the room of the murder into the streets, then into the Bois de Boulogne, a wood where the animal and the reader's imagination are both free to wander. There have been occasional comments, often tucked away in overlooked footnotes, on the "unbelievable elements" in the tale, and many of these will be mentioned; but there has not previously been any attempt made to examine and present the totality of Poe's whimsical, exuberant, utterly delightful use of inventions, odd combinations, imaginative elaborations, and seductive bypaths of situations and scenes, which result in an amazed conviction rather than incredulity or disgust. It is this combining skill that presents a basically impossible Paris, puppet-like characters, and incredible story. To avoid the need for elaborate summaries and the artificiality of studying the tale as a series of arbitrarily anatomized units in a merely logical sequence, let us consider the characters and events more or less as they flash on the screen of our awareness as projected by Poe, the ingenious maestro.

The two major characters, C. Auguste Dupin and his friend, are placed together in a most unlikely fashion. The narrator (hereafter called "N.") resides in Paris during the spring and part of the summer of 18— (it must be after 1812 when the Napoleon gold piece was first issued). N. was permitted to rent and furnish a mansion for the two of them in the Faubourg St. Germain.[9] Clearly he is English or American in background, since he designates Dupin as "the Frenchman" and occasionally interrupts the narrative to explain "affaire" or "menageais" (sic). Yet he seeks in Paris some mysterious "objects" (p. 151) never explained, a pursuit which does not prevent him from entering completely into the strange life of Dupin—reversing the hours of day and night while reading, dreaming, talking, and roaming the streets. Moreover, he has had "former associates," although the continuity of his liaison with Dupin in the spring and summer scarcely affords time to form these prior "associations"; we must assume an earlier stay in Paris, perhaps in a "hôtel garni," rather than a newly furnished "grotesque mansion." Dupin's antecedents are equally ill assorted too, for although he is a "young gentleman" (p. 150), two paragraphs later we read: "It had been many years since Dupin had ceased to know or be known in Paris" (p. 151). Yet, when convenient, he "knows G———, the Prefect of Police" (for Gisquet, prefect 1831–36, as Baudelaire surmised), and has "no difficulty in obtaining... permission" to inspect the scene of carnage (p. 167). When lined up, such fictive facts contest each other. The first of many strained coincidences is N.'s initial meeting with Dupin in an "obscure library" (presumably Poe implies the French word *librairie* for bookshop here, p. 150), where "both" are "in search of the same very rare and remarkable volume." Poe methodically imputes unusual attributes to Dupin, such as the vast extent of his reading—a characteristic of the prototype of the man, André Dupin, or a "Bi-Part Soul," which is both "creative" and "resolvent"—basic to his analytic intelligence and "vivid" imagination. Above all, Dupin extols the "attentive" faculty—i.e., the power of observation in the analytic mind, exerted in games of so-called chance, such as whist (pp. 147-49);[10] yet he declares that his own habit of "observation has become . . . of late, a species of necessity" (p. 155), as though so basic a quality can be a late acquisition in the detective hero.

This habit and correlated power are the keys, of course, to his tracing the narrator's thought, with its alleged seven "links of the chain." The opening episode really serves to demonstrate his faculty of observation and also of memory, although presented as proof of his "analytic ability" or "intelligence" (p. 152). The dramatic confrontation is well handled, as though a first example of this type of friendly interplay, but we must disregard N.'s recent statement about Dupin's being "wont" to give him "direct and very startling proofs of his intimate knowledge of my own [thoughts]" (p. 152). The "stooge" of Dupin must be able to forget almost everything, and Dupin nothing. (There are hierarchies in ignorance, however, and N. is still superior to the reader who must be, in incidental fashion, instructed in French idioms and Paris landmarks as well as in methods of detection.) The episode itself is brilliant and faulty: the links run from the fruiterer, who stumbles and pushes N. onto a pile of stones, thus setting him to thinking about an experimental pavement "affectedly" called "stereotomy." In reality, this is a joke by Poe which was inserted only in the 1845 version. The printings of 1841 and 1843 carried an associative step which too readily assumed the reader's knowledge of the rare word "stereotomy" or the science of shaping and cutting blocks of wood or stone for building material. Concerning the alley paved "with the overlapping and riveted blocks" Dupin first heard N. murmur "the word 'stereotomic.'" Poe therefore preferred an ingenious and false but impressive application of the word to a pavement. No English or French work on architecture or technology supports this "usage."[11] The next step in the chain jocularly forces or directs the reader's willing mind into an error, although Poe's Southern pronunciation of vowels may have been the cause; say "stereotomy," Poe writes, and you *must* think of "atomies" (p. 155). Since Dupin and N. both mispronounce "o" as "a" why should not the reader?

For that matter, why not use the archaic term instead of the modern "atoms," which word Poe manifestly needs as a link to Epicurus. Poe is humorously following Romeo and Juliet's "team of little atomies" (I, iv, 57). He had poetically done this in "Fairy-Land": "Its atomies however, / Into a shower dissever...."[12] But certainly it was not his "wont" when discussing physics and astronomy. "Atoms" are sprinkled all over the pages of *Eureka*, for example (16:234, 246, 248, 266–69).

One of these passages shows us—a posteriori we might say—in 1848 how Poe had originally planned to link "stereotomy, Epicurus, Dr. Nichols, Orion, and Chantilly." The good doctor, a prominent Scottish lecturer and writer on science, occupied a long footnote for his 1837 *Views of the Architecture of the Heavens*, relating it to the Nebular Hypothesis of Laplace and to the implications of astronomic observations of the "great 'nebulae' in the constellation Orion" (Harrison, 16:262); Laplace's "original idea" was "a compound of the true Epicurean atoms with the false nebulae of his contemporaries" (16:266). Thus by "indirection" Dupin would find "direction out": surely we may suspect the substantiality of a chain with a missing link, even though the orang-outang would supply a more important one later.[13] Dupin now correctly expects N. to look at the great nebula in Orion, while Poe faces the problem of turning N.'s thoughts to the stage name of "Chantilly." It is solved by learnedly citing a Latin verse from Ovid's *Fasti* (5:494) and speaking of "certain pungencies" in the explanation of the old spelling of Urion. "Pungencies" is Poe's primly veiled reference to the earthy Boeotian myth about Orion's geniture from the urine of three gods (see *The Oxford Classical Dictionary* on "Orion"). As an explanation of the cobbler's complete change of name to Chantilly, it is almost another missing link. Reality is not overly intrusive in this fictive world where a stagestruck cobbler can manage to perform the major role of Xerxes in Crébillon's tragedy. Being dazzled by Poe's use of an authentic-sounding newspaper name, the *Musée*,[14] and of a real Théâtre des Variétés, we fail to consider the impossibility of the man's role-playing or of his jocularly assuming the name "Chantilly"—a town noted for lace-making: a name which would make him neither flesh nor fowl, but small fry, according to the needs of the story-line.

Now we come to the nonexistent evening edition of a real newspaper, *Gazette des Tribunaux*, which the Parisian Mme. Meunier, unaware of Poe's method, felt duty-bound to change in her 1847 French translation.[15] The account dwells upon the three A.M. screams, which roused the inhabitants of the "Quartier" St. Roch, wrongly capitalized as though an arrondissement around the Église St. Roch, which is "véritablement" near the other streets named. Rue Morgue, on the other hand, gives us a pure and perfect invention (originally it was the less meaningful Rue Trianon-Bas). The "double assassination," as Baudelaire's famous translation presents it to English eyes, makes "Morgue" at once the most appropriate and also the least likely name for the street.[16] Indeed, even in 1846 E. D. Forgues, the very perceptive critic of Poe's *Tales*, questioned Poe's use of the unfamiliar terrain of Paris and concluded that it increased "vraisemblance" for American readers and gave to his contrived "painting" in the detective fiction "the prestige of truth." But the French readers are "flabbergasted" by the mixed-up and invented places and the overturning of social conventions, especially concerning fraternization with the police chief. Yet Forgues admires Poe's inventive daring and accepts it as no detriment.[17] Baudelaire beautifully expressed French consternation and forgiveness: "Do I need to point out à propos of the Rue Morgue and Passage Lamartine, etc. that Edgar Poe never came to Paris?"[18] There are enough "true" place names from this very "Rue Morgue" district to make it seem that Poe had a map of the Palais Royal environs before him.[19] Why then did Poe indicate "a great distance" between the murder scene and Dupin's residence (p. 167), right across the Seine, in the Faubourg St. Germain—a distance that I have frequently walked in twenty minutes? To most of his readers this was irrelevant and to the others, amusing.

Other names show the same casualness, sense of caprice, and also unverifiable personal motivation. His memory of a London school, under the Misses Dubourg, in 1816–17 (*Poems*, p. 534), led him to apply Dubourg once to a laundress (p. 158) and once to a street with a livery stable (p. 186). True, it sounds French and, probably unknown to Poe, there was a private street called Cité Dubourg. A street alongside the church of St. Roch should be Rue St. Roch, but in reality in 1836 it was called Rue Neuve St. Roch to distinguish it from an older one of that name in another district (see Plate Fourteen).[20] Poe's general dislike of Lamartine may have led him to apply the name to a "little alley" (p. 155), rather prophetically since an old street was to be renamed Lamartine in 1848. Poe invented, apparently, the Rue Deloraine (p. 161), derived perhaps from the novel of that name by William Godwin, whose writings he knew well. The map will show his general accuracy in speaking about the Rue Morgue as one of the streets "which intervene between the Rue Richelieu and the Rue St. Roch," for these are parallel (p. 167).

The names of people follow a similar pattern of interspersing the real and the imaginary. Madame L'Espanaye and her daughter Camille could derive their surname from Marshal Timoléon d'Espinay or perhaps from the more celebrated female Louise Florence Épinay, writer and

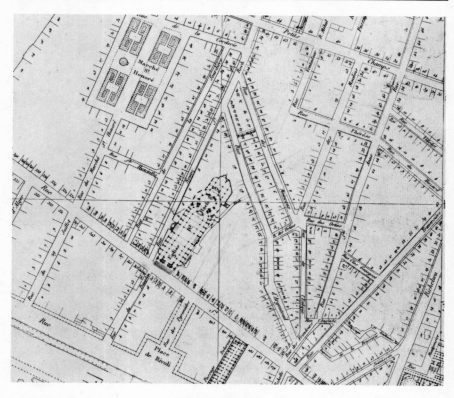

PLATE FOURTEEN

Map of the Palais Royal environs, from Théodore Jacoubet, *Atlas général de la ville, des faubourgs et des monuments de Paris* (Paris, 1836).

Courtesy Bibliothèque Nationale

intimate friend of Grimm and Rousseau. The faint aura of the déjà-vu or déjà-entendu lends enchantment and conviction to the names of various "street-people" and intermediaries involved in the plot. Strictly Gallic and even commonplace are Pierre Moreau and Jules Mignaud. What, however, should we make of ———— Odenheimer, *restaurateur*, who is "a native of Amsterdam" (p. 161)? The name is not Dutch, but German, and indeed the original was probably familiar to Poe as the Pennsylvania-born assistant rector of the Episcopalian Philadelphia Church of St. Peter's.[21] Is there not humor in the fact that Odenheimer, who must regularly deal with the public, knows no French but accurately reports four words spoken by the sailor in excitement (p. 161)? Similarly, Poe assigns the wildly unlikely name of Alfonzo Garcio to a Spaniard, "an undertaker" to boot, who "is nervous, and was apprehensive of the consequences of agitation" (p. 163). The "z" in the praenomen must, of course, be an "s" and the "o" at the end of Garcio an "a." Such facts, even though his Spanish was none of the best, Poe must have known.[22] The name of France's shrewd, energetic novelist is given to "Paul Dumas," the examining physician who makes simple-minded observations about the body: for example, the contusions of a four-story fall could have been produced by an object such as a chair (p. 164). The gendarme, Isidore Musèt, has a name which bears an unorthodox accent and which is not very far from the word *musette*, or bagpipe.[23] There is also point to Poe's naming as "Le Bon" (the Good-Man) the only suspect arrested and a man who had done the emphatically reclusive Dupin a favor—a fortuitously provided motivation for his present interest (p. 167). Consider the unlikelihood of having as separate witnesses men of five varied nationalities who just chanced to be living near or passing the house in a "by-lane" or "miserable" street at three A.M. Poe enjoys himself in other ways in this section; for example, in a fine pun: "A murder so mysterious . . . was never before committed in Paris—if indeed a murder has been committed at all. The police are entirely at fault—an unusual occurrence in affairs of this nature" (p. 165). Dupin likes the pun enough to use it again: "Putting completely at fault the boasted *acumen* of the government agents" (p. 169). Lest the reader be left mystified and to emphasize Dupin's insight, he explains later: "To use a sporting phrase, I had not been once 'at fault'" (p. 175).

I suggest that Poe knew, from the favorable reception of the tale, that a truly obvious unreality concerning the voices, as yet unnoted, had escaped everyone; they could not possibly have been heard by any of the rescuers. Consider the circumstances presented through the testimony and later through the sailor's summary (pp. 188–91). By dividing the witnesses' statements (pp. 159–65) from the final explanation, Poe blunts our discrimination and tears apart the gestalt that should determine our own critical thinking. The ape has entered the room in a most incredible way, as we shall see, followed by the sailor who is said to be dangling from a lightning rod outside the window of the fourth-floor room in which the women are "counting out their money" at three A.M. When the mayhem begins, he mutters or exclaims "Mon Dieu" and "Sacré diable," while far down within the room the ape is said to be chattering in fear, then in rage. The screams of the mother (the daughter faints at once) attract a crowd at the door who enter after Musèt breaks down the gate with a bayonet (a most unlikely feat considering the nature of Paris doors),[24] and dash up the stairs, which are placed in a well between the front and the rear rooms. The leader of the party, "upon reaching the first landing, heard two voices in loud and angry contention" (p. 160). Others report the same words, of the sailor, heard as they follow up the stairs until finally they reach the top floor. Discovering the door locked, they break it down and view the room in shambles, with the corpses appearing later. The wild unlikelihood here is (a) the lack of any possibility of the sailor's remonstrating with the ape in a frenzy of anger, especially from outside the window and (b) overhearing even on the first-floor landing the ejaculations of a sailor dangling from a rod outside one half-opened fourth-story window, through a locked door down a staircase filled with a probably noisy party of over a dozen men.[25] (More of that dangling sailor later!) This is indeed a pleasant caprice of the author's imagination—for the witnesses of the events and the readers of the tale to absorb.

There are other whimsical inventions of architecture and of technology inserted by Poe at this point. For example, a thorough search is made by the police. "Sweeps were sent up and down the chimneys"—by which, we are told, is "meant cylindrical sweeping-brushes" to be passed along the flues (pp. 162–63). Neither the *Oxford English Dictionary* nor studies of chimney-sweeping afford the slightest grounds for designating as a "sweep" anything but a man or boy who went up or down into the chimneys.[26] The explanation is a mere *plaisanterie* by Poe. Shall we thus deem the so-called "garrets (*mansardes*)" of this, the fourth story (p. 162), which have regular, large windows—two of them, in this back room, which are apparently set into the wall in regular fashion? Surely Poe knew that a mansard building had a decidedly sloping top-story wall, which required that the windows be "lucarnes" (dormer windows) set into bays. The placement of the bed inside and the swinging shutters outside made such windows impossible.[27] Again we find Poe creating an incredible setting with a straight face. While on the topic of architecture, let us take note of the second illustration drawn from the 1836 map of the district.

The police, you remember, were "at fault," since they had no idea how the body of the mother had been deposited in the court. (Poe saw fit to overlook the obvious fact that a body with the jugular vein cut would leave a trail of blood over the bed in front of the window and over the sill while being dragged and then being hurled below.[28]) No one with the slightest knowledge of Paris, especially of the Palais Royal with its lovely formal gardens, can forget the appearance of these central Paris streets—walls fronting onto the sidewalks, with entirely interior, firmly closed-off courtyards. Plate Fifteen is a map which evidences the fact that in this district the only court open to the street is in the Administration Générale des Postes (upper center, bisected by the second vertical); obviously, the horses and carts had to enter freely. This clearly shows that in 1836 one did not expose one's family

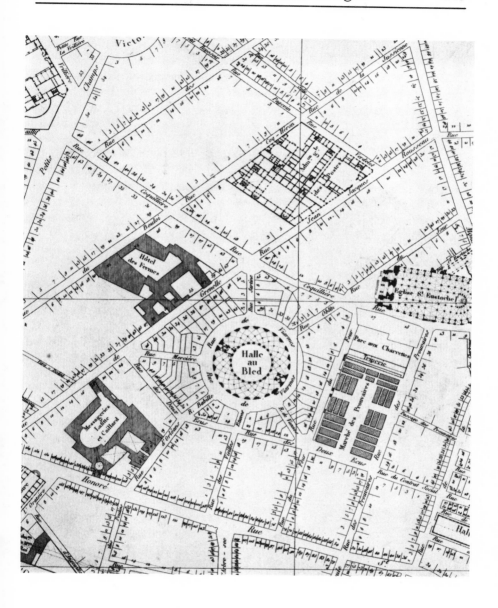

PLATE FIFTEEN

Map of the "Rue Morgue" district, from Jacoubet's *Atlas*.

Courtesy Bibliothèque Nationale

and fortune to the outside world with open courts between the rear windows and the street. It was necessary for the ape, the sailor, and then Dupin and N. to pass into the court in the rear of the building with its convenient lightning rod, where the body could be found and where, later, Dupin could find the sailor's ribbon, tied in a special way. But we must recognize that although "it was an ordinary Parisian house" in front, the rear was a house of Philadelphia. Look at the map (Plate Fifteen) to note that all the solid-line exteriors on the street designate the walls of dwellings, numbered, with their light and ventilation chiefly provided from interior courts. No house, at least in that area, consists of a front room or two and one large back room, opening onto a stone-paved rear court.

Having raised the issue of the lightning rod, let us consider this other feature of Philadelphia, very hard to find in a Paris four-story dwelling house of no great pretension.[29] Of course, Poe knew about this device; Franklin, having invented it in 1757, it had early been propagated there as a home product.[30] An effective rod had to be sturdily constructed of expensive materials, with a long chain buried in moist earth at a certain distance from the building. The early treatises that I have read on the subject speak of protecting church steeples, arsenals, and sometimes imposing mansions—never ordinary dwellings. There is good reason to believe that in France lightning rods were employed only on public buildings later in the nineteenth century, and that particular district (from personal observation) appears to me to be totally lacking in the device. Why did Poe resort to this mode of entrance into the rear window?[31] Caprice, I feel sure, since a rain pipe descending from the roof gutter would have done almost as well. Perhaps this was too common in stories of escape, and Poe, who valued originality, wished to exploit this native product; transplanted prematurely into Paris. Buy American, so to speak!

The great architectural crux in the tale, the only one ever noted, I may add, is the matter of the windows and their shutters. Poe had much to worry about in these two windows of the rear room, wherein the lady and her daughter were murdered by the orang just before his escape. He wished to throw the police off the trail—as well as the reader—and did it in three ways: (a) He suppressed all mention of the pathway of blood, as noted.[32] (b) He seriously asserted that both the stupid physicians and an equally stupid police force failed to observe that the "bruises upon the body," said to be "inflicted by some obtuse instrument," were inflicted by "the stone pavement in the yard" (p. 180). Surely Poe must have thought that an obtuse instrument was also the mind of the readers who failed to question this among other unrealities.

But he had built, and in a sense destroyed, better than he thought, and we are inclined to slip over this through distrust of "police intelligence." (c) Poe conceals the egress from the room through the tightly shut windows, until Dupin exposes the trickery.

Let us consider what is involved here: There must be a spring mechanism which automatically closes each of the windows. It must be simple enough to be worked by the two ladies from inside the room and also from behind the bedstead, placed up against the lower half of one window. (The ape *had* to land on the bed, with muffled tread, as on a trampoline, to avoid initially disturbing the busy women and also to provide time for the sailor to follow the ape up the lightning rod.) Since the spring locks the window when the sash meets the sill, it must be a fastening on or near the sill. Yet it remains "secret" from the scrutiny of the police who "have laid bare the floors, the ceilings, and the masonry of the walls, in every direction" (p. 172), while Dupin says, "Passing my hand down behind the board, I readily discovered and pressed the spring . . . identical in character with its neighbor." The neighbor had no concealing bed-headboard.[33] Having accepted this, we are also to accept the nails, one to a window, placed into a gimlet-hole driven into the frame far enough to anchor the window into the track unless released. All this, by the way, to keep down a window on the fourth floor of a "tenement" facing a stone court! There was not even a fire-escape to justify these precautions of Madame L'Espanaye! The police refuse to lift a finger to withdraw the nail from either the unobstructed window sash or its companion, and of course they fail to see the spring which, alone, holds down this window over the bed, *for* (and much depends on this causative link) in reality the nail here is broken, as Dupin by irrefutable logic deduces (p. 175). But Poe, either carelessly or deliberately, as is likely, continues to play with fictional reality: "The head, with about a quarter of an inch of the shank, came off in my fingers. The rest of the shank was in the gimlet-hole, where it had been broken off. . . . Pressing the spring, I gently raised the sash for a few inches; the head went up with it, remaining firm in its bed." This would be fine, were the window frame exactly a quarter of an inch in thickness. Obviously, a wooden frame holding the glass must be well over an inch in thickness, requiring "a very stout nail" (p. 173). Hence, there must be a second fracture in the nail, exactly at the point between the edge of the sash itself and the outer frame or track enclosing the sash. Surely Poe saw this, and surely he knew that his reader's attention would not linger over or visualize such mechanical details long enough for a mental protest.

For American readers he was on safe ground in making them ordinary sash windows that open and close up and down. French readers, probably from the beginning, hesitated to object to an American idiosyncrasy of proposing a *fenêtre à guillotine* for a Paris house of that date. They knew that any respectable French window swung inward, and closed firmly with a handle that thrust a rod into the sill. The reality of this genre has defeated the efforts of generations of uninstructed American and British tourists in French hotels, trying to shut out a sudden fall of rain. It would most certainly defeat the efforts of a departing ape, intent upon closing a window behind him, for Dupin supposes: "It must have closed the window as it passed through it" (p. 191). The inadvertent closure we, in kindly mood, imagine as the fillip of a final kick at the sash window, possibly ill hung, ready to fall in *Tristram Shandy* fashion or grazed, perhaps, by the bulk of an orang's departing body. There seems to be an increasing tendency to object to this window as a weakness in the tale, largely on cultural grounds. In actual fact, even before the French Revolution, under the name of *fenêtre-coulisse*, such a window was to be found in France, but not in the city of Paris.[34]

A delightfully whimsical invention by Poe is attached to this transplanted window, this being a transplanted shutter that Poe merrily calls the *ferrades*, to be frequently seen upon very old mansions at Lyons and Bordeaux. To be sure, as of 1842, a year after publication of the tale, according to Robert's great *Dictionnaire*, this word entered into the French tongue, *but* as a cattle-marking festival in Provence; it is to this unsuitable usage that one annotated text takes exception.[35] Perhaps Poe mistakenly alluded to the special term "ferrage" for the metal elements which work doors, according to Robert, but I doubt it. This was pure, insubstantial, paradoxical word formation (like the more than 900 instances that I have traced in *Poe, Creator of Words*); it was intended to "spoof" the serious and frolic with the knowing. Why should the *ferrades* be used in two such widely separated cities and not elsewhere; why should "Parisian carpenters" thus term them; and why should they be on the conventional mansard section of this "goodhouse—not very old" (p. 59)? As previously noted, a shutter three and one-half feet broad (p. 176) could not appear on a sloping "comble" or upper story in any event, unless there were some mechanism for retrieving it from within, once it lay flat on the outer wall (where the ape has to reach for it before his escape). But this, of course, is fantasy, since the wall of this structure had to be perpendicular, or straight, as the lightning rod helps to indicate. Needless to say, most French windows have two-leaved shutters, folding inward toward the middle to cover the standard windows—but not the *ferrades*! Poe gives other peculiarities to them: like a single door, they are of wood with lattice work on the upper half. This will enable the orang from the lightning rod to grasp one as his means of entrance, twisting his body from the wall, when he kicks off, and then, reversing the stance of his body, aiming his feet toward and into that upper portion of the lower opening of the window, which happens to be raised on the warm summer's night, while the women are gloating over their gold.[36] (Let us not wonder why they had to take it away from the safety of the bank for their flimsy coffer!) Since we do not know how high the headboard of the bed is, we cannot tell how much open-window space is left for the zooming body of the ape to clear through. If less than two feet, it would be a close scrape, but he is apparently an unerring orang, and manages it. We are to imagine also that the shutter is miraculously kicked back to its flat position against the wall (p. 189) so that the sailor, from his lightning-rod perch, can see fully into the room; otherwise the shutter would form a barrier. This *ferrade*, along with its companion on the next window, seems to be endowed with the affable vitality of an Aladdin's genius, for when the ape exits from the room, about ten minutes later, he finds this three-and-one-half-by-six-foot shutter ready for his swing back to the rod. (The surface of the window is vastly different from that of a wall, but the ape seems clever enough not to put his foot into it.) Moreover, in order to defeat the dull perception of the observing police later, these shutters "stood off at right angles from the wall" (p. 176), no doubt flapped there by a collusive wind, which would have to maintain them in this position for their separate inspections by *both* Dupin and the police. The elements cooperate under the magic wand of Poe.

Now we must return to the sailor, poised on the rod, one assumes on a stanchion fastening it to the wall. The maximum distance would be about a foot, and the sailor must maintain his feet and one hand at least on the rod while he seeks to peer into the room which lies five and one-half feet to his left. Poe grants the difficulty: "The most that he could accomplish was to reach over so as to obtain a glimpse of the interior of the room."[37] From his later account to Dupin he sees the full details of the animal's attack upon the women, sitting "with their back toward the window" well below the foot of the bed. That would be at least eight feet into the room. In practical geometric truth, the sailor's glance would be limited to a tiny portion of the wall on the left side of the room. Could Poe be serious in mentioning that the angry orang becomes fearful when its "wild glances fell... upon the head of the bed, over which the face of its master, rigid with horror, was just discernible" (p. 190)? The last two words, apparently, successfully reduce the reader's twinges of doubt about the viability of the whole scene. Our doubts presumably quieted, one paragraph later we accept the fact that "As the ape approached the casement with its mutilated burden, the sailor shrank aghast to the rod" and glided down it. We must also believe in the sailor's exclamations and the ape's "jabberings," plus the virtual destruction of the furniture, and the thrusting of the daughter's body up the chimney oddly inverted—all within the few moments between the first screams and the rescuers' arrival upstairs. (One wonders whether so intelligent a beast as the orang is said to be, now frenzied with fear, could or would have delayed his efforts by wedging a body feet first, presumably playing out the body as he thrust it upward.) Poe calls this an *"excessively outré"* manner of hiding the body (p. 179) and offers no hint of his reason for posing the difficulty for the ape.

The difficulty of position for the sailor has occasionally appealed to illustrators of the story. Of hundreds of pictures of this tale, in books and portfolios, that I have seen, only two or three have ever been able to include sash windows, rather than ordinary French windows, and usually they picture the sailor from the ape's viewpoint—this is, from within. The falsification of the text in Plate Sixteen is made inevitable through Poe's specifications about the shutter and the rod.[38] One wonders whether Felix O. C. Darley, the illustrator of "The Gold-Bug" published in June 1843,[39] was supposed to illustrate "Murders" as one of those eight mysteriously blank pages at the beginning of the *Prose Romances*, appearing at the same time.[40] Would the initial possibility of illustrations have affected such textual matters as those which we have been considering? But Poe's very modestly produced works rarely raised this question for him.[41]

Of all the visual aspects of the tale, the orang-outang was certainly the most pictorial element and one on which Poe lavished imaginative and often erroneous touches of nature lore and plot situation. We must remember that the sailor is beguiled into Dupin's apartment through an advertisement placed in *Le Monde*, which is, we are told, "a paper devoted to the shipping interest, and much sought by sailors."[42] This occurs in Paris, not in a port such as Le Havre. Poe's slight concession to the maritime background of the man is to have him speak French in accents "which, although somewhat Neufchatelish, were still sufficiently indicative of a Parisian origin," additionally ascribed (p. 186). This, I take it, means that he came from Neufchâtel near Dieppe in Seine-Maritime, famous for its *bondon* cheese and more likely to send sailors out to sea than the Swiss city of that name. I suppose his discordant Paris origin leads him to think of the famous zoological park of that city for the sale of the ferocious orang, which he has to transport

"He nearly fell from his hold through excess of horror."

PLATE SIXTEEN

Photogravure by A. D. McCormick, from *Arthur Gordon Pym, The Gold Bug, and The Murders of [sic] the Rue Morgue* (London: Downey, 1899), facing p. 214.
Collection of Burton R. Pollin

all the way from the port and lodge in his apartment while he heals its wounded foot. This wound, incidentally, is no impediment to the escapee's performances in the Rue Morgue, after he lopes there on all fours with a razor firmly clutched in one paw. These performances include such marvels as tearing out locks of the poor lady's hair, "perhaps half a million of hairs at a time." Neither the statistics nor the excessive difficulty of uprooting "even twenty or thirty hairs together" (p. 180) seems quite right to the reader who may be unaffected with numbing horror by the encompassing passage.[43]

No one, however, to my knowledge has objected to the identification by N., guided by Dupin, of the digital prints in the neck of the daughter as those of an orang, because of the manner or method by which the "facts" are presented: the facsimile drawing of the "dark bruises, and deep indentations of finger nails," and the wrapping of the drawing around a billet of wood to represent a human throat (pp. 181-82). The fact is that a man's two hands can easily close around a woman's throat, while the alleged gigantic size of an orang's hands would make the vivid indentations less, not more, noticeable, for he would truly squeeze the poor woman's throat rather than throttle it by individual finger action as described.[44] He is also given an utterly impossible task in severing with a razor the neck of the poor widow so that the head was due to fall off, even as cast onto the courtyard pavement. The overlapping bone or processes would make it difficult even for a skilled surgeon quickly to sever the vertebrae in an exposed spine.[45] For an agitated ape to perform such nice surgery is one of Poe's horrifying vagaries, a carry-over from his "Psyche Zenobia" days, with the ape wielding the scythe of time for the benefit of some hermeneutists.

The last-minute "finding" of two items concerning the ape and his master, hitherto concealed by Dupin from the reader, is not quite "cricket" and seems troublesome to modern detective story readers— although not to Poe's contemporaries. One item is the greasy ribbon for the hair, which betrays the rather irrelevant Maltese sailing-vessel past of the sailor. At least one critic doubts that there could be a peculiarly Maltese mariner's tie, and I have foregone devious research into such a knotty question. The other widely protested item is the tuft of nonhuman hair clutched in the hand of the victim, discovered not by the police but by Dupin (p. 181).[46] We shall see, in a moment, that the color of this hair is accurately reported by Dupin but *not* according to the authoritative text that he pretends to be reading from (p. 182). For that matter, we should also question the correlation between the beast's shrill and harsh sounds (pp. 160-63) and the tones of human speech. Poe is aware of the difficulty of assuming an animal's "jabberings" to be man-made, especially since he has misled us by speaking of the "intonation": hence, he prepares us by eking out a little more of the data than he had had the five witnesses reveal halfway through the tale; this sows a modicum of doubt to prepare us for the nonhuman origin: "That *very peculiar* . . . and *unequal* voice . . . in whose utterance no syllabification could be detected" (p. 177). This chances to be as adventitious as the greasy queue ribbon, waiting to be picked up by Dupin, since no witness had previously mentioned the "unequal" and "unsyllabified" sounds. What is the truth about the orang's speech? Truth here involves Dupin-Poe's fictional truth according to the narrative; second, Cuvier's record of the truth as it had been tenuously established by then, thanks to Pongo and a few other specimens;[47] and finally, less relevantly, our firmer knowledge of the orang's real capacities.

Dupin reads aloud an "account of the large fulvous Ourang-Outang of the East Indian Islands. The gigantic stature, the prodigious strength and activity, the wild ferocity, and the imitative propensities of these mammalia are . . . well known. . . . The description of the digits . . . is in exact accordance with this drawing. . . . This tuft of tawny hair too is identical . . ." (p. 182). No one, to my knowledge, has glanced into the *Règne animal* of the renowned Baron Georges Cuvier to verify this. Cuvier specifically denies the appositeness of the native name "orang," or reasonable being: "His Intelligence does not seem as high as has been claimed, being much less than that of the dog" (1:109). As for his nature: "He is a rather gentle beast, easily tamed and domesticated, who, by his structure, succeeds in imitating many of our actions." As for the fingers: "It is wrong to think that nails are missing on his rear thumbs" which are "comparatively very short" (1:108–109). Cuvier even disagrees about the hair: "His body is covered with coarse red hair," while other writers then and today ascribe tawny or reddish-brown hair to it. The voice is totally different. Cuvier wrote: "Camper has discovered and ably described two membranous sacs which communicate with the ventricles of the glottis . . . and produce a thickness and hoarseness in the voice." This vocal feature I have confirmed through conversations with those dealing directly with captive orangs; they agree that this is the quietest of the big apes, emitting occasional mumblings, low roars, or growls, with none of the detached sounds or intonation characteristics of human speech. Where then are the shrill, harsh tones of the excited, fearful orang in the garret? Obviously they exist in the fictive reality created by the ingenious Mr. Poe, who needed sounds differentiated from the gruff, Neufchatelish tones of the mariner.

What other discordant and impossible circumstances, spiced with enough of the real to be accepted if not logically acceptable, are left after the disclosure? For one thing, our sympathies are elicited for the overwrought owner of the animal; says N.: "I pitied him from the bottom of my heart" (p. 187), a stronger statement than any devoted to the two victims. Dupin exculpates him: "You were not even guilty of robbery, when you might have robbed with impunity" (that is, *if* he could have entered through the spring-locked window, while the room was filling up with over a dozen men from the street). Dupin reminds him of the need to free the innocent Le Bon by his "confession" and at this point he tells all that he knows. We see him "gladly abandoning, in his terror, all solicitude about the fate of the Ourang-Outang," but his presence in Dupin's room shows that to be merely temporary, and later the high price of an ape outweighs the chance of being executed for a double murder. Poe rewards him for his intrepidity, however, and also for his skill in retrieving a beast which roams the Paris streets and, presumably, the Bois de Boulogne undetected (if Dupin is at all prescient—p. 183).[48] Neither the sailor nor his murderous chattel is required by the abashed police, who free Le Bon merely upon Dupin's "narration of the circumstances," although they were quite capable of trapping the sailor selling the animal at the Jardin des Plantes. Whimsy, unreality, improbability are all prevalent to the very end, even though justice is not done to the criminally careless. The motto from Rousseau, applied to the "Prefect of the Police." may more fittingly be applied to Dupin as analyst and to Poe as teller of a very tall tale: "He has a way of denying what is, and explaining what is not." Whatever the origin of Dupin's name, Poe the humorist may have silently been adding to it the letter "g."

NOTES

1. The word "model" has been used by many commentators, such as Camille Mauclair, *Le Génie d'Edgar Poe* (Paris: Michel, 1925), p. 112, and Geneviève Bulli, ed., *Histoires grotesques et sérieuses* (Paris: Gallimard, 1967), p. 391, both symptomatic of a general agreement about Poe's tale among writers on detective fiction. My deep thanks are due to the American Council of Learned Societies for a travel grant making accessible to me in 1975 many of the places and materials in Paris used in this study.

2. This full-page, fine-print sketch in the 4 March 1843 Philadelphia *Saturday Museum*, purportedly written by Henry B. Hirst from material supplied by Poe but probably in part from Poe's pen, exists in a single copy in the library of the University of North Carolina at Chapel Hill, to which my thanks are due for a Xerox copy. For a few details see my study in the *New England Quarterly*, 42 (December 1969): 585–89, and Arthur Hobson Quinn, *Edgar Allan Poe* (New York: D. Appleton-Century, 1941), pp. 370–77, hereafter cited as "Quinn."

3. See his letter to Lowell of 1844, *The Letters of Edgar Allan Poe*, ed. John Ward Ostrom, 2 vols. (Cambridge: Harvard University Press, 1948), 1:258, hereafter cited as "Ostrom." For "Phantasy-Pieces" see Quinn, pp. 337–38.

4. In 16 (16 January 1847): 1. The original French article, without a translation, was provided by Rufus W. Griswold in his infamous "Memoir" which prefaced volume 3 of Poe's works (1850). The only copy of this theatrical paper appears to be in the Bibliothèque de l'Opéra, in Paris. For an account of the whole plagiarism case see William T. Bandy, *Edgar Allan Poe: Sa vie et ses ouvrages* (Toronto: University of Toronto Press, 1973), pp. xiii–xiv, Louis Seylaz, *Edgar Poe et les premiers symbolistes français* (Lausanne: La Concorde, 1923), pp. 39–45, and C. P. Cambiaire, *The Influence of Edgar Allan Poe in France* (New York: G. E. Stechert, 1927), pp. 14–34, using the material of Seylaz, and for summaries see Quinn, p. 517, A. E. Murch, *The Development of the Detective Novel* (New York: Philosophical Library, 1958), p. 79, and Sydney P. Moss, *Poe's Major Crisis* (Durham: Duke University Press, 1970), pp. 138–41, which also gives Willis' version of the Paris court case in the *Home Journal* of 30 January 1847—further proof of the contemporary American fame of Poe and of the tale. "Mr. Old Nick" in the translation and in the case was E. D. Forgues, the first appreciative critic of Poe in France (see note 17, below). Poe's "Marginalia" article may be read in *The Complete Works of Edgar Allan Poe*, ed. James A. Harrison, 17 vols. (New York: Thomas Y. Crowell, 1902), 16:104–109. Future references to this edition will be made under "Harrison."

5. For Cooke's letter, see Harrison, 17:262.

6. This was damaging enough, if taken at face value, for the unscrupulous Griswold to reprint as his own comment, without quotation marks, in the 1850 "Memoir"; Quinn notes this, p. 514.

7. For Poe's source of this idea in Godwin's works, see my *Discoveries in Poe* (Notre Dame: University of Notre Dame Press, 1970), pp. 122–25. After completing this study, I found some agreement with my views in James M. Cox, "Style as Pose," *Virginia Quarterly Review*, 44 (Winter 1968): 70–89.

8. This interesting review in the October 1845 *Aristidean*, pp. 316–19, may be consulted in the New York Public Library (Rare Books Division) in the copy generously donated by Professor Thomas O. Mabbott or in the Early American Periodicals microfilm series. As with the Hirst biography (see note 2, above), Poe supplied English with data, ideas, and sentences; Esther Hyneman, *Edgar Allan Poe: An Annotated Bibliography of Books and Articles in English 1827–1973* (Boston: G. K. Hall, 1974), pp. 13–14, ascribes it solely to English.

9. Harrison, 4:151. Hereafter references to the Harrison printing (basically of the 1845 text) will be made by page numbers alone in parentheses in the text. Besides the textual-variant notes in Harrison, I have consulted and will occasionally refer to the facsimile edition of "Murders" (Philadelphia: George Barrie, 1895), against which many readers must be warned for a few distortions apparently produced by a combination of factors: ink, lighting, and photographic methods then prevalent.

10. For the derivation of the name from an episode in the "Memoirs" of Vidocq, published in the December 1838 *Burton's Gentleman's Magazine*, see Quinn, pp. 310–11; for the prominent French politician discussed in a book recently reviewed by Poe see Pollin, *Discoveries*, p. 11, and Roger Asselineau, *Contes* (of Poe) (Paris: Aubier Flammarion, 1968), p. 373; and for the form

of the name, see *Collected Works of Edgar Allan Poe*, ed. T. O. Mabbott, 1 vol. to date (Cambridge: Harvard University Press, 1969–), vol. 1, *Poems* (1969), hereafter cited as *"Poems."* Michael Harrison, *The Exploits of the Chevalier Dupin* (Sauk City, Wis.: Mycroft and Moran, 1969), pp. 9–13, argues unconvincingly that the name of Poe's hero was derived from André's younger brother, the mathematician F. P. Charles Dupin. Poe's probable flippancy of attitude is shown in his absurd deprecation of chess; B. H. Wood, in a 1949 *Birmingham Post* article (reprinted in Fred Reinfeld, ed., *The Treasury of Chess Lore* [New York: David McKay, 1951], pp. 278–79), postulates Poe to be a beginner in chess, intent on "remembering the moves of the men," but he forgets the expertise shown in "Maelzel's Chess-Player" of April 1836 (Harrison, 14:6–37). Embarrassed for Poe's "gaffes" here, which I take to be deliberate, Paul Nougé in his posthumous *Notes sur les Échecs* (Bruxelles: Les Lèvres nues, 1969), pp. 19–67, analyzes Poe's errors and decides that he invented his own dialectic, remote from logic.

11. Aside from the definitions, with citations, in the major French and English dictionaries, see the article giving ten uses for stereotomy in *La Grande Encyclopédie* (Paris, n.d.), 30:482–83; and Émile Fourrey, *Notions de Stéréotomie* (Paris: École Spéciale de Travaux Publics, 1921). All of these and others surveyed proved negative. In 1845 Poe discussed street pavements without using the term (Harrison, 14:164–69); but see note 12, below.

12. *Poems*, p. 141. It is, however, wondrously odd to find, in "Letter V" of Poe's 15 June 1844 article in the series, "Doings of Gotham" in the Pottsville, Pennsylvania *Columbia Spy* a discussion of Brooklyn and New York with this sentence: "Of the stereatomic wooden pavement, we hear nothing, now, at all" (see the reprint, *Doings of Gotham*, ed. Jacob E. Spannuth and T. O. Mabbott [Pottsville: Jacob E. Spannuth, 1929], p. 61). Either Poe has learned to accept his own humorous spelling or a typesetter is at fault.

13. Denis Marion, *La Méthode intellectuelle d'Edgar Poe* (Paris: Éditions de Minuit, 1952), p. 116, is the only one that I have found who doubts Poe's application of stereotomy to pavement; he also questions the chain of thoughts, as does Yves Florenne in his edition of *Baudelaire: Oeuvres* (Paris: Le Club Français du livre, 1966), 2:1398, note for 162. Edward Stone, *A Certain Morbidness* (Carbondale: Southern Illinois University Press, 1969), pp. 140–52, analyzes the stereotomy chain for its associative technique and cites Galton's "discovery" of a separate idea per second in free association to protest the overlong fifteen minutes assigned by Poe to the chain, but fails to notice the absence of one of the links and other weaknesses.

14. L. E. Hatin, *Bibliographie historique et critique de la presse périodique française* (Paris: Firmin-Didot, 1866), p. 410, gives only *Le Musée pour rire*, 1839–40, three volumes of caricature designs, but no journal matching Poe's invention.

15. See Léon Lemonnier, ed., *Nouvelles Histoires Extraordinaires* (Paris: Garnier, 1961), p. xvii, for this "correction" in *La Démocratie pacifique* and also her omission of the un-French letter "C." in Dupin's name, of "le passage Lamartine" and its strange pavement, of "ferrades" (see below), and other items.

16. The comments on this name range from Harry Levin's (one of Poe's "Gallic touches . . . superficial") in *Refractions* (New York: Oxford University Press, 1966), p. 214, and Régis Messac's ("a purely imaginary name" perhaps suggested by Jules Janin, etc.) in *Le "Detective Novel" et l'influence de la pensée scientifique* (Paris: Bibliothèque de la *Revue comparée*, 1929), p. 349, to the

deeply emotional effect upon English-language readers ascribed by Ernest Boll, "The Manuscript of *The Murders in the Rue Morgue* and Poe's Revisions," *Modern Philology*, 40 (May 1945): 302–15, hereafter cited as "Boll."

17. E. D. Forgues, "Les Contes d'Edgar Poe," *Revue des deux mondes*, n.s. 5 (15 October 1846): 341–66, specifically, 353–54.

18. In *Le Pays* of 25, 26 February and 1–7 March 1855 Baudelaire published "Double assassinat dans la rue Morgue," with this note, repeated in his edition of the tales.

19. Plate Fourteen in the lower right shows these, beginning at the Théâtre Française, on a detail map taken from Théodore Jacoubet's *Atlas général de la ville, des faubourgs et des monuments de Paris* (Paris, 1836), in fifty-four large folio leaves, reproduced for me through the courtesy of the Bibliothèque Nationale, Département des Plans et des Cartes. Needless to say, Poe had no access to such aids as this.

20. This and similar facts about Paris can best be found in the *Dictionnaire Historique des Rues de Paris*, 2 vols. (Paris: Éds. de Minuit, 1963), by Jacques Hillairet (pseud. for Auguste André Coussillan). Notice the "Neuve" on Plate Fourteen, alongside the church.

21. See the article on William Henry Odenheimer, later bishop of New Jersey, in *Lamb's Biographical Dictionary of the United States*, which also ascribes to him two devotional books of 1841 about which Poe, as editor, might know. A later date is assigned to these in the *Dictionary of American Biography*.

22. It is also true that in the 1832 *Saturday Courier* Poe had published "The Bargain Lost," with a hero named Pedro Garcia who is "a metaphysician of Venice"; reprinted in J. G. Varner, *Edgar Allan Poe and the Philadelphia Saturday Courier* (Charlottesville: University of Virginia Press, 1933), p. 50. This may simply be another example of Poe's impish humor.

23. "Musèt" in the manuscript (p. 6) first bore a circumflex, like that in "Rogêt," which Harry Levin, *The Power of Blackness* (New York: Alfred A. Knopf, 1958), p. 142, terms "the purest of Poe's arabesques," but this became an equally unorthodox *grave* in 1843.

24. See Boll, 306, for Poe's last-minute changes of "door" to "gate" and "gateway," to make the Parisian architecture "more exact," he says. In reality, a gateway would admit people, via a passageway, into the central courtyard, whence stairs might lead up to the "stacks" of apartments, or into a foyer or lobby, especially for a mansion. Poe leaves vague the question of admittance onto a staircase between the front and rear rooms. Poe's changes, on p. 6, must have been early ones, for on p. 9 he uses an original "gateway"—presumably to accommodate "a glazed watch-box" for an unseen and inactive "concierge"—all part of the atmosphere.

25. Poe's figures indicate "eight or ten of the neighbors" plus "two *gendarmes*," but only Musèt is ever mentioned or cited, and Odenheimer, at least, is cited as a passer-by rather than a neighbor (pp. 156, 161).

26. See, for example, G. L. Phillips, *American Chimney Sweeps* (Trenton: The Past Times Press, 1957), which supports this usage save, perhaps, in citing "New York Cries in Rhyme" of 1825, which alludes to "Patent Sweeps" (p. 39). Contemporary encyclopedias often talk of "sweeping-machines" and "sweeping-brushes." Poe's "cylindrical" is a last-minute addition (p. 7), apparently to add the air of authenticity.

27. For the "mansarde" construction, requiring a small window, see Paul Robert,

Dictionnaire alphabétique and *La Grande Encyclopédie*, articles on "Mansarde" (22:1172) and "Lucarne" (11:725–27). See also Henry Havard, *Dictionnaire de L'Ameublement* . . . (Paris: Quantin, 1894), 3:631. Poe was able to designate the garret or top story as the "Mansarde" again in his tale of Von Kempelen (Harrison, 6:251).

28. Only Sylvester Ryan seems to have noticed the virtual absence of blood in the room (*College English*, 11 [April 1950]: 408), but he regards it as an oversight that Poe should have corrected in his revisions, disregarding its being basic to the whole structure of the tale.

29. See Noel, Carpentier, et al., eds., *Dictionnaire des Inventions* (Bruxelles: J. P. Méline, 1837), p. 400, article on "Paratonnerre" (lightning-rod), for views that since Philadelphia had adopted the device on houses, it was secure, but that only recently were they being used in France.

30. Poe humorously referred to "the originator of lightning-rods" in "Loss of Breath" (Harrison, 2:163).

31. For a clear, well-illustrated article on their construction see Ernest Bosc, *Dictionnaire Raisonné d'Architecture* (Paris: Firmin-Didot, 1876), 3:402–29, advocating their use on public buildings and others that are isolated, such as bell towers and windmills. See Oliver Lodge, *Lightning Conductors* (London: Whittaker, 1892), p. 2, for their late use in France.

32. Very well known is the engraving by Abot, after an original by the Spaniard Daniel Vierge (Urrabieta), which appeared in the sumptuous *Histoires Extraordinaires* (Paris: Quantin, 1884), 1:3, showing a cascade of blood spouting from the widow's throat. This illustration, often reproduced, has served as a gory model for many views of the scene (see a small reproduction in Harrison, 4:frontispiece).

33. Laura Riding, *Contemporaries and Snobs* (Garden City, N.Y.: Doubleday Doran, 1928), pp. 216–19, almost vituperatively takes Poe to task for his vagueness about the window and his mere "effect of great accuracy." She fails to see that Poe must have been aware of these matters too.

34. Asselineau, *Contes*, p. 372, observes that the windows are from America. For the old *fenêtre-coulisse* see Havard, *Dictionnaire*, 2:759, seeming to locate it in Poissy. Noting Poe's objections to Cooper's errors in details (11:215), Roger Forclaz, *Le Monde d'Edgar Poe* (Berne: Herbert Lang, 1975), p. 174, keenly remarks upon Poe's preferring to set his tales in Europe to avoid dissipating the illusion.

35. Asselineau, *Contes*, p. 372.

36. Boll, 310–11, noticing the manuscript changes in the seasons, remarks that the open windows, in summertime, enabled the beast to escape from the sailor and enter the Rue Morgue apartment. Somerset Maugham, *The Vagrant Mood* (London: Heinemann, 1952), p. 112, a bit facetiously, objects to Poe's supposing French women then as ready to court the night air.

37. The manuscript (p. 12) shows Poe's difficulty with this measurement, for it was first written as "six" and then "eight" feet and a half from the window. Likewise the edge of the shutter was first said to be "two" feet and a half away from the rod. Boll, 311, notes the change as putting "the performance within the abilities of an agile human being" without considering the impossibility of his seeing or being seen. In my collection of Japanese illustrated tales of Poe, I find a careful schematic drawing of the louvered and latticed shutter, in its two positions, fully marked, but devoid of its animal passenger, in *Shonen Shojyo Suiri Bungaku Zenshu*,

Collection of World Detective Literature (Tokyo: Kaiseisha, 1963), 18:101. My thanks are due to Ms. Takako Ashirai and the CUNY Research Foundation for aid in gathering this and other materials.

38. This photogravure by A. D. McCormick first appeared in *Arthur Gordon Pym, The Gold Bug, and The Murders of [sic] the Rue Morgue* (London: Downey, 1899). We note how the artist has reduced the distance, cut in two the upper shutter, and removed the looming headboard of the bed.

39. See Hervey Allen, *Israfel* (New York: Farrar and Rinehart, 1934), pp. 429 (opposite) and 453 for an account and reproduction of one of the pictures.

40. See *Prose Romances* (facsimile reprint) (New York: St. John's University Press, 1968), pp. i–vi, Introduction by George E. Hatvary, specifically, p. v.

41. Only the following works are illustrated—and very simply: "Maelzel's Chess-Player" (1836), "Journal of Julius Rodman" (1840), "Some Account of Stonehenge" (1840), "Island of the Fay" (1841), "The Elk" (1843), and *Eureka* (1848).

42. This description was added, in the margin, to the manuscript (p. 14). As Hatin shows (p. 395), only *Le Monde* of November 1836 to 1837 was published at that period, but it did include Lamennais as editor; hence, it may have been known by title to Poe.

43. Albert H. Tolman, *The Views about Hamlet* (Boston: Houghton, Mifflin, 1904), p. 402, and Yves Florenne, *Baudelaire: Oeuvres*, 2:1398, note for p. 184, both question Poe's figures here. Charles de Zemler, *Once Over Lightly: The Story of Hair* (New York: Charles de Zemler, 1939), p. 127, declares the scientific count to be about 80,000 hairs per scalp.

44. Mr. James Doherty, Curator of Mammals, New York Zoological Society, Bronx Park Zoo, assures me that the "hands" of the orang are at least twice those of a man's in spread. He has also graciously discussed for me with the keepers matters of their speech and temperament, given in my text.

45. See the diagrams in J. C. B. Grant, *An Atlas of Anatomy* (Baltimore: Williams and Wilkins, 1943), pp. 206–12; Poe probably derived the idea for the severing cut from Vidocq's *Mémoires*, according to I. V. K. Ousby, *Poe Studies*, 5 (December 1972): 52.

46. Both items are protested by B. E. Stevenson, "Supreme Moments in Detective Fiction," *Bookman*, 37 (March 1913): 49–54.

47. See Edward Griffith, et al., eds., *The Animal Kingdom* (of Cuvier), 16 vols. (London: Whittaker, 1827–35), 1:243–50, for a lengthy commentary on Cuvier's probably confusing the orang with a subspecies called the "pongo" from the name of one of the few specimens studied alive and dead in Europe. See 1:208 for a translation of the sentence concerning the "glottis" in my text (below). For my citations (below), I have used Cuvier, *Le Règne animal* (Paris: Fortin, Masson et Cie., 1835), vol. 1. For Poe's reference to this work in 1836, see Harrison, 8:210, and 3:197 and 10:26 for references to Cuvier.

48. In the margin of the manuscript (p. 14) Poe had inserted "Under the agitating circumstances . . . he could never have re-captured it" (p. 183). Left in all editions, this statement flatly contradicts the terminal fact: "It was subsequently caught by the owner himself" (p. 191).

A GUIDE TO PRIMARY SOURCE MATERIALS FOR THE STUDY OF HAWTHORNE'S OLD MANSE PERIOD

John J. McDonald

THE OLD MANSE PERIOD of Hawthorne's life has unique biographical and artistic significance. Biographically, it is important for two reasons: (1) it follows immediately on what Julian Hawthorne considered the single most important event in his father's life—marriage to Sophia Peabody; and (2) it is the first period of the author's life for which an impressive volume of primary materials exists, permitting a biographer extraordinarily detailed knowledge of what has too often been considered yet another anchorite episode for Hawthorne. Artistically, during this period Hawthorne makes a fascinating transition from the history tales and associationist sketches of his earlier life to the mature experimentation with fictional forms that leads to his composition of the major romances.

Only a handful of scholars seems to be aware of the huge primary resources available for the study of this and later periods in Hawthorne's life. Reasons for the situation are many. There is no collected edition of Hawthorne's letters. There is little awareness of the value of Sophia Hawthorne's voluminous correspondence, and hence small reliance on it for scholarly purposes. The manuscripts themselves are scattered from California to the Netherlands, making it a matter of much troublesome spadework to be reasonably sure that all extant documents of a given period have been consulted.

In particular, Sophia Hawthorne's papers yield a rarely tapped reservoir of information about Hawthorne as man and artist. They allow the specific dating of composition periods for several tales (see my article, "The Old Manse Period Canon," listed below in Part I). They contain detailed descriptions of her wedding, her husband at work, her husband's social personality (including a resounding denunciation of Emerson's knowledge of genuine married love), and the routine of daily life in the Concord parsonage. A long series of letters between Sophia and Maria Louisa Hawthorne sheds new light on the relationships between the Concord Hawthornes and their Salem forbears. Several specific questions concerning Hawthorne's finances, his relationships with publishers and with the Concord literati are all solved, wholly or partially, in this rich store of data.

It is with the hope of making all this material more accessible and of contributing to a more systematic study of Hawthorne that I have compiled this detailed guide to primary sources for the Old Manse Period. Only one kind of primary source has been entirely excluded: the bibliographic. I have attempted to list neither first publications of material written during these years, nor authorized and unauthorized reprints of earlier material. Further, I have not conducted a search for Hawthorne's literary manuscripts. Most of the known information on first publications and reprints is available in my article "The Old Manse Period Canon," and in the Centenary Edition of *Mosses from an Old Manse* (listed below in Part I). Only four of Hawthorne's literary manuscripts from the Old Manse Period seem now to be extant: "Earth's Holocaust" in the Lilly Collection at Indiana University, "The Old Manse" in the Duyckinck Collection of the New York Public Library, "Buds and Bird-Voices" in the collection of Mr. C. E. Frazer Clark, Jr., and "The Celestial Rail-road," owned by an anonymous collector (see the Centenary Edition of *Mosses from an Old Manse*).

PART I: PUBLISHED MATERIALS

Included in this list are printed sources which transcribe significant portions of manuscript material related to the Hawthornes during the Old Manse Period. A few such sources have been omitted: magazines and newspapers that print one or two letters which are more readily and reliably available elsewhere, and auction catalogues or pamphlets which are less easily obtained than photocopies of the original manuscripts. Also excluded are biographies and articles which are based on primary sources, but which do not quote them extensively. Memoirs by contemporaneous persons who mention the Hawthornes at the Manse are included.

1. Alcott, A. Bronson. *The Journals of Bronson Alcott*, ed. Odell Shepard. Boston: Little, Brown, 1938.

2. Bridge, Horatio. *Personal Recollections of Nathaniel Hawthorne*. New York: Harper & Brothers, 1893; reprint ed., New York: Haskell House Publishers, 1968.

3. Clark, C. E. Frazer, Jr., ed. *Hawthorne at Auction: 1894–1971*. Detroit: Gale Research Company, 1972.

Guide to Source Materials on the Old Manse Period 263

4. Crowley, Joseph Donald. "Nathaniel Hawthorne's *Twice-told Tales*: A Textual Study Based on an Analysis of the Tales in the Three Major Collections." Ph.D. diss., Ohio State University, 1964, 3 vols. Largely superseded by Crowley's and Fredson Bowers' work, published as the apparatus to the Centenary Edition of *Mosses from an Old Manse* (listed below), but see vol. 1, passim, and vol. 3, pp. 986–1166.

5. Curtis, George William. *Literary and Social Essays*. New York: Harper & Brothers, 1894. See especially pp. 33–49.

6. Dall, Caroline Healey. Joel Myerson, "Caroline Dall's Reminiscences of Margaret Fuller," *Harvard Library Bulletin*, 22 (October 1974): 414–28. Passing reference on p. 419.

7. Emerson, Ralph Waldo. F. B. Sanborn, "The Emerson-Thoreau Correspondence," *Atlantic Monthly*, 69 (May 1892): 577–96.

8. Emerson, Ralph Waldo. *The Journals and Miscellaneous Notebooks of Ralph Waldo Emerson*. Vol. 8, ed. William H. Gilman and J. E. Parsons, and vol. 9, ed. Ralph H. Orth and Alfred R. Ferguson. Cambridge: Harvard University Press, 1970, 1971.

9. Emerson, Ralph Waldo. *The Letters of Ralph Waldo Emerson*, ed. Ralph L. Rusk. Vol. 3. New York: Columbia University Press, 1939.

10. *First Editions of the Works of Nathaniel Hawthorne Together With Some Manuscripts, Letters, and Portraits Exhibited at the Grolier Club*. New York: The Grolier Club, 1904; reprint ed., Folcroft, Pa.: Folcroft Library Editions, 1972.

11. Gordan, John D. "Nathaniel Hawthorne, the Years of Fulfilment, 1804–1853," *Bulletin of the New York Public Library*, 59 (March, April, May, June 1955): 154–65, 198–217 (this section includes the Old Manse material), 259–69, 316–21.

12. Griswold, Rufus W. *Passages from the Correspondence and other Papers of Rufus W. Griswold*, [ed. W. M. Griswold]. Cambridge, Mass.: W. M. Griswold, 1898.

13. Harwell, Richard. *Hawthorne and Longfellow: A Guide to an Exhibit*. Brunswick, Maine: Bowdoin College, 1966.

14. Hawthorne, Julian. *Nathaniel Hawthorne and His Wife: A Biography*. 2 vols. Boston: James R. Osgood, 1884. Vol. 1 deals with the Old Manse years.

15. Hawthorne, Manning. "Maria Louisa Hawthorne," *Essex Institute Historical Collections*, 75 (April 1939): 103–34.

16. Hawthorne, Nathaniel. *The American Notebooks by Nathaniel Hawthorne*, ed. Randall Stewart. New Haven: Yale University Press, 1932. Although textually superseded by the Centenary Edition of *The American Notebooks*, Stewart's notes are still occasionally useful.

17. Hawthorne, Nathaniel. *The American Notebooks*. Vol. 8 of *The Centenary Edition of the Works of Nathaniel Hawthorne*. Columbus, Ohio: Ohio State University Press, 1972.

18. Hawthorne, Nathaniel. *The Complete Writings of Nathaniel Hawthorne: Large Paper Edition*. 22 vols. Boston: Houghton Mifflin, 1900. The text of this edition is the same as that of the "Autograph Edition." Vol. 17 prints some letters.

19. Hawthorne, Nathaniel. *Love Letters of Nathaniel Hawthorne, 1839–1841 and 1841–1863*, [ed. John R. Young]. 2 vols. Chicago: The Society of Dofobs, 1907; reprint ed., Washington, D.C.: NCR/Microcard Editions, 1972.

20. Hawthorne, Nathaniel. *Mosses from an Old Manse*. Vol. 10 of *The Centenary Edition of the Works of Nathaniel Hawthorne*. Columbus: Ohio State University Press, 1974. See especially pp. 499–536, the "Historical Commentary" by J. Donald Crowley.

21. Hawthorne, Nathaniel. *The Portable Hawthorne*, ed. Malcolm Cowley. New York: Viking Press, 1948; revised and expanded ed., 1971. Prints some letters.

22. Hawthorne, Nathaniel. Edward C. Sampson, "Three Unpublished Letters by Hawthorne to Epes Sargent," *American Literature*, 34 (March 1962): 102–105.

23. Hawthorne, Nathaniel. Randall Stewart, "Two Uncollected Reviews by Hawthorne," *New England Quarterly*, 9 (September 1936): 504–509.

24. Hawthorne, Sophia. John J. McDonald, "A Sophia Hawthorne Journal, 1843–1844," *The Nathaniel Hawthorne Journal 1974*, ed. C. E. Frazer Clark, Jr., pp. 1–30. Englewood, Colorado: Microcard Editions, 1975.

25. [Higginson, Thomas W., ed.] *The Hawthorne Centenary Celebration at the Wayside, Concord, Massachusetts, July 4–7, 1904*. Boston: Houghton, Mifflin, 1905.

26. Howe, Julia Ward. "Two Glimpses of Hawthorne," *Critic*, 1 (18 June 1881): 158.

27. Lathrop, George Parsons. "Biographical Sketch," *Tales, Sketches, and other Papers by Nathaniel Hawthorne*, pp. 441–569. Boston: Houghton, Mifflin, 1883; reprint ed., Freeport, N.Y.: Books for Libraries Press, 1972. This sketch is also printed in vol. 12 of the Riverside Edition of Hawthorne's works.

28. Lathrop, Rose Hawthorne. *Memories of Hawthorne*. Boston: Houghton, Mifflin, 1897.

29. Longfellow, Henry Wadsworth. *The Letters of Henry Wadsworth Longfellow*, ed. Andrew Hilen. Vols. 2 and 3. Cambridge: Harvard University Press, 1967, 1972.

30. Longfellow, Samuel. *Life of Henry Wadsworth Longfellow*. 2 vols. Boston: Ticknor, 1886.

Guide to Source Materials on the Old Manse Period   265

31. Lowell, James Russell. Quentin G. Johnson, "The Letters of James Russell Lowell to Robert Carter 1842–1876." M.A. thesis, University of Oregon, 1956.

32. Lowell, James Russell. George E. Woodberry, "Lowell's Letters to Poe," *Scribner's Magazine*, 16 (August 1894): 170–76.

33. McDonald, John J. "Hawthorne at the Old Manse." Ph.D. diss., Princeton University, 1971.

34. McDonald, John J. "'The Old Manse' and its Mosses: The Inception and Development of *Mosses from an Old Manse*," *Texas Studies in Literature and Language*, 16 (Spring 1974): 77–108.

35. McDonald, John J. "The Old Manse Period Canon," *The Nathaniel Hawthorne Journal 1972*, ed. C. E. Frazer Clark, Jr., pp. 13–39. Washington, D.C.: NCR/Microcard Editions, 1973.

36. Metzdorf, Robert F. "Hawthorne's Suit Against Dana and Ripley," *American Literature*, 12 (May 1940): 235–41.

37. Ossoli, Margaret Fuller. Joel Myerson, "Margaret Fuller's 1842 Journal: At Concord with the Emersons," *Harvard Library Bulletin*, 21 (July 1973): 320–40.

38. O'Sullivan, John L. Robert L. Volz, "John L. O'Sullivan to Henry A. Wise— An Unpublished Recollection of Hawthorne," *The Nathaniel Hawthorne Journal 1971*, ed. C. E. Frazer Clark, Jr., pp. 117–21. Washington, D.C.: NCR/Microcard Editions, 1971.

39. Poe, Edgar Allan. *The Letters of Edgar Allan Poe*, ed. John Ward Ostrom. 2 vols. Cambridge: Harvard University Press, 1948.

40. Roselle, Daniel. *Samuel Griswold Goodrich, Creator of Peter Parley*. Albany: State University of New York Press, 1968.

41. Sanborn, F. B. Joel Myerson, "An Ungathered Sanborn Lecture on Brook Farm," *American Transcendental Quarterly*, No. 26 (Spring 1975): Supplement 1–11.

42. Stewart, Randall. "Letters to Sophia," *Huntington Library Quarterly*, 7 (August 1944): 387–95.

43. Stewart, Randall. *Nathaniel Hawthorne: A Biography*. New Haven: Yale University Press, 1948.

44. Thoreau, Henry D. "The Emerson-Thoreau Correspondence." See above, item 7.

45. Thoreau, Henry D. *Familiar Letters of Henry David Thoreau*, ed. F. B. Sanborn. Boston: Houghton, Mifflin, 1894.

46. Tileston, Mary Wilder, ed. *Caleb and Mary Wilder Foote: Reminiscences and Letters*. Boston: Houghton Mifflin, 1918.

47. Weber, Alfred. "Hawthornes Briefe über 'The Old Manse,'" *Festschrift für*

Walter Hübner, ed. Dieter Riesner and Helmut Gneuss, pp. 234–38. Berlin: Erich Schmidt Verlag, 1964.

48. Wilson, James Harrison. *The Life of Charles A. Dana.* New York: Harper & Brothers, 1907.

PART II: CALENDAR OF CORRESPONDENCE

The following list includes all letters written by or to Nathaniel or Sophia Hawthorne, attempting to be exhaustive for the period beginning 9 July 1842 and ending 2 October 1845. Letters before or after these dates are mentioned only if they have direct reference to the Hawthornes' life in Concord or if they are related to the first publication of *Mosses from an Old Manse*. Letters known to have been written, but not now extant in manuscript or published form, are also listed. I have used a strict criterion for admissibility of such items. Only when a manuscript is unequivocally mentioned in another source have I included it in the calendar. This procedure should provide good protection against the listing of "ghost" manuscripts, although it also means that I may have excluded some items.

For more convenient reference, all material written primarily by or to Nathaniel Hawthorne has been indicated by numerals printed in boldface type. The notes given for each item contain: (1) MS location; (2) reference to at least one published source, if the item has been published; (3) a rationale for the date assigned, if a date is not provided in the author's holograph, or if the actual date differs from that given in the author's holograph; and (4) a brief indication of contents, including notation of any special features, such as postscripts and corrections written by Nathaniel in Sophia's letters. Published sources are usually cited by short titles—full bibliographical information on them appears in Part I of this article. Unless otherwise noted, all published versions should be considered incomplete, unreliable, or both. When an item has been published more than once, the Calendar mentions only the most reliable version or, if no clearly preferred version exists, the most easily accessible version.

Since several letters were written over a period of days, I have adopted the convention of listing them according to the date on which they were begun, indicating in the notes if they are continued at later dates. If the date of an item is uncertain, it is listed at the *end* of the month or year which can be assigned to it with some confidence. Thus, for example, Hawthorne's letter to [James Russell Lowell], 1843, will be found at the end of the entries for 1843, even though this letter was probably written sometime in midsummer of that year. If an uncertain date can be assigned to a day or month with good probability, I have listed the letter under that day or month. In such cases the date assigned is followed by a question mark.

Collateral correspondence—letters of persons such as Emerson, James Russell Lowell, and John L. O'Sullivan—is included in the Calendar whenever this correspondence has reference to the Hawthornes. This is the least complete part of the Calendar, since I have not systematically searched all manuscript repositories for these references. In the case of Nathaniel and Sophia's letters, on the other hand, I have made a thorough search of institutions and private collections. The results have been checked against the files of Professor Norman Holmes Pearson of Yale University, and against C. E. Frazer Clark, Jr., "Census of Nathaniel Hawthorne Letters 1813–1849," *The Nathaniel Hawthorne Journal 1971*, ed. C. E. Frazer Clark, Jr. (Washington, D.C.: NCR/Microcard Editions, 1971), pp. 257–82.

Manuscript locations are given in the format used by the National Union Catalog, with two exceptions. Because there are two important and separate collections at The New York Public Library, "NN-Berg" has been used to refer to the Henry W. and Albert A. Berg Collection, and "NN-Duyckinck" refers to the Duyckinck Collection, which is housed in the Manuscript Division. *"Berg Catalog"* refers to: *Dictionary Catalogue of the Henry W. and Albert A. Berg Collection of English and American Literature*, 5 vols. (Boston: G. K. Hall, 1969). "NH" is used for Nathaniel, and "SH" is used for Sophia Hawthorne.

1842

49. 7 May 1842, Emerson to Elizabeth Hoar, Concord.
    MS: see Emerson, *Letters*. Published: Emerson, *Letters* 3:49–50. Text reliable. Letter continues 8 May. Passing reference to NH and SH on 3:50.

50. 7 May 1842, Emerson to Charles King Newcomb, Concord.
    MS: see Emerson, *Letters*. Published: Emerson, *Letters*, 3:51–52. Text reliable. Letter continues 8 May. Passing reference to NH on 3:51.

51. 8 May 1842, Emerson to William Emerson, Concord.
    MS: see Emerson, *Letters*. Published: Emerson, *Letters* 3:52. Text reliable. Passing reference to NH.

52. 9 May 1842, Emerson to Margaret Fuller, Concord.
    MS: see Emerson, *Letters*. Published: Emerson, *Letters* 3:53–54. Text reliable. Passing reference to NH on 3:53.

53. 11 May 1842, SH to Margaret Fuller, [Boston?].
    MS: MH (fMS Am 1086, 16:29–30). Dated only Wednesday morning, 11 May, but the year is established by SH's discussion of her impending move

to Concord with NH. She says that the decision was finally made only "last evening," but she mentions a trip to Concord and visit with Emerson "last Saturday," a trip that was made in company with NH. Letter encloses a sonnet written by SH.

54. 27 May 1842, NH to SH, Boston.
MS: CSmH. Published: Hawthorne, *Love Letters*, 2:91–92. Emerson, seen yesterday at the Boston Athenæum, reported that the Hawthornes' garden in Concord was progressing well (2:92).

55. 19 June 1842, SH to Mary Caleb Foote, [Boston?].
MS: NN-Berg. Published: partially in Clark, *Hawthorne at Auction*, pp. 280–81. Mentions a trip to Concord planned for 21 or 22 June, to see how "Mary" (probably SH's sister) has arranged things sent there.

56. 20 June 1842, NH to SH, Salem.
MS: CSmH. Published: Hawthorne, *Love Letters*, 2:96–98. Hawthorne's books and furniture have already been sent to the Manse (2:98).

57. 23 June 1842, Margaret Fuller to Emerson, New Bedford.
MS: see Emerson, *Letters*. Published: Emerson, *Letters*, 3:72–73. Text reliable. Passing reference to NH on 3:72.

58. 26 June 1842, Emerson to William Emerson, Concord.
MS: see Emerson, *Letters*. Published: Emerson, *Letters* 3:67–68. Text reliable. Passing reference to NH on 3:68.

59. 30 June 1842, NH to SH, Boston.
MS: CSmH. Published: Hawthorne, *Love Letters*, 2:103–104. NH reassures SH about their imminent marriage. Some detail concerning the move to Concord (2:104).

59.5. 5 July 1842, SH to Mary Caleb Foote.
MS: unrecovered. Published: Lathrop, *Memories*, p. 49. SH assures Mary that the marriage to NH will not change her affection for long-time friends.

60. 8 July 1842, NH to "Miss Quincy," Boston.
MS: MHi. NH returns some letters to Miss Quincy, who is in Cambridge, and issues her a general invitation to visit the Hawthornes in Concord.

61. 10 July 1842, NH to Maria Louisa Hawthorne, Concord.
MS: MSaE. Published: Hawthorne, "Maria Louisa," 130–31. Text reliable. Hawthorne's famous letter to his sister describing the wedded couple's happiness on arrival at the Old Manse.

62. 10 July 1842, SH to Mrs. Peabody, Concord.
MS: NN-Berg. Published: partially in Gordan, "Nathaniel Hawthorne," 206–207. Letter was posted 11 July and was received in Boston on the morning of 12 July. Copious description of the Hawthornes' arrival in Concord after the 9 July wedding.

63. 11 July 1842, Mary Peabody to SH, Boston.
MS: NN-Berg. Published: partially in Gordan, "Nathaniel Hawthorne," 206. The letter is not dated in holograph except as Monday evening and Tuesday

Guide to Source Materials on the Old Manse Period 269

morning. Describes the SH-NH wedding from Mary's point of view and acknowledges the receipt of SH to Mrs. Peabody, 10 July 1842.

64. 12? July 1842, Mary Channing to SH.
MS: unrecovered. Mentioned as received on 13 July 1842 in SH to Mrs. Peabody, 15 July 1842.

65. 12? July 1842, Mrs. Peabody to SH, Boston.
MS: unrecovered. Published: Hawthorne, *Hawthorne & His Wife*, 1:250–51. Listed as 15 July 1842 in Julian Hawthorne, *Notebook* (see this article, Part III). The section of Julian's *Notebook* in which the letter is listed is entitled "Extracts from Letters." Julian's publication of the letter is confusing—almost certainly the material on 1:250–51 is drawn from several different letters, so that only part of the material on 1:250 would correspond with the letter here in question. I have assigned the date 12 July because SH refers to receiving a letter from her mother on 13 July (in SH to Mrs. Peabody, 15 July 1842).

66. 15 July 1842, SH to Mrs. Peabody, Concord.
MS: NN-Berg. Published: partially in Gordan, "Nathaniel Hawthorne," 207. Social details for 11–14 July—visitors to the Manse have included the Emersons, Elizabeth Hoar, and George Hillard from Boston.

67. 17 July 1842, Mary Peabody to SH, Boston.
MS: NN-Berg.

68. 28 July 1842, Mary Peabody to SH, Boston.
MS: NN-Berg. Long letter concerning NH's possible editorship of the *Boston Miscellany*.

69. 28 July 1842, Caroline Sturgis to SH.
MS: unlocated. Typescript: Professor Norman Holmes Pearson. Accompanies a wedding gift. Briefly quoted: Clark, *Hawthorne at Auction*, p. 125. Content repeats some details from SH to Caroline Sturgis, July 1842.

70. July 1842, SH to Caroline Sturgis, Concord.
MS: unrecovered. Mentioned in Caroline Sturgis to SH, 28 July 1842. Apparently written after SH's wedding, since it seems to describe the Hawthorne's first days in Concord. Hence the probable date is between 10 and 26 July 1842.

71. 2 August 1842, NH to George Hillard, Concord.
MS: NCaS. Invites Hillard and his wife to Concord for a visit "next Saturday."

72. 5 August 1842, SH to Mrs. Peabody, Concord.
MS: NN-Berg. Date is the Berg Collection's, assigned on good evidence from the text. A long, detailed letter about the kind of life lived at the Manse and in Concord.

73. 8? August 1842, Mrs. Peabody to SH.
MS: unrecovered. Mentioned as received on 9 August in SH to Mrs. Peabody, 11 August 1842.

74. 9? August 1842, George Hillard to NH.
MS: unrecovered. Mentioned as received in SH to Mrs. Peabody, 11 August

1842. Answers NH to George Hillard, 2 August 1842. Probably informs NH that the Hillards will arrive in Concord for a visit on Saturday, 13 August.

75. 11 August 1842, SH to Mrs. Peabody, Concord.
MS: NN-Berg. Published: partly in Gordan, "Nathaniel Hawthorne," 207. Details of Concord life and the *Boston Miscellany* editorship.

76. 13 August 1842, Mrs. Peabody to SH.
See Mrs. Peabody to SH, 13 August 1843.

77. 15 August 1842, NH to Maria Louisa Hawthorne, Concord.
MS: MSaE. Published: Hawthorne, "Maria Louisa," 131–32. Text reliable. NH advises Louisa about travel arrangements for her imminent visit to Concord.

78. 20 August 1842, NH to Robert Carter, Concord.
MS: NN-Berg. Published: partially in Gordan, "Nathaniel Hawthorne," 207. Details concerning NH's possible relationship with the *Boston Miscellany* and present relationship with John L. O'Sullivan of the *Democratic Review*.

79. 20 August 1842, NH to ?, Concord.
MS: unrecovered. Mentioned in SH to Mrs. Peabody, 22 August 1842.

80. 20 August 1842, SH to Dr. Walter Channing, Concord.
MS: unrecovered. Mentioned in SH to Mrs. Peabody, 22 August 1842.

81. 22 August 1842, SH to Mrs. Peabody, Concord.
MS: NN-Berg. Published: partially in Gordan, "Nathaniel Hawthorne," 207. The MS appears to be incomplete, lacking an ending. Mentions SH's nervousness and consequent inability to write any letters during the week of 15 August. Details visits by the Hillards, Margaret Fuller, and others. Maria Louisa Hawthorne arrived last Saturday (20 August).

82. 25 August 1842, NH to Margaret Fuller, Concord.
MS: CSmH (HM 11036). Published: Hawthorne, *Hawthorne & His Wife*, 1:252–56. The date is variously accepted as 28 or 25—there is often confusion between these two numerals in NH's holograph. In this case, the earlier date is correct, since Margaret had received the letter by 27 August (see Ossoli, "Margaret Fuller's 1842 Journal," 328). NH's famous rejection of Margaret's request that Ellery Channing and his new wife (Margaret's sister) be permitted to share the Manse with the Hawthornes.

83. 28? August 1842, Mrs. Peabody to SH.
MS: unrecovered. Mentioned as received on 29 August in SH to Mrs. Peabody, 30 August 1842.

84. 30 August 1842, SH to Mrs. Peabody, Concord.
MS: NN-Berg. Published: partially in Gordan, "Nathaniel Hawthorne," 207. The letter continues on 1, 2, 3, and 4 September. An eleven-page extravaganza, full of domestic and social details, including the continuing visit of Maria Louisa Hawthorne, dinner with Thoreau, and Mrs. Emerson's chronic illness.

85. August? 1842, Robert Carter to NH.
MS: unrecovered. Mentioned in NH to Robert Carter, 20 August 1842. Probably asks NH to contribute to the *Boston Miscellany*.

Guide to Source Materials on the Old Manse Period 271

86. August? 1842, SH to Margaret Fuller, Concord.
    MS: unrecovered. On 27 August, Fuller notes this letter as received "several days since." See Ossoli, "Margaret Fuller's 1842 Journal," 328. Concerns the question of Ellery Channing's sharing the Manse with the Hawthornes.

87. 1 September 1842, NH to Robert Cassie Waterston, Concord.
    MS: MHi. Gives permission to reprint "Samuel Johnson" for the Sunday School Society, but requests that Waterston clear the publication with Tappan & Dennet, who retain copyright privileges.

88. 8 September 1842, Mrs. Peabody to SH.
    MS: unrecovered. Listed in Julian Hawthorne, *Notebook* (see this article, Part III). The section of Julian's work in which the reference occurs is entitled "Extracts from Letters."

89. 17? September 1842, Maria Louisa Hawthorne to SH.
    MS: unrecovered. Mentioned as recently received in SH to Maria Louisa Hawthorne, 20 September 1842. Absolute date *a quo* is 6 September, on which day Louisa left Concord after an extended visit.

90. 20 September 1842, SH to Maria Louisa Hawthorne, Concord.
    MS: NN-Berg. Describes the Hawthornes' activities since Louisa left Concord on 6 September. Particular concentration on outings in their boat, "Pond Lily."

91. 26? September 1842, Mrs. Peabody to SH.
    MS: unrecovered. Mentioned as received on 27 September in SH to Mrs. Peabody, 29 September 1842.

92. 29 September 1842, SH to Mrs. Peabody, Concord.
    MS: NN-Berg. Mrs. Peabody has recently returned from Concord to Boston, and Mary (SH's sister) is in Concord now. Much detail, including mention of Hawthorne's two-day walking tour with Emerson to the Shaker settlement at Harvard, Massachusetts.

93. 2 October 1842, SH to Mrs. Peabody, Concord.
    MS: NN-Berg. MS is incomplete, ending in mid-sentence. Hawthorne's Salem friend, David Roberts, is visiting. SH details some trenchant comments by NH on Roberts. As usual, a good deal of domestic and social detail.

94. 3 October 1842, NH to James Munroe & Co., Concord.
    MS: MB. Requests an accounting for sales of *Twice-told Tales*.

95. 3 October 1842, SH to Mrs. Peabody, Concord.
    MS: NN-Berg. The letter appears to have been carried to Boston by Hawthorne's friend, David Roberts. Descriptions of Hawthorne fishing and entertaining Thoreau and Roberts. Sophia out to see an Indian encampment on the banks of the Concord River.

96. 4 October 1842, Mrs. Peabody to SH.
    MS: unrecovered. Listed in Julian Hawthorne, *Notebook* (see this article, Part III), section entitled "Extracts from Letters." Referred to in SH to Mrs. Peabody, 9 October 1842.

97. 5? October 1842, Mary Peabody to SH.
MS: NN-Berg. Date is the Berg Collection's, on grounds that the letter mentions the funeral of William Ellery Channing (the elder), who died 2 October 1842. The Lowells (James Russell and Maria) are planning to visit the Hawthornes in two weeks. Mention of a request for NH to do a memoir of "Laura," Samuel Gridley Howe's famous patient.

98. 9 October 1842, SH to Mrs. Peabody, Concord.
MS: NN-Berg. Published: partially in Hawthorne, *Hawthorne & His Wife*, 1:270–71. Postscript added on 10 October. SH and NH are planning to visit Boston and Salem toward the end of the month. SH makes a lengthy justification of NH's hospitable nature—she takes exception to her family's characterization of him as not very sociable.

99. 10? October 1842, Maria Louisa Hawthorne to NH.
MS: unrecovered. Mentioned as just received in NH to Louisa, 12 October 1842. Announces the death of NH's uncle, Robert Manning.

100. 12 October 1842, NH to Maria Louisa Hawthorne, Concord.
MS: MSaE. Expresses concern for the children of his uncle Robert Manning. NH cannot attend the funeral because of a writing commitment and a house guest, Frank Farley.

101. 17 October 1842, NH to Charles A. Dana, Concord.
MS: unrecovered. Published: Wilson, *The Life of Charles A. Dana*, pp. 45–46.

102. 21 October 1842, NH to Epes Sargent, Concord.
MS: NCaS. Published: Hawthorne, "Three Letters," 102–103. Text reliable. Accompanies "The Old Apple Dealer." Recommends Thoreau as a possible contributor to *Sargent's New Monthly Magazine*.

103. 9 November 1842, SH to Mrs. Peabody, Concord.
MS: NN-Berg. The Hawthornes have a new maid ("Mary," replacing "Sarah") and new airtight stoves. Visits from Thoreau and others.

104. 16 November 1842, Emerson to Margaret Fuller, Concord.
MS: see Emerson, *Letters*. Published: Emerson, *Letters*, 3:95–97. Text reliable. Passing reference to the Hawthornes on 3:97.

105. 21 November 1842, Emerson to Frederic Henry Hedge, Concord.
MS: see Emerson, *Letters*. Published: Emerson, *Letters*, 3:97–99. Letter continues on 25 November. Text reliable. Passing references to social encounters with the Hawthornes on 3:98–99.

106. 25 November 1842, Emerson to William Emerson, Concord.
MS: see Emerson, *Letters*. Published: Emerson, *Letters*, 3:100. Text reliable. Passing reference to the Hawthornes.

107. 25 November 1842, NH to Maria Louisa Hawthorne, Concord.
MS: MSaE. Lengthy, detailed letter. NH has been promised a political appointment within about six months, although it will not be the Salem Post Office. NH attended Emerson's opening Lyceum lecture (18 November). Trip to Salem is planned for late December.

Guide to Source Materials on the Old Manse Period 273

108. 26 November 1842, NH to Henry Wadsworth Longfellow, Concord.
MS: MH (bMS Am 1340.2 [2616], Folder I, Letter 11). Published: Longfellow, *Life of Longfellow*, 1:422. Asks Longfellow to lecture at the Concord Lyceum for $10.

109. November? 1842, Mary Peabody to SH.
MS: NN-Berg. Berg Collection's date is September? 1842 (see *Berg Catalog*, 3:165), but the letter mentions Charles Lane, who arrived in Boston with Bronson Alcott in mid-October 1842. The Hawthornes were in Boston and Salem during 22–31 October, so the letter was probably written in mid-November. Suggests that NH write a story based on "Schmid's Life," a story that would serve to preface some lessons in drawing which Mary is preparing.

110. 17 December 1842, NH to James Russell Lowell, Concord.
MS: NCaS. Partially published: Hawthorne, "Three Letters," 104, note 6. Short letter to accompany "The Hall of Fantasy" for *Pioneer*, Lowell's new magazine.

111. 18 December 1842, SH to Mary Caleb Foote, Concord.
MS: unrecovered. Published: Lathrop, *Memories*, pp. 50–55. The letter runs to 30 December. Recounts many details of the first six months of life at the Manse.

112. 24 December 1842, NH to Henry Wadsworth Longfellow, Concord.
MS: MH (bMS Am 1340.2 [2616], Folder I, Letter 12). Published: Longfellow, *Life of Longfellow*, 1:430–31. Regrets that he cannot now come to Cambridge to dinner, but extends cordial invitation for Longfellow to come to Concord. Comments on Longfellow's *Poems on Slavery*.

113. 27? December 1842, Mrs. Peabody to SH.
MS: unrecovered. Mentioned in SH to Mrs. Peabody, 29 December 1842. See also Emerson to SH, 29 December 1842.

114. 29 December 1842, Emerson to SH, Concord.
MS: CSmH. Published: Emerson, *Letters*, 3:225. Text reliable. Rusk's date is ca. 25? November? 1843?, but this note is unmistakably identified in SH to Mrs. Peabody, 29 December 1842, as having been received on the evening of 29 December 1842. Accompanies a bundle for the Hawthornes left at the Emerson house by Orestes Brownson, who came out from Boston to lecture in Concord on 28 December 1842.

115. 29 December 1842, SH to Mrs. Peabody, Concord.
MS: NN-Berg. Letter continues on 30 December, but the MS appears to be incomplete. Mrs. Emerson last night delivered the packet sent via Brownson. It contained money, allowing the Hawthornes to pay some debts. NH has been much attracted by skating on the Concord River.

116. December? 1842, Henry Wadsworth Longfellow to NH.
MS: unrecovered. Mentioned as having been received some time ago in NH to Longfellow, 24 December 1842. It must, however, postdate NH's letter to Longfellow dated 26 November 1842. The 26 November letter makes it clear that the two men have not corresponded since the Hawthornes' marriage.

117. 1842, Ellen S. Hooper to SH.
MS: unrecovered. Published: Lathrop, *Memories*, p. 50. A letter of congratulation on the occasion of SH's wedding, its most probable date is July 1842.

118. 1842, Mary Peabody to SH. November or December?
MS: NN-Berg. Date is the Berg Collection's (see *Berg Catalog*, 3:166).

119. 1842, Elizabeth P. Peabody? to SH?, August?
MS: unrecovered. Mentioned in NH to Robert Carter, 20 August 1842. NH may be mistaken, however, since his summary of the contents of this letter fits Mary Peabody to SH, 28 July 1842.

1843

120. 4 January 1843, SH to Maria Louisa Hawthorne, Concord.
MS: NN-Berg. Published: partially in Clark, *Hawthorne at Auction*, p. 237. NH skates at sunrise, sometimes with Emerson and Thoreau, and then works until two o'clock. Evenings are spent in reading aloud. Laconic postscript by NH.

121. 11? January 1843, Mrs. Peabody to SH.
MS: unrecovered. Mentioned as just received in SH to Mrs. Peabody, 12 January 1843.

122. 12 January 1843, SH to Mrs. Peabody, Concord.
MS: NN-Berg. Letter is sent via John L. O'Sullivan, who has been visiting the Hawthornes. O'Sullivan has met Thoreau via NH. O'Sullivan promises to give Mrs. Peabody some money for NH.

123. 15? January 1843, Mary Peabody to SH.
MS: NN-Berg. Berg Collection's date is Boston, late 1842? (see *Berg Catalog*, 3:166). The letter mentions John L. O'Sullivan as having visited the Peabody household in Boston after having completed a pleasant visit to the Old Manse. O'Sullivan left Concord for Boston on 13 January. He evidently left no money for NH with the Peabodys. Boston gossip about Bronson Alcott. Mentions SH's first pregnancy.

124. 16 January 1843, Margaret Fuller to NH, Cambridge.
MS: NN-Berg. This time Margaret requests that NH consider taking Charles Newcomb into the Manse.

125. 19 January 1843, James Russell Lowell to Robert Carter, New York.
MS: see Johnson, "Letters of Lowell to Carter." Published: Johnson, "Letters of Lowell to Carter," pp. 35–37. Refers to the need for money to pay NH for his contribution to *Pioneer*.

126. 21 January 1843, Mrs. Peabody to SH.
MS: unrecovered. Listed and quoted by Julian Hawthorne, *Notebook* (see this article, Part III), section entitled "Extracts from Letters," p. 3. Quoted section refers to Alcott's family and legal difficulties.

127. 24 January 1843, James Russell Lowell to Robert Carter, New York.
MS: see Johnson, "Letters of Lowell to Carter." Published: Johnson, "Letters of Lowell to Carter," pp. 50–53. Asks Carter to write to NH to explain financial problems of *Pioneer*.

Guide to Source Materials on the Old Manse Period 275

128. 24 January 1843, Thoreau to Emerson, Concord.
MS: unrecovered. Published: Emerson, "The Emerson-Thoreau Correspondence," 578–79. Thoreau recounts his meetings with O'Sullivan as arranged by NH. Interesting impression of O'Sullivan.

129. 28 January 1843, James Russell Lowell to Robert Carter, New York.
MS: see Johnson, "Letters of Lowell to Carter." Published: Johnson, "Letters of Lowell to Carter," pp. 54–56. NH has written another article for *Pioneer*.

130. 29 January 1843, SH to Maria Louisa Hawthorne, Concord.
MS: NN-Berg. NH is very busy writing. SH details her artistic efforts and the events of the last month. NH plans a trip to Salem in March.

131. 1 February 1843, NH to Robert Carter, Concord.
MS: MHarF. Published: facsimile in *The Flying Quill: Autographs at Goodspeed's*, October 1948. Accompanies NH's "The Birthmark" for *Pioneer*. He would like to read proof, if at all possible.

132. 1 February 1843, NH to Margaret Fuller, Concord.
MS: MH (fMS Am 1086, 16:33). Partially quoted in Hawthorne, *American Notebooks* (ed. Stewart), pp. 318–19, note 402. NH demurs at having anyone live at the Manse with them—he is writing continuously and SH is pregnant. Excellent characterization of the Hawthornes' life in Concord.

133. 17 February 1843, Mrs. Peabody to SH.
MS: unrecovered. Mentioned as received in SH to Mrs. Peabody, 22 February 1843.

134. 19? February 1843, Mary Caleb Foote to SH.
MS: unrecovered. Mentioned as received yesterday in SH to Mrs. Peabody, 22 February 1843.

135. 22 February 1843, SH to Mrs. Peabody, Concord.
MS: NN-Berg. Letter continues on 23 and 24 February. MS unsigned, appears incomplete. SH has had a miscarriage, caused by a fall. Mrs. Peabody has been to Concord to care for her. Momentarily, the Hawthornes expect money from Robert Carter—money which will allow a trip to Boston.

136. 23 February 1843, Mary Peabody to SH.
MS: unrecovered. Quoted in Julian Hawthorne, *Notebook* (see this article, Part III), section entitled "Extracts from Letters," as written in either 1842 or 1843. The latter year seems probable. "Mrs. Quincy" has been spreading some story about NH.

137. 26? February 1843, Mrs. Peabody to SH.
MS: unrecovered. Mentioned as received in SH to Mrs. Peabody, 28 February 1843.

138. 28 February 1843, SH to Mrs. Peabody, Concord.
MS: NN-Berg. Accompanies a package of NH's writing. Excellent commentary on NH's financial relationships with Lowell and Epes Sargent. NH and SH went to Concord 24 February to sign a deed before a Justice of the Peace.

139. 4 March 1843, Maria Louisa Hawthorne to SH, Salem.
MS: NN-Berg. Answers SH to Louisa, 29 January 1843. Just read NH's "The New Adam and Eve" as it was recently reprinted in the "Gazette."

140. 5 March 1843, SH to Maria Louisa Hawthorne, Concord.
MS: NN-Berg. NH has not come to Salem because he has no money—a very small amount came yesterday. NH writing furiously. SH tells Louisa about her illness, but does not mention miscarriage.

141. 12 March 1843, NH to SH, Salem.
MS: CSmH (HM 10967). Published: Hawthorne, *Love Letters*, 2:105–108. There is a slight inconsistency in the date, since it is also dated Saturday, which was the 11th of March. Long letter in which NH imagines himself back in the Manse—he is having some difficulty in getting on smoothly with his family. SH is staying with her family in Boston.

142. 12–15 March 1843, letters from SH to NH, Salem.
MSS: unrecovered. Mentioned in NH to SH, 16 March 1843. The text of this letter implies that there were at least three SH to NH letters for this period.

143. 16 March 1843, NH to SH, Salem.
MS: CSmH (HM 10968). Published: Hawthorne, *Love Letters*, 2:109–12. This publication misdates the letter 15 March—for correct date see Stewart, "Letters to Sophia." Excellent detail on financial situation and writing plans. NH is being solicited to write for a Mr. Billings, but intends to write mythological tales for O'Sullivan to publish in New York.

144. 19 March 1843, Henry Wadsworth Longfellow to NH, Cambridge.
MS: Ct. Published: Longfellow, *Letters*, 2:519. Text reliable. Reminds NH of dinner engagement for 21 March and comments on "The Birth Mark."

145. 21 March 1843, Henry Wadsworth Longfellow to Catherine Eliot Norton, Cambridge.
MS: MH. Published: Longfellow, *Letters*, 2:520–22. Recommends "The Birth Mark" for Norton's reading (2:521).

146. 23 March 1843, SH to Mrs. Peabody, Concord.
MS: NN-Berg. Letter continues on the 24th. Tells of SH's return from Boston via stage with Theodore Parker. Much detail concerning homeopathy. NH writing hard but very tired of winter.

147. 25 March 1843, NH to Horatio Bridge, Concord.
MS: MeB. Published: Bridge, *Personal Recollections*, pp. 88–91. Describes financial state, recent travels, and SH's recent illness. Plans for *Journal of an African Cruiser*.

148. 26? March 1843, Mrs. Peabody to SH.
MS: NN-Berg. Date is the Berg Collection's. This letter answers SH to Mrs. Peabody, 23 March 1843, and is, in turn, mentioned in SH to Mary Peabody, 28 March 1843. A motherly letter, encouraging SH to read (and converse) in order to encourage NH's imagination.

Guide to Source Materials on the Old Manse Period 277

149. 27? March 1843, Mary Peabody to SH.
MS: unrecovered. Mentioned as received on 28 March in SH to Mary Peabody, 28 March 1843. Announces Mary's engagement to Horace Mann.

150. 28 March 1843, SH to Mary Peabody, Concord.
MS: NN-Berg. Date is from the postmark. Congratulations on Mary's engagement to Horace Mann.

151. 29? March 1843, SH to Horace Mann.
MS: unrecovered. Mentioned as an intention in SH to Mary Peabody, 28 March 1843, and answered by Horace Mann to SH, 2 April 1843.

152. 1 April 1843, Mrs. Peabody to SH.
MS: unrecovered. Quoted in Julian Hawthorne, *Notebook* (see this article, Part III), section entitled "Extracts from Letters," pp. 3–4. Partially published in Julian Hawthorne, *Hawthorne & His Wife*, 1:266–67. For confirmation of year, see text of SH to Mary Caleb Foote, 6 April 1843. Interesting detail concerning NH's acceptance in Boston. Urges SH to be financially practical, since geniuses like NH cannot be expected to manage too well.

153. 2? April 1843, Mary Caleb Foote to SH.
MS: unrecovered. Mentioned as received on 5 April in SH to Mary Caleb Foote, 6 April 1843. Evidently concerns the death of one of Mary's children.

154. 2 April 1843, Horace Mann to SH, Boston.
MS: ViU. An affectionate reply to SH's letter dated 29? March 1843. MS defective, with a large triangular piece torn out.

155. 6 April 1843, Ellery Channing to Emerson.
MS: unrecovered. Partially published in Higginson, *Hawthorne Centenary*, pp. 183–84. Interestingly contrasts the ascetic aspirations of Bronson Alcott with the healthy sensuality of NH.

156. 6 April 1843, SH to Mary Caleb Foote, Concord.
MS: unrecovered. Published: Lathrop, *Memories*, pp. 55–57. Lengthy characterization of NH, together with good domestic and social detail.

157. 13 April 1843, SH to Mrs. Peabody.
MS: NN-Berg. Letter continues on the 14th. SH has been to Boston, without NH, to see her sister Mary, whose wedding to Horace Mann is planned for 1 May. This letter describes "bird voices" of spring, and may be a source for "Buds and Bird-Voices."

158. 13? April 1843, James Russell Lowell to NH.
MS: unrecovered. Mentioned as received this week in SH to Mrs. Peabody, 20 April 1843. Also mentioned as recently received in SH to Maria Louisa Hawthorne, 17 April 1843. Evidently solicits contributions for Poe's newly projected literary magazine.

159. 15? April 1843, NH to James Russell Lowell.
MS: unrecovered. Mentioned in James Russell Lowell to E. A. Poe, 17 April 1843. NH agrees to send a piece to Poe for his new venture, the *Stylus*, and SH may make a drawing of NH's head for the publication.

160. 16? April 1843, Mrs. Peabody to SH.
MS: unrecovered. Mentioned as recently received in SH to Mrs. Peabody, 20 April 1843.

161. 17 April 1843, SH to Maria Louisa Hawthorne, Concord.
MS: NN-Berg. Published: partially in Clark, *Hawthorne at Auction*, p. 238. Events since 22 March, including Mary Peabody's engagement and NH's offers from Poe via Lowell.

162. 17 April 1843, James Russell Lowell to E. A. Poe, Boston.
MS: unrecovered. Published: Lowell, "Lowell's Letters," 171. Relays NH's reply to Lowell's 13? April letter.

163. 19? April 1843, Mary Peabody to SH.
MS: unrecovered. Mentioned as a note received today in SH to Mrs. Peabody, 20 April 1843.

164. 20 April 1843, SH to Mrs. Peabody.
MS: NN-Berg. Published: partially in Hawthorne, *Hawthorne & His Wife*, 1:272–73. Recent news, including the Poe offer to NH. NH is writing very steadily.

165. 30 April 1843, Emerson to Charles Stearns Wheeler.
MS: ViU. Published: see Emerson, *Letters*, 3:171; *Anglia*, 12 (1889): 454–55. References to NH and his Brook Farm experience on 12:454–55.

166. 30 April 1843, Mary Peabody to SH.
MS: NN-Berg. Written on the eve of Mary's marriage to Horace Mann.

167. April? 1843, Horatio Bridge to NH.
MS: unrecovered. Mentioned as received some time ago in NH to Horatio Bridge, 3 May 1843. The letter was written in answer to NH to Horatio Bridge, 25 March 1843.

168. April? 1843, Mary Peabody to SH.
MS: NN-Berg. Their date is Boston, early April 1843 (see *Berg Catalog*, 3:166). Answers SH to Mary Peabody, 28 March 1843. Best date is ca. 31 March to 2 April. Cf. Horace Mann to SH, 2 April 1843. It cannot postdate a trip SH made to Boston, which she began on 7 April.

169. 2 May 1843, Mrs. Peabody to SH.
MS: unrecovered. Mentioned as a brief letter received yesterday and dated Tuesday in SH to Mrs. Peabody, 5 May 1843. No doubt concerns Mary's wedding and immediate departure for Europe with Horace Mann.

170. 3 May 1843, NH to Horatio Bridge, Concord.
MS: MeB. NN-Berg has a holograph copy (hand unknown) which restores a passage rendered unreadable in the original MS. Published: Hawthorne, *Portable Hawthorne*, pp. 619–20; also in Bridge, *Personal Recollections*, pp. 91–95. Lengthy account of literary successes and financial insecurity. Fascinating advice concerning the working-up of literary descriptions.

171. 5 May 1843, SH to Mrs. Peabody.
MS: NN-Berg (see *Berg Catalog*, 2:442). The letter is misdated by SH as

Guide to Source Materials on the Old Manse Period 279

5 April 1843, and is so catalogued in *Berg*. The text, however, refers to Mary P. Mann's wedding as an accomplished fact—the wedding was on 1 May. The day of the week assigned to the letter by SH—Friday—fits the May date, but not the April one. Letter continues on May 8th, also called by SH April 8th. MS appears incomplete, breaking off in mid-sentence. Good detail on financial difficulties and domestic life.

172. 6? May 1843, Mrs. Peabody to SH.
MS: unrecovered. Mentioned as received on 7 May in SH to Mrs. Peabody, 5 May 1843.

173. 8 May 1843, James Russell Lowell to E. A. Poe, Cambridge.
MS: unrecovered. Published: Lowell, "Lowell's Letters," 172. Lowell has not yet received an NH contribution for the *Stylus*.

174. 21 May 1843, Emerson to Thoreau, Concord.
MS: unrecovered. Published: Emerson, "The Emerson-Thoreau Correspondence," 585–86. Passing reference to NH being "well" on 586.

175. 23 May 1843, Thoreau to Emerson, Staten Island.
MS: unrecovered. Published: Emerson, "The Emerson-Thoreau Correspondence," 586–87. Passing reference to NH on 587.

176. 25? May 1843, SH to Mrs. Peabody.
MS: NN-Berg. Dated by SH only on a Thursday in May, but refers to a visit by her father, which terminated on Saturday, 13 May. Other possible date, therefore, is 18 May 1843. Letter continued on Friday. Long description of Concord spring. NH is planting their garden.

177. 28 May 1843, SH to Maria Louisa Hawthorne.
MS: unrecovered. Published: partially in Clark, *Hawthorne at Auction*, pp. 238, 260. Postscript by NH. Describes spring in Concord; tells recent news (including Longfellow's engagement to Fanny Appleton).

178. May? 1843, Maria Louisa Hawthorne to SH.
MS: unrecovered. Mentioned as received today in SH to Mrs. Peabody, May? 1843. Tells of Beelzebub's death (B. was a cat)—this places the letter prior to SH to Louisa, 28 May 1843.

179. May? 1843, SH to Mrs. Peabody.
MS: unrecovered. Published: Lathrop, *Memories*, pp. 57–58. Dated, in that publication, as "May." Placement in *Memories* indicates the year 1843. Other letters from SH to Mrs. Peabody during May would indicate a date for this letter ca. 12 May. Details the pleasure of Concord springtime.

180. May 1843, Mary P. Mann to SH.
MS: unrecovered. Mentioned as received yesterday in SH to Mrs. Peabody, 25? May 1843. Date is uncertain because Mary Mann embarked for Europe immediately after her wedding on 1 May.

181. May 1843, Mary Mann to SH.
MS: NN-Berg. Berg Collection's date is late May 1843 (see *Berg Catalog*, 3:166). This letter may be the same as item 180.

182. May? 1843, Mrs. Peabody to SH.
MS: unrecovered. Quoted in Julian Hawthorne, *Notebook* (see this article, Part III), section entitled "Extracts from Letters," p. 4. Partially published in Hawthorne, *Hawthorne & His Wife*, 1:267. Comments favorably on "The Celestial Rail-road," which was published in May 1843. This letter could be the same as Mrs. Peabody to SH, 2 May 1843 or 6? May 1843.

183. 28? May to 1? June 1843, several letters from Mrs. Peabody to SH.
MSS: unrecovered. Mentioned as having been received during this week in SH to Mrs. Peabody, 2 June 1843. Some "great disappointment" had apparently occurred in Concord, possibly relating to SH's health. Cf. Hawthorne, *American Notebooks* (ed. Stewart), p. 185.

184. 2 June 1843, SH to Mrs. Peabody.
MS: NN-Berg. SH details her recent reading and refers distantly to the "great disappointment" (another miscarriage?). The Hawthornes keep a domestic account book.

185. 7 June 1843, Emerson to Thoreau.
MS: unrecovered. Partially published: Higginson, *The Hawthorne Centenary*, p. 188. Favorable comment on "The Celestial Rail-road."

186. 16? June 1843, SH to Mrs. Peabody.
MS: NN-Berg. This is the last page of a letter written prior to a visit in Concord by Anna and Sarah Shaw, to which it refers in anticipation. The Shaws arrived on 22 June. The above date is assigned by the Berg Collection.

187. 17 June 1843, SH to Maria Louisa Hawthorne, Concord.
MS: NN-Berg. Published: partially in Clark, *Hawthorne at Auction*, p. 238. Postscript by NH. Urgently renews an invitation for all the Salem Hawthornes to visit Concord.

188. 20? June 1843, Maria Louisa Hawthorne to SH.
MS: unrecovered. Mentioned as received on 22 June in SH to Maria Louisa Hawthorne, 9 July 1843.

189. 29? June? 1843, Rufus W. Griswold to NH.
MS: unrecovered. Mentioned in NH to Rufus W. Griswold, 2 July 1843. Concerns contributions for *Graham's Magazine*.

190. June? 1843, Mrs. Peabody to SH.
MS: unrecovered. Quoted in Julian Hawthorne, *Notebook* (see this article, Part III), section entitled "Extracts from Letters," p. 3. Refers to "Buds and Bird-Voices," which was published in June 1843. This letter could be one of the group of letters written during the week of 28 May to 2 June.

191. 2 July 1843, NH to Rufus W. Griswold, Concord.
MS: NN-Berg. Published: Griswold, *Passages from the Correspondence*, p. 144. Tells of writing plans and seeks a permanent connection with *Graham's Magazine*.

192. 2 July 1843, John L. O'Sullivan to Thoreau, New York.
MS: NN-Berg. Refers to meeting Thoreau at NH's.

Guide to Source Materials on the Old Manse Period 281

193. 5? July 1843, Mrs. Peabody to SH.
MS: unrecovered. Mentioned as received today in SH to Mrs. Peabody, 6 July 1843.

194. 6 July 1843, SH to Mrs. Peabody.
MS: NN-Berg. The letter is misdated 6 June by SH, and is so filed at the Berg (see *Berg Catalog*, 2:422). It refers, however, to a visit that Mrs. Peabody paid the Hawthornes in Concord ca. 1–3 July. The letter continues on Friday the 7th, a date which fits July 1843, but not June. SH is pregnant; she details news since 3 July.

195. 8 July 1843, Thoreau to Emerson, Staten Island.
MS: unrecovered. Published: Emerson, "The Emerson-Thoreau Correspondence," 590–91. Nostalgia for NH's "heroic" companionship expressed on 590.

196. 9 July 1843, SH to Maria Louisa Hawthorne.
MS: NN-Berg. Published: partially in Clark, *Hawthorne at Auction*, p. 238. The letter continues on 14 July. Postscript by NH. Details of social life described by SH, who is sorry Louisa cannot visit as planned. Postscript says that NH will send money to Salem as soon as he has some.

197. 10? July 1843, Mrs. Peabody to SH.
MS: unrecovered. Quoted in Julian Hawthorne, *Notebook* (see this article, Part III), section entitled "Extracts from Letters," p. 5. Published: partially in Hawthorne, *Hawthorne & His Wife*, 1:267, 270(?). Refers to the death of Washington Allston, which occurred on 9 July 1843. Comments on "The Two Widows."

198. 20 July 1843, Emerson to Thoreau, Concord.
MS: see Emerson, *Letters*. Published: Emerson, *Letters*, 3:187. Text reliable. Passing reference to NH.

199. 20 July 1843, NH to Samuel Colman, Concord.
MS: Mr. C. E. Frazer Clark, Jr. Published: facsimile in McDonald, "The Old Manse Period Canon," p. 26. NH cannot contribute to *Boys' and Girls' Magazine*.

200. 29? July 1843, Maria Louisa Hawthorne to SH.
MS: unrecovered. Mentioned as received on 1 August in SH to Maria Louisa Hawthorne, 5 August 1843.

201. 30 July 1843, SH to Mrs. Peabody.
MS: NN-Berg (see *Berg Catalog*, 2:442). The MS is the last four pages of a letter. It continues on a date "Monday," and refers to a visit by Louisa Hawthorne that is soon expected (the date set for her arrival was 1 August). It also refers back to an earlier visit by George and Susan Hillard, which took place on 15–ca. 19 July. The fragment is directed to Boston via R. W. Emerson. See Emerson, *Letters*, 3:193, concerning this trip. SH describes her reading and social engagements.

202. 31? July 1843, John L. O'Sullivan to NH.
MS: unrecovered. Mentioned as received after 1 August in SH to Maria Louisa Hawthorne, 5 August 1843.

203. 5 August 1843, SH to Maria Louisa Hawthorne.
MS: NN-Berg. SH is disappointed at Louisa's failure to make it to Concord. She announces that she is two months' pregnant.

204. 7 August 1843, Emerson to Margaret Fuller, Concord.
MS: see Emerson, *Letters*. Published: Emerson, *Letters*, 3:193–98. Text reliable. Hawthorne is characterized as a good neighbor (3:198). Reference to SH on 3:196.

205. 8 August 1843, Emerson to Benjamin Peter Hunt, Concord.
MS: see Emerson, *Letters*. Published: Emerson, *Letters*, 3:198–200. Text reliable. Hawthorne seen as a better critic than writer. NH liked Hunt's piece in the July *Dial* ("Voyage to Jamaica").

206. 9? August 1843, SH to Mary Mann, Concord.
MS: ViU. SH's is one section—the first—of a letter written by her in concert with her sister Elizabeth and their mother to Mary Mann, who was then in Europe. The dateline of SH's section is mutilated, so the date given above is my reconstruction of it. Postmarked 1 September at Le Havre. The Barrett Library has the entire item catalogued as October 1843. Describes summer in Concord, its only problem being that NH has had to work so hard at writing.

207. 11 August 1843, SH to Mary Caleb Foote.
MS: unrecovered. Published: Lathrop, *Memories*, pp. 58–60. Lengthy description of the Concord summer, this time deemphasizing NH's writing very laboriously.

208. 13 August 1843, SH to Mrs. Peabody.
MS: NN-Berg. Letter is continued on the 14th and 15th. Refers to a visit by David Roberts which occurred in August 1843. Much detail, including mention of attending a court trial in Concord—Daniel Webster was one of the lawyers.

209. 13 August 1843, Mrs. Peabody to SH.
MS: NN-Berg. Letter is dated Sunday in the holograph; assignment to August is by the Berg Collection. SH to Mrs. Peabody, 13 August 1843, refers to this letter as having been received on 15 August. Julian Hawthorne, *Notebook* (see this article, Part III), lists a letter from Mrs. Peabody to SH on 13 August 1842, which I take to be an erroneous reference to this letter.

210. 20 August 1843, SH to Mrs. Peabody.
MS: NN-Berg. Date is the Berg Collection's. This is a three-page fragment of a much longer letter—the first page is labeled in SH's hand as the sixth sheet. Evidently the long-missing section described the Concord trial at which Daniel Webster served as one of the lawyers. Surviving pages describe social details of Concord life.

211. 26 August 1843, NH to SH, Salem.
MS: CSmH (HM 10980). Published: Hawthorne, *Love Letters*, 2:153–57. This publication misdates the letter 25 August 1845. For correct date, see Stewart, "Letters to Sophia," 389. NH recounts his twenty-four hours of

Guide to Source Materials on the Old Manse Period 283

travel with Horace Conolly toward Salem, including visits with Mrs. Peabody, George Bancroft, Longfellow, and Greene (U.S. Consul to Rome).

212. 31 August 1843, SH to NH.
MS: unrecovered. Noted and dated in the manuscript *American Notebooks* (see this article, Part III), in SH's entry for 1 September 1843.

213. August 1843, Annie Chase to SH.
MS: unrecovered. Mentioned in SH to Mary Caleb Foote, 11 February 1844.

214. August 1843, SH to Dr. Walter Channing.
MS: unrecovered. Mentioned as sent via Mrs. Peabody in SH to Mrs. Peabody, 20 August 1843.

215. 1? September 1843, Elizabeth P. Peabody to SH.
MS: unrecovered. Mentioned as received in SH to Mrs. Peabody, 3 September 1843. Evidently this letter was highly critical of NH's social habits.

216. 1? September 1843, Mrs. Peabody to SH.
MS: unrecovered. Mentioned as received in SH to Mrs. Peabody, 3 September 1843.

217. 2 September 1843, NH to Maria Louisa Hawthorne, Boston.
MS: MSaE. Arrangements for Louisa to make connections in Boston for a trip to Salem.

218. 3 September 1843, SH to Mrs. Peabody.
MS: NN-Berg. Eight pages of manuscript survive, but the letter appears to be incomplete. Almost entirely about NH's personality; a resounding denunciation of Elizabeth P. Peabody, Mary Mann, and Emerson, since they have presumed, indelicately, to criticize NH.

219. 6 September 1843, SH to Maria Louisa Hawthorne.
MS: NN-Berg. Further travel arrangements for an imminent trip to Concord by Louisa.

220. 8 September 1843, Emerson to Thoreau, Concord.
MS: unrecovered. Published: Emerson, "The Emerson-Thoreau Correspondence," 592–93. Passing reference to NH having returned from Salem (592).

221. 8 September 1843, Mary Caleb Foote to SH.
MS: not traced. Published: Tileston, *Caleb and Mary Wilder Foote*, pp. 110–11. Anecdotes about Mrs. Foote's children.

222. 15 September 1843, SH to Maria Louisa Hawthorne.
MS: NN-Berg. A testy letter on the subject of Louisa's nonappearance in Concord and on the unattractive qualities of David Roberts, NH's Salem friend. Refers to Daniel Webster in Concord.

223. 18 September 1843, Maria Louisa Hawthorne to SH, Salem.
MS: NN-Berg. Posted 19 September. Apology for not making expected visit.

224. 25? September 1843, Samuel Colman to NH.
MS: unrecovered. Mentioned in NH to Samuel Colman, 27 September 1843.

225. 27 September 1843, NH to Samuel Colman.
MS: NN-Berg. Published: partially in Roselle, *Samuel Griswold Goodrich*, p. 125. NH demurs at writing regularly for the *Boys' and Girls' Magazine*, but will send in an occasional article.

226. 15 October 1843, SH to Mary Caleb Foote.
MS: unrecovered. Published: Lathrop, *Memories*, p. 61. A moralizing, "high-toned" letter.

227. 17 October 1843, Thoreau to Emerson, Staten Island.
MS: unrecovered. Published: Emerson, "The Emerson-Thoreau Correspondence," 594–95. Passing reference to NH on 595.

228. 26 October 1843, SH to Maria Louisa Hawthorne, Concord.
MS: NN-Berg. Describes events since mid-October, when Louisa returned to Salem after completing her long-delayed visit to Concord.

229. October 1843, Evert A. Duyckinck to NH.
MS: unrecovered. Mentioned as recently received in SH to Maria Louisa Hawthorne, 26 October 1843. Includes a long quotation from a critical review of NH's work that appeared in the *Foreign Quarterly Review*.

230. 6 November 1843, Mary Mann to SH.
MS: NN-Berg. The Manns have just returned from Europe.

231. 7 November 1843, SH to Mary Mann.
MS: NN-Berg. Published: Lathrop, *Memories*, pp. 62–63. SH invites Mary and Horace to visit Concord soon. Emerson would like Horace to lecture at the Concord Lyceum.

232. 7? November 1843, Mrs. Peabody to SH.
MS: unrecovered. Mentioned as received in SH to Mrs. Peabody, 8 November 1843.

233. 8 November 1843, SH to Mrs. Peabody.
MS: NN-Berg. SH is rather put out that she learned of Mary Mann's return first through the newspapers. George Ripley (of Brook Farm) has paid the Hawthornes' interest very promptly.

234. 9 November 1843, SH to Maria Louisa Hawthorne.
MS: NN-Berg. Published: partially in Clark, *Hawthorne at Auction*, p. 238. Postscript by NH. SH copies the quotation forwarded in Evert A. Duyckinck to NH, October 1843. NH wants some pearl buttons.

235. 13? November 1843, Mary Mann to SH.
MS: unrecovered. Mentioned as received this afternoon in SH to Mrs. Peabody, 15 November 1843. For another letter from Mary Mann to SH bearing the same date, see Mary Mann to SH, December? 1843.

236. 15 November 1843, SH to Mrs. Peabody.
MS: NN-Berg. SH details preparations for her coming childbirth.

237. 17? November 1843, Mrs. Peabody to SH.
MS: unrecovered. Mentioned as received in SH to Mrs. Peabody, 19 November 1843.

Guide to Source Materials on the Old Manse Period 285

238. 19 November 1843, SH to Mrs. Peabody.
MS: NN-Berg. The manuscript appears to be incomplete. Published: partially in Lathrop, *Memories*, pp. 63–64. More details of preparation for childbirth. SH expects Mrs. Peabody to attend her.

239. 24 November 1843, John L. O'Sullivan to Henry Wise, New York.
MS: MeHi. Published: O'Sullivan, "John L. O'Sullivan." Text reliable. Lengthy and detailed character reference on behalf of NH becoming postmaster at Salem.

240. 26 November 1843, NH to Evert A. Duyckinck, Concord.
MS: NN-Duyckinck. Published: partially in Hawthorne, *American Notebooks* (ed. Stewart), p. 297. A most cordial and personal letter concerning NH's style of life and writing. Answers Duyckinck to NH, October 1843.

241. 26 November 1843, NH to George Hillard, Concord.
MS: MeHi. Published: Hawthorne, *Complete Writings*, 17:422. Acknowledges receipt of Hillard's recent Phi Beta Kappa oration, praises it and asks Hillard (NH's lawyer) to inquire after sales of *Twice-told Tales*.

242. 26 November 1843, SH to Maria Louisa Hawthorne.
MS: NN-Berg. Good details of domestic life. SH is beginning to contemplate her confinement for childbirth. NH is writing furiously.

243. 28? November 1843, Mrs. Peabody to SH.
MS: unrecovered. Mentioned as received in SH to Mrs. Peabody, 1 December 1843.

244. 1 December 1843, SH to Mrs. Peabody.
MS: NN-Berg. The manuscript is incomplete. This letter is referred to as having been long in Sophia Hawthorne, "Journal," p. 3. Domestic details and good characterization of NH.

245. 2 December 1843, Maria Louisa Hawthorne to SH, Salem.
MS: NN-Berg. Noted in Sophia Hawthorne, "Journal," p. 6, as received 5 December 1843. Replies to SH's letter dated 26 November. Louisa is readying a valise of things for the coming child.

246. 3 December 1843, NH to John L. O'Sullivan.
MS: unrecovered. Mentioned as written after dinner on 3 December in Sophia Hawthorne, "Journal," p. 5.

247. 3 December 1843, SH to Mrs. Emerson.
MS: unrecovered. Mentioned as a note written on this date in Sophia Hawthorne, "Journal," p. 4.

248. 3 December 1843, SH to Mrs. Peabody.
MS: unrecovered. Mentioned in Sophia Hawthorne, "Journal," p. 4.

249. 3 December 1843, SH to Thoreau.
MS: NNPM (M1918). A note asking Thoreau to deliver some letters in Boston.

250. 4? December 1843, Mrs. Peabody to SH.
MS: unrecovered. Mentioned as received on 5 December in Sophia Hawthorne,

"Journal," p. 6. This letter accompanied the December issue of the *United States Magazine and Democratic Review*.

251. 8 December 1843, SH to Mary Mann, Concord.
MS: NN-Berg. This letter continues on 10 December. SH is in high good spirits, and encourages Mary to be the same (Mary is also pregnant). Horace Mann is expected to lecture in Concord soon.

252. 10 December 1843, SH to Mrs. Peabody.
MS: unrecovered. Mentioned in Sophia Hawthorne, "Journal," p. 10.

253. 10 December 1843, six notes from SH to several recipients.
MSS: unrecovered. Mentioned in Sophia Hawthorne, "Journal," p. 10. These notes were in thanks for baby presents given in anticipation of the birth of Una. The recipients were Sally Gardner, Anna Shaw, Mary Shaw, Ellen S. Hooper, John L. O'Sullivan, and Rose Forbes.

254. 10? December 1843, Mary Mann to SH.
MS: unrecovered. Mentioned as received on 11 December in Sophia Hawthorne, "Journal," p. 10.

255. 10? December 1843, Mrs. Peabody to SH.
MS: unrecovered. Mentioned as received on 11 December in Sophia Hawthorne, "Journal," p. 10.

256. 15? December 1843, Sarah Clarke to SH.
MS: unrecovered. Mentioned as received on 16 December in Sophia Hawthorne, "Journal," p. 11.

257. 17 December 1843, SH to Sarah Clarke.
MS: unrecovered. Mentioned in Sophia Hawthorne, "Journal," p. 11.

258. 17 December 1843, SH to Mrs. Peabody.
MS: unrecovered. Mentioned in Sophia Hawthorne, "Journal," p. 11.

259. 17 December 1843, SH to Mrs. Sturgis.
MS: unrecovered. Mentioned in Sophia Hawthorne, "Journal," p. 11.

260. 20? December 1843, Emerson to Margaret Fuller, Concord.
MS: see Emerson, *Letters*. Published: Emerson, *Letters*, 3:231. Text reliable. Comments on NH's "Fire Worship."

261. 21 December 1843, Maria Louisa Hawthorne to SH, Salem.
MS: NN-Berg. Letter accompanies the long-awaited valise of things for the expected baby.

262. 21 December 1843, Ellen S. Hooper to SH.
MS: unrecovered. Mentioned as received on 26 December in Sophia Hawthorne, "Journal," p. 17.

263. 21 December 1843, SH to Michael O'Brien.
MS: unrecovered. Mentioned in Sophia Hawthorne, "Journal," p. 12. Michael O'Brien was the brother of the Hawthornes' maid, Mary.

Guide to Source Materials on the Old Manse Period 287

264. 21 December 1843, SH to Mrs. Peabody.
MS: unrecovered. Mentioned in Sophia Hawthorne, "Journal," p. 12.

265. 22 December 1843, SH to Mrs. Eliza Follen.
MS: unrecovered. Mentioned in Sophia Hawthorne, "Journal," p. 12. This letter accompanied the MS of NH's "A Good Man's Miracle."

266. 22? December 1843, Mary Mann to SH.
MS: unrecovered. Mentioned as received on 23 December in Sophia Hawthorne, "Journal," p. 15.

267. 22? December 1843, Mrs. Peabody to SH.
MS: unrecovered. Mentioned as received on 23 December in Sophia Hawthorne, "Journal," p. 15.

268. 25? December 1843, Ellen S. Hooper to SH.
MS: unrecovered. Mentioned as received on 26 December in Sophia Hawthorne, "Journal," p. 17. Encloses some verses on "Fire Worship."

269. 25? December 1843, Mrs. Peabody to SH.
MS: unrecovered. Mentioned as received on 26 December in Sophia Hawthorne, "Journal," p. 17.

270. 26 December 1843, SH to Mary Pickman.
MS: unrecovered. Mentioned in Sophia Hawthorne, "Journal," p. 17.

271. 27 December 1843, SH to Mrs. Peabody.
MS: unrecovered. Published: Hawthorne, *Hawthorne & His Wife*, 1:273–74. Characterization of NH as cook and housekeeper (Mary, the Hawthornes' servant, is on vacation in Boston).

272. 27? December 1843, John L. O'Sullivan to NH.
MS: unrecovered. Mentioned as received on 29 December in Sophia Hawthorne, "Journal," p. 19. The letter encloses a payment from O'Sullivan in the amount of $100.

273. 28? December 1843, Maria Louisa Hawthorne to SH.
MS: unrecovered. Mentioned as received on 30 December in Sophia Hawthorne, "Journal," p. 19. Date of reception is confirmed in SH to Louisa, 31 December 1843.

274. 28? December 1843, Mrs. Sturgis to SH.
MS: unrecovered. Mentioned as received on 29 December in Sophia Hawthorne, "Journal," p. 19.

275. 29? December 1843, George Hillard to NH.
MS: unrecovered. Mentioned as received in Sophia Hawthorne, "Journal," p. 19.

276. 31 December 1843, SH to Maria Louisa Hawthorne, Concord.
MS: NN-Berg. Published: partially in Clark, *Hawthorne at Auction*, p. 237. Detailed description of, and thanks for, each item in the valise recently sent from Salem for the new baby. Postscript dated 1 January 1844.

277. 31 December 1843, SH to Mary Mann.
MS: unrecovered. Mentioned in Sophia Hawthorne, "Journal," p. 20.

278. 31 December 1843, SH to Mrs. Peabody.
MS: unrecovered. Mentioned in Sophia Hawthorne, "Journal," p. 20. The letter continues on 1 January 1844.

279. 31 December 1843, SH to Mrs. Sturgis.
MS: unrecovered. Mentioned in Sophia Hawthorne, "Journal," p. 20.

280. December 1843, Ellery Channing to NH.
MS: unrecovered. Mentioned as received on 28 December in Sophia Hawthorne, "Journal," p. 18. Encloses $5 as partial payment of a debt.

281. December 1843, Mary Mann to SH.
MS: unrecovered. Mentioned, in SH to Mary Mann, 8 December 1843, as having been received on 7 December, although it was dated 13 November. Most likely, there was an error in dating this letter by Mary Mann. The date of the heading and the date of reception are also recorded in Sophia Hawthorne, "Journal," p. 7.

282. December 1843, ? to NH.
MS: unrecovered. Mentioned in SH to Maria Louisa Hawthorne, 31 December 1843. A long letter that was to have been forwarded with Maria Louisa Hawthorne to SH, 28? December 1843, but it was not found by the Hawthornes with that letter.

283. 1843?, Emerson to SH.
MS: NN-Berg (see *Berg Catalog*, 2:28). Published: Lathrop, *Memories*, p. 186. See Emerson, *Letters*, 3:232, for some minor corrections made in the *Memories* text.

284. 1843, NH to [James Russell Lowell].
MS: NN-Berg (see *Berg Catalog*, 2:419). The MS is the last page of a longer letter. The text bears on NH's promised contribution for E. A. Poe's planned magazine, *Stylus*. Hence the letter was certainly written in the summer of 1843. Absolute date *a quo* is ca. 8 May 1843 (see Lowell to Poe letter on that date). The fragment says that Poe will hear from NH by the first frost, so the date *ad quem* is about mid-October.

285. 1843?, SH to Mary Caleb Foote.
MS: unrecovered. Published: Lathrop, *Memories*, p. 62. The publication is confusing because it does not identify the "Mary" who is the recipient. It talks, however, of Mary Mann's engagement in a tone that seems to imply that the recipient is not Mary Mann. It does not mention Mrs. Mann's wedding, but the best guess as to the date is late May to mid-July 1843, based on the frequency of SH's letters to Mrs. Foote. Only firm date is past 28 March, when SH first learned of her sister's engagement to Horace Mann.

286. 1843?, SH to Mrs. Peabody.
MS: unrecovered. Published: Hawthorne, *Hawthorne & His Wife*, 1:256–57. Julian says that this letter and a letter from Mrs. Peabody to SH which I have dated 1845? (*Hawthorne & His Wife*, 1:258–59) were written on the

Guide to Source Materials on the Old Manse Period   289

same day, but I can make no sense out of this assertion. The present letter refers both to Margaret Fuller's "The Great Lawsuit" and Emerson's "Past and Present," two articles that were published in the July 1843 issue of *Dial*. The tone of the reference is not retrospective, so it seems most likely that the letter, if it is *one* letter rather than a composite of several, was written sometime in July, shortly after the articles appeared.

287. 1843?, Mrs. Peabody to SH.
MS: unrecovered. Quoted in Julian Hawthorne, *Notebook* (see this article, Part III). The letter is undated in Julian's notebook, but it appears in the roughly chronological list of "Extracts from Letters," p. 3, just after a paragraph about "Buds and Bird-Voices." NH's poverty, asserts Mrs. Peabody, may be a fact essential to the development of his genius.

1844

288. 5 January 1844, NH to John L. O'Sullivan.
MS: unrecovered. Mentioned in Sophia Hawthorne, "Journal," p. 23.

289. 9? January 1844, NH to Rufus W. Griswold?.
MS: unrecovered. Mentioned indirectly in SH to Mrs. Peabody, 9 January 1844. Mentioned more directly as "to Graham" in NH to George Hillard, 24 March 1844.

290. 9 January 1844, SH to Mrs. Peabody.
MS: NN-Berg. Published: partially in Lathrop, *Memories*, pp. 69–71. Extended and valuable description of NH's methods in writing, and of his relationships with publishers.

291. 19? January 1844, Mrs. Peabody to SH.
MS: unrecovered. Mentioned as received "yesterday" in SH to Mrs. Peabody, 21 January 1844.

292. 21 January 1844, SH to Mrs. Peabody.
MS: NN-Berg. Catalogued in the Berg Collection in two separate folders, one under the date given, and one labeled "Winter, 1843–44" (see *Berg Catalog*, 2:443). The letter continues on 22 January. Published: partially in Lathrop, *Memories*, pp. 71–73. Description of the cold Concord winter. SH is nearly finished with a long-wrought painting, "Endymion." NH is starved for books.

293. 30 January 1844, SH to Mary P. Mann.
MS: NN-Berg. Arrangements for Horace Mann's Concord visit.

294. January 1844, Rufus W. Griswold? to NH.
MS: unrecovered. This letter answers NH to Rufus W. Griswold?, 9? January 1844. It is mentioned as from "Graham" in NH to George Hillard, 24 March 1844.

295. January? 1844, SH to Annie Chase.
MS: unrecovered. Mentioned as written a few weeks ago in SH to Mary Caleb Foote, 11 February 1844.

296. January 1844, Mary Mann to SH.
MS: unrecovered. SH to Mary Mann, 30 January 1844, answers this letter and refers to it.

297. 4 February 1844, SH to Maria Louisa Hawthorne.
MS: NN-Berg. The letter bears an autograph of NH. SH notes NH's reading and the titles of recently completed tales. She further enumerates and describes baby presents received.

298. 4 February 1844, SH to Mrs. Peabody.
MS: NN-Berg. Published: partially in Hawthorne, *Hawthorne & His Wife*, 1:274-75. The manuscript appears to be incomplete. SH describes the cold of January at length and notes NH's recent reading. She speculates very accurately concerning the expected date of Una's arrival.

299. 4? February 1844, Mary Mann to SH.
MS: unrecovered. Mentioned as received on 5 February in SH to Mary Mann, 6 February 1844. That letter also says that SH has burned the MS of the present letter.

300. 6 February 1844, SH to Mary Mann.
MS: NN-Berg. A quarrel with Ellen Fuller Channing because of Ellen's alleged gossiping. SH is also at odds with Margaret Fuller and "Mrs. Quincy." SH asks Mary to destroy this letter. See next item.

301. 7 February 1844, SH to Mary Mann.
MS: NN-Berg. This incomplete manuscript appears to be the second half of the letter SH dated 6 February 1844, to Mary Mann. It refers to a visit by Horace Mann to occur momentarily. The visit took place on 7 February (Wednesday). The letter is currently filed, however, under the date 14 February 1844 in the Berg Collection.

302. 11 February 1844, SH to Mary Caleb Foote, Concord.
MS: NN-Berg. Published: partially in Lathrop, *Memories*, pp. 75-76. Excellent detail is here given by SH on the domestic and social routine of life in the Manse. SH includes interesting anecdotes about NH.

303. 15 February 1844, Mary Mann to SH.
MS: NN-Berg. Refers to Horace's visit in Concord and explains why he did not stay at the Manse. Mary gives SH advice about the coming child.

304. 17 February 1844, SH to Mrs. Peabody, Concord.
MS: NN-Berg. SH has not heard from Mrs. Peabody in a long time—the Hawthornes would like her to come to Concord on 23 February (in preparation for childbirth).

305. 19 February 1844, Maria Louisa Hawthorne to SH, Salem.
MS: NN-Berg. Letter continues on the 20th, is postmarked the 21st, and marked received the 22nd. News from Salem in answer to SH's letter to Louisa dated 4 February 1844.

306. 22 February 1844, Mary Mann to SH.
MS: NN-Berg.

Guide to Source Materials on the Old Manse Period 291

307. 3 March 1844, NH to Maria Louisa Hawthorne, Concord.
MS: MSaE. Announces the birth of Una at 9:30 A.M. today. SH had a long labor and NH slept not at all last night. He has not yet seen his daughter.

308. 11 March 1844, NH to "John" Frost, Concord.
MS: PPL. Published: partially in Hawthorne, *Mosses from an Old Manse* (Centenary), p. 508. Accompanies MS of "Drowne's Wooden Image." Good comments on natural development of tales.

309. 12 March 1844, George Hillard to NH, Boston.
MS: NN-Berg. Published: partially in Hawthorne, *Hawthorne & His Wife*, 1:276–77. The holograph date is confusing, appearing to read "May," but this letter is clearly answered by NH to George Hillard, 24 March 1844. The Berg Collection has the letter filed under the date 12 May. Congratulates NH on the arrival of Una, although Hillard takes some exception to her name.

310. 13? March 1844, Maria Louisa Hawthorne to NH.
MS: unrecovered. Mentioned in NH's postscript to SH to Maria Louisa Hawthorne, 15 March 1844. The manuscript was evidently destroyed because it contained unkind remarks about Una's name.

311. 15 March 1844, SH to Maria Louisa Hawthorne.
MS: NN-Berg. Published: partially in Clark, *Hawthorne at Auction*, p. 239. Long postscript by NH. Excellent description of Una as newborn infant. NH is hurt and angry at Louisa's comments about Una's name. He is troubled at not being able to send any money to Salem this winter; describes financial, literary, and travel plans.

312. 16 March 1844, SH to Mrs. Peabody.
MS: unrecovered. Published: Lathrop, *Memories*, p. 73. Details concerning Una and NH's publications.

313. 20? March 1844, Maria Louisa Hawthorne to NH.
MS: unrecovered. Mentioned as having been received "yesterday" in SH to Elizabeth Clark Manning Hawthorne, 22 March 1844. No doubt this letter "replaces" the offensive one from Louisa dated 13? March 1844.

314. 22 March 1844, SH to Elizabeth Clark Manning Hawthorne, Concord.
MS: NN-Berg. This purports to be a letter from Una (nineteen days old). Rich in detail about Una's accomplishments.

315. 24 March 1844, NH to George Hillard, Concord.
MS: MeHi. Published: Hawthorne, *Complete Writings*, 17:422–26. NH is about to give up writing for magazines—it simply does not pay enough.

316. March 1844, two letters from Horace Conolly to NH.
MSS: unrecovered. Mentioned in NH's postscript to SH to Maria Louisa Hawthorne, 15 March 1844. Both appear to have been written after 4 March, about which time news of Una Hawthorne's birth would have reached Salem. Both were "impertinent" on the subject of Una's name.

317. March? 1844, SH to Mrs. Peabody.
MS: NN-Berg. This MS is the last leaf of a longer letter. Date is the Berg

Collection's. Good commentary on the difficulty NH experiences in writing short pieces.

318. 1 April 1844, NH to Horatio Bridge, Concord.
MS: MeB. Published: Bridge, *Personal Recollections*, pp. 95–98. Noted on address page as received 8 October 1844. NH recounts Concord news, including Una's birth. Lengthy comments and advice on Bridge's letters (later edited and published as *Journal of an African Cruiser*).

319. 2? April 1844, Dr. and Mrs. Peabody to SH.
MS: unrecovered. Mentioned as received yesterday in SH to Mrs. Peabody, 4 April 1844.

320. 4 April 1844, SH to Mrs. Peabody.
MS: NN-Berg. Published: partially in Hawthorne, *Hawthorne & His Wife*, 1:277. Hawthornes are looking forward to a visit from SH's father (he arrived in Concord 10 April).

321. 12? April 1844, SH to NH.
MS: unrecovered. Mentioned as received yesterday morning in NH to SH, 14 April 1844.

322. 14 April 1844, NH to SH, Salem.
MS: CSmH (HM 10972). Published: Hawthorne, *Love Letters*, 2:124–28. NH recounts his experiences on a trip from Concord to Salem, including an encounter with R. C. Waterston, whom he much dislikes.

323. 16 April 1844, Mary Mann to SH, Wrentham.
MS: NN-Berg.

324. 17 April 1844, SH to Mrs. Peabody.
MS: NN-Berg. Filed under the date April 1844 (see *Berg Catalog*, 2:443). Published: partially in Hawthorne, *Hawthorne & His Wife*, 1:277–79. The letter was sent to Boston with Dr. Peabody, who terminated his visit to Concord on 20 April. The letter is dated only Wednesday in holograph. Continues Thursday. Details of Una and of her grandfather Peabody's hard-working visit.

325. 19? April 1844, Mrs. Peabody to SH.
MS: unrecovered. Mentioned as received recently in SH to Mrs. Peabody, 22 April 1844.

326. 22 April 1844, SH to Mrs. Peabody.
MS: NN-Berg. This letter was sent via R. W. Emerson on 23 April. NH would like the "Cuba Letters" (written by SH and Mary Mann during a visit to Cuba) for use in his work. Much detail is given concerning Una and social life in Concord.

327. April 1844, three letters by SH to Hawthorne's family.
MSS: NN-Berg. All three of these notes are dated in holograph as given above. They all purport to be letters from Una. Recipients were Maria Louisa, Elizabeth, and Elizabeth Clark Manning Hawthorne. NH took them to Salem when he went there from Concord on 10 April. All concern, mainly, Una's development.

328. 1 May 1844, Mary Mann to SH.
MS: NN-Berg.

329. 3? May 1844, Mary Caleb Foote to SH.
MS: unrecovered. Mentioned as received on 3 or 4 May in SH to Mary Caleb Foote, 4 May 1844.

330. 4 May 1844, SH to Mary Caleb Foote.
MS: NN-Berg. This purports to be a letter from Una. O'Sullivan is Una's godfather and he has just given her a Newfoundland dog, "Leo."

331. 7 May 1844, Maria Louisa Hawthorne to SH, Salem.
MS: NN-Berg. Part of the letter under this date purports to be a reply to a letter from Una, then the letter continues on 10 May in Louisa's more usual tone. Largely deals with attempts to arrange travel for Una, NH, and SH to Salem.

332. 8 May 1844, SH to Maria Louisa Hawthorne.
MS: NN-Berg. Postscript by NH. Noted as received on 9 May in Louisa to SH, 7 May 1844. The Hawthornes plan to go to Boston in June, to Salem only at the end of the summer. NH has been ill with influenza.

333. 10 May 1844, SH to Mary Mann.
MS: unrecovered. Mentioned in SH to Mrs. Peabody, 14 May 1844.

334. 10 May 1844, SH to Mrs. Peabody.
MS: unrecovered? Mentioned in SH to Mrs. Peabody, 14 May 1844. This could be the same as the fragmentary SH to Mrs. Peabody, May? 1844.

335. 12 May 1844, George Hillard to NH.
See George Hillard to NH, 12 March 1844.

336. 14 May 1844, NH to George Hillard, Concord.
MS: Mr. and Mrs. Donald Henry, Middlebury, Connecticut. Typescript: Professor Norman Holmes Pearson, Yale University. Mentions O'Sullivan's scheme to buy the remainder of *Twice-told Tales* from Munroe and other business details.

337. 14 May 1844, SH to Mrs. Peabody.
MS: NN-Berg. The letter is dated in holograph only as written on a Tuesday in May. The exact date is established because the text mainly concerns plans for a trip by SH and Una to Boston. On Monday, 20 May, Mrs. Peabody came to Concord to help SH make this trip.

338. Entry canceled.

339. 27 May 1844, NH to SH, Concord.
MS: CSmH (HM 10973). Published: Hawthorne, *Love Letters*, 2:129–31. NH details events since he left SH in Boston (he had accompanied SH, Una, and Mrs. Peabody, but had returned almost immediately to Concord).

340. 28–30? May 1844, two letters by SH to NH.
MSS: unrecovered. Mentioned as received in NH to SH, 31 May 1844.

341. 29 May 1844, NH to SH, Concord.
MS: CSmH (HM 10974). Published: Hawthorne, *Love Letters*, 2:132–33. NH describes the events of the last two days. Horace Conolly (the "Cardinal") will not be able to keep NH company any longer because of a severe cold.

342. 29 May 1844, NH to George Hillard, Concord.
MS: VtMiM. Details of the project to buy remaining 600 copies of *Twice-told Tales*. Letter sent via Horace Conolly.

343. 31 May 1844, NH to SH, Concord.
MS: CSmH (HM 10975). Published: Hawthorne, *Love Letters*, 2:134–38. Domestic details of life at the Manse without SH.

344. Entry canceled.

345. May? 1844, SH to Mrs. Peabody.
MS: NN-Berg. This is the last page of a longer letter. Date is the Berg Collection's. SH reports that Una weighs twelve pounds today.

346. May 1844, John L. O'Sullivan to NH.
MS: unrecovered. Mentioned in, and enclosed with, NH to George Hillard, 14 May 1844. Describes a method of making additional money from unsold copies of *Twice-told Tales*.

347. 1 June 1844, NH to Frank Farley.
MS: unrecovered. Mentioned in NH to SH, 2 June 1844.

348. 1? June 1844, SH to NH.
MS: unrecovered. Mentioned as received today in NH to SH, 2 June 1844.

349. 2 June 1844, NH to SH, Concord.
MS: CSmH (HM 10976). Published: Hawthorne, *Love Letters*, 2:139–43. Domestic and social details of NH's solitary life in Concord.

350. 6 June 1844, NH to SH, Concord.
MS: CSmH (HM 10977). Published: Hawthorne, *Love Letters*, 2:144–47. Frank Farley arrived yesterday to keep NH company.

351. 8? June 1844, SH to NH.
MS: unrecovered. Mentioned as received yesterday in NH to SH, 10 June 1844.

352. 10 June 1844, NH to SH, Concord.
MS: CSmH (HM 10978). Published: Hawthorne, *Love Letters*, 2:148–50. NH describes arrangements for SH's return to Concord, together with social life in Concord.

353. 12 June 1844, John L. O'Sullivan to James Munroe & Co., New York.
MS: MB. O'Sullivan proposes to buy *Twice-told Tales* and issue remainder in a new edition.

354. 24? June 1844, SH to Mrs. Peabody.
MS: unrecovered. Mentioned as received in Mrs. Peabody to SH, 25 June 1844.

355. 25 June 1844, Mrs. Peabody to SH.
MS: NN-Berg. The letter is continued on 26 June, sent to Concord on that

Guide to Source Materials on the Old Manse Period 295

date via George William Curtis, and answered by SH on the same day. Concerns SH's recent visit to Boston and comments on the Hawthornes' problem with their maid (Mary has just said that she wishes to leave immediately).

356. 26 June 1844, SH to Mrs. Peabody.
MS: NN-Berg. SH details the problem with their maid and begins to arrange for hiring a new one.

357. 1? July 1844, Maria Louisa Hawthorne to SH.
MS: unrecovered. Mentioned as received today in SH to Maria Louisa Hawthorne, 2 July 1844.

358. 2 July 1844, SH to Maria Louisa Hawthorne, Concord.
MS: NN-Berg. Postscript by NH. SH tells Louisa about recent travels and invites her to visit Concord.

359. 10? July 1844, Mrs. Peabody to SH.
MS: unrecovered. Mentioned as received just now in SH to Mrs. Peabody, 11 July 1844.

360. 11 July 1844, SH to Mrs. Peabody.
MS: NN-Berg. SH recounts domestic details.

361. 24 July 1844, Mary Mann to SH, Wrentham.
MS: NN-Berg. Mary teases SH about writing "Unaty" letters—pages almost entirely about the accomplishments of Una.

362. 26 July 1844, SH to Mary Mann.
MS: NN-Berg. More about Una.

363. July? 1844, Horatio Bridge to SH?
MS: unrecovered. Mentioned in SH to Maria Louisa Hawthorne, 4 August 1844.

364. 4 August 1844, SH to Maria Louisa Hawthorne.
MS: NN-Berg. Continues on 6 August. News concerning Una and visitors to the Manse. Mrs. Peabody is now in Concord.

365. 18 August 1844, SH to Mrs. Peabody.
MS: NN-Berg. Published: partially in Lathrop, *Memories*, pp. 73–75. The letter is dated Sunday, 19 August, but this Sunday was 18 August in 1844. Continues on 20 August. Largely about the Hawthornes' search for a new maid, with a few testy comments on the former one.

366. 18? August 1844, Mrs. Peabody to SH.
MS: unrecovered. Mentioned as received on 19 August in SH to Mrs. Peabody, 18 August 1844.

367. 19 August 1844, NH to George Hillard, Concord.
MS: NNPM (MA 611, p. 7). Published: McDonald, "'The Old Manse' and Its Mosses," p. 94. Text reliable but just short of complete. NH wants Hillard to sue some debtors on his behalf. Excellent financial detail given.

368. 27 August 1844, Maria Louisa Hawthorne to Elizabeth Clark Manning Hawthorne, Concord.

MS: not traced. Typescript: Professor Norman Holmes Pearson. Letter continues on 28 August. News of the Hawthorne household, where Louisa is now visiting.

369. August? 1844, "Miss Davis" to NH.
MS: unrecovered. Mentioned as received by NH in Maria Louisa Hawthorne to Elizabeth Clark Manning Hawthorne, 27 August 1844. A request that NH write something to be sold at a fair.

370. August 1844, Nathaniel Peabody (SH's brother) to Una Hawthorne.
MS: unrecovered. Mentioned as recently received in SH to Mrs. Peabody, 19 August 1844.

371. 16 September 1844, SH to Mary Mann.
MS: NN-Berg. SH details domestic routine since Una's birth and advises Mary concerning her new son, Horace.

372. 14 October 1844?, Mrs. Peabody to SH.
MS: unrecovered. Quoted in Julian Hawthorne, *Notebook* (see this article, Part III), section entitled "Extracts from Letters," p. 11. The year assigned to this letter seems most probable because it refers to NH making meals for Mrs. Peabody on a recent visit of hers to Concord. The Hawthornes were without a maid at this point, and the same function of NH's hospitality is mentioned in Maria Louisa Hawthorne to SH, 23 October 1844. Mrs. Peabody had visited the Hawthornes in early August 1844.

373. 19 October 1844, Mrs. Peabody to SH.
MS: unrecovered. Quoted in Julian Hawthorne, *Notebook* (see this article, Part III), section entitled "Extracts from Letters," pp. 9–10. Year is established by several internal details. Published: partially in Hawthorne, *Hawthorne & His Wife*, 1:265–66. An extended plea that NH write a memoir of Mrs. Peabody's ancestor, General Palmer.

374. 22 October 1844, Mary Mann to SH, Wrentham.
MS: NN-Berg.

375. 23 October 1844, Maria Louisa Hawthorne to SH, Salem.
MS: NN-Berg. The Salem Hawthornes want badly to have the Concord Hawthornes visit them (but without "Leo," their dog).

376. 27 October 1844, SH to Maria Louisa Hawthorne.
MS: NN-Berg. NH, SH, and Una will come to Salem as soon as NH has finished harvesting his garden and writing a tale on which he is engaged.

377. 3 November 1844, Mrs. Peabody to SH.
MS: NN-Berg. News about the Hawthorne's former maid (she is to be married soon). Mrs. Peabody still wants NH to write about General Palmer (he has declined).

378. 7 November 1844, SH to Maria Louisa Hawthorne.
MS: NN-Berg. The Hawthornes now hope to come to Salem at the end of next week—NH has not finished his article yet.

379. 19 November 1844, SH to Mrs. Peabody, Salem.
MS: unrecovered. Published: Lathrop, *Memories*, pp. 77–79. The year of this letter is established by its place of origin. The year 1844 was the first time since their marriage that SH had visited Salem with NH. The letter is an account of Una's first meeting with her paternal relatives.

380. 19? November 1844, Mrs. Peabody to SH.
MS: unrecovered. Mentioned as received this morning in SH to Mrs. Peabody, 20 November 1844.

381. 20 November 1844, SH to Mrs. Peabody.
MS: NN-Berg. A lengthy account of the social whirl in Salem. Excellent details concerning finances. Elizabeth P. Peabody is here thanked for seeing George Bancroft on NH's behalf (seeking political appointment).

382. 25 November 1844, Mary Mann to SH, Wrentham.
MS: NN-Berg.

383. 29 November 1844, NH to Horatio Bridge, Salem.
MS: MeB. Published: Bridge, *Personal Recollections*, pp. 98–99. Bridge has just returned from Africa. NH details his prospects for political appointment.

384. November 1844, Horatio Bridge to NH.
MS: unrecovered. Mentioned in NH to Horatio Bridge, 29 November 1844, as just received. No doubt this letter announces Bridge's arrival in the United States and apparently asks if NH has gotten an appointment yet.

385. November? 1844, Mary Mann to SH.
MS: NN-Berg. Berg Collection's date is between 22 October and 25 November 1844.

386. 1? December 1844, SH to NH.
MS: unrecovered. Mentioned as received this morning in NH to SH, 2 December 1844.

387. 2 December 1844, Emerson to Samuel Gray Ward, Concord?.
MS: see Emerson, *Letters*. Published: Emerson, *Letters*, 3:267–68. Passing reference to NH on 3:267.

388. 2 December 1844, NH to SH, Salem.
MS: CSmH (HM 10969). Published: Hawthorne, *Love Letters*, 2:113–16. Arrangements to meet SH in Boston (he has remained in Salem while she returned to Boston).

389. 5? December 1844, SH to NH.
MS: unrecovered. Mentioned as received "today" in NH to SH, 6 December 1844.

390. 6 December 1844, NH to SH.
MS: CSmH (HM 10970). Published: Hawthorne, *Love Letters*, 2:117–19. The manuscript of the letter is not dated in holograph; *Love Letters* dates the letter simply "December, 1844," as does the Huntington. It is, however, clearly postmarked on 6 December. NH has decided to stay in Salem a little longer. This letter is rich in details about NH's solitary life in Salem.

391. 17 December 1844, NH to Park Benjamin, Boston?.
MS: unrecovered. Listed in the files of Professor Norman Holmes Pearson. The MS was sold by the Anderson Galleries on 23 January 1924 (Sale 1798).

392. 19 December 1844, SH to NH, Boston.
MS: unrecovered. Published: Lathrop, *Memories*, pp. 79–80. Details of SH taking Una to see long-time Boston friends. SH obviously misses her husband greatly.

393. 20 December 1844, NH to SH, Salem.
MS: CSmH (HM 10971). Published: Hawthorne, *Love Letters*, 2:120–23. NH has neither written to SH nor received any letters from her since 16 December, when he left Boston after a short visit and returned to Salem. He looks forward to their return to Concord on 28 December.

394. 1844?, Horatio Bridge to SH.
MS: unrecovered. Mentioned in NH to Horatio Bridge, 1 April 1844, as having been received some time in March 1844. The date is uncertain because it was mailed from the coast of Africa, where Bridge was serving with the U.S.S. *Saratoga*.

395. 1844?, Mrs. Peabody to SH.
MS: unrecovered. Quoted in Julian Hawthorne, *Notebook* (see this article, Part III), section entitled "Extracts from Letters," p. 12, under the date 1845?. Internal detail shows that the letter must be either 1843 or 1844, probably in the month of April or May. Refers to an unnamed article by NH published in a March issue of the *Democratic Review*.

1845

396. 5 January 1845, note from Horatio Bridge to SH, Concord.
MS: unrecovered. Published: Hawthorne, *Hawthorne & His Wife*, 1:282–83. Referred to in SH to Mrs. Peabody, 12 January 1845. A graceful, long note by Bridge when an ill SH was unable to see him.

397. 10 January 1845, Maria Lowell to SH, Philadelphia.
MS: NN-Berg. Published: Hawthorne, *Hawthorne & His Wife*, 1:283–84. The proper date could be 16 January, as given in *Hawthorne & His Wife*, and in the *Berg Catalog*—the holograph is difficult to interpret. Informs SH that the Lowells are now settled in Philadelphia.

398. 12 January 1845, SH to Mrs. Peabody, Concord.
MS: NN-Berg. Letter continues on 14 January. This letter is filed in two parts in the Berg: (1) one sheet dated 12 January; (2) two sheets filed under the date 14 January. A long letter, mostly about Una, but with good detail concerning NH's writing routine and recent visitors to Concord.

399. 16? January 1845, J. H. Adams to NH.
MS: unrecovered. Quoted in SH to Maria Louisa Hawthorne, 18 January 1845. Concerns some government securities which may belong to NH's family.

400. 16 January 1845, Maria Lowell to SH, Philadelphia.
See 10 January 1845.

Guide to Source Materials on the Old Manse Period 299

401. 18 January 1845, SH to Maria Louisa Hawthorne, Concord.
MS: NN-Berg. SH has misdated this letter 1844, but its references to Una surely date it 1845. Recounts events since SH and NH returned to Concord in late December 1844. SH requests that Louisa talk to the family to see whether there is any knowledge of their having owned U.S. securities.

402. 19 January 1845, NH to Horatio Bridge, Concord.
MS: MeB. Quoted: Harwell, *Hawthorne and Longfellow*, pp. 37–38. NH reports on progress with editing *Journal of an African Cruiser*.

403. 24? January 1845, Mrs. Peabody to SH.
MS: unrecovered. Mentioned as received in SH to Mrs. Peabody, 26 January 1845.

404. 26 January 1845, SH to Mrs. Peabody, Concord.
MS: NN-Berg. Published: partially in Lathrop, *Memories*, pp. 80–82; Hawthorne, *Hawthorne & His Wife*, 1:279. Letter continues on 27 January. Mostly details concerning Una, with a description of Concord's winter.

405. January 1845, two notes from SH to Elizabeth Hawthorne and/or Maria Louisa Hawthorne and/or Elizabeth Clark Manning Hawthorne.
MSS: unrecovered. These purport to be notes from Una, and are mentioned in SH to Mrs. Peabody, 26 January 1845, with which letter they were sent.

406. January? 1845, Mary Mann to SH.
MS: NN-Berg. Berg Collection's date is late January 1845. This letter may be referred to in SH to Mary Mann, 2 February 1845. Excellent narrative of the interests and projects of Horace Mann.

407. 2 February 1845, NH to J. H. Adams, Concord.
MS: Professor Norman Holmes Pearson. A noncommittal but interested reply to Adams' proposal of a possible windfall for NH in U.S. securities.

408. 2 February 1845, SH to Mary Mann, Concord.
MS: NN-Berg. The letter appears to be unfinished. Lengthy, valuable description of the Manse routine, together with remarks on Horace Mann's public leadership.

409. 12? February 1845, Horatio Bridge to NH.
MS: unrecovered. Mentioned as received yesterday in NH to Horatio Bridge, 16 February 1845.

410. 16 February 1845, NH and SH to Horatio Bridge, Concord.
MS: MeB. Quoted: Harwell, *Hawthorne and Longfellow*, p. 37. First half of the letter was written by SH at NH's request, then NH takes over to report on the editing of *Journal of an African Cruiser*. NH asks Bridge to look into the matter of U.S. securities.

411. 16 February 1845, SH to Mrs. Peabody, Concord.
MS: NN-Berg. SH has misdated this letter 1844, but it refers to Horatio Bridge to NH, 12? February 1845. Filed under the correct date at the Berg. Concerns NH and trips that he may have to take.

412. February? 1845, SH to Mrs. Peabody.
MS: NN-Berg. Berg Collection's date is 1844. It refers, however, to Una taking a walk through a winter landscape which is very similar to that described in SH to Mrs. Peabody, 26 January 1845. The first page of the letter is missing, and there is a hiatus in sense between pp. [2] and [3], indicating at least one other missing leaf.

413. 2 March 1845, NH to Evert A. Duyckinck, Concord.
MS: NN-Duyckinck. Offers *Journal of an African Cruiser* to Wiley & Putnam for publication as a book.

414. 6 March 1845, SH to Mrs. Peabody, Concord.
MS: NN-Berg. Published: partially in Hawthorne, *Hawthorne & His Wife*, 1:279–80. Notes NH's reading and the increasingly felt difficulty of obtaining books. SH recounts NH's opinion on the annexation of Texas and on slavery.

415. 13 March 1845, SH to Maria Louisa Hawthorne.
MS: NN-Berg. NH is most upset about his financial situation. The Hawthornes must vacate the Manse next spring.

416. 21 March 1845, Evert A. Duyckinck to NH, New York.
MS: unrecovered. Autograph copy is in Duyckinck Letter Book, NN-Duyckinck. Published: partially in Hawthorne, *Mosses from an Old Manse* (Centenary), p. 512. Initial proposal, on behalf of Wiley & Putnam, for a new collection of NH's tales. A long letter, entering into much concrete detail about the proposed volume.

417. 21 March 1845, John L. O'Sullivan to NH.
MS: unrecovered. Published: Hawthorne, *Hawthorne & His Wife*, 1:284–85. Mentioned in SH to Mrs. Peabody, 23 March 1845. O'Sullivan recounts his political and literary efforts on NH's behalf.

418. 23? March 1845, NH to John L. O'Sullivan.
MS: unrecovered. Mentioned in SH to Mrs. Peabody, 23 March 1845.

419. 23 March 1845, SH to Mrs. Peabody.
MS: NN-Berg. MS ends abruptly and may be incomplete. Concerns details of NH's search for a political appointment.

420. 27 March 1845, NH to Henry Wadsworth Longfellow, Concord.
MS: MH (bMS Am 1340.2 [2616], Folder I, Letter 13). Published: partially in Hawthorne, *American Notebooks* (ed. Stewart), p. 319, note 405. Noted as received 1 April in Longfellow to Duyckinck, 2 April 1845. NH reports that he cannot come to Cambridge now, but would like to see Stephen and H. W. Longfellow in Concord.

421. 28 March 1845, Mrs. Peabody to SH, Boston.
MS: unrecovered. Published: partially in Hawthorne, *Hawthorne & His Wife*, 1:267–68. A moralizing letter, mostly about the French reformer Charles Fourier.

422. March 1845, Mrs. Peabody to SH.
MS: unrecovered. Mentioned as received in SH to Mrs. Peabody, 23 March 1845.

Guide to Source Materials on the Old Manse Period 301

423. 2 April 1845, Henry Wadsworth Longfellow to Evert A. Duyckinck, Cambridge.
MS: NN-Duyckinck. Published: Longfellow, *Letters*, 3:61. Text reliable. Longfellow wishes NH good political fortune.

424. 4? April 1845, Horatio Bridge to NH.
MS: unrecovered. Mentioned as received ca. 7 April in NH to Horatio Bridge, 17 April 1845.

425. 4? April 1845, Mary Mann to SH.
MS: NN-Berg. Answered by SH to Mary Mann, 6 April 1845. Mary has heard that the Hawthornes will leave Concord in June.

426. 5? April 1845, Mary Mann to SH.
MS: unrecovered. Mentioned as received this morning in SH to Mary Mann, 7 April 1845.

427. 6 April 1845, SH to Mary Mann.
MS: NN-Berg. Published: partially in Hawthorne, *Hawthorne & His Wife*, 1:268–69. The Hawthornes now have no idea where they might go when they leave Concord.

428. 6 April 1845, SH to Mrs. Peabody.
MS: NN-Berg. Describes reading of Fourier and unfavorably describes Theodore Parker's character.

429. 7 April 1845, NH to Evert A. Duyckinck, Concord.
MS: NN-Duyckinck. Published: partially in Hawthorne, *Mosses from an Old Manse* (Centenary), pp. 512–13. This letter accompanies the finished MS of *Journal of an African Cruiser*, and includes plans for what will eventually become *Mosses from an Old Manse*.

430. 7 April 1845, SH to Mary Mann.
MS: NN-Berg. Letter runs to 8 April. It is possible that this letter was sent with SH to Mary Mann, 6 April 1845. The latter MS was not posted. The Manns evidently plan to stay in Concord during the coming summer, and SH has found them a boarding situation.

431. 10 April 1845, Mary Mann to SH, Boston.
MS: NN-Berg. The letter answers SH to Mary Mann, 7 April 1845.

432. 15? April 1845, Evert A. Duyckinck to NH.
MS: unrecovered. Mentioned in NH to Horatio Bridge, 17 April 1845. Accepts *Journal of an African Cruiser* for publication.

433. 17 April 1845, NH to Horatio Bridge, Concord.
MS: MeB. Published: Bridge, *Personal Recollections*, pp. 100–101. NH reports the acceptance of *Journal of an African Cruiser* and the progress of his search for political appointment.

434. 19 April 1845, John L. O'Sullivan to George Bancroft.
MS: MHi. Concerns a government post for NH.

435. 19 April 1845, S. J. Thomas to George Bancroft.
MS: MHi. Thomas opposes the rumored consideration of NH for a government post.

436. 30? April 1845, Evert A. Duyckinck to NH.
MS: unrecovered. Mentioned in NH to Horatio Bridge, 2 May 1845. Reports progress with the printing of *Journal of an African Cruiser.*

437. 2 May 1845, NH to Horatio Bridge, Concord.
MS: MeB. Published: Bridge, *Personal Recollections,* pp. 101–102. Relays information furnished by Duyckinck in his 30? April letter to NH and reports NH's response to Duyckinck.

438. 2 May 1845, NH to Evert A. Duyckinck, Concord.
MS: NN-Duyckinck. NH reports lack of progress with new material for *Mosses from an Old Manse* and arranges details concerning *Journal of an African Cruiser.*

439. 4 May 1845, SH to Mary Caleb Foote, Concord.
MS: unrecovered. Published: Lathrop, *Memories,* p. 82. Description of the Concord spring and an invitation for Mary to visit.

440. 7 May 1845, NH to Horatio Bridge, Concord.
MS: MeB. Published: Bridge, *Personal Recollections,* pp. 102–103. Advice concerning the proper placement for free copies of *Journal of an African Cruiser* in order to ensure critical attention.

441. 10 May 1845, John L. O'Sullivan to George Bancroft.
MS: MHi. Concerns a government post for NH.

442. 11 May 1845, Franklin Pierce to George Bancroft.
MS: MHi. Concerns a government post for NH.

442.5. 22 May 1845, Margaret Fuller to NH and SH, New York.
MS: NN-Berg. Comments on Una and on the Hawthornes' reaction to a recent "pamphlet" which Margaret has published.

443. 23 May 1845, NH to SH, Boston.
MS: CSmH (HM 10979). Published: Hawthorne, *Love Letters,* 2:151–52. NH describes a visit to Boston and gives his arrival date for the return to Concord (next Monday—26 May).

444. 27 May 1845, SH to Mary Caleb Foote, Concord.
MS: NN-Berg. SH again invites Mary to visit Concord.

445. 31 May 1845, John L. O'Sullivan to George Bancroft.
MS: MHi. Concerns a government post for NH.

445.5 May? 1845, SH to Margaret Fuller.
MS: unrecovered. Mentioned in Margaret Fuller to NH and SH, 22 May 1845.

446. May 1845, SH to Mrs. Peabody.
MS: NN-Berg. Published: Hawthorne, *Hawthorne & His Wife,* 1:280–81. The letter is dated, in holograph, only Sunday, May 1845. Probably written either 18 or 25 May. SH recounts social details of the last week, particularly NH's meetings with Bridge and Franklin Pierce to plan strategy for seeking governmental office.

447. 4? June 1845, Horace Conolly to NH.
MS: unrecovered. Mentioned as received about a week ago in NH to Horatio Bridge, 11 June 1845.

448. 4 June 1845, John L. O'Sullivan to George Bancroft.
MS: MHi. Yet another letter about a political appointment for NH.

449. 11 June 1845, NH to Horatio Bridge, Concord.
MS: MeB. The first two pages of this letter are an undated enclosure by SH, with a postscript by NH. The whole package is sometimes dated 16 June (the MS bears this date in an unknown hand, most likely Bridge's), but the postmark is 11 June. SH recommends their maid, Mary Pray, for employment by Bridge. NH writes of political prospects.

450. 28 June 1845, NH to Pomeroy Jones, Concord.
MS: NN-Berg. Published: Hawthorne, *Complete Writings*, 17:426. NH replies to an autograph seeker.

451. 1 July 1845, NH to Evert A. Duyckinck, Concord.
MS: NN-Duyckinck. Published: partially in Hawthorne, *Mosses from an Old Manse* (Centenary), p. 514. NH describes initial plan for "The Old Manse." Interesting comments on Emerson and Thoreau.

452. 1 July 1845, SH to Caroline Sturgis.
MS: unrecovered. Mentioned as having been written in SH to Horatio Bridge, 4 July 1845.

453. 2? July 1845, Horatio Bridge to NH.
MS: unrecovered. Mentioned as just received in SH to Horatio Bridge, 4 July 1845.

454. 4 July 1845, SH to Horatio Bridge, Concord.
MS: MeB. Postmarked 5 July. Postscript by NH. SH gives her favorable commentary on *Journal of an African Cruiser* and makes arrangements for the Hawthornes to visit Bridge at Portsmouth.

455. 11 July 1845, John L. O'Sullivan to George Bancroft.
MS: MHi. O'Sullivan seeking political appointment for NH.

456. July 1845, SH to Maria Louisa Hawthorne.
MS: NN-Berg. I have assigned this date to the letter. It is filed at the Berg as no. 37 of a run of 38 A.L.S. from SH to Louisa. Its text largely concerns plans for a trip to Portsmouth to see Horatio Bridge—the trip began ca. 24 July 1845. Postscript by NH.

457. 4 August 1845, John L. O'Sullivan to George Bancroft.
MS: MHi. Another O'Sullivan salvo in the battle for an NH appointment to political office.

458. 8 August 1845, Mary Mann to SH, Concord.
MS: NN-Berg. Mary keeps SH posted on Concord doings (SH and NH are now in Portsmouth, New Hampshire).

459. 13 August 1845, Evert A. Duyckinck to NH.
MS: unrecovered. Autograph copy in Duyckinck Letter Book, NN-Duyckinck.

Mentioned as received yesterday in NH to Horatio Bridge, 19 August 1845. Amid other business, Duyckinck asks NH to write a history of New England witchcraft.

460. 13? August 1845, NH to SH.
MS: unrecovered. Mentioned in SH to NH, 15 August 1845.

461. 13? August 1845, John L. O'Sullivan to NH.
MS: unrecovered. Mentioned in SH to NH, 15 August 1845, and enclosed with this letter. Also mentioned as not yet received, but as read by SH, in NH to Horatio Bridge, 19 August 1845.

462. 15 August 1845, SH to NH, Boston.
MS: NN-Berg. Published: partially in Lathrop, *Memories*, p. 77. Mailed from Boston to Salem and then forwarded from Salem to Concord on 21 August. Interesting commentary on offers from O'Sullivan ("the Count") and Bancroft ("the Blatant Beast").

463. 16? August 1845, Horatio Bridge to NH.
MS: unrecovered. Mentioned as just now received in NH to Horatio Bridge, 19 August 1845.

464. 17 August 1845, SH to Mrs. Peabody.
MS: NN-Berg. Possibly, this letter was never sent—see next item. SH describes return to Concord and the relationship between Una and Horace Mann, Jr.

465. 17 August 1845, SH to Mrs. Peabody.
MS: NN-Berg. The letter continues on 21 August. The first part of the letter is a copy of item 464. Complains of George Ripley's (of Brook Farm) failure to pay NH a debt.

466. 19 August 1845, NH to Horatio Bridge, Concord.
MS: MeB. Published: Bridge, *Personal Recollections*, pp. 103–104. NH gives political news and relays data concerning *Journal of an African Cruiser*.

467. 24 August 1845, SH to Maria Louisa Hawthorne.
MS: NN-Berg. Postscript by NH. The Hawthornes now expect to leave Concord in November. SH asks Louisa to see if Mr. Manning will rent them part of the house in which the Salem Hawthornes now live. Excellent financial detail.

468. 24 August 1845, John L. O'Sullivan to George Bancroft.
MS: MHi. Concerns the negotiations for NH's political appointment.

469. 27? August 1845, Horatio Bridge to NH.
MS: unrecovered. Mentioned as received on 29 August in SH to Horatio Bridge, 30 August 1845.

470. 30 August 1845, SH to Horatio Bridge, Concord.
MS: MeB. Note concerning Mary Pray's employment by Bridge.

471. 30 August 1845, SH to Mary Pray.
MS: unrecovered. Mentioned in SH to Horatio Bridge, 30 August 1845.

Guide to Source Materials on the Old Manse Period 305

472. 30? August 1845, Samuel Ripley to NH.
MS: unrecovered. Mentioned as received on 1 September in SH to Maria Louisa Hawthorne, 1 September 1845.

473. August 1845, Mary Pray to SH.
MS: unrecovered. Mentioned as received this week in SH to Horatio Bridge, 30 August 1845.

474. 1 September 1845, Emerson to James Elliot Cabot, Concord.
MS: see Emerson, *Letters*. Published: Emerson, *Letters*, 3:298–99. Passing reference to NH on 3:299.

475. 1 September 1845, NH to Samuel Ripley.
MS: unrecovered. Mentioned as written in SH to Maria Louisa Hawthorne, 1 September 1845.

476. 1 September 1845, SH to Maria Louisa Hawthorne, Concord.
MS: NN-Berg. SH begins to sound a little desperate—Louisa has not answered her 24 August letter and Ripley now wants them out of the house by next week!

477. 3 September 1845, Maria Louisa Hawthorne to SH, Salem.
MS: NN-Berg. Mr. Manning is not sure that he wants to rent to the Hawthornes. Louisa is not happy with him. Discusses details of projected move.

478. 4 September 1845, SH to Maria Louisa Hawthorne.
MS: NN-Berg. The rent Mr. Manning wants to charge is exorbitant, but the Hawthornes have no choice. Details of moving plans.

479. 5? September 1845, Elizabeth P. Peabody to SH.
MS: unrecovered. Mentioned as just received in SH to Mrs. Peabody, 7 September 1845. Concerns Bancroft's political efforts on NH's behalf.

480. 5? September 1845, Mrs. Peabody to SH.
MS: unrecovered. Mentioned as just received in SH to Mrs. Peabody, 7 September 1845.

481. 6 September 1845, NH to George Hillard, Concord.
MS: NRU. Published: Metzdorf, "Hawthorne's Suit," 236. Text reliable. NH directs Hillard to sue Ripley (of Brook Farm) for collection of a debt.

482. 7 September 1845, SH to Mrs. Peabody.
MS: NN-Berg. Published: Hawthorne, *Hawthorne & His Wife*, 1:286–87. Lengthy, valuable letter summing up the Old Manse years. SH goes into much detail on NH's financial situation. A half page has been crossed out by NH (according to a note by SH) because it divulges political secrets. Crossed-out portions seem largely decipherable.

483. 12 September 1845, Maria Louisa Hawthorne to SH, Salem.
MS: NN-Berg. Published: partially in Gordan, "Nathaniel Hawthorne," 211. This letter includes a diagram of the front parlor of the Hawthornes' Herbert Street home in Salem. Upon persistent urging, Mr. Manning has agreed to rent to the Hawthornes.

484. 21? September 1845, NH to Horatio Bridge.
MS: unrecovered. Mentioned in NH to Horatio Bridge, 28 September 1845, as probably having arrived on Tuesday, 23 September, while Bridge was away from his home. NH must borrow money from Bridge.

485. 22 September 1845, SH to Maria Louisa Hawthorne.
MS: NN-Berg. SH gives details of the planned move—she plans to restrict her social life very much while living in Salem, largely, it seems, out of deference to the solitary habits of NH's mother and sister Elizabeth.

486. 28 September 1845, Horatio Bridge to NH.
MS: unrecovered. A copy in Bridge's hand is at MeB. Bridge has just received NH's letter of 21 September. He will send $150 as soon as he can get to the bank.

487. 28 September 1845, Maria Louisa Hawthorne to SH, Salem.
MS: NN-Berg. Salem is expecting NH to arrive on Friday (3 October).

488. 28 September 1845, NH to Horatio Bridge, Concord.
MS: MeB. Partially published in Hawthorne, *American Notebooks* (ed. Stewart), p. 300, note 222. A second letter concerning the requested $150 loan.

489. 2 October 1845, Evert A. Duyckinck to Emerson.
MS: see Emerson, *Letters*. Published: partially in Emerson, *Letters*, 3:308.

490. 2 October 1845, Evert A. Duyckinck to NH, New York.
MS: MeB. Autograph copy in Duyckinck Letter Book, NN-Duyckinck. Published: Bridge, *Personal Recollections*, p. 106. Duyckinck encourages NH to get on with *Mosses* and announces a second edition of *Journal of an African Cruiser*.

491. 2 October 1845, Emerson to William Emerson, Concord.
MS: see Emerson, *Letters*. Published: Emerson, *Letters*, 3:305–306. Text reliable. Announces NH's departure from Concord "today."

492. 6? October 1845, SH to NH.
MS: unrecovered. Mentioned as just arrived in NH to SH, 7 October 1845.

493. 7 October 1845, NH to Horatio Bridge, Salem.
MS: MeB. Published: Bridge, *Personal Recollections*, pp. 105–106. NH tells Bridge of the move to Salem. $100 from O'Sullivan allowed him to pay his debts in Concord. This letter enclosed Duyckinck to NH, 2 October 1845.

494. 7 October 1845, NH to SH.
MS: CSmH (HM 10952). Published: Hawthorne, *Love Letters*, 2:176–78. This publication misdates the letter as 7 October 1847. For the correct date, see Stewart, "Letters to Sophia." The letter is postmarked 8 October. NH tells SH, who is in Boston, of events since his arrival in Salem.

495. 10 October 1845, NH to Evert A. Duyckinck, Salem.
MS: NN-Duyckinck. Published: partially in Hawthorne, "Two Uncollected Reviews," 505. Also in Weber, "Hawthornes Briefe." NH is having great

Guide to Source Materials on the Old Manse Period 307

difficulty in writing the new piece needed for *Mosses*. He announces his move to Salem.

496. 29 October 1845, NH to Edmund Hosmer, Salem.
MS: NCaS. NH pays his Concord highway tax, which he had forgotten.

497. 10 November 1845, NH to SH, Salem.
MS: CSmH. Published: Hawthorne, *Love Letters*, 2:158–60. NH still having much trouble with writing.

498. 24 December 1845, NH to Evert A. Duyckinck, Salem.
MS: NN-Duyckinck. Published: partially in Hawthorne, *Mosses from an Old Manse* (Centenary), p. 516. Lengthy description of NH's difficulty in writing "The Old Manse."

499. 1845?, NH to Horatio Bridge.
MS: MeB. Published: Bridge, *Personal Recollections*, p. 108. This MS is a six-line fragment of a letter with NH's autograph attached. NH writes thanks for a gift of animal skins which Bridge sent SH just after he returned from Africa.

500. 1845?, Mrs. Peabody to SH.
MS: unrecovered. Published: Hawthorne, *Hawthorne & His Wife*, 1:258–59. This letter undoubtedly refers to Margaret Fuller's *Woman in the Nineteenth Century*, published in February 1845. July seems a probable date for the letter on the strength of Julian's statement that it was written on the same day as SH to Mrs. Peabody, 1843? (*Hawthorne & His Wife*, 1:256–57). The latter letter was almost certainly written in July.

501. 1845? (1846?), NH to Frank Farley.
MS: CtY. A short fragment concerning the imminent collapse of Brook Farm.

1846

502. 22? January 1846, Evert A. Duyckinck to NH.
MS: unrecovered. Mentioned as just received in NH to Duyckinck, 24 January 1846.

503. 24 January 1846, NH to Evert A. Duyckinck, Salem.
MS: NN-Duyckinck. Published: partially in Hawthorne, *Mosses from an Old Manse* (Centenary), p. 517. NH agrees to publish *Mosses* in two volumes, declaring that this will be the last of his short fiction.

504. 21 February 1846, NH to Horatio Bridge, Salem.
MS: MeB. Published: partially in Harwell, *Hawthorne and Longfellow*, p. 39. Political and literary news.

505. 22 February 1846, NH to Evert A. Duyckinck, Salem.
MS: NN-Duyckinck. Published: partially in Hawthorne, *Mosses from an Old Manse* (Centenary), pp. 517–18. Accompanies the first batch of copy for *Mosses* and speculates on its title.

506. 22 February 1846, SH to Mrs. Peabody.
MS: unrecovered. Published: Lathrop, *Memories*, pp. 84–85. Accompanies a package for Duyckinck (copy for *Mosses*).

507. 1 March 1846, NH to Horatio Bridge, Salem.
MS: MeB. Mentions *Mosses* as most likely in press by this time.

508. 3 March 1846, NH to Epes Sargent, Salem.
MS: NCaS. Published: Hawthorne, "Three Letters," 103–104. Text reliable. Thanks Sargent for $10 payment and for tearsheets which NH wants to use to prepare *Mosses* copy. NH also writes here of politics.

509. 13 March 1846, Evert A. Duyckinck to NH.
MS: unrecovered. Autograph copy in Duyckinck Letter Book, NN-Duyckinck. Published: partially in Jay Leyda, *The Melville Log: A Documentary Life of Herman Melville, 1819–1891* (New York: Harcourt Brace & Co., 1951), 1:206. Reports progress with the printing of *Mosses*, although he has not received copy for volume 1.

510. 15 April 1846, NH to Evert A. Duyckinck, Salem.
MS: NN-Duyckinck. Published: partially in *First Editions*, p. 25, as written on 18 April. Accompanies all remaining copy for *Mosses* and speculates on literary plans for the future.

511. 18 April 1846, NH to Wiley & Putnam, Salem.
MS: Universiteitsbibliotheek van Amsterdam. NH draws on his publishers for a $100 advance.

512. 30 April 1846, NH to Evert A. Duyckinck, Salem.
MS: NN-Duyckinck. Published: partially in Hawthorne, *Mosses from an Old Manse* (Centenary), p. 520. Directions for the distribution of fifty free copies of *Mosses*.

513. 29 May 1846, NH to Evert A. Duyckinck, Salem.
MS: NN-Duyckinck. Published: partially in *First Editions*, p. 26. Additional directions for the distribution of *Mosses* presentation copies.

514. 10 June 1846, NH to Evert A. Duyckinck, Boston.
MS: NN-Duyckinck. Published: partially in Hawthorne, *Mosses from an Old Manse* (Centenary), p. 520. Yet more instructions regarding presentation copies of *Mosses*.

515. 17 June 1846, NH to Rufus W. Griswold, Salem.
MS: PHi. Note announcing NH's gift of a copy of *Mosses*.

516. 17 June 1846, NH to E. A. Poe, Salem.
MS: Mr. H. Bradley Martin, New York City. Published: partially in Hawthorne, *Mosses from an Old Manse* (Centenary), p. 534. NH writes to announce a presentation copy of *Mosses*.

517. 18 June 1846, NH to H. T. Tuckerman.
MS: Mr. C. E. Frazer Clark, Jr. NH announces a presentation copy of *Mosses*.

518. 21 June 1846, SH to Maria Louisa Hawthorne, Boston.
MS: NN-Berg. Postscript by NH dated 22 June. SH notes a presentation copy of *Mosses* for "Miss Burley," signed by "Una." Postscript announces Julian Hawthorne's birth.

519. June 1846, Evert A. Duyckinck to NH.
MS: unrecovered. Mentioned as forwarded from Salem in NH to Evert A. Duyckinck, 10 June 1846.

520. 29 August 1846, NH to Amory Holbrook, Salem.
MS: Professor Norman Holmes Pearson. Announces a gift of *Mosses* for the Salem Athenæum.

521. 26 October 1846, NH to Horatio Bridge.
MS: NN-Berg. Published: partially in Hawthorne, *Mosses from an Old Manse* (Centenary), p. 521. Mentions the good acceptance of *Mosses*.

522. 20 December 1846, SH to Horatio Bridge.
MS: MeB. Mentions a bound copy of *Mosses* sent to Bridge a long time ago.

PART III: MISCELLANEOUS MS MATERIAL

523. Julian Hawthorne, *Notebook: Memorandum of Letters Received, etc.*
MS: NNPM (MA1375). Julian evidently used this notebook as a working record during the composition of his biography, *Nathaniel Hawthorne and His Wife*. The volume is dated June 1882, and is signed on the first leaf. It contains lists of primary documents he has seen and some extracts from material which has since disappeared, including several letters from Mrs. Peabody to her daughter. In addition, there are what appear to be first drafts of material later used in the biography. The whole amounts to about eighty-five pages in holograph.

524. Nathaniel Hawthorne. In the record book of the Concord Athenæum.
MS: MCo. Page 30 is headed "Mr N Howthorn," and contains a series of dates, evidently from 1842–43, with small amounts of money entered opposite each date. Another page, headed "Strangers," contains three NH signatures, by which method he temporarily introduced David Roberts, Francis D. Farley, and George P. Bradford to the privileges of the Athenæum.

525. Nathaniel and Sophia Hawthorne, "The American Notebooks."
MSS: NNPM. Three volumes are relevant to the Old Manse Period: (A) "American Notebooks," MA 577–9, vol. 2:1841–52; (B) "Journal," MA 580, vol. 1:1842–43; and (C) "Journal," MA 569, vol. 2:1844–54. All the NH entries in these journals and notebooks have been published reliably in *The American Notebooks*, ed. Claude Simpson (Centenary). There are considerable amounts of Sophia Hawthorne material that remain unpublished, although many of her entries have been razored out of the manuscripts, presumably by SH herself. Item "C," above, begins with ten pages of SH's description of events early in Una's life.

526. Nathaniel and Sophia Hawthorne, "Account Book."
MS: unrecovered. Mentioned in SH to Mrs. Peabody, 2 June 1843. This was evidently a complete record of income and expenses, probably begun shortly after the Hawthornes' marriage.

527. Nathaniel and Sophia Hawthorne, a deed.
DS: unrecovered. Evidently this deed was signed by both SH and NH on

24 February 1843, before a Concord Justice of the Peace named Daniel Shattuck. See SH to Mrs. Peabody, 28 February 1843.

528. Sophia Hawthorne, six pencil drawings from John Flaxman.
MSS: NNPM (MA 1843). A note by Julian Hawthorne identifies these as dating from about 1842. More exactly, they appear to have been done on 10–13 January 1843. See SH to Mrs. Peabody, 12 January 1843, and SH to Maria Louisa Hawthorne, 29 January 1843.

INDEX TO NAMES OF PERSONS

Note: The numbers listed refer to Calendar items. SH and NH are not indexed.

Adams, J. H., 399, 407
Alcott, A. Bronson, 1, 109, 123, 126, 155
Allston, Washington, 197
Appleton, Frances, 177

Bancroft, George, 211, 381, 434, 435, 441, 442, 445, 448, 455, 457, 462, 468, 479
Benjamin, Park, 391
"Billings, Mr.," 143
Bowers, Fredson, 4
Bradford, George P., 524
Bridge, Horatio, 2, 147, 167, 170, 318, 363, 383, 384, 394, 396, 402, 409, 410, 411, 424, 432, 433, 436, 437, 440, 446, 447, 449, 452, 453, 454, 456, 459, 461, 463, 466, 469, 470, 471, 473, 484, 486, 488, 490, 493, 499, 504, 507, 521, 522
Bridges, Laura, 97
Brownson, Orestes, 114, 115
"Burley, Miss," 518

Cabot, James Elliot, 474
Carter, Robert, 31, 78, 85, 119, 125, 127, 129, 131, 135
Channing, Ellen Fuller, 300
Channing, Ellery, 82, 86, 155, 280
Channing, Mary, 64, 82
Channing, Dr. Walter, 80, 214
Channing, William Ellery, 97
Chase, Annie, 213, 295
Clark, C. E. Frazer, Jr., 3, 55, 69, 120, 161, 177, 187, 196, 199, 234, 276, 311, 517
Clarke, Sarah, 256, 257
Colman, Samuel, 199, 224, 225
Conolly, Horace, 211, 316, 341, 342, 447
Cowley, Malcolm, 21
Crowley, Joseph Donald, 4, 20
Curtis, George William, 5, 355

Dall, Caroline Healey, 6
Dana, Charles A., 36, 48, 101
"Davis, Miss," 369
Duyckinck, Evert A., 229, 234, 240, 413, 416, 420, 423, 429, 432, 436, 437, 438, 451, 459, 489, 490, 493, 495, 498, 502, 503, 505, 506, 509, 510, 512, 513, 514, 519

Emerson, Mrs. Lydia, 84, 115, 247
Emerson, Ralph Waldo, 7, 8, 9, 37, 44, 49, 50, 51, 52, 53, 54, 57, 58, 66, 92, 104, 105, 106, 107, 113, 114, 120, 128, 155, 165, 174, 175, 185, 195, 198, 201, 204, 205, 218, 220, 227, 231, 260, 283, 286, 326, 387, 451, 474, 489, 491
Emerson, William, 51, 58, 106, 491

Farley, Francis D., 100, 347, 350, 501, 524
Ferguson, Alfred R., 8
Flaxman, John, 528
Follen, Mrs. Eliza, 265
Foote, Caleb, 46, 221
Foote, Mary Caleb, 46, 55, 59.5, 111, 134, 152, 153, 156, 207, 213, 221, 226, 285, 295, 302, 329, 330, 439, 444
Forbes, Rose, 253
Fourier, Charles, 421, 428
Frost, "John," 308
Fuller, Margaret: *see* Ossoli, Margaret Fuller

Gardner, Sally, 253
Gilman, William H., 8
Gneuss, Helmut, 47
Goodrich, Samuel Griswold, 40, 225
Gordan, John D., 11, 62, 63, 66, 75, 78, 81, 84, 483

Guide to Source Materials on the Old Manse Period 311

"Graham," 289, 294
Greene, Mr., 211
Griswold, Rufus W., 12, 189, 191, 289, 294, 515
Griswold, W. M., 12

Harwell, Richard, 13, 402, 410, 504
Hawthorne, Elizabeth (NH's sister), 327, 405, 485
Hawthorne, Elizabeth Clark Manning (NH's mother), 313, 314, 327, 368, 369, 405, 485
Hawthorne, Julian (NH's son), 14, 65, 82, 88, 96, 98, 126, 136, 152, 164, 182, 190, 197, 209, 271, 286, 287, 298, 309, 320, 324, 372, 373, 395, 396, 397, 404, 414, 417, 421, 427, 446, 500, 518, 523, 528
Hawthorne, Manning (NH's great-grandson), 15, 61, 77
Hawthorne, Maria Louisa (NH's sister), 15, 61, 77, 81, 84, 89, 90, 99, 100, 107, 120, 130, 139, 140, 158, 161, 177, 178, 187, 188, 196, 200, 201, 202, 203, 217, 219, 222, 223, 228, 229, 234, 242, 245, 261, 262, 273, 276, 282, 297, 305, 307, 310, 311, 313, 316, 327, 331, 332, 357, 358, 363, 364, 368, 369, 372, 375, 376, 378, 399, 401, 405, 415, 456, 467, 472, 475, 476, 477, 478, 483, 485, 487, 518, 528
Hawthorne, Una (NH's daughter), 253, 298, 307, 309, 310, 311, 312, 314, 316, 318, 324, 326, 327, 330, 331, 337, 339, 345, 361, 362, 364, 370, 371, 376, 379, 392, 398, 401, 404, 405, 412, 445.5, 464, 518, 525
Hedge, Frederic Henry, 105
Henry, Mr. and Mrs. Donald, 336
Higginson, Thomas W., 25, 155, 185
Hilen, Andrew, 29
Hillard, George S., 66, 71, 74, 81, 201, 241, 275, 289, 294, 309, 315, 335, 336, 342, 346, 367, 481
Hillard, Susan, 71, 74, 201
Hoar, Elizabeth, 49, 66
Holbrook, Amory, 520
Hooper, Ellen S., 117, 253, 268
Hosmer, Edmund, 496
Howe, Julia Ward, 26
Howe, Dr. Samuel G., 97
Hübner, Walter, 47
Hunt, Benjamin Peter, 205

Johnson, Quentin G., 31, 125, 127, 129
Jones, Pomeroy, 450

Lane, Charles, 109
Lathrop, George Parsons, 27
Lathrop, Rose Hawthorne (NH's daughter), 28, 59.5, 111, 117, 156, 179, 207, 226, 231, 238, 283, 285, 290, 292, 302, 312, 365, 379, 392, 404, 439, 462, 506, 529
Leyda, Jay, 509
Longfellow, Henry Wadsworth, 13, 29, 30, 108, 112, 116, 144, 145, 177, 211, 402, 410, 420, 423, 504
Longfellow, Samuel, 30, 108, 112
Longfellow, Stephen, 420
Lowell, James Russell, 31, 32, 97, 110, 125, 127, 129, 138, 158, 159, 161, 162, 173, 284, 397
Lowell, Maria, 97, 397, 400

McDonald, John J., 24, 33, 34, 35, 199, 367
Mann, Horace, 149, 150, 151, 154, 157, 166, 168, 169, 231, 251, 285, 293, 301, 303, 406, 408
Mann, Horace, Jr., 371, 464
Mann, Mary Peabody (SH's sister), 55, 63, 67, 68, 92, 97, 109, 118, 119, 123, 136, 148, 149, 150, 151, 157, 161, 163, 166, 168, 169, 171, 180, 181, 206, 218, 230, 231, 233, 235, 251, 254, 266, 277, 281, 285, 293, 296, 299, 300, 301, 303, 306, 323, 326, 328, 333, 361, 362, 371, 374, 382, 385, 406, 408, 425, 426, 427, 430, 431, 458
"Manning, Mr.," 467, 477, 478, 483
Manning, Robert, 99, 100
Martin, H. Bradley, 516
Melville, Herman, 509
Metzdorf, Robert F., 36, 481
Munroe, James & Co., 94, 336, 353
Myerson, Joel, 6, 37, 41

Newcomb, Charles King, 50, 124
Norton, Catherine Eliot, 145

O'Brien, Mary, 103, 263, 271, 355, 356, 365, 377
O'Brien, Michael, 263
Orth, Ralph H., 8
Osgood, James R., 14
Ossoli, Margaret Fuller, 6, 37, 52, 53, 57, 81, 82, 86, 104, 124, 132, 204, 260, 286, 300, 442.5, 445.5, 500

Ostrom, John Ward, 39
O'Sullivan, John L., 38, 78, 122, 123, 128, 143, 192, 202, 239, 246, 253, 272, 288, 330, 336, 346, 353, 417, 418, 434, 441, 445, 448, 455, 457, 461, 462, 468, 493
Palmer, General, 373, 377
Parker, Theodore, 146, 428
Parsons, J. E., 8
Peabody, Elizabeth P. (SH's sister), 119, 206, 215, 218, 381, 479
Peabody, Mrs. Elizabeth P. (SH's mother), 62, 63, 64, 65, 66, 72, 73, 74, 75, 76, 79, 80, 81, 83, 84, 88, 91, 92, 93, 95, 96, 98, 103, 113, 114, 115, 121, 122, 126, 133, 134, 135, 137, 138, 146, 148, 152, 157, 158, 160, 163, 164, 169, 171, 172, 176, 178, 179, 180, 182, 183, 184, 186, 190, 193, 194, 197, 201, 206, 208, 209, 210, 211, 214, 215, 216, 218, 232, 233, 235, 236, 237, 238, 243, 244, 248, 250, 252, 255, 258, 264, 267, 269, 271, 278, 286, 287, 289, 290, 291, 292, 298, 304, 312, 317, 319, 320, 324, 325, 326, 333, 334, 337, 339, 345, 354, 355, 356, 359, 360, 364, 365, 366, 370, 372, 373, 377, 379, 380, 381, 395, 396, 398, 403, 404, 405, 411, 412, 414, 417, 418, 419, 421, 422, 428, 446, 464, 465, 479, 480, 482, 500, 506, 523, 526, 527, 528, 529
Peabody, Nathaniel (SH's brother), 370
Peabody, Dr. Nathaniel (SH's father), 176, 319, 320, 324
Pearson, Norman Holmes, 69, 336, 368, 391, 407, 520
Pickman, Mary, 270
Pierce, Franklin, 442, 446
Poe, Edgar Allan, 32, 39, 158, 159, 161, 162, 164, 173, 284, 516
Pray, Mary, 449, 470, 471, 473

"Quincy, Miss," 60
"Quincy, Mrs.," 136, 300

Riesner, Dieter, 47
Ripley, George, 36, 233, 465, 481
Ripley, Samuel, 472, 475, 476
Roberts, David, 93, 95, 208, 222, 524
Roselle, Daniel, 40, 225
Rusk, Ralph L., 9, 114

Sampson, Edward C., 22
Sanborn, Franklin B., 7, 41, 45
"Sarah," 103
Sargent, Epes, 22, 102, 138, 508
Shattuck, Daniel, 527
Shaw, Anna, 186, 253
Shaw, Mary, 253
Shaw, Sarah, 186
Shepard, Odell, 1
Simpson, Claude, 525
Stewart, Randall, 16, 23, 42, 43, 132, 143, 183, 211, 240, 420, 488, 494
Sturgis, Mrs., 259, 274, 279
Sturgis, Caroline, 69, 70, 452

Tappan & Dennet, 87
Thomas, S. J., 435
Thoreau, Henry D., 7, 44, 45, 84, 95, 102, 103, 120, 122, 128, 174, 175, 185, 192, 195, 198, 220, 227, 249, 451
Tileston, Mary Wilder, 46, 221
Tuckerman, Henry T., 517

Volz, Robert L., 38

Ward, Samuel Gray, 387
Waterston, Robert Cassie, 87, 322
Weber, Alfred, 47, 495
Webster, Daniel, 208, 210, 222
Wheeler, Charles Stearns, 165
Wiley & Putnam, 413, 416, 511
Wilson, James Harrison, 48, 101
Wise, Henry A., 38, 239
Woodberry, George E., 32

Young, John R., 19

HAWTHORNE: THE WRITER AS DREAMER

Rita K. Gollin

NATHANIEL HAWTHORNE'S contradictory assumptions about dreams derive from his literary heritage and his assumptions about the mind itself, and they define a recurrent tension of his life. Especially during his bachelor years, he was tormented by fear that dreaming might consume him. So frequently did he describe himself as a dreamer, in relatively formal letters and prefaces as well as in intimate letters to Sophia, that we cannot attribute the term to mere sentimental whimsy. It conveys the facts of his relatively isolated life, his ambivalence about it, and his implicit hope that his dreaming might end. But even when he was married, a father, and a famous writer, he worried about the significance of his dreams.

Calling himself a dreamer, he renewed anxieties about his role as writer. He accused himself of passivity and uselessness, of falling victim to his own imagination. The indictment is fully stated in his letter acknowledging Longfellow's praise of *Twice-Told Tales*. He is an enchanted dreamer in a shadowed dungeon. "For the last ten years, I have not lived, but only dreamed about living," he wrote. He denies responsibility: "By some witchcraft or other...I have been carried apart from the main current of life, and find it impossible to get back again." Yet his passivity is itself at fault: "I have ... put me into a dungeon; and now I cannot find the key to let myself out—and if the door were open, I should be almost afraid to come out." He can barely sustain his writing: "I have nothing but thin air to concoct my stories of, and it is not easy to give a life like semblance to such shadowy stuff." With public approbation, he might have been "stimulated to greater exertions," but his writings have made no "decided impression" on the public. He will continue to be a writer only because he has "nothing else to be ambitious of."[1]

For years he called himself an enervated dreamer, repeatedly referring to the Salem bedroom of his bachelor years as a dream-haunted chamber. The image persisted in his imagination after he left home, sometimes colored by nostalgia. On a visit to Salem in 1840, he wrote to Sophia:

> This deserves to be called a haunted chamber, for thousands upon thousands of visions have appeared to me in it; and some few of them have become visible to the world. If ever I should have a biographer, he ought to make great mention of this chamber in my memoirs, because so much of my lonely youth was wasted here, and here my mind and character were formed.... By and bye, the world found me out in my lonely chamber, and called me forth... and forth I went. (4 October)

Retrospectively he could see an advantage in his solitude: it kept him "fresh" for Sophia to endow with "real life."

After his marriage, he could mock his earlier self-importance: "Here is thy husband in his old chamber, where he produced those stupendous works of fiction, which have since impressed the Universe with wonderment and awe! To this chamber, doubtless, in all succeeding ages, pilgrims will come to pay their tribute of reverence."[2] But he was not always so good-humored about it. In a letter to his friend Evert Duyckinck, he summarily condemned the room, his wasted youth, and his abortive fictions; it was "the old dingy and dusky chamber, where I wasted many good years of my youth, shaping day-dreams and night-dreams into idle stories—scarcely half of which ever saw the light; except it were their own blaze upon the hearth."[3]

Subsequently Hawthorne developed for his readers a more pastoral version of himself as an enchanted dreamer. At the end of his 1851 preface to *Twice-Told Tales*, he sentimentally recalled "the Dream-Land of his youth" with its "shadowy foliage."[4] Later that same year in the preface to *The Snow-Image*, he described himself as a kind of male Sleeping Beauty until Horatio Bridge woke him by arranging the publication of *Twice-Told Tales*:

> I sat down by the wayside of life, like a man under enchantment, and a shrubbery sprung up around me, and the bushes grew to be saplings, and the saplings became trees, until no exit appeared possible, through the entangling depths of my obscurity. And there, perhaps, I should be sitting at this moment, with the moss on the imprisoning tree-trunks, and the yellow leaves of more than a score of autumns piled above me, if it had not been for you.[5]

Yet images of imprisonment persisted. In the *English Notebooks*, he attributed a recurrent dream of failure to the "heavy seclusion in which I shut myself up, for twelve years, after leaving college, when everybody moved onward and left me behind."[6] And a year before his death, he complained that he had lived in Concord so long "that I find myself rusted into my hole, and could not get out even if I wished."[7] In each of these allusions, Hawthorne conveys the same implicit drama: he secludes himself, he finds himself enervated by his seclusion, and he is then too somnolent to escape.

His courtship letters to Sophia go beyond images of imprisonment and enchantment to define dreaming as a state of incomplete development. Life without her had been a dream, he said repeatedly, both sentimentally and in accordance with his psychological theories. Until they met, he told her, he had been absorbed by fantasies, and unable to love. He had once jotted as a story idea, "A man tries to be happy in love; he cannot sincerely give his heart; and the affair seems all a dream."[8] But Sophia had dispelled such dream-states. "Indeed, we are but shadows," he wrote Sophia in October 1840, "—we are not endowed with real life, and all that seems most real about us is but the thinnest substance of a dream—till the heart is touched. That touch creates us— then we begin to be—thereby we are beings of reality, and inheritors of eternity."[9] Even sixteen years later he repeated: "Nothing else is real, except the bond between thee and me. The people around me are but shadows. I am myself but a shadow, till thou takest me in thy arms, and convertest me into substance. Till thou comest back, I do but walk in a dream."[10]

His letters return to the word *dream* not only for his earlier life, but for all the time spent away from Sophia. From the Custom House he wrote to his fiancée, "it is a sore trial to your husband to be estranged from that which makes life a reality to him, and to be compelled to spend so many God-given days in a dream."[11] From Salem he wrote of Brook Farm, though still a member of the community: "It already looks like a dream behind me. The real Me was never an associate of the community.... This Spectre was not thy husband."[12] He echoed one of these phrases eight years later: "The life of the Custom-House lies like a dream behind me."[13]

Occasionally Hawthorne used the word *dream* in the broadest possible sense, to describe the whole of corporeal existence without Sophia: "All my life hitherto, I have been walking in a dream, among shadows which could not be pressed to my bosom," he wrote her; "but now, even in this dream of time, there is something that takes me out of it, and causes me to be a dreamer no more.... The grosser life is a dream, and the spiritual life a reality."[14] Such sentiments no doubt appealed to Sophia's simple idealism, but Hawthorne meant them. They define a profound psychological change after he met her as well as a recurrent theme of his fiction.

Even while he was declaring that dreams lack significance, he was an extraordinarily persistent observer of his own dreams. He noted them frequently in his letters and journals, sometimes as the mere fact that he had dreamed, and sometimes in more detail. In his journal for 1 December 1850 is the bare entry, "At night, dreamed of seeing Pike" (*AN*, 300). In a letter to Sophia eight months after their marriage when she was away visiting her family, he wrote, "I dreamed the other night that our house was broken open, and all our silver stolen." Without acknowledging his own repressed fears for his domestic security, he playfully reassured Sophia, "No matter though it be;—we have steel forks and German silver spoons in plenty" (15 March 1843). A few weeks later he reported dispiritedly, "I have dreamed a great deal, but to no good purpose; for all the characters and incidents have vanished" (*AN*, 376). Apparently he was by then accustomed to using his dreams as sources for his fiction. Shortly afterward he complained, "I get scarcely any sound repose, just now;—tossings and turnings, and the turmoil of dreams, consume the night" (*AN*, 390).

One dream recorded during this prolific period of his life clearly expresses his ambition for public acclaim and financial reward: "A dream, the other night, that the world had become dissatisfied with the inaccurate manner in which facts are reported, and had employed me, with a salary of a thousand dollars, to relate the things of public importance exactly as they happen" (*AN*, 244). The reference to "things of public importance" reflects his perennial worry that fiction is socially useless; and the reference to a thousand dollars touches on his anxieties about making a living. He may have been aware that this dream expressed a wish-fulfillment: about this time he commented fancifully on a bird singing at midnight, "Probably the note gushed out from the midst of a dream, in which he fancied himself in Paradise with his mate; and suddenly awaking, he found himself on a cold, leafless bough, with a New England mist penetrating through his feathers" (*AN*, 386). The same bird awakening from a wishful dream appears in "Buds and Bird-Voices," and in "The Hall of Fantasy" he explained that wishful dreams can grant temporary ease. Even so, he was reluctant to pursue the meaning of his dreams.

Unlike these laconic notations, Hawthorne's courtship letters discussing the dreams and reveries Sophia had inspired are sentimental, lyrical, often rhapsodic. In one, he describes himself sitting in his room "musing and dreaming about a thousand things, with every one of which, I do believe, some nearer or remoter thought of you was intermingled" (2 April 1839). A particularly happy night of dreaming followed a visit to her: "Did you not know, beloved, that I dreamed of you, as it seemed to me, all night long, after that last blissful meeting?" He remembered the mood of the dream but could describe none of its detail: "when I looked back upon the dream, it immediately became confused; but it had been vivid, and most happy, and left a sense of happiness in my heart." He then urged her to return to her recumbent fiancé: "Come again, sweet wife! Force your way through the mists and vapors that envelope my slumbers—illumine me with a radiance that shall not vanish when I awake. I throw my heart as wide open to you as I can."[15]

Sometimes he moved from simple description of a happy dream to whimsical speculation about it, frequently playing with fantasies about meeting Sophia in dreams. He once suggested that she deliberately try to transmit her thoughts and feelings into his mind and heart, but worried that "perhaps it is not wise to intermix fantastic ideas with the reality of our affection."[16] Nevertheless, one evening as he was about to sleep, he urged, "Sleep thou too, my beloved—let us pass at one and the same moment into that misty region, and embrace each other there" (15 March 1840). And in another letter he wondered if she ever hovered about him in her dreams, "calling to me, out of the midst of thy dream, to come and join thee there" (26 March 1840).

Sometimes Hawthorne undercut his own sentimental yearning, as when he chided Sophia for being "naughty—she would not be dreamed about" (15 March 1840). With more serious whimsy, he rejected the implications of her dream that he had addressed her as "sister" in a letter. Curiosity made him say, "I wish you had read that dream-letter through, and could remember its contents"; but he denied all responsibility: "You are to blame for dreaming such letters, or parts of letters, as coming from me. It was you that wrote it—not I" (3 May 1839). He did not inquire why she should dream such a dream. Later, responding to a letter describing a nightmare so disturbing that it made her head ache, he again ignored the dream's content, whimsically reassuring her of his protective love: "Thou shouldst have dreamed of thy husband's breast, instead of that Arabian execution" (12 January 1841).

Occasionally Hawthorne told Sophia about dreams that expressed his own known anxieties. He had terrible nightmares after she wrote of her plan to be mesmerized. "Belovedest, didst thou sleep well, last night?" he asked. "My pillow was haunted with ghastly dreams, the details whereof have flitted away like vapors, but a strong impression remains about thy being magnetised. God save me from any more such! I awoke in an absolute quake" (30 June 1842).

If a dream seemed to challenge his assurance of Sophia's love, however, he rejected it as absurd. After writing a story about a Faithless

Dove that flew away from its lover, he told her, he dreamed "the queerest dreams last night, about being deserted, and all such nonsense." Without acknowledging that both story and dream manifest the same anxiety—that he might lose his Dove—he summarily dismissed the dream as punishment for writing a "naughty romance." His disclaimer seems excessive: "It seems to me that my dreams are generally about fantasies, and very seldom about what I really think and feel." As if to assure himself that the dream was simply fantastic, he reiterated his faith in her love: "You have warmed my heart, my own wife; and never again can I know what it is to be cold and desolate, save in dreams" (3, 4 October 1839).

Yet nearly nine years later, when Sophia and their two children were visiting her mother in Newton, Hawthorne wrote of another dream that she had deserted him, a dream that left him in a state of "frozen agony." The dream expresses both distress and resentment:

> The other night, I dreamt I was at Newton, in a room with thee, and with several other people; and thou tookst occasion to announce that thou hadst now ceased to be my wife, and hadst taken another husband. Thou madest this intelligence known with such perfect composure and *sang-froid*,—not particularly addressed to me, but the company generally,—that it benumbed my thoughts and feelings, so that I had nothing to say.... But hereupon, thy sister Elizabeth, who was likewise present, informed the company that, in this state of affairs, having ceased to be thy husband, I of course became hers, and turning to me, very cooly inquired whether she or I should write to inform my mother of the new arrangement! ... I began to expostulate with thee in an infinite agony, in the midst of which I awoke.... Thou shouldst not behave so when thou comest to me in dreams.[17]

Although he narrates the dream dispassionately, its detail suggests how deeply he was disturbed. The dream confesses that he feels dependent on women (possibly including his grandmother, his Aunt Mary, his mother, his sister Elizabeth, and Sophia's sister Elizabeth, as well as Sophia herself), and it expresses his agonized acceptance of this dependence. The women in the dream are cool and composed. Possibly the woman who insists Hawthorne's mother must be told he is now her husband, and who offers to do the telling, is a version of Sophia herself, who years before had offered to tell his mother of their engagement when Hawthorne was reluctant to do so. Indisputably, the dream reveals that beneath the surface of marital security, Hawthorne was enough troubled by anxiety to revert to his old self-image as passive victim.

Two years before their marriage, Hawthorne had written to Sophia about a troublesome nightmare that seems to articulate the prospective bridegroom's uneasiness about leaving his mother and sisters:

> Dearest, thou didst not come into my dreams, last night; but on the contrary, I was engaged in assisting the escape of Louis XVI and Marie Antoinette, from Paris, during the French revolution. And sometimes, by an unaccountable metamorphosis, it seemed as if my mother and sisters were in the dream in place of the King and Queen. (27 March 1840)

This dream seems to be an attempt to resolve his guilt at deserting his mother and sisters by transferring to them his own imminent escape.[18] Hawthorne did not acknowledge the dream as an expression of his own feelings, and therefore, like Andrew Baxter theorizing that "spirits" cause dreams, he fancifully dismissed it: "I think that fairies rule over our dreams—beings who have no true reason or true feeling, but mere fantaisies [sic] instead of those endowments." This dismissal recalls his earlier dismissal of the dream of the Faithless Dove.

Yet on two occasions, one three years before his marriage and one long after, he did try to interpret the details of anxiety dreams that puzzled him, dreams in which he was the single central figure. A letter to Sophia recounts a nightmare in explicit detail and asks her to decipher it, though at the same time he calls it "silly" and tells her not to see dark meaning in it:

> ...I have been asleep; and I dreamed that I had been sleeping a whole year in the open air; and that while I slept, the grass grew around me. It seemed, in my dream, that the very bed-clothes which actually covered me were spread beneath me, and when I awoke (in my dream) I snatched them up, and the earth under them looked black, as if it had been burnt—one square place, exactly the size of the bed-clothes. Yet there was grass and herbage scattered over this burnt space, looking as fresh, and bright, and dewy, as if the summer rain and the summer sun had been cherishing them all the time. Interpret this for me my Dove—but do not draw any sombre omens from it. What is signified [by] my nap of a whole year? (it made me grieve to think that I had lost so much of eternity)—and what was the fire that blasted the spot of earth which I occupied, while the grass flourished all around?—and what comfort am I to draw from the fresh herbage amid the burnt space? But it is a silly dream, and you cannot expound any sense out of it. Generally, I cannot remember what my dreams have been—only there is a confused sense of having passed through adventures, pleasurable or otherwise. I suspect that you mingled with my dreams, but take care to flit away just before I awake, leaving me but dimly and doubtfully conscious of your visits. [Three lines are erased here.]
> Do you never start so suddenly from a dream that you are afraid to look round the room, lest your dream-personages (so strong and distinct seemed their existence, a moment before) should have thrust themselves out of dream-land into the midst of realities? I do, sometimes. (26 May 1839)

He must have recognized how close the dream was to his view of himself as an enchanted dreamer, and how clearly it expressed his fear of ineffectuality as a man and a writer. The dream, dominated by his grief at wasting time while the rest of the world was flourishing, represents him as a peculiar fusion of Sleeping Beauty and Rip Van Winkle.

He analyzed it as he frequently conceived dreams in his fiction. He assumed that each separate detail—the nap, the fire, and the grass flourishing around a burned spot—has a precise allegorical signification. The same kind of exact equivalence had just characterized Peter Goldthwaite's dream of buried treasure, and it would soon be manifested in Aylmer's dream of cutting out his wife's birthmark and Giovanni's dream identifying Beatrice and the purple flower. Further, the dream, like most of his fictional dreams, is dominated by a single idea or emotion (here, grief at wasted time). Moreover, like Giovanni, he claims that his recollection of his dreams is often confused and partial. Finally, his fear that "strong and distinct" dream phantoms might escape the confines of sleep accounts for the fictional dreamers from the first sketches to the last romances who are frightened and confused by "dream-personages" even when they are awake.

Years later, when Hawthorne was American consul in Liverpool, he again pondered a dream which expressed anxiety about his career. Once again, the dream implicitly condemns the dreamer's ineffectuality, but this time Hawthorne is concerned about his feelings within the dream. Before summarily recording it in his notebook, he remarks, "I think I have been happier, this Christmas, than ever before,—by our own fireside, and with my wife and children about me." Within this security, he could confront a recurrent nightmare:

> For a long, long while, I have occasionally been visited with a singular dream; and I have an impression that I have dreamed it, even since I have been in England. It is, that I am still at college—or, sometimes, even at School— and there is a sense that I have been there unconscionably long, and have quite failed to make such progress in life as my contemporaries have; and I seem to meet some of them with a feeling of shame and depression that broods over me, when I think of it, even at this moment. This dream, recurring all through these twenty or thiry years, must be one of the effects of that heavy seclusion in which I shut myself up, for twelve years, after leaving college, when everybody moved onward and left me behind. How strange that it should come now, when I may call myself famous, and prosperous!— when I am happy, too!—still that same dream of life hopelessly a failure! (*EN*, 98)

As always, Hawthorne tried to trace his dream to waking experience— here to his twelve years of "seclusion" while college friends like Longfellow, Pierce, and Bridge advanced in their careers. He knew that recurring worries affect dreams but cannot be confined there: the shame he felt in his dream recurred when he remembered it. Yet he was puzzled about why the dream persisted after the waking predicament had passed, why he reexperienced the shame and depression of youth "when I may call myself famous, and prosperous!—when I am happy, too!"

Like the dream of falling asleep for a year, this "singular dream" expresses concern about time passing while the dreamer makes "no progress in life." Yet it also suggests Freud's "examination dream," since it is a dream of anxiety but also of self-consolation. The dream recalls a problem that has been overcome, and so implicitly asserts that the future should hold no threats.[19] Another Freudian conjecture also seems applicable, that a dream of past unhappiness may conceal a wish for lost youth; it simultaneously expresses the wish and punishes it.[20] But most clearly, this dream expresses Hawthorne's continuing suspicion that his life was a failure.

Given his persistent fascination with his own dreams, it is not surprising that the *American Notebooks* contains suggestions for stories about dreaming. "In a dream to wander to some place where may be heard the complaints of all the miserable on earth," reads one suggestion; and another outlines the story of an old man who wishes he could relive his misspent life but happily discovers "he had only been dreaming of old age" (*AN*, 15, 182). One entry implies what Hawthorne would not acknowledge about his own dreams, that they convey truths repressed by the waking mind: a man dreams that a friend acts "the part of a most deadly enemy" and eventually discovers "that the dream-character is the true one" (*AN*, 181).

The most provocative of these notebook entries articulates a most serious literary ambition: "To write a dream, which shall resemble the real course of a dream, with all its inconsistency, its strange transformations, which are all taken as a matter of course, its eccentricities and aimlessness—with nevertheless a leading idea running through the whole. Up to this old age of the world, no such thing ever has been written" (*AN*, 240). This he accomplished repeatedly. That some details of dreams in Hawthorne's fictions resist final interpretation may be explained by Hawthorne's own experience: he knew that some dreams pierce to mysteries too painful or too profound to comprehend.

Partial, elusive, or indeterminate as Hawthorne's dreams were as reported in his letters and notebooks, they were nevertheless more detailed, more openly ambiguous, more "modern" than Sophia's. Her dreams as she reported them undoubtedly reveal more about contemporary assumptions than Hawthorne's, and allow valuable comparison. Like Hawthorne, she was curious about dreams, and wondered about their relation to real events. But she never tried to trace them to her own intimate thoughts or emotions. For Sophia, dreams were enclosed experiences, explicable and without mystery.

It is hardly surprising that as a sick young girl confined to her room, Sophia suffered from harrowing dreams. She casually reported several to her family, trying to tie them to precise waking experiences. "I dreamed that George Villiers, Duke of Buckingham, stabbed me in the bosom; and I awoke with a tremendous start, and trembled for an hour," she wrote, and then speculated ingenuously: "It was because I had been reading Shakespeare, I suppose."[21] On another occasion she merely noted: "Last night, midnight, I was awakened by a tremendous crash of thunder; and I went to sleep again to dream of all kinds of horrors."[22] Nor did she record speculation about the implications of a dream she had after waking early and drifting asleep again: she dreamed "of watching a sunrise," but "the sky was covered with clouds shaped like coffins."[23]

When she was sent to Cuba for her health a few years later, she continued to tell her family about her dreams. They all express her affection for them but also her loneliness. "You cannot think how often I dream of you, delightful dreams too," she wrote to her mother. "You always appear to me with a most happy countenance, full of hope and satisfaction. . . . I dreamed once that you and Father came to Cuba to carry me home, and last night I dreamed that Betty came."[24] The following month she wrote to her father about a dream that she had returned to Massachusetts. She wanted to relive it by writing about it: "I have been at home all night, dreaming about you and I must continue the delusion as much as possible by writing you a letter. I was again in the Church Street nest. Mother had gone to Boston, and you and I were keeping house together. All unexpectedly to me, one evening the stage drove up, and Lydia Haven and Caroline Fernandez descended from it. It was a plan of yours, to give me an agreeable surprise in our loneliness." Her pleasure in "keeping house" with her father betrays her loneliness, but Sophia seems to notice only what she finds "agreeable."[25]

Sophia's interpretations of her own dreams were usually simplemindedly literal, as when she wrote of dreaming that a friend who had been sorrowful was now happily married and visiting her, "and I told him a great many things about my foreign experiences—perfectly inspired by the recovered happiness of his countenance. . . . I hope my dream was prophetic of his present state of mind. . . ."[26] Her uneasiness about whether dreams can prophesy continued even after her marriage. "My beloved mother," she wrote in 1844, "I dreamed last night that you were very unhappy, and would not tell me why, and my heart was nearly broken. You must assure me that it was nothing but a dream when you write again; if you are happy as usual."[27]

Sophia cherished dreams she could interpret as divine messages, such as a childhood dream she was fond of recounting to her children. A dark cloud appeared and obscured the sun; but it was transformed eventually into beautiful singing birds. "This dream was doubtless interpreted symbolically by the dreamer," Julian Hawthorne said, "and the truth which it symbolized was always among the firmest articles of her faith."[28] It is easy to guess how the gentle Sophia interpreted this dream, especially after reading her four-page manuscript recording another rapturous dream.

After meditating one evening, she wrote, Morpheus embraced her, and imagination led her "to a place of exceeding loveliness, where nature was dressed in her richest drapery." It was a beautiful sunset, and spring was putting "forth her first tender leaves and blossoms." Suddenly she saw "a vision, which seemed to be the spirit of loveliness herself." After the wind seemed to "breathe upon her as upon the aeolian harp," the spirit "began to sing a sweetly plaintive lay.... It was the music of the spheres." Sophia was about to "address the angelic songstress, and request a repetition," but "my temerity met its just reward, for the moment I attempted to speak, I awoke and found the whole a *dream*!"[29]

Clearly this is not a careful account of a mental adventure, but a generalized description. Even the images—the Aeolian harp, the music of the spheres—are public and derivative. The rhapsodic tone recalls the dream poems recurrent in magazines of the 1830s and 1840s, but not the dreams in Hawthorne's tales. This does not suggest that Sophia was dishonest, but rather that her eagerness to see ideal beauty sometimes produced dreams of "loveliness," or the belief she had such dreams. Her husband knew that dreams pose distressing riddles. All the time he was reporting his dreams to Sophia, he was seeking a way to witness dreaming in process, to see his own mind reflecting profoundly on itself. His goals as a writer required it.

NOTES

1. In the long letter dated 4 June 1837, Hawthorne says he seldom leaves his room "till after dark," but is comforted to think his future must necessarily be "more varied, and therefore more tolerable than the past." He will continue to "scribble for a living," willing to "turn my pen to all sorts of drudgery." His letters to Longfellow on 16 May 1839, when he was working at the Boston Custom House, complain that "as a literary man, my new occupations entirely break me

up," and in November 1847 voice a similar complaint about work at the Salem Custom House. Unless otherwise stated, Hawthorne's letters to Longfellow (at MH) and to Sophia Peabody Hawthorne (at CSmH) are cited from typescripts prepared by Norman Holmes Pearson. All letters are quoted with permission of the respective libraries. An inaccurate text of the letters to Sophia is available in *Love Letters of Nathaniel Hawthorne*, 2 vols. (Chicago: Society of the Dofobs, 1907; rpt. ed., 1 vol., Washington: Microcard Editions, 1972).

2. The letter, dated 20 January 1842, continues the burlesque tone, as he imagines the "pilgrims" paying tribute to his washstand and looking glass.

3. The letter, written 10 October 1845, during the time Hawthorne and his family shared his mother's house in Salem, is in NN, Duyckinck Collection.

4. *The Centenary Edition of the Works of Nathaniel Hawthorne*, ed. William Charvat et al. (Columbus: Ohio State University Press, 1962–), vol. 9, *Twice-Told Tales* (1974), p. 7.

5. *The Centenary Edition of Hawthorne*, vol. 11, *The Snow-Image, and Uncollected Tales* (1974), p. 5.

6. *The English Notebooks by Nathaniel Hawthorne*, ed. Randall Stewart (New York: Modern Language Association, 1941), p. 98; hereafter cited in the text as *EN*.

7. Letter to William D. Ticknor, 6 January 1863. The correspondence with Ticknor has been separately published: *Letters of Hawthorne to William D. Ticknor, 1851–1864*, 2 vols. (Newark, N.J.: Carteret Book Club, 1910; rpt. ed., 1 vol., Washington: Microcard Editions, 1972).

8. *The Centenary Edition of Hawthorne*, vol. 8, *The American Notebooks*, ed. Claude M. Simpson (1972), p. 153; hereafter cited in the text as *AN*.

9. This letter seems to draw on Plato's cave image: "for without thy aid, my best knowledge of myself would have been merely to know my own shadow—to watch it flickering on the wall, and mistake its fantasies for my own real actions." Sophia has "taught" him about his heart, illuminated his soul, and "revealed me to myself." Sophia, describing the completion Hawthorne's love brought her, said he gave her intellectual awareness. Refuting her sister Mary's "unfounded aspersions" of her husband's "glorious, great, expanded nature," she said that "his love first awoke in me *consciousness*. I am conscious of the bliss of being now. *Before* I ignorantly lived" (3 February 1850; NN, Berg Collection).

10. The letter, dated 7 April, was written from Liverpool to Sophia who, with her daughters, had gone to Lisbon for its milder climate in the autumn of 1855. They remained until June 1856 as guests of Hawthorne's friend, J. L. O'Sullivan, American minister to Portugal.

11. He said in this letter of 18 December 1839 that the "outward show" of his life cannot "satisfy the soul that has become acquainted with truth."

12. He again assured Sophia in this letter of 3 September 1841 that only she gave life "reality and significance"; without her "all was a dream and a mockery."

13. *The Centenary Edition of Hawthorne*, vol. 1, *The Scarlet Letter* (1962), p. 44.

14. In this letter of 1 January 1840, he asks Sophia if she feels as he does that they live "above time" because their "affection diffuses eternity round about us." In a letter inviting Duyckinck to visit the Old Manse on 28 November 1843, sixteen months after his marriage, he said: "I feel as if, for the first time in my life, I was awake. I have found a reality, though it looks very much like some of my old dreams." He wistfully says he wishes only that "Providence would make it

somewhat more plain to my apprehension how I am to earn my bread" (NN, Duyckinck Collection).

15. 8 August 1839. This presentation of himself as the passive and Sophia as the aggressive partner is curiously consistent with his later image of himself as Sleeping Beauty.

16. 2 April 1839. On 11 December 1839 he whimsically observed that if there were an intellectual daguerreotype, they might exchange reveries.

17. The letter was written from Salem on 27 June 1848 and was included by Julian Hawthorne in *Nathaniel Hawthorne and His Wife* (Boston: James R. Osgood, 1885), 1:326f.

18. Sigmund Freud, in *The Interpretation of Dreams,* says kings and queens in dreams often represent the parents. For Hawthorne, whose father died when he was four, mother and sisters substitute for the king and queen (*The Basic Writings of Sigmund Freud,* trans. James Strachey [London: Hogarth Press, 1968], 5:353).

19. Freud, *Works,* 4:273.
20. Freud, *Works,* 5:473–76.
21. *Hawthorne and His Wife,* 1:76.
22. *Hawthorne and His Wife,* 1:77.
23. *Hawthorne and His Wife,* 1:81.
24. 7 April 1834; NN, Berg Collection. "Betty" is her sister, Elizabeth Peabody.
25. 25 May 1834; NN, Berg Collection.
26. 24 November 1834; NN, Berg Collection.
27. 4 February 1844; NN, Berg Collection.
28. *Hawthorne and His Wife,* 1:49.
29. n.d.; NN, Berg Collection.

DANIEL RICKETSON'S SKETCH BOOK

Thomas Blanding

HENRY THOREAU had his house at Walden Pond; Daniel Ricketson had his shanty at Brooklawn.
Daniel *who* had his shanty *where?*
Thoreau probably wondered nothing less when he received an effusive letter from this New Bedford, Massachusetts, Quaker, just a few days after Ticknor & Fields published *Walden; or, Life in the Woods* on 9 August 1854. *Walden* so delighted Ricketson, as he pored over its pages in the solitude of a rustic shanty some half-dozen rods from his Brooklawn manor, that he wrote directly to the author, hailing with pleasure "a prose poem... as simple as a running brook." Unfortunately, Ricketson's long, rambling letter was a prose poem as florid as a babbling brook. One wonders what Thoreau, who drove his own words as straight as board nails, thought when Ricketson saluted him as "Dear Mr Walden."[1]

No one, certainly not Thoreau, could have predicted that Ricketson's peculiar praise would begin one of Thoreau's fullest correspondences, surpassed only by the exchange initiated some six years earlier by a Worcester, Massachusetts, disciple, H. G. O. Blake. More than sixty letters passed between Ricketson and Thoreau between 1854 and the latter's death in 1862. Nor were letters all that sealed their friendship. Thoreau visited Ricketson at Brooklawn six times in as many years, while Ricketson made eight sorties to Concord, both often extending their stays a week or more. And later, after Thoreau's death, Ricketson continued to correspond with and visit Thoreau's sister, Sophia, and his friends, Ralph Waldo Emerson, Bronson Alcott, Ellery Channing, and F. B. Sanborn.

Thoreau and Ricketson seem strange allies. Friendship was a guarded citadel in Transcendental Concord, and Henry Thoreau was its most steadfast protector, keeping all but a few would-be pilgrims outside its gate. Daniel Ricketson was, by most accounts, a timorous dilettante who had retreated, more than retired, to the asylum of a twelve-by-fourteen-foot shanty. An unpublished passage from Thoreau's Journal, 3 April 1857, tells us just how pathetic Ricketson's phobias appeared:

> R. thought himself at last unfitted for the family relation. There was his sick wife. He knew what she wanted—that he should go in & sympathize with her—then she would have a good cry & it would be all over—but he *could not do* it— His family depended on him & it drew from him the little strength he had—some times when weakened thus with sympathy for his sick family—he had gone out & eaten his dinner on the end of a log with his workmen—cutting his meat with a jacknife & did not fail to get appetite & strength so— So sensitive is he.[2]

What sympathies then admitted to Thoreau's privileged circle a wealthy man who scribbled sentimental verses, suffered from hypochondria, feared lightning, and sickened at any allusion to death? Thoreau himself tells us something of Ricketson's appeal. Soon after the Quaker's first visit to Concord, Thoreau wrote Blake, Ricketson "is a man of very simple tastes, notwithstanding his wealth; a lover of nature; but, above all, singularly frank and plain-spoken.... Sincerity is a great but rare virtue, and we pardon to it much complaining, and the betrayal of many weaknesses."[3] Thoreau, Alcott, Channing, and others chose to overlook Ricketson's quirks and sample, rather, his virtues. Visits to Brooklawn were always a pleasurable sharing of antiquarian and nature lore, and a sympathetic communing of minds constant to the same moral principles and reforms.

The Thoreau-Ricketson friendship has been recounted often.[4] Thoreau's Journal, especially, contains ample accounts of his New Bedford excursions. Ricketson's Journal, however, has disappeared, so Thoreau's biographers have been limited in their detailing of the relationship from Ricketson's point of view.[5] Happily, though, Ricketson dabbled in another medium of record, pencil sketching. With little thought to art, he habitually dashed off sketches of relatives and friends for his own and their amusement. His caricature of Thoreau as he first presented himself at the door at Brooklawn has entertained several generations of Thoreauvians.[6]

A large cache of Ricketson's drawings has come to light in the manuscript collections of the New Bedford Whaling Museum.[7] It is a scrapbook, nine and one-half by twelve inches, into which Ricketson inserted more than 300 pencil and a few ink sketches, the result of more than fifty years' chronicling. One of the earliest drawings bears the date 1843, while the latest appears to be one of an equestrian scribbled on the back of a calendar sheet for January 1897, just a year and a half before Ricketson's death. The sketches are pasted into the

PLATE SEVENTEEN
Self-portrait of Daniel Ricketson, September 1851.
Courtesy New Bedford Whaling Museum

PLATE EIGHTEEN
Brooklawn, July 1858.
Courtesy New Bedford Whaling Museum

PLATE NINETEEN
"H. D. Thoreau returning to his Shanty from Concord."
Courtesy New Bedford Whaling Museum

Daniel Ricketson's Sketch Book

PLATE TWENTY
William Ellery Channing in 1856.
Courtesy New Bedford Whaling Museum

PLATE TWENTY-ONE
Captain Thoreau, the Great Explorer of the Middleborough Lakes, 1856.
Courtesy New Bedford Whaling Museum

PLATE TWENTY-TWO
Back view of the Brady Farm, 1856.
Courtesy New Bedford Whaling Museum

PLATE TWENTY-THREE
Amos Bronson Alcott, 1857.
Courtesy New Bedford Whaling Museum

Daniel Ricketson's Sketch Book

PLATE TWENTY-FOUR
Amos Bronson Alcott, 1857.
Courtesy New Bedford Whaling Museum

PLATE TWENTY-FIVE
William Ellery Channing in 1865.
Courtesy New Bedford Whaling Museum

PLATE TWENTY-SIX
Daniel Ricketson at age sixty.
Courtesy New Bedford Whaling Museum

PLATE TWENTY-SEVEN
"A Shanty Man": Henry Thoreau, twenty-five years later.
Courtesy New Bedford Whaling Museum

scrapbook, and many of the hidden versos contain additional, unrecovered sketches. The book itself, including self-portraits, local characters, houses and landscapes, friends, relatives, literary acquaintances, and numerous unidentified people, had its inception in 1850 at Ricketson's pre-Brooklawn estate, as Ricketson himself tells us in a note, dated 10 October 1885, on the front endpaper:

> In the winter of 1850 I became acquainted with Charles Martin of London, artist, who took crayon likenesses of Louisa and myself. On a visit at our home Woodlee, noticing I had some turn for drawing, he advised me to get a Scrap-Book, and preserve my sketch, stating also that I would be much surprised to see what improvement I made in a year or so. Taking the advice I found considerable amusement in these rude sketches, with my uncle James Thornton, Cousin Edward Brown & my family. Many of them have with the progress of time and the loss of beloved ones become valuable as reminiscences.

Henry Thoreau, too, perused Ricketson's sketch book. He spent a long rainy day in April 1857 alone in Ricketson's shanty, inventorying in his Journal its cluttered contents. There, amid volumes of verse, jackknives, canes, pipes, stuffed birds, Indian implements, and a crumpled horn, Thoreau found "A large book full of pencil sketches to be inspected by whomsoever, containing countless sketches of his friends and acquaintances and himself and of wayfaring men whom he had met, Quakers, etc., etc., and now and then a vessel under full sail or an old-fashioned house, sketched on a peculiar pea-green paper."[8] Thoreau might have noticed that Ricketson's sketch book also contained caricatures of himself and other Concord visitors.

Rude as these sketches are, they provide a glimpse of Thoreau and his friends through Ricketson's eyes. The selection which follows captures, it is hoped, something of the spirit of the Transcendentalists at Brooklawn.

NOTES ON THE SKETCHES

All drawings are reproduced through the courtesy of the New Bedford Whaling Museum

PLATE SEVENTEEN: Daniel Ricketson as drawn by himself, September 1851, projecting his appearance at age forty-five in 1858. Ricketson's sketch book contains numerous drawings of himself and his friends as he imagined they would look at some future date, often in their old age. At the time he drew this rather foppish self-portrait, Ricketson still lived at his Woodlee home in New Bedford. It would be another three years before Thoreau presented himself at Brooklawn.

PLATE EIGHTEEN: Brooklawn, July 1858, Daniel Ricketson's home on the outskirts of New Bedford. In the parlor at Brooklawn, while Bronson Alcott looked on demurely, Thoreau did an impromptu dance, complete with bacchic leaps, and was careful to tread on the philosopher's toes. Backed by thick woodland, a brook crossed the lawns about the house, thus giving the estate its name. Brooklawn became a public park later in the century, but the house continued to stand for more than a half century before it was razed by the city of New Bedford. Ricketson's shanty is now an equipment shack.

PLATE NINETEEN: "H. D. Thoreau returning to his Shanty from Concord." Thoreau moved out of his Walden house in September 1847, more than seven years before he and Ricketson met on Christmas day 1854. This sketch, then, is not an eyewitness depiction but, rather, is drawn from Ricketson's reading of *Walden*. It probably dates from 1854 or 1855 when Thoreau was still beardless. In the sketch book it appears between drawings dated 1855.

PLATE TWENTY: William Ellery Channing in 1856, when he worked on the staff of the *New Bedford Mercury*. During his sojourn in New Bedford, Channing spent long hours in Ricketson's shanty, where Ricketson hung another sketch of the Concord poet, called "The Trojan." Unfortunately, this latter drawing, probably with punning reference to Channing's work on the *Mercury*, did not find its way into the sketch book.

PLATE TWENTY-ONE: Captain Thoreau, the Great Explorer of the Middleborough Lakes, 1856. Thoreau explored the Middleboro Ponds (as they are more often called) twice with Ricketson in June 1856, on one occasion borrowing a boat shaped like a pumpkin seed to paddle on Great Quitticus. Ricketson's inventory of provisions for the one-day excursion seems drawn with characteristic whimsy: *"Expedition to Middleboro Ponds*   Buffaloes, bedding, Hair Pillow, hatchet, Matches, Spy glasses, compass, Maps, Frying pan, pork & salt, Bread, Boiled eggs, Potatoes, Indian Meal, Tin cup, tin pail, 2 plates, 3 umbrellas, 2 rollers   Halter, blanket, Corn & Hay — card sponge."

PLATE TWENTY-TWO: "Back view of the Brady Farm in company with H. D. Thoreau   August—1856—." The actual date of Thoreau's visit with Ricketson to the Brady Farm is 24 June 1856, at which time Ricketson made a sketch of the back side of the Brady house and the barn in Thoreau's notebook. The sketch reproduced here is apparently the same view two months later. Kate Brady worked as a maid at Brooklawn and became a great admirer of Thoreau after she read *Walden*. Thoreau and Ricketson visited the Bradys again the next year, and Thoreau became much taken with the twenty-year-old Irish girl, who proposed to live a Walden-like existence in the ruins of the old family homestead.

PLATES TWENTY-THREE AND TWENTY-FOUR: Two sketches of Amos Bronson Alcott. In April 1857, Thoreau, Alcott, and Channing descended on Ricketson's shanty, where they talked on high themes and smoked the pipe of friendship. The abstemious Alcott apparently did not partake of tobacco—thus Ricketson's caricature of a sour-faced philosopher puffing a pipe (Plate 23). The caption reads, "He did not smoke the pipe a joke." This was Ricketson's first meeting with Alcott, whom he erroneously calls "Asa B. Alcott," and makes one year older than his fifty-eight years. He is called "Father Alcott" doubtless because he was fourteen years Ricketson's and eighteen years Thoreau's and Channing's senior.

PLATE TWENTY-FIVE: William Ellery Channing in 1865. Ricketson captioned this sketch "Travelling Companion to Mr. Mildmay (W. E. C.)." Frank Mildmay is the protagonist of *The Naval Officer: or Scenes and Adventures in the Life of Frank Mildmay* (1829), by Captain Frederick Marryat, a writer of picaresque novels of the sea. Though the drawing is signed "W. Waterhorn," the handwriting and detail are clearly Ricketson's. Perhaps Waterhorn is another name borrowed from Captain Marryat.

PLATE TWENTY-SIX: Daniel Ricketson at age sixty. This self-portrait shows Ricketson in 1873, some eleven years after Thoreau died. In these later years Ricketson gained a modest reputation as an author in his own right, with the publication of verses in the *Liberator*, the *Commonwealth*, and in two books, *The Autumn Sheaf* (1869) 'and *The Factory Bell and Other Poems* (1873). Among these poems were touching tributes to his Concord friends.

PLATE TWENTY-SEVEN: Henry Thoreau, twenty-five years later. The caption reads only "A Shanty Man. age 70," but the aquiline nose, beard, and apparel seem unmistakable. Ricketson elsewhere had called Thoreau's Walden house a shanty. Here he imagines what his old friend would look like had he lived out the full span of his life. Daniel Ricketson's sketch book is a fitting place for such conjecture, where the likenesses, Ricketson himself tells us, "have with the progress of time and the loss of beloved ones become valuable as reminiscences."

NOTES

1. *The Correspondence of Henry David Thoreau*, ed. Walter Harding and Carl Bode (New York: New York University Press, 1958), pp. 332–35.
2. Journal of Henry D. Thoreau, 3 April 1857, NNPM, MA 1302. When Thoreau's Journal was published in 1906 in fourteen volumes, this passage was silently omitted, probably in deference to Ricketson's children.
3. *Correspondence*, p. 383.
4. See especially Walter Harding, *The Days of Henry Thoreau* (New York: Alfred A. Knopf, 1965), pp. 343–45, 349–50, 361–68, passim, and Earl J. Dias, "Daniel Ricketson and Henry Thoreau," *New England Quarterly*, 26 (September 1953): 388–96.
5. Selections from Ricketson's Journal appear in *Daniel Ricketson and His Friends*, ed. his daughter and son, Anna and Walton Ricketson (Boston: Houghton, Mifflin, 1902). The present whereabouts of the Journal is unknown. Some of Ricketson's papers and books were once in the New Bedford Public Library. For further thoughts by Ricketson on his friendship with Thoreau, see also, *Daniel Ricketson: Autobiographic and Miscellaneous*, ed. Anna and Walton Ricketson (New Bedford, Mass.: E. Anthony & Sons, Inc., 1910), Walter Harding, "Daniel Ricketson's Copy of *Walden*," *Harvard Library Bulletin*, 15 (October 1967): 401–

11, and Thomas Blanding, "Daniel Ricketson's Reminiscences of Thoreau," *Concord Saunterer*, 8 (March 1973): 7–11.

6. Ricketson's pencil sketch of Thoreau arriving at Brooklawn, 25 December 1854, first appeared in *Daniel Ricketson and His Friends*, between pp. 12 and 13. Walter Harding discovered in Ricketson's copy of *Walden*, now at the Houghton Library, Harvard University, two additional caricatures of Thoreau. Harding published one, "*An Ideal Thoreau*," in Harding, "Ricketson's *Walden*," between 404 and 405, and again in *The Thoreau Society Bulletin*, 114 (Winter 1971): 8. The second sketch, drawn on 26 December 1854 during Thoreau's first visit to Brooklawn, remains unpublished.

7. A selection from Ricketson's sketch book is reproduced here with the kind permission of the Old Dartmouth Historical Society, New Bedford, Mass. I wish to thank Richard C. Kugler, Director of the New Bedford Whaling Museum, for bringing this sketch book to my attention, and Mary Chin for assisting in the first perusal of its contents. The Thoreau Lyceum, Concord, Mass., kindly allowed me to arrange an exhibit around the Ricketson sketch book in 1972, and provided the negatives from which these sketches are reproduced.

8. *The Writings of Henry David Thoreau*, ed. Bradford Torrey and Francis H. Allen, 20 vols. (Boston: Houghton, Mifflin, 1906), *Journal*, 9:325.

MELVILLE'S CLOSET SKELETON: A NEW LETTER ABOUT THE ILLEGITIMACY INCIDENT IN *PIERRE*

Amy Puett Emmers

AN INTRIGUING LETTER hinting of unsavory secrets in the life of Herman Melville's father has been uncovered in the Lemuel Shaw collection at the Massachusetts Historical Society. Were this find merely titillating, it would remain unannounced. In fact, though, the story behind this letter from Melville's Uncle Thomas to Chief Justice Shaw, Melville's father-in-law, seems to supply the crux of a central incident in *Pierre; or The Ambiguities*—the hero's discovery of his late father's illegitimate daughter. More importantly, Melville's use of such autobiographical detail very likely contributed to his acknowledged, but largely unexplained, disquiet during the decade of the 1850s.

It happened that Herman's grandfather, Major Thomas Melvill, Sr. (Herman's mother added the final "e" after her husband's death), asked Lemuel Shaw, Sr., to be an executor of his will. Judge Shaw had of course been intimate friend and legal adviser of the Melvill family long before he became Herman's father-in-law. Following the Major's death in 1832, Shaw processed matters relating to the estate, and in doing so he several times wrote Herman's uncle, Thomas Melvill, Jr., about two women who had claims against the interests of Herman's father, Allan Melvill, in Major Melvill's estate. (Allan Melvill had died a bankrupt only a few months before his father's death, and any claims against him would have been referred to his interest in his father's estate.) It is the second reply of Thomas Melvill, Jr., to Shaw about this demand for payment which is extant and which seems relevant to *Pierre*. It should be noted that while the proliferation of identical first names in successive generations of Melville's family is sometimes baffling, the Allan mentioned in this letter is clearly Herman's father, not his brother by the same name. The complete text of the letter follows, literatim:

Dr Sir

In the letter written you, as within alluded to, I wrote you allso [sic] in answer to the first one you wrote me in relation to Mrs. A.M.A.—

> As therein stated, I feel confident that my good father *never saw*,—or at least *never knew*, or *conversed*, either with *her*, or *Mrs B.*—
> They called at the house, if I remember right, twice—just before my arrival in Boston, (after Allans decease,) and saw only my *Mother & Helen*—
> The circumstance was made known to me—& it was concluded that I should call on them, which I did, and suceeded [sic] in dispelling the erroneous ideas they had formed of *claims*, on my father—as well as the condition of my late brothers affairs—
> I well remember having paid some money to Mrs B—what the amount of it was, I do not remember,—nor, if it was a *part*, or *the whole* of what she may have claimed as due.—
> Mrs. A.M.A.—must be mistaken in stating that I *"gave her some encouragement"*.—On what foundation could I give her encouragement? I had no means of my own. My brother left none—and I had strong reasons to think, that it would not be done, by those members of my own family who might have means, should the case be made known to them;—All of whom, except Helen, are to this day, as I presume, ignorant of her existence—
> From the little I saw of her, I thought her quite an interesting young person,—that it was most unfortunate she had not been brought up different— and I most deeply regret that she too, has been called to feel the disappointments & sorrows, so generally attending our earthly sojourn—
> Very respectfully & cordially, Th Melvill[1]

While Thomas' letter does not conclusively determine the nature of the relationship between Herman Melville's father and the two women designated as Mrs. B. and Mrs. A.M.A., it does clearly establish that he had a recognized obligation to them. The fact that Thomas Melvill gave Mrs. B. any money at all indicates that he virtually accepted the justice of her claim. Further, Allan's association with the women was obviously disapproved of by the members of his family who knew about it. Interestingly, they appear to wish to protect other members of the family from the knowledge, and Thomas assumes that his other relatives would not sanction the situation should they learn of Mrs. A.M.A.'s "existence." His very use of initials as the sole means of identifying the women throughout the letter underscores his desire for concealment. Had Thomas' concern been only for secrecy, Allan's association with the women might be dismissed as an unfair business transaction, even though women of that era generally did not engage in business. However, the letter clearly implies an unacceptable personal involvement. It might be argued, therefore, that both women claimed to have been Allan's mistresses, perhaps one or both with illegitimate children. But had both women been mistresses, what legal ground would they have had for claims? Further, had both women professed to be mothers of illegitimate children, would they have been likely to associate with each other, as the initial paragraphs of this letter suggest that

Mrs. B. and Mrs. A.M.A. do? Above all, it is Thomas' defensiveness about the manner of Mrs. A.M.A.'s rearing, the woman he calls that "interesting young person," that implies a kind of concern not usually accorded mistresses. His concern, linked as it is with his shame and regret, tacitly acknowledges an obligation for Mrs. A.M.A.'s personal well-being, an obligation that would logically be felt toward a late brother's illegitimate offspring. It would appear, then, that Mrs. A.M.A. was Allan Melvill's illegitimate daughter by Mrs. B.

Herman Melville was twelve years old when his father, Allan, died. It was another twenty years before he would publish *Pierre*, and just what, in the meantime, he learned about his father's life and incorporated into his novel cannot be precisely ascertained. However, almost everyone admits the autobiographical nature of much of that novel, which Melville originally thought would be a "rural bowl of milk."[2] The work evolved rather into a scathing portrayal of a young man consciously bent on doing right—honoring an obligation to support a girl he believes to be his late father's illegitimate daughter—but unconsciously driven by his incestuous love for this same girl. Various scholars have drawn parallels between the novel and its author's life; even more to the point, family members made the same connection. In an unpublished letter now in the Harvard College Library, Melville's daughter, Mrs. Frances Thomas, asserted:

> Cousin M—[Maria Morewood, daughter of Melville's brother, Allan] wrote me that she was pretty sure she had a copy of 'Pierre' & thinks it must be at Arrowhead[.] Will [Morewood, Maria's husband] had read it & said it seemed to refer to 'family matters.'[3]

Further, Melville's granddaughter and biographer, Mrs. Eleanor Metcalf, apparently found the same enjoyment other scholars have in enumerating details from Melville's life also found in the novel. In her copy of the Constable edition of *Pierre*,[4] now in the Berg Collection of the New York Public Library, Mrs. Metcalf noted that the description of Glen Stanly's house in New York (p. 332) was like the Shaw home in Mount Vernon Street, Boston. And she also scribbled on her copy that Mr. Falsgrave's delicate hands (p. 137) resembled those of Judge Shaw's and his son Samuel's. In a novel thus acknowledged as autobiographical, it now seems likely that Melville took the incident of illegitimacy from his family history. Significantly, at one time he had thought of publishing the book anonymously or under an assumed name, perhaps partly to spare his family embarrassment.

The reaction of Melville's family circle to *Pierre* provides an important clue to the tantalizing enigma of Melville's health during the several years following the book's publication in 1852. The cryptic allusions about him in various family records of this period are all too scarce, but there is a family account of an examination for insanity about this time. An indication that his relatives were displeased with *Pierre*—and with Melville himself—comes from an uncle of Melville's, Peter Gansevoort, unable to understand an incivility on his nephew's part and thus driven to complain: "Oh Herman, Herman, Herman truly thou art an 'Ambiguity.'"[5] Further, Melville's brother-in-law, Lemuel Shaw, Jr., learning that *Pierre* had been refused by Melville's English publisher, wrote that he wished "very much he could be persuaded to leave off writing books for a few years."[6] Notably, too, after *Pierre* Melville's mother was especially determined that he should give up writing, stating as her reason that her son's health could not bear the strain of a literary career. The subject matter of *Pierre*, with its implications of illegitimacy and incest, would have been shocking to Melville's family regardless of how closely they identified with particular events and characters. Since they acknowledged that the book was about "family matters," it is probable that their embarrassment about *Pierre* made them shudder to think what he might write next. Their embarrassment, coupled with their inability to appreciate or understand the pitch of excitement into which Melville had worked himself after seven years of intensive writing, probably made them overly concerned about his health.

Thomas Melvill's letter, published here for the first time, seems to explain some of the tension that existed between Melville and his family in the 1850s. If Melville had disclosed a family skeleton in *Pierre*, as this letter strongly suggests, then his family might reasonably have wished to dissuade him from continuing along these lines. Unfortunately, their uneasiness about what he might write or do next would only have aggravated rather than alleviated any particular stress Melville experienced during this decade.

NOTES

1. No date or place of writing for this letter is indicated, MHi; quoted with permission.

2. Melville to Mrs. Nathaniel Hawthorne, 8 January 1852, *The Letters of Herman Melville*, ed. Merrell R. Davis and William H. Gilman (New Haven: Yale University Press, 1960), p. 146.

3. Mrs. Frances Thomas to Mrs. Eleanor Metcalf, 16 November 1919, MH; quoted with permission.

4. *The Complete Works of Herman Melville* (London: Constable, 1922–24), vol. 9, *Pierre*.

5. Peter Gansevoort to Maria Melville, 9 October 1852; quoted in Jay Leyda, *The Melville Log* (New York: Harcourt, Brace, 1951), 1:461.

6. Lemuel Shaw, Jr., to Mr. and Mrs. Lemuel Shaw, Sr., 13 May 1852, MHi; quoted with permission.

HARRIET BEECHER STOWE, JOHN P. JEWETT, AND AUTHOR-PUBLISHER RELATIONS IN 1853

Susan Geary

IN 1853 Harriet Beecher Stowe was probably at the height of her fame. The astounding commercial success of *Uncle Tom's Cabin* the year before, coupled with its controversial nature, had made her name a household word on both sides of the Atlantic. At home a flood of imitations and replies to her antislavery novel kept her name before the public, while piracies and translations did the same for her overseas. Although it was not selling in the electrifying quantities that *Uncle Tom* had, her new book, *A Key to Uncle Tom's Cabin*, was nonetheless selling by the tens of thousands and had reached a sale of 90,000 copies within a month of publication. And the woman who only a year previous had been the overburdened wife of an obscure and poorly paid college professor had become a literary lioness. In England, where she had gone for a protracted visit, her movements had taken on the character of a triumphal progress. In the midst of all these tangible signs of success, Mrs. Stowe quietly and abruptly changed publishers. Scarcely anyone has commented on this sudden sundering of a hitherto profitable and cordial business relationship, yet evidence that has come to light in recent years suggests that the episode may be a landmark in the history of author-publisher relations in America.

The publishing industry as a whole was in a state of transition in the early 1850s, and the changes that were under way were bound to have an impact on the profession of authorship in America. Just what these changes meant for the commerce between author and publisher has never been systematically investigated however.[1] Indeed, before the larger implications of those changes *can* be explored, more needs to be known about publishing practices in general and about the details of the working relationship between individual authors and publishers in particular. The essay which follows is not, therefore, intended to be exhaustive, merely suggestive and—at times—speculative. In it I try to place a specific episode in the history of author-publisher relations within the context of the publishing industry itself and to show how certain tensions generated by the changes that were overtaking the industry caused one such relationship to founder completely.

To understand the inner meaning of Mrs. Stowe's difficulties with John P. Jewett, we must first review the state of author-publisher relations in the period immediately preceding the publication of *Uncle Tom*. It is of course no secret that the life of the would-be professional writer in the 1840s was a hardscrabble one. Authors who could not afford to finance their own works as Irving, Cooper, and Longfellow did soon found themselves in a desperate plight if they attempted to live by their pens alone. As Caroline Kirkland wrote to the Philadelphia publishers Carey and Hart in 1843, "'I have been obliged to renounce the pen, for the present at least.... My school is not as yet very profitable, but I hope to make it much more so than writing has ever been to me—I believe that the same intellect and the same industry which authorship requires, will pay better when exerted in almost any other way.'"[2] Not all authors were driven out of the market altogether, but all felt keenly the inexorable forces that made authorship a marginal occupation. The struggles of authors like Poe and Hawthorne in these years testify to the grinding economic conditions American authors faced in the 1840s.

Yet while authors did not seem to flourish, publishers apparently did. And authors were ready to resent it. Their letters to one another are full of grumblings about the predations of the "'publishing and bookselling *species*—one of the least favorable specimens ... of the generally *not* very estimable mercantile *genus*.'"[3] On occasion a disgruntled author even erupted into print with vitriolic splendor on this subject. A case in point is a short satire entitled "The Author's Tragedy; or, The Perfidious Publisher," which appeared in April 1845 in the *Broadway Journal*. The hero of the piece—or, more accurately, its hapless victim—is a "poor devil" of an author by the name of Writefort who is subjected to the attentions of two knavish publishers. Their stock in trade is a kind of diabolical waggishness that amuses itself by trifling with the dearest hopes and direst necessities of poor Writefort:

> *1st Pub.* ... Porter, bring in that last nuisance. (*The porter brings in a roll of manuscripts. The 1st publisher shoves a reed through it and laughs.*) There, I am ready for him; and here he comes.
>
> *Enter Writefort, an American Author. He takes off his hat and bows respectfully.*
>
> *Author.* Have you examined my work, sir?
>
> *1st Pub.* (*Winks at his brother.*) I have this moment done reeding it.
>
> *Author.* Good heavens! You have read it? Little did I expect this. Sir, accept the thanks of a grateful author. I cannot doubt, then, that you will buy it.... I am partial, I know, but still, I know the work has merit.

* * *

1st Pub. . . . Pray, Mr. Writefort, what value do you put upon your work?
Author. Indeed, Sir, I am afraid to say. No price would seem too large to me who know its value, and none too small to meet my needs.
1st Pub. Would you refuse ten thousand dollars?

* * *

Author. Sir, I will take less, I will take nine thousand five hundred. Excuse my trembling, Sir, but your offer was so unexpected, it has quite unnerved me. I must go home and tell my wife. I will return again tomorrow and close the bargain. (*He shakes both Publishers by the hand, and rushes out in a wild delirium of joy.*)
1st Pub. Ha! ha! ha!
2d Pub. Ho! ho! ho!
All the clerks. He! he! he!⁴

The publishers have, of course, been leading him on. When next we see poor Writefort he has made endless visits to their office only to discover that they refuse to take his manuscript under any circumstances, let alone pay for it. (They have been putting him off with bald sarcasms: "... as for printing it now it is quite impossible—we mean to erect a new steam press *ex*-pressly for it.") When the desperate author accuses them of trifling with him, they eject him from the office forthwith. Writefort's book eventually does get published, but upon "the cheap and nasty plan" as a dingy 25¢ paperback, and so poor Writefort dies, although whether from starvation or a broken heart is hard to tell. He is, however, roused from the dead in the last act by the final indignity that is visited upon his work; it is pirated by Bentley.

The "Author's Tragedy" is obviously a highly exaggerated and humorously colored adumbration of the author-publisher relationship in the 1840s, but it does rest on a gritty substratum of fact. Authors sometimes did encounter publishers who were as high-handed as "1st Pub." Richard Henry Dana's experience with the Harper Brothers while negotiating terms for *Two Years Before the Mast* very nearly approximated that of Writefort.⁵ But the real problem was not, as the satire suggests, that publishers as a class were a bunch of bloated capitalists striding to wealth over the broken bodies of authors; it was, rather, that both the author and the publisher were engaged in trying to squeeze blood out of a stone. Publishing was almost as precarious an occupation as authorship. The book business in the 1840s was beset by cut-throat competition, a scarcity of risk capital, and low prices—all at the same time. If the publisher pressed the author hard, it was because he was hard-pressed himself. By 1850, however, conditions had eased and the book industry was about to enter a boom period the likes of which it had never seen. And American authors were beginning to be able to compete successfully with British authors even though there was still no international copyright law.[6]

One thing that we do know is that by 1850 the author was becoming more and more dependent upon the services of the publisher. The business of sending a book to market was becoming increasingly complex as that market grew and diversified. Able to check the performance of one book against another, the publisher was in a better position to know who the author's audience was and how to reach it. At the same time, the publisher's speculative investment in the author was growing.[7] This is to say that the author needed more than ever before to be able to trust his publisher at the same time that the publisher had to risk more than ever on the author. Thus although the new conditions brought about a recognition of the mutual dependence of author and publisher upon one another, they also rendered the author-publisher relationship potentially more ambiguous.

Mrs. Stowe's rupture with Jewett illuminates with a certain lurid glow the kind of problem that lurked deep in the underbrush of the author-publisher relationship in the 1850s. Her biographers have assumed in passing that she had cause to regret the bargain she made with Jewett for the book publication of *Uncle Tom's Cabin*, for in electing to take the safer 10% royalty than risk going in on a half-profits arrangement, she made far less money on the book than she might have, and far less than Jewett did. They have also assumed that her decision in the matter was a foregone conclusion, given her circumstances at the time. The Stowes had a sizable family to support, and Calvin's salary at that point was only $1,000 a year. Although he had expectations of bettering his financial situation within a year or two, it was still the case that their expenditures threatened to exceed their income. Only Harriet's writing enabled them to make both ends meet. Given this fact and the fact that she went on to publish a second book with Jewett, no one seems to have suspected that the terms of her agreement with Jewett gave her so much annoyance as to cause her to sever relations with him. However, a number of unpublished letters in the possession of the Nook Farm Research Library in Hartford and the Schlesinger Library at Radcliffe College show that although Mrs. Stowe had originally been more than pleased with the terms of her contract, she later came to believe—with some justification—that Jewett had deliberately misled her as to the relative merits of that contract. Yet up to now the letters have been largely overlooked or ignored. Indeed, where they have been noticed by scholars, they have been relegated to the obscurity of a footnote.[8]

Interestingly enough, the fact that the circumstances surrounding the termination of Mrs. Stowe's relations with Jewett have not come to light until recently may be owing in part to the deliberate suppression of the facts by the author herself. Her sister, Catharine, for instance, felt that Jewett had perpetrated "an enormous wickedness" in his dealings with Harriet, and she proposed to publish a tract similar to her "Fact Stranger than Fiction" that would expose Jewett for the scoundrel that he was. Harriet was reportedly quite distressed by sister Cate's meddling, as were the rest of the family. Mary Foote Beecher Perkins, another sister, wrote: "It will be horrible to have this matter brought out with her version & fly all over the country."[9] The family tried to head her off, and apparently succeeded to some extent, for no such tract seems to have materialized, although Catharine did try to have Jewett made the object of church discipline.[10] Harriet also refused to take *A Key to Uncle Tom's Cabin* to another publisher after Jewett had announced it, even though she had already decided to sever relations with him. She was afraid of the publicity that might ensue.[11] Her reticence seems to have continued down to the end of her life, for none of the details appear in Charles E. Stowe's biography of his mother, although he worked from her letters and journals and had her assistance in preparing it.

In his admirable biography of Mrs. Stowe, *Crusader in Crinoline*, Forrest Wilson attempted to fill out the rather truncated account of the negotiations for *Uncle Tom* contained in her son's biography, but he was often forced to fall back on inference in lieu of hard facts. Thus, while his facts are mostly accurate, the version of events he constructs from them is not. There are three important points at which Wilson goes astray: in picturing Jewett as uncertain of the outcome of the venture at the time the contract for the novel was actually drawn up and signed, in suggesting that Jewett tried to talk the Stowes into going half-profits at that time, and in hypothesizing that she changed publishers because Jewett got into financial difficulties in 1853. A reexamination of the known facts, coupled with the new information contained in the letters, shows that Jewett must have known at the time the contract was signed that the book was going to have a larger than usual sale and that under the terms finally agreed upon he therefore stood to gain far more from the sale of the book than did the author—possibly three times as much; that he persuaded her to take the 10% royalty knowing this; and that she changed publishers because she discovered what he had done. In short, Jewett was not the "unsung hero of the novel's book-publication" that Wilson depicts,[12] but—indeed—the "scoundrel" that Catharine Beecher thought him.

When Jewett first approached Mrs. Stowe about the novel in late

August or early September of 1851, *Uncle Tom's Cabin* had been running as a serial in the *National Era* for three months. There is some reason for thinking that he did not have entire confidence in the outcome of the venture at this stage in the proceedings. Phillips, Sampson & Co. had already turned the book down on the grounds that they probably could not sell even a thousand copies of it and that its publication might cause them to lose Southern patronage.[13] As an avowed abolitionist, Jewett had already incurred the latter penalty for publishing antislavery works, so he had no fears on that score, but he may have had some qualms about the book anyway. Phillips, Sampson's reaction to the novel in its early stages shows that it was not considered a sure-fire commercial property. Furthermore, Jewett reportedly did not place much faith in such "transient works as 'ladies' tales.' "[14] Certainly Mrs. Stowe's track record as an author was not encouraging. Although she was beginning to establish herself as a magazine and newspaper writer, she had not brought out a book in ten years, and her first two books, a collection of short stories and a children's geography, had not done very well.[15] According to *Norton's Literary Gazette* for 15 September 1852, Jewett may have been moved to publish the book only by pressure from his wife. A few years later, another version of the same story, a more circumstantial one, would turn up in the pages of the *Gazette*. This one reiterated the point, and stated explicitly that there was "little hope in regard to the enterprise."[16] His doubts seem to have been exacerbated by the fact that the work in question appeared to be running away with its author. As installment after installment made its way into the pages of the *National Era* with no end in sight, Jewett grew uneasy. He finally wrote to the authoress sometime that fall to warn her that the novel was getting too long. The subject was an unpopular one, he pointed out, and where one volume might have a reasonable sale, two might prove "fatal" to the success of the venture.[17] When she failed to respond to his urgings, Jewett asked a fellow publisher, J. C. Derby, to write to her about the matter also, but to no avail.[18] Jewett was obviously worried, and perhaps he had a right to be—in the fall of 1851.

But the contract for *Uncle Tom's Cabin* was not signed until 13 March 1852—just one week before the date of publication.[19] Jewett could not, of course, have predicted just how large a sale the book would eventually have, but the size, price, and format of the first edition all indicate that by this time he was expecting the book to be rather more successful than most. To quote Eugene Exman, author of the *The Brothers Harper* and an old publisher's man himself:

One of the most difficult decisions a publisher makes is the size of the first printing of a new book about ready for press. To guess the likely number of copies the book trade and the book-buying public will ingest within one year, the publisher must consider such factors as the fame of the author, the success of previous books, if any, the best possible retail price—always and of necessity figured on size of printing and royalty percentages—the state of business generally, and of professional readers' opinions particularly.[20]

When Jewett committed himself to a first printing of 5,000 copies of a two-volume work—an enormous figure in 1852—we can only presume that he thought he knew what he was doing. It was a decision to which he had had to give a great deal of thought some time previous. It also meant that he had committed himself to an investment of a little over $2,000.[21] He would hardly have risked that kind of money without good reason, no matter what kind of terms he had made with the author. He also had the book stereotyped. Since it cost twice as much to have a book stereotyped (80¢ per thousand ems) as to have it set up in movable type, publishers in the early 1850s tended to stereotype only those works that seemed destined to go through more than one printing. Ticknor and Fields, for example, did not stereotype the *Scarlet Letter* until it was ready for a third printing.[22] By that time the sales of the book had proved that stereotyping would be a worthwhile investment. It seems likely, therefore, that Jewett hoped ultimately to run off more than 5,000 copies of *Uncle Tom*. Furthermore, he went to the expense of having six engravings made for it and had the book made up in a variety of bindings, including full gilt.[23] All of this added to the cost of publishing the book—and to its retail price.

If Jewett did expect the book to be a success—as we must conclude that he did—then it is hardly to be expected that he would have tried to talk the author into going half-profits on the eve of its publication. Although the half-profits contract allowed a publisher to minimize his losses by making the author liable for half of them, it also meant that he minimized his profit too. Such a contract would have been desirable from Jewett's point of view only if the outcome of the venture had been seriously in doubt. We know, from an invoice sent to Mrs. Stowe, how much it cost to manufacture *Uncle Tom* in cloth binding, so we can actually estimate with a high degree of accuracy Jewett's potential profits under the royalty agreement as opposed to what they would have been under a half-profits contract.[24] Depending on the discount he allowed to retailers, which would have varied from 25% of the retail price on small orders to as much as 33% on large ones, Jewett would have cleared between 44¢ and 56¢ a copy under the royalty agreement, and only 29½¢ to 35½¢ under a half-profits one. Multiply the difference by 5,000 or more copies and it is easy to see why Jewett was bound to prefer paying Mrs. Stowe a 10% royalty even though he had to assume the whole burden of risk himself.

An unpublished letter from Mrs. Stowe to Jewett, written sometime after her return from England in 1853, shows that Jewett actually talked her and Calvin out of going half-profits on *Uncle Tom* and into the 10% royalty, although it raises certain questions about the sequence of events and about the extent to which the Stowes were in the dark as to how much they stood to lose under the royalty agreement:

> Were you correct in persuading me & Mr. Stowe that a ten percent contract on books that sell as mine have is better for us than a *twenty percent one*?— On that question my mind was once settled by ... you[r] representations made to me in the conversations.... hearing your statements and arguments & having none on the other side & being wholly ignorant of business, I was convinced very naturally that your opinion was the correct one.
>
> When I went to England & on many occasions subsequently I had reason to state your arguments to men of business,—as the reasons why I considered my contract an advantageous one. I found the theory disputed,—I found the most honorable publishers of England of their own accord offering me half-profits—& when I enquired if they considered this the fairest arrangement for publisher & author, answering that they did. Moreover on some occasions in my zeal to defend you from what I considered unjust implications I repeated all your arguments & statements to business men in America (not now in the trade) but men who understood its details. They brought arguments & figures, which to my mind seemed to *demonstrate* that your theory of business was not the correct one....
>
> Well then you will say—you offered me ten percent or half profits or any terms I pleased. Certainly you did, but you always offered in this way "Now I'll give you ten per cent or half-profits—or anything youl [sic] say but I do assure you you won't make so much by it—I assure you you'l [sic] lose by it."
>
> In this dilemma—seeing before my own eyes *other publishers* giving twenty per cent & even twenty-five on books where they were expecting to make very large sales, I wrote you again. I asked a reference on these points.
>
> Did you do right to persuade Mr. Stowe that it was best for him to take ten per cent on Uncle Tom when he wished to take twenty & you had offered half profits—and to persuade me afterwards to make the same for the Key & to endeavor to persuade me to adopt this as the best rule in future works.[25]

The probabilities agree with the known facts to suggest that what may have happened was that Jewett offered to publish the book on half-profits in September, when he was uncertain about it, that the Stowes declined, and that he then offered to publish it on the royalty plan (although he could not have been happy about it). But somewhere between the time Jewett first approached her about the novel and the time the contract was signed, the odds pertaining to its success or failure changed. Now the agreed-upon terms worked to Jewett's advantage and to the Stowes' disadvantage, and we might expect the latter to seek to renegotiate those terms and the former to attempt to hold them to those terms. There are several reasons for thinking that this is what may have happened.

It is unquestionably the case that Jewett sought to dissuade the Stowes from going half-profits on *Uncle Tom*. We have her letter to that effect. It would have made no sense for Jewett to have done so in September, while it would have been altogether sensible—if not altogether honorable—for him to have done so in March.[26] According to a statement quoted in Charles E. Stowe's book, the terms of the contract were still up in the air when Calvin Stowe went to Boston to close the deal for the book. Mrs. Stowe is recorded as saying, "'I did not know until a week afterward precisely what terms Mr. Stowe had made....'"[27] It is highly unlikely, as Wilson supposed, that the discussion of terms would have been left until the last minute, so it is logical to postulate that negotiations were reopened when it became clear that the book could be expected to do better than originally had been thought. From the wording of certain portions of Mrs. Stowe's letter it would appear that she and Calvin had occasion to harken back to an earlier offer and to seek the same or equivalent terms sometime later. Her question and her reproach at the end do not make sense otherwise.

In addition, it would be very hard to reconcile her letter with the account of what happened given by her son if the version of events I have proposed were to be rejected. Stowe's biography says that Jewett first offered half-profits, which the Stowes declined, and that "the agreement finally made was that the author should receive a ten per cent. royalty upon all sales."[28] While he may have had reason to suppress some of the facts, there is no reason why he should have distorted any of them significantly. It is also suggestive that when J. C. Derby reported to Mrs. Stowe many years later that Jewett had told him that she had little confidence in the book, she snappishly replied, "'What Jewett says about Uncle Tom is false. I was not altogether such a fool as he represents, although I confess I was surprised at the *extent* of the success.'"[29] Wilson's comment on this remark is that she forgot how pleased she was not to have been "enticed" into going half-profits, but it sounds more as though she had not forgotten that she had been talked into a bad bargain against her better judgment.

Wilson's reconstruction of events leaves no room for an altercation between author and publisher, so he was forced to look for some other explanation of why Mrs. Stowe changed publishers so suddenly in

1853: "John P. Jewett got into financial difficulties and sold out to the Boston house of Phillips, Sampson & Co. not only the copyrights of *Uncle Tom*, the *Key*, and the satellite volumes but his contract with the author as well."[30] It is indeed true that she did go over to Phillips, Sampson & Co., but it was of her own accord, not because Jewett had gotten into financial difficulties. If anything he was a rich man in 1853—thanks to his own acuteness in driving a bargain. Although he was to go under financially, it was not until the panic of 1857.[31] Nor is there any evidence to show that her new publishers bought the copyrights and contract at this time. If they had, they would have given notice to the trade and there is no sign in the trade journals of such a transfer of literary property. In any event, if Jewett really had gotten into such severe financial straits that he had to sell off some of his authors, he was hardly likely to have unloaded the one sure moneymaker on his list.

Whether Jewett deliberately misled Mrs. Stowe about the contract is hard to say; she does not openly accuse him of this in her letter, although she does hint that others may have. At the very least he seems to have played on her ignorance, for subsequent events show that she was laboring under some sort of misapprehension about the comparative merits of the two kinds of contracts, and she does say in her letter that she thought the 10% royalty an advantageous arrangement. She and her husband obviously had some inkling that it might be better to go half-profits on *Uncle Tom* after all, but it is not clear, despite the wording of her letter, whether they knew at the time just how unequal the bargain had become. It is hard to imagine what Jewett *could* have said that would have persuaded them that it was better to take the 10% if they knew that their share under a half-profits agreement would be equivalent to 20%. According to a letter written on 26 June 1852 by Harriet's half-sister, Isabella, who was visiting the Stowes at the time, they were more than happy with their bargain at first. They were ready to defend Jewett from sister Catharine who was outraged by the terms of the contract. She apparently had more business acumen than they:

> Poor sister Cate has taken up the matter of Hatty's bargain with the Publishers & is determined to make a fuss about it—tho' Mr. Stowe did the business in his own way & is perfectly satisfied now—Cate is making herself half-sick about it—calls Jewett a scoundrel & with her usual pertinacity says she will make the matter public unless they adopt her view of the case.... She wont rest till she has made trouble somewhere.
>
> Hatty thinks & knows that tis Jewett's efforts & outlay that have secured so large a sale—She has been behind the curtain & knows where the puffs

come from &c—& she says he has lost Southern trade before, for publishing A. Sy works & being an abolitionist & she is glad to have him rewarded. She will get 20.000 ultimately without doubt to say nothing of future works.[32]

If this version of events makes the Stowes appear a trifle unworldly, we must remember that they were overwhelmed by their sudden wealth. They seemed to understand that Jewett made more by the book than they, but they probably could not believe how much more. The fact that they made the same terms for *A Key to Uncle Tom's Cabin* makes it appear highly doubtful that Jewett had been altogether candid with them, for there was nothing to hinder them from going half-profits on the second book if they chose, except his representations. Perhaps the small fortune they made on *Uncle Tom* appeared to vindicate his arguments in favor of the 10% royalty.

In any event, Mrs. Stowe soon found reason to change her opinion of Jewett and of the merits of her contract with him. It is hard to fix upon an exact date for her awakening to the fact that she had been diddled, but from what she says in her letter to him, it was while she was in England, so it had to have been sometime between 30 March 1853, the day she set sail, and 7 September, the day she embarked for the return voyage.[33] It was probably earlier rather than later, as a letter from Calvin to the Reverend E. A. Park dated 10 May 1853 makes mention of an offer of half-profits from an English publisher.[34] It is even harder to fix on a date for her actual break with Jewett. Unable to reconcile what English publishers had told her with what Jewett had told her, she asked to have the matter of the contract arbitrated. When Jewett angrily refused to go along with the plan, preferring to break utterly, she had no choice but to seek another publisher. There seems to have been several exchanges of notes about the matter, so the affair must have extended itself over a period of several weeks at least.

In a letter to her brother Edward, Harriet says that Jewett's reply to one of her notes has set her at liberty, but that she will not take another publisher for a book that he has announced, which she elsewhere refers to as "this next book."[35] The book in question has to be *A Key*, the only other book of hers Jewett ever published. But *A Key* was published in April and that does not seem to leave enough time for her to have made the trip to England, had her discussion with the English publishers, and then have written to Jewett and received his reply. Besides, the letter to Jewett quoted earlier was written sometime after her return to America, so she was still in correspondence with him in the fall. Since by that time she was already disillusioned with him, it seems unlikely that she was thinking of giving him yet another book. Nor is there any sign that he ever announced another. The exact timing of events may just have to remain a mystery.

The controversy between Mrs. Stowe and her publisher was not simply a sordid squabble over money. As she wrote to Jewett before severing relations with him: "It has never been my intention or desire to make you pay back any part of the proceeds of Uncle Tom. I think if you review my notes you will see no statement of the kind. Neither was the question whether you had done right in making more money than I."[36] What she wanted above all was a clarification of the terms upon which Jewett had been dealing with her. She wanted to know of a certainty whether her faith in his acumen, honesty, and good will had been misplaced. She wrote to her brother Edward:

> I must say that the general character of Mr. Jewett as developed in the whole makes me feel increasingly that he is *not* the man I wish to be in business relations with. He's positive—overbearing—uneasy if crossed & unwilling to have fair inquiries made. So, it seems to me.—I greatly regret that he will not have a reference because I distrust myself & my judgment as much as him & his judgment. How far *I* may have been blinded, by personal feeling, & been consequently erroneous in judgment I do not know, & therefore it was that I did hope an amicable discussion of the matter before impartial friends—For my own part, I feel much as he does that peace of mind is worth more than money. & there can be no peace of mind in future relations with him—founded on arrangements which are subject to such difficulty— For if he offers higher percentage he does it with the assurance that I should lose by it—& if I take ten percent I have the testimony of many business men that & figures that I lose by it—On this dilemma he is unwilling to give me the light that might be gained by a reference to other businessmen—rejects it angrily & prefers to break entirely.[37]

In short, she was as much put off by his manner and his modus operandi as by anything else. She knew that if their relationship was to work, it had to be founded on trust. But, like Melville's confidence man, whose powers of smooth persuasion he seems to have possessed, Jewett refused to let his probity be tested. He demanded that she take him on trust, but offered her no assurance that he was trustworthy, thereby bringing her squarely face-to-face with the ambiguities latent in the author-publisher relationship.

The puzzling thing about the whole affair is why Jewett chose to behave as he did. Like the publishers in "The Author's Tragedy" he acted as though the author were completely unimportant, even expendable. It seems like a rather self-defeating thing to do when that author was Mrs. Stowe. Why, for instance, did he go on to talk her into believing that the 10% contract was the best for *A Key* and endeavor to persuade her that it would be best on future works? It is possible to give him the benefit of a doubt with respect to *Uncle Tom*. He may have felt that the bargain was settled, and once struck must be kept. But Mrs. Stowe was bound to find out sooner or later that the royalty arrangement was not as advantageous to her as he said it was. Indeed, she was already moving in that direction, and he had some ado to head her off. It is easy to see why he might refuse to have the matter arbitrated, but why did he choose to break with her rather than seek to deal with her on new terms? It was not an unheard of thing to do. When Abraham Hart, a Philadelphia publisher, discovered that Caroline Hentz was dissatisfied with the terms upon which he published her work and was considering an offer from another publisher, he was angry and accusative—he seemed to have felt that she had betrayed him—but he offered to match the sum tendered by his rival. Mrs. Hentz wrote back promptly: "Will you tell me exactly what I am to understand by that? On exactly the terms, the best terms on which you are willing to publish it?"[38] Like the proverbial galled jade, Hart must have winced at that, but his answer seems to have been satisfactory, for she continued to publish with his firm for several years thereafter. But Jewett chose rather to kill the goose that laid the golden eggs.

To understand what was at the heart of the contretemps over the contract for *Uncle Tom's Cabin*, we must first understand the nature of the book trade as a business and the role played by the literary contract in author-publisher relations, for the inner logic of the book trade militated against the author, and that logic worked itself out in an unexpected way in the case of *Uncle Tom*.

As publishers in the 1850s were fond of pointing out, and as authors were all too uncomfortably aware, the retailing of fiction was a risky business at best. The public was fickle, but decided, in its preferences, and there was no way to tell in advance, at least with any real certainty, which books would lose money, which would barely cover their expenses, and which would—*mirabile dictu*—turn a tidy profit for all concerned. Of course if a publisher saw no commercial value whatever in a manuscript, he would decline to publish it, but of the ones he did accept for publication, some appeared to pose more of a risk than others. The appearance of a run-away best-seller like *Uncle Tom* was an even more unpredictable event. The problem was that the publisher could not wait to see how a book would turn out before drawing up a contract for it. The best he could hope to do, therefore, was to make an informed guess and draw up an agreement in accordance with his guess. By publication day, or even before, he usually knew from advance sales and other indicators how a book would do on the market, but there were enough incalculables to preserve an indeterminate margin of uncertainty right up to the end of any venture. For months after G. P. Putnam brought out Susan Warner's *Wide, Wide World*, for instance, the publisher thought he would have to write the book up under losses, yet it eventually became one of the biggest best-sellers of the decade.[39]

The existence of this margin of uncertainty could not help but interject a certain amount of tension into the author-publisher relationship, especially in the case of a new or unproven author like Mrs. Stowe, for there was much at stake for both, not just in terms of immediate financial loss or gain, but in terms of the balance of power. An unexpected success or failure could alter their bargaining strengths almost overnight. Because the relationship between author and publisher was rendered inherently unstable by the vagaries of the book trade, the written contract was an important adjunct to it. In Ellen Ballou's words, "The contract embodies the publisher's effort to cover contingencies, the author's to secure a proportionate profit."[40] In effect, a contract is an attempt both to contain and to formalize the uncertainties governing their relative bargaining positions. Hence the nature and terms of the contract can be of vital importance to both parties. While some authors in the 1850s seem to have gotten along without a written contract, as Hawthorne did, few of them were as fortunate as he in being able to place complete and perfect trust in their publishers.[41] As George Boker wrote anxiously, if humorously, to James T. Fields in 1856:

> The want of written agreements has been the cause of so many blunders and misunderstandings in my few business transactions, that I have sworn an oath as high as heaven and as deep as hell, never to enter on any future arrangements without having the terms of the contract clearly set forth in writing. Therefore, O my Fields, do drop me a formal official note, containing your understanding of the matter, or I shall be foresworn, and the guilt will all be yours. I will reply, in due form, and my note shall be enrolled among the archives of your illustrious house.[42]

Boker was joking, but he did make a point of the occasion for the joke.

A variety of contractual arrangements were current in the 1850s, although it would appear, on the basis of available evidence, that in the large drift of events, certain ones were beginning to assume a new prominence over others. The type of contract adopted in a given situation depended on several factors: the degree of confidence the publisher had in the book, the author's past publishing record, and the author's own business sense. It goes without saying that an author who had proven himself in the marketplace was in a better position to negotiate a favorable contract than an untried one. But before he *could* negotiate successfully, he had to know what kind of contract was best under a given set of circumstances, and the author often did not have access to this kind of information except through an obliging publisher—like Jewett. As William Prescott, a shrewd bargainer himself, was to point out to a less experienced friend, "... it is not easy for an author to do the best, always—only the best, his publisher will agree to."[43] What authors did not always realize was that what was best for them and what was best for the publisher were not necessarily the same thing. In fact, they might be contrary to each other.

What was the best contract under a specific set of circumstances depended on two things: the projected performance of a book on the market and the ratio between profit and risk in a contractual arrangement. The several types of agreements can be divided into three basic categories: those in which the burden of risk is assumed solely by the author, those in which it is assumed jointly by the author and the publisher, and those in which it is assumed solely by the publisher. The first category is composed of just one type of publishing arrangement, the commission contract, in which the author agrees to bear the whole expense of publication and to pay the publisher a commission for handling the details of manufacturing and distributing the book. The half-profits contract, in which the author agrees to share equally in both losses and profits, falls into the second category, as does a rather different type of arrangement in which the author pays for the stereotype plates and leases them to the publisher for a percentage of the retail price of every copy sold. The royalty contract and the outright sale of a manuscript comprise the third category.

It can be taken as axiomatic that where the success or failure of a book are seriously in question, it is not to anybody's advantage to assume the burden of risk in full or in part. But there was a certain amount of incentive for the publisher to assume it himself as often as possible, for whoever had to take on the largest share of the risk also acquired the largest share of the proceeds if the book were successful on the market. The publisher's commission for handling a book for the author, for instance, was miniscule. It amounted to only 5% to 10% of the cost of manufacturing the book, whereas, as Irving and Cooper had shown, the author stood to realize as much as 40% to 45% of the retail price on every copy sold if his work were popular.[44] There was little to tempt an enterprising—and solvent—publisher to become a mere broker for the author, therefore, or to exert himself if he did. He could make far more money under other types of arrangements. Publishers had probably been more willing to publish on commission earlier in the century because they were short on capital, but by the 1850s they could afford to venture more in the expectation of making more, and publishing on commission was confined almost solely to vanity publishing.[45]

Somewhat more to the publisher's taste was the venture in which he and the author shared the burden of risk. Under half-profits both he and the author could each expect to realize somewhere between 15% and 25% of the retail price of each copy sold, although Mrs. Stowe's letter to Jewett indicates that the average was probably around 20%. Since the author did not actually have to put up any money, the risk involved for an author with an assured audience was virtually negligible, and he could make as much or more under this plan than if he invested in stereotype plates.[46] To be sure, Longfellow made a good thing of owning the plates to his own works. According to Charvat, the poet received gross percentages ranging from 20% to 27½% on eight of his books. But since his real royalty depended on the cost of the plates and the volume of sales, his net earnings on all eight averaged out to 18¼%.[47] And it is doubtful whether any other author could have commanded the terms Longfellow did. The case of George William Curtis ("The Howadji"), author of several popular travel books about the Near East, may be more typical. He published a number of books on this plan with Harper's, for which he was paid a gross royalty of only 18%.[48] His net earnings would naturally have been less. The point here is that the author sacrificed a considerable portion of the proceeds from the sale of his work when he assigned part of the risk of publication to the publisher.

There are indications that the half-profits contract was being edged out of favor with publishers by the straight royalty contract under which the latter assumed the whole burden of risk—at least as a standard publishing arrangement.[49] It was not simply that the publisher's take was larger than under any of the other plans that made it so attractive; it was that the author's percentage was fixed, while the publisher's was not. Since the cost per unit of manufacturing a book decreased as the size of an edition increased, that meant that the publisher's take on a popular book was larger than on an unpopular one, and could range as high as 36½%, although it was likely to average around 30%.[50] The only way the publisher was likely to lose was if he badly misjudged the demand for the book. The breaking point depended on the cost of an edition, but hovered around the halfway point. The author's royalty might be set as high as 15%, as Hawthorne's was, but that was comparatively rare. It was more likely to be 10%, although it could go as low as 8%. Since the author received his percentage on every copy sold whether the book cleared expenses or not, the royalty system was undoubtedly the safest one for him. Of course, if the book did fail, the publisher's indebtedness was increased by his payments to the author. It was to guard against this eventuality that a publisher might choose to exempt the first 1,000 copies of a book from copyright (the term then used for "royalty"). In one instance, however, Harper's went so far as to exempt the first 3,000 copies of a book, a proceeding for which there was no justification except the chance to make a larger than usual profit, for if they expected to sell that many copies the book could hardly have been considered a risky venture.[51]

When a publisher bought a manuscript outright, he was likely to offer a flat sum equivalent to no more than a 10% royalty on the least number of copies he thought he could sell, but he might well offer even less if he thought he could get away with it. Mrs. E. D. E. N. Southworth discovered this unpleasant fact while trying to arrange for the publication of one of her serials in book form. She wrote to Robert Bonner, who was acting as her agent in the matter: "As for Bride of an Evening if T. B. Peterson wont give six hundred dollars for it and any New York Publisher will give that or more, let the N. Y. publisher have it. T. B. Peterson ought to give eight hundred for it but I know he will not give one dollar more than he can help."[52] Her assessment proved only too accurate. Bonner was unable to obtain a New York publisher for the book and was forced to let it go to Peterson for $400.[53] Although the outright purchase of a manuscript meant that the publisher had to make a larger initial outlay, thereby increasing the burden of risk he assumed, he stood to reap an enormous profit if the book did well. J. C. Derby offered Sarah Parton ("Fanny Fern") 10¢ a copy or $1,000 outright for her first book. In other words, he was betting that he would sell at least 10,000 copies or more. In fact he sold between 70,000 and 80,000 copies of the book. If the author had taken the $1,000, which she was astute enough not to, Derby would have cleared between $6,000 and $7,000 over and above his usual generous margin of profit, while the author's share of the returns would have amounted to 1% of the retail price per copy or less.[54]

Since the publisher usually had the upper hand in all negotiations, it was likely to be he who determined where the burden of risk would fall. Later in the century William Dean Howells would sum up with admirable succinctness the publisher's philosophy on this point: "It is human nature, as competition has deformed human nature, for the publisher to wish the author to take all the risks...."[55] So although there was a growing tendency for publishers to publish more and more at their own risk, it was still the case that a publisher would agree to assume the full burden of risk only if he thought the odds were in his favor. If he were in doubt about a manuscript, he would try to get the author to share the risk. Failing that, he would exempt a certain number of copies from earning royalties. The latter practice of course reduced the author's share of the proceeds still further. Thus negotiations tended to work out in such a way that, for a manuscript with a given sales potential, the ideal contract in terms of the profit-to-risk ratio for the publisher was precisely the worst one for the author. It was not to an author's advantage to share the risk on a book whose commercial potential was in question, nor to accept a fixed royalty on one whose commercial value was evident. Yet that was exactly what the publisher was most likely to propose he do, unless something intervened to alter the balance of power between author and publisher. It was, with rare exceptions, a case of "heads I win, tails you lose," with the publisher calling the shots.

That Jewett, or any other publisher, should seek to drive such a hard bargain was not altogether owing to greed. It was partly owing to the precarious nature of the book business itself. Said one publisher of the period, as he sought to defend himself and his fellow publishers from the charge that they exploited authors, "Publications which prove really successful and remunerative are lamentably few in comparison with the whole number of ventures."[56] What this meant was that the successful books had to be made to subsidize the failures, as well as to cover the various business expenses that were not charged against a book in figuring the cost, such as light, heat, rent, office help, advertising, and so on. To make a go of business at all, the publisher was compelled to avoid taking any unnecessary risks. The necessary ones were already plentiful, since he had to make all of his calculations upon probabilities rather than certainties. He also had to seek as large a margin of profit as possible on ventures that looked promising.

Jewett probably knew that sooner or later Mrs. Stowe would raise the ante, just as Mrs. Hentz did, but he undoubtedly hoped to hold the line as long as possible. There is some evidence to show that other publishers adopted such a policy toward profitable new authors, although, as with Jewett, it sometimes backfired on them. Henry Peterson, cousin to the tight-fisted T. B. Peterson and publisher of the Philadelphia *Saturday Evening Post*, seems to have held out on Mrs. Southworth even though she was largely responsible for increasing the circulation of the *Post* from 1,200 to 90,000 copies.[57] Even the affable J. C. Derby was not above a little skullduggery of this sort. The 10¢ a copy he paid "Fanny Fern" for *Fern Leaves from Fanny's Portfolio* came to only 8% of the retail price, and he did not offer to raise that percentage when he decided to bring out a second series of her sketches even though the first had been a best-seller.[58] Both Mrs. Southworth and "Fanny Fern" were lured away from their publishers by promises of higher pay.

Unfortunately for Jewett, while he was playing the game strictly according to form, the situation was complicated by the fact that between the time he first opened with Mrs. Stowe for the right to publish *Uncle Tom's Cabin* and the time the contract for it was signed, the odds pertaining to the success or failure of the novel changed. It was one of those contingencies that a contract was supposed to forestall. That he had commenced negotiations with her before the book was finished—albeit unwittingly—set the stage for what happened. According to an item carried in the *National Era* for 18 September 1851, Jewett had agreed to hold off publishing the story in book form until such time as the serial should have run its course. The same item also stated that stereotyping was to begin that same week.[59] Apparently neither he nor the author realized that the serial would run another six months, picking up readers and generating excitement as it went along. (Simon Legree had not even made his entrance yet, and some of the most harrowing and lurid episodes were still to come.) This supposition is confirmed by the fact that the editor of the *Era*, Gamaliel Bailey, paid her in three uneven installments for the story, explaining as he did so that he had not planned on such an outlay when he engaged her services.[60] The shift in odds that transpired in medias res put Jewett in the awkward position of wanting to reverse himself about the desirability of the agreed-upon terms while making it impossible for him to explain why without giving the whole show away.

Jewett may well have felt justified in holding Mrs. Stowe to the 10% arrangement because of all the trouble and expense he had gone to in promoting the book. Even she acknowledged the value of his efforts. He actually hit upon a new—and expensive—marketing technique, the use of intensive advertising.[61] He traveled to Washington to talk the book up among senators and congressmen. He succeeded in getting the novel puffed in dozens upon dozens of papers. He engaged in extraordinary promotional stunts such as paying John Greenleaf Whittier to write a song about little Eva, which he then paid someone else to set to music.[62] Jewett may have made away with the lion's share of the profits, but he did do a great deal that was of lasting benefit to the author. Only in the process of learning how to exploit the mass market for books more efficiently than anyone before him, Jewett created a Frankenstein. He had helped to make Mrs. Stowe the most celebrated and sought-after author of her day, but in so doing he had also created an author who did not need him, who was entirely beyond his power to coerce or cajole. In denying her a higher percentage and denying her desire for a reference, he was also denying that the balance of power between them had shifted—if not to himself, then to her. It is entirely possible that he could not make the psychological adjustment that would have enabled him to deal with her on new and radically different terms. Her analysis of his character suggests that he was not a flexible man. Perhaps if all she had wanted from him was money, the whole affair could have been settled to both parties' satisfaction. But she called his integrity into question and there was just enough of an edge to her suspicions to make a man like Jewett feel that to agree to test the question was tantamount to admitting guilt.

NOTES

1. William Charvat set out to make a series of studies that would delineate the problem, but he died before he could complete his work. The studies that he did complete, collected and published posthumously under the title, *The Profession of Authorship in America, 1800–1870*, ed. Matthew J. Bruccoli (Columbus: Ohio State University Press, 1968), pertain, for the most part, to the period between 1800 and the late 1840s. Thus his investigation was broken off at a critical point, for it stopped short of the period in which the book trade was to undergo a dramatic transition.

2. James B. Stronks, "Author Rejects Publisher: Caroline Kirkland and *The Gift*," *Bulletin of the New York Public Library*, 64 (October 1960): 549–50.

3. Alexander Hill Everett to Lydia Sigourney, 15 May 1842; quoted in Elizabeth Evans, "Mrs. Sigourney's Friend and Mentor," *Bulletin of the Connecticut Historical Society*, 36 (July 1971): 88.

4. "The Author's Tragedy; or, The Perfidious Publisher," *Broadway Journal*, 1 (19 April 1845): 250.

5. See Eugene Exman, *The Brothers Harper* (New York: Harper & Row, 1965), pp. 127–28, for an account of Dana's troubles with Harper's.

6. John Tebbel, *A History of Book Publishing in the United States* (New York: R. R. Bowker, 1972–), 1:206–14.

7. Tebbel, *A History of Book Publishing*, 1:214, and Ellen Ballou, *The Building of the House* (Boston: Houghton Mifflin, 1970), p. 141.

8. Kathryn Kish Sklar remarks on the Nook Farm letters in the notes to *Catharine Beecher: A Study in American Domesticity* (New Haven: Yale University Press, 1973), p. 236, while Edward Wagenknecht quotes from one of the Radcliffe College letters in a note to *Harriet Beecher Stowe: The Known and the Unknown* (Princeton: Princeton University Press, 1965), pp. 242–43.

9. Mary Foote Beecher Perkins to Lyman Beecher, 22 January 1853, CtHNF.

10. Catharine Beecher to the Reverend E. N. Kirk, 4 July 1855, CtHNF.

11. Harriet Beecher Stowe to Edward Beecher, n. d. (draft), MCR-S.

12. Forrest Wilson, *Crusader in Crinoline* (Philadelphia: J. B. Lippincott, 1941), p. 277.

13. J. C. Derby, *Fifty Years Among Authors, Publishers and Books* (New York: G. W. Carleton, 1884), p. 520.
14. " 'Uncle Tom' and His Followers," *Norton's Literary Gazette*, 2 (15 September 1852): 168.
15. Charles E. Stowe, *The Life of Harriet Beecher Stowe* (Boston: Houghton, Mifflin, 1890), pp. 158–59.
16. *Norton's Literary Gazette*, n.s. 1 (1 June 1854): 275.
17. Lyman Beecher Stowe, *Saints, Sinners and Beechers* (Indianapolis: Bobbs-Merrill, 1934), p. 184.
18. Derby, *Fifty Years*, p. 457. Mrs. Stowe may well have been better able to judge the potential appeal of the book than Jewett; she was receiving "fan mail" from her readers. When Gamaliel Bailey, the editor of the *National Era*, asked his readers if they wanted her to wind up the story in a summary fashion, they demanded that she go on with the story (Wilson, *Crusader in Crinoline*, pp. 273–74).
19. Stowe, *Life of Stowe*, p. 159.
20. Exman, *The Brothers Harper*, p. 247.
21. Mrs. Stowe received an invoice from Jewett for one copy of *Uncle Tom* in cloth for which she was charged 56¢. That figure would have included not only the cost of manufacture, but also her royalty of 15¢—at least if Jewett figured the cost per unit the same way that Ticknor and Fields did. Thus the cost to manufacture one copy would have been 41¢, which when multiplied by 5,000 comes out to $2,050. Since he also put out a full gilt version, which cost somewhat more to manufacture, the total investment would have been even greater. Information about the invoice is drawn from Stowe, *Life of Stowe*, p. 159.
22. Relative costs of stereotyping and setting of type are derived from a comparison of figures for entries chosen at random from *The Cost Books of Ticknor and Fields*, ed. Warren Tryon and William Charvat (New York: Bibliographical Society of America, 1949). For information about *The Scarlet Letter*, see entries A173a, A179a, and A189a.
23. Advertisement for *Uncle Tom's Cabin, Norton's Literary Gazette*, 2 (15 March 1852): 57. Here Jewett says the book will be sold in three styles of binding—paper, cloth, and cloth gilt—but in a later advertisement he lists only the latter two (*Norton's Literary Gazette*, 2 [15 June 1852]: 120).
24. See note 21. Estimates of retailers' discounts are based on information in the introduction to *The Cost Books of Ticknor and Fields*, p. xliii.
25. Harriet Beecher Stowe to John P. Jewett, n.d. (draft), MCR–S.
26. For reasons that will be discussed later, it is highly unlikely that Jewett would have offered her a *choice* between half-profits and a 10% royalty at the outset.
27. Stowe, *Life of Stowe*, pp. 158–59.
28. Stowe, *Life of Stowe*, p. 158.
29. Wilson, *Crusader in Crinoline*, p. 622.
30. Wilson, *Crusader in Crinoline*, p. 398.
31. *Dictionary of American Biography* (New York: Scribner's, 1933), 10:69.
32. Isabella Beecher Hooker to John Hooker, 26 June 1852, CtHNF.
33. Wilson, *Crusader in Crinoline*, pp. 344, 393.
34. Calvin Stowe to the Reverend E. A. Park, 10 May 1853, MB.
35. Harriet Beecher Stowe to Edward Beecher, n.d. (draft), MCR–S.
36. Harriet Beecher Stowe to John P. Jewett, n.d. (draft), MCR–S.

37. Harriet Beecher Stowe to Edward Beecher, n.d. (draft), MCR–S.
38. Caroline Lee Hentz to Abraham Hart, 30 November 1851, MB.
39. Derby, *Fifty Years*, pp. 304–305.
40. Ballou, *The Building of the House*, p. 141.
41. See Caroline Ticknor, *Hawthorne and His Publisher* (Boston: Houghton Mifflin, 1913).
42. George Boker to James T. Fields, 27 November 1856; quoted in James C. Austin, *Fields of the Atlantic Monthly* (San Marino, Calif.: Huntington Library, 1953), p. 24.
43. Exman, *The Brothers Harper*, p. 226.
44. Ballou, *The Building of the House*, p. 141. The figures for Irving and Cooper can be found in Charvat, *The Profession of Authorship*, pp. 33, 75.
45. See *The Cost Books of Ticknor and Fields*, entries A178b, A190b, A206a, A208b, and A247b as typical examples of vanity publishing. I have discovered only one instance in which a publisher offered to publish a potentially profitable book on commission, and the offer was made under unique circumstances. When P. T. Barnum decided to bring out a second edition of his autobiography in 1854, he put the book up for bids. Twenty-one publishers bid on it. Four of the bids were offers to publish on commission, two at 5% and two at 10% (*Norton's Literary Gazette*, n.s. 1 [1 November 1854]: 554).
46. Harper's went half-profits with Melville on most of his books, and far from demanding that he put up cash, they advanced *him* money on the books (see Harrison Hayford, "Contract: *Moby-Dick*, by Herman Melville," *Proof*, 1 [1971]: 3, and Exman, *The Brothers Harper*, p. 283).
47. Charvat, *The Profession of Authorship*, p. 159.
48. "Memorandum of an Agreement made this Fourteenth Day of June, 1858, between Geo. William Curtis, Attorney, and Harper & Brothers," RPB.
49. Exman, *The Brothers Harper*, p. 331, and Tebbel, *A History of Book Publishing*, 1:275.
50. We can see to what extent the author lost out to the publisher under a straight royalty contract in the table below, which is based on the Ticknor and Fields cost book entry for Mrs. Anna Cora Mowatt Ritchie's novel, *Mimic Life* (1856). The format and design of this book were perhaps a trifle more elegant than the average run of books, but they were not unusual. Figures are expressed as a percentage of the retail price of the book.

SIZE OF EDITION	1,000	2,000	5,000	10,300
Cost	37.9%	30.0%	28.5%	23.5%
Retailer	30.0%	30.0%	30.0%	30.0%
Author	10.0%	10.0%	10.0%	10.0%
Publisher	22.1%	30.0%	31.5%	36.5%

Although the publisher's discount to the retailer would have varied from as little as 25% to as much as 33%, depending on the size of the order, I have assumed an intermediate discount of 30% for the sake of simplifying the table. I have also assumed that the two smaller editions would have been printed from movable type, the larger from stereotype plates. *Mimic Life* was actually stereotyped in an edition of 10,300 copies, hence the last figure. The cost of other (imaginary) editions was calculated from the figures given in the entry. (The cost of manufacturing *Uncle Tom* in cloth came to 27½% of the retail price.) See Tryon and Charvat, *The Cost Books of Ticknor and Fields*, entry B133.

51. Harper & Brothers Contract Book I, p. 159, NCC.
52. Mrs. Southworth to Robert Bonner, 20 July 1860, NcD.
53. Mrs. Southworth to Robert Bonner, 10 August 1860, NcD.
54. Derby, *Fifty Years*, pp. 208–209. Other sources cite different (and lower) figures as the sum offered, but the point is the same in any case.
55. William Dean Howells, "The Man of Letters as a Man of Business," *Literature and Life* (New York: Harper's, 1902), p. 13.
56. G. P. Putnam, " 'Freestone'—Authors—Publishers," *Literary World*, 10 (29 May 1852): 396. Putnam's letter is a response to an article entitled "Freestone for Authors," which appeared on 22 May (p. 363).
57. Mary Noel, *Villains Galore* (New York: Macmillan, 1954), pp. 40–41.
58. Information drawn from the author's copies of the contracts for the two books, MNS.
59. Wilson, *Crusader in Crinoline*, p. 269.
60. "A Pioneer Editor," *Atlantic Monthly*, 17 (June 1866): 748.
61. Tebbel, *A History of Book Publishing*, 1:427–28.
62. Isabella Beecher Hooker to John Hooker, 26 June 1852, CtHNF, and Wilson, *Crusader in Crinoline*, p. 284.

LOUISA M. ALCOTT IN PERIODICALS

Madeleine B. Stern

"MY FIRST STORY was printed, and $5 paid for it. It was written in Concord when I was sixteen. Great rubbish! Read it aloud to sisters, and when they praised it, not knowing the author, I proudly announced her name."[1]

As it turned out, this statement, written by Louisa May Alcott in her 1852 journal, was portentous. At the age of nineteen, writing in a house on Boston's High Street where her mother had opened an intelligence office to increase the meager family income,[2] Louisa was referring to "The Rival Painters. A Tale of Rome."[3] This was the story of Guido, a Florentine artist who fell in love with Madeline, and of his rival Count Ferdinand. Madeline's father announced he would give his daughter to the one who "hath painted a picture the most perfect in grace, and beauty of form, design and coloring." In his lesser love the count painted Madeline, but Guido sketched a portrait of his mother that won the prize. And on 8 May 1852 Louisa Alcott won the satisfaction of seeing her story, if not her name, in the *Olive Branch*. During the next fifteen years she would try her hand at a variety of occupations from sewing to washing, from domestic service to teaching. The family was poor, the cost of coal, the price of shoes high, and Bronson Alcott's lofty discourses on universal love did little to augment the family treasury. For the most part, however, Louisa Alcott wrote for her living and took her pen for her bridegroom.

Between 1852 when her first prose story was published and 1888 when she died, she would produce about 210 poems and sketches, stories and serials that would be published in some forty different periodicals. Thus the bulk of Louisa Alcott's writings appeared in the periodical literature of the day. Though some of those writings were reprinted in book form (as well as in other periodicals) many of them had solo magazine appearances and still await the research of the literary detective. Even the stories and serials that were reprinted as books—and these include several of her major works as well as most of the short-story collections—first appeared in periodicals, and so those periodicals are invested with great bibliographic and bibliophilic interest. Since most Alcott bibliographers have restricted themselves to her book publications, this really vast area of literary creation forms an unexplored mine—a mine for the bibliographer who can trace her books to their beginnings much as the philologist traces the derivation of words; a mine for the biographer who can gain from these periodical appearances all sorts of insights, from dates of composition to dealings with editors. As for the writings that were never reprinted, they include revealing autobiographical narratives, propagandist articles, and sensational tales. They employ so many varied techniques—sweetness and light, blood-and-thunder, naturalism and realism—that this great body of unread material demands rediscovery.

To the literary critic this study must prove as fruitful as to the bibliographer and the biographer. Louisa Alcott owed much to her periodical appearances. From the exigencies of serialization she learned to apply the cliffhanger technique to stories that were well paced and suspenseful, and for a variety of magazine audiences she learned to supply the demands of varied tastes. Her writings in periodicals reflect far more comprehensively and incisively than her *Little Women* series her development as a writer. Louisa Alcott was a far more complex writer than the appellation of "Children's Friend" has suggested. Her methods were diversified, and she moved slowly from a witch's cauldron to a family hearth. Those methods and those stories were aired in the periodicals of her day and to them the bibliographer-biographer-critic must turn for a fuller comprehension of a fascinating literary figure who earned a place in many niches.

Louisa's first major magazine was the *Saturday Evening Gazette*. In her early twenties she was already adopting the methods of the professional writer by studying her medium and its audience before submitting her work to the editor's scrutiny. William Warland Clapp the younger, publisher-editor of the weekly, was also an authority on the American theater, especially the Boston stage, and so had much in common with his young contributor who had a lifelong romance with greasepaint. His paper, the *Saturday Evening Gazette* (Boston), carried, besides theatrical news, "lighter gossip of Boston life," humor, and "amusing tales."[4] To it, Louisa Alcott, beginning in 1854, made fifteen contributions, one or two under the pseudonym Flora Fairfield. Most of the stories were indeed fair and flowery in the sweetness and light school, sentimental and silver-lined, although the first—"The Rival Prima Donnas"[5]—veered into violence and vengeance when one singer crushed her competitor to death by means of an iron ring placed upon her head. This effusion filled three columns of the 11 November 1854 issue where it appeared over the name Flora Fairfield.

"I sent a little tale to the 'Gazette,'" Louisa recorded in her journal, "and Clapp asked H.W. [her cousin Hamilton Willis] if five dollars would be enough. Cousin H. said yes, and gave it to me, with kind words and a nice parcel of paper, saying in his funny way, 'Now, Lu, the door is open, go in and win.'"[6]

The door of the *Gazette* opened wide to her. At prices ranging from five to ten dollars, the narratives authored by L.M.A. appeared during the next few years in its columns, and upon one occasion Louisa had the pleasure of seeing a yellow street placard announcing the publication of "Bertha"[7] by the author of "The Rival Prima Donnas." As her head spun with plots about strong-minded women and poor lost creatures, L.M.A. became the mainstay of the *Gazette*. One of those stories cast a long shadow. "The Sisters' Trial,"[8] published on 26 January 1856, described a year in the lives of four sisters: Agnes the actress, Ella the governess, Amy studying art in Europe, Nora remaining at home to write. As Louisa Alcott noted in her diary, "C. paid $6 for 'A Sister's Trial.'"[9] When the sisters were renamed March, they would earn more for their creator. Meanwhile they provide a previously unrecognized clue to those who search out literary sources.[10]

"I am in the garret with my papers round me, and a pile of apples to eat while I write my journal, plan stories, and enjoy the patter of rain on the roof, in peace and quiet."[11] When that Journal, after the bowdlerizing editorship of Ednah D. Cheney, was made public the year after Louisa Alcott's death, it was filled with cryptic references and people—especially editors—identified only by initials. It was for "F.L." that Louisa doffed the rose-colored glasses she had worn for readers of the *Saturday Evening Gazette* and turned to the unmitigated joys of sensationalism. *Frank Leslie's Illustrated Newspaper* ran the first major sensational story by Louisa Alcott and so began what might well be called a career within a career. Letting down her literary tresses, Louisa Alcott might have become the American Mrs. Radcliffe had she not at length been diverted from her gory, gruesome, and fascinating course.

In 1862, in the midst of the Civil War, *Frank Leslie's Illustrated Newspaper*, the popular New York weekly devoted to alluring pictures, gossip, and murder trials, offered a $100 prize for a story.[12] Frank Leslie had his hand on the public pulse when he supplied it with graphic cuts of murders and assassinations, prize fights and fires, and created a weekly that would dominate the field of illustrated journalism for nearly three-quarters of a century. His staff included E. G. Squier, the archeologist-scholar, and the latter's wife, Miriam Squier, who would one day divorce him and marry Frank Leslie and who was already enough of a *femme fatale* to supply Louisa Alcott with inspiration for many a sensational heroine.

It was not merely for the $100 prize, though that would help pay the family debts, that Miss Alcott wrote the first of her blood-and-thunder tales. In it she could give vent to the pent-up emotions of her thirty years: to the anger she had felt when, having gone out to service in Dedham, Massachusetts, she had been humiliated and mistreated; to the despair she had felt when, in a moment of hopeless darkness, she had contemplated suicide in the Mill Dam. She could stir in its crucible her passion for dramatics and her readings in Gothic romances. Drawing as her heroine a richly sexual *femme fatale* with a mysterious past, an electrifying present, and a revengeful future, she could bring her character to life and at the same time explode her own feminist anger at an unjust world. "Pauline's Passion and Punishment,"[13] the suspenseful tale of a proud woman's fury and its ironic consequences, set against an exotic background, was entered in competition for the Leslie prize.

In December 1862, when its author was working as a nurse in the Union Hotel Hospital, she received a letter from the editor, E. G. Squier, informing her that "Your tale 'Pauline' this morning was awarded the $100 prize for the best short tale for Mr. Leslie's newspaper, and you will hear from him in due course in reference to what you may regard as an essential part of the matter. I presume that it will be on hand for those little Christmas purchases. Allow me to congratulate you on your success and to recommend you to submit whatever you may hereafter have of the same sort for Mr. Leslie's acceptance."[14] With the new year of 1863 the newspaper announced that after deliberating over the moral tendency and artistic merit of over two hundred manuscripts, the editor had decided to award the first prize to "a lady of Massachusetts" for "Pauline's Passion and Punishment." In the next number the first half of a story of "exceeding power, brilliant description, thrilling incident and unexceptionable moral" was anonymously published with appropriate graphic illustrations.[15] "Received $100 from F.L.," Louisa commented in her Journal, "for a tale which won the prize last January; paid debts, and was glad that my winter bore visible fruit."[16] Other visible fruit ripened in the Leslie periodical: "A Whisper in the Dark"[17] and "Enigmas,"[18] a mystery about Italian refugees, a spy, and a woman disguised as a man. In 1866 Miriam Squier reminded Louisa Alcott that Frank Leslie would be glad to receive a sensational story from her every month at $50 each.[19]

By that time the prolific writer had found another periodical market for her ghoulish productions and was receiving between $2 and $3 a column for her thrillers from a Boston firm headed by another remarkable trio, Elliott, Thomes, and Talbot, publishers of the *Flag of Our Union*.[20] William Henry Thomes had been a victim of gold fever and sailed aboard an opium smuggler between China and California before forming a publishing partnership with the editor James R. Elliott in 1861—a year after the New York firm of Beadle had introduced their dime-novel series to an avid American reading public. Joined by Newton Talbot, who had sailed to New Granada, the trio operated from Boston's Washington Street and, like the House of Leslie in New York, issued a chain of periodicals to bring romance and adventure to a nation at war.

The mainstay of the firm was the *Flag of Our Union*, a miscellaneous weekly designed for the home circle. Although it scarcely lived up to the publishers' boast that it contained "not one vulgar word or line," it did specialize in violent narratives peopled with convicts and opium addicts. For that periodical Louisa M. Alcott, under the pseudonym A. M. Barnard, produced her bloodiest and most thunderous thrillers. "V.V.: or, Plots and Counterplots,"[21] "A Marble Woman: or, The Mysterious Model,"[22] "Behind a Mask: or, A Woman's Power,"[23] and "The Abbot's Ghost: or, Maurice Treherne's Temptation"[24] ran in the *Flag of Our Union* between 1865 and 1867. Both the pseudonym A. M. Barnard and the titles of her gory tales were discovered by Leona Rostenberg when, working in Harvard's Houghton Library, she hit upon a series of five remarkable letters from James R. Elliott to Louisa Alcott. The letters, citing terms and editorial reactions, are interesting enough to be quoted in part:[25]

"I forward you this evening the 3 first copies of the 'Flag' in its new form.

"I think it is now a literary paper that none need to blush for, and a credit to contribute to its columns, rather than otherwise.

"Now I have a proposition to make you. I want to publish your story 'V.V.' in it, in place of publishing it as a Novelette in cheap style, as I had intended, and will give you $25. more for the story provided I can publish it under your own name."

The author resisted the additional $25 and "V.V.: or, Plots and Counterplots," its authorship unacknowledged, appeared as a four-part serial in the *Flag of Our Union* in February 1865. An involved narrative about a danseuse, Virginie Varens, whose flesh was tattooed with the letters "V.V." above a lover's knot, it presented among its ingredients a mysterious iron ring, drugged coffee, a dancer parading as a deaf-and-dumb Indian servant, and at least two violent deaths.

The subsequent letters of editor to author continue to reflect Elliott's growing appreciation of the Alcott contributions and his repeated desire to use her real name—known now for *Hospital Sketches*—instead of A. M. Barnard. Two days after his first letter he writes: "I should be pleased to have you write me some stories for the Flag, of about 25 to 40 pages of such Ms. as 'V.V.' I want them over your own name of course, & I will give you $2.00 a column (short columns you will notice) for them." Later the same month he pursued the prolific fountainhead of thrillers with: "You may send me anything in either the sketch or Novelette line that you do not wish to 'father', or that you wish A. M. Barnard, or 'any other man' to be responsible for, & if they suit me I will purchase them.... I will give you $3,00 per column (run in inside length) for sketches under your own name."

After "A Marble Woman: or, The Mysterious Model" had titillated readers of the *Flag* with plots and counterplots revolving about an opium-eating heroine, Elliott continued his demands along with his blandishments: "Have you written anything in the novel line you would like to have me publish 'by A. M. Barnard, Author of 'V.V.' 'The Marble Woman' &c. &c.? ... my friends think the 'Marble Woman' is just splendid; & *I* think no author of novels need be ashamed to own it for a bantling." The final extant letter in this remarkable series was written in August 1866 to inform Miss Alcott that her story "Behind a Mask" was accepted: "I think it a story of peculiar power, and have no doubt but my readers will be quite as much fascinated with it as I was myself.... I will give you $65. for it." Elliott's judgment was sound, for "Behind a Mask" is indeed a suspenseful story recounted in a masterly manner, a fast-moving narrative that unlocks the past of its actress heroine and the conflicting emotions of its author. It weaves from varied threads a fabric of passion and evil, of fury and revenge, and it provides the lead story of a collection entitled *Behind a Mask: The Unknown Thrillers of Louisa May Alcott*, including four of the Alcott blood-and-thunders.

Throughout her life Louisa Alcott was intrigued by sensationalism. She confessed at one time, "I think my natural ambition is for the lurid style. I indulge in gorgeous fancies and wish that I dared inscribe them upon my pages and set them before the public."[26] Yet she was also a realist when it came to living and a professional when it came to writing. When, therefore, the opportunity arose for her not only to contribute to but to edit a magazine for young people, she discarded her Gothic horrors for simplicity and propriety. The versatile author was well on the way from the witch's cauldron to the family hearth.

In September 1867 Louisa Alcott wrote in her diary a significant notation: "Niles, partner of Roberts, asked me to write a girls' book. Said I'd try.

"F. asked me to be the editor of 'Merry's Museum.' Said I'd try.

"Began at once on both new jobs."[27]

When in 1867 "F."—Horace B. Fuller—invited Louisa Alcott to edit *Merry's Museum*, he described her to the public as "the brilliant author of 'Hospital Sketches,'—who has hardly an equal, and who has no superior as a writer for youth in the country."[28] Despite the fact that she had tried her ink-stained hand at juveniles, having produced *Flower Fables*, *The Rose Family*, and *Morning-Glories, and Other Stories*, Fuller's encomium was highly exaggerated at the time, being more prophetic than actual. So too was his description of the magazine, which he announced as "the oldest magazine for young people published in America." *Merry's Museum* had been founded in 1841 by "Peter Parley" (Samuel Griswold Goodrich) and hence was merely one of the oldest periodicals for boys and girls in the country. It had recently been acquired by Horace B. Fuller of Boston, who had long been interested in children's literature.[29] He had served an apprenticeship with the most extensive schoolbook house in New England, Hickling, Swan and Brown, before joining Walker, Wise and Company, a Unitarian publishing house that upheld the dignity and the rights not only of blacks and of women but of children. The firm included in its list several juvenile series and standard books for the young. Walker, Wise was for a short time metamorphosed into Walker, Fuller and Company until finally Horace B. Fuller set out on his own.

His primary interest was still in juvenile literature and in October 1867 he announced his purchase of *Merry's Museum*. "Several important changes," he declared, "are contemplated in the management of Merry's Museum." It would be "clearly printed, on fine white paper... prepared expressly for our own use." It would be "beautifully illustrated with original designs." Its contributors would include "some of the best and most popular writers for the young," while its editor had "hardly an equal, and... no superior as a writer for youth in the country."

That editor certainly had an indefatigable right hand, keeping up her Journal while she plunged into her new task. "Agreed with F.," she noted, "to be editor for $500 a year. Read manuscripts, write one story each month and an editorial. On the strength of this engagement went to Boston, took a room—No. 6 Hayward Place—furnished it, and set up housekeeping for myself."[30]

In the course of her editorship of *Merry's*, Louisa Alcott would not only edit stories and serials but provide the magazine with nearly thirty of her own contributions. One section of *Merry's Museum* was entitled "Merry's Monthly Chat with His Friends,"[31] and here Louisa May Alcott occupied the editorial armchair in one of the most interesting editorial corners of any juvenile periodical.

Because of that section the January 1868 issue—the first number of the "new" *Merry's*—is of more than common interest. It testified to the editor's industry, including two of her poems and two of her stories along with installments of the serials "Little Pearl" and "The Loggers; or, Six Months in the Forests of Maine," adventures and articles illustrated by Elizabeth B. Greene, bits of educational information, acrostics, and rebuses. It also contained that new editorial section, "Merry's Monthly Chat with His Friends," and there Miss Alcott under the guise of "Cousin Tribulation" contributed an episode that would later appear in *Little Women*.[32] Since it was not until July that she finished the first part of that book and not until August that she received the proofs, this first appearance of a touching incident that would be reused in *Little Women* illuminates the author's methods and at the same time gives a bibliographical significance to the January 1868 issue of *Merry's Museum*. The episode used in lieu of an editorial by "Cousin Tribulation" relates the manner in which the March girls gave their breakfast to a poor family on Christmas morning. Instead of calling the sisters Meg, Jo, Beth, and Amy, she gives them truer names, Nan, Lu, Beth, and May, and has Lu respond characteristically to mother's breakfast suggestion, "I wish we'd eaten it up."

As a sample of Louisa Alcott's writings before and during the composition of *Little Women*, all these 1868 issues of *Merry's Museum* are interesting. It is, however, for a serial that ran between April and November of that year that the periodical has become a bibliographical rarity and a mine for the publishing historian and the Alcott biographer. During those months Louisa Alcott's charming collection of animal stories for children—"Will's Wonder-Book"[33]—was published serially. Two years later *Will's Wonder Book* was also published in book form by the wily Horace B. Fuller without the author's knowledge or consent. More recently it was reprinted as the first of Clarke Historical Library's Juvenile Monographs.[34]

In the eight-part serial, "Will's Wonder-Book," Louisa Alcott made use of her readings in natural history and recalled enough of her childhood ramblings with the family neighbor Henry David Thoreau to explain in a lucid and quite enchanting manner the ways of bees and ants, spiders and crickets, butterflies and squirrels, snails and seals, cats and dogs. Will, for whom the tales are told, outgrows the minor cruelties to which he is prone at the beginning, and in the end shoots "no more song-birds, never stoned frogs, drowned cats, or whipped his pony." It was Hawthorne who in his own *Wonder-Book for Girls and Boys* advised that "Children possess an unestimated sensibility to whatever is deep or high, in imagination or feeling, so long as it is simple, likewise. It is only the artificial and the complex that bewilders them."[35] There is nothing artificial or complex about "Will's Wonder-Book," no writing down. In the serial Louisa Alcott simply re-created the nature and habits of insects and animals and made of that re-creation a colorful scrapbook of facts that take the fancy.

Will's Wonder Book certainly took the publisher's fancy. Two years later, when Louisa Alcott was reaping the rewards of *Little Women* in a grand tour abroad, he published it anonymously in book form without any consultation with his former editor. In so doing he unwittingly provided juvenile literature with a rare volume and the history of American publishing with an interesting footnote.

"Will's Wonder-Book" was perfectly adapted to the editor's dear Merrys. Her contributions to other, quite different periodicals indicate both her versatility and her ability to gauge the varieties of public taste. Despite an early and devastating rebuke from the publisher James T. Fields, who advised, "Stick to your teaching, Miss Alcott. You can't write," Louisa Alcott persisted and in 1860, with "Love and Self-Love,"[36] made her bow in his already prestigious magazine, the *Atlantic Monthly*. The same year she supplied the *Atlantic* with a story that is actually a skeleton of *Little Women*. Even more markedly than "The Sisters' Trial," "A Modern Cinderella"[37] foreshadows the book. The author began "with Nan for the heroine and John for the hero,"[38] but found it impossible to produce a story about her sister Anna's romance without introducing both her sister May and herself. And so "A Modern Cinderella" includes in its cast of characters a sister who sits picturesquely before her easel and another who can lose herself in the delights of *Wilhelm Meister* but hardly knows a needle from a crowbar. Laura is clearly a preliminary sketch of Amy; Nan needs but a touch to emerge as the capable eldest sister, Meg; and Di, corking her inkstand to plunge "at housework as if it were a five-barred gate," drowning "her idle fancies in her washtub" but determined one day to "make herself one great blot"—surely Di is an advance performance of Jo March.

Despite, or perhaps because of, the time she spent in nursing and the illness that resulted from her experience, the Civil War years were productive for Louisa Alcott. Although she offered to "write 'great guns'" for an *Atlantic Monthly* turned warlike, the principal medium she used for her war stories was the *Commonwealth*, an emancipation weekly begun by Moncure Daniel Conway and edited by her Concord friend Frank Sanborn. There her "Hospital Sketches"[39] had their trial run, along with other stories woven about the blue and the gray—and the black. In the columns of the *Commonwealth* appeared scenes Louisa Alcott had witnessed as a nurse in the Union Hotel Hospital, soldiers she had watched, the wounded she had tended. Her rewards were more than the $40 payment for the series. Among those who applauded her efforts was Henry James, Sr., who found in "Hospital Sketches" an exquisite humanity.

There was humanity in her war stories and there was truth in them. There was humor, along with perceptive observation, in the travel sketches she wrote for the *Independent*, a long-lived New York religious weekly edited by Theodore Tilton.[40] By 1868 Louisa Alcott had indeed attempted a wide variety of literary techniques, serving periodicals with divergent tastes. From sweetness and light to blood-and-thunder, from juvenilia to realistic war narratives she had explored a broad range of literary themes. When, on 14 February 1868, Robert Bonner of the *New York Ledger* appeared at 6 Hayward Place offering Miss Alcott $100 for a column of advice to young ladies, she produced a piece entitled "Happy Women,"[41] where working spinsters received the limelight. To sketches of home missionary, physician, and music teacher she added a sketch of herself—a happy writer who was finding a market for her wares.

In 1868 the first part of *Little Women* was published, in 1869 the second. The merchants of Boston, the families of New England, and in time the American public itself laughed and cried over a story destined to become a perennial best seller. The author, who had dispatched her tales to William Warland Clapp and Frank Leslie, to James R. Elliott and Frank Sanborn, to all the C.'s and L.'s and initialed editors of her Journal, had found not only a market but a style. Henceforth, while her market would widen, her themes would narrow. With *Little Women* Louisa May Alcott walked into a niche where, except for a few literary adventures, she would comfortably remain for the next twenty years.

In the spring of 1872, after her grand tour, she noted in her Journal: "Wrote another sketch for the 'Independent,'— ... and the events of my travels paid my winter's expenses. All is fish that comes to the literary net. Goethe puts his joys and sorrows into poems; I turn my adventures into bread and butter."[42] In large measure it was thanks to the abundant and varied periodical literature of the time that Louisa Alcott was able to do so. The bread and butter it provided became increasingly substantial—"$3,000 for a short serial in 1876"[43]—after the slimmer earnings of earlier years.

Her diary entry referring to Goethe was written in 1872, the year that *Merry's Museum* was absorbed by an older juvenile periodical, the *Youth's Companion*.[44] Founded in 1827 by Nathaniel Parker Willis, that monthly forty years later was controlled by Daniel Sharp Ford who invented the name "Perry Mason" for his firm and proceeded to resemble that imaginary publisher—"a benevolent old gentleman with mutton-chop whiskers." The *Youth's Companion*, with its emphasis upon premium lists, was more of a family paper than *Merry's Museum*, although its serials had a strong appeal to the young. Ford, who tabooed crime and immorality, demanded of his fiction writers "liveliness, action, humor, and convincing youthful characters"—demands easily met by the author of *Little Women*. For $35 apiece she could provide little tales written at odd moments, sometimes at the rate of two a day, while a six-part serial like her temperance story "Silver Pitchers"[45] brought $700. In time her contributions to the *Youth's Companion* outnumbered her contributions to any other periodical. The popular stories of Ford's star author appealed as widely to his family audience as the chemical cabinets and magic lanterns he offered as premiums. Alcott narratives that warned against transgression and allured to virtue were easy to manufacture. Autobiographical tales, such as "A Happy Birthday,"[46] recounting her mother's seventy-third birthday celebration or "Reminiscences"[47] of the illustrious Concord neighbor Ralph Waldo Emerson, appealed to and enlightened Daniel Ford's avid subscribers. Some of Louisa's *Companion* stories were reprinted by Roberts Brothers in Alcott collections—a volume of *Aunt Jo's Scrap-Bag* or of *Lulu's Library*. Many, however, have never been reprinted. Yet they are well worth assembling as a "new" collection of stories by Louisa May Alcott.

Second only to the *Youth's Companion* as a periodical market for Louisa was the extremely popular magazine for children begun in 1873 by Roswell Smith and named after the saint associated with Christmas. The editor of *St. Nicholas* was Mary Mapes Dodge, whose tenets regarding a children's magazine were shared by her friend Miss Alcott.[48] There should be no sermonizing, no wearisome recital of facts, no rattling of dry bones. It must not "be a milk-and-water variety of the periodical for adults. . . . it needs to be stronger, truer, bolder, more uncompromising than the other; . . . it must mean freshness and heartiness, life and joy. . . . A child's magazine is its playground." Such beliefs sat well with the former editor of *Merry's* and the author of *Little Women*. Besides, *St. Nicholas* was a handsome periodical, finely printed by the DeVinne press and profusely illustrated by distinguished artists and engravers. Although at first she refused Mrs. Dodge's request for a serial, Louisa Alcott in March of 1874 made her first appearance in *St. Nicholas* with a story, "Roses and Forget-Me-Nots,"[49] which urged kindness to the lame and the poor and which would eventually be reprinted in one of *Aunt Jo's Scrap-Bags*. "Roses and Forget-Me-Nots" was the first of a long line of contributions including short stories and serials. In 1875 "Eight Cousins"[50] ran almost concurrently in *Good Things: A Picturesque Magazine for the Young of All Ages* and in *St. Nicholas*. Here Louisa Alcott crusaded without sermonizing for sound minds in sound bodies, exalting the three great remedies of sun, air, and water. In the course of her crusade she joined the health reformers who castigated medicine and tobacco, strong coffee and hot biscuits. The serial was so successful that it was followed by another, "Under the Lilacs,"[51] which in turn was followed by "Jack and Jill"[52] written at the rate of one chapter a day—all of them illuminating the pages of *St. Nicholas* before their transformation into book form.

Besides these full-length narratives, Louisa Alcott supplied the periodical with numerous short stories. No one who had seen the operetta could fail to respond to "Jimmy's Cruise in the 'Pinafore,' "[53] where, in spite of all temptations to belong to other nations, the hero remained an "Amer-i-can," and where the author could unite the moral of industry with the pleasures of amateur theatricals. Before its reprint appearance in a *Scrap-Bag*, " 'Pinafore' " earned its indefatigable author $100. Indeed Louisa Alcott found it easier to supply Mrs. Dodge with stories and serials than with a photograph of herself. "A pleasant one does not exist," she wrote to her editor, "& the picture of the forbidding woman photographers make me will carry disappointment & woe to the bosoms of the innocents who hope to see 'Jo young & lovely with hair in two tails down her back.' "[54]

The last serial supplied to *St. Nicholas* by Louisa Alcott was a collection of old-time tales with a thread running through all from the spinning wheel introduced in the first—tales based upon Concord's revolutionary relics or Bronson Alcott's early days, stories into which a moral was tucked as one might hide pills in jelly. The Alcott pills were devoured eagerly by her young readers and in 1884 the tales that would be reprinted as *Spinning-Wheel Stories* made their monthly bow in *St. Nicholas*.[55]

Several of Louisa Alcott's major works appeared as serials in periodicals before they were issued between boards: *An Old-Fashioned Girl*[56] in *Merry's Museum*; the autobiographical *Work*[57] in the *Christian Union*; as well as *Eight Cousins, Under the Lilacs,* and *Jack and Jill* in *St.*

Nicholas—indications that the author knew how to butter her bread and spread it with jam to boot.

With *Harper's Young People*—a weekly begun in 1879—*St. Nicholas* and the *Youth's Companion* alone accounted for some seventy stories and serials produced for the young and the young in heart by L. M. Alcott.

The complex L. M. Alcott, however, had a word or two to say to those who were riper in years also, and for that purpose she made use of still another periodical whose columns were always open to her propaganda. "Yours for reforms of all kinds," she signed herself in one of her letters to the *Woman's Journal*, a Boston paper conducted by Lucy Stone and her husband, Henry B. Blackwell. Although the organ of no association it was "thoroughly identified with the interests ... of the American Woman Suffrage Association"[58] and its columns were receptive to Miss Alcott's clarion calls for woman's rights and privileges. "Woman's Part in the Concord Celebration,"[59] letters reporting local suffrage or temperance activities, a town meeting, even an account of her disappointing mind cure treatment, were welcomed by the *Woman's Journal* where they clearly reflected the feminism that had been an oblique and indirect ingredient of Louisa Alcott's early thrillers for the blood-and-thunder periodicals.

She had come a long way since she had concocted the brew in her witch's cauldron. She had turned not only her adventures but her observations, her thoughts, herself into bread and butter, finding a periodical market suited to her varied themes. Some of those periodicals survived her. Two months after her death in 1888, the *Youth's Companion* ran an article that brought her life full circle. "Recollections of My Childhood"[60] appeared in the 24 May issue and was reprinted two days later in the *Woman's Journal*. In it her audience—both youthful and mature, indeed every member of the family circle—could read how Louy Alcott had fallen into the Frog Pond, gone barnstorming in Concord, and shaken a fist at fate. She had had many names and undergone many metamorphoses. She had been called A. M. Barnard in the *Flag of Our Union*, Cousin Tribulation in *Merry's Museum*, and Louisa May Alcott in a host of periodicals. Indeed, in those periodicals, over a period of thirty-five years, her life may be read. One needs only the clues provided by the bibliographer, the insights of the biographer, and of course the periodicals themselves. We brush the dust from those weeklies and monthlies and we reanimate the past, for their pages are still alive with the stories she imagined and the stories that she lived.

APPENDIX

SUMMARY OF ALCOTT IN PERIODICALS, 1851–1888

The following list includes only first appearances; magazine reprints are not cited. In one instance only, the publication of "Eight Cousins" almost simultaneously in *Good Things* and *St. Nicholas* (Stern No. 154), is the entry included twice. Thus the total number of contributions is reduced from 213 to 212.

Stern Numbers refer to numbered items in the bibliography appended to *Louisa's Wonder Book: An Unknown Alcott Juvenile,* ed. Madeleine B. Stern (Mt. Pleasant, Mich.: Central Michigan University and Clarke Historical Library, 1975). A single asterisk indicates a poem; a double asterisk indicates a prose contribution run serially in two or more numbers.

Periodical	Number of Contributions	Years of Publications by Alcott	Stern Numbers
Peterson's Magazine	1*	1851	1
Olive Branch	1	1852	2
Dodge's Literary Museum	1	1852	3
Saturday Evening Gazette	11 + 3* + 1**	1854, 1856, 1859, 1864, 1867	4, 8–17, 20–21, 45, 63
The Little Pilgrim	2*	1858	18–19
The Liberator	1*	1860	22
The Atlantic Monthly	4 + 1*	1860, 1863	23–24, 32–34
The Monitor	1**	1862	26
Frank Leslie's Illustrated Newspaper	3**	1863–64	27, 30, 41
The Commonwealth	2 + 6**	1863–64, 1867	28–29, 31, 36, 40, 42, 44, 57
The Daily Morning Drum-Beat	1 + 1**	1864	38–39
The United States Service Magazine	1**	1864	43
The Flag of Our Union	4* + 4**	1865–67	47–48, 50–55
Our Young Folks	1	1865	49
The Independent	12 + 1**	1867–68, 1872–75, 1878, 1881	56, 59, 65, 84, 123–24, 137, 139, 148, 162, 165, 187, 201

Louisa M. Alcott in Periodicals

Periodical	Number of Contributions	Years of Publications by Alcott	Stern Numbers
Merry's Museum	20, 6* + 3**	1867–70	58, 62, 67–76, 79, 88–90, 92–93, 95–96, 98, 100–101, 103–104, 106–107, 111, 114
Boston Daily Advertiser	1	1867	61
The New York Ledger	1	1868	77
Putnam's Magazine	2	1868–69	82, 102
Frank Leslie's Chimney Corner	1 + 1**	1868–69	83, 94
National Anti-Slavery Standard	1	1868	86
The Youth's Companion	30 + 3**	1868–70, 1872–77, 1882, 1888	87, 99, 108, 110, 112, 127, 129–32, 134–36, 142, 144, 146–47, 149–50, 155, 157, 159, 161, 163–64, 169, 171–72, 177, 181, 205, 209, 265
The New World	1	1869	91
The Christian Register	2	1870, 1872	113, 118
Boston Daily Evening Transcript	2	1871, 1873	115, 138
Hearth and Home	3**	1872, 1874	119, 122, 145
The Christian Union	2**	1872–73	120, 128
Young Folks' Journal	1**	1874	141
St. Nicholas	24 + 6**	1874–88	143, 151, 154, 167–68, 184, 188–89, 195, 199, 212, 217–18, 220, 222–25, 228–33, 235, 241, 249, 256, 258, 264
The Woman's Journal	15 + 3*	1874–76, 1878–80, 1882–87	152, 156, 160, 173, 185, 190, 196, 204, 214–15, 226, 236–39, 243, 247, 253
Good Things: A Picturesque Magazine for the Young of All Ages	1**	1874–75	154

Periodical	Number of Contributions	Years of Publications by Alcott	Stern Numbers
Demorest's Monthly Magazine	2 + 1**	1876, 1881–82	170, 198, 207
Our Union	1	1877	182
Harper's Young People	6 + 2**	1880, 1882, 1884–87	197, 213, 219, 240, 244, 251, 259–60
The Sword and Pen	1**	1881	200
Concord Freeman	1	1882	206
The Union Signal	1	1883	216
The Brooklyn Magazine	2	1886	245–46
The Book Buyer	1	1886	250
The Young Crusader	1	1887	252
The Voice	1	1887	254
The Ladies' Home Journal	1	1887	255
TOTALS	42	150 + 21* + 42** (213)	

NOTES

1. *Louisa May Alcott: Her Life, Letters, and Journals*, ed. Ednah D. Cheney (Boston: Roberts, 1889), p. 68.

2. For all biographical references, see Madeleine B. Stern, *Louisa May Alcott* (Norman: University of Oklahoma Press, 1950), passim.

3. Stern No. 2. These Stern Numbers refer to the Alcott bibliography appended to *Louisa's Wonder Book: An Unknown Alcott Juvenile*, ed. Madeleine B. Stern (Mt. Pleasant, Mich.: Central Michigan University and Clarke Historical Library, 1975). See also the "Summary of Alcott in Periodicals" in the Appendix.

4. Frank Luther Mott, *A History of American Magazines 1850–1865* (Cambridge: Harvard University Press, 1957), p. 35.

5. Stern No. 4.

6. Cheney, *Alcott*, p. 73.

7. Stern No. 12.

8. Stern No. 9.

9. Cheney, *Alcott*, p. 83.

10. For preliminary studies of Alcott in periodicals, see Madeleine B. Stern, "The Witch's Cauldron to the Family Hearth," *More Books: The Bulletin of the Boston Public Library*, 18 (October 1943): 363–80, and Madeleine B. Stern, "Louisa M. Alcott's Contributions to Periodicals, 1868–1888," *More Books*, 18 (November 1943): 411–20.

11. Cheney, *Alcott*, p. 80.

12. For Frank Leslie, his staff, and his periodicals, see Madeleine B. Stern, *Imprints on History: Book Publishers and American Frontiers* (Bloomington: Indiana University Press, 1956), pp. 221–32, and Madeleine B. Stern, *Purple Passage: The Life of Mrs. Frank Leslie* (Norman: University of Oklahoma Press, 1953), passim.

13. Stern No. 27. For Louisa M. Alcott's pseudonym and her anonymous and pseudonymous thrillers, see Leona Rostenberg, "Some Anonymous and Pseudonymous Thrillers of Louisa M. Alcott," *Papers of the Bibliographical Society of America*, 37 (II Quarter 1943): 131–40, and *Behind a Mask: The Unknown Thrillers of Louisa May Alcott*, ed. Madeleine B. Stern (New York: Morrow, 1975), and *Plots and Counterplots: More Unknown Thrillers of Louisa May Alcott*, ed. Madeleine B. Stern (New York: Morrow, 1976).

14. E. G. Squier to Louisa May Alcott, ca. 18 December 1862, Rostenberg, "Some Anonymous Thrillers," n. 2; see also Stern, *Louisa May Alcott*, p. 123.

15. Stern, *Louisa May Alcott*, p. 128.

16. Cheney, *Alcott*, p. 151.

17. Stern No. 30.

18. Stern No. 41.

19. Miriam F. Squier to Louisa May Alcott, 17 September 1866, MH; see also Stern, *Purple Passage*, p. 220.

20. For Elliott, Thomes, and Talbot and their publications, see Rostenberg, "Some Anonymous Thrillers"; Stern, *Imprints on History*, pp. 206–20; and John Tebbel, *A History of Book Publishing in the United States* (New York: Bowker, 1972–), 1:438–40.

21. Stern No. 47.

22. Stern No. 51.

23. Stern No. 53.

24. Stern No. 55.

25. 5 January 1865; they are quoted in their entirety in Rostenberg, "Some Anonymous Thrillers."

26. L. C. Pickett, *Across My Path. Memories of People I Have Known* (New York: Brentano's, 1916), pp. 107–108; Madeleine B. Stern, "Louisa M. Alcott's Self-Criticism," *More Books*, 20 (October 1945): 341.

27. Cheney, *Alcott*, p. 186.

28. For quotations from *Merry's*, see *Merry's Museum*, 54 (October 1867): verso of cover; (November 1867): Prospectus for 1868 on verso of cover; and (December 1867): 1, 2.

29. For Fuller's life and career, see Stern, *Imprints on History*, pp. 45–59, 401–405.

30. Cheney, *Alcott*, p. 186.

31. Stern No. 71.

32. See Madeleine B. Stern, "The First Appearance of a 'Little Women' Incident," *American Notes & Queries*, 3 (October 1943): 99–100.

33. Stern No. 79.

34. This volume, *Louisa's Wonder Book*, contains a reprint of *Will's Wonder Book*, a detailed introduction, and an extensive Alcott bibliography by Madeleine B. Stern.

35. Nathaniel Hawthorne, *A Wonder-Book for Girls and Boys* (Boston: Ticknor, Reed and Fields, 1852), p. iv.

36. Stern No. 23.

37. Stern No. 24.
38. Cheney, *Alcott*, p. 120.
39. Stern No. 29.
40. It was the *Independent* that published (4 June 1874) the autobiographical "How I Went Out to Service" (Stern No. 148).
41. Stern No. 77.
42. Cheney, *Alcott*, p. 262.
43. Cheney, *Alcott*, p. 103.
44. For the *Youth's Companion*, see Mott, *A History of American Magazines 1850–1865*, pp. 262–74.
45. Stern No. 161.
46. Stern No. 142.
47. Stern No. 205.
48. For *St. Nicholas*, see Frank Luther Mott, *A History of American Magazines 1865–1885* (Cambridge: Harvard University Press, 1957), pp. 500–505. Mrs. Dodge's tenets are quoted on p. 501.
49. Stern No. 143.
50. Stern No. 154.
51. Stern No. 184.
52. Stern No. 195.
53. Stern No. 189.
54. Louisa May Alcott to Mary Mapes Dodge, 17 August, n.y., quoted in Stern, *Louisa May Alcott*, p. 280.
55. See Stern Nos. 220, 222–25, 228–33, 235.
56. Stern No. 103.
57. Stern No. 128.
58. Mott, *A History of American Magazines 1865–1885*, p. 94.
59. Stern No. 160.
60. Stern No. 265.

DR. RICHARD MAURICE BUCKE:
A RELIGIOUS DISCIPLE OF WHITMAN

Artem Lozynsky

DR. RICHARD MAURICE BUCKE (1837–1902) of London, Ontario, first met Walt Whitman in Camden, New Jersey, on 18 October 1877, and later that day he reported the event in a letter to his wife, Jessie Maria:

> I called this morning upon Walt Whitman and we were old friends at once. He is the most delightfull man I ever saw—I stayed over an hour at his house and then we crossed the river to Phila together[.] He made a kind of half promise that he would come and see us some time at London and spend some days—I would give anything that he would—his health has been very poor for years but it is now slowly mending[.][1]

On 24 October 1877, in a lengthy letter to his English friend Harry Buxton Forman (1842–1917), the Keats and Shelley scholar, Bucke described the meeting, adding an interpretation of its significance:

> I have just returned from a two weeks trip in the Eastern States. I was in Boston, New York and Philadelphia. When I was in the latter city I crossed the Delaware River to Camden, New Jersey and went to see Walt Whitman. We were old friends in less than two minutes and I spent a good part of the forenoon with him. We then crossed the river together to Philadelphia as he had an engagement there. I hardly know how to tell you about W. W. If I tried to say how he impressed me you would probably put it down to exaggeration. I have never seen any man to compare with him—any man the least like him—he seems more than a man and yet in all his looks and ways entirely commonplace ("Do I contradict myself"?) He is an average man magnified to the dimensions of a god—but this does not give you the least idea of what he is like and I despair of giving you any idea at all however slight—I may say that I experienced what I have heard so much about the extraordinary magnetism of his presence—I not only felt deeply in an indescrabable way towards him—but I think that that short interview has altered the attitude of my moral nature to everything—I feel differently, I feel more than I did before—this may be fancy but I do not think it is—I saw some thing of this same quality of Walt's objectively as well as subjectively during the few minutes that we were on the street together. We

> met a boy and a man who knew Walt—He said to the boy "Well Atty is that you?" hardly above his breath—without smiling, scarcely glancing at him. The boy's face reddened and lit up as I think I never saw a face—the man was a rough, dirty, dark chap—as common and common-place a man as you could find—Walt hardly looked at him and said quietly "Good day Bill"—the man smiled, his face reddened—he became transfigured instantly—there was no mistaking the affection he felt—In conversation Walt expressed no opinions—he does not praise, he never smiles—he has no trace of wit—his talk is not intellectual—but you think you could listen to it forever—but it is no use for me to try to give any idea of the man because I have no idea of him myself—I can't grasp him, I cannot take him in—he is immense—the best of it is that he half promised to come and see me in London next summer and stay awhile. I would rather Walt would make this visit than that I should receive a large legacy.[2]

Much of the remainder of Bucke's life was to be devoted to convincing his contemporaries that there lived among them "an average man magnified to the dimensions of a god." In his three books on Whitman, *Man's Moral Nature* (1879), *Walt Whitman* (1883), and *Cosmic Consciousness* (1901); in his editions of Whitman's letters, *Calamus* (1897) and *Wound Dresser* (1898);[3] and in numerous articles and lectures, Bucke set out to document the divinity of Whitman.

Bucke's meeting with Whitman in 1877 was preceded not only by years of intensive reading of the poet, but also by a mystical illumination. In the winter of 1867–68 Bucke was host to his friend Dr. T. Sterry Hunt (1826–92), a chemist and geologist from Montreal. In the course of conversation, Hunt happened to mention quite by accident the name of Whitman and went on to quote a few lines of his verse. Bucke, in a paper delivered before the Walt Whitman Fellowship in 1894, was to claim that the mention of Whitman's name was a profound experience:

> I recall as if it were yesterday the first time I ever heard pronounced the name of the author of "Leaves of Grass." ... there came to me at that moment, upon the mere mention of the poet's name, how conveyed or whence I have not the least notion, a conviction, which never afterwards left me, that the man so named was a quite exceptional person, and that a knowledge of him and of his writings was of peculiar importance to me.[4]

At this time Bucke was residing in Sarnia, Ontario, and copies of any edition of *Leaves of Grass* were hard to come by. At first he had to content himself with William Michael Rossetti's expurgated text (1868).[5] Later he borrowed a copy of the 1855 edition from Hunt, and by 1870, with the help of his brother Julius, he was busy collating various editions of *Leaves of Grass*.

That same year, Bucke wrote his first letter to Whitman:

Sarnia,
December 19, 1870.

Walt Whitman,

Dear Sir: Will you please send to the enclosed address *two* copies of "Leaves of Grass", *one* copy of "Passage to India" and *one* copy of "Democratic Vistas." Enclosed you will find $7.25–$6.75 for the books and $0.50 for postage. I do not know exactly what this last item will be but I fancy $0.50 will be enough to pay it. [—] I am an old reader of your works, and a very great admirer of them. About two years ago I borrowed a copy of the 1855 edition of "Leaves of Grass" and I have a great ambition to own a copy of this edition myself; would it be possible to get one? Before getting that the only thing I had ever seen of yours was Rossetti's selection. Lately I have got a copy of the 1867 edition of "Leaves of Grass" and I have compared the "Walt Whitman" in that with the same poem in the 1855 edition and I must say I like the earlier edition best.

I have an idea I shall be in Washington in the course of 1871; if I am it would give me much pleasure to see you, if you would not object, I am afraid, however, that, like other celebrities, you have more people call upon you than you care about seeing; in that case I should not wish to annoy you—

At all events
   Believe me
      Faithfully yours,
         R. M. Bucke—

Address
  Dr. R. Maurice Bucke
    Sarnia
      Ontario
        Canada[6]

Whitman sent Bucke the books; but there is no evidence that these were accompanied by a letter.

At about this time, Bucke's health began to suffer. The nature of his illness is difficult to determine, but it seems to have been some form of nervous prostration, caused at least in part by overwork. Bucke gave up the practice of medicine, and in an attempt to regain his health he made several extended visits to England. It was during one of these that Bucke experienced the central event of his life. His illumination occurred in the spring of 1872, either in late March or early April. Bucke has provided a detailed account of it in *Cosmic Consciousness*, narrating it in the third person:

> It was in the early spring, at the beginning of his thirty-sixth year. He and two friends [Alfred and Harry Buxton Forman] had spent the evening reading Wordsworth, Shelley, Keats, Browning, and especially Whitman. They parted at midnight, and he had a long drive in a hansom (it was in an English city [London]). His mind, deeply under the influence of the ideas,

images and emotions called up by the reading and talk of the evening, was calm and peaceful. He was in a state of quiet, almost passive enjoyment. All at once, without warning of any kind, he found himself wrapped around as it were by a flame-colored cloud. For an instant he thought of fire, some sudden conflagration in the great city; the next, he knew that the light was within himself. Directly afterwards came upon him a sense of exultation, of immense joyousness accompanied or immediately followed by an intellectual illumination quite impossible to describe. Into his brain streamed one momentary lightning-flash of the Brahmic Splendor which has ever since lightened his life; upon his heart fell one drop of Brahmic Bliss, leaving thenceforward for always an aftertaste of heaven. Among other things he did not come to believe, he saw and knew that the Cosmos is not dead matter but a living Presence, that the soul of man is immortal, that the universe is so built and ordered that without any peradventure all things work together for the good of each and all, that the foundation principle of the world is what we call love and that the happiness of every one is in the long run absolutely certain.[7]

Much of Bucke's time during the 1870s was devoted to establishing a scientific foundation for this experience of "Brahmic Bliss." But the work was slow and tortuous. Although Bucke was absolutely certain of the validity of his illumination, support in current scientific writing was hard to find. Eventually, in *Man's Moral Nature*, Bucke came up with an unwieldy system which moves from physiology to theology by way of contemporary evolutionary thought. Paralleling the evolution of our bodies, there has been the evolution of our moral nature, which has its roots in the great sympathetic nervous system. For Bucke, we are evolving at an ever increasing rate into beings whose moral nature shall one day be a continual expression of love and faith, and a mirror of the true nature of the universe. Various individuals may occasionally glimpse this truth in moments of illumination; a certain few spend their entire adult lives on this plane.

Although Bucke does not specifically discuss Whitman in *Man's Moral Nature*, the poet's supreme position in the scale of moral evolution irradiates the book. The epigraphs for the fifth and sixth chapters are drawn from Whitman, and the book is dedicated to him: "I DEDICATE THIS BOOK TO THE MAN WHO INSPIRED IT—TO THE MAN WHO OF ALL MEN PAST AND PRESENT THAT I HAVE KNOWN HAS THE MOST EXALTED MORAL NATURE—TO WALT WHITMAN."[8]

Soon after the publication of *Man's Moral Nature,* Bucke wrote to Harry Buxton Forman, on 8 July 1879, revealing its true purpose:

> What I want the book to do especially is to draw attention to "Leaves of Grass" and I believe from what I see and hear is that it will do this to a considerable extent. To assist in this object I am writing "Walt Whitman, a

sequel to Man's Moral Nature". It makes a little volume ¼ to ½ as big as "Man's Moral Nature", and will be a sort of practical application of this last. I have not settled yet what I shall do with it but I think I shall publish it in book form.⁹

Very little evidence survives to document Whitman's immediate response to *Man's Moral Nature*.¹⁰ On the whole, he seems to have retained his usual cautiousness, neither espousing Bucke's theory nor rejecting it.

Bucke went ahead with his plans of writing a sequel by asking Whitman to send him a sketch of his "interior life." Whitman's response to a request of this sort was typical.¹¹ Rather than providing any inside narrative, he sent Bucke a list of titles of published sources, including William Douglas O'Connor's *The Good Gray Poet: A Vindication* (1866), John Burroughs' *Notes on Walt Whitman as Poet and Person* (1867), and Anne Gilchrist's "An Englishwoman's Estimate of Walt Whitman" (1870).¹² It should be observed that by 1879 Whitman was satisfied with the interpretation of his life and works as presented by these authors. There was no need for a reinterpretation. All that was needed was an official biography which would collect these pieces and bring them up to date. For Whitman, Bucke's mission was to assemble the official record; the years with Horace Traubel were to be spent glossing it.

Bucke, however, was not discouraged. What he could not get through correspondence, he was sure he could through conversation. And Whitman's extended vacation with Bucke in the summer of 1880 was to provide the opportunity. Since his first meeting with Whitman in 1877, Bucke had been hoping for such a visit, and on 28 May 1880 Whitman finally consented. Bucke's joy in being with Whitman and his love and reverence for the poet are fully expressed in a letter to Harry Buxton Forman of 6 June 1880:

> I returned the day before yesterday from New York, Phila, and Washington and Walt came home with me—he will spend a large part of the summer here and we will probably go to Montreal, Ottawa, etc. together before the summer is over. I have not yet made up my mind whether Walt is human or divine—this makes associating with him a little embarrasing at times, however he is so entirely lovable that one is inclined not to care too much whether he is God or not—If one was sure he was a man one could not love him any better—and if one was sure he was a god, one could not respect and esteem him more highly—so you see the matter is simpler than it seems at first sight.¹³

On the whole, the vacation was a pleasant one, and Bucke's letters to his wife provide a detailed account. Shortly before Whitman departed for Camden, Bucke wrote, on 17 September 1880, a glowing account of the visit to Harry Buxton Forman:

> Walt is still with me. He leaves on the 28th instant, I shall go with him as far as "The Falls" and see him off from there. I can say nothing to you about him except that the three-and-a-half months' absolute intimacy in which we have just lived have made him seem greater to me than he did before, which I hardly thought possible. I have made a great many notes during his residence here of conversations, habits, manners, etc. etc. which I will go to work on after he is gone, and make into a book along with my lecture on W. W. and other material.[14]

But the promises which that summer seemed to hold were not fulfilled. Bucke had hoped that Whitman's vacation with him might become an annual event—he even had dreams of Whitman moving to Canada. But these hopes were frustrated by Bucke's wife. For her, there was nothing divine about Whitman; this poet was, in fact, something of an embarrassment. Shortly before Whitman's visit, the London (Ontario) *Advertiser* had run a series of letters to the editor accusing Bucke of having "dug up from the gutter a book stained with filth."[15] These letters were a direct response to a lecture Bucke had earlier delivered to the local Teachers Association implying that as a moral guide *Leaves of Grass* might well be the equal of if not superior to the New Testament.

By the spring of 1881 Bucke's wife had apparently made it clear that Whitman was not welcome; and Bucke was forced to choose. On 19 June 1881, he wrote his wife:

> My dearest Jessie
> I have written to Walt Whitman and have done my best to stop him from coming here without being absolutely rude to him. I wish you had said long ago that you did not want him, but I was under the impression that you liked him—you seemed to, and I knew you had good reason to. Some of our Sarnia friends have been cautioning you against him and you have been weak enough to fall into their way of thinking. You may be sure I shall never try to get Walt Whitman into any house where he is not wanted, and I am more sorry than I can say that he is likely to come here this summer—If he comes now I shall have no pleasure in his visit—at first I thought I would enclose your letter to him but that seemed too hard on you and cruel to him so I have taken a different course and one that I hope will prevent his coming without letting him see that we don't want him for I want him as little as you do now—But I will never allow yourself to imagine for a moment that you or any of you can shake my affection for Walt Whitman—If all the world stood on one side, and Walt Whitman and general contempt on the other and I had to choose which I would take

I do not think I should hesitate (I hope I should not) to choose Walt Whitman.

Do not be uneasy, you could not make me angry on such a subject but I am profoundly grieved to see that our minds are so far apart upon it—

The girls send their love to you and Mr. Beddoe wishes to be kindly remembered.

I am your affectionate
husband
R M Bucke[16]

Bucke's letter to Whitman asking him not to return to London appears not to have survived.

But more important than the cancellation of the annual reunions were the obstacles set in the way of Bucke's "sequel" to *Man's Moral Nature*. And for these, Whitman was responsible. Since Bucke wanted his biography to be the official one, he dutifully submitted drafts to Whitman, who not only edited but extensively rewrote Bucke's work.[17] Some notion of Bucke's paradoxical situation—as an obedient disciple of Whitman (a living poet), but a bold prophet of Whitman (the living god)—may be gained from his pleading letters to Whitman during the final stages of the rewriting of the biography. On 18 March 1883 he wrote Whitman:

> I like all your emendations, additions, &c so far (on the whole) very much, I can see that you are materially improving the book, for wh I feel very gratefull—But dear Walt be very carefull like a good fellow with chap iii of part ii—whatever you do dont slash it up[;][18] if you make material changes send me the M. S. with proofs that I may see exactly what they are and consider them—don't fail me in this—that chap is the pivot on which the Book turns[.][19]

And on 20 March 1883, he wrote:

> I open and read these parcels of proof in fear and trembling (you must go as easy as you can, you are the terrible surgeon with the knife & saw and I am the patient). You left out my remarks on "Children of Adam"[.][20] I believe they were good but I acquiesce—your additions are excellent as they have been all through. I shall not feel half comfortable untill I have had the proof the rest of p[t] ii and have seen how much of me will be left. Poor O'Connor too, he had to submit to the fatal shears—but you are going to make a book of it (if that be possible) so go ahead if we do flinch. But still, for Lord's sake, spare my ch iii pt ii as much as possible.[21]

To those who have read *Man's Moral Nature* and who take the trouble to read *Walt Whitman* with a careful eye for Bucke's thesis, it is possible to some extent to see the biography as a "sequel"; but for the common reader the work quite lives up to Whitman's ideal of modern biography as *"collectanea."*[22] In a letter to Franklin B. Sanborn of 14 November 1882, Whitman had commented on the latter's *Henry D. Thoreau* (1882): "The telling of Life after all refuses to be put in a polish'd formal, consecutive statement—better, living glints, samples, autographic letters above all, memoranda of friends &c—You have pursued this plan & the result justifies—."[23] To be certain there was no tampering with the biography, Whitman strongly urged Bucke to make no changes. In 1888 Whitman set out to ensure the integrity of the text of both his writings and his official biography. That year he published *Complete Poems and Prose of Walt Whitman, 1855–1888* in one volume; and on 25 September, he wrote Bucke:

> Of late I have two or three times occupied spells of hours or two hours by running over with best & alertest sense & mellowed & ripened by five years your 1883 book (biographical & critical) about me & L of G—& my very deliberate & serious mind to you is that you *let it stand just as it is*—& if you have any thing farther to write or print book shape, you do so in an *additional* or further annex (of say 100 pages to its present 236 ones)— leaving the present 1883 vol. intact as it is, any verbal errors excepted—& the further pages as (mainly) references to and furthermore &c. of *the original vol.*—the text, O'C[onnor]'s letters, the appendix—every page of the 236 left as now—This is my spinal and deliberate request—[24]

Bucke, of course, agreed. Because of the direct intervention of the poet, *Walt Whitman* is a detour on the road from *Man's Moral Nature* to *Cosmic Consciousness*.

The years between the publication of the biography and Whitman's death (1892) were devoted to helping Whitman bring out his last books—*November Boughs* (1888), *Complete Poems and Prose* (1888), *Leaves of Grass* (1889), and *Leaves of Grass* (1892)—and preparing for a future when Whitman would no longer be alive. After Whitman suffered a series of strokes between 3–4 June 1888, Bucke saw the need for officially appointing literary executors.[25] Of the three appointed— Bucke, Thomas B. Harned, and Horace L. Traubel—it was only Bucke who transcended his role. All three helped bring out *The Complete Writings of Walt Whitman* (10 vols., 1902); and Harned was faithful in attending to legal matters, while Traubel was indefatigable—and from the point of view of Whitman, no doubt, the most useful. Bucke, however, was concerned with laying the foundations of a new and universal religion.

As it became clear in the spring of 1892 that Whitman was near death, Bucke made one final and urgent attempt at having Whitman confess his divinity. As a poet, Whitman had proclaimed it in 1855—

"Divine am I inside and out, and I make holy whatever I touch or am touched from";[26] but as a man, he had said nothing about it. In the last months of Whitman's life, Bucke was writing to Traubel—who was looking in on Whitman at least once a day—almost daily. Three of these letters are especially concerned with obtaining testimony from the poet. On 7 March 1892 he asked Traubel to engage the cooperation of Whitman's attendants in listening for the poet's final words:

> I am curious to see whether he will speak of any mental experiences with the oncoming of *death*—I have asked Mrs Keller [Whitman's professional nurse] to watch him and remember any indications he might give—try to be on hand *yourself*—and to make sure speak quietly to the new nurse if an intelligent woman—it would not be amiss to have Mrs. Davis & Warry [Whitman's house-keeper and her step-son] quietly observant if you could manage it without saying too much—I can hardly imagine W. dying & making no sign but he may[.][27]

On 14 March 1892, Bucke suggested that Traubel ask direct questions.

> Do you think W. would tell you any thing about his own experience of "Cosmic Consciousness"? Tell him that the doctor says that Christ, Paul & Mohomet all had C. C. but that W. W. is the man who has it in most pronounced development—ask him something about it. Where he was and what doing at the time it first made its appearance? Did a luminous haze accompany the onset of C. C.?
> How many times has the C. C. returned? and how long remained at a time?
> It will be most important to me and interesting to thousands—to many millions in the end—but I fear he will say nothing. If I had known as much a few years ago (abt C. C.) as I do now I would have got some valuable statements from him but now I fear it is too late[.][28]

Finally, on 20 March 1892, Bucke sent Traubel a questionnaire marked "strictly *private*":

> My dear Horace:—
> As you know I am writing on what I call "Cosmic Consciousness." Of all men who have ever lived I believe Walt Whitman has had this faculty most perfectly developed. I am anxious therefore to obtain from him some confirmation or some correction of my views on the subject and I ask you to read this letter to him and get from him if possible answers (however brief) to the series of questions with which it ends.
> 1 The human mind is made up of a great many faculties and these are of all ages some dating back millions or many millions of years, others only thousands of years, others like the musical sense just coming into existence.
> 2 As main trunk and stem of all the faculties are 1 consciousness and 2 self consciousness the one many millions of years old the other dating back perhaps a few hundred thousand years.

3   What I claim is that a third stage of consciousness is now coming into existence, and that I call "C. C."
4   Of course when a new faculty comes into existence in any race at first one individual has it, then as the generations succeed one another more and more individuals have it until after say a thousand generations it becomes general in the race.
5   "C. C." dates back at least to the time of Buddha—it was this faculty that came to him under the Bo tree some two thousand five hundred years ago.
6   Christ certainly had the faculty though we have no record of how and when it came to him.
7   St Paul and Mohammed had it and we have pretty full details in both these cases of the time and manner of its onset, and we can plainly trace the effects of their illumination in their writings. P. refers to faculty fully & explicitly[.]
8   The faculty seems to be much commoner now than it used to be. I know six men who have had it in more or less pronounced development. N.B. A man may have it for half a minute or off & on for years & for days continuously[.]
9   Whatever Walt may say to you about it every page of L. of G. proves the possession of the faculty by the writer.
10 Not only so but he describes the onset of the faculty, its results and its passing away, and directly alludes to it over and over again.
11 The faculty always comes suddenly—it came to W. suddenly one June day between the years 1850 and 1855—which year was it?
12 Was the onset of the faculty accompanied by a sensation of physical illumination? As if he were in the midst of a great flame? or as if a bright light shown in his mind?
13 What did he think of the new comer at first? Was he alarmed? Did he think (or fear) he was becoming insane?
14 Here follows 15–16 &c. a brief description of the onset of "C. C."—is it fairly correct or will Walt suggest some alterations or additions?
15 The man suddenly, without warning, has a sense of being immersed in a flame or rose colored cloud or haze—' [sic] or perhaps rather a sense that the mind itself is filled with such a haze.
16 At the same instant or immediately afterwards he is bathed in an emotion of joy, exultation, triumph.
17 Along with this is what must be called for want of better words a sense of immortality and accompanying this:—
18 A clear conception (in outline) of the drift of the universe—a consciousness that the central overruling power is infinitely beneficent, also:—
19 An intellectual compentency not simply surpassing the old but on a new and higher plane.

Just as science rests on reason, just as society rests on love and friendship, and is high or low according to the presence or absence of these, so religion rests on "C. C."

It may be said indeed in a very true sense that all that is best in modern civilization depends on half a dozen men—of these few men W. W. I believe is really chief and on him will rest a higher civilization than we have yet known—but meanwhile (while this is building) "C. C." will become more and more common, and *his* prophesy of other and greater bards will be fulfilled and by means of the spread of the same faculty an audience will be supplied which will be worthy of its poets.

Tell W. that I beg him to give me through you a little light to help me forward with my present task.

With love to W. and all his friends,
    R M Bucke[29]

This list of propositions and questions provides a convenient summary of Bucke's theory of cosmic consciousness; but there is no evidence that Whitman responded to this list, or that Traubel even read it to him.

Bucke's faith was not in any degree shaken by Whitman's refusal to commit himself outside his verse on the question of his divinity—Bucke's faith rested on the foundation of his private illumination, the evidence of Whitman's writings, and the example of Whitman's life. Shortly after Whitman's death on 26 March 1892, Bucke expressed his faith in a poignant letter to J. W. Wallace and John Johnston (the leading members of a group of Whitman disciples in Bolton, England, who called themselves the "College"). Bucke wrote:

10 April [18]92

Dear Wallace and Johnston

Many thanks for your good kind letters. [−] I cannot write to you yet—My heart is as heavy as lead. But it will pass off and please God we will work for dear Walt harder than ever. [−] over and over again I keep saying to myself: The Christ is dead! Again we have buried the Christ! And for the time there seems to be an end of every thing. But I *know* he is not dead and I *know* that this pain will pass. Give my love to all the dear College fellows—*now* we are really brothers

God bless you all
    R M Bucke[30]

In *Cosmic Consciousness* (1901), Bucke presented the clearest and most mature formulation of Whitman's divinity and the nature of his own discipleship. After more than twenty-five years of meditation on the meaning of his illumination and the true significance of Whitman, Bucke arrived at a formula which raised his discipleship from a local event in the last quarter of the nineteenth century to a cosmic manifestation of the universal scheme of salvation—Whitman was Christ; and he, Bucke, was St. Paul. Freed from the emendations of Whitman, Bucke was able, at last, to prophesy.

Man's Moral Nature concluded with Bucke's assurance that "everything is really good and beautiful, and ... an all-powerful and infinitely beneficent providence holds us safe through life and death in its keeping forever...."[31] In the earlier work, Bucke's assurance about the beneficence of Providence rested on no more than an emotional conviction; but in "First Words," the opening section of *Cosmic Consciousness,* he outlines in practical terms the reasons for believing that "the immediate future of our race... is indescribably hopeful" (p. 4).

Bucke thinks that we are on the brink of three revolutions which will radically and permanently alter human existence—these are aerial navigation, socialism, and cosmic consciousness. About the latter, he writes:

> In contact with the flux of cosmic consciousness all religions known and named to-day will be melted down. The human soul will be revolutionized. Religion will absolutely dominate the race.... Religion will govern every minute of every day of all life.... The world peopled by men possessing cosmic consciousness will be as far removed from the world of to-day as this is from the world as it was before the advent of self consciousness. (pp. 4–5)

According to Bucke, it is the evolution of consciousness which accounts for our transformation from "brute to man, from man to demigod" (p. 7).

Of the fourteen extraordinary instances of cosmic consciousness Bucke examines—including Gautama, Jesus Christ, St. Paul, Mohammed, and Francis Bacon (i.e., Shakespeare)—Walt Whitman is the most remarkable. And in his examination of the poet, Bucke's procedure is significant. Just as the poet rewrote *Walt Whitman* by deleting matter having to do with moral nature, Bucke, in turn, rewrites *Walt Whitman* by reinserting matter having to do with cosmic consciousness. He introduces the biographical section of *Cosmic Consciousness* by referring to his source: "The following brief description is taken from the writer's 'Walt Whitman,' written in the summer of 1880, while he was visiting the author" (p. 215). Bucke then supplies a biographical sketch which is actually a composite of quotations from *Walt Whitman.*

He begins his analysis of Whitman by elevating the poet to a supreme position: "Walt Whitman is the best, most perfect example the world has so far had of the Cosmic Sense..." (p. 225). He goes on to explain Whitman's poetic genius in terms of cosmic consciousness. It was the onset of this faculty that altered Whitman from a mere hack to one of the most important writers in the history of the world:

> in the case of Whitman... writings of absolutely no value were immediately followed... by pages across each of which in letters of ethereal fire are written the words ETERNAL LIFE.... It is upon this instantaneous evolution of the *Titan* from the *Man,* this profound mystery of the attainment of the splendor and power of the kingdom of heaven, that this present volume seeks to throw light. (p. 226)

For biographical evidence of the phenomenon of cosmic consciousness, Bucke selects passages from Whitman's poetry and prose. As in *Walt Whitman*, Bucke quotes a few lines and then presents a commentary and paraphrase in which the underlying meaning of the text is ostensibly made clear. In *Cosmic Consciousness*, however, there is the additional refinement of presenting the text and the gloss in parallel columns. The effect, whether intended or not, is much the same as found in annotated editions of the Bible.

Whitman differs from all other instances of cosmic consciousness not only in the intensity and duration of his intuition, but most importantly in his ability to integrate this new faculty with the old ones. Whitman

> saw, what neither Gautama nor Paul saw, what Jesus saw, though not so clearly as he, that though this faculty is truly God-like, yet it is no more supernatural or preternatural than sight, hearing, taste feeling. . . . He believes in it, but he says the other self, the old self, must not abase itself to the new . . . he will see that they live as friendly co-workers together. And it may here be said that whoever does not realize this last clause will never fully understand the "Leaves." (p. 232)

It is in "Last Words," the final section of *Cosmic Consciousness*, that Bucke becomes most fully the prophet of new and loftier races of men:

> may it not well be that in the self conscious human being, as we know him to-day, we have the psychic germ of not one higher race only, but of several? . . . As for example: a cosmic conscious race; another race that shall possess seemingly miraculous powers of acting upon what we call objective nature; another with clairvoyant powers far surpassing those possessed by the best specimens so far; another with miraculous healing powers; and so on. (p. 372)

For the mass of men, the keys to these higher states of being are found in the lives and writings of those who have possessed cosmic consciousness. Indeed, these superior men have made this specific promise: "as one of them [Whitman] says: 'I bestow upon any man or woman the entrance to all the gifts of the universe'" (p. 373). Progress in this direction has been retarded by convention. Rather than accepting the sacred writings of his particular time and place, each man should seek out those which have for him the greatest effect:

> And as there are many men in the West who are . . . more benefited by Buddhistic and Mohammedan scriptures than they are by Jewish or Christian,

so, doubtless, there are thousands of men in southern Asia who . . . would be . . . more readily and profoundly stirred by the Gospels and Pauline epistles, or "Leaves of Grass." . . . (p. 374)

The most remarkable characteristic of this concluding section is the increasingly close identification of Walt Whitman with Christ. In the deification of Whitman, his achievements as a poet play no essential part: "the literary instinct (or expression of any kind) is not necessarily highly developed in the Cosmic Conscious mind, but is a faculty apart. . . . Whitman lived and died vividly conscious of his defects in expression" (p. 375). It is, rather, the supreme moral development, and other, ineffable qualities, that link Whitman with Christ:

> It is also clear that their purely moral qualities—witness especially Gautama, Jesus and Whitman—give them a rank apart from their self conscious fellows, but this is not by any means the whole story. The central point, the kernel of the matter, consists in the fact that they possess qualities for which we at present have no names or concepts. Jesus alluded to one of these when he said: "Whoever drinketh of the water that I shall give him shall never thirst; but the water that I shall give him shall become in him a well of water springing up unto eternal life." And Whitman points in the same direction when he declares that his book is not linked with the rest nor felt by the intellect, "but has to do with untold latencies" in writer and reader, and also when he states that he does not give lectures and charity—that is, either intellectual or moral gifts—but that when he gives he gives himself. (pp. 375–76)

In the opening pages of *Cosmic Consciousness*, Bucke had set up an equation: "The Savior of man is Cosmic Consciousness—in Paul's language—the Christ" (p. 6). The reasons underlying this identification are found in Bucke's glosses on St. Paul's Letter to the Galatians. For St. Paul, according to Bucke, Christ was the messiah because in him St. Paul had recognized the teachings of cosmic consciousness: "He [Paul] knew, however, enough about Jesus and his teachings to be able to recognize (when it came to him) that the teachings of Cosmic Sense were practically identical with the teachings of Jesus" (p. 116). Indeed, Christ is cosmic consciousness made flesh: "Christ is the Cosmic Sense conceived as a distinct entity or individuality" (p. 116). If such is the case, then the relationship between St. Paul and Christ is not a unique historical event; but, rather, it becomes a prototype. As the evolutionary process continues, any man who embodies the intuitions of cosmic consciousness is Christ, and any who follows him for the sake of his wisdom is St. Paul.

In St. Paul, Bucke finds not only his prototype but also his defense against the scorn of the world. He takes care to quote the apostle's famous paradox: "If any man thinketh that he is wise among you in this world, let him become a fool, that he may become wise. For the wisdom of this world is foolishness with God" (p. 117; I Corinthians 3:18–19). Bucke explicates the paradox in terms of cosmic consciousness: "Paul says the wisdom of self consciousness is not the wisdom of those who have the Cosmic Sense, and the wisdom of the latter is foolishness to the merely self conscious" (p. 117).

Cosmic Consciousness concludes with a millennial vision of a new world peopled by a "new race":

> The simple truth is, that there has lived on the earth, "appearing at intervals," for thousands of years among ordinary men, the first faint beginnings of another race; walking the earth and breathing the air with us, but at the same time walking another earth and breathing another air of which we know little or nothing, but which is, all the same, our spiritual life, as its absence would be our spiritual death. This new race is in act of being born from us, and in the near future it will occupy and possess the earth. (pp. 383–84)

It is unnecessary to report that Bucke's devotion to Whitman has met with little understanding. To his friends, it was an embarrassment; and to the less sympathetic, it was ridiculous. For the general reader, Bucke and his devotion have survived in an anecdote. Sir William Osler, a friend of Bucke, recalled the following incident:

> One evening after dinner...I drew Bucke on to tell the story of Whitman's influence.... It was an experience to hear an elderly man—looking a venerable seer—with absolute abandonment tell how "Leaves of Grass" had meant for him spiritual enlightenment, a new power in life, new joys in a new existence on a plane higher than he had ever hoped to reach. All this with the accompanying physical exaltation expressed by dilated pupils and intensity of utterance that were embarrassing to uninitiated friends.[32]

At present, *Man's Moral Nature* is unread; and *Cosmic Consciousness*, although immensely popular among various cultists and enthusiasts of mysticism, is neglected by Whitman scholars. The result has been that the very nature of Bucke's discipleship has been misunderstood. Impatient with defining modes of discipleship, readers have latched on to Bliss Perry's catchy epithet and lumped Bucke among the "hot little prophets"[33] of Whitman. It should be clear that any understanding of Bucke must begin with the primary fact that he was a religious disciple of Whitman. The corollary of this distinction is that what is excessive and even ludicrous in a *literary* disciple, is acceptable and commendable in a *religious* one.

Quite apart from doing Bucke justice, there is a further advantage in perceiving him as a religious disciple. His explication of *Leaves of Grass* provides a suitable introduction to the work as a religious text. And a reading in this fashion has much to recommend it. Not only is it in accord with the final development of Whitman's "persona," but it also begins with the healthy and corrective assumption that as a poet Whitman meant what he said.

NOTES

1. Bucke to Jessie Maria Bucke, 18 October 1877, CaOLU. I have adopted the following editorial practices for dealing with the peculiarities of Bucke's manuscripts: (1) Bucke tended to use the right-hand margin of the page as an all-purpose punctuation point. I have placed within square brackets whatever punctuation seemed suitable. I have also placed within square brackets the terminal period when Bucke has omitted it. (2) Bucke often indicated a new "paragraph" by leaving a sizable space between the end of one sentence and the opening of the next. I have indicated this space by placing a dash within square brackets. (3) I have not used *sic* to point out Bucke's habitual misspellings.
  I am grateful to Charles E. Feinberg for permission to use and to quote from materials in his outstanding Whitman collection, now at the Library of Congress, and to the D. B. Weldon Library of the University of Western Ontario for permission to quote from manuscripts in its possession.
2. Bucke to Harry Buxton Forman, 24 October 1877 (typescript copy), CaOLU.
3. *Man's Moral Nature: An Essay* (New York: G. P. Putnam's Sons); *Walt Whitman* (Philadelphia: David McKay); *Cosmic Consciousness: A Study in the Evolution of the Human Mind* (Philadelphia: Innes & Sons); *Calamus: A Series of Letters Written during the Years 1868–1880. By Walt Whitman to a Young Friend (Peter Doyle)* (Boston: Laurens Maynard); *The Wound Dresser: A Series of Letters Written from the Hospitals in Washington during the War of the Rebellion* (Boston: Small, Maynard).
4. "Memories of Walt Whitman," *Walt Whitman Fellowship Papers*, no. 6 (September 1894): 35.
5. *Poems of Walt Whitman*, sel. and ed. William Michael Rossetti (London: John Camden Hotten).
6. Bucke to Whitman, 19 December 1870, DLC.
7. *Cosmic Consciousness* (New York: E. P. Dutton, 1969), pp. 9–10. All further references are to this edition and are parenthetical.
8. *Man's Moral Nature*, p. v.
9. Bucke to Harry Buxton Forman, 8 July 1879 (typescript copy), CaOLU.
10. See Artem Lozynsky, "Whitman and *Man's Moral Nature*," *Walt Whitman Review*, 21 (March 1975): 36–37.
11. The letter or letters of Whitman to Bucke concerning the source materials for the biography appear to be lost; but Whitman's response may be deduced from Bucke's letters to him: Bucke to Whitman, 19 January 1880 and 3 February 1880, The John Rylands Library, Manchester, England.
12. William Douglas O'Connor, *The Good Gray Poet: A Vindication* (New York:

Bunce and Huntington); John Burroughs, *Notes on Walt Whitman as Poet and Person* (New York: American News Company); Anne Gilchrist, "An Englishwoman's Estimate of Walt Whitman," *The Radical*, 7 (May 1870): 345–59.

13. Bucke to Harry Buxton Forman, 6 June 1880 (typescript copy), CaOLU.

14. Bucke to Harry Buxton Forman, 17 September 1880 (typescript copy), CaOLU.

15. The charge against Bucke appeared in the *Advertiser* on 12 March 1880.

16. Bucke to Jessie Maria Bucke, 19 June 1881, CaOLU.

17. Whitman's revisions of Bucke's drafts of the biography have been studied by Harold Jaffe, "Richard Maurice Bucke's *Walt Whitman*: Edited, with an Introduction and Variant Readings" (Ph.D. diss., New York University, 1968); and Stephen Railton in *Walt Whitman's Autograph Revision of the Analysis of Leaves of Grass (for Dr. R. M. Bucke's Walt Whitman)* [ed. Quentin Anderson] (New York: New York University Press, 1974), pp. 63–191. Much still remains to be done.

18. Chpt. 3 of Pt. II is entitled "Analysis of Poems, Continued." Whitman revised this section heavily (see Anderson, *Whitman's Autograph Revision*, pp. 101, 102, 107, 111, 113, 115, 116, 119, 121, 123, 125).

19. Bucke to Whitman, 18 March 1883, DLC.

20. Bucke's remarks on "Children of Adam" are found in Jaffe, "Bucke's *Walt Whitman*," pp. 196–200.

21. Bucke to Whitman, 20 March 1883, DLC.

22. *Walt Whitman: The Correspondence*, ed. Edwin Haviland Miller, 5 vols. (New York: New York University Press, 1961–69), 3:320.

23. *The Correspondence*, 3:316.

24. *The Correspondence*, 4:215.

25. Horace Traubel, *With Walt Whitman in Camden* (Boston: Small, Maynard & Company, 1906), 1:259–312.

26. *Leaves of Grass* (New York: n.p., 1855), p. 29.

27. Bucke to Traubel, 7 March 1892, DLC.

28. Bucke to Traubel, 14 March 1892, DLC. Bucke has deleted several sentences and phrases from this letter. After the first sentence of the first paragraph, he wrote: "Would you try him some day if he was in better trim than usual? Do not say that I asked you." "Tell him" is followed by "(for instance)"; and "ask" replaces "then try and get from." The original opening of the third paragraph is: "If you could quietly induce W. to talk about this experience it would be." Since the deleted portions are quite legible it may be suggested that Bucke, who knew that Traubel was collecting for possible future publication all correspondence that Whitman received, "edited" his own letter in such a way that Traubel would clearly see what he wanted; but that future readers of the published letter would not detect undue urgency or presumption.

29. Bucke to Traubel, 20 March 1892 (typescript), DLC.

30. Bucke to Wallace and Johnston, 10 April 1892, County Borough of Bolton (England) Public Libraries.

31. *Man's Moral Nature*, p. 199.

32. Harvey Cushing, *The Life of Sir William Osler* (London: Oxford University Press, 1940), p. 266.

33. Bliss Perry, *Walt Whitman: His Life and Work* (Boston: Houghton, Mifflin, 1906), p. 286.

BOOKS RECEIVED

Robert E. Burkholder

BLASING, MUTLU KONUCK. *The Art of Life: Studies in American Autobiographical Literature*. Austin and London: University of Texas Press, [1977]. xxviii, 193pp.: ports.; 21cm. "Sources Cited": pp. [177]–185; index. LC 76–20760. ISBN 0–292–70315–5. $15.95.
Includes interpretative chapters on Thoreau's *Walden* and Whitman's "Song of Myself."

BOLGER, STEPHEN GARRETT. *The Irish Character in American Fiction, 1830–1860*. New York: Arno Press, 1976. [v], 207pp.; 23cm. (The Irish-Americans.) Bibliography: pp. 167–[196]; index. LC 76–6323. ISBN 0–405–09320–9. $14.00.
Bolger discusses Timothy Shay Arthur, John Holt Ingraham, Simms, Cooper, Hawthorne, Melville, and Poe in this facsimile reprinting of his 1971 University of Pennsylvania dissertation.

BOWDEN, HENRY WARNER. *Dictionary of American Religious Biography*. Westport, Conn.: Greenwood Press, [1977]. [xiii], 572pp.; 24cm. Appendices ("Denominational Affiliation," "Listing by Birthplace"): pp. [545]–567; index. LC 76–5258. ISBN 0–8371–8906–3. $29.95.
A compilation of 425 alphabetically arranged sketches.

BRUCCOLI, MATTHEW J., editorial director, C. E. FRAZER CLARK, JR., managing editor. *Pages: The World of Books, Writers, and Writing*. Volume 1. Detroit: Gale Research, [1976]. 304pp.: illus., facsim.; 29cm. (Pages: The World of Books, Writers, and Writing.) LC 76–203–69. ISBN 0–8103–0925–4. $24.00.
Includes "Recovering the Author's Intentions," by Fredson Bowers; "Queens of Literature," by Madeleine B. Stern, which discusses a late nineteenth-century card game which featured the faces of Stowe, Fuller, and Louisa May Alcott; and the first publication of a letter by Nathaniel Hawthorne.

CARLSON, PATRICIA ANN. *Hawthorne's Functional Settings: A Study of Artistic Method*. [Amsterdam]: Editions Rodolphi, [1977]. 208pp.; 22cm. (Melville Studies in American Culture, Volume Six.) ISBN 90–6203–428–4. Paper, $23.25.
An attempt to discover the essence of Hawthorne's fictional technique through an examination of his use of setting.

CARTER, EVERETT. *The American Idea: The Literary Response to American Optimism*. Chapel Hill: University of North Carolina Press, [1977]. [x], 276pp.; 23cm. Bibliography: pp. 265–70; index. LC 76–13867. ISBN 0–8078–1279–X. $14.95.

Carter claims that a progressive, basically optimistic abstraction which he terms "the American idea" has prompted most of America's best literature, and he includes discussions of Longfellow, Holmes, Thoreau, Whitman, Emerson, Melville, Poe, and Hawthorne to prove his point.

CASSARA, ERNEST. *History of the United States of America: A Guide to Information Sources*. Detroit: Gale Research, [1977]. xxi, 459pp.; 22cm. (Volume 3 in the American Studies Information Guide Series.) Author, short-title, and subject indices. LC 73–17551. ISBN 0–8103–1266–2. $18.00.

An annotated listing of 1,995 books arranged alphabetically by author under chronological period headings.

CONRAD, SUSAN PHINNEY. *Perish the Thought: Intellectual Women in Romantic America, 1830–1860*. New York: Oxford University Press, 1976. [x], 292pp.; 22cm. Appendices ("Regional Background and Religious Affiliation," "Professions of Fathers and Husbands"): pp. [273]–[275]; "Selected Bibliography": pp. [276]–283; index. LC 75–25463. ISBN 0–19–501995–4. $12.95.

Includes discussions of Margaret Fuller, Elizabeth Palmer Peabody, and Caroline Dall.

DAUBER, KENNETH. *Rediscovering Hawthorne*. Princeton: Princeton University Press, [1977]. xii, 235pp.; 22cm. Index. LC 76–45893. ISBN 0–691–06323–0. $13.00.

An attempt to delineate the theory of the novel that Hawthorne developed in his work, and to redefine literature employing that theory.

DOUGHERTY, JAMES J., compiler-editor; GEORGE F. WILLISS, associate compiler-editor, MARION SADER, editor. *Writings on American History, 1962–73: A Subject Bibliography of Articles*. Volumes 1 (Chronological), 2 (Geographical), 3 (Subjects), and 4 (Subjects). Washington, D.C.: American Historical Association; Millwood, N.Y.: KTO Press, 1976. xii, 583; iv, 584–909; iv, 911–1582; iv, 1583–2271pp.; 26cm. Author index (for Vols. 1–4 in Vol. 4). LC 74–18954. ISBN 0–527–00373–5. $275.00.

An important list of 33,000 citations culled from 510 journals.

DRYDEN, EDGAR A. *Nathaniel Hawthorne: The Poetics of Enchantment*. Ithaca: Cornell University Press, [1977]. 182pp.; 22cm. "Works Cited": pp. [173]–176; index. LC 76–28010. ISBN 0–8014–1028–2. $10.00.

Dryden approaches Hawthorne's work as a totality in order to discover structural principles, and finds that the alternation between enchantment and disenchantment is the dominant force in the Hawthorne canon, ultimately defining the author's relationship to his audience and his work.

EAKIN, PAUL JOHN. *The New England Girl: Cultural Ideals in Hawthorne, Stowe, Howells and James*. Athens: University of Georgia Press, [1976]. [viii], 252pp.; 24cm. Index. LC 74–185–83. ISBN 0–8203–0398–4. $11.00.

Concerned with finding the reason for the post-Civil War realists' preoccupation with the portrayal of women as keys to the national character, Eakin looks to Stowe's *The Minister's Wooing* and to Hawthorne's use of Margaret Fuller as a prototype for his heroines for the basis of this phenomenon.

EMERSON, RALPH WALDO. *The Journals and Miscellaneous Notebooks of Ralph Waldo Emerson.* Volume 12. Edited by Linda Allardt. Cambridge: The Belknap Press of Harvard University Press, 1976. xlviii, 657pp.; 24cm. (The Journals and Miscellaneous Notebooks of Ralph Waldo Emerson.) Appendices; index. LC 60–11554. ISBN 0–674–48475–4. $37.50.
Publishes nine lecture notebooks Emerson kept between 1835 and 1862, including notebooks for "The Philosophy of History" series, the "Human Culture" series, the "Present Age" series, the "Conduct of Life" series, and *Essays: Second Series.*

EMERSON, RALPH WALDO. *The Journals and Miscellaneous Notebooks of Ralph Waldo Emerson.* Volume 13. Edited by Ralph H. Orth and Alfred R. Ferguson. Cambridge: The Belknap Press of Harvard University Press, 1977. [xxii], 555pp.: illus.; 24cm. (The Journals and Miscellaneous Notebooks of Ralph Waldo Emerson.) Appendix; index. LC 60–11554. ISBN 0–674–48476–2. $35.00.
Publishes journals and notebooks kept by Emerson from 1852 to 1855, a fallow creative period between *Representative Men* and *English Traits* in which Emerson's chief literary activity was reading lectures, and which saw him grow increasingly concerned with slavery and everyday matters.

FERLAZZO, PAUL. *Emily Dickinson.* Boston: Twayne, [1976]. 168 pp.: front.; 21 cm. (Twayne's United States Authors Series: TUSAS 280.) "Selected Bibliography": pp. 157–63; index. LC 76–48304. ISBN 0–8057–7180–8. $7.95.

GILMORE, MICHAEL T., editor. *Twentieth Century Interpretations of* Moby-Dick: *A Collection of Critical Essays.* Englewood Cliffs, N.J.: Prentice-Hall, [1977]. iv, 123pp.; 21cm. (A Spectrum Book.) "Selected Bibliography": pp. 121–23. LC 76–44426. ISBN 0–13–586057–1: cloth, $6.95; ISBN 0–13–586032–6: paper, $2.45.

GOHDES, CLARENCE. *Bibliographical Guide to the Study of the Literature of the U.S.A.* Fourth edition, revised and enlarged. Durham: Duke University Press, 1976. xii, 173pp.; 24cm. Index of subjects; index of authors, editors, and compilers. LC 76–28585. ISBN 0–8223–0375–2. $8.50.
An annotated listing of 1,214 items topically arranged.

GOLEMBA, HENRY L. *George Ripley.* Boston: Twayne, [1977]. 172pp.: front.; 21cm. (Twayne's United States Authors Series: TUSAS 281.) "Selected Bibliography": pp. 164–69; index. LC 76–41768. ISBN 0–8057–7181–6. $8.95.

HOLMES, OLIVER WENDELL. *Elsie Venner: A Romance of Destiny* [New York]: Arno Press, 1976. [xviii], 487pp.: front., illus.; 22cm. (Supernatural and Occult Fiction.) LC 75–46279. ISBN 0–405–08137–5. $29.00.
Facsimile reprinting of the 1892 Standard Library Edition, published by Houghton, Mifflin.

HOOPES, JAMES. *Van Wyck Brooks: In Search of American Culture.* Amherst: University of Massachusetts Press, 1977. xviii, 346pp.: front., illus.; 24cm. "Note on Sources": pp. [307]–308; index. LC 76–8754. ISBN 0–87023–212–6. $15.00.

A study with the two-fold purpose of examining cultural transformation and a man who was at the center of the change. Hoopes' study of Brooks relies on previously unexamined medical records, interviews, and correspondence, in an attempt to discover how Brooks' cultural radicalism grew out of the genteel tradition.

HUESTON, ROBERT FRANCIS. *The Catholic Press and Nativism, 1840–1860.* New York: Arno Press, 1976. [xvi], 352pp.; 23cm. (The Irish-Americans.) Bibliography: pp. 335–[352]. LC 76–6348. ISBN 0–405–09342–X. $21.00.

Facsimile reprinting of the author's 1972 University of Notre Dame dissertation which includes discussions of Orestes Brownson's oscillating stance toward the Nativist movement.

KELLY, RICHARD M., editor, ALLISON R. ENSOR, associate editor. *Tennessee Studies in Literature.* Volume XXI, American Literature Issue. Knoxville: University of Tennessee Press, 1976. [xii], 126pp.; 24cm. (Tennessee Studies in Literature.) LC 58–63252. ISBN 0–87049–195–4. $7.50.

Includes "The Geography and Framework of Hawthorne's 'Roger Malvin's Burial,'" by John R. Byers, Jr., and "Emersonian Transcendentalism: Over-Soul or Over-Self?" by James E. Mulqueen.

MAIR, MARGARET GRANVILLE, compiler. *The Papers of Harriet Beecher Stowe.* Hartford, Conn.: The Stowe-Day Foundation, 1977. 74pp.; 27cm. (A Bibliography of the Manuscripts in the Stowe-Day Memorial Library. Vol. 1.) LC 76–56582. ISBN 0–917482–08–5. Paper, $4.00.

An annotated listing of 211 letters, 28 manuscripts, and miscellaneous documents, including autographs.

MARKI, IVAN. *The Trial of the Poet: An Interpretation of the First Edition of Leaves of Grass.* New York: Columbia University Press, 1976. [xviii], 301pp.; 23cm. "Selected Bibliography": pp. 285–95; index. LC 76–18792. ISBN 0–231–03984–0. $17.50.

An interpretative study based upon Marki's belief that the 1855 edition of *Leaves of Grass* has a structure and integrity of vision lacking in subsequent editions.

MELVILLE, HERMAN. *Poems of Herman Melville.* Edited by Douglas Robillard. New Haven, Conn.: College and University Press, [1976]. 260pp.; 20cm. (The Masterworks of Literature Series.) LC 74–18625. Paper, $3.95.

Prints *Battle-Pieces and Other Aspects of War* (1866), *John Marr and Other Sailors* (1888), *Timoleon* (1891), and other poems culled from the Constable Edition or Howard P. Vincent's edition of *Collected Poems.*

MILLER, JOHN CARL. *Building Poe Biography.* Baton Rouge: Louisiana State University Press, [1977]. [xxii], 269pp.: front., facsim.; 23cm. (Southern Literary Studies.) Appendix ("Names, Topics, Newsclippings, and Letters Frequently Mentioned in the Text"): pp. [245]–251; bibliography: pp. [253]–263; index. LC 76–47653. ISBN 0–8071–0195–8. $20.00.

A selection of letters from friends of Poe to John Henry Ingram, many published here for the first time, which were used as the raw material for Ingram's biographies of Poe. Miller's commentary explains the circumstances which prompted each letter and how the letters were used by Ingram.

MYERSON, JOEL. *Margaret Fuller: An Annotated Secondary Bibliography*. New York: Burt Franklin, [1977]. [xx], 272pp.: front.; 23cm. Index. LC 77-3187. ISBN 0-89102-026-8. $19.50.
Lists 1,306 annotated entries chronologically under three subject headings: "Writings About Fuller," "Ana," and "Manuscripts." Designed to complement Myerson's forthcoming *Margaret Fuller: A Descriptive Primary Bibliography*.

PECK, H. DANIEL. *A World By Itself: The Pastoral Moment in Cooper's Fiction*. New Haven: Yale University Press, 1977. xiv, 213pp.; 22cm. "Works Cited": pp. 191-99; index. LC 76-25868. ISBN 0-300-02027-9. $12.50.
An attempt to locate the power of Cooper's fiction in the structure of the novels rather than in Cooper's social criticism, historical importance, or pictorialism.

SPENGEMANN, WILLIAM C. *The Adventurous Muse: The Poetics of American Fiction, 1789-1900*. New Haven: Yale University Press, 1977. [x], 290pp.; 24cm. "Bibliographical Essay": pp. 277-84; index. LC 76-26936. ISBN 0-300-02042-2. $15.00.
Includes discussions of Richard Henry Dana, Jr., Poe, Melville, and Hawthorne, and the degree to which they were affected by a trio of interrelated forces: New World travel writing, European literature, and Romantic aesthetics.

STOWE, HARRIET BEECHER. *Poganuc People*. Introduction by Joseph S. Van Why. Hartford, Conn.: The Stowe-Day Foundation, 1977. [xvi], 375pp.: illus.; 22cm. (Harriet Beecher Stowe's New England Novels.) LC 76-56587. ISBN 0-917482-06-9. Paper, $6.95.
Facsimile reprinting of the 1878 Fords, Howard, & Hulbert edition.

TANSELLE, G. THOMAS, compiler. *A Checklist of Editions of* Moby-Dick, *1851-1976, Issued on the Occasion of an Exhibition at The Newberry Library Commemorating the 125th Anniversary of Its Original Publication*. Chicago: Northwestern University Press and The Newberry Library, 1976. 50pp.: illus.; 20cm. Index. Paper, $3.50.

WELTER, BARBARA. *Dimity Convictions: The American Woman in the Nineteenth Century*. Athens: Ohio University Press, 1976. 230pp.; 24cm. LC 76-8305. ISBN 0-8214-0352-4: cloth, $12.00; ISBN 0-8214-0358-3: paper, $4.50.
Welter devotes a chapter to a discussion of women novelists of religious controversy, and a chapter to Margaret Fuller's "Mystical Feminism."

WRIGHT, CONRAD. *The Beginnings of Unitarianism in America*. [Hamden, Conn.]: Archon Books, 1976. 305pp.; 22cm. "Bibliographical Note": pp. 293-94; index. LC 76-20681. ISBN 0-208-01612-0. $15.00.
Reprinting of this basic work from the 1955 Starr King Press edition.

CONTRIBUTORS

THOMAS BLANDING is a member of the Editorial Board for *The Writings of Henry D. Thoreau*, editor of *Excursions* and *Nature Essays I and II* (Thoreau's literary remains), co-editor of the *Journal*, and author of articles on Alcott, Dickinson, Emerson, and Thoreau.

ROBERT E. BURKHOLDER, a graduate student at the University of South Carolina, is the *Studies in the American Renaissance* Editorial Assistant. He is currently preparing, with Joel Myerson, an annotated secondary bibliography of Emerson to be published in 1982.

C. E. FRAZER CLARK, JR., partner in Bruccoli Clark Publishers, is editor of *The Nathaniel Hawthorne Journal*, co-editor of the *Fitzgerald/Hemingway Annual*, and compiler of *Hawthorne at Auction*. His *Nathaniel Hawthorne: A Descriptive Bibliography* was recently published.

AMY PUETT EMMERS teaches English and American Studies at Ridgewood High School, Ridgewood, New Jersey. Her dissertation was a biography of Melville's wife, Elizabeth Shaw Melville. She is a Contributing Scholar to the Northwestern-Newberry edition of *The Writings of Herman Melville*.

RICHARD FRANCIS, Lecturer in American Literature at Manchester University, England, is writing a book on the social thought of the New England Transcendentalists, and has published an article on the Fruitlands utopia in the May 1973 *American Quarterly*.

SUSAN GEARY received her Ph.D. in American Civilization from Brown University. She has published articles on Stowe in *Studies in Bibliography* and *Papers of the Bibliographical Society of America*.

RITA K. GOLLIN is Professor of English at the State University of New York's College at Geneseo. She has completed a book on dreams in Hawthorne's works and is now writing on nineteenth-century American writers' attitudes toward the Shakers.

Contributors

ROBERT N. HUDSPETH, Associate Professor of English at the Pennsylvania State University, is the author of *Ellery Channing* and several articles on British and American fiction. He is currently editing the letters of Margaret Fuller.

J. GERALD KENNEDY, author of several articles on Poe, is preparing a book on William Darby, an early nineteenth-century explorer and short story writer. He is an Assistant Professor of English at Louisiana State University.

ARTEM LOZYNSKY, Assistant Professor of English at Temple University, has recently completed an edition of Dr. Bucke's letters to Whitman and, with Gloria Francis, *Whitman at Auction*.

JOHN J. MCDONALD, Associate Professor of English at the University of Notre Dame, has published articles on Emerson and Hawthorne in *Nathaniel Hawthorne Journal*, *New England Quarterly*, and *Texas Studies in Literature and Language*.

JOSEPH J. MOLDENHAUER, Professor of English at the University of Texas at Austin, is Textual Editor of *The Writings of Henry D. Thoreau*, and volume editor of *The Maine Woods* and *Early Essays and Miscellanies*.

BURTON R. POLLIN, Professor of English Emeritus, Bronx Community College, CUNY, and a former Guggenheim Fellow, is editor of the Harvard Edition of Edgar Allan Poe, begun by the late Professor Mabbott. He is also the author of ten books (three on Poe) and over one hundred articles.

DAVID ROBINSON, Assistant Professor of English at Oregon State University, has published articles on Milton, Poe, Jones Very, T. S. Eliot, and others in various journals. He is currently engaged in a study of Emerson's philosophy of culture.

MADELEINE B. STERN, partner in Leona Rostenberg—Rare Books, has published numerous books and articles on nineteenth-century American literature, publishing history, and feminism, and has co-authored (with Leona Rostenberg) *Old & Rare: Thirty Years in the Book Business*.